CyberReader

Second Edition

◆ **Victor J. Vitanza**

UNIVERSITY OF TEXAS AT ARLINGTON

ALLYN AND BACON

Boston   London   Toronto   Sydney   Tokyo   Singapore

Vice President, Humanities: Joseph Opiela
Senior Marketing Manager: Lisa Kimball
Production Coordinator: Susan Brown
Editorial-Production Service: Matrix Productions Inc.
Designer: Seventeenth Street Studios
Cover Administrator: Linda Knowles
Composition Buyer: Linda Cox
Manufacturing Buyer: Suzanne Lareau

Credits appear on pages 506–509,
which constitutes a continuation of the copyright page.

Library of Congress Cataloging-in-Publication Data

Vitanza, Victor J.
  CyberReader / Victor J. Vitanza. — 2nd ed.
      p.   cm.
  Includes bibliographical references and index.
  ISBN 0-205-29086-8
  1. Internet (Computer network)   2. World Wide Web (Information
  retrieval system)   I. Title.
TK5105.875.I57V58   1998
302.23—dc21   98-15246
                                                          CIP

Printed in the United States of America

    9 8 7 6 5 4 3   02   01   00

■ CONTENTS

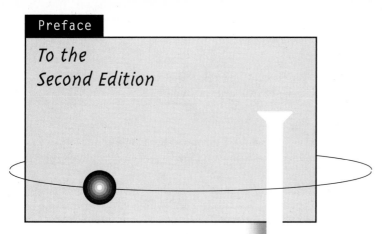

n the preface to the first edition, I wrote: "This book is about *change*. About how technology is extending our lives and everything around us geometrically. Exponentially." Ideally, to keep up with the change in technology, we would need a new book every day. Practically, I have attempted to keep up with the changing times by way of the Web page for this book (www.abacon.com/vitanza). And I have encouraged readers and surfers to use the powerful search engines to follow the unfolding of technological change as it occurs and is recorded on the Web and other electronic venues.

Now it is time for a new edition recalling what *was said* in the first edition and introducing what *is now being said* as it is anthologized in the second edition. Both editions will perhaps help us project what *will have been said* eventually. Predicting technological change, however, is like predicting where lightning will strike next.

In this edition, I have added thirteen new articles and omitted twelve. I have slightly reorganized the subjects and sequence of the chapters so that they move from the conceptual themes of

- Cyberspace and virtual reality (I omitted hyperreality)

to a new subject of

- Virtual societies and identities

and then on to the societal-legal issues of

- Freedom/censorship and

- Sexual politics

and then to the educational-legal issues of

- Virtual books and libraries (and ownership of virtual ideas)

and then on to fictional and practical experiments in changing identities as

- Cyberpunks/cyborgs

and finally to virtual places where newer forms of social, educational, and experimental identities can be explored and developed in

- MUDs and MOOs.

This sequence of themes best allows a glimpse, I think, into self-identities in terms of human-cum-virtual *bodies* in new *spaces* in an ever-changing technological-informational society.

 I more fully describe each of these themes at the beginning of each chapter and article. In an attempt to help readers deal with at times difficult subjects, I have placed questions and writing assignments at the end of each article instead of, as previously done, at the end of the chapter. (I solicited from the authors some of the questions by way of e-mail. I have included them as I received them.) Also, I have listed key terms at the beginning of each chapter and given brief definitions so as to help the reader navigate through strange seas of new terminologies and thoughts. The real "book" is out there on the Web, and it changes every nanosecond—with old links going dead and new links being established—as the world's library of babel comes into being while perpetually becoming. Finally, in some of the writing assignments, I have invited students to write for the *CyberReader* Web site. If their articles based on the readings are acceptable to me and to Allyn & Bacon, then we will publish them at the site, so that the student-readers can add to the library.

VVitanza@aol.com

To Students and Teachers/Facilitators

he purpose of this book is to introduce you to the Internet (the Net) and the World Wide Web (www). Unlike many such books on the market, however, *CyberReader* invites you to reflect on the technology that has made available this new mode of information and the rapid changes that come with it. More simply put, this book is about *change*—about how technology is extending our lives and everything around us geometrically. Exponentially.

Years ago, my family and I were invited next door to watch television. Our neighbors were the first on our block to purchase what was much later to be called the "boob tube." The screen was nine inches across and the image had a green tint. Every few minutes our neighbor had to jump up and adjust the rabbit ears (the antennae). We were all blown away. It was magic. It was as if our neighbor were pulling images out of a hat! For days on end, I gave my family no peace: we had to have a TV and that was all there was to it. But my parents kept saying that they thought it best to wait until television "was perfected." I noticed that the phrase was being repeated by a lot of people. Just about all of us were waiting for things to be perfected! (The same argument was used a few years later about color television.)

There's no doubt that things have changed and are changing so rapidly that anyone waiting for anything technological to be perfected would miss model after new improved model and perhaps the thing itself morphing into something totally different. Morphing equals metamorphosis equals "a transformation, as by magic or sorcery." Speed!

In the computer business there is "Moore's Law," which states that microcompressors double their power (speed and overall capability) and get twice as cheap (assuming the absence of a monopoly) every eighteen months. Figure out the math on that one: Where will we be technologically in five years, ten years, or twenty years?

A few years ago, I thought about getting a fax machine when I heard about the students in China during the Tiananmen Square revolt using that technology to communicate to the outside world. I never bought one. The other day, I bought a new modem with a baud rate of 28,000 and with it I was given some extra software that allows faxing. My computer (an LCIII, an outdated Mac) now has the capability to fax and to download information at a rate that seems like a blink of an eye on my black-and-white 19″ monitor. Shortly after purchasing my new modem, however, I read in the newspaper a long article on a new service known as ISDN (integrated services digital network) that would eventually be available in our area. I was crushed when the author of the article wrote: "I put an impressive Pipeline 50 router on my PC and connected to my Internet service provider at speeds up to 128 kilobits per second, nearly nine times faster than a 14.4 modem"! I read on to find exactly how much it was going to cost me to have this new thing: hundreds of $$$$. I called my service provider for my personal PPP connection (to the Internet and www) to inquire whether or not the company could provide this service. A representative said yes and for hundreds of $$$$, but to wait a few months and it would only cost hundreds of ¢¢¢¢. I decided to wait for things to be perfected! After all, I had just jumped from a 2400 baud rate to 28,000 rate! I could wait. Sure I could! And be momentarily satisfied with the speed that I had.

(As I write this, I am mocking myself. I am well aware of the stupidity of all this. At the same time, however, I am aware, as John Perry Barlow says, that there is no way to stop any of this technology and the speed it generates. If I were to say, like a good neo-Luddite, that it could be and ought to be stopped, I would equally have to mock myself for believing that I could stop with a sword what amounts to a tidal wave. I am well aware that a single human being stopped a line of tanks in Tiananmen Square, but I am also aware that technology broadcasted this event to the world over. Speaking, writing, books, fax machines, television, the Internet—all are technologies that determine our lives. As Marshall McLuhan said: the medium is the message.)

But all these examples of speed and change are child's play in comparison to other things technological. This book, at times, will introduce many readers to the bizarre or weird or what is also called the "edge" or "fringe." Besides inviting you to think about some of the most basic concepts such as freedom of expression and how to realize it on the Internet, this book will also introduce you to such fringe philosophies and sciences as

- extropianism and transhumanism
- nanotechnology
- crash culture
- cyberpunks
- hackers and crackers
- cyberdelics
- teledildonics, and so on

It can get even more bizarre, strange, and for many people wonderful (as in full of wonder). All of this wonderment (and yes, at times, hype) is the result of breathtaking speed.

It is this kind of speed—approaching that of light and beyond—that makes such a book very difficult to write and to edit. I have been painfully aware that any article or topic/theme I select may be obsolete as soon as the book appears. After all, the production of this book takes a long time—not only for me to write, edit, and get permissions from publishers and authors to reprint their work, but also for the publisher to produce the physical thing we call a "book," what you are holding in your hands. To complicate matters further, this book is about what is out on the World Wide Web, about particular websites or packets of digitized information on the www, which change so rapidly. Essentially, this book with all its URLs (uniform resource locators, telephone numbers) is somewhat comparable to a telephone directory of the world that has millions of residents listed in it who, as a way of life, are *nomadic* and constantly disconnecting and reconnecting their services and telephone numbers. Here today; gone and morphed into something else tomorrow! That's speed and change.

Are there any constants?

I would like to think that our discussions about this technology, as manifested in the articles that I have selected and on the www itself, do have some "constants." The articles deal with basic historicized issues such as time and space, the actual and the virtual, freedom of access to information versus censorship, identity and privacy, sex and gender, and the like. Our different takes on each of these may change, but as issues they have remained pretty much constant. Our URLs or e-mail addresses (eddresses) may change, but the search engines (directories) for locating our new ones only change in their increased abilities to locate the new addresses.

Therefore, while this has not been an easy book to put together, my publisher and editor and I have worked hard at anticipating problems and solving them before they arise. That is why we have decided to make this book not only an actual book in print but also a virtual, updated set of news and notes about the book at our Website <http://www.abacon.com>. That's right: with the support of Allyn & Bacon, I will be able to update this book constantly. When new articles that supplement or complement those that I have included here come out, I can cite them or, if possible with permission, place them out at the *CyberReader* Web site and make links to articles that are new on the www. Likewise, when URLs no longer reach their destination, I can put in the new URLs, if available, and constantly update the list with still newer sites on the www. Though the actual book is fixed within each edition, the virtual part of the book on the www will constantly change as required.

But there is another reason for having made this anthology both an actual book and a virtual, updated set of news and notes about the book. Books are not obsolete. Someday they may very well be in museums, but not in the foreseeable future. (This issue is discussed in chapter 5.) Books have become audiotapes and may become—and of course already are—compact disks (CDs), but magazines and books will still be around for a long while.

(There is speed, but there is nostalgia. And there is the impulse toward differences and choices.) But a book that is actual and virtual at the same time can be of great value because it allows us to see the differences between books on paper and on monitors, books with words as atoms of ink and as bits of pixels; because it allows us to see the differences among a flat presentation of words/text (as in this book itself), a simulated version of hypertext (as we have attempted in a few cases in this book, say, with the introductions and other sections), and a virtual hypertext on the www (which we have done by placing the introduction to this book at our Web site, the medium of the Web itself).

To be sure, we will not have thought of everything, and that's why we have also placed out on the *CyberReader* Web site the means for you to communicate with us, to leave us a message, to tell us what you would like to see in forthcoming editions or on the Web site. We hope that you enjoy the book and its virtual updates.

■ FAQS (FREQUENTLY ASKED QUESTIONS):

---

1. What if I know absolutely nothing about computers, e-mail, and all that? What should I do?

Well, you have done the first thing by signing up for a course. (If you are reading this book without benefit of a teacher/facilitator and a course, then you might find such a course.) What you should do is—simply put—*ask for help.* Ask your instructor/facilitator or someone in your class. There is, however, often a gender bias built into our cultural attitudes about things technological: men are supposed to know, women are not. (This issue is discussed in chapter 4.) Therefore, if you are male, and another male or a female asks for help, *help that person!* Help both yourself and others in creating an actual and a virtual community. At times, it can be very difficult to ask for help, but you must. When I wanted to learn about the Internet, I asked one of my female graduate students and she became my facilitator. In the spirit of freeware and shareware, share what you know.

---

2. What if we have only Lynx as a browsing program at our university and therefore only text without graphics or sound?

The book is written on the assumption that most people with access to the Web at various universities have only *Lynx*. If, however, you have access via a *Mosaic* or *Netscape* browser, then all this will be much easier for you. Instead of using the arrow keys ($\rightarrow \downarrow \uparrow \leftarrow$) to navigate by way of the hot links (boldface type), all you have to do is point at the icons or underlined words and click. If you still are on *Lynx*, think of it this way: the best way to learn how to drive an automobile is with a stick or standard transmission. Thereafter, when an automatic transmission is available, driving (browsing) will be a snap. Or at least that's what I told myself when I started out with *Lynx*! To research this book, I used both *Lynx* and *Netscape* 1.1.

3. How should we or I read CyberReader?

We suggest that you look through the table of contents and then skim the book. If you are already familiar with the Internet (sending e-mail) and the www, then you might want to just skim Appendix A (CyberSearch). If not, then perhaps you might want to read through this section first. After that, you can read the book from top to bottom or read the chapters in the order that interests you. (There are two possible exceptions: you might want to begin with chapter 1 and you might want to read and work on chapters 2 and 3 in succession.) The sequence that you follow in reading the book will, of course, give you a different impression of *CyberReader.* Also, you should try to read all of the material in one chapter or section together. Again, these are only sug-gestions; at times you may want to surf intuitively from one interest to another.

4. What should I do if I keep finding words (jargon) I don't understand?

Every attempt has been made to define terms, or at least to suggest, especially about elusive ones, what they might mean. But if you still find yourself at a loss when reading, we suggest you try Appendix B (the Glossary). If you do not find any help there, then you might try some of the URLs that we have supplied for dictionaries or glossaries on the www.

5. Is there a Web site on the Net where I can find FAQs about FAQs?

Yes, it's *World Wide Web FAQs* <http://sunsite.unc.edu/boutell/faq/www_faq.html>. And we will have a FAQs link on the Allyn & Bacon *(CyberReader)* Web site that will extend those already begun here. Just point your browser to <http://www.abacon.com/~cyber>, and we'll see you there.   :)>=

■ A C K N O W L E D G M E N T S

I would like to thank Jenny Bay, Collin Brooke, Diane Davis, Cynthia Haynes, Beth Kolko, Thomas Rickert, David Rieder, Alan Taylor, and my English 3371–72 classes for their suggestions and, in general, for their help. I would especially like to thank my wife, Toni, and my youngest son, Roman, for their help and understanding while I worked on this edition. I am appreciative of the assistance given me by John Perry Barlow, Jay Bolter, Amy Bruckman, Julian Dibbell, David Downing, Sen. J. James Exon, Chris Goggans, Ted Gup, Donna Haraway, Andrew Harnack, James Harrington, Michael Heim, Susan Herring, Eugene Kleppinger, Tom Maddox, Dinty Moore, Lisa Nakamura, Howard Rheingold, Douglas Rushkoff, Mark Slouka, Richard Thieme, Sherry Turkle, Janice Walker, Benjamin Wooley, and many, many others. Thanks to Kris Blair, Bowling Green State University; Susan Halter, Delgado Community College; Charles Hill, University of Wisconsin, Oshkosh; Christine Hult, Utah State University; Bob Timm, Baruch College; Cindy Wambeam, New Mexico State University; and Jay Wooten, Kent State University at Salem for their reviews. Similarly, I would like to thank Joe Opiela, Rebecca Ritchey, Susan Brown, Merrill Peterson, and everyone at Allyn & Bacon.

—Victor J. Vitanza

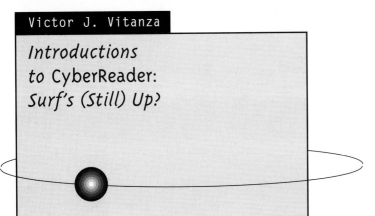

Victor J. Vitanza

Introductions to CyberReader: Surf's (Still) Up?

John Dewey worked to restore education to its primitive, pre-print phase. He wanted to get the student out of the passive role of consumer of uniformly packaged learning. In fact, Dewey in reacting against passive print culture was surf-boarding along on the new electronic wave.

—Marshall McLuhan, *The Gutenberg Galaxy*

Cyberia is frightening to everyone. Not just to technophobes, rich businessmen, midwestern farmers, and suburban house-wives, but, most of all, to the boys and girls hoping to ride the crest of the informational wave.

Surf's up.

—Douglas Rushkoff, *Cyberia*

Hi, call me Sophist@utarlg.uta.edu. I have many signatures, such as R. U. Rhetoricus?, R. U. Sophisticus?, or Vic Vit, Rotciv, saVVy, vvictor, Victa Nyanza, vEager, v///ger, Vaud-Ville, BigChief Tablet, and so on.

I am writing two introductions here: One for the traditional reader, who wants just the basic, safe, vanilla approach to using *CyberReader;* another for the off-the-wall reader, who wants to take risks and see this book in different ways. (This introduction can be found on the Allyn & Bacon Web site, under *CyberReader,* and in hypertext format, html.)

Let's call the first introduction the "Bill Gates" way; the second, the "Timothy Leary" way.

Let's **split the screen,** as————or———— Let's **split the scene,** as

"Bill" would say, so as to divide up our tasks to better control them. As "Bill" morphs into Mr. Bill, sitting in a chair, rocking back and forth, sometimes moderately while at other times intensely, he types onto his monitor:

Just think of this book that you have in your hands right now as

"Tim" would say, to dis/engage in virtual stand-up philosophy. As he puts on his datagloves and cybergoggles, and then turns on and tunes in, "Tim" boots up, up, and away:

Just don't think of this actual book that you have in your hands right

CyberReader 98+. It will provide you with everything you could ever need or desire to begin thinking about the subjects of Cyberspace and Virtual Reality—the two main concepts that *CR 98+* introduces and elaborates on. Though these concepts overlap, there are some distinguishing characteristics, which are made and elaborated on in chapter 1 of the readings. However, here's a very quick notion of how the two differ:

Cyberspace, according to William Gibson, who coined the phrase, is "consensual hallucination" and

virtual reality (VR), according to Jaron Lanier, who coined the phrase, is "post-symbolic communication."

These phrases probably tell you at this point very little, but they will begin to tell you perhaps more and more of what the future holds for all of us as you proceed through the readings and make forays on the World Wide Web (WWW or W3). And all with my help. Just follow my directions at the Web site and you will take a step into a world that will transform you!

The purpose of *CR 98+* is to introduce you to the crucial issues that are associated with each of these concepts, to introduce you specifically to a multifaceted set of "readings" on each topic, and to send you out to the WWW so as to discover more of that conversation but in a virtual community that grows by the thousands every day.

now as a book at all; think of it as a surfboard.

Now climb on top and catch this big wave I'm sending your way as Gene Roddenberry and I circle the earth in our capsule.

Back in the sixties, lots of us were, if I might say, a little leery of technology, except that which produced better things through chemistry. We were called the counterculture. I don't remember much else about the sixties. But today we sixties people live on. Now many of us take in large doses of electricity. Ecstatic electricity. We drop pixels of electronic LSD. But I wander.

I want to introduce *CyberReader* so that all of you who read and study this book can become cybernauts.

Back in the sixties, we of the counterculture knew we were embarking on an important trip into the future. Future-hacqing! If you look at the history of the development of consciousness, earlier generations moved like snails across the centuries. They surfed tiny waves. Why, it took about a century and a half for earlier generations to move from cave drawings to handwriting. Today, we surf tidal waves. · Why, in this century alone we have advanced from black-and-white television to color TVs (with colors more real than real) to virtual reality. Whereas we used to watch TV, it now watches us! While we used to sit in front of the TV, we now "sit" *in* it. We are capable of being in its virtual space. (We are beaming ourselves up and down and all over the virtualscape.) Soon we will evolve into cyborgs, a hybrid of half protoplasm and half silicon.

Back before the sixties, after WW2—oh, say, between 1950 and 1965—there were the "beats," who

Think of *CR 98+* as your gateway to cyberspace. Or think of it as your book-to-human-to-computer interface. Think of it as sort of a "Holodeck" (as you might remember from *Star Trek: The Next Generation*), a library room of a book that you enter that leads you to virtuality and increases your virtuosity as a reader of actual books and a surfer of virtual ones.

On deck you will find seven chapters and three appendices. You are presently in the introduction. Before reading any of the chapters, you might want to read very carefully, if you haven't already, the preface to *CR 98+*, and then read very quickly the appendices, both of which will give you an additional sense of what to expect.

Here are the rooms:

Introduction: "Surf's (Still) Up?"

Chapter 1: Cyberspace and Virtual Reality

Chapter 2: Virtual Communities/ Societies and Identities

Chapter 3: Freedom/Censorship

Chapter 4: Sexual Politics

Chapter 5: Virtual Books and Libraries

Chapter 6: Cyberpunk/Cyborgs

Chapter 7: MUDS/MOOS

Appendix A: CyberSearch

Appendix B: CyberGlossary

Appendix C: Bibliography of Cyberspace

were "low-tech, but early psychedelic explorers." After that generation, between 1965 and 1975, there were the hippies, who were, as I said, "psychedelic, but anti–high-tech." After that high wave, between 1975 and 1990, there were the cyberpunks, who were "high-tech electronic." Now we are getting to *you,* your generation, the biggest wave to date in the history of the development of human consciousness. Between 1990 and 2005 there is you, who I call the "New Breed" and who are "psychedelic (cyberdelic), super high-tech, with interest in smart drugs, brain machines, and the Internet."

Well, this is how I survey recent history in my book *Chaos and Cyber Culture.* VV includes a selection from that book here in *CyberReader* for you to read.

Excuse me, I keep forgetting that I am supposed to be introducing VV's *CyberReader.* Actually and virtually, it is the phirst and still revolutionary one of a kind. It's a smart book. VV nudges especially those of you who are incipiently of the "New Breed" from books as well as TV to simulated books to virtual books out to the W3. Each wave that you are asked to surf gets a little bigger. Perhaps a little more frightening.

But remember, you are the New Breed! What VV wants you to do, and your own generation wants, just as recent generations extolled, is

TFYQA.

To think for yourself; question authority! So when you read and surf with this book . . . TFYQA. Live up to that code not only in your everyday lives but especially while reading the authors in this book, many of whom themselves (by now) represent authority because they

So this is pretty cool, huh? If it's a little intimidating, remember: Don't be afraid, for I am here to help. Just think of me as your friendly lifeguard making the superhighway safe for you and others. So go ahead and paddle out, because the surf's up and ready for you to enjoy.

—"Bill"
(8-o

questioned authority. Now you must question them just as you must question me. Surfing and questing and hacking are what we cybernauts are about. Extend (hyper-) your mind, and if you think all this is only hype, then surf with that thought. TFYQA! Make VVaves!

—"Tim"
(1920–1996)

Unsplitting the page (monitor) for a moment, let's think of the names of other personages who would radically reintroduce and recombine ways of thinking about *CyberReader*. How about:

Ned Ludd?

Sandy Stone?

Christopher Columbus?

Gene Roddenberry?

Winona Ryder?

HAL?

R2D2?

Any of the replicants in *Bladerunner*?

And let's insist on *you* and your (actual/virtual/elite) class!

Etc.?

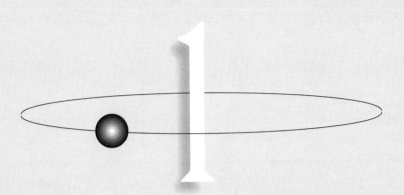

Cyberspace and Virtual Reality

Benjamin Woolley ◆ **"Cyberspace"**

Michael Heim ◆ **"The Essence of VR"**

Douglas Rushkoff ◆ **"Seeing Is Beholding"**

Richard Thieme ◆ **"Stalking the UFO Meme"**

We need first to feel comfortable—but not
too comfortable, as if we ever could—with two puzzling terms: *cyberspace*
and *virtual reality*. Before we can understand these terms and how other
authors think about them, it will be necessary to understand an ancient
distinction made by Plato among *ideal, actual,* and *sham* (virtual). Briefly put,
for Plato there had to be a realm of ideal forms for all things. His example
in the *Republic* (Bk 10) is that of a bed. There is "bedness" (as an abstraction,
an ideal, the "really real") before there can be an actual bed made by a
carpenter. In this way, an actual bed, therefore, is once removed from an
ideal, or the idea of a bed. For Plato, a painting of a bed, however, is twice
removed and hence it is a sham bed, a simulated bed, a virtual bed. And
according to him, it is of no value except to confuse matters. Consequently,
he stated that while the carpenter would be allowed in his utopia, the painter
would not.

Now for the term *cyberspace* (a.k.a. psyberspace). There is agreement that it
was coined and popularized by William Gibson in his novel *Neuromancer*. For
Gibson, it means "consensual hallucination." (Note how problematic the term
"hallucination" is.) "Consensual" means that we—many of us—agree or that
we give consent to what Gibson calls a hallucination. But what does Gibson
mean in general when he uses these words?

Perhaps the best way to answer this question is to take an example from
our everyday lives: namely, that consensual hallucination that we call the
telephone conversation. Prior to the invention of the telephone, people had
to speak in each other's presence, that is, speak face-to-face (F2F). Of
course, they could write to each other as well, but in this example we are
trying to understand speech as a mode of communication (orality), not
writing (literacy).

When people first used the telephone it was very strange, for they could
speak to each other in their spatial absence from each other. At first, the
distance was from room to room. Then from one house to another. Then

eventually from the moon to earth and back. Today we take telephone conversations for granted and specifically in relation to where the conversation is taking place.

Let's say that we are driving through city traffic and talking on our cellular phones. While we are actually in traffic, surrounded by fast-moving steel all around us, we are virtually having a conversation with a second or even three or more parties elsewhere, perhaps in other automobiles in other parts of town, in buildings in town, or even in buildings in Europe or Asia. But the question arises, Where is the conversation taking place? Gibson and others would say that it is taking place in the "matrix," which is the telephone system (that is, the wires, fiber cables, infrared rays, satellites, and so on). In other words, when we speak over the phone, our conversation is *in* the matrix in all those interconnections. However, the matrix cannot simply be reduced to this hardware (fiber cables and satellites), for as Gibson conceives it, the matrix is informational space.

As subtle as this distinction might sound, it has a profound impact on us. Plato would definitely not like the telephone, any more than he liked writing, as a substitute for face-to-face (F2F) dialogue. Both the telephone and writing are substitutes for actual, face-to-face communication, which would be only one time removed from the ideal, and Plato believed that only the philosopher was capable of knowing that ideal. In this platonic point of view then, cyberspace can be seen as simulated or sham space.

This distinction will take on many different ramifications as we move, in our considerations of cyberspace, from the telephone to the fax machine to electronic mail (e-mail) to Internet Relay Chat rooms to multiuser dungeons (MUDs) and MUD object oriented (MOO) and I see you—you see me (ICU-UCMe) communications. Moreover, the distinction will become more socially and politically clear when we consider how the U.S. Government, as well as other governments, has attempted to pass laws governing this space called cyberspace.

Setting this term aside for a while, let's look at the next term, *virtual reality* (VR), which was coined by Jaron Lanier. Whereas the term *cyberspace* may have had its origins in Gibson's cyberpunk science fiction, Howard Rheingold suggests that VR had its origins in science. It is a matter of technology that can create the illusion of actually being in another possible world while remaining in the actual world. There are many forms of VR, some that allow a person to be totally immersed and others that allow a person to be only partially immersed.

For example, a person can put on cybergloves (a.k.a. datagloves), head-mounted displays, and sometimes body suits and can by way of a computer program sense being in other environments and among other people or creatures. A person can, in other words, sense being in other possible worlds. For a while, VR was available in arcades as an amusement game. People could purchase time wearing the head-mounted displays and run around shooting at each other with rayguns. It was all an expensive game of simulation. VR games can still be found in particular venues, though they are not as popular as they used to be. Some corporations and, in general, the military find VR exceptionally important and practical.

Pilots, for example, are trained and retrained in flight simulators. Instead of donning goves, head-mounted displays, and body suits, pilots will get into what on the outside looks like a box-shaped room on pneumatic stilts. Once the pilot is inside the box, the surroundings have the actual look and feel of a real cockpit. The window, however, is a 180-degree VR screen on which various scenarios can be displayed and manipulated by an instructor sitting at a console behind the pilot. The boxlike room on stilts can be thrown in any number of directions, simulating the movements and feel of sharp turns, dives, and most frighteningly, a complete loss of control and power. (I have seen a seasoned Army Air Force pilot step out of a flight simulator all ashen in the face. I can only imagine what hostile scenarios his instructor must have put him through to better prepare him to survive and successfully complete his mission. If he did not respond in a reflex manner to the aeronautical problem that his instructor threw his way, he perhaps crashed a "virtual" crash. Though his death might have been virtual, he nonetheless must have felt close to real death.)

VR can be experienced not only in a VR suit and headgear and not only in a simulator, but also on a computer screen. Again, the military uses VR for simulated tank battles. And it uses VR for "Cool Wars," which are very real hot wars with many dead. During the Gulf War the tank battles were in some cases led and conducted from consoles at headquarters. And as we saw in television reports, pilots waged war with the same VR technology used in part for video games of war at our local arcades.

Now, what is the difference between cyberspace and virtual reality?

Our experience of cyberspace, though we have only recently begun to use the term, is older than our experience of virtual reality. The easy difference between cyberspace and virtual reality is that in VR we can *actually believe* we are *in* it. When I have talked on the telephone, I have had no sense of being *in* the matrix. I have always known where I was and known that my interlocutor was physically elsewhere. However, when I have worn a VR glove and headgear or when I have gotten into a flight simulator with my students, I have had a sense of being *in* another place that I previously was not in.

Notice that I said in the second sentence of the preceding paragraph "actually . . . in [VR]." Herein lies a confusion of not only terms but realities in

VR. While in a sense my body is *in* the glove and headgear, my mind is *in* the VR matrix, telling me—creating the illusion for me—that my body is there also. Therefore, when we are in VR, we can experience both cyberspace and virtual reality.

For many, including Plato and even Aristotle, this illusion of being elsewhere is not good. However, many people argue that when we are actually in VR we are not imitating a real action but are in a completely different, if *virtual,* reality. At this point, the differences of opinion and argument become philosophical, though nonetheless very pragmatic. Let us just say that, more than before, because of our technologies, we have not reality but realities. Hence, we get not only such phrases as Gibson's "consensual hallucination" and similarly "consensual reality," but also "designer realities" and "electronic LSD."

Many critics argue that because we are losing the distinction between reality and virtual reality, we are losing our grip on reality. They argue that we must put the brakes on VR. Others exclaim, however, that there are no brakes to apply. Still other critics argue that VR is liberating, allowing us to steer ourselves clear of would-be platonic philosopher-kings. (The Greek root *cyber-* means "steersman" or "pilot.") However, while the technology—whether it be speaking, writing, typing, word processing, simulating, or some other technology—enables us or "empowers" us in many wonderful and helpful ways, it also drives us. But to where, when we have lost our traditional notion of "where" as an actual place? Real and virtual, space and time seem to be imploding (in which differences collapse), as Jean Baudrillard and others suggest. Where has "where" gone? Have we passed through the looking glass? Can we ever find our way back to where and who we were? Or do we even want to?

I leave these questions, along with others, for your consideration after you have read the following articles. To be sure, these two concepts, as well as others, are difficult, but they are crucial to your understanding of what apparently has been and still is *taking place.*

■ SUMMARY OF KEY TERMS

actuality (reality): Our consensual perception of the world as mediated only through the senses.

cyber-: A prefix from the Greek, meaning *pilot* or *one who steers.*

cyberspace: William Gibson coined the term in the cyberpunk novel *Neuromancer* (1984). He called it a "consensual hallucination." Cyberspace is informational-data space made available by electrical circuits and computer networks. Therefore, cyberspace, or cyberreality, is mediated not just through the senses, as reality is, but also through these circuits and networks. In other words, the neural circuits of the brain and sense organs are mediated through these electrical circuits and computer networks. This informational-data space is often referred to as the matrix.

F2F: An abbreviated expression meaning a face-to-face (actual or real) meeting.

fleshmeet: Same as F2F. But the term is used in the context of that moment when people have been communicating online through e-mail or chat rooms or MOOS and finally decide to meet for the first time F2F or as a group at a real geographical site.

IRL: An abbreviated expression meaning "in real life," as opposed to cyberspace.

matrix: Etymologically, this term is feminine, referring to the mother (*mater*) and womb. In relation to cyberspace, the matrix is the wires, cables, and satellites where and through which communications over the radio, telephone, and television take place.

meme (a.k.a. metavirus): A word based on *mimesis,* imitation: ideas are like viruses as they spread from host mind to host mind. This idea of *memes* is based on Richard Dawkins's book *The Selfish Gene,* in which Dawkins says, "Memes are tunes, ideas, catch-phrases, clothes fashions, ways of making pots or of building arches. Just as genes propagate themselves in the gene pool by leaping from body to body via sperms or eggs, so memes propagate themselves in the meme pool by leaping from brain to brain via a process which . . . can be called imitation" (192).

simulation: A pretense to, feigned attempt at, or imitation of an action. A conversation over the telephone by way of cyberspace is a simulated F2F communication. Or a flight in an "Apache simulator" over enemy territory is a simulated flight in hostile territory.

virtual reality: The term was coined by Jaron Lanier. VR is a computer-simulated world. To achieve full immersion *in* VR, a person must wear a data helmet, gloves, and body suit. To achieve partial immersion, a person may enter a flight simulator, experiencing the physical movements of an airplane or helicopter flight and seeing the "actual" but *virtual* view of the terrain.

This article is chapter 6 of Benjamin Woolley's Virtual Worlds: A Journey in Hype and Hyperreality (Oxford: Blackwell, 1992). The book is one of the first investigations of the virtual for a general audience. The chapter titles include such topics as simulation, virtuality, artificial intelligence, interface, hypertext, fiction, hyperreality, and reality. It is important to note that Woolley includes reality as a topic that needs to be explained. Given the impact of the simulation and all other things virtual, reality is no longer a topic or common-sensical starting place that we can take for granted.

In the introduction to the book, Woolley writes: "On 7 May, 1987, the U.S. multinational Proctor & Gamble submitted Olestra, a new food substitute, to the American Food and Drug Administration (FDA) for approval. Olestra . . . promised what every dieter desired, the realization of an impossible dream: fat-free fat." And then, more to the point, he states:

This book is about . . . artificial-ization, of making dreams come true, of "imagineering," as the Disney Corporation calls it. What are the extent and limits of the artificial? Is there, can there be, any contact with reality when it is possible to make fat that is not fat, when the fake becomes indistinguishable from—even more authentic than—the original, when computers can create synthetic worlds that are more realistic than the real world, when technology scorns nature? (2)

Woolley's discussion is still in many ways the best all-around introduction to things virtual, simulated, artificial, sham—that is, all things that are hoped to be an improvement on the reality of nature. (2)

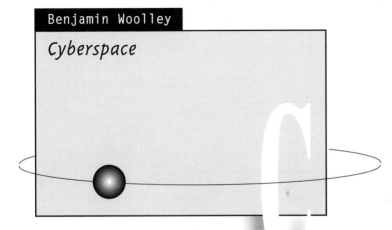

Benjamin Woolley

Cyberspace

yberspace has a nice buzz to it," said William Gibson, recalling his use of the term in his fiction, "it's something that an advertising man might of thought up, and when I got it I knew that it was slick and essentially hollow and that I'd have to fill it up with meaning."[1] By the beginning of the 1990s it was so full of meaning, it was fit to burst. In his original use of the term in *Neuromancer*, Gibson had famously described it as a "consensual hallucination"—a term he left ill defined. It was, he later said, meant to suggest "the point at which media [flow] together and surround us. It's the ultimate extension of the exclusion of daily life. With cyberspace as I describe it you can literally wrap yourself in media and not have to see what's really going on around you."

It was a fictional rendition of Ivan Sutherland's original concept of the "ultimate display," a form of display that presented information to all the senses in a form of total immersion. However, Gibson had extended Sutherland's idea of a "looking glass into a mathematical wonderland" to embrace the entire universe of information: "A graphic representation of data abstracted from the banks of every computer in the human system. Unthinkable complexity. Lines of light ranged in the nonspace of the mind, clusters and constellations of data. Like city lights receding."[2]

In the rhetoric of the virtual realists, this "nonspace" was not simply a mathematical space nor a fictional metaphor but a new frontier, a very real one that was open to exploration and, ultimately, settlement. "Cyberspace . . . is presently inhabited almost exclusively by mountain men, desperados and vigilantes, kind of a rough bunch," said John Perry Barlow. "And, as long as that's the case, it's gonna be the Law of the Wild in there. . . . Whenever you make a financial transaction, really it involves electronic data representing money. So we feel that the way to minimize anxiety, and to make certain that the freedoms we have in the so-called real world stay intact in the virtual world, is to make it inhabitable by ordinary settlers. You know, move the homesteaders in."[3] To do this, Barlow had even set up the Electronic Frontier Foundation with Mitch Kapor, the founder of the software house Lotus, one of the most successful companies to emerge out of the personal computer era and one, ironically, roundly condemned by the hacker radical Richard Stallman for its illiberal policy toward copyright.

In the twilight of the space age, cyberspace was becoming the new final frontier, and virtual reality was the Enterprise. NASA's key role in the development of the technology, right at the time of the *Challenger* and *Hubble* humiliations, when the agency no longer commanded the emblematic heights (or generous financial backing) it had enjoyed during the 1960s, was heavily symbolic. Like astronomical space, cyberspace was only dimly perceived by ordinary people, but there was a promise that technology would one day provide them with access to it. Day trips to the moon having proved unfeasible, attention was turning to mystery tours of the digital domain.

What, then, is cyberspace? The actual term is technically unimportant. Other phrases are used synonymously: cyberia, virtual space, virtual worlds, dataspace, the digital domain, the electronic realm, the information sphere. One can examine its etymological entrails for meaning—"cyber," meaning steersman, coming from "cybernetics," the study of control mechanisms—but that yields very little. A more productive strategy is to try to discover why the terms have acquired such currency. How did a word that Gibson had thrown into his work almost casually when he coined it acquire, within a few years, such value?

One interpretation of cyberspace is that it concerns the annihilation of space. "As electrically contracted," wrote Marshall McLuhan in 1964, "the globe is no more than a village."[4] "After three thousand years of explosion, by means of fragmentary and mechanical technologies, the Western world is imploding. During the mechanical ages we had extended our bodies in space. Today, after more than a century of electric technology, we have extended our central nervous system itself in a global embrace, abolishing both space and time as far as our planet is concerned."

Neglected in the 1970s, when the world was probably too diverted by shortages of energy to concern itself with ideas of electrical contraction, this concept of the global village began to become fashionable again in the 1980s. It was seen as the perfect expression of the new era of world finance and international telephone networks. In the 1980s, the financial system had migrated onto computer and communications networks, satellite and cable links that spanned the globe, capable of carrying data and voice, creating the conditions that produced the October 1987 stock market crash, where a fall in the New York stock exchange precipitated a collapse in prices that tripped off markets around the world within hours. "In principle," wrote Mark Poster, a Californian professor of history, in 1990, "information is now instantly available all over the globe and may be stored and retrieved as long as electricity is available. Time and space no longer restrict the exchange of information. McLuhan's 'global village' is technically feasible."[5]

The imagery of the "global village" is seductive, suggesting that the technology of communications will collapse dispersed urban alienation into the cozy confines of a pre-industrial age. It suggests the emergence of a whole new type of working environment, the "telecottage," set in rural surroundings, far away from the jams yet part of the world's information traffic. Telecommunications companies have even started setting up such cottages in remote areas such as the Scottish Highlands. Certain white-collar jobs, claim the global villagers, entail nothing more than the exchange of information—meetings, paperwork, making decisions—all of which can easily be communicated over the telephone network. As a result, a tele-worker's attachment to the job becomes a factor of his or her connection to the network rather than proximity to the company office.

But Marshall McLuhan expected more from the idea of the global village than a new type of post-industrial working environment. He saw technology as an extension of the body. Just as the wheel is an extension of the foot, the telescope an extension of the eye, so the communications network is an extension of the nervous system. So, as the communications network has spread across the globe, so has our neural network. Television has become our eyes, the telephone our mouths and ears; our brains are the interchange for a nervous system that stretches across the whole world—we have breached the terminating barrier of the skin.

Marshall McLuhan saw technology as an extension of the body. Just as the wheel is an extension of the foot, the telescope an extension of the eye, so the communications network is an extension of the nervous system.

The technology that has made this possible is the network. Networks are not new: there have, presumably, been social ones since the dawn of society. What is new is the technology of communication that has enabled information of any type to be carried from one place to another regardless of their distance. Such networks are electronic, and carry their messages instantly by wire, by optical fiber, by radio and microwave. In computing, it is the network that is seen as providing the next great step in the technology's inevitable progress. Personal computing will become what Steve Jobs has dubbed "interpersonal computing."

Networks first found their way into computing via the development of a system to connect computers deployed in projects funded by the American Advanced Research Projects Agency, ARPA. This ARPAnet was originally designed to allow ARPA researchers to share data, but was increasingly used to exchange messages, which in turn helped develop a sense of community between the geographically scattered centers they worked in. This was, in a sense, the world's first "virtual" community, existing only in its interaction over ARPAnet.

ARPAnet developed in two directions: it grew outward, to span the entire globe, coming to be called Internet. Internet is, for many, the model of what virtual communities can be like. Geography is irrelevant—so there are no "backwaters," no "provinces" excluded by the central metropolis. Hierarchy is irrelevant, because everyone has equal access to the network, and everyone is free to communicate with as few or as many people as they like.

ARPAnet also contracted, inspiring the development of the world's first "local area" network, "Ethernet." As the word "local" implies, geography has not quite been rendered irrelevant by telecommunication networks. The more information there is to carry and the further it has to go, the more it costs to carry it. Local area networks (LANs) were designed to carry a great deal of information across short distances—the distance between computers in the same office. Because of their carrying capacity—their "bandwidth"—they are able to create a much richer form of communication between the individual users, so rich, in fact, that on well-implemented local area networks, the distinction between each user's personal system and the network begins to blur. What belongs to whom in terms of files and facilities depends not on its physical location inside any particular machine, but upon the way it is organized across the LAN. In 1991, NeXT, the computer company set up by Steve Jobs after his departure from Apple, announced "Zilla," a program that enables a network of NeXT computers to act as a single, virtual supercomputer. A network of 100 NeXT machines was, according to Zilla's designer Richard Crandall, as powerful as a Cray 2, then the most powerful supercomputer in the world. A Zilla computer could, furthermore, have its power distributed between offices across the globe. With the development of optical fiber, which offers almost limitless bandwidth, as an alternative to wire, the possibility arose that this new form of "interpersonal" computing would truly render geography irrelevant and allow new forms of social as well as commercial interaction to emerge.

In the mid-1980s, NASA's Human Factors Research Division began working on developing what it provocatively called "telepresence." Telepresence was originally promoted as a way of controlling robots. Since it is better to send machines than humans into hazardous environments like space, the NASA research team aimed to provide a wrap-around technology that would give the machine operator the feeling of "being" in the place of the machine being operated. If, for example, a robot was being used to repair an external component on a shuttle or space station, the robot's cameras would be connected to a head-mounted display so that the wearer could see what he or she would see if actually there. Similarly, a glove or exoskeleton (that is, a series of hinges and struts clamped to the body, like an articulated splint) could be used to reproduce the wearer's movements in the robot's arm and hand or to provide tactile feedback, resisting the wearer's movements in accordance with the pressure exerted on the robot's limbs when it picks up an object. A sufficiently rich communication between the operator and the robot would, the NASA team hoped, result in the robot essentially becoming the operator's body; he or she would be "telepresent," instantly transported to wherever the robot was working.

No more watching television, but, as William Gibson put it, "doing" television. We could climb through the window of the world. Is this, then, cyberspace?

Since the communication between robot and operator is via an information link, perhaps you could be telepresent anywhere. Just plug the helmet and some sort of sensory bodysock into the telephone and television network and you would be away, literally, discovering the true meaning of McLuhan's limitless sensorium. No more watching television, but, as William Gibson put it, "doing" television. We could climb through the window of the world.

Is this, then, cyberspace? Is there really some sort of space, some sort of independent realm created by the interconnection of the world's information systems? Is this a metaphorical space or a real one?

Conventionally, we think of networks as transparent, as systems for conveying messages from one human being to another without in any way shaping their meaning.

McLuhan's other great contribution to the media age was the phrase: "The medium is the message." What he meant was that networks (or media—in other words, systems for carrying information) are not transparent. Television is not a window on the world; it does not simply show its audience pictures of events that happen to be taking place elsewhere. Rather, it actually has a role in determining what the audiences see and how they make sense of it. A game show or soap opera is not a natural event; it has been created specifically for the cameras, and only makes sense if seen on TV. (Studio audiences, one might think, are watching the event "for real," but in fact they need the prompting of an army of studio managers and warm-up artists to make up for what is, in fact, a very unreal event, constantly interrupted by retakes, filmed inserts and cutaways.)

On July 20, 1989, Wes Thomas, publicist for the magazine *Mondo 2000*, claimed that he had "unleashed the world's first media virus."[6] An unspecified source had told him of the spread of a particularly dangerous computer virus, variously called "October 12," "Datacrime" and "Columbus Day." A computer virus is extraordinarily like a biological one. A biological virus is a small strand of genetic code that uses the host organism's replicating mechanism to produce copies of itself, which are then spread to other host organisms via whatever medium they are able to use—say, the exchange of body fluids, as seems to be the case with HIV. A computer virus is similarly a strand of code, a computer program, that uses the computer's replicating mechanism to produce copies of itself, which are then spread to other host computers via whatever medium they are able to use, usually via floppy disks and the public networks used by enthusiasts to exchange software. The most significant difference between a computer virus and a biological one is that the former is written by a computer programmer for mischievous purposes, whereas the latter arises spontaneously in nature.

Thomas sent a note via electronic mail to two journalists alerting them to news of the computer virus, which he subsequently discovered would activate on October 12 in any year and wipe out the host computer's disk drives on the 13th, which in 1989 happened to fall on a Friday. As soon as the story appeared in the *San Francisco Examiner,* it was picked up by the world's press agencies. According to Thomas, the CNN cable news service (often described as the global village's local TV station) announced that "all PC computers would be wiped out at 12:01 A.M. on October 13th." The British tabloid, *Daily Star,* even featured the story on the front page of its October 5 issue, anticipating the spread of a "doomsday computer bug," and the BBC carried a news item on October 13 on the anticipated epidemic, which, as it turned out, amounted to no more than an outbreak of irregular behavior on a computer at the Royal National Institute for the Blind.

The interesting feature of the Friday the 13th virus was, of course, the way that the reporting of its spread was as much a feature of its epidemiology as the spread of the program itself. Thomas had released a story that was evidently highly contagious. Besides being a date of Christian significance (13 being the number at the Last Supper, and Friday the day of the Crucifixion), Friday the 13th had far more popular significance as the name of a successful series of Hollywood horror movies. The AIDS scare had also increased awareness of the threat of viruses. In the era of antibiotics and vaccines, the public perception of infection in countries like Britain and America had been that it was basically controllable, despite the continuous background presence of venereal disease. Few people realized just how little control medicine had over viral disease. AIDS changed all that. It also disinterred old attitudes about the links between disease and sin. The term "virus" was no longer simply a medical term, like "bacteria"; it had suddenly acquired a moral resonance. It was a resonance that was easily transferred to the computer virus. Like AIDS, we were all threatened with being tainted by the hacker's lack of moral hygiene. Infection was guilt.

The technological as well as the social climate provided the Friday the 13th virus with perfect breeding conditions. Since the international acceptance of the IBM Personal Computer as a technical standard, the vast majority of personal computers had become functionally identical: a homogeneous "species" had, in other words, emerged with very little variation to protect it from opportunistic infection. Worse, this technological monoculture was both dispersed, used across the Western world by the self-employed and the multinational alike, and highly connected by computer networks and dial-up computer services such as bulletin boards. The release of a virus capable of efficient reproduction in such an environment genuinely threatened widespread damage.

But not *that* much damage. Because the story had such mythical potency, the technical threat of the computer virus was wildly overstated by the news coverage. The world portrayed as under the greatest threat, the world of the corporate computer user, was in fact under the least threat, because most corporations get most of their software from authorized channels. The most vulnerable users were those who regularly swapped illicit software—the hackers, in other words, who were best able to spot any signs of infection and deal with them, and who in many people's eyes would be the deserving victims of any damage they caused.

More significant than the impact of the Friday the 13th virus was the increasing awareness, expressed by writers like Thomas, that the international media network was, like the computer network, not merely a passive communications system but an environment that, in many respects, had a life of its own. The virus story was a global village phenomenon. AIDS, a global village disease spread by international travel and the exchange of blood products, had created the conditions for its spread. It was introduced into an environment which was increasingly homogenized by global capitalism, and that, thanks to the sheer speed of turnover of the news agenda, was unable to build resistance. It was, in other words, evidence of the emergence of an artificial environment—something that McLuhan himself anticipated.

According to Richard Dawkins, a zoologist at Oxford University and the author of *The Selfish Gene*,[7] a feature common to all forms of life is the replicator, a mechanism that can store information and replicate it. The replicator for natural life is the gene, made up of DNA. An important distinction needs to be established in order to understand the concept of the replicator. There is the information to be replicated, called the genotype, and the product of that information being "expressed," the phenotype. The information encoded in the gene is the genotype. The organism it produces is the phenotype. The phenotype can be thought of as a set of tools which are there to make copies of the genotype. Our bodies, along with their reproductive apparatus, are the most obvious phenotypic expression of our genes. Dawkins called his book *The Selfish Gene* because, from a zoological perspective, living organisms are the product and servant of their genes. The genes that produce the most effective phenotypes for reproduction do best, because they spread. Those that do badly disappear.

Computer viruses are, like biological viruses, replicators in a special sense, because they are parasitical; they do not come packaged with the means of phenotypic expression. Nevertheless, it is easy to imagine a refinement of the computer virus that fits in exactly with the genotype/phenotype model. The virus program can be thought of as the genotype, and the effect it has on the computer when it is executed can be thought of as the phenotypic expression.

The program might even be miscopied, and the result might be a new version of the original computer virus program that, when executed, produces a phenotype that copies the virus more efficiently. The result would be the beginnings of evolution.

The unfolding scenario is a threatening one: the artificial environment created by computers will become host to a new, evolving lifeform, one that could spread uncontrolled through the world's networks. We should not, however, reassure ourselves with the thought that such a lifeform will confine itself to the realm of computers. Let us extrapolate further by introducing one of the most powerful of Dawkins's ideas: that of the extended phenotype.

The phenotypic effect of a gene is usually thought of as the body that carries the gene. But why stop there? Surely, argues Dawkins, anything that results from the gene's expression can be regarded as the phenotype.[8] Even something as large and inanimate as a beaver's dam is a genetic effect, one that contributes to the beaver gene's chances of reproduction. By the same token, could not a computer virus evolve some sort of extended phenotype? Suppose, for example, that a mutated virus caused the host system to behave in a way that prompted the computer user to indulge in some particularly vigorous file copying (perhaps it causes the system to crash a couple of times, which encourages the user to make more backup copies of infected files). Such a virus could spread further, and would do so because it, unlike other viruses, had evolved a mechanism for manipulating the world beyond the computer.

On the same day that Wes Thomas's media virus swept the globe, an event occurred that did seem to confirm that something mysterious was spreading through the global village.

There is no reason to suppose that evolution would stop there. Human users provide a perfect means of acquiring new reproductive resources. They are influenced by the computers—otherwise they would not use them—and could therefore be used in any way that escapes obvious detection to aid a particular virus's spread. This does not mean that viruses would turn computer users into mindless servants, any more than biological viruses that use us, as they surely do, to spread, have turned us into mindless servants. The point is that replicators are almost by definition opportunistic. Successful ones will take any opportunity they can to spread; that is what made them successful and is the reason they, unlike all the unsuccessful ones, have survived and evolved.

Although there is very little evidence that such replicators have yet colonized our computer systems, on the same day that Wes Thomas's media virus swept the globe, an event occurred that did seem to confirm that something mysterious was spreading through the global village.

On Friday, October 13, 1989, Wall Street went into free fall, throwing the world's financial markets into a state of chaos which, for many dealers, chillingly recalled the dark days of October 1987. The strange aspect of the 1989 crash was, however, the total absence of any apparent cause: the world economy was in pretty good shape and the European, Far Eastern as well as U.S. stock markets, until that point, appropriately stable. "Explanations abound," reported *Financial World.* "An isolated sequence, driven by events perhaps? An illogical fall with a fast return to reason? Or, a chilling thought, the reverse?"[9]

There was no possibility that the trigger was the computer virus. Computers had been implicated in the 1987 crash, when falling prices triggered systems programmed to sell shares that passed a particular price threshold, which in turn caused prices to fall further, which pushed share prices past yet lower thresholds, which triggered off yet more selling. This time, however, the computing equivalent of fire breaks should have ensured that such automatic trading systems were under control.

One possible cause, however, that the markets did not contemplate—perhaps could not contemplate—was that the 1989 crash was evidence that the world stock markets were, in effect, beyond human control. It has been increasingly hard to relate the movement of the markets to real economic conditions. Japan's Nikkei index, for example, suffered terrible falls in following years, despite the country's robust economic performance. Similarly, the British stock market reached new highs while a persistently weak economy went through one of its periodic slumps.

Though stock markets have always behaved unpredictably, the new electronic, computerized, globally networked markets are far more volatile. There seems to be a diminishing relationship between the value of a company's shares and its actual performance. The "casino economy," as leftist critics labeled it, was becoming a computer game that was under the control of no one player. Like the patterns in the computer Game of Life, unexpected patterns such as sudden rises and falls in the markets seemed to be the result of the interaction of capital, "emergent" properties of a complex system rather than the whim of individuals acting according to their best interests.

It was in 1930, the year Gödel's famous paper undermining the certainties of mathematics was published, that Britain was forced off the gold standard by increasing instability of the pound, then a major world currency. This total breakdown of the system had only happened twice before since its adoption in the early eighteenth century: during the Napoleonic and the First World Wars.[10] This time it was gone for good, killed off by the world depression that followed the first Wall Street crash of October 1929.

The gold standard was a stabilizing measure designed to provide a fixed measure of money's value by relating it to a fixed quantity of gold. It meant that the purely symbolic nature of paper money was anchored in something that was regarded as having inherent material value. However, for economic reasons, this was a system that the British government could not sustain while the economic order collapsed around it. One might have thought this was the time when something as fixed and certain as gold was worth its weight as a form of security. But, as it turned out, gold itself had no intrinsic value; it, too, could not escape the vagaries of supply and demand on the international marketplace.

The abandonment of the gold standard has turned money into a purely abstract quantity, a symbol. A deficit is no different from a surplus, except that the mathematical sign for one is a minus, for the other a plus. Exchange has become an arithmetical correlation: if my balance goes up by so much, yours must come down by the same amount. Currencies "float," their level being set by their relationship to all other currencies. There exists no material means of distinguishing "my" money from anyone else's, no need for physical possession, no stash of gold or even cash in my bank's vaults that increases or diminishes according to how much I earn or spend. In the global village, this process of abstraction has reached its purest expression. Junk bonds, paper billionaires, credit ratings—money is just a parameter in a process running on a global computer, part of the reason that for many it is now meaningless, even worthless, a form of pure abstract symbolism that bears no relation to productive effort or material rewards. It exists in another realm, the same realm as the media virus—in cyberspace.

Perhaps cyberspace, then, is—literally—where the money is. Perhaps it is also the place where events increasingly happen, where our lives and fates are increasingly determined; a place that has a very direct impact on our material circumstances—a blip in the money markets can raise bank lending rates, a blip in a multinational's productivity can close factories and throw economies into depression, a blip in the TV ratings can wipe out an entire genre of programming, a blip in an early warning system can release a missile.

Perhaps cyberspace, then, is—literally—where the money is.

The power of this realm comes from its connectedness. It is a continuum, not a series of discrete systems that act independently of each other. Blips are not isolated events. Accelerated and amplified by electronics, they are the result of the subtle interactions of the millions of bits of data that flow through the world's networks. Furthermore, anyone connected to these networks, be they a humble telephone subscriber or TV viewer, participates in such events. No one can avoid becoming active citizens of cyberspace.

To people who have been involved in computing, and in particular personal computing, in the 1980s, such citizenry is no mere matter of theoretical speculation; it is very real. In 1982, I visited California for the weekly computer trade newspaper *Datalink*. The magazine's editor, Guy Kewney, and I decided to use the trip as an opportunity to try out a new way of communicating text that would avoid the delay and inconvenience of reading the articles over the phone (this was at a time when faxes were still relatively rare, even in California).

I typed up my articles on an Osborne-1 portable microcomputer. About the size of my tightly packed suitcase, and almost as heavy, it would have probably been easier to lug around an IBM golfball typewriter, but I needed to have my text in "machine-readable," word-processed form, not typed on paper, because I was going to send it back to Britain in that form. To do this, I used a modem—a device that turns the electronic signals generated by a computer into the sort of signals carried by a telephone line—and dialed up an "electronic mail" system in the UK called "Gold." Once connected, I sent the file that contained the text of my article down the line to Gold, which filed it away in its own computer for retrieval by colleagues at the office.

The result was instant, international communication, and, in the following few years, it became a standard means for reporters to file their copy, particularly so as the weight of portable computers decreased. It was just one of a growing number of ways that computers and telecommunications combined to change working practices. Academics used the ever-spreading networks to communicate with their peers by electronic mail. Businesses began to dial up databases of stock market prices, press cuttings or company accounts. Indeed, by the late 1980s, a whole new multi-billion dollar "value added services" communications market had emerged. Businesses like AT&T were no longer telephone companies, they were "telecommunications" companies; their networks were no longer just for voice, they were for any kind of data.

Computer users were plugged straight into this growth in telecommunications. Many linked up to the ever-increasing number of electronic services at their disposal: bulletin boards, online databases, home banking, teleshopping. The experience of using such services powerfully reinforced the collective imagination of computer users that there was another "world," a world where much of their social intercourse might take place, where much of their information would come from. They also knew that it was linked into the networks of international finance, commerce and government—as demonstrated by the growing number of stories about hackers gaining unauthorized access to company and defense systems using the same basic equipment. And it was the world infected by the computer virus, spread by the exchange of pirated and "homebrew" software deposited on bulletin boards and conferencing systems.

It was the excitement of being part of this world that stoked up the computing community's interest in virtual reality. Could this be where the denizens of the global village truly belonged? Could this be a *new* reality?

■ N O T E S

1. Interview with the author, *Late Show,* BBC 2, September 26, 1990.

2. William Gibson, *Neuromancer,* London: Grafton, 1986, p. 67.

3. David Gans and R. U. Sirius, "Civilizing the electronic frontier," *Mondo 2000,* 3, Winter 1991, p. 49.

4. Marshall McLuhan, *Understanding Media: the extensions of man,* London: Routledge, 1964, p. 5.

5. Mark Poster, *The Mode of Information: poststructuralism and social context,* Cambridge: Polity Press, 1990, p. 2.

6. Wes Thomas, "How I created a media virus," *Mondo 2000,* 2, Summer 1990, p. 137.

7. Richard Dawkins, *The Selfish Gene,* 2nd edition, Oxford: Oxford University Press, 1989.

8. Richard Dawkins, *The Extended Phenotype,* Oxford: Oxford University Press, 1982, p. 200.

9. Stephen Kindel and Amy Barrett, "The crash that wasn't . . . or was it?," *Financial World,* November 14, 1989, 158 (23), p. 26.

10. E. J. Hobsbawm, *Industry and Empire,* London: Penguin, 1969, p. 236.

■ QUESTIONS FOR REREADING

1. Woolley artfully dodges having to define cyberspace. He instead is interested in why Gibson's term caught on and became common currency. Woolley refers to McLuhan's discussion of explosion (fragmentation of societies) and implosion (global village). What do these terms or images mean in this context? Or in relation to my brief introduction to this section? What do Woolley and McLuhan mean by extending our bodies, namely, by television becoming our eyes, and so on? What does Woolley mean when he uses the word *network*? What is ARPAnet?

2. Summarize Woolley's account of the development of the Net from local area networks (LANs) to the World Wide Web (WWW). How are all these questions so far connected? What do they add up to? And, most importantly, in relation to cyberspace?

3. What is "telepresence"? What is the difference between "watching" and "doing" television? What is meant by McLuhan's notion of "the medium is the message [or massage]"? What does Woolley give as an explanation for the studio audience not seeing a real-life event as opposed to the at-home viewers not seeing a real-life event? After all, is it not the case that the studio audience actually sees real people?

4. What is a computer virus? And why does Woolley discuss it? In other words, what is its relevance to a discussion that began on cyberspace? What does Woolley (and Thomas, the writer he refers to) think the Friday the 13th virus told us about the news media itself? (Are there parallels among a virus passing through the human system, the personal computer system, and the media, or mediascape? If so, what are the parallels and their significance? It might help you to find out what the word *meme* means.) Was the hacker who released the virus saying something to us, or just being mischievous or reckless?

5. What does the discussion of replicators, genotypes, and phenotypes have to do with cyberspace? What is Woolley driving at with his detailed exposition of Dawkins's discussion of a phenotypic effect of a gene? What do Dawkins and Woolley mean when they talk about the virus manipulating the world (including a PC user) around it? Is this science fiction with virus monsters, or is it reality, or can we tell the difference any more? Why does Woolley tease us with a connection between the Friday the 13th virus and the stock market crash of 1989? Why a discussion of the gold standard in Great Britain?

6. Finally, Woolley says: "Perhaps cyberspace, then, is—literally—where the money is. Perhaps it is also the place where events increasingly happen, where our lives and fates are increasingly determined; a place that has a very direct impact on our material circumstances—a blip" can change everything. We, in cyberspace, are now subject to blips (viruses and their manipulations). What is possibly meant when Woolley says it is our "connectedness" that contributes to our being subject to blips?

   After reading Woolley, what do you know? What do you fear? What do you not understand?

■ WRITING ASSIGNMENTS FOR REREADING

1. Take any of the questions, or combination of the preceding questions, and jot down or type your ideas in words, phrases, fragments, or full sentences. Do this over a period of several days. Once you have generated, say, eight to ten pages, try to locate an idea or statement that you would like to write about, that is, learn more about by researching the topic with the help of a search engine (see Appendix A). Once you have completed this assignment, go back to your notes and find another idea or statement and start again.

2. Go to your local grocery store, and while shopping look at the labels on the food products and try to determine what is natural and what is artificial. Look at the labels on cans and boxes of food in your own cupboard or pantry. Write a 250-word report on what you have consumed that is real and what you have consumed that is artificial, as well as you can determine.

3. Take a piece of paper or open a computer file and make two columns for lists of all those things in your life that are real and all those that are artificial. When doing this, begin to think in terms of cyberspace. For example, think of the money that you might have in your pockets or purse or bag. Think of the coins, the paper bills. Think of the money that you might have in your savings or checking account. Or, if you have it, in stocks. If this money, or what is called your assets, is on your person, is this money real or cyberreal? When someone writes a check, is it real or artificial (that is, once or twice removed from reality)? If your money is in the bank in an account, is it real or cyberreal? Where is the real money? Fort Knox? Discuss these issues with your classmates. If you discuss them F2F in class or on a local area network (LAN) or a listserv established by your instructor, which discussion is more real for you? Write or type your answers exploring these questions. Once you have done this, attempt to organize your writing for an essay. Or, if you wish, take the discussion with your classmates and collaboratively write an essay with them on your experiences of thinking about the differences between real and cyberreal.

"The Essence of VR" appears in the larger context of Michael Heim's book The Metaphysics of Virtual Reality *(New York: Oxford UP, 1993): 109–28. The article is especially good, for it takes, unlike other articles, an encyclopedic approach, focusing on VR variously with such "divergent concepts" as simulation, artificial reality, interactivity, immersion, full-body immersion, networked environments, and telepresence. As he proceeds in his explanation, he becomes more mythic in his approach (he speaks of the Holy Grail), and yet he remains always very pragmatic. That is, he is always concerned with the issue of how someone uses VR. In his preface, Heim writes:*

Some observers, in their first efforts to explain the phenomenon to their contemporaries, pointed to drugs or sex or entertainment. But the profundity of the VR experience calls for something of a grander stature, something philosophical and religious. The time has come to grasp the phenomenon in its depth and scope. After all, we are talking about virtual "reality," not fleeting hallucinations or cheap thrills. We are talking about a profound shift in the layers of human life and thought. We are talking about something metaphysical. (xvii)

These words will become more important and more controversial after you have read through all four articles in this chapter.

Michael Heim

The Essence of VR

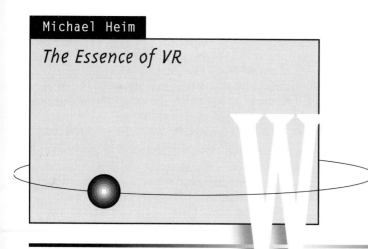

hat is virtual reality?

A simple enough question.

We might answer: "Here, try this arcade game. It's from the Virtuality series created by Jonathan Waldern. Just put on the helmet and the datagloves, grab the control stick, and enter a world of computer animation. You turn your head and you see a three-dimensional, 360-degree, color landscape. The other players see you appear as an animated character. And lurking around somewhere will be the other animated warriors who will hunt you down. Aim, press the button, and destroy them before they destroy you. Give it a few minutes and you'll get a feel for the game, how to move about, how to be part of a virtual world. That's virtual reality!"

Suppose the sample experience does not satisfy the questioner. Our questioner has already played the Virtuality game. Suppose the question is about virtual reality in general.

Reach for a dictionary. *Webster's* states:

Virtual: *"being in essence or effect though not formally recognized or admitted"*

Reality: *"a real event, entity, or state of affairs"*

We paste the two together and read: "Virtual reality is an event or entity that is real in effect but not in fact."

Not terribly enlightening. You don't learn nuclear physics from dictionaries. We need insight, not word usage.

The dictionary definition does, however, suggest something about VR. There is a sense in which any simulation makes something seem real that in fact is not. The Virtuality game combines head-tracking device, glove, and computer animation to create the "effect" on our senses of "entities" moving at us that are "not in fact real."

But what makes VR distinctive? "What's so special," our questioner might ask, "about these computer-animated monsters? I've seen them before on television and in film. Why call them 'virtual realities'?"

The questioner seeks not information, but clarification.

Pointing to the helmet and gloves, we insist: "Doesn't this feel a lot different from watching TV? Here you can interact with the animated creatures. You shoot them down or hide from them or dodge their ray guns. And they interact with you. They hunt you in three-dimensional space just as you hunt them. That doesn't happen in the movies, does it? Here you're the central actor, you're the star!"

Our answer combines hands-on demonstration with a reminder of other experiences. We draw a contrast, pointing to something that VR is not. We still have not said what it is.

To answer what VR is, we need concepts, not samples or dictionary phrases or negative definitions.

OK, so what is it?

Our next reply must be more informed: "Go to the source. Find the originators of this technology; ask them. For twenty years, scientists and engineers have been working on this thing called *virtual reality*. Find out exactly what they have been trying to produce."

When we look to the pioneers, we see virtual reality going off in several directions. The pioneers present us with at least seven divergent concepts currently guiding VR research. The different views have built camps that fervently disagree as to what constitutes virtual reality.

Here is a summary of the seven:

■ SIMULATION

Computer graphics today have such a high degree of realism that the sharp images evoke the term *virtual reality*. Just as sound systems were once praised for their high fidelity, present-day imaging systems now deliver virtual reality. The images have a shaded texture and light radiosity that pull the eye into the flat plane with the power of a detailed etching. Landscapes produced on the GE Aerospace "visionics" equipment, for instance, are photorealistic real-time texture-mapped worlds through which users can navigate. These dataworlds spring from military flight simulators. Now they are being applied to medicine, entertainment, and education and training.

The realism of simulations applies to sound as well. Three-dimensional sound systems control every point of digital acoustic space, their precision exceeding earlier sound systems to such a degree that three-dimensional audio contributes to virtual reality.

■ I N T E R A C T I O N

Some people consider virtual reality any electronic representation with which they can interact. Cleaning up our computer desktop, we see a graphic of a trash can on the computer screen, and we use a mouse to drag a junk file down to the trash can to dump it. The desk is not a real desk, but we treat it as though it were, virtually, a desk. The trash can is an icon for a deletion program, but we use it as a virtual trash can. And the files of bits and bytes we dump are not real (paper) files, but function virtually as files. These are virtual realities. What makes the trash can and the desk different from cartoons or photos on TV is that we can interact with them as we do with metal trash cans and wooden desktops. The virtual trash can does not have to fool the eye in order to be virtual. Illusion is not the issue. Rather, the issue is how we interact with the trash can as we go about our work. The trash can is real in the context of our absorption in the work, yet outside the computer work space we would not speak of the trash can except as a virtual trash can. The reality of the trash can comes from its handy place in the world woven by our engagement with a project. It exists through our interaction.

Defined broadly, virtual reality sometimes stretches over many aspects of electronic life. Beyond computer-generated desktops, it includes the virtual persons we know through telephone or computer networks. It includes the entertainer or politician who appears on television to interact on the phone with callers. It includes virtual universities where students attend classes on line, visit virtual classrooms, and socialize in virtual cafeterias.

■ A R T I F I C I A L I T Y

As long as we are casting our net so wide, why not make it cover everything artificial? On first hearing the term *virtual reality,* many people respond immediately: "Oh, sure, I live there all the time." By this they mean that their world is largely a human construct. Our environment is thoroughly geared, paved, and wired—not quite solid and real. Planet Earth has become an artifice, a product of natural and human forces combined. Nature itself, the sky with its ozone layer, no longer escapes human influence. And our public life has everywhere been computerized. Computer analysis of purchasing habits tells supermarkets how high and where to shelve the Cheerios. Advertisers boast of "genuine simulated walnut."

But once we extend the term *virtual reality* to cover everything artificial, we lose the force of the phrase. When a word means everything, it means nothing. Even the term *real* needs an opposite.

■ IMMERSION

Many people in the VR industry prefer to focus on a specific hardware and software configuration. This is the model set for virtual reality by Sutherland, Fisher, Furness, and Brooks, before whom the term *virtual reality* did not exist, since no hardware or software claimed that name.

The specific hardware first called VR combines two small three-dimensional stereoscopic optical displays, or "eye-phones"; a Polhemus head-tracking device to monitor head movement; and a dataglove or hand-held device to add feedback so the user can manipulate objects perceived in the artificial environment. Audio with three-dimensional acoustics can support the illusion of being submerged in a virtual world. That is, the illusion is immersion.

According to this view, virtual reality means sensory immersion in a virtual environment. Such systems, known primarily by their head-mounted displays (HMD) and gloves, were first popularized by Jaron Lanier's VPL (Virtual Programming Language) Incorporated. The HMD cuts off visual and audio sensations from the surrounding world and replaces them with computer-generated sensations. The body moves through artificial space using feedback gloves, foot treadmills, bicycle grips, or joysticks.

A prime example of immersion comes from the U.S. Air Force, which first developed some of this hardware for flight simulation. The computer generates much of the same sensory input that a jet pilot would experience in an actual cockpit. The pilot responds to the sensations by, for instance, turning a control knob, which in turn feeds into the computer, which again adjusts the sensations. In this way, a pilot can get practice or training without leaving the ground. To date, commercial pilots can upgrade their licenses on certain levels by putting in a certain number of hours on a flight simulator.

When you are flying low in an F-16 Falcon at supersonic speeds over a mountainous terrain, the less you see of the real world, the more control you can have over your aircraft.

Computer feedback may do more than readjust the user's sensations to give a pseudoexperience of flying. The feedback may also connect to an actual aircraft, so that when the pilot turns a knob, a real aircraft motor turns over or a real weapon fires. The pilot in this case feels immersed and fully present in a virtual world, which in turn connects to the real world.

When you are flying low in an F-16 Falcon at supersonic speeds over a mountainous terrain, the less you see of the real world, the more control you can have over your aircraft. A virtual cockpit filters the real scene and represents a more readable world. In this sense, VR can preserve the human significance of an overwhelming rush of split-second data.

The heads-up display in the cockpit sometimes permits the pilot to view the real landscape behind the virtual images. In such cases, the simulation is an augmented rather than a virtual reality.

The offshoots of this technology, such as the Waldern arcade game, should not distract us—say the immersion pioneers—from the applications being used in molecular biology (docking molecules by sight and touch), airflow simulation, medical training, architecture, and industrial design. Boeing Aircraft plans to project a flight controller into virtual space, so that the controller floats thousands of feet above the airport, looking with an unobstructed view in any direction (while actually seated in a datasuit on the earth and fed real-time visual data from satellite and multiple camera viewpoints).

A leading model of this research has been the workstation developed at NASA–Ames, the Virtual Interface Environment Workstation (VIEW). NASA uses the VIEW system for telerobotic tasks, so that an operator on earth feels immersed in a remote but virtual environment and can then see and manipulate objects on the moon or Mars through feedback from a robot. Immersion research concentrates on a specific hardware and software configuration. The immersive tools for pilots, flight controllers, and space explorers are a much more concrete meaning of VR than is the vague generalization "everything artificial."

■ TELEPRESENCE

Robotic presence adds another aspect to virtual reality. To be present somewhere yet present there remotely is to be there virtually (!). Virtual reality shades into telepresence when you are present from a distant location—"present" in the sense that you are aware of what's going on, effective, and able to accomplish tasks by observing, reaching, grabbing, and moving objects with your own hands as though they were close up. Defining VR by telepresence nicely excludes the imaginary worlds of art, mathematics, and entertainment. Robotic telepresence brings real-time human effectiveness to a real-world location without there being a human in the flesh at that location. Mike McGreevy and Lew Hitchner walk on Mars, but in the flesh they sit in a control room at NASA–Ames.

Telepresence medicine places doctors inside the patient's body without major incisions. Medical doctors like Colonel Richard Satava and Dr. Joseph Rosen routinely use telepresence surgery to remove gall bladders without the traditional scalpel incisions. The patient heals from surgery in one-tenth the usual time because telepresence surgery leaves the body nearly intact. Only two tiny incisions are needed to introduce the laparoscopic tools. Telepresence allows surgeons to perform specialist operations at distant sites where no specialist is physically present.

By allowing the surgeon to be there without being there, telepresence is a double-edged sword, so to speak. By permitting immersion, telepresence offers the operator great control over remote processes. But at the same time, a psychotechnological gap opens up between doctor and patient. Surgeons complain of losing hands-on contact as the patient evaporates into a phantom of bits and bytes.

■ FULL-BODY IMMERSION

About the same time that head-mounted displays appeared, a radically different approach to VR was emerging. In the late 1960s, Myron Krueger, often called "the father of virtual reality," began creating interactive environments in which the user moves without encumbering gear. Krueger's is come-as-you-are VR. Krueger's work uses cameras and monitors to project a user's body so it can interact with graphic images, allowing hands to manipulate graphic objects on a screen, whether text or pictures. The interaction of computer and human takes place without covering the body. The burden of input rests with the computer, and the body's free movements become text for the computer to read. Cameras follow the user's body, and computers synthesize the user's movements with the artificial environment.

I see a floating ball projected on a screen. My computer-projected hand reaches out and grabs the ball. The computer constantly updates the interaction of my body and the synthetic world that I see, hear, and touch.

In Krueger's Videoplace, people in separate rooms relate interactively by mutual body painting, free-fall gymnastics, and tickling. Krueger's Glowflow, a light-and-sound room, responds to people's movements by lighting phosphorescent tubes and issuing synthetic sounds. Another environment, Psychic Space, allows participants to explore an interactive maze in which each footstep corresponds to a musical tone, all produced with live video images that can be moved, scaled, and rotated without regard to the usual laws of cause and effect.

■ NETWORKED COMMUNICATIONS

Pioneers like Jaron Lanier accept the immersion model of virtual reality but add equal emphasis to another aspect that they see as essential. Because computers make networks, VR seems a natural candidate for a new communications medium. The RB2 (Reality Built for Two) System from VPL highlights the connectivity of virtual worlds. In this view, a virtual world is as much a shared construct as a telephone is. Virtual worlds, then, can evoke unprecedented ways of sharing, what Lanier calls "post-symbolic communication." Because users can stipulate and shape objects and activities of a virtual world, they can share imaginary things and events without using words or real-world references.

Accordingly, communication can go beyond verbal or body language to take on magical, alchemical properties. A virtual-world maker might conjure up hitherto unheard-of mixtures of sight, sound, and motion. Consciously constructed outside the grammar and syntax of language, these semaphores defy the traditional logic of verbal and visual information. VR can convey meaning kinetically and even kinesthetically. Such communication will probably require elaborate protocols as well as lengthy time periods for digesting what has been communicated. Xenolinguists will have a laboratory for experiment when they seek to relate to those whose feelings and world views differ vastly from their own.

"All right, enough!" shouts our questioner, bleary-eyed with information overload.

"I've taken your virtual-reality tour, listened to the pioneers, and now my head is spinning. These pioneers do indeed explore in different directions. There's a general drift here but no single destination. Should I go home feeling that the real virtual reality does not exist?"

Let's not lose stamina now. We cannot let the question fizzle. Too much depends on searching for the true virtual reality.

We should not get discouraged because a mention of reality, virtual or otherwise, opens several pathways in the clearing.

Let us recall for a moment just how controversial past attempts were to define the term *reality*. Recall how many wars were fought over it.

People today shy away from the *R* word. *Reality* used to be the key to a person's philosophy. As a disputed term, *reality* fails to engage scientific minds because they are wary of any speculation that distracts them from their specialized work. But a skeptical attitude will fall short of the vision and direction we need.

Here's a brief sidebar on how controversial the *R* word has been throughout Western history:

Plato holds out ideal forms as the "really real" while he denigrates the raw physical forces studied by his Greek predecessors. Aristotle soon demotes Plato's ideas to a secondary reality, to the flimsy shapes we abstract from the really real—which, for Aristotle, are the individual substances we touch and feel around us. In the medieval period, real things are those that shimmer with symbolic significance. The biblical-religious symbols add superreal messages to realities, giving them permanence and meaning, while the merely material aspects of things are less real, merely terrestrial, defective rubbish. In the Renaissance, things counted as real that could be counted and observed repeatedly by the senses. The human mind infers a solid material substrate underlying sense data but the substrate proves less real because it is less quantifiable and observable. Finally, the modern period attributed reality to atomic matter that has internal dynamics or energy, but soon the reality question was doomed by the analytical drive of the sciences toward complexity and by the plurality of artistic styles.

> **If for two thousand years Western culture has puzzled over the meaning of reality, we cannot expect ourselves in two minutes, or even two decades, to arrive at the meaning of virtual reality.**

This reminder of metaphysics should fortify us for the long haul. If for two thousand years Western culture has puzzled over the meaning of reality, we cannot expect ourselves in two minutes, or even two decades, to arrive at the meaning of virtual reality.

The reality question has always been a question about direction, about focus, about what we should acknowledge and be concerned with. We should not therefore be surprised when VR proves controversial and elusive. Creating a new layer of reality demands our best shot, all our curiosity and imagination, especially since for us, technology and reality are beginning to merge.

When we look for the essence of a technology, we are engaging in speculation, but not in airy speculation. Our speculation involves where we plant our feet, who we are, and what we choose to be. Behind the development of every major technology lies a vision. The vision gives impetus to developers in the field even though the vision may not be clear, detailed, or even practical. The vision captures the essence of the technology and calls forth the cultural energy needed to propel it forward. Often a technological vision taps mythic consciousness and the religious side of the human spirit.

Consider for a moment the development of space technology. (Keep in mind that an inner connection exists between outer space and cyberspace, as I will point out later.) The U.S. space program enjoyed its most rapid development in the 1960s, culminating in the moon walk in 1969. What was the vision behind it?

The U.S. space program was a child of the cold war. The May 1961 speech by President John F. Kennedy that set NASA's goals incorporated traditional elements of myth: heroic struggle, personal sacrifice, and the quest for national prominence. Yet the impetus for Kennedy's speech came largely from without. What launched the U.S. space program was the fear of being surpassed by the Soviets, who had made a series of bold advances in human space travel. The goal of the moon landing was for the United States an attempt not to be overtaken by the Soviet developments in manned space exploration.

Few Americans know about the vision of their Russian competitors in space exploration. Everyone knows, of course, that the Communist revolution in 1917 froze Russian public goals in the hackneyed single-party language of a Marxist-Leninist agenda. Some historians know the name of the great Russian rocket pioneer Konstantin Tsiolkovsky (1857–1935), who stands with the American Robert H. Goddard (1882–1945) and the German-born Hermann Oberth (b. 1894). But less is known about the background of Tsiolkovsky's thinking and the visionary philosophy that influenced the first generation of Soviet space explorers.

What lay behind the energetic push to send human beings into outer space? The Russians to this day have gathered far more data on human survival in outer space. The need for information was more than curiosity or a vague lust for new frontiers; it was a moral mission, a complex and imaginative grasp of human destiny in the cosmos. The early Russian rocket pioneers, who gave the impetus to the program, felt there was an essence to their space technology, a deep inner fire that inspired and directed the research. They felt an existential imperative that drew on the religious and cultural traditions coming down through the main stream of Russian history. This essence was not itself technological, and so we might call it the esoteric essence of space technology, the hidden core of ideas that in themselves are not technological. In fact, the ideas behind the first space exploration were lofty, awe inspiring, and even mystical.

The visionary ideas fueling Tsiolkovsky and the early Russian explorers came from N. F. Fedorov. Nikolai Fedorovich Fedorov (1828–1903) was a powerful inspiration to Soloviev, Dostoevsky, Tolstoy, and a whole generation of Russians who sought to understand how modernization connects with traditional religion and culture. Even the engineers of the Trans-Siberian Railway came often to sit at the feet of the famous sage. Fedorov lived an intensely spiritual life, dedicated exclusively to ideas and learning. His profound vision applied certain strands of Russian Orthodox spirituality to the harnessing of modern technology.

Sketching a national vision, Fedorov drew large. He argued that Russia should marshal its military and national strength toward a single goal: the conquest of nature. Conquering nature meant regulating the earth as a harmonious system. It meant controlling the weather so that harvests would be plentiful. It meant balancing nature so that all life-forms could thrive together in harmony.

Sketching a national vision, Fedorov drew large. He argued that Russia should marshal its military and national strength toward a single goal: the conquest of nature. Conquering nature meant regulating the earth as a harmonious system.

In his vision, Fedorov saw armies producing solar energy and harnessing the electromagnetic energy of the earth, using the energy to regulate the earth's motion in space, turning the earth into a vessel for cosmic cruises. Overpopulation would cease to be a problem as humanity colonized other planets.

Unique to Fedorov's vision is its guiding moral spark. Instead of basing the conquest of nature on dominance, aggression, and egoism, Fedorov shunned the notion that humans should rule the cosmos out of a selfish desire for material wealth and abundance. Instead, he envisioned the conquest of nature as an act of altruism. But being generous to future generations can be less than purely altruistic, for they can return the favor by their acclaim of our deeds. We must regulate the forces of nature, he believed, so altruistically that we serve those who cannot possibly return our favors: we must conquer nature in order to resurrect our ancestors, the ultimate act of altruism.

The resurrection of all our dead ancestors, and it alone, provides a lofty enough ideal to mobilize humanity to explore the entire universe, including outer space. Fedorov found this thought in Russian Orthodox Christianity. According to Christian belief, the dead will rise again so that Christ, in a final judgment, will reorganize and completely redeem the world. The bodies of all human beings will one day rise again, and this resurrection, according to Fedorov, will take place through the work of human beings who carry out the divine plan. The long-range goal of human cooperation must be to discover the laws of nature to such a depth that we can eventually reconstitute the bodies of past human beings from their remaining physical particles still floating about in the universe.

Fedorov's strategy was to channel science and technology toward the reunion of all humanity. He decried the heartless positivism that builds on the sufferings and corpses of previous generations, instead seeking a purely ideal-istic motive. Without such a high aim, a heartless science would ultimately turn against society. For him, and for the many Soviet scientists inspired by him, the ultimate aim of the space program was, quite literally, nothing less than resurrecting the dead.

Contrast this sublime—and to us incredible and bizarre—vision of the space program with current U.S. public policy. "The commercialization of space," as promoted by administrations since the late 1970s, offers civilian entrepreneurs new opportunities for investment. To cover this naked self-interest, a mythic notion from U.S. history adds the sense of a new frontier. As a mere resource for commerce, space holds little allure, but a new frontier beyond earth adds adventure to the hope for personal gain. The vision even draws on the California gold rush in the nineteenth century, the spirit of enterprise.

In fact, this last word, *enterprise,* shows us where the commercialization of space falls short. Commercialization fails to touch the essence of space explo-ration, for commercial interests will neglect the long-range research needed for space science. Commercialization also drives up the cost of information derived from space exploration so that the data from space will not be avail-able to small businesses, university scientists, farmers, state and local govern-ments, and developing countries. In short, this kind of exploration envisions no future, only short-range profit.

But for NASA, for space enthusiasts, and for the Pentagon people, *enterprise* has a capital E. The word refers to a spirit of business adventure, but it also, in many minds, has another important meaning. Many technical people today also take *enterprise* to be the proper name in a science fiction myth, that of the starship *Enterprise* in *Star Trek,* the popular science fiction television series about twenty-first-century space travelers. *Star Trek* contributed the code word, the handshake, the common inspiration for space exploration in the United States. (Shake hands informally with someone at the Pentagon or NASA and be pre-pared with an answer to the query "Are you a Trekkie?") For hundreds of tech-nicians, the space program flies on the imaginative wings of Gene Roddenberry's brainchild, born on September 8, 1966, when the TV show was first aired. But Roddenberry was no Fedorov. The sage of Pasadena created no unifying vision to direct humanity "where no one has gone before." His fic-tional productions treated only a motley collection of profound moral ques-tions pertaining to human behavior at any time, any place. But despite the limits of its lineage, *Star Trek* showed us more truly the esoteric essence, the real meaning, of space exploration than did government statements on the commercialization of space. The essence of the American space program, its heart and soul, comes from *Star Trek.*

Where in VR is a counterpart to the space program's esoteric essence? What is the essence of VR, its inner spirit, the cultural motor that propels the technology? When the first conferences met on cyberspace and on virtual reality in 1989 and 1990, respectively, two threads of shared vision ran through the diverse groups of participants. One was the cyberpunk writings of William Gibson, known to both technical and literary types as the coiner of the term *cyberspace*. The other was the Holodeck from *Star Trek: The Next Generation*.

Along with its cargo bay of imaginative treasures, the starship *Enterprise* brought the Holodeck. The Holodeck is familiar furniture in the vocabulary of virtual-reality pioneers. For most people, the Holodeck portrays the ideal human-computer interface. It is a virtual room that transforms spoken commands into realistic landscapes populated with walking, talking humanoids and detailed artifacts appearing so lifelike that they are indistinguishable from reality. The Holodeck is used by the crew of the starship *Enterprise* to visit faraway times and places such as medieval England and 1920s America. Generally, the Holodeck offers the crew rest and recreation, escape and entertainment, on long interstellar voyages.

The Holodeck is familiar furniture in the vocabulary of virtual-reality pioneers.

While not every VR pioneer explicitly agrees on goals, the Holodeck draws the research onward. Publicly, researchers try to maintain cool and reasonable expectations about VR. Hyperbole from the media often stirs grandiose expectations in the public; when presented with actual prototypes, the public turns away with scorn. So researchers play down talk of the Holodeck. At the MIT Media Lab, leaders such as David Zeltzer avoid the term *virtual reality* not only because of the specter of metaphysics it evokes, but also because of the large promises it raises. The term seems to make greater claims than do terms like *virtual environments* (preferred at MIT and NASA) and *virtual worlds* (preferred at the universities of North Carolina and Washington). But when speaking at a VR conference for the Data Processing Management Association in Washington, D.C., on June 1, 1992, Zeltzer made an intriguing aside, one that touches, I think, on the highest possibilities of virtual reality, on its esoteric essence.

Did I say "esoteric essence"? How can we expect to give our young questioner an answer to "What is virtual reality?" when we have left the public, exoteric world of clear explanations and have embarked on a search for the esoteric essence of VR, its underlying vision? Well, our questioner seems to have gotten lost some time ago, most likely during the sidebar on the history of reality. I think I see someone off in the distance pulling avidly on the trigger of the Virtuality game. Maybe more time spent in VR will eventually deliver better answers than any verbal speculation. At any rate, on to the esoteric essence. . . .

Zeltzer's remark went something like this: "True virtual reality may not be attainable with any technology we create. The Holodeck may forever remain fiction. Nonetheless, virtual reality serves as the Holy Grail of the research."

"Holy Grail?" Holy Grail!

Now when Zeltzer made this reference, he was not deliberately invoking a Jungian archetype. His remark expressed modesty and diffidence rather than alchemical arrogance. Still, archetypes do not have to hit us in the nose to wield their peculiar power. They work most powerfully at the back of the subconscious mind, and therein lies their magic. An effective archetype works its magic subtly.

David Zeltzer was calling up a mythic image far more ancient and infinitely more profound than *Star Trek. Star Trek* has, after all, become the stuff of trivia: *Star Trek* ties and boxer shorts, *Star Trek* vinyl characters and mugs ("Fill them with a hot beverage and watch Kirk and Spock beam up to an unknown world"). *Star Trek* lost any sublimity it may have had when it came to occupy Kmart shelves along with electric flyswatters and noisemaker whoopee cushions.

The Holy Grail, though, sums up the aspirations of centuries. It is an image of the Quest. From Tennyson's romantic *Idylls of the King* to Malory's King Arthur and the Knights of the Round Table, the ancient Grail legend reaches back to Christian and pre-Christian times. The Grail has always been a symbol of the quest for a better world. In pre-Christian times, the Grail was the cup that holds a cure for an ailing king who, suffering from his own wounds, sees his country turning into a wasteland. Christians believed the Grail to be both the chalice of Jesus' Last Supper and the cup that caught the Savior's blood at the Crucifixion. Medieval legend links the spear that pierced Jesus' side on the cross with the sacred cup that held his blood. Later works of art, from T. S. Eliot's *The Wasteland* to Richard Wagner's *Parsifal,* have preserved the Grail story as a symbol of spiritual quest and lofty aspiration.

VR *promises not a better vacuum cleaner or a more engrossing communications medium or even a friendlier computer interface. It promises the Holy Grail.*

Perhaps the essence of VR ultimately lies not in technology but in art, perhaps art of the highest order. Rather than control or escape or entertain or communicate, the ultimate promise of VR may be to transform, to redeem our awareness of reality—something that the highest art has attempted to do and something hinted at in the very label *virtual reality,* a label that has stuck, despite all objections, and that sums up a century of technological innovation. VR promises not a better vacuum cleaner or a more engrossing communications medium or even a friendlier computer interface. It promises the Holy Grail.

We might learn something about the esoteric essence of VR by thinking about Richard Wagner's *Parsifal.* Wagner himself was searching for a Holodeck, though he did not know it. By the time he finished *Parsifal,* his final opera, Wagner no longer considered his work to be opera. He did not want it called opera or music or theater or even "art," and certainly not entertainment. By the time he finished his last work, Wagner realized he was trying to create another reality, one that would in turn transform ordinary reality. The term he came to use was "a total work of art," by which he meant a seamless union of vision, sound, movement, and drama that would sweep the viewer to another world, not to escape but to be changed. Nor could the viewer be a mere spectator. Wagner created a specially designed building in Bayreuth, Germany, well off the beaten track, where the audience would have to assemble after a long journey because he forbade the performance of *Parsifal* in any other building. The audience would have to prepare itself well ahead of time by studying the libretto, because *Parsifal* was long, mysterious, and full of complex, significant details. (Wagner's *Ring* cycle takes over fifteen hours to present a related myth.) Looking for the right terms to express his intent, Wagner called *Parsifal* "a festival play for consecrating the stage" *(ein Bühnenweihfestspiel)*. The Bayreuth theater would become the site for a solemn, nearly liturgical celebration. The mythmaker would create a counter-reality, one reminiscent of the solemn mass of the Catholic church, which appeals to all the senses with its sights, sounds, touch, drama, even appealing to smell with incense and candles. The audiences at Bayreuth were to become pilgrims on a quest, immersed in an artificial reality.

The drama *Parsifal,* like a mysterious dream, resists easy summary, and it eludes interpretation. But the general story outline is clear. The protectors of "correct values" (the Knights) inevitably paint themselves into the corner of righteousness. Paralyzed, unable to act, their leadership suffers intense internal pain (Amfortas). They can regain the power of the Grail that they protect only through the intervention of someone who is still innocent of right and wrong, someone who is by all standards a fool. The innocent fool (Arabic, *fal parsi*) can clean out the sclerotic righteous society only after passing a test and learning to feel the sufferings of others. Once the innocent fool has acquired compassion for others and sensitivity to life's complexity, he can bring the power (the Spear) back to the righteous Knights of the Holy Grail. The Grail Knights then come to understand more deeply what the work of the Holy Grail, and their mission, means. The Grail grants its full power only to those who can be touched by compassion.

Wagner's Holodeck presents a Parsifal who mirrors the individual audience members at Bayreuth. Wagner shaped the drama with story and music so that strong sensations would engulf the audience and pierce them to the heart. Each listener begins as a naive spectator and is then gradually touched by the painful actions on stage until the listener becomes transformed into a more sensitive and compassionate member, ready to bring to a sick society some measure of healing and renewal.

Wagner hoped to do more than make music and theater; he believed that his music dramas could transform society by imparting new feelings and attitudes. This goal he shared with traditional religion; and religion returns the competition with distrust and the accusation of heterodoxy. For this reason, Wagner's work remains to this day controversial among religious people, including many artists and musicians who have strong religious faith.

How well did Wagner succeed? One of the most telling tributes to the success of Wagner's *Parsifal* comes from a Jesuit priest, Father Owen Lee, who in a radio broadcast intermission feature from the Metropolitan Opera in New York City said:

I watched as usual from the least expensive seat under the roof, hovering there with an unearthly feeling for long half-hours floating in an immense space, suffused with a sense of what Baudelaire felt listening to Wagner: "A sense of being suspended in an ecstasy compounded of joy and insight." I can remember staggering out of theaters after Parsifal, hardly aware of people applauding, the music streaming through me, carried out of myself, seeing my experience—indeed, feeling that I was seeing all experience—at a higher level of awareness, put in touch with a power greater than myself, a kind of holy fool.[1]

Another holy fool was the Finnish composer Jan Sibelius, who wrote: "Heard *Parsifal*. Nothing else in all the world has made so overwhelming an impression on me. All my heartstrings throbbed." The German composer Max Reger wrote: "Heard *Parsifal*. Cried for two weeks, then decided to become a composer."

Someday VR will elicit similar rave reviews, not mere thrills, but insight into experience. As it evolves its art form, VR will have certain advantages over Wagner's "total work of art." Certain disadvantages might also plague it where Wagnerian solutions might help.

■ ACTIVITY/PASSIVITY

VR systems, as Jaron Lanier points out, can reduce apathy and the couch-potato syndrome simply by requiring creative decisions. Because computers make VR systems interactive, they also allow the artist to call forth greater participation from users. Whereas traditional art forms struggle with the passivity of the spectator, the VR artist finds a controlled balance between passivity and activity. The model of user navigation can be balanced by the model of pilgrimage and sacred awe.

■ MANIPULATION/RECEPTIVITY

Some observers date the advent of VR to the moment when the dataglove appeared on the computer screen. At that moment, the user became visible as an active, involved force in the digital world. This implies that VR has a tilt toward manipulation, even a latent tendency toward aggressive, first-person attitudes. The VR artist will need strategies for inducing a more receptive atmosphere, so that the user can be open in all directions, receiving signals from and having empathy for other beings. The user must be able to be touched, emotionally moved, by non-first-person entities in the virtual world. The spear of manipulation must join the cup of sensitivity. If simulators serve to train hand-eye and other coordination skills, VR may take a further step and become a training tool to enhance receptivity.

▪ REMOTE PRESENCE

The visual bias of current VR brings out a possible detachment in the user's sense of the world. Seeing takes place at a distance, whereas hearing and the other senses are more intimate to our organic life. The visual bias increases the detachment of telepresence. Some VR versions stress the "looking-at" factor, such as David Gelernter's Mirror Worlds, in which, in real-time, users can zoom in on miniature shoe-box worlds containing local homes, businesses, cities, governments, or nations. VR offers the opportunity to shift the Western philosophy of presence. From Pythagoras to Aristotle, from Berkeley to Russell, our philosophical sense of presence has relied on vision, consequently putting us in the position of spectators. To be touched, we need to introduce more sensory awareness. VR may develop a kind of feedback in which presence includes an openness and sensitivity of the whole body.

▪ AUGMENTED REALITY

VR will enhance the power of art to transform reality. The picture frame, the proscenium, the movie theater all limit art by blocking it off as a section of reality. VR, with its augmented reality, allows a smoother, more controlled transition from virtual to real and back. This capability, which may frighten psychologists, will offer artists an unprecedented power to transform societies.

*VR **will enhance the power of art to transform reality.***

These are a few of the differences that make virtual reality different from traditional art forms. They belong to the essence of VR, its Holy Grail. This goal means that we need a different breed of artist as well. And where will we find these new cybersages, these virtual-world makers? I see our young questioner smiling broadly now as yet another wounded pterodactyl drops from the pink sky of Waldern's arcade game. Plenty of fledgling enthusiasm here, and a society that needs healing and renewal.

▪ NOTE

1. Father Owen Lee, "Metropolitan Opera Broadcast Intermission Feature," March 28, 1992.

▪ QUESTIONS FOR REREADING

1. Heim, like Woolley, struggles with defining virtual reality. Finally, he turns to seven different current views of VR. What are they? Explain each.

2. Why does Heim use the framing device of the person wanting to know about VR?

3. After listening to the seven explanations of VR, the questioner finally exclaims: "There's a general drift here but no single destination. Should I

go home feeling that the real virtual reality does not exist?" Why does Heim shift from a discussion of VR to one of reality, the *R* word? (Note that he inserts a sidebar on Plato.)

4. What appears to be a natural ending to the chapter, with the closing of the frame and the sidebar, is not the case, for Heim starts up his discussion again with an extended comparison between the U.S. space program and the former Soviet Union's visionary ideas. Why this comparison? What is the significance of the word *enterprise*? How does the television program *Star Trek* fit into the discussion? (At this point in the discussion, Heim brings back the frame device of the questioner: For what purpose?)

5. Explain Heim's distinction of esoteric and exoteric essences. What does he mean when he says, "VR . . . promises the Holy Grail"? Or "VR will enhance the power of art to transform reality"?

I asked Michael Heim if he had any questions that he wanted to ask you and he sent me the following:

6. Wagner's opera *Parsifal* comes from medieval legends about knights and their quest for the Holy Grail. Can you name role-playing games that use similar legends? Do you think that such interactive games can change the way that people feel about their lives?

7. What kind of VR hardware is needed to alter a person's emotional attitude? Do hardware and software make a big difference in the computer's power to transform us?

■ WRITING ASSIGNMENTS FOR REREADING

1. If you have ever gone to Disneyland (in California) or to Disney World (in Florida), write about your experiences in the theme parks in terms of your understandings of Heim's views of VR. In thinking about what you might write, concentrate on the conceptual starting places of simulation, artificial reality, interactivity, immersion, and so on. If you have not gone to either park, then write about your experiences in other parks in the same terms. When writing, think of your audience as composed of people who have never gone to Disneyland or Disney World or other theme parks.

2. Take one of Heim's questions and develop it into an article to be published on a Web page. (Your audience would be other students who might use this book, as well as students around the world who would be interested in VR.) If you and your classmates and instructor like what you have written, then e-mail me and let me know. I would like to consider your work for publication on the *CyberReader* Web site (www.abacon.com/vitanza/) that goes with this book.

"Seeing Is Beholding" comes from the larger context of Rushkoff's book Cyberia: Life in the Trenches of Hyperspace (New York: HarperCollins, 1994. Paperback edition, 1995). It is a chapter in Part 2, "Drugs: The Substances of Designer Reality." This is the first book on things cyber that I read. For me, it reads more as a social history of a group in California who created what Rushkoff calls cyberia. And what is cyberia? Rushkoff answers:

Cyberia is the place a businessperson goes when involved in a phone conversation, the place a shamanic warrior goes when traveling out of the body, the place an "acid house" dancer goes when experiencing the bliss of a techno-acid trance. Cyberia is the place alluded to by the mystical teaching of every religion, the theoretical tangents of every science, and the wildest speculations of every imagination. (5)

Rushkoff continues throughout the book investigating the question with other possible answers. Cyberia is a place created by the marriage among science, spirituality, and psychedelic drugs, at least, as cyberia evolved on the West Coast. Many of the sixties people eventually became programmers and hacked their way from one reality to the next, creating a social space Rushkoff calls cyberia.

Does all this talk about cyberia mean, then, that we have to take drugs to become a cyberian? No. What Rushkoff gives us is a historical account of what was and what contributed in great part to the technology that you are reading about in CyberReader. He writes about the 1960s "notion that we have chosen our reality arbitrarily" (7). He writes about the 1990s parallel notion that we can digitally make and choose our reality arbitrarily. In other words, from this point of view, there is no single reality, but numerous realities. Consequently, he writes about "designer reality." And when he writes he is not naively optimistic, nor does he write mere hype. He is subtly very critical of what he reports others as having seen. And yet, as he reports, seeing is always in the eyes of the beholder.

Douglas Rushkoff

Seeing Is Beholding

erence McKenna—considered by many the successor to Tim Leary's psychedelic dynasty—couldn't make it to Big Heart City Friday night for the elder's party. The bearded, lanky, forty-somethingish Irishman was deep into a Macintosh file, putting the finishing touches on his latest manuscript about the use of mind-altering plants by ancient cultures. But by Saturday evening he was ready to descend from his small mountaintop ranch house to talk about the virtual reality that has his fans so excited.

We're backstage with McKenna at a rave where he'll be speaking about drugs, consciousness, and the end of time. He's gotten famous, on the West Coast at least, as a sort of public relations manager for the plant kingdom. Part human, part gnome, and part mushroom, McKenna speaks from experience. This experience just happens to be an intimate connection with mind-altering vegetation, so his words sprawl like kudzu over the consciousness. If you listen to McKenna, that is, really listen, you can't help but get wrapped up in his rap. The luckiest of friends and mentees hang out with him in his dressing room as he prepares to go on.

"VR really is like a trip," one boy offers McKenna in the hopes of launching the Celtic Bard into one of his lyrical diatribes. Terence ponders a moment and then he's off.

"VR really is like a trip," one boy offers McKenna in the hopes of launching the Celtic Bard into one of his lyrical diatribes. Terence ponders a moment and then he's off.

"I link virtual reality to psychedelic drugs because I think that if you look at the evolution of organism and self-expression and language, language is seen to be some kind of process that actually tends toward the visible." McKenna strings his thoughts together into a breathless oral continuum. "The small mouth-noise way of communicating is highly provisional; we may be moving toward an environment of language that is beheld rather than heard."

Still, the assembled admirers hang on McKenna's every word, as if each syllable were leaving a hallucinatory aftervision on the adrenal cortex. They too dream of a Cyberia around the corner, and virtual reality is the closest simulation of what a world free of time, location, or even a personal identity might look like. Psychedelics and VR are both ways of creating a new, nonlinear reality, where self-expression is a community event.

"You mean like ESP?"

Terence never corrects anyone—he only interpolates their responses. "This would be like a kind of telepathy, but it would be much more than that: A world of visible language is a world where the individual doesn't really exist in the same way that the print-created world sanctions what we call 'point of view.' That's really what an ego is: it's a consistently defined point of view within a context of narrative. Well, if you replace the idea that life is a narrative with the idea that life is a vision, then you displace the linear progression of events. I think this is technically within reach."

To Terence, the invention of virtual reality, like the resurgence of psychoactive drugs, serves as a kind of technological philosopher's stone, bringing an inkling of the future reality into the present. It's both a hint from our hyperdimensional future and an active, creative effort by cyberians to reach that future.

"I like the concept of the philosopher's stone. The next messiah might be a machine rather than a person. The philosopher's stone is a living stone. It is being made. We are making it. We are like tunnelers drilling toward something. The overmind is drilling toward us, and we are drilling toward it. And when we meet, there will be an enormous revelation of the true nature of being. I think every person who takes five or six grams of psilocybin mushrooms in silent darkness is probably on a par with Christ and Buddha, at least in terms of the input."

So, according to McKenna, the psychedelic vision provides a glimpse of the truth cyberians are yearning for. But have psychedelics and virtual reality really come to us as a philosopher's stone, or is it simply that our philosopher's stoned?

▪ MORPHOGENETIC FIELDS FOREVER

Cyberians share a psychedelic common ground. To them, drugs are not simply a recreational escape but a conscious and sometimes daring foray into new possible realities. Psychedelics give them access to what McKenna is calling the overmind and what we call Cyberia. However stoned they might be when they get there, psychedelic explorers are convinced that they are experiencing something real, and bringing back something useful for themselves and the rest of us.

Psychedelic exploration, however personal, is thought to benefit more than the sole explorer. Each tripper believes he is opening the door between humanity and hyperspace a little wider. The few cyberians who haven't taken psychedelics still feel they have personally experienced and integrated the psychedelic vision through the trips of others, and value the role of these chemicals in the overall development of Cyberia. It is as if each psychedelic journey completes another piece of a universal puzzle.

But, even though they have a vast computer net and communications infrastructure at their disposal, psychedelic cyberians need not communicate their findings so directly. Rather, they believe they are each sharing and benefiting from a collective experience. As we'll see, one of the most common realizations of the psychedelic trip is that "all is one." At the euphoric peak of a trip, all people, particles, personalities, and planets are seen as part of one great entity or reality—one big fractal.

It may have been that realization that led Cambridge biologist Rupert Sheldrake to develop his theory of morphogenetic fields, now common knowledge to most cyberians. From *morph,* meaning "forms," and *genesis,* meaning "birth," these fields are a kind of cumulative record of the past behaviors of species, groups, and even molecules, so that one member of a set can learn from the experience of all the others.

A failed animal-behavior test is still one of the best proofs of Sheldrake's idea. Scientists were attempting to determine if learned skills could be passed on from parents to children genetically. They taught adult mice how to go through a certain maze, then taught their offspring, and their offspring, and so on for twenty years and fifty generations of mice. Indeed, the descendants of the taught mice knew how to get through the maze very quickly without instruction, but so did the descendants of the control group, who had never seen the maze at all! Later, a scientist decided to repeat this experiment on a different continent with the same mouse species, but they already knew how to go through the maze, too! As explained by morphic resonance, the traits need not have been passed on genetically. The information leak was due not to bad experimental procedure but to the morphogenetic field, which stored the experience of the earlier mice from which all subsequent mice could benefit.

Similarly, if scientists are developing a new crystalline structure, it may take years to "coax" atoms to form the specific crystal. But once the crystal is developed in one laboratory, it can be created instantly in any other laboratory in the world. According to Sheldrake, this is because, like the mice, the atoms are all "connected" to one another through morphogenetic fields, and they "learn" from the experiences of other atoms.

Sheldrake's picture of reality is a vast fractal of resonating fields. Everything, no matter how small, is constantly affecting everything else. If the tiniest detail in a fractal pattern echoes the overall design of the entire fractal, then a change to (or the experience of) this remote piece changes the overall picture (through the principles of feedback and iteration). Echoing the realizations of his best friends, Ralph Abraham and Terence McKenna, Sheldrake is the third member of the famous "Trialogues" at Esalen, where the three elder statesmen (by cyberian standards) discuss onstage the ongoing unfolding of reality before captivated audiences of cyberians. These men are, quite consciously, putting into practice the idea of morphogenetic fields. Even if these Trialogues were held in private (as they were for years), Cyberia as a whole would benefit from the intellectual developments. By pioneering the new "headspace," the three men leave their own legacy through morphic resonance, if not direct communication through their publishing, lectures, or media events.

Likewise, each cyberian psychedelic explorer feels that by tripping he is leaving his own legacy for others to follow, while himself benefiting from the past psychedelic experiences of explorers before him. For precisely this reason, McKenna advises using only organic psychedelics, which have well-developed morphogenetic fields: "I always say there are three tests for a drug. It should occur in nature. That gives it a morphogenetic field of resonance to the life of the planet. It should have a history of shamanic usage [which gives it a morphogenetic field of resonance to the consciousness of other human beings]. And it should be similar to or related to neurotransmitters in the brain. What's interesting about that series of filters is that it leaves you with the most powerful hallucinogens there are: psilocybin, DMT, ayahuasca, and, to some degree, LSD."

These are the substances that stock the arsenal of the drug-using cyberian. Psychedelics use among cyberians has developed directly out of the drug culture of the 1960s. The first tripsters—the people associated with Leary on the East Coast, and Ken Kesey on the West Coast—came to startling moral and philosophical conclusions that reshaped our culture. For today's users, drugs are part of the continuing evolution of the human species toward greater intelligence, empathy, and awareness.

From the principle of morphogenesis, cyberians infer that psychedelic substances have the ability to reshape the experience of reality and thus— if observer and observed are one—the reality itself. It's hardly disputed

From the principle of morphogenesis, cyberians infer that psychedelic substances have the ability to reshape the experience of reality and thus—if observer and observed are one—the reality itself.

that, even in a tangible, cultural sense, the introduction of psychedelics into our society in the 1960s altered the sensibilities of users and nonusers alike. The trickle-down effect through the arts, media, and even big business created what can be called a postpsychedelic climate, in which everything from women's rights, civil rights, and peace activism to spirituality and the computer revolution found suitable conditions for growth.

As these psychoactive plants and chemicals once again see the light of day, an even more self-consciously creative community is finding out about designer reality. While drugs in the 1960s worked to overcome social, moral, and intellectual rigidity, drugs now enhance the privileges of the already free. Cyberians using drugs do not need to learn that reality is arbitrary and manipulable, or that the landscape of consciousness is broader than normal waking-state awareness suggests. They have already learned this through the experiences of men like Leary and Kesey. Instead, they take chemicals for the express purpose of manipulating that reality and exploring the uncharted regions of consciousness.

■ INTEGRATING THE BELL CURVE

LSD was the first synthesized chemical to induce basically the same effect as the organic psychedelics used by shamans in ancient cultures. Psychedelics break down one's basic assumptions about life, presenting them instead as arbitrary choices on the part of the individual and his society. The tripper feels liberated into a free-form reality, where his mind and point of view can alter his external circumstances. Psychedelics provide a way to look at life unencumbered by the filters and models one normally uses to process reality. (Whether psychedelics impose a new set of their own filters is irrelevant here. At least the subjective experience of the trip is that the organizing framework of reality has been obliterated.)

Nina Graboi, the author of *One Foot in the Future,* a novel about her own spiritual journey, was among the first pioneers of LSD in the 1960s. Born in 1918 and trained as an actress, she soon became part of New York's bohemian subculture, and kept company with everyone from Tim Leary to Alan Watts. She now works as an assistant to mathematician Ralph Abraham, and occasionally hosts large conferences on psychedelics. She spoke to me at her Santa Cruz beach apartment, over tea and cookies. She believes from what she has seen over the past seven decades that what psychedelics do to an individual, LSD did to society, breaking us free of cause-and-effect logic and into an optimistic creativity.

"Materialism really was at its densest and darkest before the sixties and it did not allow us to see that anything else existed. Then acid came along just at the right time—I really think so. It was very important for some people to reach states of mind that allowed them to see that there is more, that we are more than just these physical bodies. I can't help feeling that there were forces at work that went beyond anything that I can imagine. After the whole LSD craze, all of a sudden, the skies opened up and books came pouring down and wisdom came. And something started happening. I think by now there are enough of us to have created a morphogenetic field of awareness, that are open to more than the materialists believe."

But Graboi believes that the LSD vision needs to be integrated into the experience of America at large. It's not enough to tune in, turn on, and drop out. The impulse now is to recreate reality consciously—and that happens both through a morphogenetic resonance as well as good old-fashioned work.

"I don't think we have a thing to learn from the past, now. We really have to start creating new forms, and seeing real ways of being. This was almost like the mammalian state coming to a somewhat higher octave in the sixties, which was like a quantum leap forward in consciousness. It was a gas. The end of a stage and the beginning of a new one. So right now there are still these two elements very much alive: the old society wanting to pull backward and keep us where we were, and the new one saying, 'Hey, there are new frontiers to conquer and they are in our minds and our hearts.' "

Nina does not consider herself a cyberian, but she does admit she's part of the same effort, and desperately hopes our society can reach this "higher octave." As with all psychedelics, "coming down" is the hardest part. Most would prefer simply to "bring up" everything else . . . to make the rest of the world conform to the trip.

The acid experience follows what can be called a bell curve: the user takes the drug, goes up in about an hour, stays up for a couple of hours, then comes down over a period of three or four hours. It is during the coming-down time—which makes up the majority of the experience—that the clarity of vision or particular insight must be integrated into the normal waking-state consciousness. Like the Greek hero who has visited the gods, the tripper must figure out how the peak of his Aristotelian journey makes sense. The integration of LSD into the sixties' culture was an analogous process. The tripping community had to integrate the truth of their vision into a society that could not grasp such concepts. The bell curve of the sixties touched ground in the form of political activism, sexual liberation, the new age movement, and new scientific and mathematical models.

Cyberians today consider the LSD trip a traditional experience. Even though there are new psychedelics that more exactly match the cyberian checklist for ease of use, length of trip, and overall intensity, LSD provides a uniquely epic journey for the tripper, where the majority of time and energy in the odyssey is spent bringing it all back home. While cyberians usually surf the waves of consciousness for no reason but fun, they take acid because there's work to be done.

When Jaida and Cindy, two twenty-year-old women from Santa Cruz, reunited after being away from each other for almost a year, they chose LSD because they wanted to go through an intense experience of reconnection.

Besides, it was the only drug they could obtain on short notice. They began
by smoking some pot and hitch hiking to a nearby beach town. By the time
they got there, the girls were stoned and the beach was pitch black. They
spent the rest of the night talking and sleeping on what they guessed was a
sand dune, and decided to "drop" at dawn. As the sun rose,
the acid took effect.

While cyberians usually surf the waves of consciousness for no reason but fun, they take acid because there's work to be done.

When the girls stood up, Jaida accidentally stepped on a
crab claw that was sticking out of the sand. Blood flowed out
of her foot. As she describes it now:

"The pain was just so . . . incredible. I could feel the movement of the pain all the way up to my brain, going up the
tendrils, yet it was very enjoyable. And blood was coming out,
but it was incredibly beautiful. At the same time, there was
still the part of me that said 'you have to deal with this,'
which I was very grateful for."

Once Jaida's foot was bandaged, the girls began to walk
together. As they walked and talked, they slipped into a commonly experienced acid phenomenon: shared consciousness.
"It's the only time I've ever been psychic with Cindy. It's like
one of those things that you can't believe . . . there's no evidence or anything. Whatever I was thinking, she would be
thinking. We were making a lot of commentary about the people we were
looking at, and there'd be these long stretches of silence and I would just be
sort of thinking along, and then she would say word for word what I was
thinking. Like that. And then I would say something and it would be exactly
what she was thinking. And we just did that for about four or five hours.
She's a very different physical type from me, but it reached the point where I
could feel how she felt in her body. I had the very deep sensation of being
inside her body, hearing her think, and being able to say everything that she
was thinking. We were in a reality together, and we shared the same space.
Our bodies didn't separate us from each other. We were one thing."

But then came the downside of the bell curve. The girls slowly became
more "disjointed." They began to disagree about tiny things—which way to
walk, whether to eat. "There was this feeling of losing it. I could feel we were
moving away from it with every step. There was a terrible disappointment
that set in. We couldn't hold on to that perfect attunement."

By the time the girls got back to their campsite on the sand dune, their
disillusionment was complete. The sand dune was actually the local trash
dump. As they climbed the stinking mound of garbage to gather their sleeping bags, they found the "crab claw" on which Jaida had stepped. It was really
a used tampon and a broken bottle. And now Jaida's foot was beginning to
smart.

Jaida's reintegration was twofold: She could no more bring back her
empathic ability than she could the belief that she had stepped on a crab
claw. What Jaida retained from the experience, though, came during the
painful crash landing. She was able to see how it was only her interpretation

that made her experience pain as bad, or the tampon and glass as less natural than a crab claw. As in the experience of a Buddha, the garbage dump was as beautiful as a sand dune . . . until they decided it was otherwise. Losing her telepathic union with her friend symbolized and recapitulated the distance that had grown between them over the past year. They had lost touch, and the trip had heightened both their friendship and their separation.

Most acid trippers try to prolong that moment on the peak of the bell curve, but to do so is futile. Coming down is almost inevitably disillusioning to some degree. Again, though, like in a Greek tragedy, it is during the reintegration that insight occurs, and progress is made—however slight—toward a more all-encompassing or cyberian outlook. In order to come down with a minimum of despair and maximum of progress, the tripper must guide his own transition back to normal consciousness and real life while maintaining the integrity of whatever truths he may have gleaned at the apogee of his journey. The LSD state itself is not an end in itself. While it may offer a brief exposure to post-paradigm thinking or even hyperdimensional abilities, the real value of the LSD trip is the *change* in consciousness, and the development of skills in the user to cope with that change. Just as when a person takes a vacation, it is not that the place visited is any better than where he started. It's just different. The traveler returns home changed.

Eugene Schoenfeld, M.D., is the Global Village Town Physician. A practicing psychologist, he wrote the famous "Dr. Hip" advice column in the sixties; he now treats recovering drug addicts. It's easy to see why he has become such a trusted friend and counselor to Cyberia's many chemical casualties. His rich eyes seem to absorb the anxiety of whoever stares into them. One gentle nod of his large, shiny head shows he understands. This man has been there. This man groks. The doctor believes that the desire to alter consciousness, specifically psychedelically, is a healthy urge.

"I think what happens is that it allows people to sense things in a way that they don't ordinarily sense them because we couldn't live that way. If our brains were always the way that they are under the influence of LSD, we couldn't function. Perhaps it is that when babies are born—that's the way they perceive things. Gradually they integrate their experience because we cannot function if we *see music,* for example. We can't live that way.

"Part of the reason why people take drugs is to change their sense of reality, change their sensation, change from the ordinary mind state. And if they had *that* state all the time, they would seek to change *it.* It seems that humans need to change their minds in some way. There's a reason why people start talking about 'tripping.' It's related to trips people take when they physically change their environment. I'm convinced that if there were a way to trip all the time on LSD, they would want to change their reality to something else. That is part of the need."

The sense of being on a voyage, of "tripping," is the essence of a classic psychedelic experience. The user is a traveler, and an acid or mushroom trip is a heroic journey or visionquest through unexplored regions, followed by a reentry into mundane reality. Entry to the psychedelic realm almost always

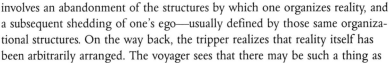

involves an abandonment of the structures by which one organizes reality, and a subsequent shedding of one's ego—usually defined by those same organizational structures. On the way back, the tripper realizes that reality itself has been arbitrarily arranged. The voyager sees that there may be such a thing as an objective world, but whatever it is we're experiencing as reality on a mass scale sure isn't it. With the help of a psychedelic journey, one can come back and consciously choose a

> *On the way back, the tripper realizes that reality itself has been arbitrarily arranged.*

different reality from the one that's been agreed upon by the incumbent society. This can be manifest on a personal, theoretical, political, technological, or even spiritual level.

As Dr. Schoenfeld, who once served as Tim Leary's family physician and now shares his expertise with cyberians as co-host of the DRUGS conference on the WELL, explains, "that quality—that nonjudgmental quality could be carried over without the effects of the drug. After all, one hopes to learn something from a drug experience that he can use afterward. (All this interest in meditation and yoga, all these various disciplines, it all began with people taking these drugs and wanting to recreate these states without drugs.) So, to the extent that they can, that is a useful quality. And this nonjudgmental quality is something I think that can be carried over from a drug experience."

■ OVER THERE

So, the use of psychedelics can be seen as a means toward experiencing free-flowing designer reality: the goal, and the fun, is to manipulate intentionally one's objectivity in order to reaffirm the arbitrary nature of all the mind's constructs, revealing, perhaps, something truer beneath the surface, material reality. You take a trip on which you go nowhere, but everything has changed anyway.

To some, though, it is not just the change of consciousness that makes psychedelics so appealing, but the qualitative difference in the states of awareness they offer. The place people "go" on a trip—the psychedelic corridors of Cyberia—may even be a real space. According to Terence McKenna's frontline correspondence from that place, it is quite different from normal waking-state consciousness:

The voyager journeys "into an invisible realm in which the causality of the ordinary world is replaced with the rationale of natural magic. In this realm, language, ideas, and meaning have greater power than cause and effect. Sympathies, resonances, intentions, and personal will are linguistically magnified through poetic rhetoric. The imagination is invoked and sometimes its forms are beheld visibly. Within the magical mind-set of the shaman, the ordinary connections of the world and what we call natural laws are deemphasized or ignored."

As McKenna describes it, this is not just a mindspace but more of a netherworld, where the common laws of nature are no longer enforced. It is a place where cause-and-effect logic no longer holds, where events and objects function more as icons or symbols, where thoughts are beheld rather than verbalized, and where phenomena like morphic resonance and the fractal reality become consciously experienced. This is the description of Cyberia.

As such, this psychedelic world is not something experienced personally or privately, but, like the rest of Cyberia, as a great group project. The psychedelic world each tripper visits is the same world, so that changes made by one are felt by the others. Regions explored by any traveler become part of the overall map. This is a hyperdimensional terrain on which the traditional solo visionquest becomes a sacred community event.

This feeling of being part of a morphogenetic unfolding is more tangible on psilocybin mushrooms than on LSD. McKenna voices Cyberia's enchantment with the ancient organic brain food: "I think that people should grow mushrooms. They are the real connector back into the archaic, even more so than LSD, which was largely psychoanalytical. It didn't connect you up to the greeny engines of creation. Psilocybin is perfect."

Like LSD, mushrooms provide an eight-hour, bell-curve trip, but it is characterized by more physical and visual "hallucinations" and a much less intellectual edge. Users don't overanalyze their experiences, opting instead to revel in them more fully. Mushrooms are thought to have their own morphogenetic field, which has developed over centuries of their own evolution and their use by ancient cultures. The mushroom trip is much more predictable, cyberians argue, because its morphogenetic field is so much better established than that of acid, which has only been used for a couple of decades, and mostly by inexperienced Western travelers.

Students at U.C. Santa Cruz have developed a secret section of woods dedicated to mushroom tripping called Elf Land (the place just behind Ralph Abraham's office).

As a result, mushroom experiences are, in many ways, less intensely disorienting than LSD trips; the "place" one goes on mushrooms is more natural and user-friendly than the place accessed on acid or other more synthetic psychedelics. Likewise, 'shroomers feel more tangibly a part of the timeless, locationless community of other users, or even animals, fairies, or the "greeny engines" of the spirit of Nature herself.

For this feeling of morphic community and interconnection with nature to become more tangible, groups of 'shroomers often choose to create visionquest hot spots. Students at U.C. Santa Cruz have developed a secret section of woods dedicated to mushroom tripping called Elf Land (the place just behind Ralph Abraham's office). Some students believe that fairies prepared and maintain the multidimensional area of the woods for 'shroomers. Others even claim to have found psilocybin mushrooms—which these fairies are said to leave behind them—growing in Elf Land. Most of all, Elf Land serves as a real-world reference plane for the otherworldly, dimensionless mushroom plane. And, like the morphogenetic mushroom field, Elf Land is shared and modified by everyone who trips there, making the location a kind of cumulative record of a series of mushroom trips.

Mariah is tripping in Elf Land for the first time. A sophomore at U.C. Santa Cruz, the English major had heard of Elf Land since she began taking mushrooms last year, but never really believed in it as a real, physical place. She eats the mushrooms in her dorm with her friends Mark and Rita, then the trio head out to the woods. It's still afternoon, so the paths are easy to follow, but Rita—a much more plugged-in, pop-cultural, fashion-conscious communications major than one would expect to find tripping in the woods of Santa Cruz—suddenly veers off into a patch of poison oak.

Mark, a senior mathematics major and Rita's boyfriend, grabs Rita by the arm, afraid that she's stoned and losing her way.

"It's a pathless path, Mariah," Rita assures the younger girl, without even looking at Mark. Rita knows that Mariah's fears are the most pressing, and that Mark's concerns will be answered by these indirect means. Rita has made it clear that this trip is for Mariah.

"It's the perfect place to trip." Rita puts her arm around Mariah. "People continually put things there. Some of it's very subtle, too. Every time you go there, there's different stuff there. And it's all hidden in the trees up past the fire trails, up in the deep woods there." She points a little farther up the hill.

Then Mariah sees something—a little rock on the ground with an arrow painted on it. "Lookee here!" She stops, picks it up, and turns it over. Painted on the back are the words "This way to Elf Land."

"Someone left this for me?" Mariah asks, the mushrooms taking full effect now, and the fluorescent words on the gray rock beginning to vibrate.

"Just for you, Mariah," Rita whispers, "and for everyone. Come on."

"Here's another one!" Mark is at an opening to the deeper woods, standing next to another sign, this one carved into the side of a tree: "Welcome to Elf Land."

As the three pass through the opening, they walk into another world. It's a shared state of consciousness, not just among the three trippers but among them and everyone else who has ever tripped in Elf Land or anywhere else.

Mariah is thinking about her name; how she got it, how it's shaped her, how it's like the name Mary from the Bible, but changed somehow, too. Updated. At the same moment as these thoughts, she comes upon a small shrine that has been set up in a patch of ferns between two tall trees. The two-foot statue is of the Virgin Mary, but she has been decorated—updated— with a Day-Glo costume.

"How'd that get there?" Mariah wonders out loud.

Meanwhile, Mark has wandered off by himself. He's been disturbed about his relationship with Rita. She seems so addicted to popular culture—not the die-hard Deadhead he remembers from their freshman year. Should they stay together after graduation? Get married, even?

He stands against a tree and leans his head against its trunk, looking up into the branches. He looks at the way each larger branch splits in two. Each smaller branch then splits in two, and so and so on until the branches become leaves. Each leaf, then, begins with a single vein, then splits, by two, into smaller and smaller veins. Mark is reminded of chaos math theory, in which ordered systems, like a river flowing smoothly, become chaotic through a process called bifurcation, or dividing by twos. A river splits in two if there's a rock in its path, the two separate sections preserving—between the two of them—the order and magnitude of the original. A species can bifurcate into two different mutations if conditions require it. And a relationship can break up if....

As Mark stares at the bifurcated pairs of branches and leaves, he realizes that bifurcation is the nature of decision making. He's caught in the duality of a painful choice, and the tree is echoing the nature of decision-making itself.

"Making a decision?" Mariah asks innocently. She has read the small sign nailed into the side of the tree: "Tree of Decision."

"I wonder who left that there?" Mark wonders aloud.

"Doesn't matter," answers Rita, emerging from nowhere. "Someone last week, last year. A tripper, an elf . . . whoever."

As if on a visionquest, Mark and Mariah were presented with a set of symbols in material form that they could analyze and integrate into a pattern. They were "beholding" their thoughts in physical form. The reality of their trip was confirmed not just by their fantasies but by the totems and signs left for them by other trippers experiencing the same things at different times.

Mushrooms very often give users the feeling of being connected with the past and the future. Whether the 'shroomers know about morphogenetic fields, they do feel connected with the spirit of the woods, and everyone who has traveled before in the same space. Going up is the voyage to that space, peaking is the unself-conscious experience of the new world, and coming down is the reintegration during which the essence of the peak experience is translated into a language or set of images a person can refer to later, at base-line reality.

■ QUESTIONS FOR REREADING

1. Why does Rushkoff title this reading "Seeing Is Beholding"?

2. Rushkoff begins his take on VR with an anecdote about Terence McKenna, the philosopher of the psychedelic plant world. For what purpose does Rushkoff begin with this discussion? Can you tell from Rushkoff's tone (that is, the author's voice or attitude) what his purpose might be? What is the analogy or parallel, as Rushkoff reports it, between psychedelic (mind-expanding) drugs and VR or cyberspace? (Recall the passage that I quoted from Heim in my brief introduction to Heim's article.)

3. What do McKenna and his cohorts believe is beneficial in their taking drugs? What scientific experiments are cited by Rushkoff that might explain the benefits? What is the "unity" that Rushkoff talks about? The morphogenetic field? How does the taking of drugs, and by analogy trekking in cyberspace, change reality? (Are there parallels here between

what Woolley says about McLuhan's thinking and McKenna's and others'? And what about parallels with what Heim says about VR?)

4. In discussing Nina Graboi's views of LSD, Rushkoff reports that the so-called bell curve of intelligence, and so on, improves when taking psyche-delic drugs, and most notably, it improved and manifested its upward movement dramatically in the 1960s and 1970s in terms of political protests against the war in Vietnam, sexual liberation, concern for the envi-ronment, and new mathematical systems and designs (fractals). What is Rushkoff suggesting by relating the story of Jaida and Cindy? (This is a very difficult question that I am asking. Talk about it carefully in the light of what Rushkoff is variously saying.)

5. What is your overall assessment of Rushkoff's account of *seeing is beholding?*

■ WRITING ASSIGNMENTS FOR REREADING

1. Have a class or online discussion with your classmates about Rushkoff's attitude toward the parallel between drugs and virtual reality. Try to deter-mine whether Rushkoff is serious about the parallel, and if so, whether he is consistently serious. When discussing this issue, try to plot out the details of the mini-narratives and descriptions in the article, and try to determine how they can serve as evidence of Rushkoff's attitude toward drugs and VR. During the discussion, begin a journal and take notes of what is said. Then write an essay on your attitudes toward this chapter and the whole issue of drugs that change the perception of reality. If your atti-tude has changed, explain why; if not, then explain.

2. If you have a chance, try to read all of the book *Cyberia,* from which this chapter comes. Remember that your reading of the chapter is a reading out of context. Perhaps you might like to write a book report for your class-mates. Perhaps several of you might want to write book reports individu-ally or collaboratively.

Richard Thieme's article "Stalking the UFO Meme" first appeared as "How to Build a UFO... Story" in Internet Underground 1:12 (November 1996): 36–41. Besides being republished here under its present title, it has been republished online by Arthur and Marilouise Kroker at CTHEORY and in the Kroker's Digital Delirium. (Richard Thieme ‹rthieme@thiemeworks.com› speaks, consults, and writes on organizational change and the impact of computer technology on individuals, organizations, and society ‹http://www.thiemeworks.com›.)

While Thieme is much concerned with the idea of what constitutes evidence for something having happened, he is simultaneously concerned with the concept of reality. In his article, he is concerned specifically with the famous "Roswell incident." And what is this incident? It is a set of beliefs (or memes) about what happened in Roswell back in 1947 near the Roswell Army Air Field. The question is whether an alien spaceship crashed there. For many people, it is no longer a question but an answer that the government would keep quiet.

For Thieme, what counts as reality demands evidence. At best, for Thieme, "Roswell"—not the city in New Mexico, but the "incident"—is a virtual reality, a meme. But it is a reality that potentially threatens any sense of reality and evidence. After the first newspaper report was published about the "incident," a meme spread across the land, across the world. The "Roswell incident" is a new reality.

"There is Thingumbob shouting!" the Bellman said. "He is shouting like mad, only hark! He is waving his hands, he is waggling his head, He has certainly found a Snark!"

—Lewis Carroll,
The Hunting of the Snark

"We are convinced that Roswell took place. We've had too many high ranking military officials tell us that it happened, that told us that it was clearly not of this earth."

—Don Schmitt, co-author, "The Truth About the UFO Crash at Roswell," in an interview by Ed Mar and Jody Mecanic for *Lumpen Magazine* on the Internet

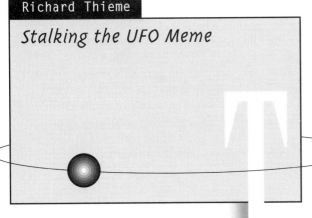

Richard Thieme

Stalking the UFO Meme

hat "interview with a real X-Filer" can be found on one of the hundreds of Web sites—in addition to Usenet groups, gopher holes stuffed with hundreds of files, and clandestine BBSs where abductees meet to compare "scoop marks"—that make up the virtual world of flying saucers.

The UFO subculture or—for some—the UFO religion on the Internet is a huge supermarket of images and words. Everything is for sale—stories and pictures, membership in a community, entire belief systems. But what are we buying? The meal? Or the menu?

■ THE BRICKS THAT BUILD THE HOUSE

When Don Schmitt uses the word "Roswell," he is not merely identifying a small town in New Mexico that put itself on the tourist map with a terrific

UFO story. He uses it to mean the whole story—the one that says a UFO crashed in 1947 near the Roswell Army Air Field, after which alien bodies were recovered, eyewitnesses rewarded with new pickup trucks or threatened with death, and a cosmic Watergate—as Stanton Friedman, another Roswell author, calls it—initiated. Schmitt uses the word "Roswell" the way Christian evangelists use "Jesus," to mean everything believed about "Roswell." Like an evangelist, he counts on his audience to fill in the details. Every good Roswellite knows them—it's the story, after all, that defines them as a community.

That story is scattered on the Internet like fragments of an exploding spaceship. Do the pieces fit together to make a coherent puzzle? Or is something wrong with this picture?

■ STALKING THE UFO MEME ON THE INTERNET

Memes are contagious ideas that replicate like viruses from mind to mind. The Internet is like a petri dish in which memes multiply rapidly. Fed by fascination, incubated in the feverish excitement of devotees transmitting stories of cosmic significance, the UFO meme mutates into new forms, some of them wondrous and strange.

"The Roswell incident" is but one variation of the UFO meme. On the Internet, Schmitt's words are hyperlinked to those of other UFO sleuths and legions of interested bystanders like myself, as fascinated by the psychodynamics of the subculture as by the "data" exchanged as currency in that marketplace.

Before we examine a few fragments, let's pause to remember what the Internet really is.

■ COPIES OF COPIES—OR COPIES OF ORIGINALS?

The Internet represents information through symbols or icons. So does speech, writing, and printed text, but the symbols on the Net are even further removed from the events and context to which they point.

The power of speech gave us the ability to lie, then writing hid the liar from view. That's why Plato fulminated at writing—you couldn't know what was true if you didn't have the person right there in front of you, he said, the dialogue providing a necessary check.

The printing press made it worse by distancing reader and writer even more. Now we put digital images and text on the Net. Pixels can be manipulated. Without correlation with other data, no digital photo or document can be taken at face value. There's no way to know if we're looking at a copy of an original, a copy of a copy, or a copy that has no original.

But wait. It gets worse.

■ THE WORLD IS A BLANK SCREEN

Certain phenomena, including UFOs and religious symbols, elicit powerful projections. We think we're seeing "out there" what is really inside us. Because projections are unconscious, we don't know if we're looking at iron filings obscuring a magnet or the magnet itself.

Carl Jung said UFOs invite projections because they're mandalas—archetypal images of our deep Selves. Unless we separate what we think we see from what we see, we're bound to be confused.

Repetition makes any statement seem true. Hundreds of cross-referenced links on the Web create a matrix of even greater credibility. In print, we document assertions with references. Footnotes are conspicuous by their absence on the Web. Information is self-referential. Symbols and images point to themselves like a ten-dimensional dog chasing its own tails.

"Roswell" may be the name of the game, but what does the name really say?

■ WHAT'S IN A NAME?

Everything.

Names reveal our beliefs about things.

Was there a "Roswell incident"? Or was there a "so-called Roswell incident"?

Are Don Schmitt and his former partner Kevin Randle "the only two professional investigators in the field" as Schmitt claims in that interview? Or are they in fact "self-styled professional UFO investigators"? (UFO investigators accredit themselves, then reinforce their authority by debating one another and showing up at the same forums. Refuting or attacking another "investigator" does him a favor by acknowledging his importance.)

Names reveal our beliefs about things.

Are there "eight firsthand witnesses who saw the bodies," "many high-ranking military officials who said it was not of this earth," or "550 witnesses stating that this was not from this earth"? All of those statements are made in the same interview.

Words like "self-styled" and "alleged" do more than avoid lawsuits. They make clear that the speaker states or believes something rather than knows it to be true. Schmitt uses the word "witness" the way Alice in Wonderland uses words, to mean exactly what she wants them to mean—instead of letting witness mean . . . well, *witness.*

Dan Kagan and Ian Summers have written a masterful investigation of "cattle mutilation." (*Mute Evidence,* Bantam Books, New York: 1984), detailing how predator damage became "cattle mutilation" conducted with "surgical precision," i.e., in straight lines, through the distortion of the media, "professional experts" who kept everyone one step away from the evidence (common in UFO research), and true believers who suspended their capacity for critical judgment.

"The Roswell incident" also consists of words repeated often enough to turn them into pseudo-facts which are then used to weave a scenario. When enough people believe the scenario, they focus on the minutiae of the story—did it crash on the Plains of San Augustin, as Stanton Friedman claims, or north of Roswell as Schmitt and Randle claim?—instead of the basics, i.e., did anything other than a balloon crash at all? Science turns quickly into theology.

■ CAN A FACT MOVE AT THE SPEED OF LIGHT?

The way sites are connected on the www tends to obliterate our historical sense. Everything on the Web seems to be happening *now*. Without a point of reference, all information seems equal. Lining up texts side-by-side and evaluating discrepancies feels like hard work.

Surf to the Cambridge Cybercafé, for example, and you'll find a laudatory article about Schmitt written by Milwaukee writer Gillian Sender.

Sender says the piece was purloined without her permission. Like much on the Net, it's an unauthorized copy of a copy.

Sender did a follow-up piece for *Milwaukee Magazine* in which she confessed her subsequent disillusionment with Schmitt. In interviews he misrepresented his educational background and occupation. Sender concluded that those misrepresentations undermined his credibility across the board.

You won't learn that on the Web, because the second piece isn't there. The Cybercafé Web site also has a newsletter written by Schmitt and Randle but no link to information about their later split, when Randle denounced Schmitt for deceiving him as well as others.

■ THE SOUL OF THE WEB

According to Jung, when the psyche projects its contents onto an archetypal symbol, there is always secrecy, fascination, and high energy. When a Webmaster finds an article like Sender's he gets excited, plucks it out of cyberspace, and puts it on his site. Come across it four or five times, you start to believe it.

Tracking down the truth about the "Roswell incident" is like hunting the mythical Snark in the Carroll poem. The closer one gets to the "evidence," the more it disappears.

There is in fact not one living "witness" to the "Roswell incident" in the public domain, not one credible report that is not filtered through a private interview or other privileged communication.

There are, though, lots of people making a living from it.

■ WHO ARE THESE GUYS?

Karl Pflock is another "Roswell investigator." Stick his name into a search engine and you'll find him on the UFOlogist roster at Glenn Campbell's Area 51 Web site. The text of an online interview with Pflock and Stanton Friedman is reproduced there.

What effect does this have?

By appearing with him, Friedman lends credibility to Pflock's status. Their disagreement over details (Pflock thinks the Roswell debris was the remains of a Project Mogul balloon, as the Air Force claims) is less important than the fact of their debate, which implies that the details are important, the debate worth having. That ensures future bookings for both.

Get the idea? In the virtual world, the appearance of reality becomes reality. Then you can buy and sell words, icons, symbols as if the menu is the meal.

Pflock is not new to the world of UFOs. Kagan and Summers first encountered him as a man named "Kurt Peters" who appropriated a story he knew was fabricated about "cattle mutilations," then tried to pass it off as his own and sell it to a New York publisher. When the authors confronted Pflock "with the Kurt Peters gambit, he was shaken that we had found him out."

What might we infer, therefore, about Pflock's credibility? On the Web, however, the context created by juxtaposition with Friedman makes it seem as if he is a real "professional."

■ F O L L O W   T H E   M O N E Y

The UFO game needs teams so the game can be played. The "for-team" and the "against-team" are essential to each other. The famous "alien autopsy film" exploited by Ray Santilli illustrates this.

This film allegedly showed the autopsy of an alien retrieved from a crash site. Many Web sites were devoted to this film; Usenet groups hummed with endless conversation about the details. One major thread was devoted to finding the cameraman. (Once again, the key player or detail was absent, the audience addressed by a "spokesperson for the event.")

A great deal of money was made by debating the film, regardless of which side one was on. Stanton Friedman was off to Italy for a screening, Schmitt to England to "examine the evidence," and so on. Meanwhile reports like that by Dr. Joseph A. Bauer on CSICOP's Web site that exposed the film's "overwhelming lack of credibility" were ignored. The lack of credibility was obvious from the beginning, but had it been acknowledged, there would have been no game to play—no Fox-TV special, no books or debates, no conferences in Europe.

The Santilli episode is about played out, but other "evidence" is taking its place. At the moment, an anonymous tipster claims to have a fragment of the crashed saucer. The story is spreading on the Web, mutating as it grows. Now, fifty years after the alleged crash, others claim to have fragments too.

The good thing about fragments of crashed saucers is that they are endless. Even better are the claims made by "professional investigators" that they are negotiating with shadowy figures who have fragments but are afraid of being killed if they go public. Those stories are endless too.

To know someone's motivation, follow their checkbook. Look, for example, at the heated rivalry in the town of Roswell between museums competing for tourist dollars with trips to rival crash sites. You can even sign up for the tour on the Web.

■ INFORMATION? MISINFORMATION? DISINFORMATION?

The Santilli film could be dismissed as a non-event, did it not reveal a deeper dimension of life in the UFO world. What were its effects?

Energy was displaced, the focus of the debate shifted, and the "Roswell incident"—ironically—reinforced.

When someone says "These are not the real crown jewels" they imply that real crown jewels exist. If this is a fake autopsy film, where is the *real* autopsy film? That implies a real autopsy, which implies real aliens and a real crash.

Or was the film an ingenious piece of disinformation by the government? Was it designed to throw investigators off the track? See how we responded to news of real aliens? Hide some real data among a snowstorm of false data?

Is all this confusion . . . intentional?

It's X-files time.

■ READY FOR A HEADACHE?

Now we're closing in on the Snark.

Are government agents using the subculture to manipulate or experiment with public opinion? To cover up what they know? Are the investigators "useful idiots," as they're known in the spy trade, real spies, or just in it for the buck?

One of my online adventures illustrates the difficulty of getting answers to these questions.

A woman in Hamilton, Montana, was speaking to Peter Davenport, head of the National UFO Reporting Center in Seattle, about a UFO she said was hanging around her neighborhood. She said she could hear strange beeps on the radio when it was hovering. Then, while they spoke, some beeps sounded.

"There!" she said. "You hear that? What **is** that?"

Peter played the beeps over the telephone. I recorded them. Then I posted a message on alt.2600—a hacker's Usenet group—asking for help.

I received several offers of assistance. One came from LoD.

Plato was right. We need to know who is speaking.

LoD! The Legion of Doom! I was delighted. If anybody can get to the bottom of this, the LoD can. These guys are the best hackers in the business.

I recorded the beeps as a .wav file and e-mailed them to LoD. They asked a few questions and said they'd see what they could find.

Meanwhile I received another e-mail. This writer said he had heard similar tones over telephone lines and shortwave radio in his neighborhood, which happened to be near a military base.

Then he wrote, "I have some info that would be of great interest. Government documents. . . ." He mentioned friends inside the base who told him about them.

Meanwhile the LoD examined the switching equipment used by the telco and reported that they were evaluating the data.

A third e-mail directed me to a woman specializing in the "beeps" frequently associated with UFOs. She sent me a report she had written about their occurrence and properties.

LoD asked for my telephone number and someone called the following week. They could affirm, the caller said, that the signals did not originate within the telephone system. They could say what the signals were not, but not what they were. One negative did not imply a positive.

Then the correspondent near the military base sent a striking communication.

"The documentation and info that I am getting are going to basically confirm what a member of the team has divulged to me."

"They are here and they are not benign."

He gave me information about other things he had learned, then acknowledged that all he said was either worthless hearsay or serious trouble. Therefore, he concluded, "I am abandoning this account and disappearing back into the ether."

■ THE TWILIGHT ZONE

There you have it. Without corroboration or external evidence to use as a triangulating point, that's as far as the Internet can take us.

Words originate with someone—but who? Is the name on the e-mail real? Is the domain name real? Is the account real?

Secrecy. Fascination. High energy.

Maybe it's a sign of the times that I was pleased to have the help of the LoD. While I would have dismissed a government or telco statement as maybe true, maybe not, I trusted LoD.

They did a solid piece of work. Technically they're the best, but more than that, I knew they'd be true to their code. Like me, they're need-to-know machines and they love a good puzzle.

What about the next-door-to-the-military source? Was he who he said he was? Were his contacts telling the truth? Are "they" here and are "they" not benign? Or was he a government agent trying to learn what I knew? Or just a bored kid who felt like killing a little time?

How do we separate fact from fiction? Jacques Vallée, a respected writer and researcher, recently authored a work of fiction about UFOs. Is he really writing fiction so he can disguise the truth, as some say? Or is he just another guy selling a book? Or a serious investigator who has blurred his own credibility by writing fiction that's hard to distinguish from his theories?

Or is he a secret agent working for the government?

The UFO world is a hall of mirrors. The UFO world on the Internet is a simulation of a hall of mirrors. The truth is out there, all right . . . but how can we find it?

Plato was right. We need to know who is speaking. We need to stay with the bottom-line data that won't go away.

■ THE BOTTOM LINE

What does it look like?

One piece looks like this. I know a career Air Force officer, recently retired as a full colonel. He worked at the Pentagon and the War College. He is a terrific guy who has all the "right stuff." He's the kind of guy you'd willingly follow into battle. Many did.

A fellow B47 pilot in the sixties told him of an unusual object that flew in formation with him for a while, then took off at an incredible speed he could not match. The copilot independently verified the incident. Neither wanted to report it and risk damage to their careers.

When he first told me that account in the 1970s, I remember how he looked. He usually looked confident, even cocky. That time he looked puzzled, maybe a little helpless. I knew he was telling me the truth.

I have seen that look many times as credible people told me their account of an anomalous experience. They don't want publicity or money. They just want to know what's happening on their planet.

Data has accumulated for at least fifty years. Some of it is on the Internet. Some of it, like e-mail from that retired Air Force officer, is trustworthy. Much of it isn't.

Are we hunting a Snark, only to be bamboozled by a boojum? Or are we following luminous breadcrumbs through the darkening forest to the Truth that is Out There? The Net is one place to find answers, but we'll find them only if our pursuit of the truth is rigorous, disciplined, and appropriately skeptical.

■ QUESTIONS FOR REREADING

1. What is it that you have to know to understand what someone is saying? Thieme's article requires that you bring to it a basic understanding of the allusions of events that have occurred since the 1950s. Therefore, to understand this important article, you need to know something about the following:

   a. Roswell
   b. Carl Jung
   c. Alice in Wonderland
   d. Project Mogul Balloon
   e. Alien autopsy film
   f. LoD (Legion of Doom)

g. Watergate

h. *The Twilight Zone* versus *The X-Files*

and what else?

How would you find out about these persons, places, and things? Often when we read someone's work, we find references or allusions to things we have no knowledge about. It is easy to blame the author instead of ourselves. All understanding of others' writings, and so on, is based on commonly shared knowledge or experience. Therefore, we need to do a quick "inspectional" reading to discover what we do not know so that we can prepare ourselves to know finally what the author is attempting to say. Reading is not passive; it requires that you actively inquire. So get to work and find out!

2. Notice how Thieme refers to Plato, as Heim does in his article and as I do in my introduction to this section. What Plato said is a shared commonplace among many readers. What is the difference, if any, between the ways that Heim and Thieme use Plato? Do they express different attitudes toward Plato?

3. What is the point of Thieme's article? Is it a simple, yet complex, question of whether there have been aliens visiting Earth? Or is he concerned primarily with memes and how they spread and replicate? Now, what I think is the most important question in the context of this chapter is, What is the relationship between a meme (the UFO meme) and virtual reality? Recall what Woolley says about memes and computer viruses. Recall that Heim and Rushkoff say that VR has religious (metaphysical, spiritual) overtones and that Thieme writes about the "UFO religion on the Internet." What other parallels do you find between what Heim says in characterizing VR and what Thieme has to say about the UFO meme?

I asked Richard Thieme if he had any questions that he wanted to ask you and he sent the following:

4. I quote an interview with Don Schmitt that was on the World Wide Web. Is it still there? If not, how can you determine the accuracy of my quotes? Are there archives of www sites anywhere? If you locate them, how can you know they have not been altered?

5. I quote e-mail from a hacker revealing information from inside an American military base. Do you think it is accurate? How can you know?

6. I quote a career Air Force officer who reported an encounter with a UFO. Is the sort of experience the officer described—being paced by an object with aerodynamic capabilities beyond our best jets at the time—unique? Are there reports from Air Force pilots and commercial airline pilots that are similar? Does it matter that this was an American? Do other countries have archives of similar UFO reports?

7. I turned to the Legion of Doom, a loose confederation of hackers, for help with some electronic tones recorded in Montana. Why didn't he speak to the telephone company in Montana or ask the U.S. Air Force? Has any serious research been done on sounds associated with UFO sightings?

8. I seem to expose a lot of chicanery in the UFO domain, but I also seem to take UFO reports seriously. Where do you think I stand on the subject? What's your evidence?

■ WRITING ASSIGNMENT FOR REREADING

For a collaborative project, six or so students might do some basic research into one specific aspect of Thieme's article and divide the group into two sub-groups, with one researching in the library (books, articles, and so on) and the other group searching by way of search engines such as Hotbot and AltaVista. (See Appendix A, CyberSearch.) What you search for in the two ways must be *the same thing,* and you must make sure that you continue to coordinate your search, for the point is to compare what you find that is in common and what is uncommon and then to try to determine what is credible and not credible. Ask your instructor/facilitator to help you maintain a parallel search and to think about the criteria for determining credibility. (Recall that Thieme writes: "Footnotes are conspicuous by their absence on the Web.") When you have made your search and arrived at a set of criteria, then write a collaborative essay reporting your findings and put it, as best as you can, in hypertext for-mat at a Web site. When you have finished and are satisfied with it, have your instructor let me know by sending me the URL (uniform resource locator, or Web address) so that I can consider it for inclusion at the *CyberReader* Web site.

Virtual Communitie

(Societies and Identities)

"The new electronic
interdependence recreates the
world in the image of a global
village."
—Marshall McLuhan,
The Medium Is the Message

There are so many theories and explanations for what makes a community. One simple explanation is kinship by biology (birth) or custom (marriage). Another is any shared interest. Still another is the desire and need for conviviality. Or for self-identity. Each of us is who we are by virtue of our connections with others. These connections make a community and society.

There are many *places* or venues for the establishment of community. In fact, without those places set aside for being social, there might not be any community at all. Such places are the home, the fireplace, the television, the church, the town hall, the courtroom, the school, the office, the farmers' market, the beach, the arcade, the pub, and the coffee house. (And the prison, the most unsocial of social communities.) The list goes on. There is a place for every occasion of communication—and all are for the sake of community. Besides place, there are *manners* of communication. There is a way to sit around a campfire. A way of sitting in a circle. Of telling a story. Of listening and observing as the story is told. There are ways of sitting in front of a television and watching it with others, and those ways vary from group to group, person to person, culture to culture, though there are overlappings among them.

All of these examples are from our real or actual world, which leads to the question, Is there a corresponding series of examples for the virtual world? The answer is yes. For every real city or society, there is, so to speak, a soft(ware) city or *soft city*. All of the interconnected computers through nodes that are linked to the Internet make up one virtual global city, around which those of us who have computers sit *as if* at a café or around a campfire, swapping stories; *as if* in a classroom, taking lessons and giving them; *as if* in a town hall, advocating a public policy; *as if* at the market, selling our goods. We visit each other's *home* pages. And so on. Though we may be physically alone when online, we are virtually with others, most of whom we have never met nor will ever meet face-to-face (F2F). And when online with others, we have manners and customs to follow, which contribute to the idea of a virtual community.

But besides a virtual place and manners of communication, which more often than not are analogous with places and manners in the real world, there is a third aspect of the comparison between real and virtual places and societies, and that is the difference between actual and virtual *self-identity*. Being in real places demands that we maintain a stable self-identity. Being in virtual places, however, invites people to be fluid, unfixed, ever-changing, and multiple. For example, if people want to change their names and identities in real places and want this change to have legal status, they must ask and give cogent reasons in court to a judge. When people go to virtual places and communities, however, they are less concerned with the legal status of the real world and can take and use their so-called real names, but they also can seek anonymity, taking other identities, ranging from such apparently minor changes as in social class and vocation to such radical changes as in gender (cross-dressing), race, and species. In other words, virtual places invite people to be other than they are. They invite people to experiment by way of role-playing.

For many critics of cyber and virtual communities, this fluid identity is too radical and threatening to real places and manners in real communities and societies. For other people this multiplicity of identities, this role-playing, can be therapeutic and make people sympathetic to and have empathy for others. It can make people appreciate differences and be more tolerant toward others. Often it is forgotten that this difference of views makes for societies themselves, both real and simulated. It is difference and debate among *citizens* and *netizens* that keep the two possible worlds separate and distinct. But there is more to be said about whether or not the differences between the two can be maintained.

The virtual or soft city cum *bit city* has arisen almost catastrophically, as if overnight, spanning the world. Every day, as more and more miles of fiber optics are laid, more and more bandwidth is created through which we can move from place to place collapsing *here* and *there,* collapsing four dimensions and great distances at the speed of light. As William J. Mitchell says in *City of Bits,* every day more and more protoplasm is turned, so to speak, into bits and bytes. In cyber places. In virtual places. Every day we are getting closer and closer to leaving the real world-community as we have come to know and experience it. When sitting at our monitors, Mitchell says, "we will not just look *at* [cyber places]; we will feel present *in* them" (Mitchell's emphasis). Perhaps this is just a silly idea from a science-fiction movie such as *Tron.* For Mitchell, however, this is no silly idea; he believes in a balance between the two worlds, but sees great advantages for communities and societies in what he calls—instead of the virtual or the public sphere—the *bitsphere*. He writes: "The task of the twenty-first century will be to build the bitsphere—a world-wide, electronically mediated environment in which networks are every-where."

But many people want to know if this will *really* happen—this feeling of being more *in* the virtual world rather than in the real world. In the bitsphere. And many of the same people are afraid of computer networks everywhere. (Simply recall the fear of Big Brother.) Moreover, many people compare being *in* VR to being *on* drugs. To being antisocial.

There are so many answers and arguments pro and con. Perhaps the more prudent answer to the question of the value of virtual communities is *to wait and see* whether we will feel more present and alive and more politically free when *in* virtual communities. Or perhaps it is not a matter of either/or, but a matter of being *in between* the real and the virtual, shuttling in practical ways between. But many people do not want to wait and see or do not want to think in terms of *in-betweens,* for they want to apply the brakes immediately, so as to stay in the real world. The three articles in this chapter and throughout the rest of the book very generally and progressively take up the issue in either optimistic or pessimistic terms or in rather cautiously balanced views.

■ S U M M A R Y   O F   K E Y   T E R M S

BBSS: Bulletin board systems. Constructed by hobbyists, a BBS is an electronic conferencing or bulletin board that is established in some-one's hard disk within a computer by way of special software that allows for the communicating and posting of messages on a modem across telephone lines.

bitsphere: A term, coined by William J. Mitchell, that stands in contrast to the term *public sphere.* The bitsphere is a worldwide, electronically mediated environment with everything electronically connected to everything else and therefore is what constitutes a virtual community.

CMC: Computer-mediated communication.

Luddite, neo-Luddite: The term derives from Ned Ludd, an apparent leader of an early nineteenth-century radical agrarian movement against the industrial revolution. A contemporary manifestation, by analogy, is the neo-Luddite move-ment against high technology and computers.

netizen: A citizen of a virtual community. (Sometimes the term *cyberzen* is used.)

soft city: Short for soft(ware) city. A virtual city or community. A simulated city (or simcity).

Usenet: User's Net or the Inter-net. A collection of interconnected computers that are sites for CMC such as BBSS and larger groups.

virtual community: A computer-mediated social group or groups.

virtual identity: A computer-mediated persona that is fluid and multiple. In a virtual environment, people feel free to take on any persona that they wish, whether male or female or another, whether human or some other species.

WELL: The Whole Earth 'Lectronic Link is a computer network <www.well.com/> in the San Francisco area that can be sub-scribed to from anywhere. It is the site of many well-known and published discussions among hackers, technophilosophers, Internet enthusiasts, and the like.

Howard Rheingold is perhaps the best-known advocate for all things virtual. His genre and style of writing are journalistic, which in great part contributes to his popularity among readers. Things virtual are not easy to explain to a general audience of readers, so his contributions and skill in explaining difficult concepts are always much welcomed.

He has been the Editor of The Whole Earth Review and Editor-in-Chief of The Millennium Whole Earth Catalog. He is on the Board of Directors of the WELL, and he was the founding Executive Editor of HotWired, which is associated with Wired magazine. In his own words: "He's a participant-observer in the design of new technologies, a pioneer, critic and forecaster of technology's impacts, and a speaker who involves his audience in an interactive adventure in group futurism."

The selection included here is the Introduction to The Virtual Community: Homesteading on the Electronic Frontier (New York: Addison-Wesley, 1993): 1–16. Rheingold's is the first book-length account of whether there is any such thing as a virtual community; his account is from his own experiences online at the WELL and elsewhere.

Rheingold believes in the hacker ethic that information wants to be free. His entire book can be found on the Web for everyone's free-of-charge reading: ‹http://www.well.com/user/hlr/vcbook/›.

We know the rules of community; we know the healing effect of community in terms of individual lives. If we could somehow find a way across the bridge of our knowledge, would not these same rules have a healing effect upon our world? We human beings have often been referred to as social animals. But we are not yet community creatures. We are impelled to relate with each other for our survival. But we do not yet relate with the inclusivity, realism, self-awareness, vulnerability, commitment, openness, freedom, equality, and love of genuine community. It is clearly no longer enough to be simply social animals, babbling together at cocktail parties and brawling with each other in business and over boundaries. It is our task—our essential, central, crucial task—to transform ourselves from mere social creatures into community creatures. It is the only way that human evolution will be able to proceed.

—The Different Drum:
Community-Making and Peace

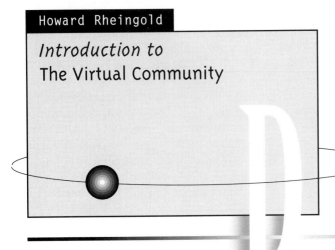

Howard Rheingold

Introduction to
The Virtual Community

addy is saying 'Holy moly!' to his computer again!"

Those words have become a family code for the way my virtual community has infiltrated our real world. My seven-year-old daughter knows that her father congregates with a family of invisible friends who seem to gather in his computer. Sometimes he talks to them, even if nobody else can see them. And she knows that these invisible friends sometimes show up in the flesh, materializing from the next block or the other side of the planet.

Since the summer of 1985, for an average of two hours a day, seven days a week, I've been plugging my personal computer into my telephone and making contact with the WELL (Whole Earth 'Lectronic Link)—a computer conferencing system that enables people around the world to carry on public conversations and exchange private electronic mail (e-mail). The idea of a community accessible only via my computer screen sounded cold to me at first, but I learned quickly that people can feel passionately about e-mail and computer conferences. I've become one of them. I care about these people I met through my computer, and I care deeply about the future of the medium that enables us to assemble.

I'm not alone in this emotional attachment to an apparently bloodless technological ritual. Millions of people on every continent also participate in the computer-mediated social groups known as virtual communities, and this population is growing fast. Finding the WELL was like discovering a cozy little world that had been flourishing without me, hidden within the walls of my house; an entire cast of characters welcomed me to the troupe with great merriment as soon as I found the secret door. Like others who fell into the WELL, I soon discovered that I was audience, performer, and scriptwriter, along with my companions, in an ongoing improvisation. A full-scale subculture was growing on the other side of my telephone jack, and they invited me to help create something new.

The virtual village of a few hundred people I stumbled upon in 1985 grew to eight thousand by 1993. It became clear to me during the first months of that history that I was participating in the self-design of a new kind of culture. I watched the community's social contracts stretch and change as the people who discovered and started building the WELL in its first year or two were joined by so many others. Norms were established, challenged, changed, reestablished, rechallenged, in a kind of speeded-up social evolution.

The WELL felt like an authentic community to me from the start because it was grounded in my everyday physical world. WELLites who don't live within driving distance of the San Francisco Bay Area are constrained in their ability to participate in the local networks of face-to-face acquaintants. By now, I've attended real-life WELL marriages, WELL births, and even a WELL funeral. (The phrase "in real life" pops up so often in virtual communities that regulars abbreviate it to IRL.) I can't count the parties and outings where the invisible personae who first acted out their parts in the debates and melodramas on my computer screen later manifested in front of me in the physical world in the form of real people, with faces, bodies, and voices.

I remember the first time I walked into a room full of people IRL who knew many intimate details of my history and whose own stories I knew very well. Three months after I joined, I went to my first WELL party at the home of one of the WELL's online moderators. I looked around at the room full of strangers when I walked in. It was one of the oddest sensations of my life. I had contended with these people, shot the invisible breeze around the electronic watercooler, shared alliances and formed bonds, fallen off my chair laughing with them, become livid with anger at some of them. But there wasn't a recognizable face in the house. I had never seen them before.

My flesh-and-blood family long ago grew accustomed to the way I sit in my home office early in the morning and late at night, chuckling and cursing, sometimes crying, about words I read on the computer screen. It might have looked to my daughter as if I were alone at my desk the night she caught me chortling online, but from my point of view I was in living contact with old and new friends, strangers and colleagues.

I was in the Parenting conference on the WELL, participating in an informational and emotional support group for a friend who had just learned that his son had been diagnosed with leukemia.

I was in MicroMUSE, a role-playing fantasy game of the twenty-fourth century (and science education medium in disguise), interacting with students and professors who know me only as "Pollenator."

I was in TWICS, a bicultural community in Tokyo; CIX, a community in London; CalvaCom, a community in Paris; and Usenet, a collection of hundreds of different discussions that travel around the world via electronic mail to millions of participants in dozens of countries.

I was browsing through Supreme Court decisions, in search of information that could help me debunk an opponent's claims in a political debate elsewhere on the Net, or I was retrieving this morning's satellite images of weather over the Pacific.

I was following an eyewitness report from Moscow during the coup attempt, or China during the Tiananmen Square incident, or Israel and Kuwait during the Gulf War, passed directly from citizen to citizen through an ad hoc network patched together from cheap computers and ordinary telephone lines, cutting across normal geographic and political boundaries by piggybacking on the global communications infrastructure.

I was monitoring a rambling real-time dialogue among people whose bodies were scattered across three continents, a global bull session that seems to blend wit and sophomore locker-room talk via Internet relay chat (IRC), a medium that combines the features of conversation and writing. IRC has accumulated an obsessive subculture of its own among undergraduates by the thousands from Adelaide to Arabia.

People in virtual communities use words on screens to exchange pleasantries and argue, engage in intellectual discourse, conduct commerce, exchange knowledge, share emotional support, make plans, brainstorm, gossip, feud, fall in love, find friends and lose them, play games, flirt, create a little high art and a lot of idle talk. People in virtual communities do just about everything people do in real life, but we leave our bodies behind. You can't kiss anybody and nobody can punch you in the nose, but a lot can happen within those boundaries. To the millions who have been drawn into it, the richness and vitality of computer-linked cultures is attractive, even addictive.

There is no such thing as a single, monolithic, online subculture.

There is no such thing as a single, monolithic, online subculture; it's more like an ecosystem of subcultures, some frivolous, others serious. The cutting edge of scientific discourse is migrating to virtual communities, where you can read the electronic pre-preprinted reports of molecular biologists and cognitive scientists. At the same time, activists and educational reformers are using the same medium as a political tool. You can use virtual communities to find a date, sell a lawnmower, publish a novel, conduct a meeting.

Some people use virtual communities as a form of psychotherapy. Others, such as the most addicted players of Minitel in France or multiuser dungeons (MUDs) on the international networks, spend eighty hours a week or more pretending they are someone else, living a life that does not exist outside a computer. Because MUDs not only are susceptible to pathologically obsessive use by some people but also create a strain on computer and communication resources, MUDding has been banned at universities such as Amherst and on the entire continent of Australia.

Scientists, students, librarians, artists, organizers, and escapists aren't the only people who have taken to the new medium. The U.S. senator who campaigned for years for the construction of a National Research and Education Network that could host the virtual communities of the future is now vice president of the United States. As of June 1993, the White House and Congress have e-mail addresses.

Most people who get their news from conventional media have been unaware of the wildly varied assortment of new cultures that have evolved in the world's computer networks over the past ten years. Most people who have not yet used these new media remain unaware of how profoundly the social, political, and scientific experiments under way today via computer networks could change all our lives in the near future.

I have written this book to help inform a wider population about the potential importance of cyberspace to political liberties and the ways virtual communities are likely to change our experience of the real world, as individuals and communities. Although I am enthusiastic about the liberating potentials of computer-mediated communications, I try to keep my eyes open for the pitfalls of mixing technology and human relationships. I hope my reports from the outposts and headquarters of this new kind of social habitation, and the stories of the people I've met in cyberspace, will bring to life the cultural, political, and ethical implications of virtual communities both for my fellow explorers of cyberspace and for those who never heard of it before.

The technology that makes virtual communities possible has the potential to bring enormous leverage to ordinary citizens at relatively little cost—intellectual leverage, social leverage, commercial leverage, and most important, political leverage. But the technology will not in itself fulfill that potential; this latent technical power must be used intelligently and deliberately by an informed population. More people must learn about that leverage and learn to use it, while we still have the freedom to do so, if it is to live up to its potential. The odds are always good that big power and big money will find a way to control access to virtual communities; big power and big money always found ways to control new communications media when they emerged in the past. The Net is still out of control in fundamental ways, but it might not stay that way for long. What we know and do now is important because it is still possible for people around the world to make sure this new sphere of vital human discourse remains open to the citizens of the planet before the political and economic big boys seize it, censor it, meter it, and sell it back to us.

The potential social leverage comes from the power that ordinary citizens gain when they know how to connect two previously independent, mature, highly decentralized technologies: It took billions of dollars and decades to develop cheap personal computers. It took billions of dollars and more than a century to wire up the worldwide telecommunication network. With the right knowledge, and not too much of it, a ten-year-old kid today can plug these two vast, powerful, expensively developed technologies together for a few hundred dollars and instantly obtain a bully pulpit, the Library of Congress, and a world full of potential coconspirators.

Computers and the switched telecommunication networks that also carry our telephone calls constitute the technical foundation of *computer-mediated communications* (CMC). The technicalities of CMC, how bits of computer data move over wires and are reassembled as computer files at their destinations, are invisible and irrelevant to most people who use it, except when the technicalities restrict their access to CMC services. The important thing to keep in mind is that the worldwide, interconnected telecommunication network that we use to make telephone calls in Manhattan and Madagascar can also be used to connect computers together at a distance, and you don't have to be an engineer to do it.

The Net is an informal term for the loosely interconnected computer networks that use CMC technology to link people around the world into public discussions.

Virtual communities are social aggregations that emerge from the Net when enough people carry on those public discussions long enough, with sufficient human feeling, to form webs of personal relationships in cyberspace.

Cyberspace, originally a term from William Gibson's science-fiction novel *Neuromancer,* is the name some people use for the conceptual space where words, human relationships, data, wealth, and power are manifested by people using CMC technology.

Although spatial imagery and a sense of place help convey the experience of dwelling in a virtual community, biological imagery is often more appropriate to describe the way cyberculture changes. In terms of the way the whole system is propagating and evolving, think of cyberspace as a social petri dish, the Net as the agar medium, and virtual communities, in all their diversity, as the colonies of microorganisms that grow in petri dishes. Each of the small colonies of microorganisms—the communities on the Net—is a social experiment that nobody planned but that is happening nevertheless.

We now know something about the ways previous generations of communications technologies changed the way people lived. We need to understand why and how so many social experiments are coevolving today with the prototypes of the newest communications technologies. My direct observations of online behavior around the world over the past ten years have led me to conclude that whenever CMC technology becomes available to people anywhere, they inevitably build virtual communities with it, just as microorganisms inevitably create colonies.

I suspect that one of the explanations for this phenomenon is the hunger for community that grows in the breasts of people around the world as more and more informal public spaces disappear from our real lives. I also suspect that these new media attract colonies of enthusiasts because CMC enables people to do things with each other in new ways, and to do altogether new kinds of things—just as telegraphs, telephones, and televisions did.

Because of its potential influence on so many people's beliefs and perceptions, the future of the Net is connected to the future of community, democracy, education, science, and intellectual life—some of the human institutions people hold most dear, whether or not they know or care about the future of computer technology. The future of the Net has become too important to leave to specialists and special interests. As it influences the lives of a growing number of people, more and more citizens must contribute to the dialogue about the way public funds are applied to the development of the Net, and we must join our voices to the debate about the way it should be administered. We need a clear citizens' vision of the way the Net ought to grow, a firm idea of the kind of media environment we would like to see in the future. If we do not develop such a vision for ourselves, the future will be shaped for us by large commercial and political powerholders.

The Net is so widespread and anarchic today because of the way its main sources converged in the 1980s, after years of independent, apparently unrelated development, using different technologies and involving different populations of participants. The technical and social convergences were fated, but not widely foreseen, by the late 1970s.

The wide-area CMC networks that span continents and join together thousands of smaller networks are a spinoff of American military research. The first computer network, ARPAnet, was created in the 1970s so that Department of Defense–sponsored researchers could operate different computers at a distance; computer data, not person-to-person messages, were the intended content of the network, which handily happened to serve just as easily as a conduit for words. The fundamental technical idea on which ARPAnet was based came from RAND, the think tank in Santa Monica that did a lot of work with top-secret thermonuclear war scenarios; ARPAnet grew out of an older RAND scheme for a communication, command, and control network that could survive nuclear attack by having no central control.

Computer conferencing emerged, also somewhat unexpectedly, as a tool for using the communication capacities of the networks to build social relationships across barriers of space and time. A continuing theme throughout the history of CMC is the way people adapt technologies designed for one purpose to suit their own, very different, communication needs. And the most profound technological changes have come from the fringes and subcultures, not the orthodoxy of the computer industry or academic computer science. The programmers who created the first computer network installed electronic mail features; electronic mail wasn't the reason ARPAnet was designed, but it was an easy thing to include once ARPAnet existed. Then, in a similar, ad hoc, do-it-yourself manner, computer conferencing grew out of the needs of U.S. policymakers to develop a communications medium for dispersed decision making. Although the first computer conferencing experiments were precipitated by the U.S. government's wage-price freeze of the 1970s and the consequent need to disseminate up-to-date information from a large number of geographically dispersed local headquarters, computer conferencing was quickly adapted to commercial, scientific, and social discourse.

The hobbyists who interconnect personal computers via telephone lines to make computer bulletin-board systems, known as BBSs, have home-grown their part of the Net, a true grassroots use of technology. Hundreds of thousands of people around the world piggyback legally on the telecom network via personal computers and ordinary telephone lines. The most important technical attribute of networked BBSs is that it is an extremely hard network to kill—just as the RAND planners had hoped. Information can take so many alternative routes when one of the nodes of the network is removed that the Net is almost immortally flexible. It is this flexibility that CMC telecom pioneer John Gilmore referred to when he said, "The Net interprets censorship as damage and routes around it." This way of passing information and communication around a network as a distributed resource with no central control manifested in the rapid growth of the anarchic global conversation known as Usenet. This invention of distributed conversation that flows around obstacles—a grassroots adaptation of a technology originally designed as a doomsday weapon—might turn out to be as important in the long run as the hardware and software inventions that made it possible.

The big hardwired networks spend a lot more money to create high-speed information conduits between high-capacity computing nodes. Internet, today's U.S. government–sponsored successor to ARPAnet, is growing in every dimension at an astonishing pace. These "data superhighways" use special telecommunication lines and other equipment to send very large amounts of information throughout the network at very high speeds. ARPAnet started around twenty years ago with roughly one thousand users, and now Internet is approaching ten million users.

The portable computer on my desk is hundreds of times less expensive and thousands of times more powerful than ARPAnet's first nodes. The fiber-optic backbone of the current Internet communicates information millions of times faster than the first ARPAnet. Everything about Internet has grown like a bacterial colony—the raw technical capacity to send information, the different ways people use it, and the number of users. The Internet population has grown by 15 percent a month for the past several years. John Quarterman, whose book *The Matrix* is a thick guide to the world's computer networks, estimates that there are nine hundred different networks worldwide today, not counting the more than ten thousand networks already linked by the Internet "network of networks."

Real grassroots, the kind that grow in the ground, are a self-similar branching structure, a network of networks. Each grass seed grows a branching set of roots, and then many more smaller roots grow off those; the roots of each grass plant interconnect physically with the roots of adjacent plants, as any gardener who has tried to uproot a lawn has learned. There is a grassroots element to the Net that was not, until very recently, involved with all the high-tech, top-secret doings that led to ARPAnet—the BBSers.

The population of the grassroots part of the Net, the citizen-operated BBSs, has been growing explosively as a self-financed movement of enthusiasts, without the benefit of Department of Defense funding. A BBS is the simplest, cheapest infrastructure for CMC: you run special software, often available inexpensively, on a personal computer, and use a device known as a *modem* to plug the computer into your regular telephone line. The modem converts computer-readable information into audible beeps and boops that can travel over the same telephone wires that carry your voice; another modem at the other end decodes the beeps and boops into computer-readable bits and bytes. The BBS turns the bits and bytes into human-readable text. Other people use their computers to call your BBS, leave and retrieve messages stored in your personal computer, and you have a virtual community growing in your bedroom. As the system operator (sysop) of the BBS, you contribute part of your computer's memory and make sure your computer is plugged into the telephone; the participants pay for their own communication costs.

Boardwatch magazine estimates that sixty thousand BBSs operated in the United States alone in 1993, fourteen years after the first BBSs opened in Chicago and California. Each BBS supports a population of a dozen to several hundred, or even thousands, of individual participants. There are religious BBSs of every denomination, sex BBSs of every proclivity, political BBSs from all parts of the spectrum, outlaw BBSs, law enforcement BBSs, BBSs for the disabled, for educators, for kids, for cults, for nonprofit organizations—a list of the different flavors of special-interest BBSs is dozens of pages long. The BBS culture has spread from the United States to Japan, Europe, Central and South America.

Each BBS started out as a small island community of a few people who dialed into a number in their area code; by their nature, like a small-wattage radio station, BBSs are localized. But that's changing, too. Just as several different technologies converged over the past ten years to create CMC—a new medium with properties of its own—several different online social structures are in the process of converging and creating a kind of international culture with properties of its own.

Technical bridges are connecting the grassroots part of the network with the military-industrial parts of the network. The programmers who built the Net in the first place, the scholars who have been using it to exchange knowledge, the scientists who have been using it for research, are being joined by all those hobbyists with their bedroom and garage BBSs. Special "gateway" computers can link entire networks by automatically translating communications from the mechanical languages used in one network to the languages (known as protocols) used in another network. In recent years, the heretofore separate groups of Internet and BBS pioneers worked together to gateway the more than ten thousand computers of the worldwide FidoNet, the first network of small, private BBSs, with Internet's millions of people and tens of thousands of more powerful computers.

The Net and computer conferencing systems are converging too, as medium-size computer conferencing communities like the WELL join Internet. When the WELL upgraded to a high-speed connection to Internet, it became not just a community-in-progress but a gateway to a wider realm, the worldwide Net-at-large. Suddenly, the isolated archipelagos of a few hundred or a few thousand people are becoming part of an integrated entity. The small virtual communities still exist, like yeast in a rapidly rising loaf, but increasingly they are part of an overarching culture, similar to the way the United States became an overarching culture after the telegraph and telephone linked the states.

The WELL is a small town, but now there is a doorway in that town that opens onto the blooming, buzzing confusion of the Net, an entity with properties altogether different from the virtual villages of a few years ago. I have good friends now all over the world whom I never would have met without the mediation of the Net. A large circle of Net acquaintances can make an enormous difference in your experience when you travel to a foreign culture. Wherever I've traveled physically in recent years, I've found ready-made communities that I met online months before I traveled; our mutual enthusiasm for virtual communities served as a bridge, time and again, to people whose language and customs differ significantly from those I know well in California.

I routinely meet people and get to know them months or years before I see them—one of the ways my world today is a different world, with different friends and different concerns, from the world I experienced in premodem days. The places I visit in my mind, and the people I communicate with from one moment to the next, are entirely different from the content of my thoughts or the state of my circle of friends before I started dabbling in virtual communities. One minute I'm involved in the minutiae of local matters such as planning next week's bridge game, and the next minute I'm part of a debate raging in seven countries.

Entire cities are coming online.

Not only do I inhabit my virtual communities; to the degree that I carry around their conversations in my head and begin to mix it up with them in real life, my virtual communities also inhabit my life. I've been colonized; my sense of family at the most fundamental level has been virtualized.

I've seen variations of the same virtualization of community that happened to me hitting other virtual groups of a few hundred or a few thousand, in Paris and London and Tokyo. Entire cities are coming online. Santa Monica, California, and Cleveland, Ohio, were among the first of a growing number of American cities that have initiated municipal CMC systems. Santa Monica's system has an active conference to discuss the problems of the city's homeless that involves heavy input from homeless Santa Monica citizens who use public terminals. This system has an electronic link with COARA, a similar regional system in a remote province of Japan. Biwa-Net, in the Kyoto area, is gatewayed to a sister city in Pennsylvania. The Net is only beginning to wake up to itself.

Watching a particular virtual community change over a period of time has something of the intellectual thrill of do-it-yourself anthropology, and some of the garden-variety voyeurism of eavesdropping on an endless amateur soap opera where there is no boundary separating the audience from the cast. For the price of a telephone call, you can take part in any kind of vicarious melo-drama you can dream of; as a form of escape entertainment, the Minitel addicts in Paris and the MUDders of Internet and the obsessive IRC participants on college campuses everywhere have proved that CMC has a future as a seri-ous marketplace for meterable interactive fantasies.

CMC might become the next great escape medium, in the tradition of radio serials, Saturday matinees, soap operas—which means that the new medium will be in some way a conduit for and reflector of our cultural codes, our social subconscious, our images of who "we" might be, just as previous media have been. There are other serious reasons that ordinary nontechnical citizens need to know something about this new medium and its social impact. Some-thing big is afoot, and the final shape has not been determined.

In the United States, the Clinton administration is taking measures to amplify the Net's technical capabilities and availability manyfold via the National Research and Education Network. France, with the world's largest national information utility, Minitel, and Japan, with its stake in future telecommunications industries, have their own visions of the future. Albert Gore's 1991 bill, the High Performance Computing Act, signed into law by President Bush, outlined Gore's vision for "highways of the mind" to be stim-ulated by federal research-and-development expenditures as a national intel-lectual resource and carried to the citizens by private enterprise. The Clinton-Gore administration has used the example of the ARPA (Advanced Research Projects Agency) venture of the 1960s and 1970s that produced the Net and the foundations of personal computing as an example of the way they see government and the private sector interacting in regard to future communications technologies.

In the private sector, telecommunication companies, television networks, computer companies, cable companies, and newspapers in the United States, Europe, and Japan are jockeying for position in the nascent "home interactive information services industry." Corporations are investing hundreds of mil-lions of dollars in the infrastructure for new media they hope will make them billions of dollars. Every flavor of technological futurist, from Alvin Toffler and John Naisbitt to Peter Drucker and George Gilder, base utopian hopes on "the information age" as a techno-fix for social problems. Yet little is known about the impact these newest media might have on our daily lives, our minds, our families, even the future of democracy.

CMC has the potential to change our lives on three different, but strongly interinfluential, levels. First, as individual human beings, we have perceptions, thoughts, and personalities (already shaped by other communications tech-nologies) that are affected by the ways we use the medium and the ways it uses us. At this fundamental level, CMC appeals to us as mortal organisms with certain intellectual, physical, and emotional needs. Young people around the world have different communication proclivities from their pre-McLuhanized elders. MTV, for example, caters to an aesthetic sensibility that is closely tuned to the vocabulary of television's fast cuts, visually arresting images, and special effects. Now, some of those people around the world who were born in the television era and grew up in the cellular telephone era are beginning to migrate to CMC spaces that better fit their new ways of experiencing the world. There is a vocabulary to CMC, too, now emerging from millions and millions of individual online interactions. That vocabulary reflects something about the ways human personalities are changing in the age of media saturation.

The second level of possible CMC-triggered change is the level of person-to-person interaction where relationships, friendships, and communities happen. CMC technology offers a new capability of "many to many" communication, but the way such a capability will or will not be used in the future might depend on the way we, the first people who are using it, succeed or fail in applying it to our lives. Those of us who are brought into contact with each other by means of CMC technology find ourselves challenged by this many-to-many capability—challenged to consider whether it is possible for us to build some kind of community together.

The question of community is central to realms beyond the abstract networks of CMC technology. Some commentators, such as Bellah et al. (*Habits of the Heart, The Good Society*), have focused on the need for rebuilding community in the face of America's loss of a sense of a social commons.

Social psychologists, sociologists, and historians have developed useful tools for asking questions about human group interaction. Different communities of interpretation, from anthropology to economics, have different criteria for studying whether a group of people is a community. In trying to apply traditional analysis of community behavior to the kinds of interactions emerging from the Net, I have adopted a schema proposed by Marc Smith, a graduate student in sociology at the University of California at Los Angeles, who has been doing his fieldwork in the WELL and the Net. Smith focuses on the concept of "collective goods." Every cooperative group of people exists in the face of a competitive world because that group of people recognizes there is something valuable that they can gain only by banding together. Looking for a group's collective goods is a way of looking for the elements that bind isolated individuals into a community.

The three kinds of collective goods that Smith proposes as the social glue that binds the WELL into something resembling a community are social network capital, knowledge capital, and communion. Social network capital is what happened when I found a ready-made community in Tokyo, even though I had never been there in the flesh. Knowledge capital is what I found in the WELL when I asked questions of the community as an online brain trust representing a highly varied accumulation of expertise. And communion is what we found in the Parenting conference, when Phil's and Jay's children were sick, and the rest of us used our words to support them.

The third level of possible change in our lives, the political, derives from the middle, social level, for politics is always a combination of communications and physical power, and the role of communications media among the citizenry is particularly important in the politics of democratic societies. The idea of modern representative democracy as it was first conceived by Enlightenment philosophers included a recognition of a living web of citizen-to-citizen communications known as civil society or the public sphere. Although elections are the most visible fundamental characteristics of democratic societies, those elections are assumed to be supported by discussions among citizens at all levels of society about issues of importance to the nation.

If a government is to rule according to the consent of the governed, the effectiveness of that government is heavily influenced by how much the governed know about the issues that affect them. The mass-media–dominated public sphere today is where the governed now get knowledge; the problem is that commercial mass media, led by broadcast television, have polluted with barrages of flashy, phony, often violent imagery a public sphere that once included a large component of reading, writing, and rational discourse. For the early centuries of American history, until the telegraph made it possible to create what we know as news and sell the readers of newspapers to advertisers, the public sphere did rely on an astonishingly literate population. Neil Postman, in his book about the way television has changed the nature of public discourse, *Amusing Ourselves to Death,* notes that Thomas Paine's *Common Sense* sold three hundred thousand copies in five months in 1775. Contemporary observers have documented and analyzed the way mass media ("one to many" media) have "commoditized" the public sphere, substituting slick public relations for genuine debate and packaging both issues and candidates like other consumer products.

The political significance of CMC lies in its capacity to challenge the existing political hierarchy's monopoly on powerful communications media, and perhaps thus revitalize citizen-based democracy. The way image-rich, sound-bite–based commercial media have co-opted political discourse among citizens is part of a political problem that communications technologies have posed for democracy for decades. The way the number of owners of telecommunication channels is narrowing to a tiny elite, while the reach and power of the media they own expand, is a converging threat to citizens. Which scenario seems more conducive to democracy, which to totalitarian rule: a world in which a few people control communications technology that can be used to manipulate the beliefs of billions, or a world in which every citizen can broadcast to every other citizen?

Ben Bagdikian's often-quoted prediction from *The Media Monopoly* is that by the turn of the century "five to ten corporate giants will control most of the world's important newspapers, magazines, books, broadcast stations, movies, recordings and videocassettes." These new media lords possess immense power to determine which information most people receive about the world, and I suspect they are not likely to encourage their privately owned and controlled networks to be the willing conduits for all the kinds of information that unfettered citizens and nongovernmental organizations tend to disseminate. The activist solution to this dilemma has been to use CMC to create alternative planetary information networks. The distributed nature of the telecommunications network, coupled with the availability of affordable computers, makes it possible to piggyback alternate networks on the mainstream infrastructure.

We temporarily have access to a tool that could bring conviviality and understanding into our lives and might help revitalize the public sphere. The same tool, improperly controlled and wielded, could become an instrument of tyranny. The vision of a citizen-designed, citizen-controlled worldwide communications network is a version of technological utopianism that could be called the vision of "the electronic agora." In the original democracy, Athens, the agora was the marketplace, and more—it was where citizens met to talk, gossip, argue, size each other up, find the weak spots in political ideas by debating about them. But another kind of vision could apply to the use of the Net in the wrong ways, a shadow vision of a less utopian kind of place—the Panopticon.

Panopticon was the name for an ultimately effective prison, seriously proposed in eighteenth-century Britain by Jeremy Bentham. A combination of architecture and optics makes it possible in Bentham's scheme for a single guard to see every prisoner, and for no prisoner to see anything else; the effect is that all prisoners act as if they were under surveillance at all times. Contemporary social critic Michel Foucault, in *Discipline and Punish,* claimed that the machinery of the worldwide communications network constitutes a kind of camouflaged Panopticon; citizens of the world brought into their homes, along with each other, the prying ears of the state. The cables that bring information into our homes today are technically capable of bringing information out of our homes, instantly transmitted to interested others. Tomorrow's version of Panoptic machinery could make very effective use of the same communications infrastructure that enables one-room schoolhouses in Montana to communicate with MIT professors, and enables citizens to disseminate news and organize resistance to totalitarian rule. With so much of our intimate data and more and more of our private behavior moving into cyberspace, the potential for totalitarian abuse of that information web is significant and the cautions of the critics are worth a careful hearing.

The wise revolutionary keeps an eye on the dark side of the changes he or she would initiate. Enthusiasts who believe in the humanitarian potential of virtual communities, especially those of us who speak of electronic democracy as a potential application of the medium, are well advised to consider the shadow potential of the same media. We should not forget that intellectuals and journalists of the 1950s hailed the advent of the greatest educational medium in history—television.

Because of its potential to change us as humans, as communities, as democracies, we need to try to understand the nature of CMC, cyberspace, and virtual communities in every important context—politically, economically, socially, cognitively. Each different perspective reveals something that the other perspectives do not reveal. Each different discipline fails to see something that another discipline sees very well. We need to think together here, across boundaries of academic discipline, industrial affiliation, nation, if we hope to understand and thus perhaps regain control of the way human communities are being transformed by communications technologies.

We can't do this solely as dispassionate observers, although there is certainly a strong need for the detached assessment of social science. Community is a matter of emotions as well as a thing of reason and data. Some of the most important learning will always have to be done by jumping into one corner or another of cyberspace, living there, and getting up to your elbows in the problems that virtual communities face.

I care about what happens in cyberspace, and to our freedoms in cyberspace, because I dwell there part of the time. The author's voice as a citizen and veteran of virtual community-building is one of the points of view presented in this book: I'm part of the story I'm describing, speaking as both native informant and as uncredentialed social scientist. Because of the paucity of first-person source material describing the way it feels to live in cyberspace, I believe it is valuable to include my perspective as participant as well as observer. In some places, like the WELL, I speak from extensive experience: in many of the places we need to examine in order to understand the Net, I am almost as new to the territory as those who never heard about cyberspace before. Ultimately, if you want to form your own opinions, you need to pick up a good beginner's guidebook and plunge into the Net for yourself. It is possible, however, to paint a kind of word-picture, necessarily somewhat sketchy, of the varieties of life to be found on the Net.

I am almost as new to the territory as those who never heard about cyberspace before.

Much of this book is a tour of widening circles of virtual communities as they exist today. I believe that most citizens of democratic societies, given access to clearly presented information about the state of the Net, will make wise decisions about how the Net ought to be governed. But it is important to look in more than one corner and see through more than one set of lenses. Before we can discuss in any depth the way CMC technology is changing us as human beings, as communities, and as democracies, we need to know something about the people and places that make the Net what it is.

Our journey through the raucous immensity of Usenet, the subcultures of the MUDs and IRC channels, the BBSs, mailing lists, and e-journals, starts with a glimpse over my shoulder at the WELL, the place where cyberspace started for me. The ways I've witnessed people in the virtual community I know best build value, help each other through hard times, solve (and fail to solve) vexing interpersonal problems together, offer a model—undoubtedly not an infallible one—of the kinds of social changes that virtual communities can make in real lives on a modestly local scale. Some knowledge of how people in a small virtual community behave will help prevent vertigo and give you tools for comparison when we zoom out to the larger metropolitan areas of cyberspace. Some aspects of life in a small community have to be abandoned when you move to an online metropolis; the fundamentals of human nature, however, always scale up.

■ QUESTIONS FOR REREADING

1. Rheingold begins with a quote from his daughter: "Daddy is saying 'Holy moly!' to his computer again!" His gloss on this statement is "Those words have become a family code for the way my virtual community has infiltrated our real world." In a number of passages, Rheingold is very careful to talk about the relationship and balance between his real and virtual communities. Notice, for example, how he is careful to make clear, "The WELL felt like an authentic community to me from the start because it was grounded in my everyday physical world." Identify and discuss this and other similar passages.

2. How does Rheingold's view of a virtual community compare to Rushkoff's view of cyberia? You might want to read Rheingold's section titled "Media Warp and Mystery Religions in the 1990s" in his book *Virtual Reality* (353–57), in which he discusses the question "Is virtual reality going to be electronic LSD?" In this section he discusses both brother Jerry Garcia and uncle Tim Leary.

■ WRITING ASSIGNMENT FOR REREADING

If you have access to a computer and a modem, and you have an account with your university or Internet service provider (ISP), then keep a *daily journal* of your communitarian and social experiences on a list or lists. Try to write in the manner that Rheingold writes about his experiences, for example, anecdotally. Take special care to report what effect the virtual has on your actual life, and vice versa. And try to write for an audience of readers who will take the class that your are taking now or a similar one. Leave an actual and virtual legacy for those who will follow. This is how we will have built communities together. If you and your instructor/facilitator especially like what you have written and one or the other of you can place your project on your Web site, then send me (vvitanza@aol.com) your URL for the site so that I can consider it for possible inclusion at the *CyberReader* Web site.

Sherry Turkle's "Identity Crisis" is chapter 10 of her book Life on the Screen: Identity in the Age of the Internet *(New York: Simon & Schuster, 1995): 255–69. Turkle is Professor of Sociology of Science at MIT. She is a licensed clinical psychologist.*

In "Identity Crisis," Turkle writes about the border between real life and virtual life. She is an advocate for the value of role-playing in virtual environments and for a multiplicity of identities. The "crisis" of the chapter title is one of getting in alignment with the times of multiple selves, the postmodern times. Being multiple allows people, Turkle reports, to get in touch with their various selves in real life. It is a step toward health and well-being. Turkle makes it very clear, however, that "multiplicity is not viable if it means shifting among personalities that cannot communicate. Multiplicity is not acceptable if it means being confused to a point of immobility." And so the question that she is dealing with is, "How can we be multiple and coherent at the same time?" (258). Much that she writes about will cast light on the readings in later chapters of CyberReader, especially chapters 6 and 7.

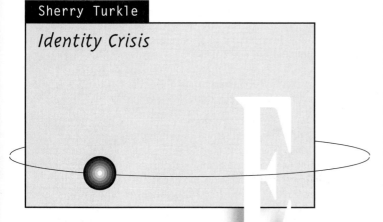

Sherry Turkle

Identity Crisis

very era constructs its own metaphors for psychological well-being. Not so long ago, stability was socially valued and culturally reinforced. Rigid gender roles, repetitive labor, the expectation of being in one kind of job or remaining in one town over a lifetime, all of these made consistency central to definitions of health But these stable social worlds have broken down. In our time, health is described in terms of fluidity rather than stability. What matters most now is the ability to adapt and change—to new jobs, new career directions, new gender roles, new technologies.

In *Flexible Bodies,* the anthropologist Emily Martin argues that the language of the immune system provides us with metaphors for the self and its boundaries.[1] In the past, the immune system was described as a private fortress, a firm, stable wall that protected within from without. Now we talk about the immune system as flexible and permeable. It can only be healthy if adaptable.

The new metaphors of health as flexibility apply not only to human mental and physical spheres, but also to the bodies of corporations, governments, and businesses. These institutions function in rapidly changing circumstances; they too are coming to view their fitness in terms of their flexibility. Martin describes the cultural spaces where we learn the new virtues of change over solidity. In, addition to advertising, entertainment, and education, her examples include corporate workshops where people learn wilderness camping, high-wire walking, and zip-line jumping. She refers to all of these as flexibility practicums.

In her study of the culture of flexibility, Martin does not discuss virtual communities, but these provide excellent examples of what she is talking about. In these environments, people either explicitly play roles (as in MUDs) or more subtly shape their online selves. Adults learn about being multiple and fluid—and so do children. "I don't play so many different people online—only three," says June, an eleven-year-old who uses her mother's Internet account to play in MUDs. During our conversation, I learn that in the course of a year in RL, she moves among three households—that of her biological mother and stepfather, her biological father and stepmother, and a much-loved "first stepfather," her mother's second husband. She refers to her mother's third and current husband as "second stepfather." June recounts that in each of these three households the rules are somewhat different and so is she. Online switches among personae seem quite natural. Indeed, for her, they are a kind of practice. Martin would call them practicums.

■ "LOGINS R US"

On a WELL discussion group about online personae (subtitled "boon or bête-noire") participants shared a sense that their virtual identities were evocative objects for thinking about the self. For several, experiences in virtual space compelled them to pay greater attention to what they take for granted in the real. "The persona thing intrigues me," said one. "It's a chance for all of us who aren't actors to play [with] masks. And think about the masks we wear every day."[2]

In this way, online personae have something in common with the self that emerges in a psychoanalytic encounter. It, too, is significantly virtual, constructed within the space of the analysis, where its slightest shifts can come under the most intense scrutiny.[3]

What most characterized the WELL discussion about online personae was the way many of the participants expressed the belief that life on the WELL introduced them to the many within themselves. One person wrote that through participating in an electronic bulletin board and letting the many sides of ourselves show, "We start to resemble little corporations, 'Logins R Us,' and like any company, we each have within us the beancounter, the visionary, the heart-throb, the fundamentalist, and the wild child. Long may they wave."[4] Other participants responded to this comment with enthusiasm. One, echoing the social psychologist Kenneth Gergen,[5] described identity as a "pastiche of personalities" in which "the test of competence is not so much the integrity of the whole but the apparent correct representation appearing at the right time, in the right context, not to the detriment of the rest of the internal 'collective.' "[6] Another said that he thought of his ego "as a hollow tube, through which, one at a time, the 'many' speak through at the appropriate moment. . . . I'd like to hear more . . . about the possibilities surrounding the notion that what we perceive as 'one' in any context is, perhaps, a conglomerate of 'ones.' " This writer went on:

Hindu culture is rooted in the "many" as the root of spiritual experience. A person's momentary behavior reflects some

influence from one of hundreds of gods and/or goddesses. I am
interested in . . . how this natural assumption of the "many"
creates an alternative psychology.[7]

Another writer concurred:

Did you ever see that cartoon by R. Crumb about "Which is the
real R. Crumb?" He goes through four pages of incarnations,
from successful businessman to street beggar, from media
celebrity to gut-gnawing recluse, etc. etc. Then at the end
he says, "Which is the real one?" . . . "It all depends on
what mood I'm in!"
   We're all like that on-line.[8]

Howard Rheingold, the member of the WELL who began the discussion
topic, also referred to Gergen's notion of a "saturated self," the idea that communication technologies have caused us to "colonize each other's brains." Gergen describes us as saturated with the many "voices of humankind—both
harmonious and alien." He believes that as "we absorb their varied rhymes
and reasons, they become part of us and we of them. Social saturation furnishes us with a multiplicity of incoherent and unrelated languages of the
self." With our relationships spread across the globe and our knowledge of
other cultures relativizing our attitudes and depriving us of any norm, we
"exist in a state of continuous construction and reconstruction; it is a world
where anything goes that can be negotiated. Each reality of self gives way to
reflexive questioning, irony, and ultimately the playful probing of yet another
reality. The center fails to hold."[9]

Although people may at first feel anguish at what they sense as a breakdown of identity, Gergen believes they may come to embrace the new possibilities. Individual notions of self vanish "into a stage of relatedness. One
ceases to believe in a self independent of the relations in which he or she is
embedded."[10] "We live in each other's brains, as voices, images, words on
screens," said Rheingold in the online discussion. "We are multiple personalities and we include each other."[11]

Rheingold's evocation of what Gergen calls the "raptures of multiplicitous
being" met with support on the WELL. One participant insisted that all pejora-
tive associations be removed from the notion of a saturated self. "Howard,
I *like* being a saturated self, in a community of similarly saturated selves.
I grew up on TV and pop music, but it just ain't enough. Virtual communities are, among other things, the co-saturation of selves who have been,
all their lives, saturated in isolation."[12] To which Rheingold could only
reply, "I like being a saturated self too."[13] The cybersociety of the WELL is
an object-to-think-with for reflecting on the positive aspects of identity as
multiplicity.

■ IDENTITY AND MULTIPLICITY

Without any principle of coherence, the self spins off in all directions. Multiplicity is not viable if it means shifting among personalities that cannot communicate. Multiplicity is not acceptable if it means being confused to a point of immobility.[14] How can we be multiple and coherent at the same time? *In The Protean Self,* Robert Jay Lifton tries to resolve this seeming contradiction. He begins by assuming that a unitary view of self corresponded to a traditional culture with stable symbols, institutions, and relationships. He finds the old unitary notion no longer viable because traditional culture has broken down and identifies a range of responses. One is a dogmatic insistence on unity. Another is to return to systems of belief, such as religious fundamentalism, that enforce conformity. A third is to embrace the idea of a fragmented self.[15] Lifton says this is a dangerous option that may result in a "fluidity lacking in moral content and sustainable inner form." But Lifton sees another possibility, a healthy protean self. It is capable, like Proteus, of fluid transformations but is grounded in coherence and a moral outlook. It is multiple but integrated.[16] You can have a sense of self without being one self.

Lifton's language is theoretical. Experiences in MUDs, on the WELL, on local bulletin boards, on commercial network services, and on the World Wide Web are bringing his theory down to earth. On the Web, the idiom for constructing a "home" identity is to assemble a "home page" of virtual objects that correspond to one's interests. One constructs a home page by composing or "pasting" on it words, images, and sounds, and by making connections between it and other sites on the Internet or the Web. Like the agents in emergent AI, one's identity emerges from whom one knows, one's associations and connections. People link their home page to pages about such things as music, paintings, television shows, cities, books, photographs, comic strips, and fashion models. As I write this book I am in the process of constructing my own home page. It now contains links to the text of my curriculum vitae, to drafts of recent papers (one about MUDs, one about French psychoanalysis), and to the reading lists for the two courses I shall teach next fall. A "visitor" to my home page can also click a highlighted word and watch images of Michel Foucault and Power Rangers "morph," one into the other, a visual play on my contention that children's toys bring postmodernism down to earth. This display, affectionately referred to as "The Mighty Morphin' Michel Foucault," was a present from my assistant at MIT, Cynthia Col. A virtual home, like a real one, is furnished with objects you buy, build, or receive as gifts.

On the Web, the idiom for constructing a "home" identity is to assemble a "home page."

My future plans for my home page include linking to Paris (the city has a home page), the bot Julia, resources on women's studies, Imari china, and recent research on migraines. I am not limited in the number of links I can create. If we take the home page as a real estate metaphor for the self, its decor is postmodern. Its different rooms with different styles are located on computers all over the world. But through one's efforts, they are brought together to be of a piece.

Home pages on the Web are one recent and dramatic illustration of new notions of identity as multiple yet coherent; in this book we have met others. Recall Case, the industrial designer who plays the female lawyer Mairead in MedievalMUSH. He does not experience himself as a unitary self, yet says that he feels in control of "himselves" and "herselves." He says that he feels fulfilled by his real and virtual work, marriage, and friendships. While conventional thinking tends to characterize multiple personae in pathological terms, this does not seem to capture what is most meaningful about Case playing Mairead or Garrett (introduced in chapter 8) playing Ribbit.

Within the psychoanalytic tradition, there have been schools that departed from the standard unitary view of identity. As we have seen, the object-relations theorists invented a language for talking about the many voices that we bring inside ourselves in the course of development. Jungian psychology encouraged the individual to become acquainted with a whole range of personae and to understand them as manifestations of universal archetypes, such as innocent virgins, mothers and crones, eternal youths and old men.[17] Jung believed that for each of us, it is potentially most liberating to become acquainted with our dark side, as well as the other-gendered self called anima in men and animus in women. Jung was banished from the ranks of orthodox Freudians for such suggestions. The object-relations school, too, was relegated to the margins. As America became the center of psychoanalytic politics in the mid-twentieth century, ideas about a robust executive ego became the psychoanalytic mainstream.

Through the fragmented selves presented by patients and through theories that stress the decentered subject, contemporary psychology confronts what is left out of theories of the unitary self. Now it must ask, What is the self when it functions as a society?[18] What is the self when it divides its labors among its constituent "alters"?[19] Those burdened by post-traumatic dissociative disorders suffer these questions; here I have suggested that inhabitants of virtual communities play with them.

Ideas about mind can become a vital cultural presence when they are carried by evocative objects-to-think-with.[20] I said earlier that these objects need not be material. For example, dreams and slips of the tongue were objects-to-think-with that brought psychoanalytic ideas into everyday life. People could play with their own and others' dreams and slips. Today, people are being helped to develop ideas about identity as multiplicity by a new practice of identity as multiplicity in online life. Virtual personae are objects-to-think-with.

When people adopt an online persona they cross a boundary into highly charged territory. Some feel an uncomfortable sense of fragmentation, some a sense of relief. Some sense the possibilities for self-discovery, even self-transformation. Serena, a twenty-six-year-old graduate student in history, says, "When I log on to a new MUD and I create a character and know I have to start typing my description, I always feel a sense of panic. Like I could find out something I don't want to know." Arlie, a twenty-year-old undergraduate, says, "I am always very self-conscious when I create a new character. Usually, I end up creating someone I wouldn't want my parents to know about. It takes me, like, three hours. But that someone is part of me." In these ways and others, many more of us are experimenting with multiplicity than ever before.

With this last comment, I am not implying that MUDs or computer bulletin boards are causally implicated in the dramatic increase of people who exhibit symptoms of multiple personality disorder (MPD), or that people on MUDs have MPD, or that MUDding is like having MPD. What I am saying is that the many manifestations of multiplicity in our culture, including the adoption of online personae, are contributing to a general reconsideration of traditional, unitary notions of identity.

The history of a psychiatric symptom is inextricably tied up with the history of the culture that surrounds it. When I was in graduate school in psychology in the 1970s, clinical psychology texts regarded multiple personality as so rare (perhaps one in a million) as to be barely worthy of mention. In these rare cases, there was typically one alter personality in addition to the host personality.[21] Today, cases of multiple personality are much more frequent and typically involve up to sixteen alters of different ages, races, genders, and sexual orientations.[22] In multiple personality disorder, it is widely believed that traumatic events have caused various aspects of the self to congeal into virtual personalities, the "ones" often hiding from the "others" and hiding too from that special alter, the host personality. Sometimes, the alters are known to each other and to the host; some alters may see their roles as actively helping others. Such differences led the philosopher Ian Hacking to write about a "continuum of dissociation."[23] These differences also suggest a way of thinking about the self in terms of a continuum of how accessible its parts are to each other.

At one extreme, the unitary self maintains its oneness by repressing all that does not fit. Thus censored, the illegitimate parts of the self are not accessible. This model would of course function best within a fairly rigid social structure with clearly defined rules and roles. At the other extreme is the MPD sufferer whose multiplicity exists in the context of an equally repressive rigidity. The parts of the self are not in easy communication. Communication is highly stylized; one personality must speak to another personality. In fact, the term "multiple personality" is misleading, because the different parts of the self are not full personalities. They are split-off, disconnected fragments. But if the disorder in multiple personality disorder is the need for the rigid walls between the selves (blocking the secrets those selves protect), then the study of MPD may begin to furnish ways of thinking about healthy selves as nonunitary but with fluid access among their many aspects. Thus, in addition to the extremes of unitary self and MPD, we can imagine a flexible self.

The essence of this self is not unitary, nor are its parts stable entities. It is easy to cycle through its aspects and these are themselves changing through constant communication with each other. The philosopher Daniel Dennett speaks to the flexible self in his multiple drafts theory of consciousness.[24] Dennett's notion of multiple drafts is analogous to the experience of having several versions of a document open on a computer screen where the user is able to move between them at will. The presence of the drafts encourages a respect for the many different versions while it imposes a certain distance from them. No one aspect can be claimed as the absolute, true self. When I got to know French Sherry I no longer saw the less confident English-speaking Sherry as my one authentic self. What most characterizes the model of a flexible self is that the lines of communication between its various aspects are open. The open communication encourages an attitude of respect for the many within us and the many within others.

The essence of this self is not unitary.

As we sense our inner diversity we come to know our limitations. We understand that we do not and cannot know things completely, not the outside world and not ourselves. Today's heightened consciousness of incompleteness may predispose us to join with others. The historian of science Donna Haraway equates a "split and contradictory self" with a "knowing self." She is optimistic about its possibilities: "The knowing self is partial in all its guises, never finished, whole, simply there and original; it is always constructed and stitched together imperfectly; and *therefore* able to join with another, to see together without claiming to be another."[25]

When identity was defined as unitary and solid it was relatively easy to recognize and censure deviation from a norm. A more fluid sense of self allows a greater capacity for acknowledging diversity. It makes it easier to accept the array of our (and others') inconsistent personae—perhaps with humor, perhaps with irony. We do not feel compelled to rank or judge the elements of our multiplicity. We do not feel compelled to exclude what does not fit.

■ VIRTUALITY AS TRANSITIONAL SPACE

In a journal published on the Internet, Leslie Harris speculates on how virtual experiences become part of the perceptual and emotional background "that changes the way we see things."[26] Harris describes an episode of *Star Trek: The Next Generation* in which Captain Picard plays Caiman, an inhabitant of the virtual world Catanh. On Catanh, Picard lives the experiences he had to forgo in order to make a career in Starfleet. He has a virtual experience of love, marriage, and fatherhood. He develops relationships with his community that are not possible for him as a Starfleet commander. "On" Catanh, the character Caiman "learns" to play the Ressiccan flute. Harris says, "He can eventually fall in love with a fellow crew member in his 'real life' because he experienced the feelings of love, commitment, and intimacy 'on' Catanh."[27] When in his real life Picard plays the flute with a fellow Starfleet officer he realizes that he is in love with her. Picard is aware that he has projected his desire for music and sensuality onto his virtual world. It is this awareness that lets him use music to link the "real" Captain Picard to the emotional growth he was able to experience as the virtual Caiman.

Here, virtuality is powerful but transitional. Ultimately, it is put in the service of Picard's embodied self. Picard's virtual Catanh, like the space created within psychoanalysis, operates in a time out of normal time and according to its own rules. In a successful psychoanalysis, the meetings between analyst and analysand come to an end, although the analytic process goes on forever. It is internalized within the person, just as Picard brought Catanh inside himself. Buddhists speak of their practice as a raft to get to the other shore, liberation. But the raft, like an analytic treatment, is thought of as a tool that must be set aside, even though the process of crossing the river is conceived of as never-ending. Wittgenstein takes up a similar idea in *The Tractatus,* when he compares his work to a ladder that is to be discarded after the reader has used it to reach a new level of understanding.

In April 1995, a town meeting was held at MIT on the subject "Doing Gender on the Net." As the discussion turned to using virtual personae to try out new experiences, a thirty-year-old graduate student, Ava, told her story. She had used a MUD to try out being comfortable with a disability. Several years earlier, Ava had been in an automobile accident that left her without a right leg. During her recuperation, she began to MUD. "Without giving it a lot of advance thought," Ava found herself creating a one-legged character on a MUD. Her character had a removable prosthetic limb. The character's disability featured plainly in her description, and the friends she made on the MUD found a way to deal with her handicap. When Ava's character became romantically involved, she and her virtual lover acknowledged the "physical" as well as the emotional aspects of the virtual amputation and prosthesis. They became comfortable with making virtual love, and Ava found a way to love her own virtual body. Ava told the group at the town meeting that this experience enabled her to take a further step toward accepting her real body. "After the accident, I made love in the MUD before I made love again in real life," she said. "I think that the first made the second possible. I began to think of myself as whole again." For her, the Internet had been a place of healing.

Virtual reality gave Ava choices. She could have tried being one of this MUD's many FabulousHotBabes. If so, she might have never felt safe leaving the anonymity of the virtual world. But instead she was able to reimagine herself not as whole but as whole-in-her-incompleteness. Each of us in our own way is incomplete. Virtual spaces may provide the safety for us to expose what we are missing so that we can begin to accept ourselves as we are.

Virtuality need not be a prison. It can be the raft, the ladder, the transitional space, the moratorium, that is discarded after reaching greater freedom. We don't have to reject life on the screen, but we don't have to treat it as an alternative life either. We can use it as a space for growth. Having literally written our online personae into existence, we are in a position to be more aware of what we project into everyday life. Like the anthropologist returning home from a foreign culture, the voyager in virtuality can return to a real world better equipped to understand its artifices.

■ CYBORG DREAMS

I have argued that Internet experiences help us to develop models of psychological well-being that are in a meaningful sense postmodern: They admit multiplicity and flexibility. They acknowledge the constructed nature of reality, self, and other. The Internet is not alone in encouraging such models. There are many places within our culture that do so. What they have in common is that they all suggest the value of approaching one's "story" in several ways and with fluid access to one's different aspects. We are encouraged to think of ourselves as fluid, emergent, decentralized, multiplicitous, flexible, and ever in process.[28] The metaphors travel freely among computer science, psychology, children's games, cultural studies, artificial intelligence, literary criticism, advertising, molecular biology, self-help, and. artificial life. They reach deep into the popular culture. The ability of the Internet to change popular understandings of identity is heightened by the presence of these metaphors.

For example, a recent *Newsweek* article reports on a new narrative movement in psychotherapy, describing the trend as consistent with the "postmodernist idea that we don't so much perceive the world as interpret it." "The psyche," says *Newsweek*, "is not a fixed objective entity, but a fluid, social construct—a story that is subject to revision."[29] The new therapeutic movement described by *Newsweek* draws on deconstructionist literary criticism and on recent currents of psychoanalytic thought that emphasize conflicting narratives as a way of thinking about the analytic experience.[30] But its breezy and accessible newsmagazine coverage makes it clear that psychotherapy, too, can bring postmodernism down to earth.

The literary scholar Katherine Hayles, writing on the cultural resonances of chaos theory, has made the circulation of dominant metaphors a central theme of her work. She suggests that similarities arise in diverse scholarly disciplines and within popular culture "because of broadly based movements within the culture which made the deep assumptions underlying the new paradigms thinkable, perhaps inevitable, thoughts."[31] These assumptions carry a sense of the times that manifests itself in one place and then another, here as developmental psychology and there as a style of engineering, here as a description of our bodies and there as a template for corporate organization, here as a way to build a computer network and there as a manifesto of political ideals.

We are all dreaming cyborg dreams. While our children imagine "morphing" humans into metallic cyber-reptiles, our computer scientists dream themselves immortal. They imagine themselves thinking forever, downloaded onto machines. The AI researcher W. Daniel Hillis says,

I have the same nostalgic love of human metabolism that everybody else does, but if I can go into an improved body and last for 10,000 years I would do it in an instant, no second thoughts. I actually don't think I'm going to have that option, but maybe my children will.[32]

Hillis's musings exemplify the mythic side of cybernetics, apparent from its earliest days. Norbert Wiener, a pioneer in the field, once wrote, "This is an idea with which I have toyed before—that it is conceptually possible for a human being to be sent over a telegraph line."[33] Today, the cyborg, in which human and machine are one, has become a postmodern myth.[34] The myth is fed by the extravagances of Robocop, the Terminator, and Power Rangers as well as by the everyday reality of children plugged into video games. When William Gibson was asked about his sources of inspiration for *Neuromancer,* he described the merging of human and machine as he watched a teenager playing a video game in a downtown arcade.

Video games weren't something I'd done much, and I'd have been embarrassed to actually go into these arcades because everyone was so much younger than I was, but when I looked into one, I could see in the physical intensity of their postures how rapt these kids were. It was like one of those closed systems out of a Pynchon novel: you had this feedback loop, with photons coming off the screen into the kids' eyes, the neurons moving through their bodies, electrons moving through the computer. And these kids clearly believed in the space these games projected.

Everyone who works with computers seems to develop an intuitive faith that there's some kind of actual space behind the screen.[35]

The video game player is already a cyborg.

Thus, for Gibson, the video game player has already merged with the computer. The video game player is already a cyborg, an insight Gibson spun into a postmodern mythology. Over the past decade, such mythologies have been recasting our sense of collective identity.

For Will, a thirty-seven-year-old writer who has recently gone online, the Internet inspires a personal mythology in which he feels part of something far larger than himself: "The Internet is like a giant brain. . . . It's developing on its own. And people and computers are its neural net." This view puts human brains and computers in a provocative symmetry and together they contribute to a larger evolving structure. Will tells me that his new idea about the Internet as a brain made up of human and computer parts "felt like an epiphany." In an age where we feel fragmented as individuals, it is not surprising to see the emergence of popular mythologies that try to put the world back together again.

Will creates his unity by treating both people and machines as Internet nodes, sites through which information travels. like the fantasies of Wiener and Hillis, his epiphany depends on a central notion of artificial intelligence and artificial life: Emergent or not, when reduced to our most basic elements, we are made up, mind and body, of information. Some believe that thinking about people as information carries the possibility for leveling the playing field.[36] For example, if all people are ultimately thought to be information, then such categories as race, class, and gender may be stripped of their cultural charge. But thinking about people as information also carries the serious risk of impoverishing our sense of the human. Even as we recognize the risks of reducing people to strings of code, we must remember that we are peculiarly vulnerable to the message (whether from scientists, futurists, novelists, or filmmakers) that we and machines are kin. In this book we've seen many examples of people treating even a very primitive computer as an other, worthy of relationship.

At the MIT Artificial Intelligence Laboratory, Rodney Brooks has embarked on a project to build an artificial two-year-old. Brooks calls his new "creature" Cog in order to evoke both the mechanical nature of this two-year-old (and perhaps others) and its aspiration to cognition. Brooks's artificial life research, inspired by Herbert Simon's description of the ant walking across a sand dune, takes as a starting assumption that much of what we see as complex behavior is actually simple responses to a complex environment. After over fifteen years of using this strategy to build robots that aspired to insect-level intelligence, Brooks decided, in his words, "to go for the whole enchilada." Cog is being designed to "learn" from its interaction with its environment—most particularly from its interaction with the many researchers who will dedicate themselves to its education. Cog is controversial: for some a noble experiment that takes seriously the notion of embodied, emergent intelligence, for others a grandiose fantasy. When I heard about Cog, I was extremely skeptical. I decided to pay a visit.

Cog's mobile torso, neck, and head stand on a pedestal. Trained to track the largest moving object in its field (because this will usually be a human being) Cog "noticed" me soon after I entered its room. Its head turned to follow me and I was embarrassed to note that this made me happy. I found myself competing with another visitor for its attention. At one point, I felt sure that Cog's eyes had "caught" my own. My visit left me shaken—not by anything that Cog was able to accomplish but by my own reaction to "him." For years, whenever I had heard Rodney Brooks speak about his robotic "creatures," I had always been careful to mentally put quotation marks around the word. But now, with Cog, I had found that the quotation marks disappeared. Despite myself and despite my continuing skepticism about this research project, I had behaved as though in the presence of another being.

In the introduction to this book I quoted Ralph Waldo Emerson: "Dreams and beasts are two keys by which we are to find out the secrets of our nature. . . .They are test objects."[37] And I said that if he lived today, Emerson would have added computers to his list. But computers are more than a simple addition. Through virtual reality they enable us to spend more of our time in our dreams. And through "beings" like Cog they revise what we understand as "beast." Not only are computers evocative in their own right but they have transformed the nature of the test objects that have come before.

■ D W E L L E R S   O N   A   T H R E S H O L D

In the past decade, the computer culture has been the site of a series of battles over contested terrains. There have been struggles between formal logic and bricolage, about profound disruptions in our traditional ways of categorizing people and things, and about the nature of the real in a culture of simulation. These struggles marked the three sections of this book, in which we have seen the computer as tool, as mirror, and as gateway to a world through the looking glass of the screen. In each of these domains we are experiencing a complex interweaving of modern and postmodern, calculation and simulation. The tensions are palpable.

In the struggle of epistemologies, the computer is caught between its natural pluralism and the fact that certain styles of computing are more culturally resonant than others. On one hand, the computer encourages a natural diversity of responses. Different people make the computer their own in their own ways. On the other hand, computers are increasingly expressing a constellation of ideas associated with postmodernism, which has been called our new cultural dominant.[38] We have moved in the direction of accepting the postmodern values of opacity, playful experimentation, and navigation of surface as privileged ways of knowing.

In the contest over where the computer fits into categories such as what is or is not intelligent, alive, or person-like, the game is still very much in play. Here, too, we saw tension. In one context, people treat the machine as sentient, an other; in a different context, they insist on its difference from us, its "other-*ness*." As people have become more comfortable psychologizing computers and have come to grant them a certain capacity for intelligence, the boundary dispute between people and machines now falls on the question of life.

The final contest concerns the notion of the real. In simulated science experiments, virtual chemicals are poured from virtual beakers, and virtual light bounces off virtual walls. In financial transactions, virtual money changes hands. In film and photography, realistic-looking images depict scenes that never took place between people who never met. And on the networked computers of our everyday lives, people have compelling interactions that are entirely dependent on their online self-representations. In cyberspace, hundreds of thousands, perhaps already millions, of users create online personae who live in a diverse group of virtual communities where the routine formation of multiple identities undermines any notion of a real and unitary self. Yet the notion of the real fights back People who live parallel lives on the screen are nevertheless bound by the desires, pain, and mortality of their physical selves. Virtual communities offer a dramatic new context in which to think about human identity in the age of the Internet. They are spaces for learning about the lived meaning of a culture of simulation. Will it be a separate world where people get lost in the surfaces or will we learn to see how the real and the virtual can be made permeable, each having the potential for enriching and expanding the other? The citizens of MUDs are our pioneers.

As we stand on the boundary between the real and the virtual, our experience recalls what the anthropologist Victor Turner termed a liminal moment, a moment of passage when new cultural symbols and meanings can emerge.[39]

Liminal moments are times of tension, extreme reactions, and great opportunity. In our time, we are simultaneously flooded with predictions of doom and predictions of imminent utopia. We live in a crucible of contradictory experience. When Turner talked about liminality, he understood it as a transitional state—but living with flux may no longer be temporary. Donna Haraway's characterization of irony illuminates our situation: "Irony is about contradictions that do not resolve into larger wholes . . . about the tension of holding incompatible things together because both or all are necessary and true."[40] It is fitting that the story of the technology that is bringing postmodernism down to earth itself refuses modernist resolutions and requires an openness to multiple viewpoints.

Multiple viewpoints call forth a new moral discourse.

Multiple viewpoints call forth a new moral discourse. I have said that the culture of simulation may help us achieve a vision of a multiple but integrated identity whose flexibility, resilience, and capacity for joy comes from having access to our many selves. But if we have lost reality in the process, we shall have struck a poor bargain. In Wim Wenders's film *Until the End of the World,* a scientist develops a device that translates the electrochemical activity of the brain into digital images. He gives this technology to his family and closest friends, who are now able to hold small battery-driven monitors and watch their dreams. At first, they are charmed. They see their treasured fantasies, their secret selves. They see the images they otherwise would forget, the scenes they otherwise would repress. As with the personae one can play in a MUD, watching dreams on a screen opens up new aspects of the self.

However, the story soon turns dark. The images seduce. They are richer and more compelling than the real life around them. Wenders's characters fall in love with their dreams, become addicted to them. People wander about with blankets over their heads the better to see the monitors from which they cannot bear to be parted. They are imprisoned by the screens, imprisoned by the keys to their past that the screens seem to hold.

We, too, are vulnerable to using our screens in these ways. People can get lost in virtual worlds. Some are tempted to think of life in cyberspace as insignificant, as escape or meaningless diversion. It is not. Our experiences there are serious play. We belittle them at our risk. We must understand the dynamics of virtual experience both to foresee who might be in danger and to put these experiences to best use. Without a deep understanding of the many selves that we express in the virtual we cannot use our experiences there to enrich the real. If we cultivate our awareness of what stands behind our screen personae, we are more likely to succeed in using virtual experience for personal transformation.

The imperative to self-knowledge has always been at the heart of philosophical inquiry. In the twentieth century, it found expression in the psychoanalytic culture as well. One might say that it constitutes the ethic of psychoanalysis. From the perspective of this ethic, we work to know ourselves in order to improve not only our own lives, but those of our families and society. I have said that psychoanalysis is a survivor discourse. Born of a modernist worldview, it has evolved into forms relevant to postmodern times. With mechanistic roots in the culture of calculation, psychoanalytic ideas become newly relevant in the culture of simulation. Some believe that we are at the end of the Freudian century. But the reality is more complex. Our need for a practical philosophy of self-knowledge has never been greater as we struggle to make meaning from our lives on the screen.

■ N O T E S

1. Emily Martin, *Flexible Bodies* (Boston: Beacon Press, 1994), pp. 161–225.

2. mcdee, The WELL, conference on virtual communities (vc.20.17), 18 April 1992.

3. The sentiment that life online could provide a different experience of self was seconded by a participant who described himself as a man whose conversational abilities as an adult were impaired by having been a stutterer as a child. Online he was able to discover the experience of participating in the flow of a conversation.

   I echo [the previous contributor] in feeling that my online persona differs greatly from my persona offline. And, in many ways, my online persona is more "me." I feel a lot more freedom to speak here. Growing up, I had a severe stuttering problem. I couldn't speak a word without stuttering, so I spoke only when absolutely necessary. I worked through it in my early 20s and you wouldn't even notice it now (except when I'm stressed out), but at 37 I'm still shy to speak. I'm a lot more comfortable with listening than with talking. And when I do speak I usually feel out of sync: I'll inadvertently step on other people's words, or lose people's attention, or talk through instead of to. I didn't learn the dynamic of conversation that most people take for granted, I think. Here, though, it's completely different: I have a feel for the flow of the "conversations," have the time to measure my response, don't have to worry about the balance of conversational space—we all make as much space as we want just by pressing "r" to respond. It's been a wonderfully liberating experience for me. (Anonymous)

4. spoonman, The WELL, conference on communities (vc.20.65), 11 June 1992.

5. Kenneth Gergen, *The Saturated Self: Dilemmas of Identity in Contemporary Life* (New York: Basic Books, 1991).

6. bluefire (Bob Jacobson), The WELL, conference on virtual reality (vr.85.146), 15 August 1993.

7. The WELL, conference on virtual reality (vr.85.148), 17 August 1993.

8. Art Kleiner, The WELL, conference on virtual reality (vr.47.41), 2 October 1990.

9. Gergen, *The Saturated Self,* p. 6.

10. Gergen, *The Saturated Self,* p. 17.

11. hlr (Howard Rheingold), The WELL, conference on virtual reality (vr.47.351), 2 February 1993.

12. McKenzie Wark, The WELL, conference on virtual reality (vr.47.361), 3 February 1993.

13. hlr (Howard Rheingold), The WELL, conference on virtual reality (vr.47.362), 3 February 1993.

14. James M. Glass, *Shattered Selves: Multiple Personality in a Postmodern World (Ithaca, N.Y.: Cornell University Press, 1993).*

15. Robert Jay Lifton, *The Protean Self: Human Resilience in an Age of Fragmentation* (New York: Basic Books, 1993), p. 192.

16. Lifton, *The Protean Self,* pp. 229–32.

17. See, for example, "Aion: Phenomenology of the Self," in *The Portable Jung,* ed. Joseph Campbell, trans. R. F. C. Hull (New York: Penguin, 1971).

18. See, for example, Marvin Minsky, *The Society of Mind* (New York: Simon & Schuster, 1985).

19. See, for example, Colin Ross, *Multiple Personality Disorder: Diagnosis, Clinical Features, and Treatment* (New York: John Wiley & Sons, 1989).

20. Claude Lévi-Strauss, *The Savage Mind* (Chicago: University of Chicago Press, 1960).

21. Ian Hacking, *Rewriting the Soul: Multiple Personality and the Sciences of Memory* (Princeton, N.J.: Princeton University Press, 1995), p. 21.

22. Hacking, *Rewriting the Soul,* p. 29.

23. See Hacking, *Rewriting the Soul,* pp. 96ff.

24. Daniel C. Dennett, *Consciousness Explained* (Boston: Little, Brown and Company, 1991).

25. Donna Haraway, "The Actors Are Cyborg, Nature Is Coyote, and the Geography Is Elsewhere: Postscript to 'Cyborgs at Large'" in *Technoculture,* eds. Constance Penley and Andrew Ross (Minneapolis: University of Minnesota Press, 1991), p. 22.

26. Leslie Harris, "The Psychodynamic Effects of Virtual Reality," *The Arachnet Electronic Journal on Virtual Culture* 2, 1 (February 1994), abstract.

27. Harris, "The Psychodynamic Effects of Virtual Reality," section 14.

28. Allucquere Rosanne Stone has referred to our time in history as the close of the mechanical age, underscoring that we no longer look to clockwork or engines to build our images of self and society. See *The War of Desire and Technology at the Close of the Mechanical Age* (Cambridge, Mass.: MIT Press, 1995).

29. *Newsweek,* 17 April 1995: 70.

30. See, for example, Barbara Johnson, *A World of Difference* (Baltimore: Johns Hopkins University Press, 1987); Donald P. Spence, *Narrative Truth and Historical Truth: Meaning and Interpretation in Psychoanalysis* (New York: W. W. Norton & Company, 1982; and Humphrey Morris, ed., *Telling Facts: History and Narration in Psychoanalysis* (Baltimore: Johns Hopkins University Press, 1992).

31. N. Katherine Hayles, *Chaos Bound: Orderly Disorder in Contemporary Literature and Science* (Ithaca, N.Y.: Cornell University Press, 1990), p. 3.

32. W. Daniel Hillis quoted in Steven Levy, *Artificial Life: The Quest for a New Creation* (New York: Pantheon Books, 1992), p. 344.

33. Norbert Wiener, *God and Golem, Inc.: A Comment on Certain Points Where Cybernetics Impinges on Religion* (Cambridge, Mass.: MIT Press, 1964), p. 36.

34. "A Cyborg Manifesto: Science, Technology, and Socialist-Feminism in the Late Twentieth Century" in Donna Haraway, *Simians, Cyborgs, and Women: The Reinvention of Nature* (New York: Routledge, 1991), pp. 149–81.

35. Colin Greenland, "A Nod to the Apocalypse: An Interview with William Gibson," *Foundation* 36 (Summer): 5–9.

36. In *Chaos Bound,* Katherine Hayles refers to Donna Haraway's language of cyborgs when describing the positive and negative sides of how information technology has contributed to reconceptualizing the human:

    Haraway argues that information technology has made it possible for us to think of entities (including human beings) as conglomerations that can be taken apart, combined with new elements, and put together again in ways that violate traditional boundaries.

    From one perspective this violation is liberating, for it allows historically oppressive constructs to be deconstructed and replaced by new kinds of entities more open to the expression of differences. The problem, of course, is that these new constructs may also be oppressive, albeit in different ways. For example, much feminist thought and writing since the 1940s has been directed toward deconstructing the idea of "man" as a norm by which human experience can be judged. To achieve this goal, another construction has been erected, "woman." Yet as it has been defined in the writing of white, affluent, heterosexual, Western women, this construct has tended to exclude the experiences of black women, Third World women, poor women, lesbian women, and so on. [p. 283]

37. Joel Porte, ed., *Emerson in His Journals* (Cambridge, Mass,: Belknap Press, 1982), p. 81.

38. Fredric Jameson calls these ideas our new "cultural dominant." See Fredric Jameson, "Postmodernism, or the Cultural Logic of Late Capitalism," *New Left Review* 146 (July–August 1984): 53–92. I thank Jim Berkley for directing my attention to the parallels between Jameson's position and consequent developments in personal computation.

39. Victor Turner, *The Ritual Process: Structure and Antistructure* (Chicago: Aldine, 1966).

40. Donna Haraway, "A Cyborg Manifesto," p. 148.

■ Q U E S T I O N S   F O R   R E R E A D I N G

1. What do you think Turkle means by her section heading "Logins R Us"? What is Kenneth Gergen's notion of the "saturated self"? And why is it so important in the discussion on the WELL that Turkle writes about? How does the saturated self contribute to your understanding of a new social identity in VR?

2. It can be argued that we each in varying degrees play different roles or have different identities in our actual lives. I am many different kinds of people to others: A father, a spouse, a teacher, a facilitator, a friend, a tax-payer, an author, a moderator of lists, and so on. So in a sense, I and each of you play many different roles. But what is Turkle talking about that is different in terms of being other people or playing roles? What do you understand from Turkle's references to Carl Jung?

3. What is "Cog"? Why does Turkle mention Cog?

4. What does "dwellers on a threshold" refer to? What does Victor Turner's concept "liminal" mean? (This closing section of Turkle's chapter will be especially helpful as you read about cyborgs and MOOs.)

■ W R I T I N G   A S S I G N M E N T S   F O R   R E R E A D I N G

1. If you know some people—perhaps in your class—who spend a lot of time online playing games or socializing, interview them in terms of the various roles that they play. Inquire into whether the role playing has been beneficial to them. When you have finished with the interviews, write them in the form of a column for your college or university newspaper.

2. If you are taking a psychology or sociology or comparable course, see if you can do some basic research into role playing and apply it to Turkle's discussion. Specifically, first take notes; then make sure that you under-stand what Turkle says; and finally, write an essay-review of Turkle's chap-ter, in which you find authorities that would agree or disagree with her position on role playing in computer-mediated environments.

Mark Slouka's discussion "The Road to Unreality" is the introduction to his book War of the Worlds: Cyberspace and the High-Tech Assault on Reality (New York: Basic Books, 1995): 1–16. Throughout his book, Slouka raises provocative questions about the value of and the possible threat of computer-mediated communication to the actual/real world in which we live. Immediately, he tells his reader that he is concerned with our "growing separation from reality," with some of us accepting "the copy as reality" (1). As a case in point, the title of his book is an allusion to Orson Welles's radio broadcast of H. G. Wells's War of the Worlds, during which many listeners actually believed that the drama was real—that, in fact, Martians had landed on Earth. To be sure, this radio broadcast was no computer-mediated communication; but for Slouka, its broadcast and people's responses indicate our willingness to be taken in. Slouka sees the broadcast as the defining moment when "an electronic illusion triumphed easily over common sense and reality" (6). He makes it very clear that he is not against technology, but that he is against the lack of concern for how computers are changing the world. He says that he is no Neo-Luddite.

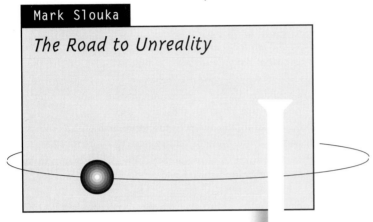

Mark Slouka

The Road to Unreality

I n 1990, a reporter for the *New York Times,* following the famous case of a man accused of murdering his pregnant wife and then blaming the assault on an unknown black assailant, asked a neighbor of the couple for her thoughts on the tragedy. Do you accept his story? she was asked. Does it seem possible to you, knowing this man, that he made up the whole thing? "I don't know," the woman replied, "I'm dying for the movie to come out so I can see how it ends."[1]

I don't think this woman was joking. Or being cynical. Or even evasive. I think she simply meant what she said. For her, a TV movie about the tragedy would tell her—more accurately than her own experience—what to believe. It would settle for her what was real. Less than a year later, the made-for-television movie "Good Night, Sweet Wife: A Murder in Boston" presumably did just that.

I bring up this episode for the light it sheds on an important cultural trend, a trend so pervasive as to be almost invisible: our growing separation from reality.[2] More and more of us, whether we realize it or not, accept the copy as the original. Increasingly removed from experience, overdependent on the representations of reality that come to us through television and the print media, we seem more and more willing to put our trust in intermediaries who "re-present" the world to us.

The problem with this is one of communication; intermediaries are notoriously unreliable. In the well-known children's game of telephone, a whispered message is passed along from person to person until it is garbled beyond recognition. If we think of that original message as truth, or reality, we stand today at the end of a long line of interpreters. It's a line that's been growing longer throughout the century. And now, accustomed to our place at the end of that line, we've begun to accept the fictions that reach us as the genuine article. This is not good news. For one thing, it threatens to make us stupid. For another, it makes us, collectively, gullible as children: we believe what we are told. Finally, it can make us dangerous.

When did we start accepting abstractions for the real thing? Most answers point roughly to the beginning of this century. Before 1900, daily life for the majority of individuals was agrarian, static, local—in other words, not that different from what it had been for centuries. The twentieth century, however, altered the pace and pattern of daily life forever. Within two generations, the old world (for better and worse) was gone. Its loss meant the loss of two things that had always grounded us: our place within an actual community and our connection to a particular physical landscape.[3]

What started us on the road to unreality? Though the catalog reads like a shopping list of many of the century's most dramatic trends—urbanization, consumerism, increasing mobility, loss of regionality, growing alienation from the landscape, and so on—technology, their common denominator, was the real force behind our journey toward abstraction.

A single example may make my point. As everyone knows, unreality increases with speed. Walking across a landscape at six miles an hour, we experience the particular reality of place: its smells, sounds, colors, textures, and so on. Driving at seventy miles an hour, the experience is very different. The car isolates us, distances us; the world beyond the windshield—whether desert mesa or rolling farmland—seems vaguely unreal. At supersonic speeds, the divorce is complete. A landscape at 30,000 feet is an abstraction, as unlike real life as a painting.

. . . unreality increases with speed.

It's an unreality we've grown used to. Habit has dulled the strangeness of it. We're as comfortable with superhuman speed—and the level of abstraction it brings with it—as we are with, say, the telephone, which in a single stroke distanced us from a habit as old as our species: talking to one another face-to-face. We forget that initial users of the telephone (our grandmothers and grandfathers) found it nearly impossible to conceptualize another human being beyond the inanimate receiver; in order to communicate, they had to personify the receiver and speak *to* it, as to some mechanical pet, rather than *through* it to someone else. Today, that kind of instinctive attachment to physical reality seems quaint.

We've come a long way, very quickly. What surprises us now, increasingly, is the shock of the real: the nakedness of face-to-face communication, the rough force of the natural world. We can watch hours of nature programming, but place us in a forest or a meadow and we don't know quite what to do with ourselves. We look forward to hanging out at The Brick with Chris on *Northern Exposure* but dread running into our neighbor while putting out the trash. There has come to be something almost embarrassing about the unmediated event; the man or woman who takes out a musical instrument at a party and offers to play is likely to make everyone feel a bit awkward. It's so naked, somehow. We're more comfortable with its representation: Aerosmith on MTV, Isaac Stern or Eric Clapton on CD.

And now, as we close out the century, various computer technologies threaten to take our long journey from reality to its natural conclusion. They are to TV or videoconferencing what the Concorde is to the car. They have the capacity to make the partially synthetic environments we already inhabit complete—to remove us, once and for all, from reality.

Let me state my case as directly as possible: I believe it is possible to see, in a number of technologies spawned by recent developments in the computer world, an attack on reality as human beings have always known it. I believe this process has been under way for some time, that it will be aided immeasurably by the so-called digital revolution currently sweeping through the industrialized world, and that its implications for our culture are enormous.

I'm the first to admit that this may seem an absurd contention. Most of us, after all, have little trouble separating reality from illusion. We know, for example, that Homer Simpson is a cartoon character on TV, while our neighbor, however much he may act like one, is not; that the highway during our morning commute, the sky at noon, or the bird on the wire at dusk, are not hallucinations; that a drawing of a two-by-four does not a two-by-four make.

Within a few years, however, distinctions such as these will be less automatic. We'll be able to pick up an electronically generated two-by-four. Feel its weight. Swing it around. Whack somebody with it. And yet none of it—not the two-by-four, the person we hit, or the landscape in which this takes place—will be real, in the usual, physical sense. We'll be able to immerse ourselves in an entirely synthetic world, a world that exists only as a trick of the senses, a computer-induced hallucination. And when we emerge from cyberspace—that strange nonplace beyond the computer screen—all indicators suggest that we will find it increasingly difficult to separate real life (already demoted to the acronym RL on computer Nets around the world) from virtual existence. Or worse, that we will know the difference but opt for the digitized world over the real one.

However futuristic all this may sound, it's not all that new. In May 1938, in an essay written for *Harper's Magazine,* E. B. White predicted the encroachment of technology on what we might call the territory of the real. "Clearly," he noted, "the race today is . . . between the things that are and the things that seem to be, between the chemist at RCA and the angel of God." Already, he pointed out, sound effects had begun taking the place of sound itself. Television and radio were enlarging the eye's range, advertising an abstract place, an Elsewhere, that would grow to seem increasingly real. In time, he concluded, *representations* of life, seen on radio and television and in the movies, would come to seem more lifelike to us than their originals.[4]

White called it perfectly. Only months after his prediction, citizens up and down the Eastern seaboard of the United States were heading for the hills, panicked by Orson Welles's radio adaptation of H. G. Wells's *War of the*

Worlds into believing that sixteen-tentacled Martians had landed on Earth. It was a dramatic victory for the chemist at RCA and a defining moment for the New Age. For the thousands who rushed north to escape the Martians' onslaught, Welles's electronic illusion easily triumphed over common sense *and* reality.

The Martians (or the forces of electronic illusion) have been rolling on ever since. The war of the worlds—pitting physical reality against the forces of Elsewhere—continues, and reality continues to take it on the chin. In Yugoslavia recently, an actor who had portrayed the deceased dictator Marshal Tito in a docudrama found himself applauded, and reviled, by ordinary citizens on the streets of Belgrade. In Rio de Janeiro, when a soap opera villain murdered his co-star in real life, the actual homicide and the tortured plot of the *telenovela* fused seamlessly in the public mind. When the National Weather Service interrupted daytime programming to issue a tornado warning for a county in Kansas, the local TV station was flooded with phone calls from outraged citizens incensed over having to miss their soaps.[5]

But television's transgressions on the territory of the real are just minor skirmishes compared to the all-out assault being conducted by the digital avant-garde. The race, you see, is no longer between the angel of God and the chemist at RCA. It's between the angel of God and the computer visionary at Microsoft. Or Apple. Or MIT. And he's not interested in imitating reality; he's out to replace it altogether. What the computer world is doing, says John Perry Barlow, Greatful Dead lyricist-turned-computer-cowboy, "is taking material and making it immaterial: Now is the flesh made word, in many respects."[6]

Reduced to its essentials, it comes down to this: only a decade after White's death, we stand on the threshold of turning life itself into computer code, of transforming the experience of living in the physical world—every sensation, every detail—into a product for our consumption. "We now have the ability," says Barlow, "to take the sum of human experience and give it a medium in which to flow." What this means, simply, is that computer simulations may soon be so pervasive (and so realistic) that life itself will require some sort of mark of authenticity. Reality, in other words, may one day come with an asterisk.[7]

None of which should come as much of a surprise. These, after all, are the days of miracle and wonder, of "telepresence" and "immersion technology" (which promise to submerge us in a fully sensual, synthetic world), of intelligent software, artificial life, and virtual damn-near everything. Entire virtual communities, some numbering ten thousand citizens and more, are now accessible through the conceptual window of your computer screen. Many have homes, prostitutes, tree houses for your children. Within five years, according to John Quarterman, a cyberspace cartographer, the digital world will be inhabited by over a billion individuals worldwide. Those of us still on the outside, Professor Timothy Ferris of Berkeley informs us, will be able to "watch grandmothers be shot by snipers in Sarajevo from six camera angles" without leaving our couches.[8]

Even for the technologically literate, it can all seem vaguely surreal, a strange mixture of hard science and science fiction, binary code and bubble gum, Our home computers, to take just one example, will soon come with a face capable of responding to our expressions, understanding our gestures, even reading our lips. Its eyes will follow us around the room. We'll be able to talk with it, argue with it, flirt with it. We'll be able to program it to look like our husband or our child. Of the Holy See, I suppose. Will it have emotions? You bet. Scream at it and it will cower, or cringe. Maybe even cry. "What we want is not intelligence," says Akikazu Takeuchi, a researcher at the Sony Computer Science Laboratory, "but humanity."[9]

What are we to make of this large-scale tinkering with the human mind and its time-tested orbit? What should those of us in RL make of the dizzying proliferation (and ever-increasing sophistication) of cyberspace communities—the so-called MUDS and MOOS and MUSHES? Or of the fact that an entire generation of *computerjugen*[10] is now spending its leisure time in electronically generated space, experiencing what cyberspace theorists like to call "lucid dreaming in an awake state"?[11] Or that cyberization—the movement to animate everyday objects in order to make them more responsive to our needs—is making rapid progress? In a word, how seriously should we be taking all this?

I'd like to suggest that we take it *very* seriously. Why? Because technology is never a neutral force: it orders our behavior, redefines our values, reconstitutes our lives in ways we can't always predict. Like a political constitution or a legislative act, as Langdon Winner, professor of political science at Rensselaer Polytechnic Institute, has noted, technology establishes the rules by which people live.[12] The digital revolution is technology with a capital T. And its rules, I suspect, may not be to everyone's liking.

Given the enormous effect the digital revolution may come to have on our lives (the digerati, as Steve Lohr has called them,[13] routinely liken its impact to that of the splitting of the atom, the invention of the Gutenberg Press, and the discovery of fire), there is something downright eerie about the lack of debate, the conspicuous absence of dissenting voices, the silence of the critics. Congress seems uninterested; watchdog groups sleep. Like shined deer, we seem to be wandering en masse onto the digital highway, and the only concern heard in the land, by and large, is that some of us may be left behind.[14] Under the circumstances, some caution is surely in order, particularly if we consider that the digital revolution is having its greatest effect on the young. Think of this book as a speed bump on the fiber-optic highway.

I'm a humanist, not a Luddite.

My gripe, I should point out, is not so much with the technologies themselves as with the general lack of concern over the consequences that many new applications may come to have. I'm a humanist, not a Luddite. Though I'll admit to a certain fondness for old-fashioned pastimes (I'll take a book or a musical instrument over a Mac and a modem), I'm not incapable of appreciating the contemporary wonders—from gene splicing to lasers—that everywhere crowd in on our attention. I'm not insensitive to the benefits and beauties of technology; without them, my wife and my son would have died during childbirth.

So let me be as clear as possible: I have no problem with what Andrew S. Grove, President and CEO of the Intel Corporation, has called "the ubiquitous PC."[15] I own and use one. Nor do I have any argument, for example, with the millions of people who crowd the "chat groups" available on the Net (many of whom I've found to be no more or less decent and interesting than people in the real world). My quarrel is with a relatively small but disproportionately influential group of self-described "Net religionists" and "wannabe gods" who believe that the physical world can (and should) be "downloaded" into a computer, who believe that the future of mankind is not in RL (real life) but in some form of VR (virtual reality); who are working very hard (and spending enormous amounts of both federal and private money) to engineer their very own version of the apocalypse. As intelligent as they are single-minded, these people have been ignored by the majority of humanists for too long; it's time we started listening.

The *real* issue here, as the novelist and technoevangelist Robert Coover has pointed out, is how we answer the question, "What's human?" For some, he explains, humanity "has to do with souls and 'depth' and the search for meaning and purpose; with tradition, ritual, mystery and individualism." For others, like himself, it has more to do with the spiritualism of the hive: the increasingly interlinked system of computers and computer technologies about to subsume (as Kevin Kelly, the executive editor of *Wired* magazine, recently put it) the "millions of buzzing, dim-witted personal computers" (that's us) into one grand organism/machine immeasurably greater than the sum of its parts. For Coover (as for others, including Speaker of the House of Representatives Newt Gingrich), our "evolution" into this hive state is inevitable. "I regret," he says, "having to give up the comforting fairy tales of the past: I, too, want to be unique, significant, connected to a 'deeper truth,' canonized. I want to *have* an 'I.' Too bad."[16]

Of course, shedding "fairy tales" like tradition, individualism, and identity, Coover admits, may have its downside. "If creatures of the past were hived under queen bees like Alexander the Great or Genghis Khan," he points out (quite reasonably, I think), "it seems unlikely that hived creatures of the future will escape their own hive-masters." And what, one might wonder, will happen to the "unhived"? "No doubt they will get stepped on," says Coover; "the Sophist principle 'knowledge is power' will make them mere meat at the fringe."

The expression "meat at the fringe," I think, comes close to explaining what this book is about. When a significant number of powerful individuals— scientists, academics, authors, engineers, computer programmers—following the scent of a potential $3.5 *trillion* industry[17] begin referring to the human body as meat (the expression is a common one among the digerati), it's time for those still foolishly attached to theirs to start paying attention. When a subculture of enthusiasts yearning for the technological equivalent of rapture begins labeling the unhived (in a weak attempt at digital wit) PONAs (people of no account), the PONAs may want to start asking what counts and what doesn't.

"When the yearning for human flesh has come to an end," asks Barlow, referring to the human touch, not to cannibalism, "what will remain?" Good question. "Mind," he says hopefully, "may continue, uploaded into the Net, suspended in an ecology of voltage as ambitiously capable of self-sustenance as was that of its carbon-based forebears."[18] To unhived PONAs like myself, this is hardly encouraging. I *like* my carbon-based body and the carbon-based bodies of my wife and children and friends. I like my carbon-based dog and my carbon-based garden. Nor, to pick up on Coover's "meat on the fringe" image, do I particularly fancy myself as roadkill on the digital highway.

My uneasiness with the new transcendentalists, I suppose, springs from my own instinctive allegiance to the physical world, to the present moment, to the strengths and limitations of the human mind. I'm suspicious of whatever tends to improve or displace these. I believe we all should be. I believe that tampering with the primary things in life (our sense of reality, for example, or individual identity) is not to be undertaken lightly, that technological progress sometimes is and sometimes ain't, and that the cloak of inevitability (the technologists' time-tested method for steamrollering dissent or even debate) has been known to conceal both miracles and monsters.

Coover and Co. may find my timidity quaint, my values hopelessly sentimental. I can live with that. What it comes down to, it seems to me, is this: human culture depends on the shared evidence of the senses, always has; we can communicate with one another because a hurled rock will always break skin, a soap bubble always burst. A technology designed to short-circuit the senses, a technology capable of providing an alternate world—abstract, yet fully inhabitable, real to our senses yet accessible only through a computer screen—would take away this common ground and replace it with one manufactured for us by the technologists.

And this is not a good thing. Why? Because human history, in the largest sense, has been of our debate with the world. Because reality has been and continues to be the great touchstone for the world's ethical systems. Because, simply put, the world provides context, and without context, ethical behavior is impossible. It is the physical facts of birth and pain and pleasure and death that force us (enable us) to make value judgments: *this* is better than *that.* Nourishment is better than hunger. Compassion is better than torture. Virtual systems, by offering us a reality divorced from the world, from the limits and responsibilities of presence, offer us as well a glimpse into an utterly amoral universe. Consider an obvious example: in Night Trap, a CD-ROM video game recently popular among prepubescent boys, vampires drill holes into the necks of their barely clad female victims and hang them from meat hooks; virtual reality (coming soon to a modem near you) will allow you to *be* the vampire. To inflict pain. Without responsibility. Without consequences. The punctured flesh will heal at the touch of a button, the scream disappear into cyberspace. You'll be able to resurrect the digital dead and kill them again.

The implications of these new technologies are social; the questions they pose, broadly ethical; the risks they entail, unprecedented. They are the cultural equivalent of genetic engineering, except that in this experiment, even more than in the other one, *we* will be the potential new hybrids, the two-pound mice.

What will technologies that alter our sense of reality mean, in the long run? What will they do to us? No one knows. Ask the technovisionaries how human beings (who have evolved over millions of years in response to the constraints and pressures of the physical world) might respond to existence in aphysical environments, or to the wholesale cyberization of the human environment, and they'll fall over one another in their willingness to admit that they have no idea. Does this concern them just a little? Frighten them, maybe? Not a bit. "The best things in life are scary," Kevin Kelly told me recently, "I'm serious."[19] Unfortunately for the rest of us, he probably is. So on we go, blindfolded, pedal to the floor, over the canyonlands.

"It's happening and will continue to. If I could stop it I would."

Does my concern spring from a lack of vision? Apparently not. Not long ago, I asked John Perry Barlow what the advantages might be to leaving the physical world behind. "Damned few," he wrote back, "for any individual as presently configured. But advantage," he went on, "has nothing to do with it. There are many evolutionary forces at work here, most of them working against us. All of them inexorable." But what about all that business of leaving the flesh behind, I asked, of uploading ourselves into the Net? "Again," he answered, "it's less a matter of advantage than inevitability. It's happening and will continue to. If I could stop it I would." But what, I asked, would you say to those who might be terrified by this prospect (of transcending the meat, so to speak)? "They're right," said Barlow, wrapping up with a philosophical shrug. "But when you're about to be swept over the falls, you might as well try to enjoy the ride."[20]

I am no Oliver Stone. I have no interest in conspiracy theories. Nor do I wish to gloss over the very real benefits the digital New Age may bring; technology, as I have said, is never a wholly one-sided affair. My concern, rather, is based on a small number of well-worn truths: that the free market can unleash forces difficult to control; that technological innovation has its own logic, often separate from questions of value and ethics; and that *some* technologies—particularly those that promise (or threaten) to transform human culture as we know it—bear watching.

■ NOTES

1. Constance L. Hays, "Illusion and Tragedy Coexist After a Couple Dies," *New York Times,* 7 January 1990.

2. I am aware, of course, that the term *reality,* problematic since Plato, has lately become a political minefield. So as not to be misunderstood, then, let me be as clear as possible. I have no problem with those who argue

that reality, like taste, is subjective—a product of one's race, gender, economic class, education, and so on. These qualifications strike me as good and true. At the same time, however, I believe that under the strata of subjectivity, of language and perspective, lies a bedrock of fact: neo-Nazis in Koln or California may define the Holocaust differently than I do, yet the historical *fact* stands firm. It is *this* kind of reality—immutable, empirical, neither historically nor culturally relative–that I refer to here.

3. The rapid acceleration of cultural change in the twentieth century, of course, is a historical truism. One of the most vivid documents recording this transformation in American culture (it originally appeared in 1929) is Robert S. and Helen M. Lynd, *Middletown: A Study in Contemporary American Culture* (New York: Harcourt Brace Jovanovich, 1959).

4. E. B. White, "Removal," reprinted in *One Man's Meat* (New York: Harper Colophon, 1983), 2–3.

5. Roger Cohen, "Tito Lives Again But Like Ex-Nation, Is Bewildered," *New York Times*, April 30, 1994, 4; Alma Guillermoprieto, "Obsessed in Rio," *The New Yorker* (August 16, 1993): 44–45. Guillermoprieto quotes a friend of hers as saying, "Brazilians discovered virtual reality years ago. They never know when they are entering the [television] screen and when they are leaving it."

6. Interview, Julian Dibbell, "Net Prophet," *Details* (August 1994):100.

7. Ibid. "It's eerie," says Barlow's friend and editor of *Wired* magazine, Kevin Kelly, "how much of life *can* be transferred. So far, some of the traits of the living that have successfully been transported to mechanical systems include self-replication, self-governance, limited self-repair, mild evolution, and partial learning." Kevin Kelly, *Out of Control: The Rise of Neo-Biological Civilization* (Reading, Mass.: Addison-Wesley, 1994), 2. Kelly's science, as suggested by terms like "mild evolution," is suspect. More interesting, I think, is the sensibility behind the assertion.

8. Quarterman quoted in Peter H. Lewis, "Cyberspace Is Looking a Lot Like Christmas," *New York Times*, 25 December 1993. Timothy Ferris, "The Future Is Coming," *New York Times*, 12 November 1993.

9. Quoted in Andrew Pollack, "Japanese Put a Human Face on Computers," *New York Times*, 28 June 1994.

10. The term is from Allucquere Rosanne Stone, "Will the Real Body Please Stand Up?" in *Cyberspace: First Steps*, ed. Michael Benedikt (Cambridge, Mass.: MIT Press, 1991), 92.

11. Ibid., 94.

12. Langdon Winner, "Do Artifacts Have Politics?" in *Technology and Politics*, ed. Michael E. Kraft and Norman J. Vig (Durham, N.C.: Duke University Press, 1988), 43.

13. Steve Lohr, "For Computer Convention, Be Sure to Pack Vision," *New York Times*, 24 September 1993.

14. There are notable exceptions, of course. Both Bill McKibben and Neil Postman, continuing in the honorable tradition of humanist/skeptics like Thomas Carlysle and H. G. Wells, have recently argued that technological advances have begun to separate us from the "information" available only through direct, unmediated contact with the natural world (McKibben) and the values inherent in what we might broadly term humanistic culture (Postman). See Bill McKibben, *The Age of Missing Information* (New York: Random House, 1992), and Neil Postman, *Technopoly: The Surrender of Culture to Technology* (New York: Vintage Books, 1992).

15. The term is from the Intel Corporation's official videotape of Andrew S. Grove's keynote address at the PC Expo on 28 June 1994.

16. Kevin Kelly, "Embrace It," from "The Electronic Hive: Two Views," *Harper's Magazine* 288 (May 1994): 21. Kelly elaborates on his notion of the electronic hive, in *Out of Control,* esp. pp. 11–28, and I elaborate on Kelly in chapter 4. Quote is from a letter by Robert Coover to *Harper's Magazine* 289 (August 1994): 4.

17. The estimate quoted here is from Steve Lohr, "For Computer Convention, Be Sure to Pack Vision," *New York Times,* 23 September 1993.

18. Quote is from a letter by John Perry Barlow to *Harper's Magazine* 289 (August 1994): 5.

19. Kevin Kelly, personal e-mail, 27 July 1994. The amusement park attitude is a common one among the digerati.

20. John Perry Barlow, personal e-mail, 22 July 1994.

■ QUESTIONS FOR REREADING

1. In the light of your reading of Slouka, ask yourself how much of your time is taken up with copies of reality. That is, how much time do you spend listening to records, watching and listening to television, using your computer, and so on, instead of attending a live concert to listen to music, going to the actual event that might be broadcast on television, and writing or computing on paper with pencil or ink? Or how often do you, as Slouka suggests, simply take a walk out into the real world?

2. Put forth the clearest oral exposition of what Slouka means by *the attack on reality.* Once you and your classmates arrive at a general agreement of the accuracy of the exposition, try to decide, based on your experiences, whether Slouka is right about this attack. If you disagree with Slouka, do you think that your age (assuming that you're under 21) and your being born within the time of the advanced technology have made it impossible for you to distinguish what is virtual from what is real, since you now might live in nothing but a virtual (copy-of-reality) world? Or at least, perhaps advanced technology has made it difficult for you to distinguish the difference as, say, a parent or grandparent might?

3. If you are not familiar with Orson Welles's radio broadcast of H. G. Welles's *War of the Worlds,* find out what you can about the event. Then discuss the full implications of what Slouka might be alluding to in his comparison.

■ WRITING ASSIGNMENTS FOR REREADING

1. After reading Slouka's article and rereading Thieme's article (in chapter 1), write an essay arguing for their similarities and differences.

2. Write an imagined meeting between Rheingold and Slouka. Let's say that they meet at a real café and discuss their differences. What would the dialogue or exchange between them read like? Write it out. First give the setting, then the dialogue. If there is an audience of people around them interjecting comments from time to time, describe those people and place their comments in the dialogue. Then write an imagined dialogue between them online. Write it out just as it might appear online, with others commenting.

Freedom/Censorship

*(Security, Hackers/Crackers,
and the Communications Decency Act[s]):*

I

n this section as well as into the next one, we will be reading, for the most part, indirectly about the U.S. Constitution—a document written a couple of centuries ago and whose principles and laws have spread from New England all across what is known today as the United States. As our map grew from colonies to territories to states, so grew the reach of the Constitution. As we attempt today, however, to stretch our map to include cyberspace, so grows our confusion. Moving from the colonization of the original thirteen to the colonization of the rest of the country is not at all comparable, we are finding out, to the colonization of cyberspace. The principles of the *actual* world are difficult, if not finally impossible, to apply to the *virtual* world. And yet, many legislators and citizens are trying to apply the Constitution to virtual world(s).

In a 1995 issue of *Newsweek* ("TechnoMania," Feb. 27, 1995), the editors write: "The revolution has only just begun, but already it's starting to overwhelm us. It's outstripping our capacity to cope, antiquating our laws, transforming our mores, reshuffling our economy, reordering our priorities, redefining our workplaces." The editors say we are in the "Bit Bang." Not the Big Bang of Creation, but the Bang of a terminal revolution that challenges us with problems that we have no idea how to deal with. The major problem is how to apply the Constitution to the New Virtual World. For many citizens of the actual world, this is not a problem: They say, just apply the Constitution as we do to the actual world. For others, however, this kind of thinking is part of the problem: Just applying it to a virtual world, they argue, is an unjust application that really, in the long run, cannot be implemented, and they remind us that applying the Constitution to the actual world itself has been no easy, uncontested task.

The media have touted the problem as "crimes of the Net." Some argue, however, that the term "criminal" activity is too broadly applied and is used by the state and federal governments as a pretext to extend their powers over those people living in the Internet communities. The issue has become, therefore, one of freedom of expression versus censorship on the Internet, of private versus public, of freedom on the virtual range versus being fenced in and restricted by legislation that would post actual and virtual signs warning of "illegal" trespassing.

Transgressions on the Net can range from spamming subscribers on a list with junk mail, through enticing people to meet with the intent to harm or hurt a person, to hacking into government or corporate computers. In the first of these, a handful of netizens have taken it into their own hands to police the Net by sending "cancelbots" destroying messages that they do not want sent. In the second, groups of netizens police the net by setting up criminals for arrest, criminals who would lure children and adults into dangerous liaisons. (There is one group called CyberAngels that is comparable to the New York City subway group known as the Guardian Angels.)

In the third, hacking into government or corporate computers, netizens have a rather different, mixed attitude, for they do not see hackers as all bad. A distinction is often made by netizens and digerati between hackers and crackers. What hackers in general challenge us with is an ethic, as Steven Levy in his *Hackers* phrases it, that says "information wants to be free." Hackers, as Bruce Sterling depicts them in *The Hacker Crackdown,* "are absolutely soaked through with heroic antibureaucratic sentiment. Hackers long for recognition as a praiseworthy cultural archetype, the postmodern electronic equivalent of the cowboy and mountain man." What is considered cybertheft can be considered by a hacker *in some cases* as "sharing" (hence the term *shareware*). Crackers, however, are seen as outright criminals who want to steal information for private gain—information such as credit card numbers.

While many other netizens and digerati might make this distinction between hackers and crackers, many citizens and governments at all levels—local, state, and federal—do not. Therefore, as a result of citizens' alarm around the country, lobbyists of special-interest groups and U.S. legislators have become especially interested in regulating and making the Net and all things electronically communicated safe. The netizens and digerati who would make a distinction between hackers and crackers and who are concerned with protecting civil liberties have resisted the attempt to legislate what they see to be unconstitutional laws.

Both sides have met recently in battling over what was called the *Communications Decency Act* (CDA) which was an amendment to the 1996 Telecommunications Bill. The amendment was an attempt to protect children from obscene language. The Electronic Freedom Foundation (EFF) as well as other civil liberties groups started the Blue Ribbon Campaign <http://www.eff.org/blueribbon.html> to stop Sen. James Exon and Congress from passing the act, which the coalition was not successful in doing. On June 12, 1996, however, a three-judge panel in Philadelphia ruled the CDA unconstitutional and issued an injunction, stopping the U.S. Justice Department from enforcing the amendment to the law. The department has appealed the the ruling to the U.S. Supreme Court. Therefore, the struggle for protection and justice continues on both sides. There is no rest. And the outcome, whatever it might eventually be, will affect all of us in ways that we have not even begun to understand.

■ SUMMARY OF KEY TERMS

cancelbot: A computer-programmed message that functions like a guided missile and that will destroy another computer's electronic messages.

Communications Decency Act (CDA): An amendment to the 1996 Telecommunications Bill that became a law. Originally proposed by Sen. James Exon, the amendment was a broad provision that made it illegal to use obscene language in electronic media where children might be exposed to it. The bill, when rewritten and passed as law, would punish anyone up to $250,000. A panel of three judges in Philadelphia placed an injunction on the U.S. Department of Justice, forbidding it to enforce the law. The department appealed the law to the U.S. Supreme Court.

crackers (kraqrz): People who break computer code with the sole purpose of being malicious and damaging code or stealing and using information such as credit card or telephone numbers for private gain. (See definition in "Is Computer Hacking a Crime?")

digirati: The term echoes "literati," which refers to people who have expert knowledge about literature. A person who has expert knowledge about things virtual and about computers.

Electronic Frontier Foundation (EFF): In its own words: "A non-profit civil liberties organization working in the public interest to protect privacy, free expression, and access to public resources and information online, as well as to promote responsibility in new media" <www.eff.org>. The EFF was founded in 1990 by John Perry Barlow and Mitchell Kapor.

hackers (haqr, haqrz): People who program efficiently, create their own programs to solve computer problems, believe in the ethic that information wants to be free, and therefore create software that they call freeware, or in some cases shareware, and appreciate the aesthetic nature of the Net. (See definition in "Is Computer Hacking a Crime?")

Michael Meyer's "Crimes of the 'Net'" was published in Newsweek (November 14, 1994): 46–47. It is one of the very first articles reporting in a national magazine about crimes in cyberspace. Meyer focuses on the problem of theft on the info-highway. (As we proceed through CyberReader this theme and its various ramifications will build into such areas as copyright issues.)

Michael Meyer with Anne Underwood

Crimes of the "Net"

Software: Hackers call it "sharing." But theft on the Internet is costing companies billions, and the high-tech industry is struggling to stop it.

Ray Curci is an earnest, diligent guy. He spends days off with his wife, but works from home every weekend. One recent Saturday he settled himself in front of the computer in his den—and noticed something odd. Dozens of people were logging on to a seldom-used computer that Curci, a systems administrator, runs at Florida State University. More puzzling was that most of the users were from abroad. And, once logged in, they seemed to just . . . disappear.

Hackers, Curci realized. Quickly, he tracked the intruders to their destination—a so-called invisible directory, or data bank lacking any identifiable name or listing. He was astonished by what he found: a vast cache of proprietary software, including test versions of Windows 95 and OS/2, the new operating systems being developed by Microsoft Corp. and IBM. He had no idea who secreted it within the university's computers. But it was obviously a pirate's treasure trove. There were games and word-processing programs, even "tools" to help hackers break passwords and conceal their digital trespasses. Curci scrambled the purloined programs to make them unusable, even as a dozen hackers swarmed to download copies. But, he guesses, hundreds of cybersurfers beat him to the punch. Many more are still trying.

Such is the dark side of the Internet, the ubiquitous electronic web linking as many as 40 million computers worldwide. As anyone not wholly techno-illiterate knows by now, the Net is growing gangbusters. It's our new frontier, a digital Wild West. As befits such a rough-and-ready place, it's populated by lots of bad guys. Want the latest computer games from Broderbund or 3DO? Interested in previewing Microsoft's vaunted Windows 95, nine months before it hits a store near you? Tap into the Net, find the right bulletin board, and you can probably secure a free copy. Telephone credit cards, copyrighted music, even digital *Playboy* centerfolds are being electronically pilfered, too. Hackers call it "sharing." Others consider it theft, pure and simple. "It's like shoplifting," says Bruce Lehman, U.S. commissioner of patents and trademarks, no different from letting your fingers do the walking at your local CD store.

It's hard to gauge the scope of the phenomenon or its economic impact. But numbers tell part of the story. By some estimates, roughly $2 billion worth of software was stolen over the Internet last year, a growing portion of the total $7.4 billion the Software Publishers Association reckons was lost to piracy in 1993. Just last month the leader of an international piracy ring operating out of Majorca, Spain, pleaded guilty to a brand of fraud destined to become commonplace. According to U.S. investigators, the racketeers stole 140,000 telephone credit-card numbers, then sold them to computer bulletin boards in the United States and Europe. Hackers used the numbers to make a whopping $140 million worth of long-distance phone calls—sometimes merely to pay for their time online, other times to tap into remote computers and download hijacked software. Who ate the loss? GTE Corp., AT&T, Bell Atlantic and MCI, among others.

It was not an isolated incident. Police have arrested half a dozen bulletin-board operators in recent months on charges of illegally distributing software over the Internet. "This is only the tip of the iceberg," says Sandra Sellers of the Software Publishers Association. The association has identified 1,600 bulletin boards carrying bootleg software, she claims. Last week authorities in North Carolina indicted nine alleged members of a nationwide piracy ring, known digitally by code names like Phone Stud, Major Theft and Killerette. Like the hackers of the Majorca network, they have been charged with stealing as many as 100,000 telephone credit-card numbers—as well as pirating an array of software. The cost to the phone companies has been estimated at $50 million.

The thievery isn't likely to stop with software and phone cards. Not so far in the future, the Internet will become a well-traveled avenue of commerce. Already retailers are using it to hawk everything from computer parts to flowers and teddy bears. Since anyone with a modem and a computer can go into

Theft on the Infohighway

October 1994 Hackers bust into computers at Florida State University and upload pirated versions of a dozen new programs, including Windows 95.

September 1994 Max Louarn, 22, is arrested for masterminding a plot to sell 140,000 pilfered phone-card numbers in the United States and abroad via computer bulletin boards. He later pleads guilty.

August 1994 Richard D. Kenadek, 43, is indicted for reportedly allowing pirated programs to be traded on his bulletin board, Davey Jones Locker.

April 1994 David LaMacchia, 20 and a student at MIT, is indicted for conspiracy to commit wire fraud, after allegedly permitting the distribution of more than $1 million worth of copyrighted software over the Internet.

December 1993 Playboy wins its suit against George Frena, who allowed copyrighted nude photos to be distributed on his computer billboard.

November 1993 Frank Music Corp. files a class-action suit against CompuServe for allegedly permitting subscribers to post more than 500 copyrighted songs, including Frank's "Unchained Melody."

business, the possibilities for abuse are almost endless. *Playboy* magazine, for instance, has sued half a dozen bulletin boards over the last two years for baring its Bunny pix. CompuServe, the major online information service, has been sued by 140 music publishers for allegedly permitting subscribers to download popular songs. Cybertheft as yet accounts for an indiscernible share of the $400 million lost annually to record piracy, but that's partly because of technical difficulties. Taping a popular single takes only a few moments; pirating a digital version can require anywhere from 30 minutes to several hours, depending on your equipment. But that will change as digital transmission technology improves. Before long, says David Leibowitz at the Recording Industry Association of America, "you will be able to download an entire album in seconds." Then, watch out.

Businesses are moving to protect themselves. Perhaps because it's so obviously part of a trend, the Florida break-in provoked an unusually tough response. Microsoft posted a $10,000 bounty for information leading to the arrest and conviction of the perpetrators. DeScribe Inc., a computer-software company whose new word-processing program was found among the pirated software, offered a $20,000 reward. IBM is investigating, in cooperation with federal authorities. But tracking the cybercrooks won't be easy. The Internet is a chaotic place. Hackers go from computer to computer, vaulting borders and leaving few traces. Before entering a computer at Florida State University, they might pass through another computer in Finland, say, that strips any names or addresses from their communications. Even when uncovered, pirates can disavow wrongdoing. For instance, many of the Florida intruders hailed from Asia, where piracy is not always considered a crime.

Legality collides with practicality when battling cybertheft. As part of its plan for a "national information infrastructure," the Clinton administration proposes tightening the federal Copyright Act to explicitly cover transmissions over the Internet. New laws would also make it clear that electronic property rights are as sacrosanct as any other. But to what effect? The rules of commerce and fair play that govern real-world business are alien to the anarchic "Wild West" culture of the Internet. There, the prevailing ethic is "shareware." Knowledge is to be disseminated. Anything found in etherspace is widely considered to be "mine" as well as "yours"—"ours," in other words. Digital socialism rules the Net, not copyrightable capitalism. Few Interneters would disagree that stealing and reselling software or credit cards is wrong. But fewer still would feel guilty about copying the latest game version of Doom, or some such, rather than forking out $39.95. Unfortunately, that often admirable ethos makes it easier for genuine crooks to perpetrate—and justify—their crimes.

■ Q U E S T I O N S   F O R   R E R E A D I N G

1. How do you think that crime in cyberspace compares to crime in the actual world? Is there more or less? If there is less, is it really all that important to us? Why should we expect our law enforcers to even bother?

Who pays for cyberthefts? If a company loses millions of dollars because its software has been "lifted" and placed on a BBS for all to download, who pays for this loss?

2. Is economics the only issue? Or are there other issues in relation to what is called cybertheft? What about the hacker ethic that information wants to be free? What do you make of Meyer's distinction between "digital social-ism" and "copyrightable capitalism"? Which do you agree with? How would your choice, if it were to become the law of cyberspace, affect your life and the lives of those around you? (There will be another chance to discuss this issue in chapter 5.)

■ WRITING ASSIGNMENTS FOR REREADING

1. With several of your classmates, discuss and draft a law for cyberspace. When doing so, be sure to take into consideration that your law *can* be implemented. You might begin this difficult assignment by taking one aspect—say, software placed online at BBSs for the taking. And then move on to other kinds of "sharing" or "stealing."

2. Interview a staff member or members at your university who work in the area of academic computer services. Ask them a series of questions that you have developed in terms of your readings on cybertheft. Try to find out their attitudes toward piracy of software. Once you have completed the interviews, write them as a brief article—say, about 600 words.

Peter H. Lewis

No More "Anything Goes": Cyberspace Gets Censors

Peter H. Lewis's "No More 'Anything Goes':
Cyberspace Gets Censors" was published in
The New York Times (June 29, 1994): A1, D5.
Lewis's article is one of the first of its kind
in a major U.S. newspaper. In many ways,
like Meyer's article, it sounds the closing of
the Wild West electronic frontier, where
anything used to go.

Freedom of expression has always been the rule in
the fast-growing web of public and private computer networks known as
cyberspace. But even as thousands of Americans each week join the several
million who use computer networks to share ideas and "chat" with others, the
companies that control the networks and sometimes individual users are
beginning to play the role as censor.

Earlier this month, the American Online network shut several feminist discussion forums, saying it was concerned that the subject matter might be
inappropriate for young girls who would see the word "girl" in the forum's
headline and "go in there looking for information about their Barbies," a
spokeswoman said.

Users on other networks have been banished, censored or censured this
year for the widespread posting of messages like "Jesus Is Coming," "Your
Armenian Grandfathers Are Guilty of Genocide." The third case brought to
cyberspace the long conflict between Turks and Armenians, and, according to
some network users, produced a counterattack by an unknown Armenian
sympathizer who programmed his or her computer to sniff out any message
on the system containing the word "turkey" and substitute "genocide," even in
forums discussing Thanksgiving meals.

On Prodigy, the country's largest commercial network, with more than
two million users, supervisors have been expanding the use of what they call
"George Carlin software," which finds messages with certain objectionable
words and warns those who sent them to erase them or their messages will be
censored. The nickname refers to the comedian who does a monologue about
censorship in broadcasting titled "Seven Dirty Words." Prodigy's list of
offending words has grown into the dozens.

A University of Florida student's access to the giant network known as the
Internet was revoked this month after the student used university computers
to repeatedly post copies of a political polemic. Outrage and calls for censorship arose among users of the Usenet network after racist messages appeared
on forums set up to discuss O. J. Simpson's arrest on murder charges.

Then there is the case of Arnt Gulbrandsen, a 25-year-old Norwegian
computer programmer who was enraged earlier this month when he saw that
a Phoenix law firm, Canter & Siegel, was once again advertising its services

over the worldwide Usenet computer network, despite pleas from many users to cease and desist. From his keyboard halfway around the world, Mr. Gulbrandsen launched the electronic equivalent of a Patriot missile: each time the law firm sent out an electronic advertisement, his computer automatically sent out a message that caused the network system to intercept and destroy the firm's transmissions.

"I was somewhat surprised that I only got positive feedback," Mr. Gulbrandsen said. "I expected more than a little 'flaming,' " as personal attacks and complaints, transmitted electronically, are known among networks users.

▪ TROUBLESOME ISSUES

Even longtime networks users who applaud such a use of what they call a "cancelbot" acknowledge that the situation raises broad and troubling issues about censorship in cyberspace.

But because the wide use of computer networks is so new, no established case law moderates the debate over censorship in such cases, the way it does for publishing, broadcasting and speech.

For some networks, the legal questions hinge on whether they are to be considered common carriers, much like telephone companies or even bookstores, which are not responsible for the content of the messages they carry, or to be regarded as private networks that have the right to establish and enforce standards of language and ethics for all users.

In recent court cases involving the computer network Compuserve, a division of the H&R Block Company, the network has argued that it is protected as a common carrier. But that raises the question of whether Compuserve has been right to enforce its own standards for content.

▪ NO ONE SOURCE

The responsibility for any censorship rests not with a central authority but with the administrators of the thousands of private and public computer networks. Many of those administrators offer guidelines for users, but enforcement is usually left to peer pressure—criticism from others using the network. While some networks will act to stop a potentially objectionable message before it is distributed, others will take action only after a message is posted and users complain about it.

Because of their international nature, the networks operate outside the framework of First Amendment protections familiar to most Americans. "What First Amendment?" Wolfgang Schelongowski, a Usenet user in Bochum, Germany, transmitted during a network debate on such issues. "No such thing here, or in any country besides the U.S.A."

Laurence A. Canter and Martha S. Siegel, the lawyers who are Mr. Gulbrandsen's target, said his actions amounted to censorship. "What does this mean, that everyone on Usenet will have to meet the standards of this

Gulbrandsen guy or he will take it upon himself to cancel their messages?" Ms. Siegel asked. "If anything is going to bring down the net, it'll be things like robot cancelers and self-styled censors."

The conflict is most intense on Usenet, a cooperative anarchy of private and public computers comprising more than 8,000 discussion groups, used by an estimated six million people worldwide. Usenet is most commonly reached through the Internet, an even larger web that links some 25 million people worldwide.

■ A SHIFT IN PURPOSE

The technology that enables messages to be canceled was built into Usenet originally to allow an individual to withdraw a message he or she had written. As a safeguard, the command was designed so that only the writer could withdraw a message. In practice, however, canceling was occasionally used by computer system administrators to remove offensive or outdated messages.

Canceling someone else's message is controversial, said Ron Newman, a programmer who helped develop a technology used on many Internet computers, "because the person who issues the cancel message has to write a message claiming, falsely, to be the sender of the original message." In other words, the canceler must commit electronic forgery.

"The cancel facility was not intended to be used this way, and it could easily be abused by people who want to set themselves up as censors," Mr. Newman said.

Mr. Gulbrandsen and Internet technical experts acknowledged that it would be easy to create "cancelbots" that wipe out messages from a given company, or even a certain country.

But even with its potential for abuse, Mr. Gulbrandsen's action against Canter & Siegel seems to have met with popular support among users, many of whom object to advertising on the network. "C. & S. illustrates a potential vulnerability of the net," Mike Godwin, legal counsel for the Electronic Frontier Foundation, a lobbying group in Washington, said of the law firm. "They are pushing it to the extreme. If everyone did what they did," the system would be clogged with unwanted messages and there would be "nothing worth reading."

Mr. Godwin added: "The EFF believes very strongly that censorship is the wrong way to approach net problems. But we also believe there are rules of the road that limit what you can do on the net, rules that don't amount to censorship."

Daniel P. Dern of Newton Center, Mass., author of *The Internet Guide for New Users,* said even well-intentioned action could drift into censorship. "There is a danger of the cancel wars shifting from inappropriate resource use to canceling based on 'I don't like your opinion,'" he said. "At what point does somebody say, 'I don't like this person, and I'm going to cancel them'?"

To most users of the Internet, unbridled freedom, even anarchy, are guiding principles.

"Usenet has principles, it has a social structure, but it has no government," said Brad Templeton, publisher at the Clarinet Communications Corporation, an electronic-newspaper company in San Jose, California. "People who study such things have said that a real anarchy, like a commune, starts breaking down at about 100 people. Somehow we have managed to grow a community of several million people. Now people see the fringes of that system breaking down. Is the answer to impose a government, or is the answer to be found within the system? The idea of a cancelbot is actually something working within the system."

■ QUESTIONS FOR REREADING

1. What are the differences among Compuserve, Arnt Gulbrandsen, and the U.S. Government when each interferes (by way of, so to speak, a "cancelbot") with the free passage of information? Are there differences in these authorities on the Net? If so, how would you verify (or if you must, justify) these differences?

2. There is much indirect talk about the U.S. Constitution and the First Amendment as well as other amendments. Since the Internet moves beyond the boundaries of the United States, what does the Constitution have to do with how netizens discourse with each other and move about on the Web? If there is going to be a law regulating the movement of information across national boundaries, should it be a set of individual laws written for and by each country or an international law applying to all countries (or as many as would ratify it)?

■ WRITING ASSIGNMENT FOR REREADING

Write a defense for the freedom of expression on the Net. Once you have completed a draft, write against a so-called free expression of whatever someone might want on the Net. Now once you have completed this draft, go back and rewrite the defense of freedom of expression in the light of your statement against it. And yes, once again rewrite the statement against it. It is this kind of movement back and forth—pro and con—that can help you find your own position on the issue. As you read more and discuss the issues with people who are interested, you will be further refining your position.

Matthew Ebnet

Vigilantes Patrol Cyberspace

Matthew Ebnet's "Vigilantes Patrol Cyberspace" first appeared in The Kansas City
Star (June 8, 1997): A1. What Ebnet reports is
that in the absence of laws for the Net,
vigilantes, comparable to neighborhood
patrols, have become netizen police,
enforcing actual law in cyberspace and
imposing online order.

KANSAS CITY, Mo.—Randall Sluder stared at his computer screen almost in a trance as the man who just entered an online chat room said he was looking for sex with young girls.

Then it came to Sluder: He could catch the man.

It was fairly simple. Sluder logged off his computer and created a false profile of a 13-year-old girl, Maggie284. When he logged back on, he was bombarded with prurient messages; some men sent him kiddie porn. For days Sluder swooned and flirted and played, until he started a relationship with a man on the Internet who was interested in fooling around.

It didn't take long: The man asked Maggie284 to meet him and suggested that they would "play together." Sluder called the police.

"It felt so good," he said.

Officers in Kissimmee, Florida, arrested a Johnson County, Kansas, businessman on a charge of using a computer to solicit sex from a minor. Billy Charles Burgess of Stilwell is awaiting trial in August.

Sluder, who lives in St. Cloud, Florida, and works at Walt Disney World, is an example of a trend that experts say is the latest step in the evolution of the Internet: Civilians are taking it upon themselves to impose law and order on a largely unregulated Internet. Cyber crime has galled computer users into forming virtual "special forces" to show bad guys that there is a sheriff in town.

From a woman in Federal Way, Washington, who used an online service to catch a man she believed molested her son, to the computer enthusiast who "mail bombs" an especially fiendish "spammer," computer users are justifying their actions by asking the same question Sluder did when he appointed himself a quasi cop: "Who else is going to do it?"

"The Internet especially depends on people who are willing to do the right thing," said Colin Gabriel Hatcher, the head of Cyberangels, an offshoot of the New York City Guardian Angels. "You also need to have some people out there who are willing to go out of their way to do the right thing. There are two issues: one is law, and one is moral conscience. One is hard to enforce; one is absolutely necessary."

In the past year, several Web pages—such as whoa.femail.com (Women Halting Online Abuse) or webpolice.org (the Web Police)—were created to spy on chicanery on the Net. The Web Police has hundreds of members. There are roughly more than a hundred other groups, but they are more informal. A few outposts fade on- and off-line to keep their vigilante creators anonymous.

Some are trying to turn a profit, but most self-styled Internet police said they're doing it for the greater good and don't want money.

"It's personal," said Katherine Griffis-Greenberg, a lawyer who teaches a course about Internet harassment. "This is the mentality that enables people to go out and fight back with the same energy. Their knee-jerk reaction is to fight back. It's personal."

Donna Parker, who lives in Alabama, represents perhaps the largest contingent of Internet police: those who are out to protect women and children. Parker said that after she puts the kids to bed, she gets online to look for pedophiles. She adds them to her America Online Buddy List, which informs her when another user is signed on.

"I always make sure I know where they are. . . . If I see a connection, I'll call the DA," she said. "Nothing can replace good, old-fashioned detective work."

Sluder is no fusspot. The Internet probably will always traffic in dirty pictures, he said, and that won't send him screaming for the cops. But then again, he said, what he saw wasn't just dirty pictures.

Masquerading as the 13-year-old, Sluder found that men didn't bother with niceties like romance and woo. They demanded what they wanted in no graceful terms. Several sent him pictures of nude children or themselves. Sluder was horrified.

But it wasn't his disapproval that led him to try to catch a man looking for unlawful sex with kids. Earlier, a customer service representative for his online service refused to help, and Sluder also knew from his neighbor, a law officer, that police departments often don't have the time to catch Internet villains.

"It upset me and my morals," Sluder said. "It's kind of your patriotic duty. I felt like I had to do it. Nobody else is going to do it."

He's probably right. Law enforcement officials say police and the FBI have a difficult time keeping track of the Internet, which is by design an abstract maze of computer connections and data bits.

Jeff Lanza, an FBI special agent in Kansas City, said many police departments don't have enough people to handle traditional police work. A department with enough officers who are Internet savvy and able to spend time surfing the Web is rare.

"We are behind the power curve," Lanza said.

Said Detective Alan Lacy in Mercer Island, Washington: "There never seems to be a cop around when you need one. So they said, 'I'll just be a detective.'"

Not everybody is hopeful about the idea of self-regulation. Dennis Derryberry, one of the founders of the Electronic Frontier Foundation in San Francisco, said that, for the most part, people on the Internet shouldn't be trusted to act unselfishly.

"Responsible behavior in real life is hard enough," he said.

What's more, self-styled Internet police are notorious in the cyber community for being too aggressive and often self-righteous. Experts wonder whether, in the end, they will ever accomplish anything.

■ QUESTIONS FOR REREADING

1. How does all this talk about freedom and the law sound like an old Western film? There's talk about the Wild West nature of the Net and of vigilantes, and so on. Is this analogy very helpful, or does it confuse matters?

2. If you agree with Ebnet when he says "self-styled Internet police are notorious in the cyber community for being too aggressive and often self-righteous," do you think they themselves should be curbed in some fashion? Take into consideration that there are not enough police for the actual world and even fewer for the cyberworld that many of us live in. What to do? Must we just wait until the wild cyberfrontier is completely settled before we can expect the law to be there to keep us all safe?

■ WRITING ASSIGNMENT FOR REREADING

If your class is connected by way of a local area network (LAN) or a wide area network (WAN), with access to a listserv for the class, study the exchanges in discussions among classmates online. Assuming that your instructor or facilitator does not intervene unless absolutely necessary, do you find that sometimes the exchanges get out of line, that there is flaming (that is, personal attacks) online? If so, write a document with your classmates stating what is permissible and not permissible, and decide on a method of deliberating over whether a person has broken the "law" and, if so, what the punishment should be. Remember that everyone in the class will have to agree to the document, since they will all live by it.

Hacker's Manifesto, or The Conscience of a Hacker

The Mentor published "Hacker's Manifesto, or The Conscience of a Hacker," in the online hacker's e-journal Phrack. 1.7 (September 25, 1986): File 3 of 10, which is located at ‹http://www.fc.net/phrack/files/p07/p07-3.html›. As The Mentor tells us, he wrote it shortly after his arrest.

The following was written shortly after my arrest, January 8, 1986.

Another one got caught today, it's all over the papers. "Teenager Arrested in Computer Crime Scandal," "Hacker Arrested after Bank Tampering" . . .

Damn kids. They're all alike.

But did you, in your three-piece psychology and 1950s technobrain, ever take a look behind the eyes of the hacker? Did you ever wonder what made him tick, what forces shaped him, what may have molded him?

I am a hacker, enter my world . . .

Mine is a world that begins with school . . . I'm smarter than most of the other kids, this crap they teach us bores me . . .

Damn underachiever. They're all alike.

I'm in junior high or high school. I've listened to teachers explain for the fifteenth time how to reduce a fraction. I understand it. "No, Ms. Smith, I didn't show my work. I did it in my head . . ."

Damn kid. Probably copied it. They're all alike.

I made a discovery today. I found a computer. Wait a second, this is cool. It does what I want it to. If it makes a mistake, it's because I screwed it up. Not because it doesn't like me . . .

Or feels threatened by me . . .

Or thinks I'm a smart ass . . .

Or doesn't like teaching and shouldn't be here . . .

Damn kid. All he does is play games. They're all alike.

And then it happened . . . a door opened to a world . . . rushing through the phone line like heroin through an addict's veins, an electronic pulse is sent out, a refuge from the day-to-day incompetencies is sought . . . a board is found.

"This is it . . . this is where I belong . . ."

I know everyone here . . . even if I've never met them, never talked to them, may never hear from them again . . . I know you all . . .

Damn kid. Tying up the phone line again. They're all alike . . .

You bet your ass we're all alike . . . we've been spoon-fed baby food at school when we hungered for steak . . . the bits of meat that you did let slip through were pre-chewed and tasteless. We've been dominated by sadists, or ignored by the apathetic. The few that had something to teach found us willing pupils, but those few are like drops of water in the desert.

This is our world now . . . the world of the electron and the switch, the beauty of the baud. We make use of a service already existing without paying for what could be dirt-cheap if it wasn't run by profiteering gluttons, and you call us criminals. We explore . . . and you call us criminals. We seek after knowledge . . . and you call us criminals. We exist without skin color, without nationality, without religious bias . . . and you call us criminals. You build atomic bombs, you wage wars, you murder, cheat, and lie to us and try to make us believe it's for our own good, yet we're the criminals.

Yes, I am a criminal. My crime is that of curiosity. My crime is that of judging people by what they say and think, not what they look like. My crime is that of outsmarting you, something that you will never forgive me for.

I am a hacker, and this is my manifesto. You may stop this individual, but you can't stop us all . . . after all, we're all alike.

—The Mentor

■ QUESTIONS FOR REREADING

1. What does "The Mentor" mean when he writes: "We make use of a service already existing without paying for what could be dirt-cheap if it wasn't run by profiteering gluttons, and you call us criminals"? What is the ethic that The Mentor is putting forth? Do you agree with him? If so, why? If not, why not?

2. Is a good way to understand what "The Mentor" is talking about by way of Meyer's distinction (in "Crimes of the 'Net' ") between "digital socialism" and "copyrightable capitalism"? If so, how? If there are other ways of understanding The Mentor, then share and discuss them in class.

3. Do you find it a problem that The Mentor does not use his "real" name? Recall the previous discussions in chapter 2 on cyber identities. How would you find out who The Mentor actually is? How old do you think The Mentor was when he wrote his manifesto?

■ WRITING ASSIGNMENT FOR REREADING

Write a manifesto against The Mentor's manifesto. What is the genre of a manifesto? What are its conventions? Notice how The Mentor takes great care and with much subtlety shapes his persona in the writing. How do you think that he achieves the persona? How will you achieve yours against that of The Mentor? (Why do I refer to The Mentor as a male? Could The Mentor be female? How could you determine the answer to this question?)

Hackers (roundtable) "Is Computer Hacking a Crime?" first appeared in Harper's Magazine (March 1990: 45–55; 57. Though the editors' introduction to the roundtable is informative, it does not tell enough. Throughout the discussion, if the reader is aware of what has taken place following it, is a great

concern for what Bruce Sterling refers to as the "hacker crackdown" (in his book of the same title) on the hackers. A truncated version of the crackdown story goes like this: There was much concern shown by John Perry Barlow and hackers across the country about the number of federal crackdowns, and in December 1989 they were invited by Harper's Magazine to discuss the issue on the WELL. Such

hackers (crackers?) as "Phiber Optik" and "Acid Phreak" made their appearance to discuss such questions as whether there is a "hacker ethic" and whether hacking is a crime. Shortly thereafter, on January 24, 1990, the federal government and New York State police raided the homes of Phiber Optik, Acid Phreak, and another hacker. Optik (Mark Abene) was not charged in this raid until a year later and then only with a misdemeanor. The raids escalated: March 1, 1991, has come to be known as the day of the "Steve Jackson Games" raid in Austin, Texas; and then, on May 7 through 9, came the "Operation Sundevil" raids all across the country.

These raids make up the hacker crackdown; in June of the same year, they led to the creation of the EFF by Barlow and Mitchell Kapor.

Is Computer Hacking a Crime?

he image of the computer hacker drifted into public awareness in the mid-seventies, when reports of Chinese-food-consuming geniuses working compulsively at keyboards began to issue from MIT. Over time, several of these impresarios entered commerce, and the public's impression of hackers changed: They were no longer nerds but young, millionaire entrepreneurs.

The most recent news reports have given the term a more felonious connotation. Early this year, a graduate student named Robert Morris, Jr., went on trial for releasing a computer program known as a worm into the vast Internet system, halting more than 6,000 computers. The subsequent public debate ranged from the matter of proper punishment for a mischievous kid to the issue of our rapidly changing notion of what constitutes free speech—or property—in an age of modems and data bases. In order to allow hackers to speak for themselves, *Harper's Magazine* recently organized an electronic discussion and asked some of the nation's best hackers to "log on," discuss the protean notions of contemporary speech, and explain what their powers and talents are.

The following forum is based on a discussion held on the WELL, a computer bulletin-board system based in Sausalito, California. The forum is the result of a gradual accretion of arguments as the participants—located throughout the country—opined and reacted over an eleven-day period. *Harper's Magazine* senior editor Jack Hitt and assistant editor Paul Tough served as moderators.

ADELAIDE is a pseudonym for a former hacker who has sold his soul to the corporate state as a computer programmer.

BARLOW is John Perry Barlow, a retired cattle rancher, a former Republican county chairman, and a lyricist for the Grateful Dead, who currently is writing a book on computers and consciousness entitled *Everything We Know Is Wrong.*

BLUEFIRE is Dr. Robert Jacobson, associate director of the Human Interface Technology Laboratory at the University of Washington and a former information-policy analyst with the California legislature.

BRAND is Russell Brand, a senior computer scientist with Reasoning Systems, in Palo Alto, California.

CLIFF is Clifford Stoll, the astronomer who caught a spy in a military computer network and recently published an account of his investigation entitled *The Cuckoo's Egg.*

DAVE is Dave Hughes, a retired West Pointer who currently operates his own political bulletin board.

DRAKE is Frank Drake, a computer-science student at a West Coast university and the editor of *W.O.R.M.,* a cyberpunk magazine.

EDDIE JOE HOMEBOY is a pseudonym for a professional software engineer who has worked at Lucasfilm, Pyramid Technology, Apple Computer, and Autodesk.

EMMANUEL GOLDSTEIN is the editor of *2600,* the "hacker's quarterly."

HANK is Hank Roberts, who builds mobiles, flies hang gliders, and proof-reads for the *Whole Earth Catalog.*

JIMG is Jim Gasperini, the author, with TRANS Fiction Systems, of Hidden Agenda, a computer game that simulates political conflict in Central America.

JRC is Jon Carroll, daily columnist for the *San Francisco Chronicle* and writer-in-residence for the Pickle Family Circus, a national traveling circus troupe based in San Francisco.

KK is Kevin Kelly, editor of the *Whole Earth Review* and a cofounder of the Hacker's Conference.

LEE is Lee Felsenstein, who designed the Osborne-1 computer and cofounded the Homebrew Computer Club.

MANDEL is Tom Mandel, a professional futurist and an organizer of the Hacker's Conference.

RH   is Robert Horvitz, Washington correspondent for the *Whole Earth Review.*

RMS   is Richard Stallman, founder of the Free Software Foundation.

TENNEY   is Glenn Tenney, an independent-systems architect and an organizer of the Hacker's Conference.

ACID PHREAK and PHIBER OPTIK   are both pseudonyms for hackers who decline to be identified.

■ THE   DIGITAL   FRONTIER

HARPER'S [Day 1, 9:00 A.M.]: When the computer was young, the word *hacking* was used to describe the work of brilliant students who explored and expanded the uses to which this new technology might be employed. There was even talk of a "hacker ethic." Somehow, in the succeeding years, the word has taken on dark connotations, suggesting the actions of a criminal. What is the hacker ethic, and does it survive?

ADELAIDE [Day 1, 9:25 A.M.]: The hacker ethic survives, and it is a fraud. It survives in anyone excited by technology's power to turn many small, insignificant things into one vast, beautiful thing. It is a fraud because there is nothing magical about computers that causes a user to undergo religious conversion and devote himself to the public good. Early automobile inventors were hackers too. At first the elite drove in luxury. Later practically everyone had a car. Now we have traffic jams, drunk drivers, air pollution, and suburban sprawl. The old magic of an automobile occasionally surfaces, but we possess no delusions that it automatically invades the consciousness of anyone who sits behind the wheel. Computers are power, and direct contact with power can bring out the best or the worst in a person. It's tempting to think that everyone exposed to the technology will be grandly inspired, but, alas, it just ain't so.

BRAND [Day 1, 9:54 A.M.]: The hacker ethic involves several things. One is avoiding waste; insisting on using idle computer power—often hacking into a system to do so, while taking the greatest precautions not to damage the system. A second goal of many hackers is the free exchange of technical information. These hackers feel that patent and copyright restrictions slow down technological advances. A third goal is the advancement of human knowledge for its own sake. Often this approach is unconventional. People we call crackers often explore systems and do mischief. They are called hackers by the press, which doesn't understand the issues.

KK [Day 1, 11:19 A.M.]: The hacker ethic went unnoticed early on because the explorations of basement tinkerers were very local. Once we all became connected, the work of these investigators rippled through the world. Today the hacking spirit is alive and kicking in video, satellite TV, and radio. In some fields they are called chippers, because they modify and peddle altered chips. Everything that was once said about "phone phreaks" can be said about them too.

DAVE [Day 1, 11:29 A.M.]: Bah. Too academic. Hackers hack. Because they want to. Not for any higher purpose. Hacking is not dead and won't be as long as teenagers get their hands on the tools. There is a hacker born every minute.

ADELAIDE [Day 1, 11:42 A.M.]: Don't forget ego. People break into computers because it's fun and it makes them feel powerful.

BARLOW [Day 1, 11:54 A.M.]: Hackers hack. Yeah, right, but what's more to the point is that humans hack and always have. Far more than just opposable thumbs, upright posture, or excess cranial capacity, human beings are set apart from all other species by an itch, a hard-wired dissatisfaction. Computer hacking is just the latest in a series of quests that started with fire hacking. Hacking is also a collective enterprise. It brings to our joint endeavors the simultaneity that other collective organisms—ant colonies, Canada geese— take for granted. This is important, because combined with our itch to probe is a need to *connect*. Humans miss the almost telepathic connectedness that I've observed in other herding mammals. And we want it back. Ironically, the solitary sociopath and his 3:00 A.M. endeavors hold the most promise for delivering species reunion.

EDDIE JOE HOMEBOY [Day 1, 4:44 P.M.]: Hacking really took hold with the advent of the personal computer, which freed programmers from having to use a big time-sharing system. A hacker could sit in the privacy of his home and hack to his heart's and head's content.

LEE [Day 1, 5:17 P.M.]: "Angelheaded hipsters burning for the ancient heavenly connection to the starry dynamo in the machinery of night" (Allen Ginsberg, "Howl"). I still get an endorphin rush when I go on a design run— my mind out over the edge, groping for possibilities that can be sensed when various parts are held in juxtaposition with a view toward creating a whole object: straining to get through the epsilon-wide crack between What Is and What Could Be. Somewhere there's the Dynamo of Night, the ultra-mechanism waiting to be dreamed, that we'll never get to in actuality (think what it would *weigh!*) but that's present somehow in the vicinity of those mental wrestling matches. When I reemerge into the light of another day with the design on paper—and with the knowledge that if it ever gets built, things will never be the same again—I know I've been where artists go. That's hacking to me: to transcend custom and to engage in creativity for its own sake, but also to create objective effects. I've been around long enough to see the greed creeps take up the unattended reins of power and shut down most of the creativity that put them where they are. But I've also seen things change, against the best efforts of a stupidly run industry. We cracked the egg out from under the Computer Priesthood, and now everyone can have omelets.

RMS [Day 1, 5:19 P.M.]: The media and the courts are spreading a certain image of hackers. It's important for us not to be shaped by that image. But there are two ways that it can happen. One way is for hackers to become part of the security-maintenance establishment. The other, more subtle, way is for a hacker to become the security-breaking phreak the media portray. By shaping ourselves into the enemy of the establishment, we uphold the establishment. But there's nothing wrong with breaking security if you're accomplishing something useful. It's like picking a lock on a tool cabinet to get a screwdriver to fix your radio. As long as you put the screwdriver back, what harm does it do?

ACID PHREAK [Day 1, 6:34 P.M.]: There is no one hacker ethic. Everyone has his own. To say that we all think the same way is preposterous. The hacker of old sought to find what the computer itself could do. There was nothing illegal about that. Today, hackers and phreaks are drawn to *specific,* often corporate, systems. It's no wonder everyone on the other side is getting mad. We're always one step ahead. We were back then, and we are now.

CLIFF [Day 1, 8:38 P.M.]: RMS said, "There's nothing wrong with breaking security if you're accomplishing something useful." Huh? How about, There's nothing wrong with entering a neighbor's house if you're accomplishing something useful, just as long as you clean up after yourself. Does my

A Hacker's Lexicon

Back door: A point of entry into a computer system—often installed there by the original programmer—that provides secret access.

Bomb: A destructive computer program, which, when activated, destroys the files in a computer system.

Chipper: A hacker who specializes in changing the programming instructions of computer chips.

Cracker: A hacker who breaks illegally into computer systems and creates mischief; often used pejoratively. The original meaning of *cracker* was narrower, describing those who decoded copyright-protection schemes on commercial software products either to redis-tribute the products or to modify them; sometimes known as a software pirate.

Hacker: Originally, a compulsive computer programmer. The word has evolved in meaning over the years. Among computer users, *hacker* carries a positive connotation, meaning anyone who creatively explores the operations of computer systems. Recently, it has taken on a negative connotation, primarily through confusion with *cracker.*

Phone phreak: One who explores the operations of the phone system, often with the intent of making free phone calls.

Social engineering: A nontechnical means of gaining informa-tion simply by persuading people to hand it over. If a hacker wished to gain access to a computer system, for example, an act of *social engineering* might be to contact a system operator and to convince him or her that the hacker is a legitimate user in need of a password; more colloquially, a con job.

Virus: A program that, having been introduced into a system, replicates itself and attaches itself to other programs, often with a variety of mischievous effects.

Worm: A destructive program that, when activated, fills a computer system with self-replicating information, clogging the system so that its operations are severely slowed, sometimes stopped.

personal privacy mean anything? Should my personal letters and data be open to anyone who knows how to crack passwords? If not my property, then how about a bank's? Should my credit history be available to anyone who can find a back door to the private computers of TRW, the firm that tracks people's credit histories? How about a list of AIDS patients from a hospital's data bank? Or next week's prime interest rate from a computer at the Treasury Department?

BLUEFIRE [Day 1, 9:20 P.M.]: Computers are everywhere, and they link us together into a vast social "cybernetia." The grand skills of the hackers, formidable though they may have been, are incapable of subverting this automated social order. The networks in which we survive are more than copper wire and radio waves: They are *the* social organization. For every hacker in revolt, busting through a security code, ten thousand people are being wired up with automatic call-identification and credit-checking machines. Long live the Computer Revolution, which died aborning.

JRC [Day 1, 10:28 P.M.]: We have two different definitions here. One speaks of a tinkerer's ecstasy, an ecstasy that is hard to maintain in the corporate world but is nevertheless at the heart of Why Hackers Hack. The second is political, and it has to do with the free flow of information. Information should flow more freely (how freely is being debated), and the hacker can make it happen because the hacker knows how to undam the pipes. This makes the hacker ethic—of necessity—antiauthoritarian.

EMMANUEL GOLDSTEIN [Day 2, 2:41 A.M.]: It's meaningless what we call ourselves: hackers, crackers, techno-rats. We're individuals who happen to play with high tech. There is no *hacker community* in the traditional sense of the term. There are no leaders and no agenda. We're just individuals out exploring.

BRAND [Day 2, 9:02 A.M.]: There are two issues: invariance and privacy. Invariance is the art of leaving things as you found them. If someone used my house for the day and left everything as he found it so that there was *no way* to tell he had been there, I would see no problem. With a well-run computer system, we can assure invariance. Without this assurance we must fear that the person picking the lock to get the screwdriver will break the lock, the screwdriver, or both. Privacy is more complicated. I want my medical records, employment records, and letters to *The New Republic* private because I fear that someone will do something with the information that is against my interests. If I could trust people not to do bad things with information, I would not need to hide it. Rather than preventing the "theft" of this data, we should prohibit its collection in the first place.

HOMEBOY [Day 2, 9:37 A.M.]: Are crackers really working for the free flow of information? Or are they unpaid tools of the establishment, identifying the holes in the institutional dike so that they can be plugged by the authorities, only to be tossed in jail or exiled?

DRAKE [Day 2, 10:54 A.M.]: There is an unchallenged assumption that crackers have some political motivation. Earlier, crackers were portrayed as failed revolutionaries; now Homeboy suggests that crackers may be tools of the establishment. These ideas about crackers are based on earlier experiences with subcultures (beats, hippies, yippies). Actually, the contemporary cracker is often middle-class and doesn't really distance himself from the "establishment." While there are some anarcho-crackers, there are even more right-wing crackers. The hacker ethic crosses political boundaries.

MANDEL [Day 2, 11:01 A.M.]: The data on crackers suggests that they are either juvenile delinquents or plain criminals.

BARLOW [Day 2, 11:34 A.M.]: I would far rather have *everyone* know my most intimate secrets than to have noncontextual snippits of them "owned" by TRW and the FBI—and withheld from me! Any cracker who is entertained by peeping into my electronic window is welcome to the view. Any institution that makes money selling rumors of my peccadilloes is stealing from me. Anybody who wants to inhibit that theft with electronic mischief has my complete support. Power to the techno-rats!

EMMANUEL [Day 2, 7:09 P.M.]: Calling someone on the phone is the equivalent of knocking on that person's door, right? Wrong! When someone answers the phone, you are *inside* the home. You have already been *let in.* The same with an answering machine, or a personal computer, if it picks up the phone. It is wrong to violate a person's privacy, but electronic rummaging is not the same as breaking and entering. The key here is that most people are unaware of *how easy it is* for others to invade their electronic privacy and see credit reports, phone bills, FBI files, Social Security reports. The public is grossly underinformed, and that's what must be fixed if hackers are to be thwarted. If we had an educated public, though, perhaps the huge—and now common—data bases would never have been allowed to exist. Hackers have become scapegoats: We discover the gaping holes in the system and then get blamed for the flaws.

HOMEBOY [Day 2, 7:41 P.M.]: Large, insular, undemocratic governments and institutions need scapegoats. It's the first step down the road to fascism. *That's* where hackers play into the hands of the establishment.

DAVE [Day 2, 7:55 P.M.]: If the real criminals are those who leave gaping holes in their systems, then the real criminals in house burglaries are those who leave their windows unlatched. Right? Hardly. And Emmanuel's analogy to a phone being answered doesn't hold either. There is no security protection in making a phone call. A computer system has a *password,* implying a desire for security. Breaking into a poorly protected house is still burglary.

CLIFF [Day 2, 9:06 P.M.]: Was there a hacker's ethic and does it survive? More appropriately, was there a vandal's ethic and does it survive? As long as there are communities, someone will violate the trust that binds them. Once, our computers were isolated, much as eighteenth-century villages were. Little was exchanged, and each developed independently. Now we've built far-flung electronic neighborhoods. These communities are built on trust: people believing that everyone profits by sharing resources. Sure enough, vandals crept in, breaking into systems, spreading viruses, pirating software, and destroying people's work. "It's okay," they say. "I can break into a system because I'm a hacker." Give me a break!

BARLOW [Day 2, 10:41 P.M.]: I live in a small town. I don't have a key to my house. Am I asking for it? I think not. Among the juvenile delinquents in my town, there does exist a vandal's ethic. I know because I once was one. In a real community, part of a kid's rite of passage is discovering what walls can be breached. Driving 110 miles per hour on Main Street is a common symptom of rural adolescence, publicly denounced but privately understood. Many teenagers die in this quest—two just the night before last—but it is basic to our culture. Even rebellious kids understand that risk to one's safety is one thing, wanton vandalism or theft is another. As a result, almost no one locks anything here. In fact, a security system is an affront to a teenage psyche. While a kid might be dissuaded by conscience, he will regard a barricade as an insult and a challenge. So the CEOs who are moving here (the emperor of PepsiCo and the secretary of state among them) soon discover that over the winter people break into their protected mansions just to hang out. When systems are open, the community prospers, and teenage miscreants are satisfied to risk their own lives and little else. When the social contract is enforced by security, the native freedom of the adolescent soul will rise up to challenge it in direct proportion to its imposition.

HANK [Day 2, 11:23 P.M.]: Barlow, the small town I grew up in was much like yours—until two interstate highways crossed nearby. The open-door style changed in one, hard summer because our whole *town* became unlocked. I think Cliff's community is analogous to my little town—confronted not by a new locked-up neighbor who poses a challenge to the local kids but by a sudden, permanent opening up of the community to many faceless outsiders who owe the town no allegiance.

EMMANUEL [Day 3, 1:33 A.M.]: Sorry, I don't buy Dave's unlatched-window analogy. A hacker who wanders into a system with the ease that it's done today is, in my analogy, walking into a house without walls—and with a cloaking device! Any good hacker can make himself invisible. If housebreaking were this easy, people would be enraged. But we're missing the point. I'm not referring to accessing a PC in someone's bedroom but about accessing credit reports, government files, motor vehicle records, and the megabytes of data piling up on each of us. Thousands of people legally can see and use this ever-growing mountain of data, much of it erroneous. Whose rights are we violating when we peruse a file? Those of the person we look up? He doesn't even know that information exists, that it was compiled without his consent, and that it's not his property anymore! The invasion of privacy took place long before the hacker ever arrived. The only way to find out how such a system works is to break the rules. It's not what hackers do that will lead us into a state of constant surveillance; it's allowing the authorities to impose on us a state of mock crisis.

MANDEL [Day 3, 9:27 A.M.]: Note that the word *crime* has no fixed reference in our discussion. Until recently, breaking into government computer systems wasn't a crime; now it is. In fact, there is some debate, to be resolved in the courts, whether what Robert Morris, Jr., did was actually a crime [see "A Brief History of Hacking"]. *Crime* gets redefined all the time. Offend enough people or institutions and, lo and behold, someone will pass a law. That is partly what is going on now: Hackers are pushing buttons, becoming more visible, and that inevitably means more laws and more crimes.

ADELAIDE [Day 3, 9:42 A.M.]: Every practitioner of these arts knows that at minimum he is trespassing. The English "country traveler ethic" applies: The hiker is always ethical enough to close the pasture gates behind him so that no sheep escape during his pastoral stroll through someone else's property. The problem is that what some see as gentle trespassing others see as theft of service, invasion of privacy, threat to national security—take your pick.

BARLOW [Day 3, 2:38 P.M.]: I regard the *existence* of proprietary data about me to be theft—not just in the legal sense but in a faintly metaphysical one, rather like the belief among aborigines that a photograph steals the soul. The crackers who maintain access to that data are, at this level, liberators. Their incursions are the only way to keep the system honest.

RMS [Day 3, 2:48 P.M.]: Recently, a tough anti-hacker measure was proposed in England. In *The Economist* I saw a wise response, arguing that it was silly to treat an action as worse when it involves a computer than when it does not. They noted, for example, that physical trespassing was considered a civil affair, not a criminal one, and said that computer trespassing should be treated likewise. Unfortunately, the U.S. government was not so wise.

BARLOW [Day 3, 3:23 P.M.]: The idea that a crime is worse if a computer is involved relates to the gathering governmental perception that computer viruses and guns may be related. I know that sounds absurd, but they have more in common than one might think. For all its natural sociopathy, the virus is not without philosophical potency—like a gun. Here in Wyoming guns are part of the furniture. Only recently have I observed an awareness of their political content. After a lot of frothing about prying cold, dead fingers from triggers, the sentiment was finally distilled to a bumper sticker I saw on a pickup the other day: "Fear the Government That Fears Your Gun." Now I've read too much Gandhi to buy that line without misgivings, but it would be hard to argue that Tiananmen Square could have been inflicted on a populace capable of shooting back. I don't wholeheartedly defend computer viruses, but one must consider their increasingly robust deterrent potential. Before it's over, the War on Drugs could easily turn into an Armageddon

between those who love liberty and those who crave certainty, providing just the excuse the control freaks have been waiting for to rid America of all that constitutional mollycoddling called the Bill of Rights. Should that come to pass, I will want to use every available method to vex and confuse the eyes and ears of surveillance. The virus could become the necessary instrument of our freedom. At the risk of sounding like some digital *posse comitatus,* I say: Fear the Government That Fears Your Computer.

"The virus could become an instrument of freedom. At the risk of sounding like some digital **posse comitatus,** *I say:* **Fear the Government That Fears Your Computer."**

TENNEY [Day 3, 4:41 P.M.]: Computer-related crimes are more feared because they are performed remotely—a crime can be committed in New York by someone in Los Angeles—and by people not normally viewed as being criminals—by teenagers who don't look like delinquents. They're very smart nerds, and they don't look like Chicago gangsters packing heat.

BARLOW [Day 4, 12:12 A.M.]: People know so little of these things that they endow computers and the people who *do* understand them with powers neither possesses. If America has a religion, its ark is the computer and its covenant is the belief that Science Knows. We are mucking around in the temple, guys. It's a good way to catch hell.

DAVE [Day 4, 9:18 A.M.]: Computers *are* the new American religion. The public is in awe of—and fears—the mysteries and the high priests who tend them. And the public reacts just as it always has when faced with fear of the unknown—punishment, burning at the stake. Hackers are like the early Christians. When caught, they will be thrown to the lions before the Roman establishment: This year the mob will cheer madly as Robert Morris is devoured.

KK [Day 6, 11:37 A.M.]: The crackers here suggest that they crack into systems with poor security *because* the security is poor. Do more sophisticated security precautions diminish the need to crack the system or increase it?

ACID [Day 6, 1:20 P.M.]: If there was a system that we knew was uncrackable, we wouldn't even try to crack it. On the other hand, if some organization boasted that its system was impenetrable and we knew that was media hype, I think it would be safe to say we'd have to "enlighten" them.

EMMANUEL [Day 6, 2:49 P.M.]: Why do we insist on cracking systems? The more people ask those kinds of questions, the more I want to get in! Forbid access and the demand for access increases. For the most part, it's simply a mission of exploration. In the words of the new captain of the starship *Enterprise,* Jean-Luc Picard, "Let's see what's out there!"

BARLOW [Day 6, 4:34 P.M.]: Tell us, Acid, *is* there a system that you know to be uncrackable to the point where everyone's given up?

ACID [Day 6, 8:29 P.M.]: CICIMS is pretty tough.

PHIBER OPTIK [Day 7, 2:36 P.M.]: Really? CICIMS is a system used by Bell operating companies. The entire security system was changed after myself and a friend must have been noticed in it. For the entire United States, there is only one such system, located in Indiana. The new security scheme is flawless *in itself,* and there is no chance of "social engineering," i.e., bullshitting someone inside the system into telling you what the passwords are. The system works like this: You log on with the proper account and password; then, depending on who you are, the system asks at random three of ten questions that are unique to each user. But the system *can* be compromised by entering forwarding instructions into the phone company's switch for that exchange, thereby intercepting every phone call that comes in to the system over a designated period of time and connecting the call to your computer. If you are familiar with the security layout, you can emulate its appearance and fool the caller into giving you the answers to his questions. Then you call the system yourself and use those answers to get in. There are other ways of doing it as well.

BLUEFIRE [Day 7, 11:53 P.M.]: I can't stand it! Who do you think pays for the security that the telephone companies must maintain to fend off illegal use? I bet it costs the ratepayers around $10 million for this little extravaganza. The cracker circus isn't harmless at all, unless you don't mind paying for other people's entertainment. Hackers who have contributed to the social welfare should be recognized. But cracking is something else—namely, fun at someone else's expense—and it ain't the folks who own the phone companies who pay; it's us, me and you.

BARLOW [Day 8, 7:35 A.M.]: I am becoming increasingly irritated at this idea that you guys are exacting vengeance for the sin of openness. You seem to argue that if a system is dumb enough to be open, it is your moral duty to violate it. Does the fact that I've never locked my house—even when I was away for months at a time—mean that someone should come in and teach me a good lesson?

ACID [Day 8, 3:23 P.M.]: Barlow, you leave the door open to your house? Where do you live?

BARLOW [Day 8, 10:11 P.M.]: Acid, my house is at 372 North Franklin Street in Pinedale, Wyoming. Heading north on Franklin, go about two blocks off the main drag before you run into a hay meadow on the left. I'm the last house before the field. The computer is always on. But do you really mean to imply what you did with that question? Are you merely a sneak looking for easy places to violate? You disappoint me, pal. For all your James Dean-on-Silicon rhetoric, you're not a cyberpunk. You're just a punk.

EMMANUEL [Day 9, 12:55 A.M.]: No offense, Barlow, but your house analogy doesn't stand up, because your house is far less interesting than a Defense

Department computer. For the most part, hackers don't mess with individuals. Maybe we feel sorry for them; maybe they're boring. Institutions are where the action is, because they are compiling this mountain of data—without your consent. Hackers are not guardian angels, but if you think we're what's wrong with the system, I'd say that's precisely what those in charge want you to believe. By the way, you left out your zip code. It's 82941.

BARLOW [Day 9, 8:34 A.M.]: Now that's more like it. There is an ethical distinction between people and institutions. The law makes little distinction. We pretend that institutions are somehow human because they are made of humans. A large bureaucracy resembles a human about as much as a reef

A Brief History of Hacking

September 1970 John Draper takes as his alias the name Captain Crunch after he discovers that the toy whistle found in the cereal of the same name perfectly simulates the tone necessary to make free phone calls.

March 1975 The Homebrew Computer Club, an early group of computer hackers, holds its first meeting in Menlo Park, California.

July 1976 Homebrew members Steve Wozniak, twenty-six, and Steve Jobs, twenty-one, working out of a garage, begin selling the first personal computer, known as the Apple.

June 1980 In one week, errors in the computer system operating the U.S. air-defense network cause two separate false reports of Soviet missile launches, each prompting an increased state of nuclear readiness.

December 1982 Sales of Apple personal computers top one billion dollars per year.

November 1984 Steven Levy's book *Hackers* is published, popu-

larizing the concept of the "hacker ethic": that "access to computers, and anything that might teach you something about the way the world works, should be unlimited and total." The book inspires the first Hacker's Conference, held that month.

January 1986 The "Pakistani Brain" virus, created by a software distributor in Lahore, Pakistan, infects IBM computers around the world, erasing data files.

June 1986 The U.S. Office of Technology Assessment warns that massive, cross-indexed government computer records have become a "de facto national data base containing personal information on most Americans."

March 1987 William Gates, a Harvard dropout who founded Microsoft Corporation, becomes a billionaire.

November 1988 More than 6,000 computers linked by the nationwide Internet computer network are infected by a destructive computer program known as a worm and are crippled for two

days. The worm is traced to Robert Morris, Jr., a twenty-four-year-old Cornell University graduate student.

December 1988 A federal grand jury charges Kevin Mitnick, twenty-five, with stealing computer programs over telephone lines. Mitnick is held without bail and forbidden access to any telephones without supervision.

March 1989 Three West German hackers are arrested for entering thirty sensitive military computers using home computers and modems. The arrests follow a three-year investigation by Clifford Stoll, an astronomer at the Lawrence Berkeley Laboratory who began tracing the hackers after finding a seventy-five-cent billing error in the lab's computer system.

January 1990 Robert Morris, Jr., goes on trial in Syracuse, New York, for designing and releasing the Internet worm. Convicted, he faces up to five years in prison and a $250,000 fine.

resembles a coral polyp. To expect an institution to have a conscience is like expecting a horse to have one. As with every organism, institutions are chiefly concerned with their own physical integrity and survival. To say that they have some higher purpose beyond their survival is to anthropomorphize them. You are right, Emmanuel. The house analogy breaks down here. Individuals live in houses; institutions live in mainframes. Institutions are functionally remorseless and need to be checked. Since their blood is digital, we need to be in their bloodstreams like an infection of humanity. I'm willing to extend limitless trust to other human beings. In my experience they've never failed to deserve it. But I have as much faith in institutions as they have in me. None.

OPTIK [Day 9, 10:19 A.M.]: In other words, Mr. Barlow, you say something, someone proves you wrong, and then you agree with him. I'm getting the feeling that you don't exactly chisel your views in stone.

HANK [Day 9, 11:18 A.M.]: Has Mr. Optik heard the phrase "thesis, antithesis, synthesis"?

BARLOW [Day 10, 10:48 A.M.]: Optik, I do change my mind a lot. Indeed, I often find it occupied by numerous contradictions. The last time I believed in absolutes, I was about your age. And there's not a damn thing wrong with believing in absolutes at your age either. Continue to do so, however, and you'll find yourself, at my age, carrying placards filled with nonsense and dressing in rags.

ADELAIDE [Day 10, 6:27 P.M.]: The flaw in this discussion is the distorted image the media promote of the hacker as "whiz." The problem is that the one who gets caught obviously isn't. I haven't seen a story yet on a true genius hacker. Even Robert Morris was no whiz. The genius hackers are busy doing constructive things or are so good no one's caught them yet. It takes no talent to break into something. Nobody calls subway graffiti artists geniuses for figuring out how to break into the yard. There's a difference between genius and ingenuity.

BARLOW [Day 10, 9:48 P.M.]: Let me define my terms. Using *hacker* in a mid-spectrum sense (with crackers on one end and Leonardo da Vinci on the other), I think it does take a kind of genius to be a truly productive hacker. I'm learning PASCAL now, and I am constantly amazed that people can spin those prolix recursions into something like PageMaker. It fills me with the kind of awe I reserve for splendors such as the cathedral at Chartres. With crackers like Acid and Optik, the issue is less intelligence than alienation. Trade their modems for skateboards and only a slight conceptual shift would occur. Yet I'm glad they're wedging open the cracks. Let a thousand worms flourish.

OPTIK [Day 10, 10:11 P.M.]: You have some pair of balls comparing my talent with that of a skateboarder. Hmm. . . . This was indeed boring, but nonetheless: [*Editors' Note: At this point in the discussion, Optik—apparently having hacked into TRW's computer records—posted a copy of Mr. Barlow's credit history. In the interest of Mr. Barlow's privacy—at least what is left of it—*Harper's Magazine *has not printed it.*] I'm not showing off. Any fool knowing the proper syntax and the proper passwords can look up a credit history. I just find your high-and-mighty attitude annoying and, yes, infantile.

HOMEBOY [Day 10, 10:17 P.M.]: Key here is "any fool."

ACID [Day 11, 1:37 P.M.]: For thirty-five dollars a year anyone can have access to TRW and see his or her own credit history. Optik did it for free. What's wrong with that? And why does TRW keep files on what color and religion we are? If you didn't know that they kept such files, who would have found out if it wasn't for a hacker? Barlow should be grateful that Optik has offered his services to update him on his personal credit file. Of course, I'd hate to see my credit history up in lights. But if you hadn't made our skins crawl, your info would not have been posted. Everyone gets back at someone when he's pissed; so do we. Only we do it differently. Are we punks? Yeah, I guess we are. A punk is what someone who has been made to eat his own words calls the guy who fed them to him.

■ HACKING THE CONSTITUTION

HARPER'S [Day 4, 9:00 A.M.]: Suppose that a mole inside the government confirmed the existence of files on each of you, stored in the White House computer system, PROFS. Would you have the right to hack into that system to retrieve and expose the existence of such files? Could you do it?

TENNEY [Day 4, 1:42 P.M.]: The proverbial question of whether the end justi-fies the means. This doesn't have much to do with hacking. If the file were a sheet of paper in a locked cabinet, the same question would apply. In that case you could accomplish everything without technological hacking. Con-sider the Pentagon Papers.

EMMANUEL [Day 4, 3:55 P.M.]: Let's address the hypothetical. First, I need to find out more about PROFS. Is it accessible from off site, and if so, how? Should I update my 202-456 scan [a list of phone numbers in the White House's exchange that connect incoming calls to a computer]? I have a listing for every computer in that exchange, but the scan was done back in 1984. Is PROFS a new system? Perhaps it's in a different exchange? Does anybody know how many people have access to it? I'm also on fairly good terms with a White House operator who owes me a favor. But I don't know what to ask for. Obviously, I've already made up my mind about the *right* to examine this material. I don't want to debate the ethics of it at this point. If you're with me, let's do something about this. Otherwise, stay out of the way. There's hacking to be done.

ACID [Day 4, 5:24 P.M.]: Yes, I would try to break into the PROFS system. But first I'd have someone in the public eye, with no ties to hacking, request the info through the Freedom of Information Act. Then I'd hack in to verify the information I received.

DRAKE [Day 4, 9:13 P.M.]: Are there a lot of people involved in this anti-hacker project? If so, the chances of social engineering data out of people would be far higher than if it were a small, close-knit group. But yes, the simple truth is, if the White House has a dial-up line, it can be hacked.

EMMANUEL [Day 4, 11:27 P.M.]: The implication that a trust has been betrayed on the part of the government is certainly enough to make me want to look a little further. And I know I'm doing the right thing on behalf of others who don't have my abilities. Most people I meet see me as an ally who can help them stay ahead of an unfair system. That's what I intend to do here. I have a small core of dedicated hackers who could help. One's specialty is the UNIX system, another's is networks, and another's is phone systems.

TENNEY [Day 5, 12:24 A.M.]: PROFS is an IBM message program that runs on an operating system known as VM. VM systems usually have a fair number of holes, either to gain access or to gain full privileges. The CIA was working on, and may have completed, a supposedly secure VM system. No ethics here, just facts. But a prime question is to determine what system via what phone number. Of course, the old inside job is easier. Just find someone who owes a favor or convince an insider that it is a moral obligation to do this.

BARLOW [Day 5, 2:46 P.M.]: This scenario needs to be addressed in four parts: ethical, political, practical I (from the standpoint of the hack itself), and practical II (disseminating the information without undue risk).

Ethical: Since World War II, we've been governed by a paramilitary bureaucracy that believes freedom is too precious to be entrusted to the people. These are the same folks who had to destroy the village in order to save it. Thus the government has become a set of Chinese boxes. Americans who believe in democracy have little choice but to shred the barricades of secrecy at every opportunity. It isn't merely permissible to hack PROFS. It is a moral obligation.

Political: In the struggle between control and liberty, one has to avoid action that will drive either side to extreme behavior. The basis of terrorism, remember, is excess. If we hack PROFS, we must do it in a way that doesn't become a pretext for hysterical responses that might eventually include zero tolerance of personal computers. The answer is to set up a system for entry and exit that never lets on we've been there.

Practical I: Hacking the system should be a trivial undertaking.

Practical II: Having retrieved the smoking gun, it must be made public in such a way that the actual method of acquisition does not become public. Consider Watergate: The prime leaker was somebody whose identity and information-gathering technique is still unknown. So having obtained the files, we turn them over to the *Washington Post* without revealing our own identities or how we came by the files.

EMMANUEL [Day 5, 9:51 P.M.]: PROFS is used for sending messages back and forth. It's designed *not* to forget things. And it's used by people who are not computer literate. The document we are looking for is likely an electronic-mail message. If we can find out who the recipient or sender is, we can take it from there. Since these people frequently use the system to communicate, there may be a way for them to dial into the White House from home. Finding that number won't be difficult: frequent calls to a number local to the White House and common to a few different people. Once I get the dial-up, I'll have to look at whatever greeting I get to determine what kind of system it is. Then we need to locate someone expert in the system to see if there are any built-in back doors. If there aren't, I will social engineer my way into a working account and then attempt to break out of the program and explore the entire system.

BRAND [Day 6, 10:06 A.M.]: I have two questions: Do you believe in due process as found in our Constitution? And do you believe that this "conspiracy" is so serious that extraordinary measures need to be taken? If you believe in due process, then you shouldn't hack into the system to defend our liberties. If you don't believe in due process, you are an anarchist and potentially a terrorist. The government is justified in taking *extreme* action to protect itself and the rest of us from you. If you believe in the Constitution but also that this threat is so extreme that patriots have a duty to intercede, then you should seek one of the honest national officials who can legally demand a copy of the document. If you believe that there is no sufficiently honest politician and you steal and publish the documents, you are talking about a revolution.

ACID [Day 6, 1:30 P.M.]: This is getting too political. Who says that hacking has to have a political side? Generalizing does nothing but give hackers a false image. I couldn't care less about politics, and I hack.

LEE [Day 6, 9:01 P.M.]: Sorry, Acid, but if you hack, what you do is inherently political. Here goes: Political power is exercised by control of information channels. Therefore, any action that changes the capability of someone in power to control these channels *is* politically relevant. Historically, the one in power has been not the strongest person but the one who has convinced the goon squad to do his bidding. The goons give their power to him, usually in exchange for free food, sex, and great uniforms. The turning point of most successful revolutions is when the troops ignore the orders coming from above and switch their allegiance. Information channels. Politics. These days, the cracker represents a potential for making serious political change if he coordinates with larger social and economic forces. Without this coordination, the cracker is but a techno-bandit, sharpening his weapon and chuckling about how someday. . . . Revolutions often make good use of bandits, and some of them move into high positions when they're successful. But most of them are done away with. One cracker getting in won't do much good. Working in coordination with others is another matter—called politics.

JIMG [Day 7, 12:28 A.M.]: A thought: Because it has become so difficult to keep secrets (thanks, in part, to crackers), and so expensive and counterproductive (the trade-off in lost opportunities is too great), secrets are becoming less worth protecting. Today, when secrets come out that would have brought down governments in the past, "spin-control experts" shower the media with so many lies that the truth is obscured despite being in plain sight. It's the information equivalent of the Pentagon plan to surround each real missile with hundreds of fake ones, rendering radar useless. If hackers managed to crack the White House system, a hue and cry would be raised—not about what the hackers found in the files but about what a threat hackers are to this great democracy of ours.

HARPER'S [Day 7, 9:00 A.M.]: Suppose you hacked the files from the White House and a backlash erupted. Congressmen call for restrictions, arguing that the computer is "property" susceptible to regulation and not an instrument of "information" protected by the First Amendment. Can we craft a manifesto setting forth your views on how the computer fits into the traditions of the American Constitution?

"*I don't want any Congressional King Georges treading on my cursor. We must continue to have absolute freedom of electronic speech!*"

DAVE [Day 7, 5:30 P.M.]: If Congress ever passed laws that tried to define what we do as "technology" (regulatable) and *not* "speech," I would become a rebellious criminal immediately—and as loud as Thomas Paine ever was. Although computers are part "property" and part "premises" (which suggests a need for privacy), they are supremely instruments of *speech.* I don't want any congressional King Georges treading on my cursor. We must continue to have *absolute* freedom of electronic speech!

BARLOW [Day 7, 10:07 P.M.]: Even in a court guided by my favorite oxymoron, Justice Rehnquist, this is an open-and-shut case. The computer is a printing press. Period. The only hot-lead presses left in this country are either in museums or being operated by poets in Vermont. The computer cannot fall under the kind of regulation to which radio and TV have become subject, since computer output is not broadcast. If these regulations amount to anything more than a fart in the congressional maelstrom, then we might as well scrap the whole Bill of Rights. What I am doing with my fingers right now is "speech" in the clearest sense of the word. We don't need no stinking manifestos.

JIMG [Day 8, 12:02 A.M.]: This type of congressional action is so clearly unconstitutional that "law hackers"—everyone from William Kunstler to

Robert Bork—would be all over it. The whole idea runs so completely counter to our laws that it's hard to get worked up about it.

ADELAIDE [Day 8, 9:51 A.M.]: Not so fast. There used to be a right in the Constitution called "freedom from unreasonable search and seizure," but, thanks to recent Supreme Court decisions, your urine can be demanded by a lot of people. I have no faith in the present Supreme Court to uphold any of my rights of free speech. The complacent reaction here—that whatever Congress does will eventually be found unconstitutional—is the same kind of complacency that led to the current near-reversals of *Roe* v. *Wade.*

JRC [Day 8, 10:05 A.M.]: I'd forgo the manifestos and official explanations altogether: Fight brushfire wars against specific government incursions and wait for the technology to metastasize. In a hundred years, people won't have to be told about computers because they will have an instinctive understanding of them.

KK [Day 8, 2:14 P.M.]: Hackers are not sloganeers. They are doers, take-things-in-handers. They are the opposite of philosophers: They don't wait for language to catch up to them. Their arguments are their actions. You want a manifesto? The Internet worm was a manifesto. It had more meaning and symbolism than any revolutionary document you could write. To those in power running the world's nervous system, it said: Wake up! To the underground of hackers, crackers, chippers, and techno-punks, it said: You have power; be careful. To the mass of citizens who find computers taking over their telephone, their TV, their toaster, and their house, it said: Welcome to Wonderland.

BARLOW [Day 8, 10:51 P.M.]: Apart from the legal futility of fixing the dam after it's been breached, I've never been comfortable with manifestos. They are based on the ideologue's delusion about the simplicity, the figure-outability, of the infinitely complex thing that is Life Among the Humans. Manifestos take reductionism for a long ride off a short pier. Sometimes the ride takes a very long time. Marx and Engels didn't actually crash until last year. Manifestos fail because they are fixed and consciousness isn't. I'm with JRC: Deal with incursions when we need to, on our terms, like the guerrillas we are. To say that we can outmaneuver those who are against us is like saying that honeybees move quicker than Congress. The future is to the quick, not the respectable.

RH [Day 8, 11:43 P.M.]: Who thinks computers can't be regulated? The Electronic Communications Privacy Act of 1986 made it a crime to own "any electronic, mechanical, or other device [whose design] renders it primarily useful for the purpose of the surreptitious interception of wire, oral, or electronic communication." Because of the way Congress defined "electronic communication," one could argue that even a modem is a surreptitious interception device (SID), banned by the ECPA and subject to confiscation. It's not that Congress intended to ban modems; it was just sloppy drafting. The courts will ultimately decide what devices are legal. Since it may not be possible to draw a clear bright line between legal and illegal interception devices, the gray area—devices with both legitimate and illegitimate uses—may be subject to regulation.

BARLOW [Day 9, 8:52 A.M.]: I admit with some chagrin that I'm not familiar with the ECPA. It seems I've fallen on the wrong side of an old tautology: Just because all saloon keepers are Democrats, it doesn't follow that all Democrats are saloon keepers. By the same token, the fact that all printing presses are computers hardly limits computers to that function. And one of the other things computers are good at is surreptitious monitoring. Maybe there's more reason for concern than I thought. Has any of this stuff been tested in the courts yet?

RH [Day 9, 10:06 P.M.]: My comments about surreptitious interception devices are not based on any court cases, since there have not been any in this area since the ECPA was enacted. It is a stretch of the imagination to think that a judge would ever find a stock, off-the-shelf personal computer to be a "surreptitious interception device." But a modem is getting a little closer to the point where a creative prosecutor could make trouble for a cracker, with fallout affecting many others. An important unknown is how the courts will apply the word *surreptitious*. There's very little case law, but taking it to mean "by stealth; hidden from view; having its true purpose physically disguised," I can spin some worrisome examples. I lobbied against the bill, pointing out the defects. Congressional staffers admitted privately that there was a problem, but they were in a rush to get the bill to the floor before Congress adjourned. They said they could patch it later, but it is a pothole waiting for a truck axle to rumble through.

JIMG [Day 10, 8:55 A.M.]: That's sobering information, RH. Yet I still think that this law, if interpreted the way you suggest, would be found unconstitutional, even by courts dominated by Reagan appointees. Also, the economic cost of prohibiting modems, or even restricting their use, would so outweigh conceivable benefits that the law would never go through. Finally, restricting modems would have no effect on the phreaks but would simply manage to slow everybody else down. If modems are outlawed, only outlaws will have modems.

RH [Day 10, 1:52 P.M.]: We're already past the time when one could wrap hacking in the First Amendment. There's a traditional distinction between words—expressions of opinions, beliefs, and information—and deeds. You can shout "Revolution!" from the rooftops all you want, and the post office will obligingly deliver your recipes for nitroglycerin. But acting on that information exposes you to criminal prosecution. The philosophical problem posed by hacking is that computer programs transcend this distinction: They are pure language that dictates action when read by the device being addressed. In that sense, a program is very different from a novel, a play, or even a recipe: Actions result automatically from the machine reading the words. A computer has no independent moral judgment, no sense of responsibility. Not yet, anyway. As we program and automate more of our lives, we undoubtedly will deal with more laws: limiting what the public can know, restricting devices that can execute certain instructions, and criminalizing the possession of "harmful" programs with "no redeeming social value." Blurring the distinction between language and action, as computer programming does, could eventually undermine the First Amendment or at least force society to limit its application. That's a very high price to pay, even for all the good things that computers make possible.

HOMEBOY [Day 10, 11:03 P.M.]: HACKING IS ART. CRACKING IS REVO-LUTION. All else is noise. Cracks in the firmament are by nature threatening. Taking a crowbar to them is revolution.

■ QUESTIONS FOR REREADING

1. In terms of upstaging others, which hackers come out ahead in "Is Computer Hacking a Crime?" What are your criteria for making this decision?

2. What valuable services to you and me, to corporations, and to governments do hackers provide? There is a point in the exchange when Barlow takes issue with the hackers. What do you take his argument to be? Emmanuel Goldstein disagrees with Barlow's analogy based on the open door of his house. In doing so he says, "Hackers are not guardian angels, but if you think we're what's wrong with the system, I'd say that's precisely what those in charge want you to believe." Can hackers be seen as good vigilantes standing in between the would-be corporate criminals and the would-be system of law enforcement agencies? In other words, how do you think Goldstein wants Barlow and others to take what he is saying?

3. What is your attitude toward Phiber Optik when he discloses Barlow's credit history before all online?

4. What does Homeboy mean when he closes the exchange by saying, "HACKING IS ART. CRACKING IS REVOLUTION. All else is noise. Cracks in the firmament are by nature threatening. Taking a crowbar to them is revolution"? Is Homeboy echoing something said earlier in the discussion and making something new of it?

■ WRITING ASSIGNMENT FOR REREADING

After reading the exchange from beginning to end, write an essay stating what you think the hacker's ethic is. State specific examples in the transcript of *why* you think what you think about their exchange on ethics.

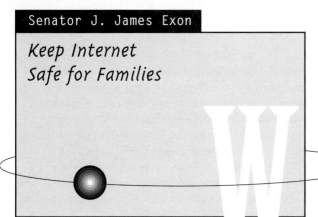

Senator J. James Exon

Keep Internet Safe for Families

Senator J. James Exon's "Keep Internet Safe for Families" and James Harrington's "Beware of Chilling Freedom of Expression" were originally published in the Dallas Morning News (April 9, 1995): J1, J10. Both the senator and Harrington (of the American Civil Liberties Union) take pro and con positions on protecting people on the Net, which they divide in terms of protecting the family *versus* protecting freedom of expression.

When a youngster logs onto a computer terminal, he or she is welcomed into a vast new world of information that will revolutionize how we all learn and work in the future. This worldwide web of computer connections represents an information explosion unprecedented in world history. This information revolution may rival the invention of the printing press and broadcasting in terms of how it will affect our daily lives.

The evolving telecommunications infrastructure known as the Internet will link homes, businesses, schools, hospitals and libraries to each other and to a vast array of electronic information resources. Imagine a student in Hastings, Nebraska, being able to tap into the computer database of a University in Budapest, Hungary, more easily than walking down to the local library.

But there are some dark side roads on the information superhighway that contain material that would be considered unacceptable by any reasonable standard.

The U.S. Senate will consider my proposal, the Communications Decency Amendment, to lay down some basic guidelines on the information superhighway. I want to make this exciting new highway as safe as possible for kids and families to travel. Just as we have laws against dumping garbage on the interstate, we ought to have similar laws for the information superhighway.

My amendment to the Telecommunications Reform Bill will toughen penalties for people who actively "transmit" pornographic and harassing material, boosting the maximum fine from $50,000 to $100,000 and increasing the maximum jail sentence from six months to two years. We need this added deterrent so that those who would pervert the network will think twice. We already have laws to prohibit obscenity over the telephone or pornography through the mail. My amendment extends to computer users the very same protections against obscenity or harassment that now partially protect telephone users.

The legislation does not make innocent "carriers" of electronic messages liable for inappropriate messages, nor does it by any stretch of the imagination require system operators to "eavesdrop" on electronic messages. To do so would be the equivalent of holding the mailman liable for the packages he delivers.

Many critics say that on the Internet, anything should go, no matter how outrageous. I say the framers of the Constitution never intended for the First Amendment to protect pornographers and pedophiles.

There are documented cases of computer misuse all over the country. These include incidents of electronic stalking, inappropriate contact with children and computer breaking and entering.

Last summer, the *Los Angeles Times* reported that a computer at the Lawrence Livermore National Laboratory in California was being used to store and distribute hard-core pornography. Despite the lab's elaborate security precautions, investigators found more than 1,000 pornographic pictures. The computer was shut down and the FBI called in.

The *Washington Post* reported on a case where a group of investigators signed on to a major computer service with false identifications and pretended to be children. They posted a few innocuous messages on teen bulletin boards and the next day they had "solicitations for nude pictures, phone sex and offers to meet in person for sex."

Computers are a unique medium because children often have much more knowledge about how they operate than their parents. My amendment would pass the standard outlined by the U.S. Supreme Court that Congress may take action to protect children from obscenity, pornography and indecency in areas like radio or television broadcasts where youngsters have unique access.

Does anyone really think that a parent can stand over their child's shoulder and monitor them all of their waking hours of every day? If anyone thinks that this material is hard for youngsters to come by, they don't know youngsters.

We have laws against murder and we have laws against speeding. We still have murder and we still have speeding. But I think most reasonable people would agree that we very likely would have more murders and more speeders if we didn't have laws as a deterrent.

In a recent newspaper article, a computer "hacker" who viewed some of this pornography on the Internet said 98 percent of it is no worse than you might find in an "adult video rental store." That weird admission makes my point. Is material that is okay for an adult video store okay for kids to see on their home computers?

To those who are critical of my suggestions I say, "Come, let us reason together." Nothing is etched in stone and I am open to any constructive proposals. I have suggested, for example, a parental lock-out mechanism as a possible solution to make certain areas of the Internet inaccessible to youngsters.

We are talking about our most important and precious commodity—our children. We cannot simply throw up our hands and say a solution is impossible or the First Amendment is so sacrosanct that we must stand idly by while our children are inundated with pornography and smut on the Internet. The public needs to be aware of the problem and direct its correction.

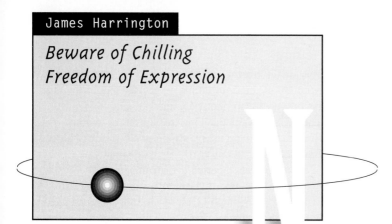

James Harrington

Beware of Chilling
Freedom of Expression

one of our founders who gathered together more than 200 years ago to write the Constitution and eventually author its Bill of Rights could have imagined an electronic communication system such as the Internet. Yet, even if the drafters could have peered into the future, they probably would not have framed the First Amendment any differently. They would apply the principles in the First Amendment with as much vitality to today's debate about obscenity, children and access to the Internet, as they did to King George's suppression of colonial newspapers.

Today's debate comes courtesy of U.S. Sen. J. James Exon (D-Neb.). Mr. Exon is sponsor of the Communications Decency Amendment that could punish electronic communicators who transmit "obscene, lewd, lascivious, filthy, or indecent" language and images—rather broad and vague terms that could apply to what most of us might speak or write to another. The new law, if passed, would punish Internet use of the "seven dirty words" we might speak in daily life; the penalty is a $100,000 fine and/or two years jail time.

This attempt to censor cyberspeech raises two major constitutional problems: Can the government limit access to sexually explicit information on the Internet to adults who want it, and, if so, who decides what is "offensive" and thus punishable?

The Internet can bring to our homes instantly accessible art, literature, music, science and just general communication from around the globe; the Internet also can be a conduit for obscenity, and for children who know how to find it. Not that obscenity is new to human existence, even for minors. Nor is salacious and vulgar material easy to locate on the Internet; ferreting it out requires a certain adeptness, even for seasoned Internet surfers. Its availability alone should not set the stage for cybercensorship.

Three general philosophical arguments support strong constitutional guarantees of free speech, assembly and press. The most favored is the concept of full and unlimited access to the "marketplace of ideas." If an idea has value, then arguments in its favor will carry the day by the force of their logic. On the other hand, ideas of no (or bad) consequence will fall of their own dead weight. Democracy strengthens itself through this intellectual free market. Government intervention is counterproductive because it impedes communication;

and, since people naturally resent repressive measures, state censorship under-cuts political legitimacy.

Self-development is a second rationale for the constitutional communica-tion protections: Absent causing real harm to another person, individuals should live unfettered by government and free to develop the kind of autonomous character they desire. That, after all, is one purpose of a democ-racy, and often the wellspring of culture and scientific advance.

Freedom to criticize government at will is the third reason for constitution-ally protected speech and press. We rarely see government move against the press these days, the last memorable time being its failed attempt during the Vietnam War to block publication of the Pentagon Papers. Lack of govern-ment activity in this area is due in part to the shallow critical and analytical quality of today's print and electronic media.

The Internet has expanded the "marketplace of ideas" beyond the wildest imaginations of Thomas Jefferson, who had to wait months for learned books from Europe. Now he could surf around the world, in minutes admiring museum art in Sydney, Australia, or accessing the human rights law library at the University of Genoa. Imagine how the Internet could have fueled Benjamin Franklin's creativity and might have fed his prurient interests as well. This latter choice, though, Mr. Franklin would have argued, was his, not the government's.

If an adult wants to access sexual materials on the Internet, that right belongs to the adult. Individuals have the liberty to define their own personal autonomy and development; they may err, even seriously, but the mistake is theirs, not ours. We simply don't trust the government making private deci-sions for us and what we may read or freely say to each other.

The Internet has made the obscenity problem more difficult, however; and the media have played it up because of its uniqueness. Many facets of the Internet operate as repositories ("billboards" or "mail boxes") of communica-tions and materials that other users may "visit" and from which they may take an item at will and even download it.

Obviously, because of the country's diversity, something stored on a per-sonal billboard might be viewed as "indecent" in Waco, Texas, but not in Los Angeles. Yet Mr. Exon's bill would allow prosecution of the originator of alleged indecency (which includes using the "f" word) in any jurisdiction where the electronic mail is downloaded. Thus, an Internet user in rural Ten-nessee may visit the billboard of a Hollywood Internetter, take and download some "lascivious" material, and thus make the billboard owner criminally liable.

This leads to the second problem. Mr. Exon's proposed Communications Decency Amendment not only punishes offensive sexual material, but it allows the most conservative community in the nation to hold the rest of the country hostage to its very narrow definitions of "obscene, lewd, lascivious, filthy or indecent."

This frightening scenario has occurred already under another obscenity law. A Tennessee jury convicted a couple in Milpitas, California, on 11 counts of obscenity. They now face 55 years in prison and a $2.75 million fine, thanks to a Memphis postal inspector, who found out they stored sexually explicit material on their electronic billboard and set out to prosecute them halfway across the country.

Mr. Exon's proposal also could punish us for writing a racy Internet love note to a spouse, even though we would speak the words on the telephone without fear, and whether what we write is offensive might be judged by a jury a thousand miles away from us.

A few years back the U.S. Supreme Court ruled that prevailing community standards should measure what is, and is not, obscene in a given locale. That case sought to protect rural and conservative communities from imposition of standards acceptable in large urban communities such as New York. Mr. Exon's bill, however, enforces the converse; it allows rural, conservative communities to set standards for the rest of the nation.

As to the problem of children possibly finding scatological material on the Internet, efforts would be better directed toward technology, such as filters and bowdlerizers that parents can use if needed. Some technology already exists: university Internet systems lock out pornographic materials; and commercial on-line services can do the same. All in all, though, parental guidance is key; there is no effective substitute. For some reason, cybercensors find this alternative uncomfortable.

We ought to exult in the explosion of Internet's unrestrained expression; the passionate desire to convey ideas and expand creativity is a hundred times better than commercial media's suffocating programs, milquetoast news and boring sound-bites.

Mr. Exon's misguided proposal would send a message to Internet users around the world that the United States is more interested in being a cyber-cop rather than fostering a global marketplace of ideas where all can speak without fear and in the hope of bettering the human condition.

■ QUESTIONS FOR REREADING

1. How would you summarize Exon's and Harrington's positions? Are they arguing in terms of the same criteria for judging the issue of the law and the Net? If they are not, then are they speaking at cross-purposes? What are their purposes?

2. Are Exon and Harrington attempting to inform or persuade each other or their readers? In what ways are their arguments different? Start thinking about these questions by determining Exon's and Harrington's predispositions toward the problem at hand. What are their basic assumptions?

■ WRITING ASSIGNMENT FOR REREADING

What was your position on the law and cyberspace, if you had one, prior to reading the articles in this chapter? If your position has changed or been strengthened, write a brief account (say, 600 words) of what specifically moved you to change or hold firm to your position.

John Perry Barlow's "Crime and Puzzlement" was originally published in Whole Earth Review *68 (Fall 1990): 44–57. It can be found online at ‹http://www.eff.org/~barlow/barlow.html›.*

At his Home(Stead) Page, Barlow tells us: "John Perry Barlow is a retired Wyoming cattle rancher, a lyricist for the Grateful Dead, and co-founder of the Electronic Frontier Foundation. He is also a member of The WELL *Board of Directors. He was born in Wyoming in 1947, was educated there in a one-room schoolhouse, and graduated from Wesleyan University in Middletown, Connecticut, with an honors degree in comparative religion in 1969."*

His article is a history of the early days—and really not so long ago—of the struggle for freedom of expression in cyberspace. He records the events that led up to the founding of the EFF. *In fact, this essay is the founding document of the* EFF. *(A parallel document was written by Mitchell Kapor.)*

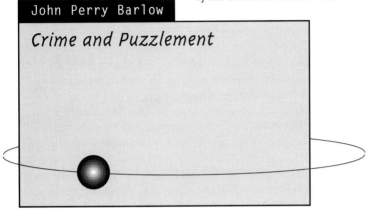

John Perry Barlow

Crime and Puzzlement

■ DESPERADOS OF THE DATASPHERE

So me and my sidekick Howard, we was sitting out in front of the 40 Rod Saloon one evening when he all of a sudden says, "Lookee here. What do you reckon?" I look up and there's these two strangers riding into town. They're young and got kind of a restless, bored way about 'em. A person don't need both eyes to see they mean trouble . . .

Well, that wasn't quite how it went. Actually, Howard and I were floating blind as cave fish in the electronic barrens of the WELL, so the whole incident passed as words on a display screen:

HOWARD: Interesting couple of new users just signed on. One calls himself acid and the other's optik.

BARLOW: Hmmm. What are their real names?

HOWARD: Check their finger files.

And so I typed !finger acid. Several seconds later the WELL's Sequent computer sent the following message to my Macintosh in Wyoming:

```
Login name: acid                    In real life: Acid Phreak
```

By this, I knew that the WELL had a new resident and that his corporeal analog was supposedly called Acid Phreak. Typing !finger optik yielded results of similar insufficiency, including the claim that someone, somewhere in the real world, was walking around calling himself Phiber Optik. I doubted it.

However, associating these sparse data with the knowledge that the WELL was about to host a conference on computers and security rendered the conclusion that I had made my first sighting of genuine computer crackers. As the arrival of an outlaw was a major event to the settlements of the Old West, so was the appearance of crackers cause for stir on the WELL.

The WELL (or Whole Earth 'Lectronic Link) is an example of the latest thing in frontier villages, the computer bulletin board. In this kind of small town, Main Street is a central minicomputer to which (in the case of the WELL) as many as 64 microcomputers may be connected at one time by phone lines and little blinking boxes called modems.

In this silent world, all conversation is typed. To enter it, one forsakes both body and place and becomes a thing of words alone.

You can see what your neighbors are saying (or recently said), but not what either they or their physical surroundings look like. Town meetings are continuous and discussions rage on everything from sexual kinks to depreciation schedules.

There are thousands of these nodes in the United States, ranging from PC clone hamlets of a few users to mainframe metros like CompuServe, with its 550,000 subscribers. They are used by corporations to transmit memoranda and spreadsheets, universities to disseminate research, and a multitude of factions, from apiarists to Zoroastrians, for purposes unique to each.

Cyberspace, in its present condition, has a lot in common with the 19th Century West.

Whether by one telephonic tendril or millions, they are all connected to one another. Collectively, they form what their inhabitants call the Net. It extends across that immense region of electron states, microwaves, magnetic fields, light pulses and thought which sci-fi writer William Gibson named Cyberspace.

Cyberspace, in its present condition, has a lot in common with the 19th Century West. It is vast, unmapped, culturally and legally ambiguous, verbally terse (unless you happen to be a court stenographer), hard to get around in, and up for grabs. Large institutions already claim to own the place, but most of the actual natives are solitary and independent, sometimes to the point of sociopathy. It is, of course, a perfect breeding ground for both outlaws and new ideas about liberty.

Recognizing this, *Harper's Magazine* decided in December 1989 to hold one of its periodic Forums on the complex of issues surrounding computers, information, privacy, and electronic intrusion or "cracking." Appropriately, they convened their conference in Cyberspace, using the WELL as the "site."

Harper's invited an odd lot of about 40 participants. These included: Clifford Stoll, whose book *The Cuckoo's Egg* details his cunning efforts to nab a German cracker. John Draper or "Cap'n Crunch," the granddaddy of crackers whose blue boxes got Wozniak and Jobs into consumer electronics. Stewart Brand and Kevin Kelly of Whole Earth fame. Steven Levy, who wrote the seminal *Hackers*. A retired Army colonel named Dave Hughes. Lee Felsenstein, who designed the Osborne computer and was once called the "Robespierre of computing." A UNIX wizard and former hacker named Jeff Poskanzer. There was also a score of aging techno-hippies, the crackers, and me.

What I was doing there was not precisely clear since I've spent most of my working years either pushing cows or song-mongering, but I at least brought to the situation a vivid knowledge of actual cow-towns, having lived in or around one most of my life.

That and a kind of innocence about both the technology and morality of Cyberspace which was soon to pass into the confusion of knowledge.

At first, I was inclined toward sympathy with Acid 'n' Optik as well as their colleagues, Adelaide, Knight Lightning, Taran King, and Emmanuel. I've always been more comfortable with outlaws than Republicans, despite having more certain credentials in the latter camp.

These kids were fractious, vulgar, immature, amoral, insulting, and too damned good at their work.

But as the *Harper's* Forum mushroomed into a boom-town of ASCII text (the participants typing 110,000 words in 10 days), I began to wonder. These kids were fractious, vulgar, immature, amoral, insulting, and too damned good at their work.

Worse, they inducted a number of former kids like myself into Middle Age. The long feared day had finally come when some gunsel would yank my beard and call me, too accurately, an old fart.

Under ideal circumstances, the blind gropings of bulletin board discourse force a kind of Noh drama stylization on human commerce. Intemperate responses, or "flames" as they are called, are common even among conference participants who understand one another, which, it became immediately clear, the cyberpunks and techno-hippies did not.

My own initial enthusiasm for the crackers wilted under a steady barrage of typed testosterone. I quickly remembered I didn't know much about who they were, what they did, or how they did it. I also remembered stories about crackers working in league with the Mob, ripping off credit card numbers and getting paid for them in (stolen) computer equipment.

And I remembered Kevin Mitnick. Mitnick, now 25, recently served federal time for a variety of computer and telephone related crimes. Prior to incarceration, Mitnick was, by all accounts, a dangerous guy with a computer. He disrupted phone company operations and arbitrarily disconnected the phones of celebrities. Like the kid in *Wargames,* he broke into the North American Defense Command computer in Colorado Springs.

Unlike the kid in *Wargames,* he is reputed to have made a practice of destroying and altering data. There is even the (perhaps apocryphal) story that he altered the credit information of his probation officer and other enemies. Digital Equipment claimed that his depredations cost them more than $4 million in computer downtime and file rebuilding. Eventually, he was turned in by a friend who, after careful observation, had decided he was "a menace to society."

His spectre began to hang over the conference. After several days of strained diplomacy, the discussion settled into a moral debate on the ethics of security and went critical.

The techno-hippies were of the unanimous opinion that, in Dylan's words, one "must be honest to live outside the law." But these young strangers apparently lived by no code save those with which they unlocked forbidden regions of the Net.

They appeared to think that improperly secured systems deserved to be violated and, by extension, that unlocked houses ought to be robbed. This latter built particular heat in me since I refuse, on philosophical grounds, to lock my house.

Civility broke down. We began to see exchanges like:

DAVE HUGHES: Clifford Stoll said a wise thing that no one has commented on. That networks are built on trust. If they aren't, they should be.

ACID PHREAK: Yeah. Sure. And we should use the "honor system" as a first line of security against hack attempts.

JEFF POSKANZER: This guy down the street from me sometimes leaves his back door unlocked. I told him about it once, but he still does it. If I had the chance to do it over, I would go in the back door, shoot him, and take all his money and consumer electronics. It's the only way to get through to him.

ACID PHREAK: Jeff Poskanker (Puss? Canker? yechh) Anyway, now when did you first start having these delusions where computer hacking was even *remotely* similar to murder?

Presented with such a terrifying amalgam of raw youth and apparent power, we fluttered like a flock of indignant Babbitts around the Status Quo, defending it heartily. One former hacker howled to the *Harper's* editor in charge of the forum, "Do you or do you not have names and addresses for these criminals?" Though they had committed no obvious crimes, he was ready to call the police.

They finally got to me with:

ACID: Whoever said they'd leave the door open to their house . . . where do you live? (the address) Leave it to me in mail if you like.

I had never encountered anyone so apparently unworthy of my trust as these little nihilists. They had me questioning a basic tenet, namely that the greatest security lies in vulnerability. I decided it was time to put that principle to the test . . .

BARLOW: Acid. My house is at 372 North Franklin Street in Pinedale, Wyoming. If you're heading north on Franklin, you go about two blocks off the main drag before you run into hay meadow on the left. I've got the last house before the field. The computer is always on . . .

And is that really what you mean? Are you merely just the kind of little sneak that goes around looking for easy places to violate? You disappoint me, pal. For all your James Dean-on-silicon rhetoric, you're not a cyberpunk. You're just a punk.

ACID PHREAK: Mr. Barlow: Thank you for posting all I need to get your credit information and a whole lot more! Now, who is to blame? ME for getting it or YOU for being such an idiot?! I think this should just about sum things up.

BARLOW: Acid, if you've got a lesson to teach me, I hope it's not that it's idiotic to trust one's fellow man. Life on those terms would be endless and brutal. I'd try to tell you something about conscience, but I'd sound like Father O'Flannigan trying to reform the punk that's about to gutshoot him. For no more reason than to watch him die.

But actually, if you take it upon yourself to destroy my credit, you might do me a favor. I've been looking for something to put the brakes on my burgeoning materialism.

I spent a day wondering whether I was dealing with another Kevin Mitnick before the other shoe dropped:

BARLOW: . . . With crackers like acid and optik, the issue is less intelligence than alienation. Trade their modems for skateboards and only a slight conceptual shift would occur.

OPTIK: You have some pair of balls comparing my talent with that of a skateboarder. Hmmm . . . This was indeed boring, but nonetheless:

Optik had hacked the core of TRW, an institution which has made my business (and yours) their business, extracting from it an abbreviated (and incorrect) version of my personal financial life.

At which point he downloaded my credit history.

Optik had hacked the core of TRW, an institution which has made my business (and yours) their business, extracting from it an abbreviated (and incorrect) version of my personal financial life. With this came the implication that he and Acid could and would revise it to my disadvantage if I didn't back off.

I have since learned that while getting someone's TRW file is fairly trivial, changing it is not. But at that time, my assessment of the crackers' black skills was one of superstitious awe. They were digital brujos about to zombify my economic soul.

To a middle-class American, one's credit rating has become nearly identical to his freedom. It now appeared that I was dealing with someone who had both the means and desire to hoodoo mine, leaving me trapped in a life of wrinkled bills and money order queues. Never again would I call The Sharper Image on a whim.

I've been in redneck bars wearing shoulder-length curls, police custody while on acid, and Harlem after midnight, but no one has ever put the spook in me quite as Phiber Optik did at that moment. I realized that we had problems which exceeded the human conductivity of the WELL's bandwidth. If someone were about to paralyze me with a spell, I wanted a more visceral sense of him than could fit through a modem.

I e-mailed him asking him to give me a phone call. I told him I wouldn't insult his skills by giving him my phone number and, with the assurance conveyed by that challenge, I settled back and waited for the phone to ring. Which, directly, it did.

In this conversation and the others that followed I encountered an intelligent, civilized, and surprisingly principled kid of 18 who sounded, and continues to sound, as though there's little harm in him to man or data. His cracking impulses seemed purely exploratory, and I've begun to wonder if we wouldn't also regard spelunkers as desperate criminals if AT&T owned all the caves.

The terrifying poses which Optik and Acid had been striking on screen were a media-amplified example of a human adaptation I'd seen before: One becomes as he is beheld. They were simply living up to what they thought we, and, more particularly, the editors of *Harper's,* expected of them. Like the televised tears of disaster victims, their snarls adapted easily to mass distribution.

Months later, *Harper's* took Optik, Acid and me to dinner at a Manhattan restaurant which, though very fancy, was appropriately Chinese. Acid and Optik, as material beings, were well-scrubbed and fashionably clad. They looked to be dangerous as ducks. But, as *Harper's* and the rest of the media have discovered to their delight, the boys had developed distinctly showier personae for their rambles through the howling wilderness of Cyberspace.

Months later, Harper's took Optik, Acid and me to dinner at a Manhattan restaurant.

Glittering with spikes of binary chrome, they strode past the klieg lights and into the digital distance. There they would be outlaws. It was only a matter of time before they started to believe themselves as bad as they sounded. And no time at all before everyone else did.

In this, they were like another kid named Billy, many of whose feral deeds in the pre-civilized West were encouraged by the same dime novelist who chronicled them. And like Tom Horn, they seemed to have some doubt as to which side of the law they were on. Acid even expressed an ambition to work for the government someday, nabbing "terrorists and code abusers."

There is also a frontier ambiguity to the "crimes" the crackers commit. They are not exactly stealing VCRs. Copying a text file from TRW doesn't deprive its owner of anything except informational exclusivity. (Though it may be said that information has monetary value only in proportion to its containment.)

There was no question that they were making unauthorized use of data channels. The night I met them, they left our restaurant table and disappeared into the phone booth for a long time. I didn't see them marshalling quarters before they went.

And, as I became less their adversary and more their scoutmaster, I began to get "conference calls" in which six or eight of them would crack pay phones all over New York and simultaneously land on my line in Wyoming. These deft maneuvers made me think of sky-diving stunts where large groups convene geometrically in free fall. In this case, the risk was largely legal.

Their other favorite risky business is the time-honored adolescent sport of trespassing. They insist on going where they don't belong. But then teen-age boys have been proceeding uninvited since the dawn of human puberty. It seems hard-wired. The only innovation in the new form of the forbidden zone is the means of getting in it.

In fact, like Kevin Mitnick, I broke into NORAD when I was 17. A friend and I left a nearby "woodsie" (as rustic adolescent drunks were called in Colorado) and tried to get inside the Cheyenne Mountain. The chrome-helmeted Air Force MP's held us for about 2 hours before letting us go. They weren't much older than us and knew exactly our level of national security threat. Had we come cloaked in electronic mystery, their alert status certainly would have been higher.

Their other favorite risky business is the time-honored adolescent sport of trespassing. They insist on going where they don't belong.

Whence rises much of the anxiety. Everything is so ill-defined. How can you guess what lies in their hearts when you can't see their eyes? How can one be sure that, like Mitnick, they won't cross the line from trespassing into another adolescent pastime, vandalism? And how can you be sure they pose no threat when you don't know what a threat might be?

And for the crackers some thrill is derived from the meta-morphic vagueness of the laws themselves. On the Net, their effects are unpredictable. One never knows when they'll bite.

This is because most of the statutes invoked against the crackers were designed in a very different world from the one they explore. For example, can unauthorized electronic access be regarded as the ethical equivalent of old-fashioned trespass? Like open range, the property boundaries of Cyberspace are hard to stake and harder still to defend.

Is transmission through an otherwise unused data channel really theft? Is the trackless passage of a mind through TRW's mainframe the same as the passage of a pickup through my Back 40? What is a place if Cyberspace is everywhere? What are data and what is free speech? How does one treat property which has no physical form and can be infinitely reproduced? Is a computer the same as a printing press? Can the history of my business affairs properly belong to someone else? Can anyone morally claim to own knowledge itself?

If such questions were hard to answer precisely, there are those who are ready to try. Based on their experience in the Virtual World, they were about as qualified to enforce its mores as I am to write the Law of the Sea. But if they lacked technical sophistication, they brought to this task their usual conviction. And, of course, badges and guns.

■ OPERATION SUN DEVIL

Recently, we have witnessed an alarming number of young
people who, for a variety of sociological and psychological
reasons, have become attached to their computers and are
exploiting their potential in a criminal manner. Often, a
progression of criminal activity occurs which involves
telecommunications fraud (free long distance phone calls),
unauthorized access to other computers (whether for profit,
fascination, ego, or the intellectual challenge), credit card
fraud (cash advances and unauthorized purchases of goods),
and then move on to other destructive activities like
computer viruses.

Our experience shows that many computer hacker suspects are
no longer misguided teenagers mischievously playing games
with their computers in their bedrooms. Some are now high
tech computer operators using computers to engage in unlawful
conduct.

> —excerpts from a statement by Garry M. Jenkins,
> Assistant Director, U.S. Secret Service

The right of the people to be secure in their persons,
houses, papers, and effects, against unreasonable searches
and seizures, shall not be violated, and no warrants shall
issue but upon probable cause, support by oath or
affirmation, and particularly describing the place to be
searched, and the persons or things to be seized.

> —Amendment IV, U.S. Constitution

On January 24, 1990, a platoon of Secret Service agents entered the apartment which Acid Phreak shares with his mother and 12-year-old sister. The latter was the only person home when they burst through the door with guns drawn. They managed to hold her at bay for about half an hour until their quarry happened home.

On January 24, 1990, a platoon of Secret Service agents entered the apartment which Acid Phreak shares with his mother and 12-year-old sister.

By then, they were nearly done packing up Acid's worldly goods, including his computer, his notes (both paper and magnetic), books, and such dubiously dangerous tools as a telephone answering machine, a ghetto blaster and his complete collection of audio tapes. One agent asked him to define the real purpose of the answering machine and was frankly skeptical when told that it answered the phone. The audio tapes seemed to contain nothing but music, but who knew what dark data Acid might have encoded between the notes . . .

When Acid's mother returned from work, she found her apartment a scene of apprehended criminality. She asked what, exactly, her son had done to deserve all this attention and was told that, among other things, he had caused the AT&T system crash several days earlier. (Previously AT&T had taken full responsibility.) Thus, the agent explained, her darling boy was thought to have caused over a billion dollars in damage to the economy of the United States.

This accusation was never turned into a formal charge. Indeed, no charge of any sort was filed against Mr. Phreak then and, although the Secret Service maintained resolute possession of his hardware, software, and data, no charge had been charged four months later.

Across town, similar scenes were being played out at the homes of Phiber Optik and another colleague code-named Scorpion. Again, equipment, notes, disks both hard and soft, and personal effects were confiscated. Again no charges were filed.

Thus began the visible phase of Operation Sun Devil, a two-year Secret Service investigation which involved 150 federal agents, numerous local and state law enforcement agencies, and the combined security resources of PacBell, AT&T, Bellcore, Bell South MCI, U.S. Sprint, Mid-American, Southwestern Bell, NYNEX, U.S. West and American Express.

The focus of this impressive institutional array was the Legion of Doom, a group which never had any formal membership list but was thought by the members with whom I spoke to number less than 20, nearly all of them in their teens or early twenties.

I asked Acid why they'd chosen such a threatening name. "You wouldn't want a fairy kind of thing like Legion of Flower Pickers or something. But the media ate it up too. Probing the Legion of Doom like it was a gang or something, when really it was just a bunch of geeks behind terminals."

Sometime in December 1988, a 21-year-old Atlanta-area Legion of Doomster named The Prophet cracked a Bell South computer and downloaded a three-page text file which outlined, in bureaucrat-ese of surpassing opacity, the administrative procedures and responsibilities for marketing, servicing, upgrading, and billing for Bell South's 911 system.

A dense thicket of acronyms, the document was filled with passages like:

In accordance with the basic SSC/MAC strategy for provisioning, the SSC/MAC will be Overall Control Office (OCO) for all Notes to PSAP circuits (official services) and any other services for this customer. Training must be scheduled for all SSC/MAC involved personnel during the pre-service stage of the project.

And other such.

At some risk, I too have a copy of this document. To read the whole thing straight through without entering coma requires either a machine or a human who has too much practice thinking like one. Anyone who can understand it fully and fluidly has altered his consciousness beyond the ability to ever again read Blake, Whitman, or Tolstoy. It is, quite simply, the worst writing I have ever tried to read.

Since the document contains little of interest to anyone who is not a student of advanced organizational sclerosis . . . that is, no access codes, trade secrets, or proprietary information . . . I assume The Prophet only copied this file as a kind of hunting trophy. He had been to the heart of the forest and had returned with this coonskin to nail to the barn door.

Furthermore, he was proud of his accomplishment, and since such trophies are infinitely replicable, he wasn't content to nail it to his door alone. Among

the places he copied it was a UNIX bulletin board (rather like the WELL) in Lockport, Illinois, called Jolnet.

It was downloaded from there by a 20-year-old hacker and pre-law student (whom I had met in the *Harper's* Forum) who called himself Knight Lightning. Though not a member of the Legion of Doom, Knight Lightning and a friend, Taran King, also published from St. Louis and his fraternity house at the University of Missouri a worldwide hacker's magazine called *Phrack*. (From phone phreak and hack.)

Phrack was an unusual publication in that it was entirely virtual. The only time its articles hit paper was when one of its subscribers decided to print out a hard copy. Otherwise, its editions existed in Cyberspace and took no physical form.

When Knight Lightning got hold of the Bell South document, he thought it would amuse his readers and reproduced it in the next issue of Phrack.

When Knight Lightning got hold of the Bell South document, he thought it would amuse his readers and reproduced it in the next issue of *Phrack*. He had little reason to think that he was doing something illegal. There is nothing in it to indicate that it contains proprietary or even sensitive information. Indeed, it closely resembles telco reference documents which have long been publicly available.

However, Rich Andrews, the systems operator who oversaw the operation of Jolnet, thought there might be something funny about the document when he first ran across it in his system. To be on the safe side, he forwarded a copy of it to AT&T officials. He was subsequently contacted by the authorities, and he cooperated with them fully. He would regret that later.

On the basis of the foregoing, a grand jury in Lockport was persuaded by the Secret Service in early February to hand down a seven-count indictment against The Prophet and Knight Lightning, charging them, among other things, with interstate transfer of stolen property worth more than $5,000. When The Prophet and two of his Georgia colleagues were arrested on February 7, 1990, the Atlanta papers reported they faced 40 years in prison and a $2 million fine. Knight Lightning was arrested on February 15.

The property in question was the aforementioned blot on the history of prose whose full title was "A Bell South Standard Practice (BSP) 660-225-104SV-Control Office Administration of Enhanced 911 Services for Special Services and Major Account Centers, March, 1988."

And not only was this item worth more than $5,000.00, it was worth, according to the indictment and Bell South, precisely $79,449.00. And not a penny less. We will probably never know how this figure was reached or by whom, though I like to imagine an appraisal team consisting of Franz Kafka, Joseph Heller, and Thomas Pynchon . . .

In addition to charging Knight Lightning with crimes for which he could go to jail 30 years and be fined $122,000.00, they seized his publication,

Phrack, along with all related equipment, software and data, including his list of subscribers, many of whom would soon lose their computers and data for the crime of appearing on it.

I talked to Emmanuel Goldstein, the editor of *2600,* another hacker publication which has been known to publish purloined documents. If they could shut down *Phrack,* couldn't they as easily shut down *2600?*

He said, "I've got one advantage. I come out on paper and the Constitution knows how to deal with paper."

In fact, nearly all publications are now electronic at some point in their creation. In a modern newspaper, stories written at the scene are typed to screens and then sent by modem to a central computer. This computer composes the layout in electronic type and the entire product is transmitted electronically to the presses. There, finally, the bytes become ink.

Phrack merely omitted the last step in a long line of virtual events. However, that omission, and its insignificant circulation, left it vulnerable to seizure based on content. If the 911 document had been the Pentagon Papers (another proprietary document) and *Phrack* the *New York Times,* a completion of the analogy would have seen the government stopping publication of the *Times* and seizing its every material possession, from notepads to presses.

Not that anyone in the newspaper business seemed particularly worried about such implications. They, and the rest of the media who bothered to report Knight Lightning's arrest, were too obsessed by what they portrayed as actual disruptions of emergency service and with marvelling at the sociopathy of it. One report expressed relief that no one appeared to have died as a result of the "intrusions."

Meanwhile, in Baltimore, the 911 dragnet snared Leonard Rose, aka Terminus. A professional computer consultant who specialized in UNIX, Rose got a visit from the government early in February. The G-men forcibly detained his wife and children for six hours while they interrogated Rose about the 911 document and ransacked his system.

Rose had no knowledge of the 911 matter. Indeed, his only connection had been occasional contact with Knight Lightning over several years . . . and admitted membership in the Legion of Doom. However, when searching his hard disk for 911 evidence, they found something else. Like many UNIX consultants, Rose did have some UNIX source code in his possession. Furthermore, there was evidence that he had transmitted some of it to Jolnet and left it there for another consultant.

UNIX is a ubiquitous operating system, and though its main virtue is its openness to amendment at the source level, it is nevertheless the property of AT&T. What had been widely distributed within businesses and universities for years was suddenly, in Rose's hands, a felonious possession.

Finally, the Secret Service rewarded the good citizenship of Rich Andrews by confiscating the computer where Jolnet had dwelt, along with all the e-mail, read and unread, which his subscribers had left there. Like the many others whose equipment and data were taken by the Secret Service subsequently, he wasn't charged with anything. Nor is he likely to be. They have already inflicted on him the worst punishment a nerd can suffer: data death.

Andrews was baffled. "I'm the one that found it, I'm the one that turned it in. . . . And I'm the one that's suffering," he said.

One wonders what will happen when they find such documents on the hard disks of CompuServe. Maybe I'll just upload my copy of Bell South Standard Practice (BSP) 660-225-104SV and see . . .

In any case, association with stolen data is all the guilt you need. It's quite as if the government could seize your house simply because a guest left a stolen VCR in an upstairs bedroom closet. Or confiscate all the mail in a post office upon finding a stolen package there. The first concept of modern jurisprudence to have arrived in Cyberspace seems to have been Zero Tolerance.

Early on March 1, 1990, the offices of a role-playing game publisher in Austin, Texas, called Steve Jackson Games were visited by agents of the United States Secret Service.

Rich Andrews was not the last to learn about the Secret Service's debonair new attitude toward the 4th Amendment's protection against unreasonable seizure.

Early on March 1, 1990, the offices of a role-playing game publisher in Austin, Texas, called Steve Jackson Games were visited by agents of the United States Secret Service. They ransacked the premises, broke into several locked filing cabinets (damaging them irreparably in the process) and eventually left carrying three computers, two laser printers, several hard disks, and many boxes of paper and floppy disks.

Later in the day, callers to the Illuminati BBS (which Steve Jackson Games operated to keep in touch with role-players around the country) encountered the following message:

So far we have not received a clear explanation of what the Secret Service was looking for, what they expected to find, or much of anything else. We are fairly certain that Steve Jackson Games is not the target of whatever investigation is being conducted; in any case, we have done nothing illegal and have nothing whatsoever to hide. However, the equipment that was seized is apparently considered to be evidence in whatever they're investigating, so we aren't likely to get it back any time soon. It could be a month, it could be never.

It's been three months as I write this and, not only has nothing been returned to them, but, according to Steve Jackson, the Secret Service will no longer take his calls. He figures that, in the months since the raid, his little company has lost an estimated $125,000. With such a fiscal hemorrhage, he can't afford a lawyer to take after the Secret Service. Both the state and national offices of the ACLU told him to "run along" when he solicited their help.

He tried to go to the press. As in most other cases, they were unwilling to raise the alarm. Jackson theorized, "The conservative press is taking the attitude that the suppression of evil hackers is a good thing and that anyone who happens to be put out of business in the meantime . . . well, that's just their tough luck."

In fact, *Newsweek* did run a story about the event, portraying it from Jackson's perspective, but they were almost alone in dealing with it.

What had he done to deserve this nightmare? Role-playing games, of which Dungeons and Dragons is the most famous, have been accused of creating obsessive involvement in their nerdy young players, but no one before had found it necessary to prevent their publication.

It seems that Steve Jackson had hired the wrong writer. The managing editor of Steve Jackson Games is a former cracker, known by his fellows in the Legion of Doom as The Mentor. At the time of the raid, he and the rest of Jackson's staff had been working for over a year on a game called GURPS Cyberpunk, High-Tech Low-Life Role-Playing.

At the time of the Secret Service raids, the game resided entirely on the hard disks they confiscated. Indeed, it was their target. They told Jackson that, based on its author's background, they had reason to believe it was a "handbook on computer crime." It was therefore inappropriate for publication, 1st Amendment or no 1st Amendment.

I got a copy of the game from the trunk of The Mentor's car in an Austin parking lot. Like the Bell South document, it seemed pretty innocuous to me, if a little inscrutable. Borrowing its flavor from the works of William Gibson and Austin sci-fi author Bruce Sterling, it is filled with silicon brain implants, holodecks, and gauss guns.

It is, as the cover copy puts it, "a fusion of the dystopian visions of George Orwell and Timothy Leary." Actually, without the gizmos, it describes a future kind of like the present its publisher is experiencing at the hands of the Secret Service.

An unbelievably Byzantine world resides within its 120 large pages of small print. (These role-players must be some kind of idiots savants . . .) Indeed, it's a thing of such complexity that I can't swear there's no criminal information in there, but then I can't swear that Grateful Dead records don't have satanic messages if played backward. Anything's possible, especially inside something as remarkable as Cyberpunk.

The most remarkable thing about Cyberpunk is the fact that it was printed at all. After much negotiation, Jackson was able to get the Secret Service to let him have some of his data back. However, they told him that he would be limited to an hour and a half with only one of his three computers. Also, according to Jackson, "They insisted that all the copies be made by a Secret Service agent who was a two-finger typist. So we didn't get much."

In the end, Jackson and his staff had to reconstruct most of the game from neural rather than magnetic memory. They did have a few very old backups, and they retrieved some scraps which had been passed around to game testers. They also had the determination of the enraged.

Despite government efforts to impose censorship by prior restraint, Cyberpunk is now on the market. Presumably, advertising it as "the book that was seized by the U.S. Secret Service" will invigorate sales. But Steve Jackson Games, the heretofore prosperous publisher of more than a hundred role-playing games, has been forced to lay off more than half of its employees and may well be mortally wounded.

Any employer who has heard this tale will think hard before he hires a computer cracker. Which may be, of course, among the effects the Secret Service desires.

On May 8, 1990, Operation Sun Devil, heretofore an apparently random and nameless trickle of Secret Service actions, swept down on the Legion of Doom and its ilk like a bureaucratic tsunami. On that day, the Secret Service served 27 search warrants in 14 cities from Plano, Texas, to New York, New York.

On May 8, 1990, Operation Sun Devil, heretofore an apparently random and nameless trickle of Secret Service actions, swept down on the Legion of Doom and its ilk like a bureaucratic tsunami.

The law had come to Cyberspace. When the day was over, transit through the wide open spaces of the Virtual World would be a lot trickier.

In a press release following the sweep, the Secret Service boasted having shut down numerous computer bulletin boards, confiscated 40 computers, and seized 23,000 disks. They noted in their statement that "the conceivable criminal violations of this operation have serious implications for the health and welfare of all individuals, corporations, and United States Government agencies relying on computers and telephones to communicate."

It was unclear from their statement whether "this operation" meant the Legion of Doom or Operation Sun Devil. There was room to interpret it either way.

Because the deliciously ironic truth is that, aside from the 3-page Bell South document, the hackers had neither removed nor damaged anyone's data. Operation Sun Devil, on the other hand, had "serious implications" for a number of folks who relied on "computers and telephones to communicate." They lost the equivalent of about 5.4 million pages of information. Not to mention a few computers and telephones.

And the welfare of the individuals behind those figures was surely in jeopardy. Like the story of the single mother and computer consultant in Baltimore whose sole means of supporting herself and her 18-year-old son was stripped away early one morning. Secret Service agents broke down her door with sledge hammers, entered with guns drawn, and seized all her computer equipment. Apparently her son had also been using it . . .

Or the father in New York who opened the door at 6:00 A.M. and found a shotgun at his nose. A dozen agents entered. While one of them kept the man's wife in a choke-hold, the rest made ready to shoot and entered the

bedroom of their sleeping 14-year-old. Before leaving, they confiscated every piece of electronic equipment in the house, including all the telephones.

It was enough to suggest that the insurance companies should start writing policies against capricious governmental seizure of circuitry.

In fairness, one can imagine the government's problem. This is all pretty magical stuff to them. If I were trying to terminate the operations of a witch coven, I'd probably seize everything in sight. How would I tell the ordinary household brooms from the getaway vehicles?

But as I heard more and more about the vile injustices being heaped on my young pals in the Legion of Doom, not to mention the unfortunate folks nearby, the less I was inclined toward such temperate thoughts as these. I drifted back into a 60's-style sense of the government, thinking it a thing of monolithic and evil efficiency and adopting an up-against-the-wall willingness to spit words like "pig" or "fascist" into my descriptions.

In doing so, I endowed the Secret Service with a clarity of intent which no agency of government will ever possess. Despite almost every experience I've ever had with federal authority, I keep imagining its competence.

For some reason, it was easier to invest the Keystone Kapers of Operation Sun Devil with malign purpose rather than confront their absurdity straight on. There is, after all, a twisted kind of comfort in political paranoia. It provides one such a sense of orderliness to think that the government is neither crazy nor stupid and that its plots, though wicked, are succinct.

I was about to have an experience which would restore both my natural sense of unreality and my unwillingness to demean the motives of others. I was about to see firsthand the disorientation of the law in the featureless vastness of Cyberspace.

■ IN SEARCH OF NUPROMETHEUS

I pity the poor immigrant . . .

—Bob Dylan

Sometime last June, an angry hacker got hold of a chunk of the highly secret source code which drives the Apple Macintosh. He then distributed it to a variety of addresses, claiming responsibility for this act of information terrorism in the name of the NuPrometheus League.

Apple freaked. NuPrometheus had stolen, if not the Apple crown jewels, at least a stone from them. Worse, NuPrometheus had then given this prize away. Repeatedly.

All Apple really has to offer the world is the software which lies encoded in silicon on the ROM chip of every Macintosh. This set of instructions is the cyber-DNA which makes a Macintosh a Macintosh.

Worse, much of the magic in this code was put there by people who not only do not work for Apple any longer, but might only do so again if encouraged with cattle prods. Apple's attitude toward its ROM code is a little like that of a rich kid toward his inheritance. Not actually knowing how to create wealth himself, he guards what he has with hysterical fervor.

Time passed, and I forgot about the incident. But one recent May morning, I learned that others had not. The tireless search for the spectral heart of NuPrometheus finally reached Pinedale, Wyoming, where I was the object of a two-hour interview by Special Agent Richard Baxter, Jr., of the Federal Bureau of Investigation.

Poor Agent Baxter didn't know a ROM chip from a Vise-grip when he arrived, so much of that time was spent trying to educate him on the nature of the thing which had been stolen. Or whether "stolen" was the right term for what had happened to it.

You know things have rather jumped the groove when potential suspects must explain to law enforcers the nature of their alleged perpetrations.

I wouldn't swear Agent Baxter ever got it quite right. After I showed him some actual source code, gave a demonstration of e-mail in action, and downloaded a file from the WELL, he took to rubbing his face with both hands, peering up over his fingertips and saying, "It sure is something, isn't it," or, "Whooo-ee."

Or, "My 8-year-old knows more about these things than I do." He didn't say this with a father's pride so much as an immigrant's fear of a strange new land into which he will be forcibly moved and in which his own child is a native. He looked across my keyboard into Cyberspace and didn't like what he saw.

We could have made it harder for one another, but I think we each sensed that the other occupied a world which was as bizarre and nonsensical as it could be. We did our mutual best to suppress immune response at the border.

You'd have thought his world might have been a little more recognizable to me. Not so, it turns out. Because in his world, I found several unfamiliar features, including these:

1. The Hacker's Conference is an underground organization of computer outlaws with likely connections to, and almost certainly sympathy with, the NuPrometheus League. (Or as Agent Baxter repeatedly put it, the "New Prosthesis League.")

2. John Draper, the aforementioned Cap'n Crunch, in addition to being a known member of the Hacker's Conference, is also CEO and president of Autodesk, Inc. This is of particular concern to the FBI because Autodesk has many top-secret contracts with the government to supply Star Wars graphics imaging and "hyperspace" technology. Worse, Draper is thought to have Soviet contacts.

He wasn't making this up. He had lengthy documents from the San Francisco office to prove it. And in which Autodesk's address was certainly correct.

On the other hand, I know John Draper. While, as I say, he may have once distinguished himself as a cracker during the Pleistocene, he is not now, never has been, and never will be CEO of Autodesk. He did work there for a while last year, but he was let go long before he got in a position to take over.

Nor is Autodesk, in my experience with it, the Star Wars skunk works which Agent Baxter's documents indicated. One could hang out there a long time without ever seeing any gold braid.

Their primary product is something called AutoCAD, by far the most popular computer-aided design software but generally lacking in lethal potential. They do have a small development program in Cyberspace, which is what they call Virtual Reality. (This, I assume is the "hyperspace" to which Agent Baxter's documents referred.)

However, Autodesk had reduced its Cyberspace program to a couple of programmers. I imagined Randy Walser and Carl Tollander toiling away in the dark and lonely service of their country. Didn't work. Then I tried to describe Virtual Reality to Agent Baxter, but that didn't work either. In fact, he tilted. I took several runs at it, but I could tell I was violating our border agreements. These seemed to include a requirement that neither of us try to drag the other across into his conceptual zone.

Agent Baxter looked at my list of Hacker's Conference attendees and read their bios. "These are the people who actually design this stuff, aren't they?" He was incredulous. Their corporate addresses didn't fit his model of outlaws at all well.

I fared a little better on the Hacker's Conference. Hardly a conspiracy, the Hacker's Conference is an annual convention originated in 1984 by the Point Foundation and the editors of *Whole Earth Review.* Each year it invites about a hundred of the most gifted and accomplished of digital creators. Indeed, they are the very people who have conducted the personal computer revolution. Agent Baxter looked at my list of Hacker's Conference attendees and read their bios.

"These are the people who actually design this stuff, aren't they?" He was incredulous. Their corporate addresses didn't fit his model of outlaws at all well.

Why had he come all the way to Pinedale to investigate a crime he didn't understand which had taken place (sort of) in five different places, none of which was within 500 miles?

Well, it seems Apple has told the FBI that they can expect little cooperation from Hackers in and around the Silicon Valley, owing to virulent anti-Apple sentiment there. They claim this is due to the Hacker belief that software should be free combined with festering resentment of Apple's commercial success. They advised the FBI to question only those Hackers who were as far as possible from the twisted heart of the subculture.

They did have their eye on some local people, though. These included a couple of former Apple employees, Grady Ward and Walter Horat, Chuck Farnham (who has made a living out of harassing Apple), Glenn Tenney (the purported leader of the Hackers), and, of course, the purported CEO of Autodesk.

Other folks Agent Baxter asked me about included Mitch Kapor, who wrote Lotus 1-2-3 and was known to have received some of this mysterious source code. Or whatever. But I had also met Mitch Kapor, both on the WELL and in person. A less likely computer terrorist would be hard to come by.

Actually, the question of the source code was another area where worlds but shadow-boxed. Although Agent Baxter didn't know source code from Tuesday, he did know that Apple Computer had told his agency that what had been stolen and disseminated was the complete recipe for a Macintosh computer. The distribution of this secret formula might result in the creation of millions of Macintoshes not made by Apple. And, of course, the ruination of Apple Computer.

In my world, NuPrometheus (whoever they, or more likely, he might be) had distributed a small portion of the code which related specifically to Color QuickDraw. QuickDraw is Apple's name for the software which controls the Mac's on-screen graphics. But this was another detail which Agent Baxter could not capture. For all he knew, you could grow Macintoshes from floppy disks.

I explained to him that Apple was alleging something like the ability to assemble an entire human being from the recipe for a foot, but even he knew the analogy was inexact. And trying to get him to accept the idea that a corporation could go mad with suspicion was quite futile. He had a far different perception of the emotional reliability of institutions.

When he finally left, we were both dazzled and disturbed. I spent some time thinking about Lewis Carroll and tried to return to writing about the legal persecution of the Legion of Doom. But my heart wasn't in it. I found myself suddenly too much in sympathy with Agent Baxter and his struggling colleagues from Operation Sun Devil to get back into a proper sort of pig-bashing mode.

Given what had happened to other innocent bystanders like Steve Jackson, I gave some thought to getting scared. But this was Kafka in a clown suit. It wasn't precisely frightening. I also took some comfort in a phrase once applied to the administration of Frederick the Great: "Despotism tempered by incompetence."

Of course, incompetence is a double-edged banana. While we may know this new territory better than the authorities, they have us literally out-gunned. One should pause before making well-armed paranoids feel foolish, no matter how foolish they seem.

■ THE FEAR OF WHITE NOISE

Neurosis is the inability to tolerate ambiguity.
　　　　　　　—Sigmund Freud, appearing to me in a dream

I'm a member of that half of the human race which is inclined to divide the human race into two kinds of people. My dividing line runs between the people who crave certainty and the people who trust chance.

You can draw this one a number of ways, of course, like Control vs. Serendipity, Order vs. Chaos, Hard answers vs. Silly questions, or Newton, Descartes & Aquinas vs. Heisenberg, Mandelbrot & the Dalai Lama. Etc.

Large organizations and their drones huddle on one end of my scale, busily trying to impose predictable homogeneity on messy circumstance. On the other end, freelancers and ne'er-do-wells cavort about, getting by on luck if they get by at all.

I'm a member of that half of the human race which is inclined to divide the human race into two kinds of people.

However you cast these poles, it comes down to the difference between those who see life as a struggle against cosmic peril and human infamy and those who believe, without any hard evidence, that the universe is actually on our side. Fear vs. Faith.

I am of the latter group. Along with Gandhi and Rebecca of Sunnybrook Farm, I believe that other human beings will quite consistently merit my trust if I'm not doing something which scares them or makes them feel bad about themselves. In other words, the best defense is a good way to get hurt.

In spite of the fact that this system works very reliably for me and my kind, I find we are increasingly in the minority. More and more of our neighbors live in armed compounds. Alarms blare continuously. Potentially happy people give their lives over to the corporate state as though the world were so dangerous outside its veil of collective immunity that they have no choice.

I have a number of theories as to why this is happening. One has to do with the opening of Cyberspace. As a result of this development, humanity is now undergoing the most profound transformation of its history. Coming into the Virtual World, we inhabit Information. Indeed, we become Information. Thought is embodied and the Flesh is made Word. It's weird as hell.

Beginning with the invention of the telegraph and extending through television into Virtual Reality, we have been, for over a century, experiencing a terrifying erosion in our sense of both body and place. As we begin to realize the enormity of what is happening to us, all but the most courageous have gotten scared.

And everyone, regardless of his psychic resilience, feels this overwhelming sense of strangeness. The world, once so certain and tangible and legally precise, has become an infinite layering of opinions, perceptions, litigation, camera-angles, data, white noise, and, most of all, ambiguities. Those of us who are of the fearful persuasion do not like ambiguities.

Indeed, if one were a little jumpy to start with, he may now be fairly humming with nameless dread. Since no one likes his dread to be nameless, the first order of business is to find it some names.

For a long time here in the United States, Communism provided a kind of catch-all bogeyman. Marx, Stalin and Mao summoned forth such a spectre that, to many Americans, annihilation of all life was preferable to the human portion's becoming Communist. But as Big Red wizened and lost his teeth, we began to cast about for a replacement.

Finding none of sufficient individual horror, we have draped a number of objects with the old black bunting which once shrouded the Kremlin. Our current spooks are terrorists, child abductors, AIDS, and the underclass. I would say drugs, but anyone who thinks that the War on Drugs is not actually the War on the Underclass hasn't been paying close enough attention.

There are a couple of problems with these Four Horsemen. For one thing, they aren't actually very dangerous. For example, only seven Americans died in worldwide terrorist attacks in 1987. Fewer than 10 (out of about 70 million) children are abducted by strangers in the U.S. each year. Your chances of getting AIDS if you are neither gay nor a hemophiliac nor a junkie are considerably less than your chances of getting killed by lightning while golfing. The underclass is dangerous, of course, but only, with very few exceptions, if you are a member of it.

The other problem with these perils is that they are all physical. If we are entering into a world in which no one has a body, physical threats begin to lose their sting.

And now I come to the point of this screed: The perfect bogeyman for Modern Times is the Cyberpunk! He is so smart he makes you feel even more stupid than you usually do. He knows this complex country in which you're perpetually lost. He understands the value of things you can't conceptualize long enough to cash in on. He is the one-eyed man in the Country of the Blind.

The perfect bogeyman for Modern Times is the Cyberpunk!

In a world where you and your wealth consist of nothing but beeps and boops of micro-voltage, he can steal all your assets in nanoseconds and then make you disappear.

He can even reach back out of his haunted mists and kill you physically. Among the justifications for Operation Sun Devil was this chilling tidbit:

"Hackers had the ability to access and review the files of hospital patients. Furthermore, they could have added, deleted, or altered vital patient information, possibly causing life-threatening situations."

Perhaps the most frightening thing about the Cyberpunk is the danger he presents to The Institution, whether corporate or governmental. If you are frightened, you have almost certainly taken shelter by now in one of these collective organisms, so the very last thing you want is something which can endanger your heretofore unassailable hive.

And make no mistake, crackers will become to bureaucratic bodies what viruses presently are to human bodies. Thus, Operation Sun Devil can be seen as the first of many waves of organizational immune response to this new antigen. Agent Baxter was a T-cell. Fortunately, he didn't know that himself and I was very careful not to show him my own antigenic tendencies.

I think that herein lies the way out of what might otherwise become an Armageddon between the control freaks and the neo-hip. Those who are comfortable with these disorienting changes must do everything in our power to convey that comfort to others. In other words, we must share our sense of hope and opportunity with those who feel that in Cyberspace they will be obsolete eunuchs for sure.

It's a tall order. But, my silicon brothers, our self-interest is strong. If we come on as witches, they will burn us. If we volunteer to guide them gently into its new lands, the Virtual World might be a more amiable place for all of us than this one has been.

Of course, we may also have to fight.

Defining the conceptual and legal map of Cyberspace before the ambiguo-phobes do it for us (with punitive overprecision) is going to require some effort. We can't expect the Constitution to take care of itself. Indeed, the precedent for mitigating the Constitutional protection of a new medium has already been established. Consider what happened to radio in the early part of this century.

Under the pretext of allocating limited bandwidth, the government estab-lished an early right of censorship over broadcast content which still seems directly unconstitutional to me. Except that it stuck. And now, owing to a large body of case law, looks to go on sticking.

New media, like any chaotic system, are highly sensitive to initial condi-tions. Today's heuristical answers of the moment become tomorrow's perma-nent institutions of both law and expectation. Thus, they bear examination with that destiny in mind.

Earlier in this article, I asked a number of tough questions relating to the nature of property, privacy, and speech in the digital domain. Questions like: "What are data and what is free speech?" or "How does one treat property which has no physical form and can be infinitely repro-duced?" or "Is a computer the same as a printing press?" The events of Operation Sun Devil were nothing less than an effort to provide answers to these questions. Answers which would greatly enhance governmental ability to silence the future's opinionated nerds.

In over-reaching as extravagantly as they did, the Secret Service may actually have done a service for those of us who love liberty.

In overreaching as extravagantly as they did, the Secret Service may actually have done a service for those of us who love liberty. They have provided us with a devil. And devils, among their other galvanizing virtues, are just great for clari-fying the issues and putting iron in your spine. In the presence of a devil, it's always easier to figure out where you stand.

While I previously had felt no stake in the obscure conun-dra of free telecommunication, I was, thanks to Operation Sun Devil, suddenly able to plot a trajectory from the current plight of the Legion of Doom to an eventual constraint on opinions much dearer to me. I remembered Martin Neimoeller, who said:

In Germany they came first for the Communists, and I didn't speak up because I wasn't a Communist. Then they came for the Jews, and I didn't speak up because I wasn't a Jew.

They came for the trade unionists, and I didn't speak up because I wasn't a trade union-
ist. Then they came for the Catholics, and I didn't speak up because I was a Protestant.
Then they came for me, and by that time no one was left to speak up.

I decided it was time for me to speak up.

The evening of my visit from Agent Baxter, I wrote an account of it which I placed on the WELL. Several days later, Mitch Kapor literally dropped by for a chat.

Also a WELL denizen, he had read about Agent Baxter and had begun to meditate on the inappropriateness of leaving our civil liberties to be defined by the technologically benighted. A man who places great emphasis on face-to-face contact, he wanted to discuss this issue with me in person. He had been flying his Canadair bizjet to a meeting in California when he realized his route took him directly over Pinedale.

We talked for a couple of hours in my office while a spring snowstorm swirled outside. When I recounted for him what I had learned about Operation Sun Devil, he decided it was time for him to speak up, too.

He called a few days later with the phone number of a civil libertarian named Harvey Silverglate, who, as evidence of his conviction that everyone deserves due process, is currently defending Leona Helmsley. Mitch asked me to tell Harvey what I knew, with the inference that he would help support the costs which are liable to arise whenever you tell a lawyer anything.

I found Harvey in New York at the offices of that city's most distinguished constitutional law firm, Rabinowitz, Boudin, Standard, Krinsky, and Lieberman. These are the folks who made it possible for the *New York Times* to print the Pentagon Papers. (Not to dwell on the unwilling notoriety which partner Leonard Boudin achieved back in 1970 when his Weathergirl daughter blew up the family home . . .)

In the conference call which followed, I could almost hear the skeletal click as their jaws dropped. The next day, Eric Lieberman and Terry Gross of Rabinowitz, Boudin met with Acid Phreak, Phiber Optik, and Scorpion.

As of today (in early June of 1990), Mitch and I are legally constituting the Electronic Frontier Foundation.

The maddening trouble with writing this account is that *Whole Earth Review,* unlike, say, *Phrack,* doesn't publish instantaneously. Events are boiling up at such a frothy pace that anything I say about current occurrences surely will not obtain by the time you read this. The road from here is certain to fork many times. The printed version of this will seem downright quaint before it's dry.

But as of today (in early June of 1990), Mitch and I are legally constituting the Electronic Frontier Foundation, a two (or possibly three) man organization which will raise and disburse funds for education, lobbying, and litigation in the areas relating to digital speech and the extension of the Constitution into Cyberspace.

Already, on the strength of preliminary stories about our efforts in the *Washington Post* and the *New York Times,* Mitch has received an offer from Steve

Wozniak to match whatever funds he dedicates to this effort. (As well as a fair amount of abuse from the more institutionalized precincts of the computer industry.)

The Electronic Frontier Foundation will fund, conduct, and support legal efforts to demonstrate that the Secret Service has exercised prior restraint on publications, limited free speech, conducted improper seizure of equipment and data, used undue force, and generally conducted itself in a fashion which is arbitrary, oppressive, and unconstitutional.

In addition, we will work with the Computer Professionals for Social Responsibility and other organizations to convey to both the public and the policy-makers metaphors which will illuminate the more general stake in liberating Cyberspace.

Not everyone will agree. Crackers are, after all, generally beyond public sympathy. Actions on their behalf are not going to be popular no matter who else might benefit from them in the long run.

Nevertheless, in the litigations and political debates which are certain to follow, we will endeavor to assure that their electronic speech is protected as certainly as any opinions which are printed or, for that matter, screamed. We will make an effort to clarify issues surrounding the distribution of intellectual property. And we will help to create for America a future which is as blessed by the Bill of Rights as its past has been.

■ Q U E S T I O N S   F O R   R E R E A D I N G

1. What is Barlow's attitude toward the hackers in the *Harper's* forum when he writes of them in "Crime and Puzzlement"? Does his attitude remain the same throughout? Toward the end of his article, Barlow refers to the "Pentagon Papers." What is he referring to and what is its relevance?

2. How does Barlow's account of the *Harper's Magazine* roundtable differ from yours, if it does?

3. Barlow, in comparing himself to Kevin Mitnick, says that he, too, attempted to break into NORAD when he was young. But what was the difference between Mitnick's motive and the young Barlow's? And how does this difference add to the "crime" committed by Mitnick?

4. What is your response to Barlow's account of "Operation Sun Devil"? Begin by examining the opening paragraph of that section: "On January 24, 1990, a platoon of Secret Service agents entered the apartment which Acid Phreak shares with his mother and 12-year-old sister. . . ."

5. What is the NuPrometheus? What do you make of the depiction of "Agent Baxter"?

6. Barlow says he, along with others, divides the world into those "people who crave certainty and the people who trust chance." What does he mean by this division? And what does he attempt to gain by it in terms of understanding how people respond to Cyberspace? Where do you fit in this division?

7. Who is "the bogeyman of modern times"? Are you convinced by Barlow's characterization and rationale for this bogeyman? If not, why not? How would you characterize this bogeyman?

8. Barlow puts some questions to us: "What are data and what is free speech?" "How does one treat property which has no physical form and can be infinitely reproduced?" "Is a computer the same as a printing press?" What are your answers, provisional though they may be?

■ WRITING ASSIGNMENTS FOR REREADING

1. Read Bruce Sterling's account of "Operation Sun Devil" (in *The Hacker Crackdown*) and compare it with Barlow's account. Write a paper comparing the two accounts. If they are radically different or the same, point that out and explain in detail how in a book review of the two works. As a follow-up, discover who else has written about the operation and compare their work with the two previous authors' works. When studying the accounts, look not only for detail but how that detail is characterized— how style of writing shapes content.

2. Both Barlow and Newt Gingrich are Republicans. Do some basic research and see what you can find out about the two men and their attitudes toward computers. After your research, write a report on what you find.

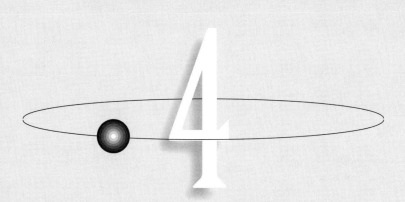

Sexual Politics

T here is a growing concern about gender dif-
ferences in cyberspace. It is argued that when on-line, whether someone is on
a BBS or newsgroup or even on academic lists or especially at a MOO, gender
stereotypes are greatly amplified. (A MOO is short for MUD *object oriented* and is
a virtual place where people can talk by typing to each other in real time; it is
comparable to Internet Relay Chat [IRC] "rooms" provided by some commercial on-line services.) Males tend to dominate the talk or make sexual
advances toward females (or those whom they take to be females). Females
tend to lurk on lists or to be annoyed—and understandably so—when males
hit on them at MOOs. In cyberspace, it is generally argued, males are active,
while females are passive. Males tend to flame, while females tend to be
silenced publicly, causing them either to unsubscribe from the discussion list
or post to each other privately. It should be understood, however, that there
are exceptions to this general claim, but many who study exchanges on the
Net insist that the exceptions are few and far between. Though we may not
especially like stereotypes, we human beings tend to live by them in a major
way in cyberspace.

This raises the question of whether the two sexes are predisposed to
active/passive or agonistic/nurturing roles by biology or culture, by gene or
scene. For some commentators, men and women are not biologically determined in this way, which means, then, that women are not naturally passive in
respect to things computerized, but culturally passive.

Sexual differences lead to discussions of sexual politics in cyberspace and
to attempts to legislate laws against sexual harassment and pornography and
to enforce them. As discussed in chapter 3, the Internet has been like the
Wild West before law and order was brought to it. We are at that juncture
now when Congress is talking in very specific terms about putting a stop to
"cyberporn" on the Net so as to protect not only women but also children or
"the family."

Women (or Grrls, a.k.a. gURLs) are creating special places for themselves on the Net and the Web. There are more and more discussion lists designed for women and more e-journals for women. But to think in terms of "more than before" can be terribly misleading, for it assumes that women are having to catch up with men and their interests in computers and the Net. To dispel such notions as "catching up," many women point to Ava Lovelace as the first computer programmer and the person who got Charles Babbage's Difference Engine to work. Consequently, many women have established computer associations and organizations in her name. From the beginning there have been as many innovative women as men working in technology. Most recently, Sadie Plant in her book *Zeros + Ones: Digital Women + the New Technoculture* has demonstrated that women have always been involved in the development and use of new technologies and are now immensely involved in cyberspace. Plant's book makes us totally rethink women's place in technology and the new technoculture.

Along with the serious side of sexual politics comes a lighter side. Tragedy demands a comic relief from time to time. The idea of having sex in cyberspace or having it virtually is offered in many instances as a serious project, but often has a comic side to it. As you read through the articles on sexual politics, you will find occasionally much to laugh at. (We will return to the issue of cybersex when we read about MUDs and MOOs in chapter 7.)

■ SUMMARY OF KEY TERMS AND PERSONS

Babbage, Charles (1791–1871): Inventor of the first computer, known as the Difference Engine, and then later a completely different Analytical Engine.

to flame, flaming: To post a nasty, ugly, or harassing message via e-mail.

Grrls: A respelling of *girls* in a more appropriate way to signify women working with computers.

Variations of the spellings include Webgrrls, Cybergrrl, GeekGirl, Modem Grrls, Urrl Grrl, and gURLs.

Lovelace, Ada (1815–1852): Wrote the first computer programs while working with Charles Babbage.

MOO: Short for *Mud Object Oriented.* A MOO is a virtual place on the Net where people can talk by typing to each other in real

time; it is comparable to Internet Relay Chat "rooms" provided by some commercial on-line services, though it differs greatly in that people on-line can build rooms and objects. (See chapter 7.)

teledildonics (dildonics): Howard Rheingold added the prefix *tele-* to Ted Nelson's *dildonics* to coin a term signifying the possibilities of cybersex.

Barbara Kantrowitz's "Men, Women, and Computers" appeared in Newsweek (May 16, 1994): 48–52, 54–55. Kantrowitz works from the presumption that while at an early age males are generally encouraged to be aggressive, assertive, and interested in things mechanical, females at the same age are cul- turally encouraged to be passive and invested in things nonme- chanical. Kantrowitz argues that males generally learn to play Nintendo games, while females are encouraged to play with Barbie: "Computer culture is created, defined and con- trolled by men. Women often feel about as welcome as a sys- tem crash." For Kantrowitz, this difference can be and needs to be corrected.

Barbara Kantrowitz

Men, Women, and Computers

Cyberspace, it turns out, isn't much of an Eden after all. It's marred by just as many sexist ruts and gender conflicts as the Real World.

As a longtime *Star Trek* devotee, Janis Cortese was eager to be part of the Trekkie discussion group on the Internet. But when she first logged on, Cortese noticed that these fans of the final frontier devoted megabytes to such profound topics as whether Troi or Crusher had bigger breasts. In other words, the purveyors of this *Trek* dreck were all *guys.* Undeterred, Cortese, a physicist at California's Loma Linda University, figured she'd add perspective to the electronic gathering place with her own momen- tous questions. Why was the male cast racially diverse while almost all the females were young, white and skinny? Then, she tossed in a few lustful thoughts about the male crew members.

After those seemingly innocuous observations, "I was chased off the net by rabid hounds," recalls Cortese. Before she could say "Fire phasers," the Trekkies had flooded her electronic mailbox with nasty messages—a practice called "flaming." Cortese retreated into her own galaxy by starting the all- female Starfleet Ladies Auxiliary and Embroidery/Baking Society. The private electronic forum, based in Houston, now has more than 40 members, includ- ing psychologists, physicians, students and secretaries. They started with Trek- talk, but often chose to beam down and go where no man had ever wandered before—into the personal mode. When Julia Kosatka, a Houston computer scientist, got pregnant last year, she shared her thoughts with the group on weight gain, sex while expecting and everything else on her mind. Says Kosatka: "I'm part of one of the longest-running slumber parties in history."

From the Internet to Silicon Valley to the PC sitting in the family room, men and women often seem like two chips that pass in the night. Sure, there are women who spout techno-speak in their sleep and plenty of men who think a hard drive means four hours on the freeway. But in general, computer culture is created, defined and controlled by men. Women often feel about as welcome as a system crash.

About a third of American families have at least one computer, but most of those are purchased and used by males. It may be new technology, but the old rules still apply. In part, it's that male-machine bonding thing, reincarnated in the digital age. "Men tend to be seduced by the technology itself," says Oliver Strimpel, executive director of The Computer Museum in Boston. "They tend to get into the faster-race-car syndrome," bragging about the size of their discs or the speed of their microprocessors. To the truly besotted, computers are a virtual religion, complete with icons (on-screen graphics), relics (obsolete programs and machines) and prophets (Microsoft's Bill Gates, outlaw hackers). This is not something to be trifled with by mere . . . females, who seem to think that machines were meant to be *used,* like the microwave oven or the dishwasher. Interesting and convenient on the job but not worthy of obsession. Esther Dyson, editor of *Release 1.0,* an influential software-industry newsletter, has been following the computer field for two decades. Yet when she looks at her own computer, Dyson says she still doesn't "really care about its innards. I just want it to work."

Men tend to be seduced by the technology. . . . Women are much more practical, much more interested in the machine's utility.

Blame (a) culture (b) family (c) schools (d) all of the above. Little boys are expected to roll around in the dirt and explore. Perfect training for learning to use computers, which often requires hours in front of the screen trying to figure out the messy arcanum of a particular program. Girls get subtle messages—from society if not from their parents—that they should keep their hands clean and play with their dolls. Too often, they're discouraged from taking science and math—not just by their schools but by parents as well (how many mothers have patted their daughters on the head and reassured them: "Oh, I wasn't good at math, either").

The gender gap is real and takes many forms.

▪ BARBIE VS. NINTENDO

Girls' technophobia begins early. Last summer, Sarah Douglas, a University of Oregon computer-science professor, took part in a job fair for teenage girls that was supposed to introduce them to nontraditional occupations. With great expectations, she set up her computer and loaded it with interesting programs. Not a single girl stopped by. When she asked why, the girls "told me computers were something their dads and their brothers used," Douglas sadly recalls. "Computer science is a very male profession . . . When girls get involved in that male world, they are pushed away and belittled. Pretty soon, the girls get frustrated and drop out."

Computer games usually involve lots of shooting and dying. Boy stuff. What's out there for girls? "If you walk down the street and look in the computer store, you will see primarily male people as sales staff and as customers," says Jo Sanders, director of the gender-equity program at the Center for Advanced Study in Education at the City University of New York Graduate Center.

Boys and girls are equally interested in computers until about the fifth grade, says University of Minnesota sociologist Ronald Anderson, who coauthored the recent report "Computers in American Schools." At that point, boys' use rises significantly and girls' use drops, Anderson says, probably because sex-role identification really kicks in. Many girls quickly put computers on the list of not-quite-feminine topics, like car engines and baseball batting averages. It didn't have to be this way. The very first computer programmer was a woman, Ada Lovelace, who worked with Charles Babbage on his mechanical computing machines in the mid-1800s. If she had become a role model, maybe hundreds of thousands of girls would have spent their teenage years locked in their bedrooms staring at screens. Instead, too many are doing their nails or worrying about their hair, says Marcelline Barron, an administrator at the Illinois Mathematics and Science Academy, a publicly funded coed boarding school for gifted students. "You're not thinking about calculus or physics when you're thinking about that," says Barron. "We have these kinds of expectations for young girls. They must be neat, they must be clean, they must be quiet."

Despite great strides by women in other formerly male fields, such as law and medicine, women are turning away from the computer industry. Men earning computer-science degrees outnumber women 3 to 1 and the gap is growing, according to the National Science Foundation. Fifteen years ago, when computers were still new in schools, they hadn't yet been defined as so exclusively male. But now girls have gotten the message. It's not just the technical and cultural barrier. Sherry Turkle, a Massachusetts Institute of Technology sociologist who teaches a course on women and computers, says that computers have come to stand for "a world without emotion," an image that seems to scare off girls more than boys.

The vast majority of videogame designers are men: they make games they want to play. Why do you think it's called Game Boy?

In the past decade, videogames have become a gateway to technology for many boys, but game manufacturers say few girls are attracted to these small-screen shoot-'em-ups. It's not surprising that the vast majority of videogame designers are men. They don't call it Game *Boy* for nothing. Now some manufacturers are trying to lure girls. In the next few months, Sega plans to introduce "Berenstein Bears," which will offer players a choice of boy or girl characters. A second game, "Crystal's Pony Tale," involves coloring (there's lots of pink in the background). Neither game requires players to "die," a common videogame device that researchers say girls dislike. Girls also tend to prefer nonlinear games, where there is more than one way to proceed. "There's a whole issue with speaking girls' language," says Michealene Cristini Risley, group director of licensing and character development for Sega. The company would like to hook girls at the age of 4, before they've developed fears of technology.

Girls need freedom to explore and make mistakes. Betsy Zeller, a 37-year-old engineering manager at Silicon Graphics, says that when she discovered computers in college, "I swear I thought I'd seen the face of God." Yet she had to fend off guys who would come into the lab and want to help her work through problems or, worse yet, do them for her. "I would tell them to get lost," she says. "I wanted to do it myself." Most women either asked for or accepted proffered help, just as they are more likely to ask for directions when lost in a strange city. That may be the best way to avoid driving in circles for hours, but it's not the best way to learn technical subjects.

Schools are trying a number of approaches to interest girls in computers. Douglas and her colleagues are participating in a mentorship program where undergraduate girls spend a summer working with female computer scientists. Studies have shown that girls are more attracted to technology if they can work in groups: some schools are experimenting with team projects that require computers but are focused on putting out a product, like a newspaper or pamphlet. At the middle and high-school level, girls-only computer classes are increasingly popular. Two months ago Roosevelt Middle School in Eugene, Ore., set up girls-only hours at the computer lab. Games were prohibited and artists were brought in to teach girls how to be more creative with the computer. Students are also learning to use e-mail, which many girls love. Says Debbie Nehl, the computer-lab supervisor: "They see it as high-tech note-passing."

■ POWER NETWORKS

As a relatively new industry, the leadership of computerdom might be expected to be more gender-diverse. Wrong: few women have advanced beyond middle-management ranks. According to a study conducted last year by the *San Jose Mercury News,* there are no women CEOs running major computer-manufacturing firms and only a handful running software companies. Even women who have succeeded say they are acutely conscious of the differences between them and their male coworkers. "I don't talk the same as men," says Paula Hawthorn, an executive at Montage Software, in Oakland, California. "I don't get the same credibility." The difference, she says, "is with you all the time."

Women who work in very technical areas, such as programming, are often the loneliest. Anita Borg, a computer-systems researcher, remembers attending a 1987 conference where there were so few women that the only time they ran into each other was in the restroom. Their main topic of discussion: why there were so few women at the conference. That bathroom cabal grew into Systers, an on-line network for women with technical careers. There are now 1,740 women members from 19 countries representing 200 colleges and universities and 150 companies. Systers is part mentoring and part consciousness-raising. One graduate student, for example, talked about how uncomfortable she felt sitting in her shared office when a male graduate student and a professor put a picture of a nude woman on a computer. The problem was resolved when a couple of female faculty members, also on the Systers network, told their offending colleagues that the image was not acceptable.

Women have been more successful in developing software, especially when their focus is products used by children. Jan Davidson, a former teacher, started Davidson & Associates, in Torrance, California, with three programs in 1982. Now it's one of the country's biggest developers of kids' software, with 350 employees and $58.6 million in revenues. Multimedia will bring new opportunities for women. The technology is so specialized that it requires a team—animators, producers, scriptwriters, 3-D modelers—to create state-of-the-art products. It's a far cry from the stereotype of the solitary male programmer, laboring long into the night with only takeout Chinese food for company. At Mary Cron's Rymel Design Group in Palos Verdes, California, most of the software artists and designers are women, Cron says. "It's like a giant puzzle," she adds. "We like stuff we can work on together."

As more women develop software, they may also help create products that will attract women consumers—a huge untapped market. Heidi Roizen, a college English major, cofounded T/Maker Co. in Mountain View, California, a decade ago. She says that because women are often in charge of the family's budget, they are potential consumers of personal-finance programs. Women are also the most likely buyers of education and family-entertainment products, a fast-growing segment of the industry. "Women are more typically the household shopper," Roizen says. "They have tremendous buying power."

■ WIRED WOMEN

The Infobahn—a.k.a. the Information Superhighway—may be the most hyped phenomenon in history—or it could be the road to the future. In any case, women want to get on. But the sign over the access road says CAUTION. MEN WORKING. WOMEN BEWARE. Despite hundreds of thousands of new users in the last year, men still dominate the Internet and commercial services such as Prodigy or CompuServe. The typical male conversation on line turns off many women. "A lot of time, to be crude, it's a pissing contest," says Lisa Kimball, a partner in the Meta Network, a Washington, D.C., on-line service that is 40 percent female. Put-downs are an art form. When one woman complained recently in an Internet forum that she didn't like participating because she didn't have time to answer all her e-mail, she was swamped with angry responses, including this one (from a man): "Would you like some cheese with your whine?"

Some men say the on-line hostility comes from resentment over women's slowly entering what has been an almost exclusively male domain. Many male techno-jocks "feel women are intruding into their inner sanctum," says André Bacard, a Silicon Valley, California, technology writer. They're not out to win sensitivity contests. "In the computer world, it's 'Listen, baby, if you don't like it, drop dead'," says Bacard. "It's the way men talk to guys. Women aren't used to that."

Many men on the net aren't out to win sensitivity contests.

Even under more civilized circumstances, men and women have different conversational styles, says Susan Herring, a University of Texas at Arlington professor who has studied women's participation on computer networks. Herring found that violations of long-established net etiquette—asking too many basic questions, for example—angered men. "The women were much more tolerant of people who didn't know what they were doing," Herring says. "What really annoyed women was the flaming and people boasting. The things that annoy women are things men do all the time."

Like hitting on women. Women have learned to tread their keyboards carefully in chat forums because they often have to fend off sexual advances that would make Bob Packwood blush. When subscribers to America Online enter one of the service's forums, their computer names appear at the top of the screen as a kind of welcome. If they've chosen an obviously female name, chances are they'll soon be bombarded with private messages seeking detailed descriptions of their appearance or sexual preferences. "I couldn't believe it," recalls 55-year-old Eva S. "I said, 'Come on, I'm a grandmother'."

More and more women are signing on to networks that are either coed and run by women, or are exclusively for women. Stacy Horn started ECHO (for East Coast Hang Out) four years ago because she was frustrated with the hostility on line. About 60 percent of ECHO's 2,000 subscribers are men; among ECHO's 50 forums, only two are strictly for women. "Flaming is nonexistent on ECHO," Horn says. "New women get on line and they see that. And then they're much more likely to jump in." Women's Wire in San Francisco, started in January, has 850 subscribers, only 10 percent of them men—the reverse of most on-line services. "We wanted to design a system in which women would help shape the community from the floor up," says cofounder Ellen Pack. The official policy is that there is no such thing as a dumb question—and no flaming.

Male subscribers say Women's Wire has been a learning experience for them, too. Maxwell Hoffmann, a 41-year-old computer-company manager, says that many men think that only women are overly emotional. But men lose it, too. A typical on-line fight starts with two guys sending "emotionally charged flames going back and forth" through cyberspace (not on Women's Wire). Then it expands and "everybody starts flaming the guy. They scream at each other and they're not listening."

If only men weren't so *emotional*, so *irrational*, could we all get along on the net?

■ TOYS AND TOOLS

In one intriguing study by the Center for Children and Technology, a New York think tank, men and women in technical fields were asked to dream up machines of the future. Men typically imagined devices that could help them "conquer the universe," says Jan Hawkins, director of the center. She says women wanted machines that met people's needs, "the perfect mother."

Someday, gender-blind education and socialization may render those differences obsolete. But in the meantime, researchers say both visions are useful. If everyone approached technology the way women do now, "we wouldn't be pushing envelopes," says Cornelia Bruner, associate director of the center. "Most women, even those who are technologically sophisticated, think of machines as a means to an end." Men think of the machines as an extension of their own power, as a way to "transcend physical limitations." That may be why they are more likely to come up with great leaps in technology, researchers say. Without that vision, the computer and its attendant industry would not exist.

Men typically imagine devices that could help them conquer the universe. . . . Women want machines that meet people's needs, the perfect mother.

Ironically, gender differences could help women. "We're at a cultural turning point," says MIT's Turkle. "There's an opportunity to remake the culture around the machine." Practicality is now as valued as invention. If the computer industry wants to put machines in the hands of the masses, that means women—along with the great many men who have no interest in hot-rod computing. An ad campaign for Compaq's popular Presario line emphasizes the machine's utility. After kissing her child good night, the mother in the ad sits down at her Presario to work. As people start to view their machines as creative tools, someday women may be just as comfortable with computers as men are.

■ QUESTIONS FOR REREADING

1. Take a poll in class between the genders to see if what Kantrowitz says about upbringing (boys get computer games; girls get Barbie) is true to the experiences of most classmates. Do you think that men are in general genetically wired to excel at computers and women are not? Or do you think, like Kantrowitz, that encouragement and cultural roles have more to do with determining which sex does what?

2. What is the gender ratio in your computer writing class? In your other computer classes, if you are taking them, such as programming or engineering courses? Is the ratio in line with what Kantrowitz reports? (When I teach computers and writing or hypertext or even multimedia, the ratio is greatly in favor of females over males. But the gender populations in my classes may not be typical.)

■ WRITING ASSIGNMENT FOR REREADING

See if you can get some figures on male/female enrollment from departments at your college or university that teach computer courses (English, journalism, computer science, fine arts, and so on). If the figures are available, *write a report* for your classmates and perhaps your university. If they are not available, then put together a basic questionnaire that will help you determine the male/female ratio and interest and see if instructors will distribute it to their students. You might formulate some questions based on the readings in this chapter.

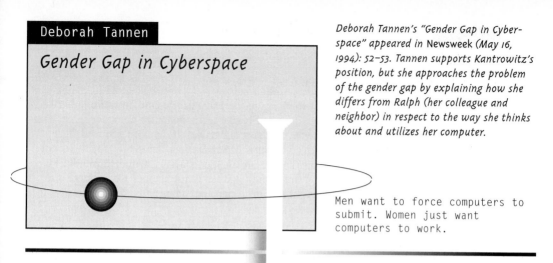

Deborah Tannen

Gender Gap in Cyberspace

Deborah Tannen's "Gender Gap in Cyberspace" appeared in Newsweek (May 16,
1994): 52–53. Tannen supports Kantrowitz's
position, but she approaches the problem
of the gender gap by explaining how she
differs from Ralph (her colleague and
neighbor) in respect to the way she thinks
about and utilizes her computer.

Men want to force computers to
submit. Women just want
computers to work.

was a computer pioneer, but I'm still something
of a novice. That paradox is telling.

I was the second person on my block to get a computer. The first was my
colleague Ralph. It was 1980. Ralph got a Radio Shack TRS-80; I got a used
Apple II+. He helped me get started and went on to become a maven, reading computer magazines, hungering for the new technology he read about,
and buying and mastering it as quickly as he could afford. I hung on to old
equipment far too long because I dislike giving up what I'm used to, fear
making the wrong decision about what to buy and resent the time it takes to
install and learn a new system.

My first Apple came with videogames: I gave them away. Playing games
on the computer didn't interest me. If I had free time I'd spend it talking on
the telephone with friends.

Ralph got hooked. His wife was often annoyed by the hours he spent at
his computer and the money he spent upgrading it. My marriage had no such
strains—until I discovered e-mail. Then I got hooked. E-mail draws me the
same way the phone does: it's a souped-up conversation.

E-mail deepened my friendship with Ralph. Though his office was next to
mine, we rarely had extended conversations because he is shy. Face to face he
mumbled so, I could barely tell he was speaking. But when we both got on e-
mail, I started receiving long, self-revealing messages: we poured our hearts
out to each other. A friend discovered that e-mail opened up that kind of
communication with her father. He would never talk much on the phone (as
her mother would), but they have become close since they both got on line.

Why, I wondered, would some men find it easier to open up on e-mail?
It's a combination of the technology (which they enjoy) and the obliqueness
of the written word, just as many men will reveal feelings in dribs and drabs
while riding in the car or doing something, which they'd never talk about sitting face to face. It's too intense, too bearing-down on them, and once you
start you have to keep going. With a computer in between, it's safer.

It was on e-mail, in fact, that I described to Ralph how boys in groups
often struggle to get the upper hand whereas girls tend to maintain an
appearance of cooperation. And he pointed out that this explained why boys
are more likely to be captivated by computers than girls are. Boys are

typically motivated by a social structure that says if you don't dominate you will be dominated. Computers, by their nature, balk: you type a perfectly appropriate command and it refuses to do what it should. Many boys and men are incited by this defiance: "I'm going to whip this into line and teach it who's boss! I'll get it to do what I say!" (and if they work hard enough, they always can). Girls and women are more likely to respond, "This thing won't cooperate. Get it away from me!"

Although no one wants to think of herself as "typical"—how much nicer to be sui generis—my relationship to my computer is—gulp—fairly typical for a woman. Most women (with plenty of exceptions) aren't excited by tinkering with the technology, grappling with the challenge of eliminating bugs or getting the biggest and best computer. These dynamics appeal to many men's interest in making sure they're on the top side of the inevitable who's-up-who's-down struggle that life is for them. E-mail appeals to my view of life as a contest for connections to others. When I see that I have 15 messages I feel loved.

I once posted a technical question on a computer network for linguists and was flooded with long dispositions, some pages long. I was staggered by the generosity and expertise, but wondered where these guys found the time—and why all the answers I got were from men.

Like coed classrooms and meetings, discussions on e-mail networks tend to be dominated by male voices, unless they're specifically women-only, like single-sex schools. On line, women don't have to worry about getting the floor (you just send a message when you feel like it), but, according to linguists Susan Herring and Laurel Sutton, who have studied this, they have the usual problems of having their messages ignored or attacked. The anonymity of public networks frees a small number of men to send long, vituperative, sarcastic messages that many other men either can tolerate or actually enjoy, but turn most women off.

The anonymity of networks leads to another sad part of the e-mail story: there are men who deluge women with questions about their appearance and invitations to sex. On college campuses, as soon as women students log on, they are bombarded by references to sex, like going to work and finding pornographic posters adorning the walls.

■ TAKING TIME

Most women want one thing from a computer—to work. This is significant counterevidence to the claim that men want to focus on information while women are interested in rapport. That claim I found was often true in casual conversation, in which there is no particular information to be conveyed. But with computers, it is often women who are more focused on information, because they don't respond to the challenge of getting equipment to submit.

Once I had learned the basics, my interest in computers waned. I use it to write books (though I never mastered having it do bibliographies or tables of contents) and write checks (but not balance my checkbook). Much as I'd like to use it to do more, I begrudge the time it would take to learn.

Ralph's computer expertise costs him a lot of time. Chivalry requires that he rescue novices in need, and he is called upon by damsel novices far more often than knaves. More men would rather study the instruction booklet than ask directions, as it were, from another person. "When I do help men," Ralph wrote (on e-mail, of course), "they want to be more involved. I once installed a hard drive for a guy, and he wanted to be there with me, wielding the screwdriver and giving his own advice where he could." Women, he finds, usually are not interested in what he's doing: they just want him to get the computer to the point where they can do what they want.

Which pretty much explains how I managed to be a pioneer without becoming an expert.

■ QUESTION FOR REREADING

How do you differ from others in class in your *attitude* toward a computer? Do you want, in the words of Tannen, to force your computer to submit, or just want it to work? If you have a computer at home, what do you have around it? Have you decorated it in some way? Do you have small decorative items on top of the monitor or stuck to the side or front? Do you have a "pet" name for your computer? Share this information with everyone in class.

■ WRITING ASSIGNMENT FOR REREADING

Depending on the answers to the first question above, write an essay reporting the various attitudes that were expressed. And, in response, express your attitude or the attitudes expressed by your classmates. If you did not have a particular attitude—other than "it's like my telephone!"—has your attitude changed after hearing others express their attitudes toward computers? Do you think that to have a special attitude is silly? Sentimental? Or just basically human? After all, a computer is nothing but a dumb machine, right?

David Nicholson

Cyber-Gender Stereotypes Just Don't Compute

David Nicholson's "Cyber-Gender Stereotypes Just Don't Compute" first appeared in The Washington Post Book World and was republished in The Dallas Morning News (March 13, 1996): B1. Nicholson supports both Kantrowitz and Tannen's views, but adds that for the most part it is a stereotype that women are not interested in computers. His interviews with women suggest that women not only have different attitudes from men but that they also are just as involved with using computers.

Computing has always seemed a guy thing to me. I've always seen it as a heavily male province, like sports cars, baseball and expensive stereo equipment, an activity women have little interest in or aptitude for.

Lately, however, I've exchanged e-mail with several women who've challenged my sexist assumptions. To their great credit, they've been remarkably patient, perhaps because it wasn't the first time they'd confronted those kinds of assumptions.

Sara Henry, a freelance writer and editor in Herndon, Virginia, tells of going shopping for a new computer a few years ago. In one store, the salesman ignored her and began to speak to her male companion—who knew far less than she did about computers—assuming he was the one interested in buying.

"I just kind of thought, 'You idiot,'" Ms. Henry says. "I felt really angry. When I immediately butted in and came out with my questions, the salesman couldn't even answer me. He didn't know what I was talking about."

■ MARKETING AND MEDIA BIAS

Bianca Floyd, an editorial assistant at the *Chronicle of Higher Education,* says computing is perceived as a male activity because "it has been marketed that way," with ads primarily directed toward male users.

Moreover, she blames the popular media for reinforcing the stereotype that women aren't interested in computers. The media, she says, perpetuate the skewed view of "computer whizzes as white, male, geeks and nerds."

Nothing could be further from the truth, as far as she's concerned. Each of the ten women in her family owns at least one computer, and Ms. Floyd, who is black, owns three—two DOS/Windows machines and a Macintosh.

A self-described "heavy user," Ms. Floyd first learned about computers from a supervisor at an earlier job who built her a PC, encouraged her to use it, and showed her how to troubleshoot problems. (Ms. Henry also had a mentor—a twelve-year-old boy who gave her tips on how to improve her computer's performance.)

But what proved even more important for these two women than having somebody to show them the ropes was their willingness to experiment. They'd ask, "What if?" and see if they could, or "How do I do that? and then try.

Reading the computing stories they and others sent me and listening to their tales, I was filled with more than a little chagrin and envy. They're doing things I can't, or have been reluctant to try. So much for stereotypes.

■ CALL IT HARD DRIVE ENVY

Yet I still think women are less likely to be fascinated by new technologies in the same way men are. When I talk about computers with other men, we chat about them the way we do—or used to—about cars. We boast about the speed of our processors and the size of our hard drives. We derive a certain satisfaction from having the newest, best things on our desks, even if we're using it only to process words.

On the other hand, I think most women are less easily seduced by mega-hertz (the units used to measure processor speed) and megabytes (the units used to measure a computer's storage space).

Instead, like Ms. Henry, they're more interested in whether the computer works well enough to do what they want it to do. "I want to have a good system, but I want to use it, not admire it," she says. "The fun for me is using it."

But I don't think it's accurate to say that women are more technophobic, or even less receptive to technology. In fact, I'm no longer sure that gender is the all-important marker for someone's interest in PCs or Macs that I once thought it was.

Ms. Henry says her experience just might show that women may be more adaptable then men.

"Among the people I've worked with, I've noticed about equal numbers of men and women who were unable or unwilling to use computers easily," she says. "The two people I have worked with who were completely unwilling to view the computer as much more than a typewriter—and literally closed off their minds to learning more—were both male. . . . The women I've worked with, in contrast, seem willing to learn when I explained things to them or showed them an easier way to do things."

And maybe that's the point. In the end, as Ms. Henry said, what really matters is curiosity, a willingness to explore and, not least of all, to make mistakes. If we all had that, we just might find ourselves changing our minds—about computers, and about stereotypes.

■ QUESTION FOR REREADING

When interviewed by Nicholson, Bianca Floyd says that working with computers only appears to be a male activity because they are "marketed that way." Have you noticed that advertisements for computers are aimed exclusively or slanted toward men? If aimed toward women, are the advertisements demeaning? Look through magazines that are not aimed specifically at either men or women, but for a general audience, and search for ads for computers so as to test this proposition that advertising creates the stereotype. Then look in magazines that are published exclusively for men or for women and search for ads. What do you find?

■ WRITING ASSIGNMENTS FOR REREADING

1. If you find some interesting advertisements when investigating the question above, put together a Web site, with a series of links, showing your results. Make this a collaborative project that is approved and facilitated with and by your instructor. Try to get permission from the copyright owner (which will most likely be the company that is advertising) to scan graphic files and place them on your Web site. Make sure that the files are small enough to load quickly. (Try to convert them to GIF files and compress them as much as you can.) If you are happy with the project, drop me a note at VVitanza@aol.com.

2. Develop and design collaboratively an advertisement for computers that would express no sexist attitude toward males or females. Include a balance of words and images.

Susan Herring

Bringing Familiar Baggage to the New Frontier: Gender Differences in Computer-Mediated Communication

Susan Herring's "Bringing Familiar Baggage to the New Frontier: Gender Differences in Computer-Mediated Communication" was originally published on the Web at a number of sites; it is first published in print in CyberReader. Herring reports on her empirical study of several discussion lists, giving representative examples and statistics to back up her claim—very similar to that of Kantrowitz and Tannen—that males dominate the Net.

■ INTRODUCTION

lthough research on computer-mediated communication (CMC) dates back to the early days of computer network technology in the 1970s, researchers have only recently begun to take the gender of users into account.[1] This is perhaps not surprising considering that men have traditionally dominated the technology and have comprised the majority of users of computer networks since their inception, but the result is that most of what has been written about CMC incorporates a very one-sided perspective. However, recent research has been uncovering some eye-opening differences in the ways men and women interact "on-line," and it is these differences that I will address here.

My basic claim has two parts: first, that women and men have recognizably different styles in posting electronic messages to the Internet, contrary to claims that CMC neutralizes distinctions of gender, and second, that women and men have different communication ethics—that is, they value different kinds of on-line interactions as appropriate and desirable. I illustrate these differences—and some of the problems that arise because of them—with specific reference to the phenomenon of "flaming."

■ BACKGROUND

Since 1991 I've been lurking (or what I prefer to call "carrying out ethnographic observation") on various computer-mediated discussion lists, downloading electronic conversations and analyzing the communicative behaviors of participants. I became interested in gender shortly after subscribing to my first discussion list, LINGUIST-L, an academic forum for professional linguists. Within the first month after I began receiving messages, a conflict arose on the list (what I would later learn to call a "flame war") in which the two major theoretical camps within the field became polarized around an issue of central interest. My curiosity was piqued by the fact that very few women were contributing to this important professional event; they seemed to be sitting on the sidelines while men were airing their opinions and getting all the attention. In an attempt to understand the women's silence, I made up an anonymous survey which I sent to LINGUIST-L asking subscribers what they thought of the discussion and, if they hadn't contributed, why not.

■ INITIAL OBSERVATIONS

The number one reason given by both men and women for not contributing to the LINGUIST discussion was "intimidation"—as one respondent commented, participants were "ripping each other's lungs out." Interestingly, however, men and women responded differently to feeling intimidated. Men seemed to accept such behavior as a normal feature of academic life, making comments to the effect that "Actually, the barbs and arrows were entertaining, because of course they weren't aimed at me." In contrast, many women responded with profound aversion. As one woman put it: "That is precisely the kind of human interaction I committedly avoid. . . . I am dismayed that human beings treat each other this way. It makes the world a dangerous place to be. I dislike such people and I want to give them WIDE berth."

When I analyzed the messages in the thread itself, another gender difference emerged, this time relating to the linguistic structure and rhetoric of the messages. A daunting 68 percent of the messages posted by men made use of an adversarial style in which the poster distanced himself from, criticized, and/or ridiculed other participants, often while promoting his own importance. The few women who participated in the discussion, in contrast, displayed features of attenuation—hedging, apologizing, asking questions rather than making assertions—and a personal orientation, revealing thoughts and feelings and interacting with and supporting others.

One respondent commented, participants were "ripping each other's lungs out."

It wasn't long before I was noticing a similar pattern in other discussions and on other lists. Wherever I went on mixed-sex lists, men seemed to be doing most of the talking and attracting most of the attention to themselves, although not all lists were as adversarial as LINGUIST. I started to hear stories about and witness men taking over and dominating discussions even of women-centered topics on women-centered lists.[2] In contrast, on the few occasions when I observed women attempting to gain an equal hearing on male-dominated lists, they were ignored, trivialized, or criticized by men for their tone or the inappropriateness of their topic.[3] It wasn't until I started looking at lists devoted to women's issues, and to traditionally "feminized" disciplines such as women's studies, teaching English as a second language, and librarianship, that I found women holding forth in an amount consistent with their numerical presence on the list. I also found different interactional norms: little or no flaming, and cooperative, polite exchanges.

■ DIFFERENT STYLES

As a result of these findings, I propose that women and men have different characteristic on-line styles. By characteristic styles, I do not mean that all or even the majority of users of each sex exhibit the behaviors of each style, but rather that the styles are recognizably—even stereotypically—gendered. The male style is characterized by adversariality: putdowns, strong, often contentious assertions, lengthy and/or frequent postings, self-promotion, and sarcasm. Below are two examples, one from an academic list (LINGUIST) and the other from a nonacademic list (POLITICS).[4]

1. [Jean Linguiste's] proposals towards a more transparent
   morphology in French are exactly what he calls them: a
   farce. Nobody could ever take them seriously—unless we
   want to look as well at pairs such as *pe're-me're*, *coq-
   poule* and defigure the French language in the process.

[strong assertions ("exactly," "nobody"), putdowns ("JL's proposals are a farce"; implied: "JL wants to defigure the French language")]

The male style is characterized by adversariality: putdowns, strong, often contentious assertions, lengthy and/or frequent postings, self-promotion, and sarcasm.

2. >yes, they did . . . . This is why we must be
   allowed to remain armed . . .
     >who is going to help us if our government
   becomes a tyranny?
   >no one will.

oh yes we *must* remain armed. anyone see day one
last night abt charlestown where everyone/s so
scared of informing on murderers the cops have
given up? where the reply to any offense is a
public killing? knowing you/re not gonna be
caught cause everyone/s to afraid to be a witness?

yeah, right, twerp.

>—[RON] "THE WISE"—

what a joke.

[sarcasm, name calling, personal insults]

The second example would be characterized as a "flame" by most readers because of its personally offensive nature.

Less exclusively male-gendered but still characteristic of male postings is an authoritative, self-confident stance whereby men are more likely than women to represent themselves as experts, e.g., in answering queries for information. The following example is from NOTIS-L.

3. The NUGM Planning meeting was cancelled before all of this
   came up. It has nothing to do with it. The plans were simply proceeding along so well that there was no need to
   hold the meeting. That is my understanding from talking to
   NOTIS staff just last week.

[authoritative tone, strong assertions ("nothing," "simply," "just")]

The female-gendered style, in contrast, has two aspects which typically co-
occur: supportiveness and attenuation. "Supportiveness" is characterized by
expressions of appreciation, thanking, and community-building activities that
make other participants feel accepted and welcome. "Attenuation" includes
hedging and expressing doubt, apologizing, asking questions, and contributing ideas in the form of suggestions. The following examples from a nonacademic list (WOMEN) and an academic list (TESL-L) illustrate each aspect:

4. >[AILEEN],

>

>I just wanted to let you know that I have really enjoyed all

>your posts about Women's herstory. They have been

>extremely informative and I've learned alot about the

>women's movement. Thank you!

>

>—[ERIKA]

DITTO!!!! They are wonderful!

Did anyone else catch the first part of a Century of Women? I
really enjoyed it. Of course, I didn't agree with everything
they said. . . . but it was really informative.

[ROBERTA]~~~~~~~~~~~~~~~~~~~~~~~~~~~~

[appreciates, thanks, agrees, appeals to group]

5. [. . .] I hope this makes sense. This is kind of what I
   had in mind when I realized I couldn't give a real definitive answer. Of course, maybe I'm just getting into the
   nuances of the language when it would be easier to just
   give the simple answer. Any response?

[hedges, expresses doubt, appeals to group]

The female style takes into consideration what the sociologist Erving
Goffman called the "face" wants of the addressee—specifically, the desire of

the addressee to feel ratified and liked (e.g., by expressions of appreciation)
and her desire not to be imposed upon (e.g., by absolute assertions that don't
allow for alternative views). The male style, in contrast, confronts and threatens the addressee's "face" in the process of engaging him in agonistic debate.

Although these styles represent in some sense the extremes of gendered
behavior, they have symbolic significance above and beyond their frequency
of use. For example, other users regularly infer the gender of message posters
on the basis of features of these styles, especially when the self-identified gender of a poster is open to question. Consider the following cases, the first
involving a male posting as a female, the second a suspected female posting
as a male:

i. A male subscriber on SWIP-L (Society for Women in Philosophy list)
    posted a message disagreeing with the general consensus that discourse on
    SWIP-L should be nonagonistic, commenting, "There's nothing like a
    healthy denunciation by one's colleagues every once in a while to get
    one's blood flowing, and spur one to greater subtlety and exactness of
    thought." He signed his message with a female pseudonym, however, caus-
    ing another (female) subscriber to comment later, "I must confess to look-
    ing for the name of the male who wrote the posting that [Suzi] sent
    originally and was surprised to find a female name at the end of it." The
    female subscriber had (accurately) inferred that anyone actively advocating
    "denunciation by one's colleagues" was probably male.

ii. At a time when one male subscriber had been posting frequent messages to
    the WOMEN list, another subscriber professing to be a man posted a mes-
    sage inquiring what the list's policy was toward men participating on the
    list, admitting, "I sometimes feel guilty for taking up bandwidth." The
    message, in addition to showing consideration for the concerns of others
    on the list, was very attenuated in style and explicitly appreciative of the
    list: "I really enjoy this list (actually, it's the best one I'm on)." This
    prompted another (female) subscriber to respond, "Now that you've posed
    the question . . . how's one to know you're not a woman posing this ques-
    tion as a man?" Her suspicion indicates that on some level she recognized
    that anyone posting a message expressing appreciation and consideration
    for the desires of others was likely to be female.

The existence of gendered styles has important implications, needless to
say, for popular claims that CMC is anonymous, "gender blind," and hence
inherently democratic. If our on-line communicative style reveals our gender,
then gender differences, along with their social consequences, are likely to
persist on computer-mediated networks.[5]

Entire lists can be gendered in their style as well. It is tacitly expected
that members of the nondominant gender will adapt their posting style in
the direction of the style of the dominant gender. Thus men on women's
special interest lists tend to attenuate their assertions and shorten their messages, and women, especially on male-dominated lists such as LINGUIST

and PAGLIA-L, can be contentious and adversarial. Arguably, they must adapt in order to participate appropriately in keeping with the norms of the local list culture. Most members of the nondominant gender on any given list, however, end up style mixing, that is, taking on some attributes of the dominant style while preserving features of their native style—for example, with men often preserving a critical stance and women a supportive one at the macro-message level. This suggests that gendered communication styles are deeply rooted—not surprising, since they are learned early in life—and that some features are more resistant to conscious reflection and modification than others.

■ DIFFERENT COMMUNICATION ETHICS

The second part of this essay concerns the value systems that underlie and are used to rationalize communicative behavior on the net. In particular, I focus on the phenomenon of flaming, which has been variously defined as "the expression of strong negative emotion," use of "derogatory, obscene, or inappropriate language," and "personal insults." A popular explanation advanced by CMC researchers[6] is that flaming is a by-product of the medium itself—the decontextualized and anonymous nature of CMC leads to "disinhibition" in users and a tendency to forget that there is an actual human being at the receiving end of one's emotional outbursts. However, until recently CMC research has largely overlooked gender as a possible influence on behavior, and the simple fact of the matter is that it is virtually only men who flame. If the medium makes men more likely to flame, it should have a similar effect on women, yet if anything the opposite appears to be the case. An adequate explanation of flaming must therefore take gender into account.

Why do men flame? The explanation, I suggest, is that women and men have different communication ethics, and flaming is compatible with male ethical ideals. I stumbled upon this realization recently as a result of a survey I conducted on politeness on the Internet. I originally hypothesized that the differences in the extremes of male and female behavior online—in particular, the tendency for women to be considerate of the "face" needs of others while men threaten others' "face"—could be explained if it turned out that women and men have different notions of what constitutes appropriate behavior. In other words, as a woman I might think adversarial behavior is rude, but men who behave adversarially might think otherwise. Conversely, men might be put off by the supportive and attenuated behaviors of women.

In the survey, I asked subscribers from eight Internet discussion lists to rank their like or dislike for 30 different on-line behaviors, including "flaming," "expressing thanks and appreciation," and "overly tentative messages," on a scale of 1 (like) to 5 (dislike). The survey also asked several open-ended questions, including most importantly: "What behaviors bother you most on the net?"

My initial hypothesis turned out to be both correct and incorrect. It was incorrect in that I found no support whatsoever for the idea that men's and women's value systems are somehow reversed. Both men and women said they liked expressions of appreciation (avg. score of 2), were neutral about tentative messages (avg. about 3), and disliked flaming (although women expressed a stronger dislike than men, giving it a score of 4.3 as compared with only 3.9 for men). This makes male flaming behavior all the more puzzling. Should we conclude, then, that men who flame are deliberately trying to be rude?

The answers to the open-ended questions suggest a different explanation. These answers reveal a gender contrast in values that involves politeness but cannot be described in terms of politeness alone. It seems women place a high value on consideration for the wants and needs of others, as expressed in the following comment by a female net user:

If we take responsibility for developing our own sensitivities to others and controlling our actions to minimize damage—we will each be doing [good deeds] for the whole world constantly.

Men, in contrast, assign greater value to freedom from censorship (many advocate absolute free speech), forthright and open expression, and agonistic debate as a means to advance the pursuit of knowledge. Historically, the value on absolute freedom of speech reflects the civil libertarian leanings of the computing professionals who originally designed the net and have con-tributed much of the utopian discourse surrounding it; the value on agonistic debate is rooted in the Western (male) philosophical tradition.

These ideals are stirringly evoked in the following quote from R. Hauben (1993) praising the virtues of the Usenet system, on which 95 percent of the contributors are estimated to be male:

The achievement of Usenet News demonstrates the importance of facilitating the develop-ment of uncensored speech and communication—there is debate and discussion—one person influences another—people build on each other's strengths and interests, differ-ences, etc.

One might think that uncensored speech if abused could cause problems, but M. Hauben (1993) explains that there is a democratic way of handling this eventuality:

When people feel someone is abusing the nature of Usenet News, they let the offender know through e-mail. In this manner . . . people fight to keep it a resource that is helpful to society as a whole.

In daily life on the Internet, however, the ideal of "people fight[ing] to keep [the net] a resource that is helpful to society as a whole" often translates into violent action. Consider, for example, the response of a male survey respondent to the question: "What behaviors bother you most on the net?" (typos are in the original):

As much as I am irritated by [incompetent posters], I don't want imposed rules. I would prefer to "out" such a person and let some public minded citizen fire bomb his house to imposing rules on the net. Letter bombing a annoying individual's feed is usually prefer-able to building a formal heirarchy of net cops.

Another net vigilante responds graphically as follows:

I'd have to say commercial shit. Whenever someone advertises some damn get-rich-quick scheme and plasters it all over the net by crossposting it to every newsgroup, I reach for my "gatling gun mailer crasher" and fire away at the source address.

These responses not only evoke an ideal of freedom from external author-ity, they provide an explicit justification for flaming—as a form of self-appointed regulation of the social order, a rough and ready form of justice on the virtual frontier. Thus a framework of values is constructed within which flaming and other aggressive behaviors can be interpreted in a favorable (even prosocial) light. This is not to say that all or even most men who flame have the good of net society at heart, but rather that the behavior is in princi-ple justifiable for men (and hence tolerable) in ways that it is not for most women.

■ NETIQUETTE

Further evidence that flaming is tolerated and justified within a system of male values comes from the content of written rules of network etiquette, or "netiquette," such as are available on many public FTP sites and in introduc-tory messages to new members of some discussion lists. I analyzed the con-tent of netiquette rules from six lists, along with those found in the guidelines for Usenet and in the print publication *Towards an Ethics and Etiquette for Elec-tronic Mail,* by Norman Shapiro and Robert Anderson (1985). What do neti-quette rules have to say about flaming?

The answer is: remarkably little, given that it is one of the most visible and frequently complained about "negatives" cited about the Internet. One might even say there is a striking *lack* of proscription against flaming, except on a few women-owned and women-oriented lists. And in the rare instances where flaming is mentioned, it is implicitly authorized. Thus the guidelines for new subscribers to the POLITICS list prohibit "flames of a personal nature," and Shapiro and Anderson advise, "Do not insult or criticize third parties without giving them a chance to respond." While on the surface appearing to oppose flaming, these statements in fact implicitly authorize "flames other than of a personal nature" (for example, of someone's ideas or values) and "insulting or criticizing third parties" (provided you give them a chance to respond!). Nor-mative statements such as these are compatible with male values and male adversarial style; the intimidating rhetoric on LINGUIST and many other lists is not a violation of net etiquette according to these rules.[7] Yet these are behaviors that female survey respondents say intimidate them and drive them away from lists and newsgroups. Can the Internet community afford to toler-ate behaviors that intimidate and silence women? This is a question that urgently needs to be raised and discussed netwide.

■ CONCLUSIONS

To sum up, I have argued that women and men constitute different discourse communities in cyberspace—different cultures, if you will—with differing communicative norms and practices. However, these cultures are not "separate but equal," as recent popular writing on gender differences in communication has claimed. Rather, the norms and practices of masculine net culture, codified in netiquette rules, conflict with those of the female culture in ways that render cyberspace—or at least many "neighborhoods" in cyberspace—inhospitable to women. The result is an imbalance whereby men control a disproportionate share of the communication that takes place via computer networks.

This imbalance must be redressed if computer-mediated communication is ever to live up to its much-touted democratic potential. Fortunately, there are ways in which women can promote their concerns and influence the discourse of the net;[8] I will mention three here. First and foremost is to participate, for example in women-centered lists. Such lists provide supportive fora for women on line and are frequently models of cooperative discourse whose norms can spread if subscribers participate in other lists as well. But separatism has its disadvantages, among them the risk of ghettoization. Women must not let themselves be driven by flame throwers away from mainstream, mixed-sex fora, but rather should also actively seek to gain influence there, individually and collectively, especially in fora where metadiscourse about the net itself takes place.

The second way to promote women's interests netwide is to educate on-line communities about the rhetorical strategies used in intimidating others, and to call people on their behavior and its consequences when they use such strategies.[9] This is already happening on some women-centered lists such as WMST-L and SWIP-L—aware of the tendency for a single man or group of men to dominate discussions, female subscribers call attention to this behavior as soon as they realize it is happening; interestingly, it is happening less and less often on these lists. Group awareness is a powerful force for change, and it can be raised in mixed-sex fora as well.

Finally, women need to contribute in any way they can to the process that leads to the encoding of netiquette rules. They need to instigate and participate persuasively in discussions about what constitutes appropriate and inappropriate behavior on line—seeking to define in concrete terms what constitutes "flaming," for instance, since women and men are likely to have different ideas about this. They must be alert to opportunities (or make their own opportunities) to write out guidelines for suggested list protocol (or modifications to list protocol if guidelines already exist) and post them for discussion. No greater power exists than the power to define values, and the structure of the Internet—especially now, while it is still evolving and seeking its ultimate definition—provides a unique opportunity for individual users to influence the normative process.

Indeed, it may be vital that we do so if women's on-line communication styles are to be valued along with those of men, and if we are to ensure women the right to settle on the virtual frontier on their own—rather than on male-defined—terms.

■ N O T E S

This essay was originally delivered as a speech to the American Library Association as part of a panel entitled "Making the Net*Work*: Is there a Z39.50 in gender communication?", Miami, June 27, 1994. Copyright rests with the author.

1. A notable exception to this generalization is the work of Sherry Turkle in the 1980s on how women and men relate to computers.

2. For an extreme example of this phenomenon that took place on the soc.feminism Usenet newsgroup, see Sutton (1994).

3. Herring, Johnson, and DiBenedetto (1992, in press).

4. All names mentioned in the messages are pseudonyms.

5. This problem is discussed in Herring (1993a).

6. For example, Kiesler et al. (1984), Kim and Raja (1990), and Shapiro and Anderson (1985).

7. The discussion of politeness and communication ethics here is an abbreviated version of that presented in Herring (In press a, In press b).

8. For other practical suggestions on how to promote gender equality in networking, see Kramarae and Taylor (1993).

9. Cases where this was done, both successfully and unsuccessfully, are described in Herring, Johnson, and DiBenedetto (In press).

■ R E F E R E N C E S

Hauben, Michael. 1993. "The social forces behind the development of Usenet News." Electronic document. (FTP weber.ucsd.edu, directory /pub/usenet.hist)

Hauben, Ronda. 1993. "The evolution of Usenet News: The poor man's ARPANET." Electronic document. (FTP weber.ucsd.edu, directory /pub/usenet.hist)

Herring, Susan. 1992. "Gender and participation in computer-mediated linguistic discourse." Washington, DC: ERIC Clearinghouse on Languages and Linguistics, document no. ED345552.

Herring, Susan. 1993a. "Gender and democracy in computer-mediated communication." *Electronic Journal of Communication* 3(2), special issue on

Computer-Mediated Communication, T. Benson, ed. Reprinted in R. Kling (ed.), *Computerization and Controversy*, 2nd ed. New York: Academic (In press).

Herring, Susan. 1993b. "Men's language: A study of the discourse of the Linguist list." In A. Crochetihre, J. -C. Boulanger, and C. Ouellon (eds.), *Les Langues Menacies: Actes du XVe Congres International des Linguistes*, Vol. 3. Quebec: Les Presses de l'Université Laval, 347–350.

Herring, Susan. In press a. "Politeness in computer culture: Why women thank and men flame." In M. Bucholtz, A. Liang and L. Sutton (eds.), *Communicating In, Through, and Across Cultures: Proceedings of the Third Berkeley Women and Language Conference*. Berkeley Women and Language Group.

Herring, Susan. In press b. "Posting in a different voice: Gender and ethics in computer-mediated communication." In C. Ess (ed.), *Philosophical Perspectives on Computer-Mediated Communication*. Albany: SUNY Press.

Herring, Susan. In press c. "Two variants of an electronic message schema." In S. Herring (ed.), *Computer-Mediated Communication: Linguistic, social, and cross-cultural perspectives*. Amsterdam/Philadelphia: John Benjamins.

Herring, Susan, Deborah Johnson, and Tamra DiBenedetto. 1992. "Participation in electronic discourse in a 'feminist' field." In M. Bucholtz, K. Hall, and B. Moonwomon, eds., *Locating Power: Proceedings of the Second Berkeley Women and Language Conference*. Berkeley Women and Language Group.

Herring, Susan, Deborah Johnson, and Tamra DiBenedetto. In press d. " 'This discussion is going too far!' Male resistance to female participation on the Internet." In M. Bucholtz and K. Hall, eds., *Gender Articulated: Language and the Socially-Constructed Self*. New York: Routledge.

Kiesler, Sara, Jane Seigel, and Timothy W. McGuire. 1984. "Social psychological aspects of computer-mediated communication." *American Psychologist*, 39, 1123–1134.

Kim, Min-Sun and Narayan S. Raja. 1990. "Verbal aggression and self-disclosure on computer bulletin boards." ERIC document (ED334620).

Kramarae, Cheris and H. Jeanie Taylor. 1993. "Women and men on electronic networks: A conversation or a monologue?" In Taylor, Kramarae and Ebben, eds., *Women, Information Technology and Scholarship*, 52–61. Urbana, IL: Center for Advanced Study.

Rheingold, Howard. 1993. *The Virtual Community: Homesteading on the Electronic Frontier*. Reading, MA: Addison-Wesley.

Seabrook, John. 1994. "My first flame." *The New Yorker*, June 6, 1994, 70–79.

Shapiro, Norman Z. and Robert H. Anderson. 1985. *Toward an Ethics and Etiquette for Electronic Mail*. The Rand Corporation.

Sutton, Laurel. 1994. "Using USENET: Gender, power, and silencing in electronic discourse." *Proceedings of the 20th Annual Meeting of the Berkeley Linguistics Society* (BLS-20). Berkeley: Berkeley Linguistics Society, Inc.

Turkle, Sherry. 1984. *The Second Self: Computers and the Human Spirit.* London: Granada.

■ QUESTIONS FOR REREADING

Here are Susan Herring's questions:

1. Are the gender patterns I describe consistent with your own experiences of computer-mediated communication? How or how not? Recall that the groups I studied were asynchronous (e-mail based) and mostly academic in focus. From your own observations of on-line communication, are there similar gender differences in other kinds of CMC—for example, in real-time chat, groups whose purpose is mainly nonserious or social, private e-mail?

2. I've noticed when I present the results of this research that women tend to agree with my observations and conclusions while men are more likely to take issue with me. (This isn't true of all women and all men, of course, but it is a definite pattern.) What might the reasons for this be, and do they support or undermine the basic claims of this essay?

3. Some people attempt to argue against the gender patterns I describe on the grounds that they know a woman (or women) who dominates on-line discussions, posts frequent messages, has an aggressive style, and is not easily intimidated—in short, who doesn't fit the pattern. Is the existence of such exceptions sufficient to invalidate the generalization of gender differences, in your opinion? Why or why not?

■ WRITING ASSIGNMENT FOR REREADING

If you are a male—or even if you are a female—and you are inclined to attack someone on-line who has attacked you or said something that you feel is "stupid," then instead of attacking that person, simply open your word-processing program or *notepad* or *simpletext* and write your attack. When finished, *the urge to attack should be gone.* Do this several times when you are on-line and feel the urge to attack, but *don't ever send the message.* The object of this exercise is to get the hostility that you might feel out of your mind, through your arms into your typing fingers and onto your monitor, and finally to delete it. Some people who are veterans at sending e-mail will actually write the message on-line and then cancel it. I would advise you, however, if you are not that experienced, to write it off-line. After all, you could make a mistake and actually send the message. Then what? After a while, perhaps you will no longer have to write attacks and delete them, but just let the urge that fosters them simply be *no longer a part of your life.*

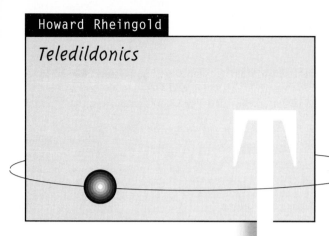

Howard Rheingold

Teledildonics

Howard Rheingold's "Teledildonics" is a selection from his book Virtual Reality (New York: Simon and Schuster, 1991):346–53. Rheingold is not for the banning of sex but for its legitimization in terms of "Teledildonics" (which is an extension of Ted Nelson's word "dildonics"). In discussing various aspects of the technology, Rheingold writes: "The tool that I am suggesting is much more than a fancy vibrator, but I suggest we keep the archaic name. A more sober formal description of the technology would be 'interactive tactile telepresence.' " (What Rheingold is describing in the article is total immersion into VR.)

he first fully functional teledildonics system will be a communication device, not a sex machine. You probably will *not* use erotic telepresence technology in order to have sexual experiences with machines. Thirty years from now, when portable telediddlers become ubiquitous, most people will use them to have sexual experiences with other *people,* at a distance, in combinations and configurations undreamed of by precybernetic voluptuaries. Through a marriage of virtual reality technology and telecommunication networks, you will be able to reach out and touch someone—or an entire population—in ways humans have never before experienced. Or so the scenario goes.

The word "dildonics" was coined in 1974 by that zany computer visionary Theodore Nelson (inventor of hypertext and designer of the world's oldest unfinished software project, appropriately named "Xanadu"™), to describe a machine (patent #3,875,932) invented by a San Francisco hardware hacker by the name of How Wachspress, a device capable of converting sound into tactile sensations. The erotogenic effect depends upon where you, the consumer, decide to interface your anatomy with the tactile stimulator. VR raises the possibility of a far more sophisticated technology.

The word "dildonics" was coined in 1974 by that zany computer visionary Theodor Nelson.

Picture yourself a couple of decades hence, dressing for a hot night in the virtual village. Before you climb into a suitably padded chamber and put on your 3D glasses, you slip into a lightweight (eventually, one would hope, diaphanous) bodysuit, something like a body stocking, but with the kind of intimate snugness of a condom. Embedded in the inner surface of the suit, using a technology that does not yet exist, is an array of intelligent sensor-effectors—a mesh of tiny tactile detectors coupled to vibrators of varying degrees of hardness, hundreds of them per square inch, that can receive and transmit a realistic sense of tactile presence, the way the visual and audio displays transmit a realistic sense of visual and auditory presence.

You can reach out your virtual hand, pick up a virtual block, and by running your fingers over the object, feel the surfaces and edges, by means of the effectors that exert counterforces against your skin. The counterforces correspond to the kinds of forces you would encounter when handling a nonvirtual object of the specified shape, weight, and texture. You can run your cheek over (virtual) satin, and feel the difference when you encounter (virtual) flesh. Or you can gently squeeze something soft and pliable and feel it stiffen under your touch.

Now, imagine plugging your whole sound-sight-touch telepresence system into the telephone network. You see a lifelike but totally artificial visual representation of your own body and of your partner's. Depending on what numbers you dial and which passwords you know and what you are willing to pay (or trade or do), you can find one partner, a dozen, a thousand, in various cyberspaces that are no farther than a telephone number. Your partner(s) can move independently in the cyberspace, and your representations are able to touch each other, even though your physical bodies might be continents apart. You will whisper in your partner's ear, feel your partner's breath on your neck. You run your hand over your partner's clavicle, and 6000 miles away, an array of effectors are triggered, in just the right sequence, at just the right frequency, to convey the touch exactly the way you wish it to be conveyed. If you don't like the way the encounter is going, or someone requires your presence in physical reality, you can turn it all off by flicking a switch and taking off your virtual birthday suit.

Now, imagine plugging your whole sound-sight-touch telepresence system into the telephone network.

Before plunging into questions about whether it is ethical to build or moral to use teledildonic technology, it pays to ask how far today's technology seems to be from achieving such capabilities, because the answer appears to be: very far. Fiberoptic networks will be required to handle the very high bandwidth that tactile telepresence requires, perhaps including the kind of hybrid circuit and packet-switched technology NTT is installing in Japan as "broadband ISDN"; fortuitously, it looks like the world is going to be webbed with fiberoptic bundles for other reasons. Carrying information back and forth across town, continent, or hemisphere in large amounts, fairly quickly, will not be a problem. Until the speed of light barrier is broken, the physical size of the planet precludes a truly instantaneous on-line shared cyberspace; the larger your cyberspace is distributed geographically, the larger your system lag time is likely to be. The computation load generated by such a system is definitely a problem, too, a show-stopper, in fact, in terms of today's computing capabilities. The most serious technical obstacles that make teledildonics an early-to-mid-twenty-first-century technology rather than next year's fad lie in the extremely powerful computers needed to perform the enormous number of added calculations required to monitor and control hundreds of thousands of sensors and effectors. Every nook and protuberance, every plane and valley and knob of your body's surface, will require its own processor.

Transducers are a real problem, as well. It will take decades to develop the mesh of tiny, high-speed, safe but powerful tactile effectors: today's vibrators are in the ENIAC era. The engineering problems in building the transducers, the parts of the system that communicate in a form that people can squeeze and scratch, stroke and probe, may be formidable, but they are already the subject of focused effort on three continents. Hennequin with his pneumatics and Johnson with his shape memory alloy are not the only ones. The researchers who were showing me their demonstrations at ATR in Japan were very interested in the transmission of touch. Researchers in Italy may have just made a big step toward the kind of intimate cybergarment described above. A very crude prototype of the lightweight sensor-effector mesh has already been developed, according to these passages quoted from a 1990 article by Shawna Vogel, "Smart Skin":

> One of the most sophisticated approaches to this goal is being developed at the University of Pisa by Italian engineer Danilo De Rossi, who has closely modeled an artificial skin on the inner and outer layers of human skin: the dermis and epidermis. His flexible, multilayered sheathing even has the same thickness as human skin—roughly that of a dime.
> De Rossi's artificial dermis is made of a water-swollen conducting gel sandwiched between two layers of electrodes that monitor the flow of electricity through the squishy middle. Like the all-natural human version, this dermis senses the overall pressure being exerted on an object. As pressure deforms the gel, the voltage between the electrodes changes; the harder the object being pressed, the greater the information. By keeping tabs on how the voltage is changing, a skin-clad robot could thus distinguish between a rubber ball and a rock.
> For resolving the finer details of surface structure, De Rossi has created an epidermal layer of sensor-studded sheets of plastic placed between thin sheets of rubber. The sensors are pinhead-size disks made of piezoelectric substances, which emit an electric charge when subjected to pressure. These disks can sense texture as fine as the bumps on a braille manuscript.

These scientific frontiers provide the jumping-off point for the VR sex fantasy: Put together a highly refined version of "smart skin" with enough computing power, cleverly designed software, some kind of effector system, and a high-speed telecommunication network, and you have a teledildonics system. The tool I am suggesting is much more than a fancy vibrator, but I suggest we keep the archaic name. A more sober formal description of the technology would be "interactive tactile telepresence."

Teledildonics seems to be a thought experiment that got out of control. The quantum physicists had used this technique of imagining a certain set of conditions as a kind of mental scenario, a *gedankenexperiment,* a "thought experiment." The idea is to induce people to put themselves into an appropriate mindset for seeing the implications of a new discovery. I made the mistake of performing my gedankenexperiment on my local node of the Worldnet.

I wrote a short riff on teledildonics, not too different in content from this chapter, and posted it on the WELL; I used my modem to send the electronic

version of that essay from my home computer to the larger computer a few miles from my home that stores the electronic record of conversations and publications that constitute the WELL. It's a cheap way of getting instant feedback from a few dozen respondents out of a local readership of a couple of thousand people. Anybody whose home computer is communicating with the WELL a moment after I post it, or in the middle of the night, or six months later, can tell me what they think publicly in the public conversation, or privately via e-mail. People can also do other things, like copy documents and send them places. I thought that my piece would stimulate discussion that could help me think through the various implications of sex at a distance. The weird part came when I started receiving electronic mail from around the country within hours of posting that essay. I did not take special measures to prevent anybody from duplicating the file.

Teledildonics seems to be a thought experiment that got out of control.

Apparently, one of the several thousand people who had access to the WELL had sent my teledildonics riff elsewhere via electronic mail; it only takes a few keystrokes to send an existing file on your host computer to any other computer in the Worldnet.

The piece seems to have struck a nerve. I noticed that an editor who interviewed me in Tokyo for one of Japan's largest computer magazines had a printed copy. I got calls from London and Amsterdam. People seemed to skip over all of my verbal qualifications and descriptions of technical difficulties, and almost all the people who contacted me for information seemed to believe that such a device actually exists somewhere and that I've seen it or tested it in some fulsome way. Among the other experiences my thought experiment led me into was a dinner with a German journalist. A young reporter for *Der Spiegel,* one of Germany's two largest news magazines, was traveling in search of the next computer revolution, and that had led him to VR. After our dinner, he wrote an article; it was published several months later. My name was mentioned. There was a photo. My agent sent me a very rough translation, which apparently was too rough, or else I failed to read it thoroughly enough. A month after that, I got a call from a woman in Augsburg, Germany, who was quite insistent that I should come to address a convention for NCR, within a few days. She persuaded me to speak, as specifically or vaguely as I wanted, about "future prospects for virtual reality." When I arrived in Augsburg, I was immediately whisked to a reception given by the mayor at the splendidly gilded, restored Augsburg City Hall. Then we retired to the municipal ratskeller for beer, sausage, and an interminable bilingual skit about Augsburg's history. It was at this point that NCR's German marketing communications director told me that I was a hot commodity in Germany at that time, because of what *Der Spiegel's* story had said, or what they thought it said.

"What do you mean?" I asked.

"The part where they said you were experimenting with ways to have sex with computers," the marketing communications director replied.

No wonder the vice presidents who introduced themselves to me were smiling the way they were when they told me they were looking forward to my talk. So I opened my presentation with John von Neumann's limerick.

The teledildonics story was also published in *Mondo 2000,* an avant-garde, technology-oriented "mutazine." I got even more weird phone calls after that. I can't help believing, from the reaction I've received in response to an essay I wrote in ten minutes, for fun, that the interest in this possibility will remain high. When people seem to want a technology to develop, to literally lust for a possible new toy, that need can take on a force of its own, especially given the rates of progress in the enabling technologies and the enormous market-driven forces that will be unleashed when sex at a distance becomes possible. Yes, teledildonics is a titillating fantasy, far from the serious human realities of medical imaging or teleoperated machine guns. But once you start thinking about sex at a distance, it's amazing how many other questions about future possibilities present themselves, questions about big changes that might be in store for us. Given the rate of development of VR technologies, we don't have a great deal of time to tackle questions of morality, privacy, personal identity, and even the prospect of a fundamental change in human nature. When the VR revolution really gets rolling, we are likely to be too busy turning into whatever we are turning into to analyze or debate the consequences.

One side effect of technological power seems to be that human culture is growing more mechanized. We wake up and eat and sleep and arrange our days according to the dictates of the machines that make our lives easier—or at least difficult in different ways—than our grandparents' lives. At the same time, human desires have been progressively stimulated, confused, and ulti-mately numbed by the barrage of provocative images, sounds, words thrown our way via electronic media; McLuhan didn't tell us that the global village would be experienced primarily by most people as an overdose of beautifully crafted advertisements, based largely on sexual innuendo, for the products of multinational corporations. Electronic media have been used thus far by a few to manipulate the desires of many, resulting in unprecedented financial profit. It is possible that telepresence technology, if linked with an inherently distrib-uted network system such as the telecommunications infrastructure, will give this power to many, rather than reserving it for a few. Whether that is true and whether it is a good idea are both questions that remain to be settled.

To many, the idea of literally "embracing technology" seems repugnant. Computer ethicist Joseph Weizenbaum, author of *Computing Power and Human Reason,* I am sure, would consider it antihuman. And perhaps it is. We should think about those deep moral reservations of a few less than optimistic prophets very hard and very long. But there is no doubt that people every-where in the world are fascinated by the prospect. And why not? Contempo-rary philosophers have pointed to progressive mechanization of human culture and the future of sexual expression as the site of a potential cultural collision of immense dimensions.

Think about a few fundamental assumptions about the way things are that might have to change if teledildonics becomes practical. If everybody can look as beautiful, sound as sexy, and feel as nubile and virile as everybody else, then what will become the new semiotics of mating? What will have erotic meaning? In the area of sexual-cultural coding, much can be learned by the way people seem to be using other electronic communication technologies to construct artificial erotic experience. "Telephone sex," in which paying customers are metered for the number of minutes they have a conversation about their choice of sexually charged topics, with a real human of the gender of their choice, might offer clues. So says Allucquére Rosanne Stone, a scholar of such matters. I met her on the net, and we knew each other's opinions pretty well by the time we met "ftf" ("face to face"), as the computer conferencing habituees say. Stone had been spending her time interviewing VR programmers, telephone sex workers, and amputees, because they all shared the experience of disembodiment and of feeling sensations from a body that does not exist physically.

"Telephone sex" . . . might offer clues.

When she found out about my quest into all the odd corners of VR research, Stone made contact with me via e-mail. In an electronic mail exchange, Stone sent me some provocative observations about telephone sex, part of a work-in-progress named "Sex and Death Among the Disembodied," which seemed to have direct bearing on the idea that people might use the telecommunication infrastructure for erotic gratification:

Phone sex is the process of constructing desire through a single mode of communication. In the process, participants draw on a repertoire of cultural codes to construct a scenario that compresses large amounts of information into a very small space. The worker verbally codes for gesture, appearance, and proclivity, and expresses these as tokens, sometimes in no more than a word. The client uncompresses the tokens and constructs a dense, complex interactional image. In these interactions desire appears as a product of the tension between embodied reality and the emptiness of the token, in the forces that maintain the preexisting codes for body in the modalities that are not expressed in the token; that is, tokens in phone sex are purely verbal, and the client uses cues in the verbal token to construct a multimodal object of desire with attributes of shape, tactility, etc. This act is thoroughly individual and interpretive; out of a highly compressed token of desire the client constitutes meaning that is dense, locally situated, and socially particular.

The secondary social effects of technosex are potentially revolutionary. If technology enables you to experience erotic frissons or deep physical, social, emotional communion with another person with no possibility of pregnancy or sexually transmitted disease, what then of conventional morality, and what of the social rituals and cultural codes that exist solely to enforce that morality? Is disembodiment the ultimate sexual revolution and/or the first step toward abandoning our bodies? Whenever I think of the vision of billions of earthlings of the future, all plugged into their home reality sets, I think of E. M. Forster's dystopia of a future in which people remain prisoners of their cubicles, entranced by their media, not even aware of the possibility of physical escape. And then I think that it is good to beware of looking at the future through the moral lens of the present: in a world of tens of billions of people, perhaps cyberspace is a better place to keep most of the population relatively happy, most of the time.

Back to thought-provocative implications of telesex. If you can map your hands to your puppet's legs, and let your fingers do the walking through cyberspace, as it is possible to do in a crude way with today's technology, there is no reason to believe you won't be able to map your genital effectors to your manual sensors and have direct genital contact by shaking hands. What will happen to social touching when nobody knows where anybody else's erogenous zones are located?

Privacy and identity and intimacy will become tightly coupled into something we don't have a name for yet. In UNIX computer systems, such as those used by the host computers of Worldnet, files (documents, databases, graphics, encoded sounds and programs) and categories of users who have access to those files can be grouped into nested hierarchies by a system of "permissions," like hiding information behind doors of encryption that can be opened only by those who know the key. People who use UNIX systems today often have publicly accessible file areas, in which everyone with access to the computer system has the key (a secret combination of numbers and letters and punctuation marks) to read and copy these files, and private areas for which only a small group of associates or one trusted partner knows the key. In cyberspace, if a parallel structure emerges, your most public persona—the way you want the world to see you—will be "universally readable," in UNIX terms. If you decide to join a group at a collegial or peer level, or decide to become informationally intimate with an individual or group of individuals, you will share the public keys to your identity permission access codes. It might be that the physical commingling of genital sensations will come to be regarded as a less intimate act than the sharing of the data structures of your innermost self-representations.

Potential psychosocial effects of present state-of-the-art VR technology were cannily anticipated thirty years ago by Marshall McLuhan in *Understanding Media,* which seems to make more sense in the 1990s than it did at the time it was published. But future cyberspace spinoffs are getting into territory beyond the McLuhan horizon. With all those layers of restricted access to self-representations that may differ radically from layer to layer, what happens to the self? Where does identity lie? What new meanings will "intimacy" and "morality" accrete? And with our information machines and our bodily sensations so deeply "intertwingled," as Theodore Nelson might say, will our communication devices be regarded as "it"s or will they be part of "us"?

■ Q U E S T I O N S   F O R   R E R E A D I N G

1. What is the *tone* of the article? (By tone, I mean Rheingold's attitude toward his subject and what he is saying about it.) Is Rheingold being humorous, satirical, serious, or all of these, or what?

2. In the light of Rheingold's discussion, what do you take to be the differences between *telephone sex* and *teledildonics?* Is the difference in terms of place—that is, *where* the sexual exchange is taking place? (It can certainly be argued, and has been, that sex takes place in the mind of the beholder, but Rheingold is talking about sex as a communicative, participatory act, which by definition requires at least two people interacting.) Is the difference in terms of *place* the same difference between the places of *cyberspace* and *virtual reality?* Does Rheingold's report of his discussion with Allucquére Rosanne Stone help answer this latter question?

■ WRITING   ASSIGNMENT   FOR   REREADING

Does your college or university have a policy about posting on e-mail lists to other students at your institution or even to outside places? If so, obtain a copy and examine it carefully. If it does not seem adequate, then write a collaborative critique of it and offer a better policy. If your college does not have a policy, then collaboratively write a policy and try to get it accepted by your college by taking it to your student representative.

Would You View This with Your Mother?

Dr. Emilio Bombay's "Would You View This with Your Mother?" appeared in Dr. Bombay's "Techno Talk" advice column (Fort Worth Star-Telegram [August 21, 1997]: C3) in answer to a question sent in by a reader. The answer raises issues not only about the appropriateness of sexual imagery called up on a browser (and therefore loaded in cache) but also the fact that there is no privacy when on-line or searching Web sites.

Dear Dr. Bombay: What is the law regarding the viewing of sexually explicit material on the Internet? I don't want to get dragged off to jail by the cyberpolice.

—Not a pervert

Dear Not: Well, I'm no lawyer, but I'd say it's pretty much legal until your mother catches you.

Actually, in a rebuke to all those well-meaning dunderheads in Congress who seem to think this whole First Amendment thing has gotten way out of hand, last June the Supreme Court said the Constitution's guarantee of freedom of speech extends to the Internet.

But before you go shooting off any fireworks and singing *God Bless America,* here's something to consider. Just because it's now a God-given right to be able to post pictures of barnyard animals in compromising positions on the Internet doesn't mean it's legal for you to collect them. If your community outlaws, say, pictures of Pamela Anderson's unnaturally large and obviously surgically enhanced lips, your collection of lip pix is contraband, and you could be looking at hard time in the Chap Stick Hilton.

Even if you don't consciously save all the dirty pictures you accidentally come across on your Web wanderings, most of them are probably still in your hard-drive cache, waiting for some ambitious prosecutor who wants to hear his name on CNN. The cache saves graphics and stuff from any Web page you visit so your browser doesn't take so long to display it the next time you visit. If you think you have things you shouldn't have in there—purely by accident, of course—it never hurts to empty it, just in case the ACLU doesn't think your case will get enough good publicity to bother with it. And don't expect Woody Harrelson to play you in the movie.

And, if you *are* a perv, and you think that ruling gives you the right to collect patently illegal smut like child porn, just send me your address and I'll come over and perform a little reprogramming your computer will never forget.

Oh, and just to heighten the paranoia level a bit, any time you visit a Web page—any page—the geeks in charge get a pretty good snapshot of who you are and where you are, and your own Internet provider probably has the capability of tracking exactly where you visit and what you look at while you're there.

And your mother knows what you're doing, too. You're not fooling anybody when you close that door.

■ QUESTIONS FOR REREADING

1. What is Dr. Bombay's tone (the attitude) in the letter to "Not a Pervert"? Do you find it appropriate and productive? If so, how so? What do you make of the headline "Would You View This with Your Mother?"

2. Recall the readings in chapter 3 about freedom of expression and censorship. What is Dr. Bombay alluding to when he says that it might be OK to place certain images on the Web but not to collect them, when he speaks of the ACLU and CNN and the cache in your computer? Besides the possible humor, is there a serious side to what Dr. Bombay is saying?

■ WRITING ASSIGNMENT FOR REREADING

Respond in writing—as Dr. Bombay does, but not necessarily like him—to "Not a Pervert." If by chance you see nothing wrong with porn, and so on, and you should include in your response some URLs to porn sites that you want "NAP" to check out, I'm not a lawyer but I would not print out the letter or distribute it to your classmates and instructor. Nor would I delete it in the Trash and to the inner, inner caches of your computer! Catch my drift?

Dinty W. Moore

The Night Thoreau
Had Cybersex
Or, Once You're On,
How Do You Get Off?

Dinty W. Moore's "The Night Thoreau Had Cybersex" was originally chapter 11 in his book The Emperor's Virtual Clothes: The Naked Truth about Internet Culture (Chapel Hill, NC: Algonquin Books, 1995): 149–72. Throughout his book, Moore uses Henry David Thoreau as his guide to (the dark side of) the Internet.

Late one evening, as I was nearing the end of my one-year journey into the Internet's deep, uncharted electronic woods, Thoreau came to me in a dream. He had dark, tousled hair and one of those beards that rings the bottom of the jaw, and his mouth was drawn into a scowl. He looked surprisingly like Abe Lincoln, only shorter.

"We are conscious of an animal in us," he said out of nowhere, his voice soft and deep. "It is reptile and sensual, and perhaps cannot be wholly expelled."

"What?" I asked.

"An animal in us," he repeated. "Reptile and sensual."

It was only then I noticed that Thoreau was carrying a dead otter, tethered on a rope. The otter was wet, and there was an unpleasant smell. "I don't know what you're asking me," I said.

"What is chastity?" Thoreau grunted back. "How shall a man know if he is chaste?"

"I don't know," I insisted, "but that otter has to go."

■　■　■

It was only a dream, of course, but he had a good point. Here I was, close to finishing this book, with only the barest mention of sex and the Net. Why?

I'm basically a shy person, easily embarrassed. My idea of a good, long discussion about sex is saying, "I want to, do you want to?" Yet it seems like most everyone else on the planet would rather discuss sex than any other topic available. People talk about sex on television. People pay to talk about sex with strangers on the telephone. Senators from Utah talk about sex at hearings of the Judiciary Committee. People cannot get enough, it seems, so why should the information superhighway be any different?

Well, it isn't.

Net users have devised countless ways to talk about sex, and even a few ways to have sex (assuming actual bodily contact is not a high priority). The proliferation of sex discussion groups on the Net has been a source of amusement for some and outrage for others, but none of this has slowed it down.

At last count, there were 42 separate sex discussion groups within Usenet, including such oddities as:

```
alt.sex
alt.sex.bestiality
alt.sex.bestiality.barney
alt.sex.bondage
alt.sex.breast
alt.sex.fetish.feet
alt.sex.fetish.hair
alt.sex.fetish.startrek
alt.sex.magazines
alt.sex.movies
alt.sex.spanking
alt.sex.woody-allen
```

And I have left out the ones that I'm too embarrassed to even mention. For instance, alt.sex.fetish.diapers, which I hope is someone's idea of a joke, and alt.sex.fetish.watersports, which has nothing at all to do with swim meets. Frankly, I'm having trouble even thinking of a topic that *isn't* covered.

The alt.sex assortment is not only one of the raciest neighborhoods on the Net, it is also one of the most popular. Computer wizards with fancy software and lots of free time compile statistics on how many people send messages to a particular newsgroup and how many people read those messages. Near the top of the monthly Top 40, consistently, are alt.sex, alt.sex.stories, alt.sex.bondage, rec.arts.movies, and misc.jobs.offered.

This seems, perhaps, to be a fairly representative illustration of what people want to do with their lives: talk about sex, go to the movies, and if there is any time left over, find a good-paying job.

Thoreau returned the next night, and the night after that. In some of the dreams, he had a fishing pole and a lopsided grin; in others he was holding a quill pen to his temple, looking quite the studious author. His jacket was always black, but needed a good dry cleaning. He wanted to know more than I could tell him.

"I fear," he rumbled, "that we are such gods or demigods only as fawns and satyrs, the divine allied to beasts, the creatures of appetite, and that, to some extent, our very life is our disgrace."

"What?" I asked again.

He shook his head, as if I had disappointed him. "I would fain know," he repeated, "how shall a man know if he is chaste?"

The easiest way to shame a writer is to accuse him of insufficient research, and Thoreau was writer enough to know that. His words did not make total sense to me, but I think he was suggesting I had ducked the issue, that I had not probed deeply enough. I had no choice but to meet his challenge.

So I went, notebook at my side, read the main sex group thoroughly, recorded my field observations, and here is what I found: Alt.sex is fairly docile. A typical evening's sample of subjects might include condom use, various methods of female birth control, breast size preference, the importance of male magnitude, the perpetual "What Do Women Really Want?" query, and assorted helpful little tips to improve one's performance, duration, or accuracy.

For instance, one nervous novice posted a question to alt.sex about basic boudoir technique. How, he wondered, if the situation should ever present itself, would he know if he was doing it right? He specifically wanted to "make her go crazy."

A presumably more experienced practitioner responded with this advice, "There is no one way to do it, so instructions wouldn't help. The main thing to keep in mind is simply how she reacts to what you do. Listen for changes in her breathing, or the sudden contraction of muscles."

Notwithstanding the fact that this advice applies just as well to cardiopulmonary resuscitation as lovemaking, I thought the guy did a pretty good job of explaining a fairly complicated subject in simple, basic terms. He might, in fact, do very well in a technical writing class. Most everyone else responded with fanciful boasts about how *they* did it, and how deliciously insane they managed to drive their sex partner. I believed none of them.

People post fiction to the group as well, but most of the stories seem to be little more than the endlessly banal fantasies of desperate young men (more men than women post here)—the types of "true" stories that get published in *Penthouse* Forum: "I was hot, I was ready, and my landlady didn't seem to mind."

A few—very few—alt.sex posters have read their Anaïs Nin, however, and try, at least, for metaphor. Let me quote from one, in which the female has been mysteriously transformed into a white horse:

"He looked about for a saddle. There was none. He heard a soft, feminine voice whisper, 'Ride me. Ride me till morning.' He became suddenly aware of an erection. He cleared his throat."

It was about that time I cleared my screen.

"My gratitude for that," Thoreau said on his next visit. He looked long and hard at my bedroom curtains, picked at his teeth with a twig he had carried into my dream, then turned in my direction and smiled. "The generative energy invigorates and inspires us."

"What?"

He smiled again, nodded cheerfully, insistently. He clearly wanted to know more.

To be honest, I started to suspect old Thoreau of something beyond simple intellectual curiosity here, but that is just conjecture. I do know that he spent an awful lot of time alone in that cabin.

In any case, I tried to locate some less-traveled corner of the woods for him, something to further invigorate and inspire him, and I found that it was but a short walk from alt.sex to alt.sex.fetish.feet.

To be honest, I started to suspect old Thoreau of something beyond simple intellectual curiosity . . .

Oddly, or at least to my naïve surprise, the alt.sex.fetish.feet people seemed more serious than the plain old alt.sex people. The amateurs had been left behind, perhaps. There was an immediately apparent urgency to the postings on alt.sex.fetish.feet. Topics on the night I visited included a foot fetish quiz and discussions of leather shoes; of high heels; of toenails (painted and unpainted); of leg fetishes, shoe catalogs, voyeurism, and "celebrity feet."

The hot question while I was reading this male-dominated group was voiced thusly, "If a man has dorky feet, we can still develop a business or social relationship. With a woman on the other hand, I might have a business or semisocial relationship, but it is doubtful a sensual attraction would develop. I wonder if this fetish of ours is replicated in the female species?"

The messages that followed seemed to share the original poster's sentiments, but no women came forward to offer their opinion, so the question was ultimately unresolved.

Then there is bondage.

I was raised Catholic, attended Catholic school for twelve interminable years. My educational background perhaps explains my discomfort with all aspects of sex talk, and many aspects of sex, and given this, the mere idea of a sadomasochistic or bondage relationship is extremely difficult for me to fathom. At this stage of my life, bondage is just not a personal priority. When I go shopping, I shop for pants that fit more loosely around the waist, not ones that bind. The only thing tying me down right now is too much work and my daughter's kindergarten schedule. If I wish to be lightly flogged, I have an editor.

But alt.sex.bondage is certainly impressive. These people are immeasurably brave. I wouldn't even think of some of this stuff, much less type it onto a computer screen and send it to a worldwide newsgroup where potentially thousands might read it and figure out who I am. Nicknames are the norm here, but accounts can sometimes be traced.

Topics on alt.sex.bondage range from the technical, as in "Cleaning procedures for whips," to shopping queries such as "Looking for locking buckles," to information on bondage clubs and private parties, and on to people's own stories of S&M encounters, real and imagined.

In a message titled "Essences of Spanking," a person who did not reveal his or her gender wrote about the proper use of a frame and block. "I kneel naked on the bench and place my hands and head in a stock at the front of the frame. My body is hinged over the rear block and my waist is strapped down. Then my legs are spread and strapped. This forces me to arch my back and stick my bottom out in the air." The message goes on awhile to describe the actual spanking, with a British cane. The description is offered in all seriousness.

Another writer, again with no hint of irony or wit, posted a message titled "50 Ways to Tie Your Lover." He listed all fifty, in cold detail, with no further comment. "Arms crossed behind," one read, "wrists bound to each other by a tether." Oddly enough, that was how Thoreau had tied the otter, the one he carried into my room that first night.

But when I came across a long, thoughtful discussion on gagging, and the suggestion that a golf ball with eye screws in opposite sides and a raw-hide strap might work well as a muzzle, giving a "durable, and playful texture," I figured it was time for me to go.

By the end of the week, Thoreau was coming into my dreams more and more often, seeming more and more agitated. He shuffled his big boots nervously on my bedroom floor (I would check in the mornings, but there were never any scuff marks or other outward proof). He bit nervously at his nails, all ashen-faced and disheveled, scowled repeatedly but didn't speak.

He just kept blinking his eyes, open and shut, open and shut, as if it were some signal. I could only guess, but I eventually surmised what the man wanted were pictures, something to look at.

And yes, there are pictures on the Net, plenty of them, from the suggestive, to the erotic, to the obscene. The technology to scan photographs into electronic form, transmit them across phone lines, and download them into our homes is fast becoming widespread. On the Net, these pictures are called binaries, referring to the basic logical "on-off" language of computers. (The more usual definition of binary is "something made up of two parts," but the joke here is too obvious.) The other Internet term is GIF, short for Graphic Interchange Format—more of that jargon that keeps technoids from actually making sense. The pictures come across the electronic lace doily as numbers—ones and zeros—and special software is needed to transform them back into recognizable shapes.

Within Usenet, there is alt.binary.pictures.erotica.females, alt.binary.pictures.erotica.male, alt.binaries.pictures.erotica.blondes, and many more. A good number of the photos found on these groups are scanned in illegally from popular skin magazines, and the sophistication of your computer's graphics card and software will determine whether what you see is erotic or just fuzzy.

Many people are truly upset, though, about the very real possibility that an eleven-year-old could conceivably search, find, and stare at these pictures. But I look at it this way—any kid with enough technical savvy to hook up a modem, find an Internet connection, dial in, negotiate the software, download binary files, decode them, and make them appear as intended on the screen, could probably figure out how to come up with five dollars and locate a magazine rack. Sure, kids could potentially find some pretty raw stuff here, but they would find it much faster under their older brother's mattress. Mom and Pop should probably just keep an eye on the computer room.

And there is another sexual outlet on the Net—cybersex, the evil twin of cyberspace. Cybersex is sex without touching, sex without seeing, sex without even hearing the other person's voice. It is sex by typing, and reading, and lots of folks are all hot up about it.

People tried to explain cybersex to me back when I was unacquainted with the term, and I ended up just staring at them blankly. Then, after imagining that perhaps I understood, I tried to explain cybersex to others, and they ended up just staring at me blankly. Cybersex, admittedly, is hard to describe, but get your blank stares ready, because I am going to try.

Cybersex is talking dirty in real time, describing various sexual acts in chronological and intimate detail, with a partner who could be anything or anyone you could possibly imagine. Here is how it is done:

1. Two people sit alone in front of their respective computers, anywhere in the world.

2. They type onto the screen a description of what they might be doing to one another if they were not separated by three thousand miles, marriage, total lack of acquaintance, and the fact that one of them is really just a thirteen-year-old boy pretending to be a voluptuous blonde woman of twenty-five.

3. When they type these descriptions, such as "I am ripping off your blouse in a passionate frenzy," the description is read almost immediately by the other person and that person types a response. "Careful, it's faux silk."

4. They sometimes do things in the privacy of their own homes that would embarrass me, but maybe not Joycelyn Elders.

I just read that step-by-step description, and now *I* have that blank stare again.

Let me try to clear this up by example.

I noticed that a woman named Martha was posting to the alt.sex group frequently, often discussing the positive aspects of her cybersexual interludes. I sent Martha an electronic mail message and asked her to tell me what she found so attractive about computer sex.

"Some may consider it adultery," she wrote back. "Others, like me, see it as a means of release and pure, innocent sexual gratification, for both involved. In fact, if anything, it *stops* me from having an affair in the physical sense."

Martha is a twenty-nine-year-old graphic artist from Chicago, and she is married. I asked her to explain how a cybersex relationship develops.

"Although Cybersex allows one to have 'sex' with whomever they please," she told me, "I've found that I can't just jump into sex with just anyone. That's too unfeeling, and not at all satisfying. How can I imagine the person if I don't know anything about him? I have to develop a mental image of him, by knowing what his general appearance is . . . hair, eye color, height, build . . . just a general portrait. Then, through hours of conversation, I allow my instincts to take over."

She explained that her "most satisfying scenario" is corresponding with someone for weeks or months before anything happens. She met one fellow that way, began to chat quite casually, and eventually felt a strong attraction. "Night after night we'd talk—learning everything there was to know about each other. Every secret, every thought, every detail was revealed. We'd tell each other things that we could barely tell ourselves, let alone anyone else!"

Then, despite embarrassment and reservations, they tried it. They joked around, pretending to be having sex in a burning house, or during a cyclone. But eventually, she wrote, "our crazy sex began to calm down. It began to grow more sensuous, more tender, more *real.* Each occasion, we became closer and closer, and when it was over, we'd hold each other in our arms, whispering and touching each other softly. These became magical moments for us both."

They joked around, pretending to be having sex in a burning house . . .

Understand, they've never met.

She even sent me a transcript of a cybersex encounter, but first—*first,* so relax for a moment—I have to explain yet another technical marvel: Internet Relay Chat, or IRC, or just "chat." Usenet postings and e-mail both have certain time lags. While the mail or bulletin board message you type and send may reach its destination in seconds or minutes, it will usually then sit there for anywhere from hours to days to weeks before it is read. Usenet messages are stored on a machine somewhere until you and I retrieve the message. Electronic mail sits on the hard disk of your access provider in what is known as an e-mail queue, until you decide to read your e-mail.

But chat messages don't sit anywhere. When you log into a chat system (and how you do it differs widely, depending on software and whom you have chosen for an access provider, so I will spare you the technical details), you type in a command to join a "channel." Every IRC channel has a name, like "chatzone," or "wasteland," or "hottub," and depending on the channel and the time of day, there might be ten or twenty other people hooked in. When you type, "Hello, how are you wild and crazy guys?" onto your screen, that message appears on the screens of the ten or twenty others on the channel almost at once, whether they are three blocks away or in Oulu, Finland. If the guy in Finland, a guy named Heikki, types back, "I'm just fine, thanks," that will appear on everyone's screen as well. Of course, if Heikki were that polite, he wouldn't be on IRC.

There are two sides to the IRC. To its credit, the relay chat system was used to dramatic effect during the 1993 coup attempt against Russian president Boris Yeltsin, keeping the world instantaneously updated on troop movements and Stolichnaya shipments. To its discredit, IRC is used much of the rest of the time by college students, geeks, weirdos, and bores who have nothing to say and can't stop saying it.

But IRC is where cybersex happens, because cybersex needs to be spontaneous and instantaneous, not remote and sporadic. Cybersex happens on IRC because when a man rips away a woman's faux silk blouse, he wants her to know it, and he wants her to know it right away.

So, without further ado, here is the transcript Martha sent me of her cybersexual interlude with Guy (name changed). It is none of our business really, but here it is:

```
<Guy> okay—light the fire

<Martha> throwing kindling on newspapers . . . striking
match . . . Poof! Blaze.

<Guy> You're wearing a sheer negligee—a present from your
hubby which you've saved to two-time him.

<Martha> Of course . . . he's never seen me in it. . . .

<Guy> it's a teddy, with G-string

<Martha> Yes, and that string is starting to rub against
me . . . turning me on . . .

<Guy> a long one would catch fire from the fire lapping at
our feet. I'm just wearing a towel, after a long, hot shower

<Martha> You smell so so good, as I nuzzle your neck and kiss
your ear

<Guy> you put your hands on my shoulders, my hands go to your
hips

<Martha> Looking up at you . . . into your amazing green
eyes, I kiss you . . . deeply . . .

<Guy> I bring my face around to kiss your neck, you lift your
head & pull it back

<Guy> my hand kneads your hip, playing with the string

<Martha> fingering my string, I place my hands on your ass,
and pull you into me . . . then I rip off your towel

<Guy> you press against me, feeling me through the thick
towel

<Martha> No, the towel is gone now . . . but I feel your rock
hard penis against me

<Guy> my hardness is up against you, you press into it. You
bring your hands to take it all
```

Martha herself did some editing here before sending the transcript along to me, explaining that matters had gotten too graphic. We pick up some moments later:

```
<Martha> I can feel you begin to slow . . . our mouths
together . . . our sweaty bodies rubbing against each other

<Guy> I can smell your sweet, musky smell between us and
breathe it in deeply

<Martha> So can I! and we lay down together, still breathing
heavily . . . and kiss, and look at each other, and giggle!
oh how sweet you are!!!!!!

<Guy> It's quite an amazing sight

<Guy> we hold each other tenderly, and holding each other,
drift gently off to sleep.

<Martha> You are, without a doubt, the most amazing person.
You turn me on so much, its scary!

<Guy> it's all in the mind, darling
```

Sweet, tender, electronic, unreal. That's cybersex. But Martha swears by it, and she and Guy stay in touch, even though she tells me the affair is over. "Seeing his sweet name on my e-mail list always brings a smile to my face," she writes. "And now, here we are, two lovers, painfully separated by a half of a country, and marriages, kids, lifestyles. The fact that we've never physically met or have never spoken to each other orally is insignificant. We fell in love with our minds, not our physical bodies. But oh, how frustrating it can be! Just to have him hold me for real, to make love to him and his body would probably ruin me for sex for the rest of my life."

She doesn't even know the man's name, just the name he has chosen for Internet correspondence. They will probably never meet, yet it seems obvious she is carrying a big torch for him. For some, at least, cybersex is a tangible thing.

■ ■ ■

But Thoreau? Well the old philosopher, it turns out, surely did spend too much time alone in that small cabin, reading Homer, staring out at the ever-frozen pond, contemplating lives of quiet desperation, because the next thing I knew, he was standing over my bed again.

"I care not how obscene my *words* are," he shouted, jumping up and down like a schoolboy. "We discourse freely without shame of one form of sensuality, and are silent about another. From exertion comes wisdom and purity."

It took me a moment to get his meaning, but I eventually did. "You want me to *try* it?" I shouted back. "You want me to actually try this stuff?"

He quieted down, nodded, then gave me a wink. "It is neither the quality nor the quantity, but the devotion to sensual savors," he whispered. "I would fain know."

I awoke at that moment, and of course there was no one there. The dream had gone *poof.* Thoreau was conveniently gone, but not my writerly guilt. He was eager to know, and perhaps my readers would be as well.

So I found my way into Chat and typed the commands to enter a channel called Netsex, which seemed promising enough.

When you log into the IRC system, by the way, the first thing you do is choose a nickname (by typing nick=<whatever>). I considered the nickname <Henry David> but doubted that would elicit much sensual interest, so I opted instead for the nickname <Lover>, presuming that would make my intentions perfectly clear.

What follows is a transcript of my first cybersexual experience, with a woman named <Chris>, and numerous interruptions from a guy named <Bulge>:

<Bulge> Is everyone having a cigarette? Where's all the sex?

<Chris> How about you?

<Bulge> Nope.

<Chris> Oh well

<Bulge> Is this the sex channel?

<Chris> Yep.

<Bulge> Are you m or f Chris?

<Chris> f

<Bulge> How old?

<Chris> 24

I jumped in here, realizing that there was an alleged female on the channel, and feeling a strong urge to complete my research. I will explain the alleged part later.

<Lover> Can you tell me how to have cybersex?

<Chris> Okay, first go and find a girl . . .

<Bulge> Will a blow up doll do?

<Chris> No a blow up doll is too passive.

<Lover> Can we have cybersex?

<Chris> You don't even know me.

<Lover> I know, but I'm really interested in learning how cybersex works.

<Chris> I know how it works. I've done it nine or ten times.

<Lover> How is it done?

<Chris> Have you ever masturbated in front of another person?

<Lover> That is too embarrassing to even think about answering.

<Chris> Why? Are you fat?

<Lover> No, I play lots of tennis.

<Chris> Then you'd have nothing to be embarrassed about. Or is your penis too small?

<Lover> Are we going to have cybersex, or are you just teasing me?

<Chris> Let's start again, but don't rush. Go slowly.

<Lover> Okay. I think you are nice.

<Chris> Thank you.

<Lover> I am six foot tall, sandy hair. You?

<Chris> I am 5'10", brown hair, 36C breasts, and a cute butt.

<Lover> You sound pretty.

But, unfortunately, immediately at the mention of Chris's posterior, something strange happened. A crowd of Chat types whose nicknames were <JoyBoy>, <Lucifer>, <Lonewolf>, and <SpErM> hurriedly joined the channel and began the Chat-channel equivalent of wolf whistling. Perhaps they had been listening in all along; I don't fully understand how they would do that, but I know enough to know that clever computer users can do a lot that the normal user cannot. In any case, <Chris>, understandably put off by such an assembly, began to insist that the only way we could really have sex was if I drove to Cincinnati. The other men started to harass her, saying they wanted sex, too, and demanding information on other parts of her anatomy.

Seconds later, this message showed up at the bottom of my screen:

*** <Chris> parts channel #Netsex

She was gone, and who could blame her?

Sad, really. Perhaps <Chris> was a woman with whom I might have found happiness. Perhaps we were destined for one another's arms. Perhaps we might have had something very, very special.

Or perhaps she was a guy.

For all I know, <Chris> may have been <Bulge> logging in somehow under twin nicknames. <Chris> might have been anything, or anyone, but chances are she was not actually a woman. You see, there is a well-documented dearth of females on IRC, for two reasons. One is that there are still more male computer whizbangs in the world than there are female computer whizbangs, though that is changing. The second reason is that any woman who does show up to chat is immediately surrounded by a large crowd of men asking her rude and insensitive questions. Women tend to have two intelligent reactions to this onslaught of unwanted notice: they leave, or they adopt a new nickname like <Bruiser> and never tell a soul.

In response to this, countless men have pretended to be women on IRC, just as some of them do in the other areas of the Internet. There is often no way to tell, and it is an excellent way to get attention.

My first attempt at cybersex frustrated, Thoreau's words still ringing in my ears, I had no alternative it seemed but to gender-switch myself. Heck, they do it in Shakespeare's plays all the time. It is almost a literary tradition.

Since a clever computer navigator could probably find out my university account number, and thus my initials, I chose <Deb> as my new nickname. Soon after that, my Deb persona wandered onto the Netsex channel of IRC, just to see what was happening.

I felt almost immediately like a bright light in a field of mosquitoes. I could hardly keep up with the high number of greetings blinking on my monochrome monitor. I had countless suitors within minutes, but I chose a fellow nicknamed <By-Tor> to be my sex partner. He came on to me like a barrel of beer-drunk monkeys, and gosh, he sounded kinda cute.

He even persuaded me to leave the Netsex channel and, through the wizardry of IRC, created a whole new channel on which we could meet in privacy. He called it Lovechild.

Here, then, is our complete encounter, in all its ludicrous glory:

```
<By-tor> undresses Deb

<Deb> My button is stuck

<By-tor> pulls button off

<Deb> Ping!

<By-tor> pulls deb's dress? blouse? off

<Deb> Okeedokee

<By-tor> What are you wearing now?

<Deb> Just my jeans

<By-tor> unzippers your jeans with his teeth

<Deb> Yikes

<By-tor> caresses your supple breasts

<Deb> With what?

<By-tor> notices the erect nipples

<Deb> Good observation skills
```

<By-tor> licks in circles around the erect nipples

<Deb> Don't make yourself dizzy!

<By-tor> grabs the massage oil and turns down the lights

<Deb> Yikes. I can't see. That oil is hot.

<By-tor> thinks you'll grow to like it. He puts on soft music.

<Deb> Is that Barry Manilow I hear?

<By-tor> Yes, Barry baby.

<Deb> By-tor you big, wild boy you.

<By-tor> whispers sweet nothings in your ear

<Deb> Like what, for instance?

<By-tor> pops open the best bottle of champagne

<Deb> Can't drink. Allergies.

<By-tor> The champagne is for me then

<Deb> Are you just telling me these things to get sex?

<By-tor> would never do that

<Deb> I'm totally naked and running around the room screaming.

<By-tor> notices your heavy breathing

<Deb> I think I'm freaking out

<By-tor> grabs you and licks your hot spot

<Deb> My parents are home! My parents are home!

<By-tor> No they aren't

<Deb> They're coming up the stairs. Hide, By-tor, under the bed.

<By-tor> hides under the bed

<Deb> Hi, Ma!

<By-tor> is scared

<Deb> No, Ma, no one was here. That was the radio.

At this point, by typing the chat command "nick=<Ma>," I instantaneously switch my nickname to <Ma>. <By-tor> remains huddled under the bed, understandably confused.

<Ma> You little whore! Slap!

I switch back to <Deb>.

<Deb> Ssssssh, By-tor, if Ma hears you she will kill you.

I switch back to <Ma>.

<Ma> Who's under the bed, Deb?

I switch back to <Deb>.

<Deb> No one, Ma. I was reading the Bible.

<By-tor> eats some soap

<Deb> Ohmigod, Ma has the belt!

<By-tor> runs

<Deb> Swack! Swack! Swack!

<By-tor> streaks from the room, naked.

<Deb> Swack! Swack! Swack!

*** <By-tor> parts channel #Lovechild

    I don't really blame him for leaving in such a rush. Frankly, I was amazed that young <By-tor> stuck around as long as he did.
    Personally, I was having a wonderful time, but I'm not sure I would compare it to sex.
    Perhaps I was not compliant enough.
    Here, in any case, is what I think this episode reveals:

1. Male cybersex partners don't care how obviously sarcastic the female becomes, because they are just too lust-driven to notice, and

2. I would probably have made a very histrionic female.

I will get professional help soon.

    I don't really know why <By-tor> put up with all of my silliness and smart-aleck remarks. Perhaps he thought I was just living out my sexual fantasy.
    Perhaps I was.
    I will get professional help soon.
    But I have done it now, Mr. Thoreau. I have lived deep and sucked all the marrow of cyberlife. I have experienced cybersex, and you have, too, I suppose, by proxy. I didn't like it much, as a replacement for sex, but it did make me giggle.
    A fair number of people, though, such as Martha, seem to like it quite a bit.
    Why? Well, the most obvious answer would be safety. Net sex is the ultimate in safe sex, and I don't just mean from HIV and other transmitted diseases. Net sex leaves us safe from commitment, from entanglement, from having others witness our embarrassment. Sure, there are weirdos, but they

are thousands of electronic miles away, they can't hurt us. They can't even see us, they can only type words, and words are easy to ignore.

If we choose to talk about sex on the Net, or even engage in a sort of sex, we can do it without fear. No one really knows who we are, no one but ourselves needs to know that we are doing it, and if anything goes wrong, if an affair turns ugly or inconvenient, we can just switch it off. The perfect answer in a society that is increasingly busy, and increasingly unsafe.

Easy in, easy out, no regrets in the morning.

I have seen the future.

I already miss the past.

■ QUESTIONS FOR REREADING

1. Compare Rheingold's description of *virtual sex* and Moore's description of *cybersex*. What's the difference? Does it better explain—if not sex on-line itself—at least the difference between VR and cyberspace?

2. Why does Moore use Thoreau appearing to him in dreams as the motive for his going to sex sites? This question can be interpreted in several ways. For example, Why Thoreau and not someone else? Why Thoreau or anyone else?

I asked Dinty if he had any questions for you and he sent me this post:

3. Martha, the graphic artist from Chicago, insists that her cybersexual relationship with Guy does no harm. "Some may see it as adultery," she says. "Others, like me, see it as a means of release, and pure, innocent sexual gratification." Do you agree that such a relationship, where the two people involved never actually meet in person but become very intimate with words and descriptions, is not adultery? How does the "virtual" nature of this sex act differ morally from an actual, physical relationship? How would you feel if your husband or wife were involved in such a relationship?

4. Net sex, I believe, is the ultimate in safe sex. It keeps you safe not just from disease, but from commitment, entanglement, and embarrassment. But if you make a relationship too safe, if you take away these consequences of misbehavior or mistake, isn't the relationship lessened? Psychologists have proven that we value most those things for which we work the hardest. If we take away what is most difficult and frightening about forming a relationship—sexual or just friendly—is the relationship less valuable?

5. Do you believe the part where Henry David Thoreau appears to me in a dream carrying a dead otter?

■ WRITING ASSIGNMENT FOR REREADING

Dinty Moore says that he does not mind your writing to him via e-mail. So why don't you drop him a note with answers to his questions? Better still, so as to make all this efficient, I would recommend that the class, after discussion, formulate together some answers to his questions and then send them to him. <Dinty@psu.edu>

Virtual Books and Libraries

(Hypertext, Multimedia, Copyright versus Copyleft)

W

hat are virtual books in virtual libraries? The best way to think about answering this question is to first be concerned with, What is a virtual library?

In Jorge Luis Borges's "The Library of Babel," the narrator says: "I affirm that the Library is interminable." With this statement in mind, I remember not too many years ago being in very large research libraries and seeing rows and rows of card catalogs with hundreds of drawers filled with hundreds of cards on which were printed or even written bibliographical references and call letters. Today, in the same libraries where these catalogs used to be, are tables and chairs, taking up much of the space but leaving much empty space that is sparsely filled with a dozen or so computer terminals. To begin my research, all that I do is type the name of the book or author or subject matter, execute the request, and wait to see if the library has what I want. (It is not necessary for me to do this *in* the library at all, for I can follow the same procedure from my office or home or wherever I am, as long as I have a terminal, a modem, and a telephone.) While checking, I can also query other libraries in the immediate area, or throughout the state, the country, the Library of Congress, or the world.

What happened is that they carted off those old card catalogs after putting all the references into the database, and then linked up the databases by way of the World Wide Web (the matrix), and now I have access to all this information—this library that is interminable (in the terminal). I can now virtually reach many of the volumes or articles that previously I had to retrieve from the stacks or order through interlibrary loan. I can display them on my screen and place them in a file in my hard disk. I can search through them quickly with the Find command. Cut and paste from them. Delete what I don't want.

Just a couple of years ago our library had about a million books; now it has billions, virtually an indefinite number. (Just a couple of years ago, my study was crammed to the ceiling with tons of books; now many of them are potentially accessible in my hard drive!)

Am I stretching a point to make a point? Perhaps. But in no time at all, this opening statement will not be an exaggeration, but a reality . . . will have become a virtuality.

So the card catalogs are gone and, in my exaggerated statement, many of the articles and books are on-line or are just a computer search or *uniform research locater* (URL) away. But how does all of this—by way of the computer—happen? The answer, to begin with, is that this transition from real to virtual takes place by way of the technology of *hypertext.* This answer is going to need some explaining. I am not using the term *hypertext* in any exclusive sense. Let me simplify matters and say that I have at least two senses in mind: On the one hand, the *death* of the actual book and the *birth* of the virtual book, and on the other, that form of writing (that is, hypertextual writing) that has no sense of a beginning or ending, as we commonly experience such conventions in narratives (whether they be in books or films or our so-called everyday lives). Notice how the first sense speaks of *beginning* and *ending* (birth/death) and the second, by implication, speaks of *only middles* and "everywhere" middles.

From *real books* to *virtual books.* From *text* to *hypertext.* (And let's not forget, from real libraries to virtual ones.) This distinction is abstract (just as the difference between *actual* and *virtual* is), but the distinction can be understood if we take a look at the readings in this chapter about virtual books and virtual libraries.

First, we have Neil Postman speaking for books and Camille Paglia speaking for TV, or so the title of the exchange leads us to believe. Upon closer examination of the "printed" transcript of the dinner conversation, we can see otherwise: Postman favors books over television; Paglia, however, favors the book and the television and other media—*all of them simultaneously.* She says: "When I wrote my book, I had earphones on, blasting rock music or Puccini and Brahms. The soap operas—with the sound turned down—flickered on my TV. I'd be talking on the phone at the same time." (She explains this difference with Postman in terms of being born before or after World War II.)

Now juggle this image of being in tune with one thing versus many things or with one linear thing versus many nonlinear yet laterally associated things, while we go on to Sven Birkerts's point of view. (If you were born after WWII, you should be able to juggle this image!) Birkerts makes a distinction among

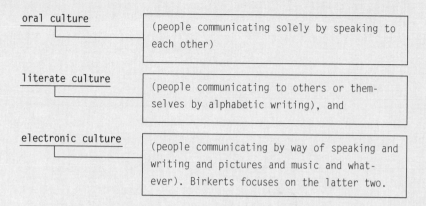

oral culture

(people communicating solely by speaking to each other)

literate culture

(people communicating to others or themselves by alphabetic writing), and

electronic culture

(people communicating by way of speaking and writing and pictures and music and whatever). Birkerts focuses on the latter two.

He further distinguishes literate (print) culture in terms of

linear thinking,

logic/concepts, and

vertically cumulative

and electronic culture as not an unbroken line or thread of thought but a

network (a web), not logical but

impressionistic and **imagistic** (television commercials), not vertically cumulative but

laterally associative....

What am I doing? Has this not become a joke (an irony, a paradox)? Here I am in a book (literate culture), trying to explain virtual books, hypertext, multimedia (electronic culture), and eventually a virtual library! Notice how in the previous paragraph I (and the people who helped me produce this book) tried to create a simulation of electronic culture while explaining it. That is, we, as so many other authors/publishers before us—such as in *Wired* magazine, or *Mondo 2000* or *.Net* or even special issues of *Time* and *Newsweek*— tried to fool your eyes and brain into believing you were *actually* reading a *virtual* text, *hypertext*. The simulation is of the World Wide Web (www). The simulation is an attempt to create what is called a hot link **[link]** and then what would be a linked text, replacing altogether the previous text on the screen, but on the actual printed page would be an actual virtual box of text out in the margin. A perfect example of this is found in my introduction to this very book (with the two introductions splitting and going in two different directions); other examples of this kind of formatting are found in *Mondo 2000: A User's Guide to the New Edge.*

It is important to stress that in this book we can only simulate hypertext. Is our attempt at simulation to be criticized? Perhaps. As you will see when

you read Birkerts and others, however, we readers are not yet in an electronic
culture as much as we are in a literate culture. Birkerts calls the period we are
in "proto-electronic," which will "not require a transition period of two centuries" as did the transition from oral culture into literate culture. He says:
"Fifty years, I'm sure, will suffice." Until we pass over into electronic culture,
we will talk about such a culture and about hypertext itself by way of literate
culture. But so as to have our book and consume hypertext also, we have in
each section of this book, such as this one, begun with traditional, literate
introductions to the readings but expect you at the end of each section to go
to the Web site that complements this book <www.abacon.com/vitanza> and
to jump into the middle of the beginnings of electronic culture.

In that light, then, I again ask, What is hypertext? Put simply, let me point
each of you to the www. When you are out on the Web, you are *in* the conditions of an electronic culture, *in* hypertext, which has no beginning or ending,
but is all middle. You can jump in anywhere and move in the direction of
your interests as your interests change from one site to another. It's not like
picking up a book and reading it the way that we traditionally have been
taught to consume it, from beginning to end. When you begin to do research
out on the Web—when you are supposed to be focused toward a particular
linear goal—you will discover that your interests might change rather quickly
and capriciously, and more importantly, that the technology of hypertext
allows you to pursue those interests very easily. Hypertext (to be hypertext)
does not have to follow the logic of linear thought but can follow (and some
insist *should* follow) lateral or associative thought. (Linear, discursive, proposi-
tional thought, we say in terms of brain hemispheres, is from the left brain;
associative thought is from the right brain.)

With some understanding now of what hypertext is, let's get a working
understanding of what is a virtual book. In its grandest form, it is the Web.
(Other examples are forthcoming in the readings.) And, what is multimedia?
If you are using the program Lynx as the means of browsing the Web, you
will get only text (that is, words); if you are using Internet Explorer or
Netscape, you will get not only text but also pictures (graphics) and sound
(voice, music, and so on). Lynx gives you only hypertext; Internet Explorer
and Netscape and whatever the next browser program is will give you multimedia (which is, again hypertext plus pictures and sound). Therefore, multimedia, like hypertext and graphics and sound, is the Web. As you *read* (back
to the irony) Jay David Bolter, you will better understand, in a bookish-linear
sense, what hypertext and multimedia can be.

We started by talking about the virtual library and then to how the actual
library was reconstructed into a virtual library by way of the technology of
hypertext and multimedia, which are technologies used for the construction of

virtual books. We are confronted now with asking again the question, What is the virtual library? Simply put, a virtual library is a collection of virtual books, right? Well, yes, but *where is* the virtual library in which these virtual book are to be located? An answer is the World Wide Web, just as it has been to all the questions that we have thus far asked. However, the library is not only to be found *in* the World Wide Web but *it is* also the entire World Wide Web. It is, in a manner of speaking, the electronic reconstruction of the lost library of Alexandria, while it is also the realization *cum* virtualization of Borges's Library of Babel. Yes, like the narrator of Borges's tale, I, too, affirm that *the Library is interminable.* And so are its spinoff problems!

When libraries and books become electronic, for example, the principles of copyright and royalties (that is, ownership) inevitably must be reassessed. The problem or question is, How can someone own a virtual, nontangible object? But the question concerning ownership of the virtual becomes so problematic that people begin to requestion ownership of any actual object itself. (This spinoff problem takes the shape of the return of the unexamined hacker's ethic, but this time in terms of *copyleft* or digital socialism.)

■ S U M M A R Y   O F   K E Y   T E R M S   A N D   P E R S O N S

Alexandria: A city in Egypt (founded by Alexander the Great) that had the great but lost "universal library." On February 12, 1990, the Aswan Declaration was signed, which is an agreement to rebuild the library. The text of the agreement has this phrasing in it: The library will be "a *link* with the past and opening on to the future" <www.unesco.org/webworld/alex/aswdecl.htm> (emphasis mine).

Borges, Jorge Luis: Argentinian author of fiction. Some commentators liken Borges's fiction to proto-hypertext. Most famous are Borges's collections of stories entitled *Ficciones* and *Labyrinths,* and most famous are his stories "The Library of Babel" and "The Garden of Forking Paths."

copyleft: The opposite of *copyright.* Copyleft argues that no one can claim ownership of ideas and things. Copyleft is a form of "digital socialism" and is often associated with the hacker's ethic that information "wants" to be free. (See *plagiarism.*)

cultural hacker: A pirate and stealer of other people's copyrighted material. Or from a copyleft point of view, a hacker of the culture, and not by taking other people's things, but the culture's things, and taking them in strange, previously unknown directions of thought.

hypertext: Literally, "extended text," a form of nonsequential discourse used on the World Wide Web or other computer environments. Constructed at the surface similarly to sequential discourse, hypertext features *links* or *hotlinks* (in boldface or underlined), which when activated (that is, clicked on) display on the monitor embedded discourse, which in turn can have links to more embedded discourse, *ad infinitum.*

multimedia: A hypertext that can feature not only text but also audio and video.

plagiarism: The act of stealing someone else's ideas. (See *copyleft.*)

uniform resource locators (URLs): The addresses to Web sites. Such an address begins, for example, with <http://> (hypertext transfer protocol), which is one type of access method. A complete URL is composed of <access method://host.domain/path/filename>. Other access methods are file transfer protocol (ftp), gopher protocol (gopher), and wide-area information servers (wais).

Neil Postman and Camille Paglia

She Wants Her TV!
He Wants His Book!

Neil Postman and Camille Paglia's "She Wants Her TV! He Wants His Book!" was originally published in Harper's Magazine (March 1991): 44–51, 54–55. The format is that of a forum, comparable to the hackers' forum, but this time with only two people battling it out. The issue is books versus television, or print culture versus electronic culture.

hat I see as dangerous here," he said "is the discontinuity of emotion that television promotes, its unnatural evocation, every five minutes, of different and incompatible emotions."

"You leave a restaurant," she said, "and get killed by a falling air conditioner. A tornado hits a picnic. There is no sense to reality. Television is actually closer to reality than anything in books. The madness of TV is the madness of human life."

So went the conversation between two cultural critics, Neil Postman and Camille Paglia, taking up an argument that has vexed nearly everyone in this century—the struggle for preeminence between words and pictures, today between books and television. This conflict is uniquely American—debate so dense with prejudices that it has turned almost all of us into liars: "I don't watch TV" is now so common a dissembling among those who read that it has become a kind of mantra. And "I read that book" is a euphemism acceptable among recent generations to mean simply that one has heard of the title.

Neil Postman is one of the most original writers in defense of the book. A professor of communication arts at New York University and the author of *Amusing Ourselves to Death: Public Discourse in the Age of Show Business,* Postman is a scholar, raised in the pretelevision world, whose eloquence owes much to the classical declarative prose of Strunk and White. He argues that reading is an ordered process requiring us to sit at a table, consume ideas from left to right, and make judgments of truth and falsehood. By its nature, reading teaches us to reason. Television, with its random unconnected images, works against this linear tradition and breaks the habits of logic and thinking. Postman has said that the two most dangerous words in this century are "Now . . . this"—that strange verbal doodad uttered by television anchors to ease the transition from a report on a natural disaster to a commercial about your need—desperate need, in fact—for an electric toothbrush.

Those who argue from the other side usually make a weak and unconvincing case. With the possible exception of Marshall McLuhan, anyone writing about television has done so with apologies. Recently, a new critic has emerged named Camille Paglia. She is a professor of humanities at the Philadelphia College of the Arts and is currently finishing a critical history of culture that ranges from the cave paintings of Altamira to the Rolling

Stones concert at Altamont. Volume One, entitled *Sexual Personae: Art and Decadence from Nefertiti to Emily Dickinson,* was recently nominated for a National Book Critics Circle Award. Paglia was born after World War II, an accident to which she ascribes great significance. To hear her talk is to confirm her theory about the influence of the modern media: She speaks in a rush of images, juxtapositions, and verbal jump cuts. She argues that instead of criticizing television, most academics and other cultural critics simply turn up their noses dismissively at its enormous power—a kind of intellectual denial. Television, Paglia says, is the culture. And, she asks, by what and whose criteria is the latest Madonna any less meaningful an icon than the last? To those who argue that kids who watch television can't recall any of the facts mentioned on it, she wonders whether we have ever watched television. Perhaps we are doing something else when we stare at the screen; perhaps the remembrance of facts has nothing to do with television's significance or effect.

Since no two thinkers have in recent time made such compelling cases, *Harper's Magazine* decided to introduce them. We sent each author a copy of the other's book and asked each to read it. One cold winter night in December, we asked them to dine in the Private Tasting Room of New York City's Le Bernardin restaurant—a small, glass room located inside the kitchen of Chef Gilbert Le Coze. Throughout the conversation Bruno Jourdaine served a *menu dégustation* beginning with seviche of black bass and poured glasses of St. Veran Trenel (1988). We began the dinner with a blessing in the form of two readings from the Bible.

Thou shalt not make unto thee any graven image.

—Exodus 20:4

In the beginning was the Word, and the Word was with God, and the Word was God.

—John 1:1

CAMILLE PAGLIA: But John got it all wrong. "In the beginning was nature." That's the first sentence of *my* book. Nature—violent, chaotic, unpredictable, uncontrollable—predates and stands in opposition to the ordered, structured world created by the word, by the law, by the book-centered culture of Judeo-Christianity. The image—which is pagan and expressive of nature's sex and violence—was outlawed by Moses in favor of the word. That's where our troubles began.

Remember that when the Ten Commandments were handed down on Mount Sinai, Moses had just led the Jews out of Egypt. They had followed Joseph down there several hundred years before and had become resident workers, then slaves. Over time, Judaism had gotten a little mixed up with the local Egyptian cults—a syncretism not unlike Santería in the Caribbean, with its blend of voodoo and Catholicism. When Moses tried to get his people to leave Egypt, there was resistance: "What are we *doing?* Moses, you're crazy. What homeland are you talking about?" The Ten Commandments were an attempt to clarify what is Hebrew, what is Jewish.

The Second Commandment implies that the Hebrew God has no shape, that He is pure spirit. Egyptian gods often appeared in animal form. The pagan cults of Egypt, Babylon, and Canaan worshiped such idols—for example, the Golden Calf. So Moses is saying, "We do not worship the gods of nature but a God who is above nature, a God who *created* nature. The ultimate God."

And the prohibition against images didn't forbid just pagan idols. It banned *all* visual imagery, of anything on earth or in the heavens. Moses knew that once a people begin to make images of any kind, they fall in love with them and worship them. Historically, the Second Commandment diverted Jewish creative energy away from the visual arts and into literature, philosophy, and law.

NEIL POSTMAN: It is curious that of the first three, so-called establishing commandments, two of them concern communications: the prohibitions against making graven images and taking the Lord's name in vain. Yet this makes sense if you think about the problems of constructing an ethical system 3,000 years ago. It was critical to tell the members of the tribe how to symbolize their experience. That is why Moses chose writing—using a phonetic alphabet, which the Jews no doubt borrowed from the Egyptians—to conceptualize this nonvisual, nonmaterial God. Writing is the perfect medium because, unlike pictures or an oral tradition, the written word is a symbol system *of* a symbol system, twice removed from reality and perfect for describing a God who is also far removed from reality: a nonphysical, abstracted divinity. Moses smartly chose the right communications strategy. With the Second Commandment, Moses was the first person who ever said, more or less, "Don't watch TV; go do your homework."

Most important, the written word allows for the development of a God who is, above all things, *mobile.* To invent a God who exists only in the word and through the word is to make a God that can be taken anyplace. Just as writing is portable speech, Moses' God is a portable God, which is fitting for a people setting forth on a long journey.

PAGLIA: That is why Jewish culture is one of the founts of Western tradition and why Western culture is so intellectually developed. Jewish thought is highly analytical, as is Greco-Roman philosophy. Both are very Apollonian. But the Greco-Roman tradition is also one of pagan idolatry. Early Christianity, which first proselytized among the poor, outcast, and unlearned, needed to use visual imagery, which became more and more pronounced in the Middle Ages and early Renaissance. Out of this came the renegade priest Martin Luther, who correctly diagnosed a lapse from authentic early Christianity in medieval Catholicism. Catholics are never told to read the Bible. Instead, they have to listen to the priest commenting on excerpts from the Bible, usually just the New Testament.

POSTMAN: Luther called the invention of the printing press the "supremist act of grace by which the Gospel can be driven forward." And it was. As a result of Luther's Reformation, the intellectual geography of Europe flipped. Until then Venice, in the south of Europe, was the leading printing center and one of the world's intellectual capitals. Then the Catholic Church got nervous about it, because of the possibilities of further heresy, and began to restrict the printing press. And then, within a year of each other, Galileo died and Newton was born. The intellectual power of Europe moved from the south to the north. England, Scandinavia, Germany became the realm of the word, and the south returned to spectacle. Catholicism resorted increasingly to ornament and beautiful music and painting. To this day we think of Spain, Italy, and southern France as centers of great visual arts, from the Escorial to the Sistine Chapel. The north, home of the austere Protestant, concentrated on the word, until it found its greatest fulfillment here in the first political system built on the word alone: no divine right of kings, no mysticism, just a few pages of written text, the American Constitution.

PAGLIA: The polarity in Europe got more and more rigid. In the north, book, book, book; but in the Counter-Reformation of southern Europe, unbelievably lurid images—like Bernini's St. Teresa having a spiritual orgasm. My first childhood memories are of images, fantastic images, created by the Catholic Church. The statues are polychromatic, garish. In my church stood a statue of St. Sebastian, nude, arrows piercing his flesh, red blood dripping down. Who can wonder where *my* mind came from? Here were spectacular pagan images standing right next to the altar. In the beginning, you see, were sex and violence.

Early Christianity was very masculine. Just two male gods and a neuter— the Father, the Son, and the Holy Ghost. But the popular imagination couldn't tolerate that, so in the Middle Ages it added the Virgin Mary. Go reread the Bible and see how small a role Mary plays in the Gospels. Almost none. She is a survivor of the great goddess cults of antiquity. I interpret the most essential elements of Italian Catholicism as pagan. Martin Luther saw the latent paganism of the Catholic Church and rebelled against it. The latest atavistic discoverer of the pagan heart of Catholicism is Madonna. This is what she's up to. She doesn't completely understand it herself. When she goes on *Nightline* and makes speeches about celebrating the body, as if she's some sort of Woodstock hippie, she's way off. She needs *me* to tell her. But this is what she's doing—revealing the eroticism and sadomasochism, the pagan ritualism and idolatry in Italian Catholicism.

Protestantism today continues to be based on the word and the book. That's why Protestant ministers in church or on television always stress the Bible. They shout, "*This* is all you need." And they wave it, they flap it, they even slam it around. The Protestant needs no priest, no hierarchy. There is nothing between you and God. Protestants want a close and chatty relationship with Jesus: "Have you accepted Christ as your *personal* Savior?" And they sing, "He walks with you and He talks with you." For Protestants, Jesus is a friend, the Good Shepherd.

The Italian Catholic Jesus can't speak. He's either preliterate—a baby in the arms of Mary—or comatose—a tortured man on a cross. The period when Christ is literate, when he can speak, is edited out of southern Catholicism.

■ . . . B A K E D   S E A   U R C H I N . . .

POSTMAN: It helps to understand your point if we remember what happens every time Moses leaves. He comes back and the whole tribe has lapsed into idol worship. He is always complaining to Aaron, "What the hell did you do while I was gone?" The image is so seductive. Catholics are known for keeping little images on the dashboard of their cars, and nowadays you find them among Jews as well. Many reform temples now have more and more interesting visual designs. The Second Commandment held for a long time. Jews weren't known for their achievements in the visual arts until this century.

This proves my point about the life of the word and the image: Humans are not biologically programmed to be literate. In John Locke's essay on education, he insists that the body must become a slave to the mind. One of my students, upon hearing that quotation, said, "I know just what he means." And she told me how she can only read lying on her side while holding the book against the wall and, as a result, only reads the right-hand page of any book. This is the challenge of literacy: to get children accustomed to sitting still, to abiding in a realm that is unnaturally *silent*. That is the world of the word. How can silence compete with television?

This is the challenge of literacy: to get children accustomed to sitting still, to abiding in a realm that is unnaturally silent.

PAGLIA: But, Neil, people who are naturally disposed to reading may not be as physically active as others. There is an important difference here. I teach dancers. They are sometimes poor readers or even dyslexic. But they are brilliant at other, older forms of feeling and expression. Some people are inclined to the sedentary life that reading requires, others are not. That is why the entire discourse on sex and gender in academe and in the media is so off, because teachers and writers are not nearly as athletic or rambunctious as others.

POSTMAN: The literate person does pay a price for literacy. It may be that readers become less physically active and not as sensitive to movement, to dance, and to other symbolic modes. That's probably true. It's a Faustian bargain. Literacy gives us an analytic, delayed response in perceiving the world, which is good for pursuits such as science or engineering. But we do lose some part of the cerebral development of the senses, the sensorium.

PAGLIA: And some people have more developed sensoriums than others. I've found that most people born before World War II are turned off by the modern media. They can't understand how we who were born after the war can read a book and watch TV at the same time. But we *can*. When I wrote my book, I had earphones on, blasting rock music or Puccini and Brahms. The soap operas—with the sound turned down—flickered on my TV. I'd be talking on the phone at the same time. Baby boomers have a multilayered, multitrack ability to deal with the world. I often use the metaphor of a large restaurant stove to describe the way the mind works. There are many burners, and only one of them is the logical, analytical burner. And, Neil, I think we agree that our contemporary education system neglects it.

One reason American academic feminism is so mediocre is that these women can't think their way out of a wet paper bag. They have absolutely no training in logic, philosophy, or intellectual history, so they're reduced to arguing that we should throw out Plato and Aristotle because they're dead white males, or some such nonsense. That's so dopey and ignorant. People born before World War II can't understand those of us raised in the fragmented, imagistic world of TV. We can shut off one part of the brain and activate another. Scientists, psychologists, and IQ testers haven't caught up with these new ways of perception.

"With the commandment forbidding graven images, Moses became the first to say, 'Don't watch TV; do your homework.'"

POSTMAN: Camille, I think we actually agree on the evidence. Only you think it is all just fine and will be a liberating development. Television and the other visual media will enlarge the sensorium and give people a fuller repertoire of means of expression. Marshall McLuhan used to refer to people like me and others as POBS: Print-Oriented Bastards—literates who had their right hemispheres amputated or atrophied. You should adopt the term, Camille; your analysis is absolutely correct. Only I tend to see this development as ominous.

Bertrand Russell used to utter a lovely phrase. He said that the purpose of education was to teach each of us to defend ourselves against the "seductions of eloquence." In the realm of the word, we learn the specific techniques used to resist these seductions: logic, rhetoric, and literary criticism. What worries me is that we have not yet figured out how to build defenses against the seductions of imagery. The Nazi regime was only the most recent example of seducing, through words and images, one of the most *literate* populations on earth. I remember Hitler's rantings. Now, I won't ask you how old you are.

PAGLIA: I'm forty-three. I was born in 1947. And you graduated from college in 1953. I checked! I wanted to know, because I think this information is absolutely critical to how one views the mass media. I graduated from college in 1968. There are only fifteen years between us, but it's a critical fifteen years, an unbridgeable chasm in American culture.

■ . . . S H R I M P   A N D   B A S I L   B E I G N E T S . . .

POSTMAN: I remember the imagery of the 1940s, when an entire political machine was pressed into the service of imagistic propaganda. In America it is somewhat different. There *is* a machine producing such images, but it is capitalism, and the output is the commercial. The process is the same. Have you seen the commercial for Hebrew National frankfurters? It shows Uncle Sam while a narrator declares how good and healthy frankfurters are because

Uncle Sam maintains such high standards. Then Uncle Sam looks up as the narrator adds that Hebrew Nationals are even better than other frankfurters because they must answer to a higher authority.

PAGLIA: I love that ad! It's wonderful. Hilarious.

POSTMAN: Here is what bothers me. Symbols *are* infinitely repeatable, but they are not inexhaustible. If you use God to sell frankfurters, or if you use the face of George Washington to sell discount car tires, you drain the symbol of the very meanings, Camille, that you so astutely discover and explicate in your book. You look at a painting and analyze its levels of meaning, its ambiguities, its richness. But what happens if people see the same image a thousand times, and always to sell tight jeans?

PAGLIA: I would argue exactly the opposite. In the Hebrew National ads the invocation of Uncle Sam and God reinforces their symbolic meaning and helps young people have a historical perspective on their own culture.

Ads shaped the imagination of my generation. The Hebrew National image of Jehovah—that he's invisible, a voice inspiring his children to high standards—is faithful to tradition. It's a fabulous ad. And, by the way, it's true—kosher franks *are* better! I believed this ad and bought the franks! I love ads as an art form. To me, there is no degradation in this particular ad at all.

POSTMAN: Perhaps you're not taking it seriously enough, Camille. By age twenty, the average American has seen 800,000 television advertisements, about 800 a week. I am not talking about radio, print, or any other kind of advertisement. I am referring only to television advertisements. Television commercials are now the most powerful source of socialization, and the schools ought to take them seriously.

Some advertisements are good, of course. I don't think Madonna would serve too well. But I think of Jimmy Stewart selling soup. In that advertisement, the producers used his voice only because that voice is sufficient to symbolize what he stands for—the embodiment of the thoroughly decent American. So the use of that imagery is fine. But in the Hebrew National advertisement, a sense of the sacred is being eliminated, or exploited by redirecting it to the profane world.

PAGLIA: If Jehovah had never expressed Himself about table manners, I would support you. But the Bible shows that Jehovah instructed the Jews at great length about what foods to eat and how to prepare and serve them.

POSTMAN: And, of course, Jehovah also forbade shellfish—everything we're eating tonight!

PAGLIA: This is the point. Kosher ritual preparation is dictated by the Bible. Nothing in the Hebrew National ad distorts or lies about Jewish tradition.

POSTMAN: Suppose you saw a commercial that showed Jesus looking at a bottle of Gallo wine and saying, "When I turned the water into wine in Cana, it wasn't nearly as good as this Gallo Pinot Noir." What does that do to the meaning of Jesus Christ for Christians? You seem very enthusiastic about the use of these images, but I think the *secularization* of these symbols and religious icons is dangerous.

PAGLIA: To you, coming from the Judeo-Christian tradition, this looks secular. If you look at it from my perspective, popular culture is an eruption of paganism—which is also a sacred style. In your book, you skip from 1920 to television. I think you leap over a critical period—the great studio era of Hollywood movies in the 1930s and 1940s. Cinema then was a pagan cult full of gods and goddesses, glamour and charisma. It was a style devoted to the sacred and the numinous. So it's not that the sacred has been lost or is being trivialized. We are steeped in idolatry. The sacred is everywhere. I don't see any secularism. We've returned to the age of polytheism. It's a rebirth of the pagan gods.

What I argue in my book is that Judeo-Christianity never defeated paganism but rather drove it underground, from which it constantly erupts in all kinds of ways. Ancient Greco-Roman culture harnessed the dynamic duality of the Apollonian and the Dionysian principles. We've inherited the Apollonian element of the Greco-Roman tradition. The history of Western civilization has been a constant struggle between these two impulses, an unending tennis match between cold Apollonian categorization and Dionysian lust and chaos.

That's why you can always tell whether a critic was born before or after World War II by the way he or she speaks of the twentieth century. To you who grew up knowing life as narrative exposition and who saw the end of an era with Fitzgerald and Hemingway—and you're right, there was a great shift, and the novel is now dead as a doornail—it's the Age of Anxiety. But the death of the novel was also the beginning of movies. I date the modern age from the first sound pictures in 1928. I call the twentieth century the Age of Hollywood.

There's a huge generational difference here. For those of us born after the war, our minds were formed by TV. Take Susan Sontag, born in 1933. There are fourteen years between her and me. It doesn't seem like much, but it's like an abyss between us. In the 1960s she was writing briefly about popular culture, but then she backed off and has spent the rest of her life saying, "I'm serious, I'm serious. Gotta find that ultimate Eastern European writer!" A few years ago, she boasted in *Time* that she had no TV and had to rent one when a guest came to visit. My TV is constantly fluttering. It's a hearth fire in the modern home. TV is not something you *watch;* it is simply on, all the time.

■ ...SEARED SCALLOPS IN TRUFFLE VINAIGRETTE...

POSTMAN: If you keep this up, Camille, I'm going to need either more wine or a cigarette. Do you mind if I smoke?

PAGLIA: Not at all. Neil, in your book you mentioned tests in which people didn't remember any facts from a news program they had watched thirty minutes earlier on TV. But they weren't testing the right part of the brain.

Watching TV has nothing to do with thought or analysis. It's a passive but highly efficient process of storing information to be used later. The proper analogy is to interstate driving or football. You know, baseball was *the* sport of the pre–World War II era. Academics love it. It's the ultimate academic sport—linear, logical, slow. Football, especially as *remade* for TV with slow motion and replays, is the sport of my generation. There's a lot of writing about baseball but hardly any good stuff about football. When a quarterback pulls back from the line and quickly checks out the field, he's not thinking, he's *scanning,* the very thing we do when we watch TV. It's like the airline pilot sweeping his eyes across his bank of instruments or the driver cruising down the interstate at high speed, always scanning the field, looking for the drunk, the hot rod, the police, or the slow old lady in the Cadillac—watch out for *her.* None of these people—the quarterback, the pilot, the driver—is thinking. They're only reading the field and working by instinct, deciding in an instant where to throw the ball or steer the jet or car. The decision is made by intuition, not by ratiocination.

POSTMAN: It's called pattern recognition.

PAGLIA: Oh, really? Perfect! And that's why you can't picture Susan Sontag driving a car. You know what I mean? Can you imagine Susan Sontag behind the wheel? Forget it. It's like a *New Yorker* cartoon: *Susan Sontag buys her first car!*

POSTMAN: Of course, I agree: Reading a book and "reading" television are two completely different cerebral activities. I can remember hearing print-oriented people complain that the problem with a show like *Charlie's Angels* is that it didn't honor the Aristotelian unities of time, place, and action. Or that it didn't have any *true* character development.

PAGLIA: You liked *Charlie's Angels?*

POSTMAN: As a matter of fact, I did, but I am bringing it up as an example of how people misread television. Print-oriented people can't understand such a show because they try to judge it by the measures of literature. I came to understand *Charlie's Angels* when I realized that the entire show was about *hair.*

Do you remember that at the end of the show there was a two-minute segment in which the disembodied voice of Charlie explained to the angels *what the entire show had been about?* I imagine that the show was written by a bunch of former English majors. And I see them confounded by the fact that they have just written a show that is basically about hair and doesn't fit any of the categories that they have been taught count. So at the end, they shoehorn in a vestigial narrative. Once I saw an episode in which, in order to explain everything, the voice at the end had to mention characters and action that hadn't even been *in* the program: "She killed him because years ago he had stolen money and given it to a third person . . ." Those sixty seconds before the credits—when the show was actually already over—were meant to give a show about hair a sense of logic or coherence.

PAGLIA: *TV Guide* once said about the actresses on *Knots Landing*—my favorite prime-time show—that "they act with their hair." I love it! Soap operas also are mainly about hair, you know. Very pagan—the worship of beauty. And do you realize that the Farrah Fawcett hairdo of *Charlie's Angels* can still be seen today in every shopping mall in America? Though that show has been off the air for ten years, it has this incredible ongoing influence. Farrah herself has moved on to battered-wife roles, but her old Seventies hairstyle is still the dominant look for boy-crazy girls in American high schools. Awesome, really.

"Print-oriented people judged Charlie's Angels by the measures of a literature, but it was a show entirely about hair."

POSTMAN: We agree on the influence of popular culture as expressed through visual images. Everyone has a right to defend his or her own culture, and I feel sure there will be a cost to the kind of culture I value. It may be that your sensorium has been enlivened while mine has atrophied. But let's look at my tradition and see what it has accomplished. Consider that in 1776 Thomas Paine sold, by the most conservative estimates, 300,000 copies of *Common Sense*. That is the equivalent of selling 30,000,000 copies—a feat attainable only today by Danielle Steel or Tom Wolfe. Camille, do you think we will pay a price for this more fully developed sensorium?

PAGLIA: In your book you say that there was a high literacy rate during the American Revolution. But does that mean people actually *read* books? Political and literary books? Or was it that they could just sign their names? Your portrait of the highly literate nineteenth century also sort of ignores the trashy sentimental novels, ladies' fashion magazines, and the dime western. I agree with you that our country was founded as an Enlightenment experiment. The framers of the American Constitution were true intellectuals. But I think your book puts undue stress on that period, which was, as I see it, a kind of privileged moment. Comparing our period with that one—when there was a high degree of cultural awareness and political activity—makes us think we're slipping into a decline. But maybe we're just returning to the norm. I think the world as it is now is the way it always was.

■ . . . B L A C K   B A S S   I N   C O R I A N D E R   N A G E . . .

POSTMAN: I'm not certain it was only a privileged moment, although you are right in suggesting that a high literacy rate creates a somewhat abstracted view of the world. Our culture paid a price for literacy, and it will pay a price for its transformation into a visual culture. We are, for example, rapidly losing any sense of sacrality. The reason the Ayatollah Khomeini struck most Americans as either a complete riddle or a lunatic is that he was actually a *truly religious person*. And we can no longer understand what such a person is like.

PAGLIA: Exactly. Whenever Qaddafi would spend days in his tent, the Western media would sneer and ridicule him. I couldn't believe it. Does no one understand the ethical meaning of the desert in Bedouin culture? It's like our Walden Pond. Hasn't the media ever seen *Lawrence of Arabia?* There are two lessons in the Salman Rushdie case. First, artistic freedom is a value only in the democratic Western tradition. Second, to millions of people in the world, religion is a matter of life and death.

POSTMAN: Camille, I think these observations support my argument that what I call the secularization of imagery depletes religious symbolism: not only the frequency of the image but also the ignominious tie between the image and commercialization. That is why we in the West can't understand why someone would risk his life in an attempt to kill Salman Rushdie. To us, it's crazy. To the martyr, it is the path to heaven.

PAGLIA: Rather than your total secularization, I see the repaganization of Western culture. In the realm of politics, I think pop culture—the vehicle of the pagan eruption—plays a crucial role. Popular culture has the function of purging politics of many of its potential demagogues. Elvis Presley, an enormously charismatic figure, was able to build his empire in the politically neutral realm of pop culture.

POSTMAN: Are you saying that Hitler might have been a Hollywood star in America?

PAGLIA: Today, you have other ways for extraordinarily charismatic people to create their worlds. There are other ways to rule the universe. Before popular culture, the only realm that allowed that kind of power of personality was politics.

POSTMAN: I see the confluence between television and politics a little differently. The first television president was, obviously, John Kennedy. But the first *image* president was Ronald Reagan. They were very different figures. Kennedy, Jimmy Carter, even Mario Cuomo are very much identified with regions of the country. They were and are developed personalities that play well on television. But Reagan and even Bush are different. Remember how no one knows what state Bush is from and how Reagan's being from California seemed irrelevant. These are personalities onto whom a full spectrum of voters are able to project their personal image of a president. Whatever a president is supposed to be, then that is what Reagan or Bush is.

PAGLIA: As a television persona, Reagan was avuncular and nostalgic—a return to the happy, innocent, pre–World War II era of baseball, before the chaos and disasters of the Sixties. He was simple, kindly, even-tempered, sometimes goofy. He got into his pajamas right after dinner. He ate jelly beans. He called his wife "Mommy." He never aged. His hair never got gray. To liberal writers and academics, these things seemed stupid and ludicrous.

They were off reading his policy papers, missing the whole point of his popularity. Our president is both the political and the symbolic head of our government, serving in jobs that in England, for example, are separately represented by the prime minister and the queen. The president symbolizes the nation in psychodramatic form.

POSTMAN: A nation as heterogeneous as ours gropes to find comprehensive symbols and icons to pull us together. Ronald Reagan was such an image. Every Christmas you hear people say, "Happy Holidays." We try to be so polite and inclusive. We are a fragile polity desperate for unifying images. But, paradoxically, we can destroy ourselves by exhausting the available icons.

PAGLIA: Another such image is the national weather map, which is shown, naturally, on TV. Here's this patchwork country of Chinese and Chicanos and African-Americans and Jews and Italians, and then there's this map with beautifully sweeping curved lines of air pressure stretching from sea to shining sea, pulling us together. The weatherman and the president are our two titular heads.

These images and their meaning become obvious once you know how to read TV. One more example. Remember, during the 1988 election, how everyone was calling George Bush a wimp? And he *was* a wimp, constantly trotting after Reagan and in his shadow. What a ninny, I would think; he'll never win the election. Then came the day when Ronald Reagan made his last visit to the Republican convention, and Bush named Dan Quayle as his running partner for vice president. It was the most stunning moment of TV transformation I've ever seen, but no one in the media picked it up. After Reagan left, remember the outdoor scene when Bush named Quayle? The press hysterically rushed off to report the story of how silly, stupid, and rich Quayle was. But the story was not that George had picked a jerk. The story was that George Bush, emerging as a new man, had picked a *son*. Bush had made a complete *rite de passage* on television and for television. Remember how Quayle was jumping around acting like a puppy—even grabbing Bush by the shoulder? Later that day at the indoor press conference, Bush was amazingly stern and confident. He cut reporters off, he was completely in charge. He was this totally new person, a man no one had seen before. It was then I knew he was going to be president. I called people up and told them, but no one believed me. If you didn't know how to read TV or weren't watching, you missed it completely.

POSTMAN: And my point, Camille, which you are overlooking, is that Roger Ailes engineered that entire effect. We were all manipulated into having just that very perception.

PAGLIA: What I am talking about is nothing that Roger Ailes could have created. It was a side of Bush that predated Roger Ailes. We all have many personas, and we can pick and choose which to make public. But we cannot create them. Roger Ailes could not have saved Michael Dukakis.

■ . . . R O A S T   M O N K F I S H   O N   S A V O Y   C A B B A G E . . .

POSTMAN: Granted. If you read Bush's résumé, it is one of the most macho documents of recent times—first baseman at Yale, youngest Navy pilot, shot down in combat, head of the CIA. But when Ailes saw him acting like a ninny on television—and television does have a way of showing the authentic soul—I agree, he went to work on the indecisive wimp and promoted the image of the macho guy so that you and others would pick it up. And then that image was repeated and repeated, washing away any memory of a past impression.

PAGLIA: In your book you speak of television as being a medium of flashing images with only an eternal present and no past. I disagree. It's just the opposite. TV is a genre of reruns, a formulaic return to what we already know. Everything is familiar. Ads and old programs are constantly recycled. It's like mythology, like the Homeric epics, the oral tradition, in which the listener hears pasages, formulae, and epithets repeated over and over again. There is a joy in repetition, as children know when they say, "Mommy, tell me that story again." TV is a medium that makes us feel "at home."

"Pop culture purges politics of demagogues: A charismatic figure such as Elvis could build his empire in the pop realm."

If you go back to the Fifties, when movies lost their cultural centrality to TV, you'll see that the great sacred images— the huge, cold images of cinema—were being miniaturized, familiarized, and domesticated by the television screen. The box became part of the family, and the shows reflected it: *Father Knows Best* and *Leave it to Beaver*. Ads are the same way. I put one of my favorite ads in my book—Luciana Avedon crooning, "Camay has coconut-enriched lather." I adored that ad! Of course, ads you hate are like torture. You want to die.

So TV is about repetition and compulsion. It's like prayer, like the Catholic Rosary, repeated over and over again. That's what ads are: soothing litanies that make us feel safe and familiar and at home in the strange modern world.

POSTMAN: So idolatry has triumphed. I think Luther would join Moses in saying that the cult of the word is defenseless in the face of the image.

PAGLIA: Moses got his people out of Egypt, out of the land of the pagan image. That was the only way. Judaism could not have flourished in Egypt. Today, either you live in a cabin in northern Canada or you try to control TV. And I believe we *should* try to control it, by the way. Liberals are wrong when they say, "Parents should just turn off the TV set." You can't. TV is everywhere. It's bigger than politics. It's bigger than the Church.

POSTMAN: This is where education comes in, Camille. I believe that educational theory should be what I call "ecological"; that is, education should supply what the rest of the culture is not supplying. In this case, I think the only defense against the seductions of imagery is a literate education. If children are educated in the traditions of the word, then perhaps they will be able to make discriminating choices in the chaotic realm of the image.

PAGLIA: To me the ideal education should be rigorous and word-based—logocentric. The student must learn the logical, hierarchical system. Then TV culture allows the other part of the mind to move freely around the outside of that system. This is like the talent you need for internal medicine. An internist has to be intuitive. He knows there are about a half dozen different systems in the body, all interrelated. His mind has to weave in and out and around them and more or less guess what's wrong. This is the mental flexibility that a word-based education and a TV-based culture can develop. All parents should read to their children, from infancy on. Education is, by definition, repressive. So if you're going to repress, then repress like hell. I don't believe in the Dewey or Montessori methods—"We want to make this pleasant." There is nothing pleasant about learning to read or to think. The teachers used to shake me and yell at me to stay in line or sit still in my seat. I didn't like it, but I recommend it.

PAGLIA: *Well, Neil, that's life.*

POSTMAN: *That's insanity.*

PAGLIA: *Not to me.*

POSTMAN: In *Aspects of the Novel,* E. M. Forster wrote that if you say the king died and the queen died, you don't have a story. But if you say that the king died *because* the queen died, you have a story. I find that television undermines these simple word-based connections. The whole idea of language is to provide a world of intellectual and emotional continuity and predictability. But many of my students no longer understand, for example, the principle of contradiction. I was talking to one student the other day about a paper in which he asserted one thing to be true in the first paragraph and the exact opposite to be true three paragraphs later. He said, "What's the problem?"

This habit derives from television, which tells you that there was a rape in New York and then it tells you there was an earthquake in Chile and then it tells you that the Mets beat the Cardinals.

PAGLIA: Well, Neil, that's life.

POSTMAN: That's insanity.

PAGLIA: Not to me. In your book you say TV is Dadaist in its random, nihilistic compilation of unrelated events. I say it's surrealist—because *life* is surreal! You leave a restaurant and get killed by a falling air conditioner. A tornado hits a picnic. There's no sense to reality. It simply happens. Television is actually closer to reality than anything in books. The madness of TV is the madness of human life.

POSTMAN: Here is what I would like: When our young student is watching Dan Rather say that 5,000 people died in an earthquake in Chile and then Dan says, "We'll be right back after this word from United Airlines," I would like our student to say, "Hey, wait a second, how could he ask me to make such an emotional switch?"

PAGLIA: My answer is this: Buddha smiles. He sees the wheel of reincarnation and accepts the disasters of the universe. That's the way it should be. There's no way we can possibly extend our compassion to 5,000 dead people. By juxtaposing such jarring images, TV is creating a picture of the world that is simply true to life. We are forced to contemplate death the way farmers do—as just another banal occurrence, no big deal. Nature can crack the earth open and swallow thousands, and then the sun shines and the birds sing. It's like going from an airplane crash to a hemorrhoids ad. In TV, as in nature, all have equal weight.

■ . . . C A R O U S E L   O F   C A R A M E L   D E S S E R T S

POSTMAN: What I am focusing on is our emotional response to those things. We all know that nurses who work in hospitals make jokes. They see the absurdity of death routinely. But they don't see anywhere near the number of deaths the television viewer sees. What I see as dangerous here is a discontinuity of emotion that television promotes, its unnatural evocation, every five minutes, of different and incompatible emotions.

PAGLIA: By moving from disaster to commercial, TV creates the effect of Greek tragedy: emotion, then detachment; contemplation of loss, then philosophical perspective. At the end of *Hamlet,* there are four corpses strewn all over the stage.

POSTMAN: But no one is laughing—although I will admit that in the graveyard scene, when Hamlet makes the "Alas, poor Yorick" speech, he *is* laughing. But my point is, just after Horatio's final soliloquy, at least on television, we would then see the Hebrew National spot, or perhaps a commercial for Danish pastry.

"Jesus was a brilliant Jewish stand-up comedian, a phenomenal improvisor. His parables are great one-liners."

PAGLIA: To make that radical switch from disaster to detachment is, I think, a maturing process. If you fully responded emotionally to every disaster you saw, you'd be a mess. In fact, you'd be a perpetual child, a psychological cripple. Wisdom by definition is philosophical detachment from life's disasters.

POSTMAN: Injecting humor into otherwise insane catastrophes is comic relief. It is what we must do unless we want to go mad. But the effect I am talking about on the television news is different.

PAGLIA: I know that you see "amusement" as a bad thing wherever it shows up. You said in your book that teaching has finally been reduced to a branch of popular entertainment and that students won't sit still for anything that's not as funny as Big Bird on Sesame Street. And you cite Plato, Cicero, and Locke as educational philosophers who would insist on seriousness. I respectfully disagree. Plato's dialogues, which follow the Socratic method, a conversational give-and-take such as we're having here, are in fact very entertaining. There's a lot of comedy in Plato. Socrates is always pretending to be the most ignorant person there, and so on.

I think Jesus was a brilliant Jewish stand-up comedian, a phenomenal improvisor. His parables are great one-liners. When an enemy, trying to trap him, asks him about paying taxes, Jesus says, "Show me the coin of the tribute. Whose image is on it?" "Caesar's," the guy replies. "Then render unto Caesar the things that are Caesar's and unto God the things that are God's." I think that line got applause and laughs.

POSTMAN: You studied with Harold Bloom too long.

PAGLIA: Bloom used to say, "Teaching's a branch of show biz!" One last point—there are the koans, the teachings of the great Buddhist masters. They often took the form of slapstick. The novice comes in and says, "Tell me about life, master," and the elder whacks him on the head. Or says something surreal, like "Beanstalk!" So we do have many examples of teaching by great sages using humor or stand-up improv—Plato, Jesus, Buddha.

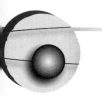

POSTMAN: *You studied with Harold Bloom too long.*

PAGLIA: *Bloom used to say, "Teaching's a branch of show biz!"*

POSTMAN: No one is saying not to use humor in the classroom. I guess we are talking about magnitude. It is one thing to use humor to reveal an idea you are developing. But now it is used simply to win the student's attention. Consequently, drawing an audience—rather than teaching—becomes the focus of education, and that is what television does. School is the one institution in the culture that should present a different worldview: a different way of knowing, of evaluating, of assessing. What worries me is that if school becomes so overwhelmed by entertainment's metaphors and metaphysics, then it becomes not content-centered but attention-centered, like television, chasing "ratings" or class attendance. If school becomes that way, then the game may be lost, because school is using the same approach, epistemologically, as television. Instead of being something different from television, it is reduced to being just another *kind* of television.

PAGLIA: Our dialogue has reached one major point of agreement. I want schools to stress the highest intellectual values and ideals of the Greco-Roman and Judeo-Christian traditions. Nowadays, "logocentric" is a dirty word. It comes from France, where deconstruction is necessary to break the stranglehold of centuries of Descartes and Pascal. The French *have* something to deconstruct. But to apply Lacan, Derrida, and Foucault to American culture is absolutely idiotic. We are born into an imagistic and pagan culture ruled by TV. We don't need any more French crap from ditsy Parisian intellectuals and their American sycophants. Neil, we agree on this: We need to reinforce the logocentric and Apollonian side of our culture in the schools. It is time for enlightened repression of the children.

■ Q U E S T I O N S   F O R   R E R E A D I N G

1. What is the significance of beginning the dinner discussion between Neil Postman and Camille Paglia with two passages as "a blessing" from the Bible? (Did you notice that the meal is punctuated with fish courses?) Map out the step-by-step images and analogies that Paglia uses as she proceeds on the opening pages of the discussion. How does Postman respond to the images? (Perhaps you might want, first, to concentrate on the advertisement for Hebrew National frankfurters and then work your way back to the start of the discussion.)

2. Trace how Postman and Paglia both weave in and out of the discussion with each other and how, occasionally, Postman will say, "Camille, I think these [your] observations support my argument" about "secularization." And then Paglia talks about "repaganization." What's the difference?

3. What does Paglia mean by the logocentric and Apollonian side of culture and the Dionysian side? Paglia points to her agreement with Postman at the very end ("enlightened repression of the children"), but what leads to the differences in terms of Postman's favoring books and Paglia's favoring all media including books?

4. How do you respond to Paglia's attitude that terrible things happen to human beings and we just have to learn to live with them? Would you charge her with political quietism (indifference to suffering) when she makes this kind of statement?

5. When you wake up in the morning or arrive home, do you turn on the television right away? Do you do your homework with the television on? With music blasting? With the television on *and* music blasting, and so on?

■ W R I T I N G   A S S I G N M E N T   F O R   R E R E A D I N G

Try an experiment: Half of the class do an assignment, which includes writing, in complete silence and without any other intrusion. And the other half do the same assignment with the television and stereo (or Walkman) going on and any other "natural" intrusion imaginable. Do the same writing assignment and take the same amount of time to do it. Then compare the two by placing examples on a class Web site and writing a collaborative essay that compares and reports on the two different ways, perhaps better known as the Postman way and the Paglia way. If you like what you did, then have your instructor contact me with your URL. I would like to consider establishing a link to the site. (vvitanza@aol.com)

Ted Gup

The End
of Serendipity

Ted Gup's "The End of Serendipity" first appeared in The Chronicle of Higher Education (November 21, 1997): A52. He recalls having a twenty-two-volume printed encyclopedia and compares it to the CD-ROM that his two sons have of the same encyclopedia. His claim is that the printed version allowed for unintended discoveries that the CD version will not allow for. And therein lies a major reconfiguration of the conditions for education.

When I was a young boy, my parents bought me a set of *The World Book Encyclopedia*. The twenty-two burgundy-and-gold volumes lined the shelves above my bed. On any given day or night I would reach for a book and lose myself for hours in its endless pages of maps, photographs, and text. Even when I had a purpose in mind—say, for instance, a homework assignment on salamanders—I would invariably find myself reading instead of Salem and its witch hunts or of Salamis, where the Greeks routed the Persians in the fifth century B.C. Like all encyclopedias of the day, it was arranged alphabetically, based on sound and without regard to subject. As a child, I saw it as a system wondrously whimsical and exquisitely inefficient. Perfect for exploration. The "S" volume alone could lead me down 10,000 unconnected highways.

The world my two young sons inherit is a very different place. That same encyclopedia now comes on CD-ROM. Simply drop the platinum disk into the A-drive and type in a key word. In a flash the subject appears on the screen. The search is perfected in a single keystroke—no flipping of pages, no risk of distraction, no unintended consequences. And therein lies the loss.

My boys belong to an age vastly more efficient in its pursuit of information but oblivious to the pleasures and rewards of serendipity. From Silicon Valley to M.I.T., the best minds are dedicated to refining our search for answers. Noble though their intentions may be, they are inadvertently smothering the opportunity to find what may well be the more important answers—the ones to questions that have not yet even occurred to us. I wish, then, to write on behalf of random epiphanies and the virtues of accidental discovery—before they, too, go the way of my old Remington manual.

My boys are scarcely aware that they are part of a grand experiment in which the computer, the Internet, and the World Wide Web are redefining literacy and reshaping the architecture of how they learn. These innovations are ushering in a world that, at least to my tastes, is entirely too purposeful—as devoid of romance as an arranged marriage. Increasingly, we hone our capacity to target the information that we seek. More ominous still, we weed out that which we deem extraneous. In a world of information overload, this ability to filter what reaches us has been hailed as an unqualified good. I respectfully disagree.

Consider, for example, those of my sons' generation who are learning to read the newspaper on a computer screen. They do not hold in their hands a cumbersome front page but instead see a neat menu that has sliced and diced the news into user-friendly categories. They need not read stories but merely scan topical headings—sports, finance, entertainment. The risk that they or any readers will inadvertently be drawn into a story afield from their peculiar interests, or succumb to some picture or headline, grows ever more remote. The users define their needs while the computer, like an overly eager waiter, stands ready to deliver, be it the latest basketball scores, updates of a personal stock portfolio, or tomorrow's weather. In my youth, information was a smorgasbord. Walking past so irresistible an array of dishes, I found it impossible not to fill my plate. Today, everything is à la carte.

There are moral consequences to being able to tailor the information that reaches us. Like other journalists, I have spent much of my life writing stories that I knew, even as I worked on them, would not be welcomed by my readers. Accounts of war, of hardship or want seldom are. But those stories found their way first into readers' hands and then into their minds. They were read sometimes reluctantly, sometimes with resentment, and, most often, simply because they appeared on the printed page. Doubtless the photo of a starving child or a string of refugees stretching above the morning's shredded wheat and orange juice may be viewed as an unsightly intrusion, but it is hard to ignore.

In cyberspace, such intrusions will become less frequent. There will be fewer and fewer uninvited guests. Nothing will come unless summoned. Unless the mouse clicks on the story, the account will not materialize. And who will click on the story headlined "Rwandans Flee," "Inner-City Children Struggle," or even "Endangered Butterflies Fight for Survival"? If the mouse is a key, it is also a padlock to keep the world out.

"If the mouse is a key, it is also a padlock to keep the world out."

Those already on the margins of our consciousness—the homeless, the weak, the disenfranchised—are being pushed right off the page, exiled into cyberspace and the ever-expanding domain of the irrelevant. Already the phrase "That's not on my screen" has found its way into common parlance. In the end, self-interest may be the most virulent form of censorship, inimical to compassion and our sense of community. It is the ultimate V-chip, this power to sanitize reality, to bar unpleasantries. "Technology," the Swiss playwright Max Frisch once observed, is "the knack of so arranging the world that we don't have to experience it."

It would be ironic if the computer, this great device of interconnectivity, should engender a world of isolationists. Yet increasingly we use its powers to read about ourselves and to feed our own parochial self-interests. Instead of a global village, we risk a race of cyber-hermits. And the World Wide Web, the promised bridge to that which is beyond ourselves, may be yet another moat to protect the self-absorbed.

A friend of mine recently joined Microsoft. He was struck by the youthfulness of those around him and the absolute faith they had that every question had an answer, every problem a solution. It is the defining character of the Microsoft Culture, its celebration of answers. Within that church, there are few Luthers to challenge its orthodoxy. So much energy is spent to produce the right answers that little time is left to ponder the correctness of the questions.

I find it amusing that Bill Gates, shrewd investor that he is, has emerged as one of the world's premier art collectors, acquiring the notebooks of Leonardo da Vinci, the consummate figure of the Renaissance. I wonder: Does he indentify with that genius, or, perhaps recognizing the peril in which that humanistic tradition is now placed, is he simply attempting to corner the market on its artifacts?

This is not a revolution but an evolution. In ancient caves can be found flakes of flint left by early humans, evidence of the first impulse to put a point on our tools, to refine them. The computer, with its search engines, is simply an extension of that primal urge. From the Olduvai Gorge to Silicon Valley, we have always been obsessed with bringing our tools to a perfect point. But where knowledge of the world is concerned, I suspect there is some virtue to possessing a blunter instrument. Sometimes a miss produces more than a hit.

Ironically, we continue to call entrées to cyberspace "Web browsers," but increasingly they are used not to browse but to home in on a narrow slice of the universe. We invoke mystery with corporate names such as "Oracle," but we measure progress in purely quantitative terms—gigabits and megahertz, capacity and speed. Our search engines carry names such as "Yahoo" and "Excite," but what they deliver is ever more predictable. The parameters of the universe shrink, defined by key words and Boolean filters, sieves that—with each improvement in search engines—increasingly succeed in siphoning off anything less than responsive to our inquiries. The more precise the response, the more the process is hailed as a success.

What has been billed as the information superhighway has, like all superhighways, come with a price. We have shortened the time between departure and arrival, but gone is all scenery in between, reduced to a Pentium blur. We settle for information at the expense of understanding and mistake retrieval for exploration. The vastness of the Internet's potential threatens to shrink into yet another utility. As the technology matures, the adolescent exuberance of surfing the Web yields to the drudgery of yet another commute.

One need not be a Luddite or technophobe to sound a cautionary word in the midst of euphoria over technology. I have a fantasy that one day I will produce a computer virus and introduce it into my own desktop, so that when my sons put in their key word—say, "salamander"—the screen will erupt in a brilliant but random array of maps and illustrations and text that will divert them from their task. This I will do so that they may know the sheer joy of finding what they have not sought. I might even wish for this virus to spread from computer to computer. And I would name this virus for that which ought not to be lost—serendipity.

1. Gup's position that serendipity—chance discoveries—are not possible, or are less possible, with electronic books, challenges much that I say in my introduction to this chapter about particular hypertext documents being radically associative and much that others say in the readings. For example, Gup writes: "In my youth, information was a smorgasbord. . . . Today, everything is à la carte." How does Gup set up the terms for not discovering something unintended and not new? What are the terms that I established? Is what he says about most CD-ROM encyclopedias or dictionaries true? What about the searches that you make when you look for the location of a book in your library via the computer? Or when you use a search engine on the Web? The issue here is how links or connections are established. Are all links predetermined for you? While there may be a team of collaborative authors establishing and directing all the links in an encyclopedia on a CD-ROM, is there such a team on the Web?

2. Gup extends his claim to searching on the Internet for information. For example, let's say that you want to find out something about "the lost library of Alexandria" and you go to the search engine *AltaVista*. One of the things that your instructor will tell you is that you must refine and focus your search by way of, say, boolean logic, which allows you to say what you want and don't want. Okay, so using AltaVista, type in what you want and see what you get. Probably you will get far too much. So you will have to start narrowing down by excluding what you do not want, right? You will have to use boolean logic, after the fact, right? What conclusions do you draw from this experience? Can you think of any instances, however, that would not work from general search to particular search, but straight to particular search?

3. Having conducted the preceding search and reasoning through the questions, do you still think that there is merit in what Gup says? (As an author or editor of this book, I am not supposed to intrude my answer into the asking of the question, but I do think that there is much merit to Gup's claim. If you agree or disagree, then why? Give the specifics of an argument.)

Write me and let me know what your extended answer is to question 3. (vvitanza@aol.com)

Computers Should Supplement Textbooks, Not Replace Them

Gerry Barker's [subscribers respond to question] "Computers Should Supplement Textbooks, Not Replace Them" originally appeared in The Fort Worth Star-Telegram *(December 7, 1997): D3. Each week, Barker puts forth an issue in the form of a question and has readers comment and vote on it. The issue of computers replacing textbooks is a hot one in Texas, for it is a real proposed change being considered by the state for the academic year 1998–99.*

This week's question:

Do you support replacing textbooks in Texas public schools with laptop computers?

Yes: 35.

No: 218.

Not sure: 11.

- "The school system can't control where the money goes now. What's gonna happen if we start pumping that kind of money towards laptops? Besides, we need to keep the idea of books around for as long as we can."

- "Sounds good, but there is no way a computer can replace textbooks. Books don't 'crash' or fail due to dead batteries or power failures. Before we replace textbooks, we had better teach kids to read them. If they can't read a book, how can they read data on a screen?"

- "I think someone has lost their mind to even consider such a thing. The current crop of teen-agers can't seem to do the simplest math in their heads because they grew up with calculators, and it is very frustrating to see someone use pencil and paper to figure 10 percent! There is such a thing as too much technology and too little common sense."

- "Stay with textbooks."

- "*Absolutely not!* Children need to learn the basics first. Computers in schools shouldn't happen, on an individual basis, until middle school."

- "I think kids have already become quite lazy. Some lads don't even know basic multiplication without their calculators. Why encourage more 'electronic knowledge'? I agree that learning about computers is a great tool, and an invaluable skill in today's growing world; however, I feel that basic reading, writing and math skills are needed as a basis for anyone's success."

- "First of all, can we play 'dropsy' with these high-tech electronics? That's what's going to happen. Second, more temptation and neat little packages means you need more security to protect your investment. Third—why? Let's get to first base with the 'three R's' before we look for ever fancier ways to soak the taxpayer. I have worked with computers for 30 years, and I guarantee you don't need one to get a first-rate education."

- "For some classes, but not for all of them."

- "Since my kindergartener entered school this year, we have been bombarded with every kind of marketing/sales effort to raise money for her school—i.e., computers, books, etc. It has been explained to me that the schools are grossly underfunded, unable to afford even the most basic things. My tax money would be better spent on giving teachers better pay! All the technology in the world will never replace a top-notch teacher and her love of children and the world they desire to open up to young minds."

- "*No way!* We already have a problem with our students not being able to read. Books are the fundamental vehicle to reading and comprehension skills in life."

- "Can you imagine the cost? 'The dog ate my laptop!' "

- "Computers should supplement textbooks, not replace them. Reading skills will diminish significantly without textbooks, and the joy of reading will be completely vitiated."

- "No. We can't afford textbooks for all our children in school. How can we buy laptops and pay for the upkeep?"

- "Generally I do support replacing textbooks with laptop computers. Why? Well, the time it takes for a book to go from written to published text, especially in the newer technologies, is just too long! The printed books are obsolete before the students use them to learn from, and our teachers are just not able to fill the gaps from printed book to current events. No blame to lay—the technology is just moving too fast for the current system of printed text!"

- "I support mandatory inclusion of visual arts in the standard K–12 curriculum and the installation of art facilities in existing schools."

- "*No!* The public education system cannot even afford enough books for all of the kids. How could it possibly afford a laptop for each one? Just imagine the amount of vandalism and lost laptops that would result."

- "*Yes,* by all means! I can't find a single pawnshop that will buy my textbooks, but I know I can unload my laptop at the nearest one for at least 50 bucks. If I can get my hands on enough laptops, I might even stay in school a few extra years and earn a living by hocking my computers."

- "Computers should be a vital part of education. However, they should not replace textbooks. Ninety percent of the graduating seniors do not know how to read as it is, and they sure won't learn how to read on a computer screen."

- "The cost of maintaining, updating and providing equipment to all students is not worth what little benefit they might gain in computer expertise."

- "What would be on the laptops? Complete textbooks? Word processors?"

- "Yes, but we must first upgrade teaching skills and related tech and educational support to where the teachers can tailor programs to the individual needs and skills of each student. Until then, laptops would be a waste of time and money for most students."

- "The cost of such a practice would not be practical. Also, textbooks do not require special training beyond learning to read, and textbooks do not crash or require batteries or electrical outlets to operate."

- "Yes, and I also support replacing teachers with a video hookup that would have a very qualified teacher in that particular subject, with a monitor in the classroom—who could/should be a teacher. But the 'main' teacher would be the best in the field."

- "First, young people must master the art of reading. Then they are taught computer skills. The computer is a big part of our daily lives. However, textbooks should remain the foundation for learning."

- "Absolutely not for it. We have already dumbed down a lot of our youth by allowing them to use calculators to solve problems. Many of them do not even know how to make change unless the cash register tells them what to give you. And why learn to spell? If you have a computer, it has spell-check."

- "No. Let's get the kids familiar with books and their many delights. *Then* the laptops would be in order. First things first!"

QUESTIONS FOR REREADING

1. Discuss the merits of using virtual books in elementary and secondary schools instead of actual books. After discussing the merits, argue for keeping actual books and not using virtual ones at all.

2. After the discussing the pros and cons, take a tally (Yes, No, Not Sure) so as to see what the results are in your class.

WRITING ASSIGNMENT FOR REREADING

After the discussion and tally, write a position paper on the value, or lack thereof, in using virtual books, CD-ROMs, over actual books. You may write this individually or collaboratively.

Into the Electronic Millennium

Sven Birkerts's "Into the Electronic Millennium" is a chapter from The Gutenberg Elegies: The Fate of Reading in an Electronic Age (Boston: Faber and Faber, 1994). Birkerts has become one of the canonized authors lamenting the loss of print culture. Much like Slouka (in chapter 2) he cautions his reader about what to expect in our moving from a print culture to an electronic culture.

ome years ago, a friend and I comanaged a used and rare book shop in Ann Arbor, Michigan. We were often asked to appraise and purchase libraries—by retiring academics, widows, and disgruntled graduate students. One day we took a call from a professor of English at one of the community colleges outside Detroit. When he answered the buzzer I did a double take—he looked to be only a year or two older than we were. "I'm selling everything," he said, leading the way through a large apartment. As he opened the door of his study I felt a nudge from my partner. The room was wall-to-wall books and as neat as a chapel.

The professor had a remarkable collection. It reflected not only the needs of his vocation—he taught nineteenth- and twentieth-century literature—but a book lover's sensibility as well. The shelves were strictly arranged, and the books themselves were in superb condition. When he left the room we set to work inspecting, counting, and estimating. This is always a delicate procedure, for the buyer is at once anxious to avoid insult to the seller and eager to get the goods for the best price. We adopted our usual strategy, working out a lower offer and a more generous fallback price. But there was no need to worry. The professor took our first offer without batting an eye.

As we boxed up the books, we chatted. My partner asked the man if he was moving. "No," he said, "but I am getting out." We both looked up. "Out of the teaching business, I mean. Out of books." He then said that he wanted to show us something. And indeed, as soon as the books were packed and loaded, he led us back through the apartment and down a set of stairs. When we reached the basement, he flicked on the light. There, on a long table, displayed like an exhibit in the Space Museum, was a computer. I didn't know what kind it was then, nor could I tell you now, fifteen years later. But the professor was keen to explain and demonstrate.

While he and my partner hunched over the terminal, I roamed to and fro, inspecting the shelves. It was purely a reflex gesture, for they held nothing but thick binders and paperbound manuals. "I'm changing my life," the ex-professor was saying. "This is definitely where it's all going to happen." He told us that he already had several good job offers. And the books? I asked. Why was he selling them all? He paused for a few beats. "The whole profession represents a lot of pain to me," he said. "I don't want to see any of these books again." The scene has stuck with me. It is now a kind of marker in my mental life. That afternoon I got my first serious inkling that all was not well in the world of print and letters. All sorts of corroborations followed. Our professor was by no means an isolated case. Over a period of two years we met with several others like him. New men and new women who had glimpsed the future and had decided to get out while the getting was good. The selling off of books was sometimes done for financial reasons, but the need to burn bridges was usually there as well. It was as if heading to the future also required the destruction of tokens from the past.

A change is upon us—nothing could be clearer. The printed word is part of a vestigial order that we are moving away from—by choice and by societal compulsion. I'm not just talking about disaffected academics, either. This shift is happening throughout our culture, away from the patterns and habits of the printed page and toward a new world distinguished by its reliance on electronic communications.

A change is upon us— nothing could be clearer. The printed word is part of a vestigial order that we are moving away from—by choice and by societal compulsion.

This is not, of course, the first such shift in our long history. In Greece, in the time of Socrates, several centuries after Homer, the dominant oral culture was overtaken by the writing technology. And in Europe another epochal transition was effected in the late fifteenth century after Gutenberg invented movable type. In both cases the long-term societal effects were overwhelming, as they will be for us in the years to come.

The evidence of the change is all around us, though possibly in the manner of the forest that we cannot see for the trees. The electronic media, while conspicuous in gadgetry, are very nearly invisible in their functioning. They have slipped deeply and irrevocably into our midst, creating sluices and circulating through them. I'm not referring to any one product or function in isolation, such as television or fax machines or the networks that make them possible. I mean the interdependent totality that has arisen from the conjoining of parts—the disk drives hooked to modems, transmissions linked to technologies of reception, recording, duplication, and storage.

Numbers and codes and frequencies. Buttons and signals. And this is no longer "the future," except for the poor or the self-consciously atavistic—it is now. Next to the new technologies, the scheme of things represented by print and the snail-paced linearity of the reading act looks stodgy and dull. Many educators say that our students are less and less able to read, or analyze, or write with clarity and purpose. Who can blame the students? Everything they meet with in the world around them gives the signal: That was then, and electronic communications are now.

Do I exaggerate? If all this is the case, why haven't we heard more about it? Why hasn't somebody stepped forward with a bow tie and a pointer stick to explain what is going on? Valid questions, but they also beg the question. They assume that we are all plugged into a total system—

where else would that "somebody" appear if not on the screen at the communal hearth?

Media theorist Mark Crispin Miller has given one explanation for our situation in his discussions of television in *Boxed In: The Culture of TV*. The medium, he proposes, has long since diffused itself throughout the entire system. Through sheer omnipresence it has vanquished the possibility of comparative perspectives. We cannot see the role that television (or, for our purposes, all electronic communications) has assumed in our lives because there is no independent ledge where we might secure our footing. The medium has absorbed and eradicated the idea of a pretelevision past; in place of what used to be we get an ever-new and ever-renewable present. The only way we can hope to understand what is happening, or what has already happened, is by way of a severe and unnatural dissociation of sensibility.

Do I exaggerate?

To get a sense of the enormity of the change, you must force yourself to imagine—deeply and in nontelevisual terms—what the world was like a hundred, even fifty, years ago. If the feat is too difficult, spend some time with a novel from the period. Read between the lines and reconstruct. Move through the sequence of a character's day and then juxtapose the images and sensations you find with those in the life of the average urban or suburban dweller today.

Inevitably, one of the first realizations is that a communications net, a soft and pliable mesh woven from invisible threads, has fallen over everything. The so-called natural world, the place we used to live, which served us so long as the yardstick for all measurements, can now only be perceived through a scrim. Nature was then; this is now. Trees and rocks have receded. And the great geographical Other, the faraway rest of the world, has been transformed by the pure possibility of access. The numbers of distance and time no longer mean what they used to. Every place, once unique, itself, is strangely shot through with radiations from every other place. "There" was then; "here" is now.

One of the first realizations is that a communications net, a soft and pliable mesh woven from invisible threads, has fallen over everything.

Think of it. Fifty to a hundred million people (maybe a conservative estimate) form their ideas about what is going on in America and in the world from the same basic package of edited images—to the extent that the image itself has lost much of its once-fearsome power. Daily newspapers, with their long columns of print, struggle against declining sales. Fewer and fewer people under the age of fifty read them; computers will soon make packaged information a custom product. But if the printed sheet is heading for obsolescence, people are tuning in to the signals. The screen is where the information and entertainment wars will be fought. The communications conglomerates are waging bitter takeover battles in their zeal to establish global empires. As Jonathan Crary has written in "The Eclipse of the Spectacle," "Telecommunications is the new arterial network, analogous in part to what railroads were for capitalism in the nineteenth century. And it is this electronic substitute for geography that corporate and national entities are now carving up." Maybe one reason why the news of the change is not part of the common currency is that such news can only sensibly be communicated through the more analytic sequences of print.

To underscore my point, I have been making it sound as if we were all abruptly walking out of one room and into another, leaving our books to the moths while we settle ourselves in front of our state-of-the-art terminals. The truth is that we are living through a period of overlap; one way of being is pushed athwart another. Antonio Gramsci's often-cited sentence comes inevitably to mind: "The crisis consists precisely in the fact that the old is dying and the new cannot be born; in this interregnum a great variety of morbid symptoms appears." The old surely is dying, but I'm not so sure that the new is having any great difficulty being born. As for the morbid symptoms, these we have in abundance.

The overlap in communications modes, and the ways of living that they are associated with, invites comparison with the transitional epoch in ancient Greek society, certainly in terms of the relative degree of disturbance. Historian Eric Havelock designated that period as one of "proto-literacy," of which his fellow scholar Oswyn Murray has written:

To him [Havelock] the basic shift from oral to literate culture was a slow process; for centuries, despite the existence of writing, Greece remained essentially an oral culture. This culture was one which depended heavily on the encoding of information in poetic texts, to be learned by rote and to provide a cultural encyclopedia of conduct. It was not until the age of Plato in the fourth century that the dominance of poetry in an oral culture was challenged in the final triumph of literacy.

Our historical moment, which we might call "proto-electronic," will not require a transition period of two centuries. . . . Fifty years, I'm sure, will suffice.

That challenge came in the form of philosophy, among other things, and poetry has never recovered its cultural primacy. What oral poetry was for the Greeks, printed books in general are for us. But our historical moment, which we might call "proto-electronic," will not require a transition period of two centuries. The very essence of electronic transmissions is to surmount impedances and to hasten transitions. Fifty years, I'm sure, will suffice. As for what the conversion will bring—and *mean*—to us, we might glean a few clues by looking to some of the "morbid symptoms" of the change. But to understand what these portend, we need to remark a few of the more obvious ways in which our various technologies condition our senses and sensibilities.

I won't tire my reader with an extended rehash of the differences between the print orientation and that of electronic systems. Media theorists from Marshall McLuhan to Walter Ong to Neil Postman have discoursed upon these at length. What's more, they are reasonably commonsensical. I therefore will abbreviate.

The order of print is linear, and is bound to logic by the imperatives of syntax. Syntax is the substructure of discourse, a mapping of the ways that the mind makes sense through language. Print communication requires the active engagement of the reader's attention, for reading is fundamentally an act of translation. Symbols are turned into their verbal referents and these are in turn interpreted. The print engagement is essentially private. While it does represent an act of communication, the contents pass from the privacy of the sender to the privacy of the receiver. Print also posits a time axis; the turning of pages, not to mention the vertical descent down the page, is a forward-moving succession, with earlier contents at every point serving as a ground for what follows. Moreover, the printed material is static—it is the reader, not the book, that moves forward. The physical arrangements of print are in accord with our traditional sense of history. Materials are layered; they lend themselves to rereading and to sustained attention. The pace of reading is variable, with progress determined by the reader's focus and comprehension.

The electronic order is in most ways opposite. Information and contents do not simply move from one private space to another, but they travel along a network. Engagement is intrinsically public, taking place within a circuit of larger connectedness. The vast resources of the network are always there, potential, even if they do not impinge on the immediate communication. Electronic communication can be passive, as with television watching, or interactive, as with computers. Contents, unless they are printed out (at which point they become part of the static order of print) are felt to be evanescent. They can be changed or deleted with the stroke of a key. With visual media (television, projected graphs, highlighted "bullets") impression and image take precedence over logic and concept, and detail and linear sequentiality are sac-rificed. The pace is rapid, driven by jump-cut increments, and the basic move-ment is laterally associative rather than vertically cumulative. The presentation structures the reception and, in time, the expectation about how information is organized.

Further, the visual and nonvisual technology in every way encourages in the user a heightened and ever-changing awareness of the present. It works against historical perception, which must depend on the inimical notions of logic and sequential succession. If the print medium exalts the word, fixing it into permanence, the electronic counterpart reduces it to a signal, a means to an end.

Transitions like the one from print to electronic media do not take place without rippling or, more likely, *reweaving* the entire social and cultural web. The tendencies outlined above are already at work. We don't need to look far to find their effects. We can begin with the newspaper headlines and the mil-lennial lamentations sounded in the op-ed pages: that our educational systems are in decline; that our students are less and less able to read and comprehend their required texts, and that their aptitude scores have leveled off well below those of previous generations. Tag-line communication, called "bite-speak" by some, is destroying the last remnants of political discourse; spin doctors and media consultants are our new shamans. As communications empires fight for

control of all information outlets, including publishers, the latter have suc-
cumbed to the tyranny of the bottom line; they are less and less willing to
publish work, however worthy, that will not make a tidy profit. And, on every
front, funding for the arts is being cut while the arts themselves appear to be
suffering a deep crisis of relevance. And so on.

Every one of these developments is, of course, overdetermined, but there
can be no doubt that they are connected, perhaps profoundly, to the transition
that is underway.

Certain other trends bear watching. One could argue, for instance, that the
entire movement of postmodernism in the arts is a consequence of this same
macroscopic shift. For what is postmodernism at root but an aesthetic that
rebukes the idea of an historical time line, as well as previously uncontested
assumptions of cultural hierarchy. The postmodern artifact manipulates its
stylistic signatures like Lego blocks and makes free with combinations from
the formerly sequestered spheres of high and popular art. Its combinatory
momentum and relentless referencing of the surrounding culture mirror perfectly the associative dynamics of electronic media.

One might argue likewise, that the virulent debate within academia over
the canon and multiculturalism may not be a simple struggle between the
entrenched ideologies of white male elites and the forces of formerly disenfranchised gender, racial, and cultural groups. Many of those who would
revise the canon (or end it altogether) are trying to outflank the assumption
of historical tradition itself. The underlying question, avoided by many, may
be not only whether the tradition is relevant, but whether it might not be too
taxing a system for students to comprehend. Both the traditionalists and the
progressives have valid arguments, and we must certainly have sympathy for
those who would try to expose and eradicate the hidden assumptions of bias
in the Western tradition. But it also seems clear that this debate could only
have taken the form it has in a society that has begun to come loose from its
textual moorings. To challenge repression is salutary. To challenge history
itself, proclaiming it to be simply an archive of repressions and justifications,
is idiotic.*

Then there are the more specific sorts of developments. Consider the
multibillion-dollar initiative by Whittle Communications to bring commercially sponsored education packages into the classroom. The underlying

---

*The outcry against the modification of the canon can be seen as a plea for old reflexes and
routines. And the cry for multicultural representation may be a last-ditch bid for connection to
the fading legacy of print. The logic is simple. When a resource is threatened—made scarce—
people fight over it. In this case the struggle is over textual power in an increasingly nontextual
age. The future of books and reading is what is at stake, and a dim intuition of this drives the
contending factions.

As Katha Pollitt argued so shrewdly in her much-cited article in *The Nation*: If we were a
nation of readers, there would be no issue. No one would be arguing about whether to put Toni
Morrison on the syllabus because her work would be a staple of the reader's regular diet anyway.
These lists are suddenly so important because they represent, very often, the only serious works
that the student is ever likely to be exposed to. Whoever controls the lists comes out ahead in the
struggle for the hearts and minds of the young.

premise is staggeringly simple: If electronic media are the one thing that the young are at ease with, why not exploit the fact? Why not stop bucking television and use it instead, with corporate America picking up the tab in exchange for a few minutes of valuable airtime for commercials? As the *Boston Globe* reports:

> *Here's how it would work:*
> *Participating schools would receive, free of charge, $50,000 worth of electronic paraphernalia, including a satellite dish and classroom video monitors. In return, the schools would agree to air the show.*
> *The show would resemble a network news program, but with 18- to 24-year-old anchors.*
> *A prototype includes a report on a United Nations Security Council meeting on terrorism, a space shuttle update, a U2 music video tribute to Martin Luther King, a feature on the environment, a "fast fact" ('Arachibutyrophobia is the fear of peanut butter sticking to the roof of your mouth') and two minutes of commercial advertising.*
> *"You have to remember that the children of today have grown up with the visual media," said Robert Calabrese (Billerica School Superintendent). "They know no other way and we're simply capitalizing on that to enhance learning."*

A collective change of sensibility may already be upon us. We need to take seriously the possibility that the young truly "know no other way," that they are not made of the same stuff that their elders are.

Calabrese's observation on the preconditioning of a whole generation of students raises troubling questions: Should we suppose that American education will begin to tailor itself to the aptitudes of its students, presenting more and more of its materials in newly packaged forms? And what will happen when educators find that not very many of the old materials will "play"—that is, capture student enthusiasm? Is the *what* of learning to be determined by the *how*? And at what point do vicious cycles begin to reveal their viciousness?

A collective change of sensibility may already be upon us. We need to take seriously the possibility that the young truly "know no other way," that they are not made of the same stuff that their elders are. In her *Harper's* magazine debate with Neil Postman, Camille Paglia observed:

> *Some people have more developed sensoriums than others. I've found that most people born before World War II are turned off by the modern media. They can't understand how we who were born after the war can read and watch TV at the same time. But we can. When I wrote my book, I had earphones on, blasting rock music or Puccini and Brahms. The soap operas—with the sound turned down—flickered on my TV. I'd be talking on the phone at the same time. Baby boomers have a multilayered, multitrack ability to deal with the world.*

I don't know whether to be impressed or depressed by Paglia's ability to disperse her focus in so many directions. Nor can I say, not having read her book, in what ways her multitrack sensibility has informed her prose. But I'm baffled by what she means when she talks about an ability to "deal with the world." From the context, "dealing" sounds more like a matter of incessantly repositioning the self within a barrage of onrushing stimuli.

Paglia's is hardly the only testimony in this matter. A *New York Times* article on the cult success of Mark Leyner (author of *I Smell Esther Williams* and *My Cousin, My Gastroenterologist*) reports suggestively:

His fans say, variously, that his writing is like MTV, or rap music, or rock music, or simply like everything in the world put together: fast and furious and intense, full of illusion and allusion and fantasy and science and excrement.

Larry McCaffery, a professor of literature at San Diego State University and co-editor of Fiction International, *a literary journal, said his students get excited about Mr. Leyner's writing, which he considers important and unique: "It speaks to them, somehow, about this weird milieu they're swimming through. It's this dissolving, discontinuous world." While older people might find Mr. Leyner's world bizarre or unreal, Professor McCaffery said, it doesn't seem so to people who grew up with Walkmen and computers and VCR's, with so many choices, so much bombardment, that they have never experienced a sensation singly.*

The article continues:

There is no traditional narrative, although the book is called a novel. And there is much use of facts, though it is called fiction. Seldom does the end of a sentence have any obvious relation to the beginning. "You don't know where you're going, but you don't mind taking the leap," said R. J. Cutler, the producer of "Heat," who invited Mr. Leyner to be on the show after he picked up the galleys of his book and found it mesmerizing. "He taps into a specific cultural perspective where thoughtful literary world view meets pop culture and the TV generation."

My final exhibit—I don't know if it qualifies as a morbid symptom as such—is drawn from a *Washington Post Magazine* essay on the future of the Library of Congress, our national shrine to the printed word. One of the individuals interviewed in the piece is Robert Zich, so-called "special projects czar" of the institution. Zich, too, has seen the future, and he is surprisingly candid with his interlocutor. Before long, Zich maintains, people will be able to get what information they want directly off their terminals. The function of the Library of Congress (and perhaps libraries in general) will change. He envisions his library becoming more like a museum: "Just as you go to the National Gallery to see its Leonardo or go to the Smithsonian to see the Spirit of St. Louis and so on, you will want to go to libraries to see the Gutenberg or the original printing of Shakespeare's plays or to see Lincoln's hand-written version of the Gettysburg Address."

Zich is outspoken, voicing what other administrators must be thinking privately. The big research libraries, he says, "and the great national libraries and their buildings will go the way of the railroad stations and the movie palaces of an earlier era which were really vital institutions in their time . . . Somehow folks moved away from that when the technology changed."

And books? Zich expresses excitement about Sony's hand-held electronic book, and a miniature encyclopedia coming from Franklin Electronic Publishers. "Slip it in your pocket," he says. "Little keyboard, punch in your words and it will do the full text searching and all the rest of it. Its limitation, of course, is that it's devoted just to that one book." Zich is likewise interested in the possibility of memory cards. What he likes about the Sony product is the portability: one machine, a screen that will display the contents of whatever electronic card you feed it.

I cite Zich's views at some length here because he is not some Silicon Valley research and development visionary, but a highly placed executive at what might be called, in a very literal sense, our most conservative public institution. When men like Zich embrace the electronic future, we can be sure it's well on its way.

Others might argue that the technologies cited by Zich merely represent a modification in the "form" of reading, and that reading itself will be unaffected, as there is little difference between following words on a pocket screen or a printed page. Here I have to hold my line. The context cannot but condition the process. Screen and book may exhibit the same string of words, but the assumptions that underlie their significance are entirely different depending on whether we are staring at a book or a circuit-generated text. As the nature of looking—at the natural world, at paintings—changed with the arrival of photography and mechanical reproduction, so will the collective relation to language alter as new modes of dissemination prevail.

Whether all of this sounds dire or merely "different" will depend upon the reader's own values and priorities. I find these portents of change depressing, but also exhilarating—at least to speculate about. On the one hand, I have a great feeling of loss and a fear about what habitations will exist for self and soul in the future. But there is also a quickening, a sense that important things are on the line. As Heraclitus once observed, "The mixture that is not shaken soon stagnates." Well, the mixture is being shaken, no doubt about it. And here are some of the kinds of developments we might watch for as our "proto-electronic" era yields to an all-electronic future:

1. *Language erosion.* There is no question but that the transition from the culture of the book to the culture of electronic communication will radically alter the ways in which we use language on every societal level. The complexity and distinctiveness of spoken and written expression, which are deeply bound to traditions of print literacy, will gradually be replaced by a more telegraphic sort of "plainspeak." Syntactic masonry is already a dying art. Neil Postman and others have already suggested what losses have been incurred by the advent of telegraphy and television—how the complex discourse patterns of the nineteenth century were flattened by the requirements of communication over distances. That tendency runs riot as the layers of mediation thicken. Simple linguistic prefab is now the norm, while ambiguity, paradox, irony, subtlety, and wit are fast disappearing. In their place, the simple "vision thing" and myriad other "things." Verbal intelligence, which has long been viewed as suspect as the act of reading, will come to seem positively conspiratorial. The

greater part of any articulate person's energy will be deployed in dumbing-down her discourse.

Language will grow increasingly impoverished through a series of vicious cycles. For, of course, the usages of literature and scholarship are connected in fundamental ways to the general speech of the tribe. We can expect that curricula will be further streamlined, and difficult texts in the humanities will be pruned and glossed. One need only compare a college textbook from twenty years ago to its contemporary version. A poem by Milton, a play by Shakespeare—one can hardly find the text among the explanatory notes

Language will grow increasingly impoverished through a series of vicious cycles.

nowadays. Fewer and fewer people will be able to contend with the so-called masterworks of literature or ideas. Joyce, Woolf, Soyinka, not to mention the masters who preceded them, will go unread, and the civilizing energies of their prose will circulate aimlessly between closed covers.

2. *Flattening of historical perspectives.* As the circuit supplants the printed page, and as more and more of our communications involve us in network processes—which of their nature plant us in a perpetual present—our perception of history will inevitably alter. Changes in information storage and access are bound to impinge on our historical memory. The depth of field that is our sense of the past is not only a linguistic construct, but is in some essential way represented by the book and the physical accumulation of books in library spaces. In the contemplation of the single volume, or mass of volumes, we form a picture of time past as a growing deposit of sediment; we capture a sense of its depth and dimensionality. Moreover, we meet the past as much in the presentation of words in books of specific vintage as we do in any isolated fact or statistic. The database, useful as it is, expunges this context, this sense of chronology, and admits us to a weightless order in which all information is equally accessible.

If we take the etymological tack, history (cognate with "story") is affiliated in complex ways with its texts. Once the materials of the past are unhoused from their pages, they will surely *mean* differently. The printed page is itself a link, at least along the imaginative continuum, and when that link is broken, the past can only start to recede. At the same time it will become a body of disjunct data available for retrieval and, in the hands of our canny dream merchants, a mythology. The more we grow rooted in the consciousness of the now, the more it will seem utterly extraordinary that things were ever any different. The idea of a farmer plowing a field—an historical constant for millennia—will be something for a theme park. For, naturally, the entertainment industry, which reads the collective unconscious unerringly, will seize the advantage. The past that has slipped away will be rendered ever more glorious, ever more a fantasy play with heroes, villains, and quaint settings and props. Small-town American life returns as "Andy of Mayberry"—at first enjoyed with recognition, later accepted as a faithful portrait of how things used to be.

3. *The waning of the private self.* We may even now be in the first stages of a process of social collectivization that will over time all but vanquish the ideal of the isolated individual. For some decades now we have been edging away from the perception of private life as something opaque, closed off to the world; we increasingly accept the transparency of a life lived within a set of systems, electronic or otherwise. Our technologies are not bound by season or light—it's always the same time in the circuit. And so long as time is money and money matters, those circuits will keep humming. The doors and walls of our habitations matter less and less—the world sweeps through the wires as it needs to, or as we need it to. The monitor light is always blinking; we are always potentially on-line.

I am not suggesting that we are all about to become mindless, soulless robots, or that personality will disappear altogether into an oceanic homogeneity. But certainly the idea of what it means to be a person living a life will be much changed. The figure-ground model, which has always featured a solitary self before a background that is the society of other selves, is romantic in the extreme. It is ever less tenable in the world as it is becoming. There are no more wildernesses, no more lonely homesteads, and, outside of cinema, no more emblems of the exalted individual.

> *I am not suggesting that we are all about to become mindless, soulless robots, or that personality will disappear altogether into an oceanic homogeneity.*

The self must change as the nature of subjective space changes. And one of the many incremental transformations of our age has been the slow but steady destruction of subjective space. The physical and psychological distance between individuals has been shrinking for at least a century. In the process, the figure-ground image has begun to blur its boundary distinctions. One day we will conduct our public and private lives within networks so dense, among so many channels of instantaneous information, that it will make almost no sense to speak of the differentiations of subjective individualism.

We are already captive in our webs. Our slight solitudes are transected by codes, wires, and pulsations. We punch a number to check in with the answering machine, another to tape a show that we are too busy to watch. The strands of the web grow finer and finer—this is obvious. What is no less obvious is the fact that they will continue to proliferate, gaining in sophistication, merging functions so that one can bank by phone, shop via television, and so on. The natural tendency is toward streamlining: The smart dollar keeps finding ways to shorten the path, double-up the function. We might think in terms of a circuit-board model, picturing ourselves as the contact points. The expansion of electronic options is always at the cost of contractions in the private sphere. We will soon be navigating with ease among cataracts of organized pulsations, putting out and taking in signals. We will bring our terminals, our modems, and menus further and further into our former privacies; we will implicate ourselves by degrees in the

unitary life, and there may come a day when we no longer remember that
there was any other life.

While I was brewing these somewhat melancholy thoughts, I chanced to
read in an old *New Republic* the text of Joseph Brodsky's 1987 Nobel Prize
acceptance speech. I felt as though I had opened a door leading to the great
vault of the nineteenth century. The poet's passionate plea on behalf of the
book at once corroborated and countered everything I had been thinking.
What he upheld in faith were the very ideals I was saying good-bye to.
I greeted his words with an agitated skepticism, fashioning from them something more like a valediction. Here are four passages:

*If art teaches anything . . . it is the privateness of the human condition. Being the most
ancient as well as the most literal form of private enterprise, it fosters in a man, know-
ingly or unwittingly, a sense of his uniqueness, of individuality, of separateness—thus
turning him from a social animal into an autonomous "I."*

*The great Baratynsky, speaking of his Muse, characterized her as possessing an
"uncommon visage." It's in acquiring this "uncommon visage" that the meaning of
human existence seems to lie, since for this uncommonness we are, as it were, prepared
genetically.*

*Aesthetic choice is a highly individual matter, and aesthetic experience is always a
private one. Every new aesthetic reality makes one's experience even more private; and
this kind of privacy, assuming at times the guise of literary (or some other) taste, can in
itself turn out to be, if not a guarantee, then a form of defense, against enslavement.*

*In the history of our species, in the history of Homo sapiens, the book is an anthropo-
logical development, similar essentially to the invention of the wheel. Having emerged in
order to give us some idea not so much of our origins as of what that sapiens is capable
of, a book constitutes a means of transportation through the space of experience, at the
speed of a turning page. This movement, like every movement, becomes flight from the
common denominator . . . This flight is the flight in the direction of "uncommon visage,"
in the direction of the numerator, in the direction of autonomy, in the direction of
privacy.*

Brodsky is addressing the relation between art and totalitarianism, and
within that context his words make passionate sense. But I was reading from a
different vantage. What I had in mind was not a vision of political totalitarianism, but rather of something that might be called "societal totalism"—that
movement toward deindividuation, or electronic collectivization, that I discussed above. And from that perspective our era appears to be in a headlong
flight *from* the "uncommon visage" named by the poet.

Trafficking with tendencies—extrapolating and projecting as I have been
doing—must finally remain a kind of gambling. One bets high on the validity of a notion and low on the human capacity for resistance and for unpredictable initiatives. No one can really predict how we will adapt to the
transformations taking place all around us. We may discover, too, that language is a hardier thing than I have allowed. It may flourish among the beep
and the click and the monitor as readily as it ever did on the printed page.
I hope so, for language is the soul's ozone layer and we thin it at our peril.

■ QUESTIONS FOR REREADING

1. What is an elegy? Is Birkerts simply caught up with the problem of not changing with the times? Or is he making another point by lamenting the loss of literate book culture? What similarities do you see between Neil Postman and Birkerts? Are they both neo-Luddites?

2. Do you know of anyone who is giving away or selling his or her books and going completely digital? Does your instructor/facilitator have any colleagues who are going strictly digital?

3. Note how Birkerts cites Paglia's discussion about doing and listening to the world around her in multiple ways. Why does Birkerts cite Paglia? And then Mark Leyner? And then Robert Zich? What do you make of Zich's prospects for the Library of Congress in the light of my introduction to this chapter? If I exaggerated about all books and journals being on-line and no longer in the library, do you think that Zich is exaggerating also?

4. List and discuss what Birkerts refers to as the "morbid symptoms" of the proto-electronic age. Reflecting on the shift from a literate, book-reading culture to an electronic one, Birkerts says: "I find these portents of change depressing, but also exhilarating—at least to speculate about." What does Birkerts mean by "depressing" *and* "exhilarating"? (In thinking about this question, you might want to examine the meaning of *spasm* in the glossary, Appendix B.)

5. Why does Birkerts end with the discussion on and quote from Joseph Brodsky? What rhetorically strategic significance does it have to the conclusion of the chapter?

■ WRITING ASSIGNMENTS FOR REREADING

1. Write an essay on what Birkerts considers to be the fate of reading.

2. Read Birkerts's book and write a report on it for your classmates.

Jay David Bolter

The Computer as a New Writing Space

"The Computer as a New Writing Space" is a chapter in Jay David Bolter's book Writing Space (Hillsdale, NJ: Lawrence Erlbaum, 1991). Bolter's book is the best general and scholarly book on the fate of writing in the new computer environments. He takes both a historical approach (examining the changes that writing the "book" has undergone) and a prognostic approach (projecting the changes to come). In his discussion of the new writing space, he focuses on topographical and hypertextual writing.

onsider this simple example of electronic writing. (See Fig. 1.) The text is a continuous prose paragraph, displayed on the computer screen for the reader to read in the traditional way. Some of the words are in boldface; the style indicates that there is a note on that word or phrase, something more to be said. To retrieve the note, the reader points with the cursor at the text in boldface and presses a button. A second window then opens on the screen and presents a new paragraph for the reader to consider. The reader examines the note and may then return to the original paragraph.

In one sense this is simply the electronic equivalent of the footnote used in printed books for hundreds of years. Instead of looking to the bottom of the page or the end of the book, the reader aims the cursor and the computer retrieves and displays the reference. The machine is merely handling the

FIGURE 1
(a) To examine a note, the reader points to and activates a phrase in boldface. (b) A new window appears and presents the associated text, which contains boldface phrases of its own.

(a)

Nature of writing

Writing has been called "visible language." The name suggests that the spoken word is the primary human experience and that writing merely visualizes speech. **Eric Havelock** carries this suggestion to its extreme when he insists **that writing should be reduced to a functional minimum.** To insist upon pure phonetic writing is to ignore the possibility that visible signs may convey messages that cannot be spoken. A broader definition of writing would include any system of visual symbols—even systems like those of **mathematics** **or computer programming**, which are hard to speak, and **picture writing**, which does not immediately correspond to spoken language

(b)

Nature of writing

Note

"Strictly speaking, written orthography should behave solely as the servant of the spoken tongue, reporting its sounds as accurately and swiftly as possible. It need not and should not have a nature of its own.... [T]he artistic fascination of the Chinese **with the calligraphy of the ideogram** has had its counterpart in the development of scripts and their elaboration in European and Arabic countries. This visual development of the written signs has nothing to do with the purpose of language, namely **instantaneous communication** between members of a human group." (Eric A. Havelock, <u>The Literate Revolution in Greece and its Cultural Consequences</u>, 53).

mechanics of reading footnotes. But there is this important difference: the second window can also contain boldface phrases that in turn lead the reader to other paragraphs. The process can continue indefinitely as the reader moves from one window to another through a space of paragraphs. The second paragraph is not necessarily subordinate to the first. A phrase in boldface may lead the reader to a longer, more elaborate paragraph. One paragraph may be linked to many and serve in turn as the destination for links from many others. In a printed book, it would be intolerably pedantic to write footnotes to footnotes. But in the computer, writing in layers is quite natural, and reading the layers is effortless. All the individual paragraphs may be of equal importance in the whole text, which then becomes a network of interconnected writings. The network is designed by the author to be explored by the reader in precisely this peripatetic fashion.

Such a network is called a *hypertext,* and, as we shall see, it is the ability to create and present hypertextual structures that makes the computer a revolution in writing. The computer as hypertext invites us to write with symbols that have both an intrinsic and extrinsic significance. That is, the symbols have a meaning that may be explained in words, but they also have meaning as elements in a larger structure of verbal gestures. Both words and structures are visible, writeable, and readable in the electronic space.

■ W R I T I N G   P L A C E S

With or without the computer, whenever we write, we write topically. We conceive of our text as a set of verbal gestures, large and small. To write is to do things with topics—to add, delete, and arrange them. The computer changes the nature of writing simply by giving visual expression to our acts of conceiving and manipulating topics.

With or without the computer, whenever we write, we write topically. To write is to do things with topics—to add, delete, and arrange them.

A writer working with a word processor spends much of the time entering words letter by letter, just as he or she does at a typewriter. Revising is a different matter. With most word processors, writers can delete or replace an entire word; they can highlight phrases, sentences, or paragraphs. They can erase a sentence with a single keystroke; they can select a paragraph, cut it from its current location, and insert it elsewhere, even into another document. In using these facilities, the writer is thinking and writing in terms of verbal units or topics, whose meaning transcends their constituent words. The Greek word *topos* meant literally a place, and ancient rhetoric used the word to refer to commonplaces, conventional units or methods of thought. In the Renaissance, topics became headings that could be used to organize any field of knowledge, and these headings were often set out in elaborate diagrams. (See Ong, 1958, pp. 104–130.) Our English word *topic* is appropriate for the computer because its etymology suggests the spatial character of electronic writing: topics exist in a writing space that is not only a visual surface but also a data structure in the computer. The programmers who designed word processors recognized the importance of topical writing, when they gave us operations for adding or deleting sentences and paragraphs as units. They did not, however, take the further step of allowing a writer to associate a name or a visual symbol with such topical units. This important step lends the unit a conceptual identity. The unit symbol becomes an abiding element in the writer's thinking and expression, because its constituent words or phrases can be put out of sight.

On a printed or typed page, we indent and separate paragraphs to indicate the topical structure. Within each paragraph, however, we have only punctuation, occurring in the stream of words, to mark finer structure. A better representation of topical writing is the conventional outline, in which major topics are designated by Roman numerals, subtopics by capital letters, sub-subtopics by Arabic numerals, and so on. Each point of an outline serves to organize and situate the topics subordinate to it, and the outline as a whole is a static representation, a snapshot, of the textual organization. The conventions of outlining turn the writing surface into a tiered space in which the numbering and indentation of lines represent the hierarchy of the author's ideas. A paragraphed text is the flattening or linearization of an outline.

The word processor, which imitates the layout of the typed page, also flattens the text.

The word processor, which imitates the layout of the typed page, also flattens the text. It offers the writer little help in conceiving the evolving structure of the text. Although the word processor allows the writer to define a verbal unit in order to move or delete it, the definition lasts only until the operation is complete. But if the word processor offers the writer only temporary access to his or her structure, another class of programs called outline processors makes structure a permanent feature of the text. An outline processor sets the traditional written outline in motion. A writer can add points to an electronic outline in any order, while the computer continually renumbers to reflect additions or deletions. The writer can promote minor points to major ones, and the computer will again renumber. The writer can collapse the outline in order to see only those points above a certain level, an action that gives an overview of the evolving text. In short the writer can think globally about the text: one can treat topics as unitary symbols and write with those symbols, just as in a word processor one writes with words. (See Fig. 2.)

Writing in topics is not a replacement for writing with words; the writer must eventually attend to the details of his or her prose. The outline processor contains within it a conventional word processor, so that the writer can attach text to each of the points in the outline. But in using an outline processor, writers are not aware of a rigid distinction between outlining and prose writing: they move easily back and forth between structure and prose. What is new is that the points of the outline become functional elements in the text,

(a)

Electronic Writing Space

  I. Introduction

  II. Writing places

  III. Electronic trees

  IV. Hypertext

  V. Hypermedia

  VI. The First Hypertext

  VII. Writers and Readers

(b)

Electronic Writing Space

  I. Introduction
    A. Example
      1. Figure 1
    B. Footnote
    C. Hypertext
  II. Writing places
    A. Topos
    B. Print format
    C. Word processor
      1. Conventional
      2. Desktop publishing
    D. Outline processor
      1. Figure 2
    E. Topical writing
      1. With the computer
      2. In print

(c)

  II. Writing places
    A. Topos

> With or without the computer, whenever we write, we write topically.
> We conceive of our text as a set of verbal gestures, large and small.
> To write is to do things with topics—to add, delete, and arrange
> them. The computer changes the nature of writing simply by giving
> visual expression to our acts of conceiving and manipulating topics.
> A writer working with a word processor spends much of his time
> entering words letter by letter, just as he does at a typewriter.
> Revising is a different matter. With most word processors, the

    B. Print format

> On a printed or typed page, we indent and separate paragraphs to
> indicate the topical structure. Within each paragraph, however, we
> have only punctuation, occurring in the stream of words, to mark finer
> structure. A better representation of topical writing is the
> conventional outline, in which major topics are designated by Roman
> numerals, subtopics by capital letters, sub-subtopics by Arabic
> numerals, and so on. Each point of an outline serves to organize and
> situate the topics subordinate to it, and the outline as a whole is a

    C. Word processor

> The word processor, which imitates the layout of the typed page, also
> flattens the text. It offers the writer little help in conceiving the
> evolving structure of his text. Although the word processor allows

---

F I G U R E   2

An outline processor can reveal or hide detail as the writer requires. It may show only the
major points (a), the full outline (b), or the prose paragraph attached to each point of the outline (c).

because when the points move, the words move with them. In this way the computer makes visible and almost palpable what writers have always known: that the identifying and arranging of topics is itself an act of writing. Outline processing is writing at a different grain, a replication on a higher level of the conventional act of writing by choosing and arranging words. The symbols of this higher writing are simply longer and more complicated "words," verbal gestures that may be whole sentences or paragraphs.

In an outline processor, then, the prose remains, but it is encased in a formally operative structure. With a pen or typewriter, writing meant literally to form letters on a page, figuratively to create verbal structures. In an electronic writing system, the figurative process becomes a literal act. By defining topical symbols, the writer can, like the programmer or the mathematician, abstract himself or herself temporarily from the details of the prose, and the value of this abstraction lies in seeing more clearly the structural skeleton of the text. It is not possible or desirable that the prose writer should become a mathematician or that human language should be reduced to a system of logical symbols. The result of giving language wholeheartedly over to formalism would simply be the impoverishment of language. On the other hand, the electronic medium can permit us to play creatively with formal structures in our writing without abandoning the richness of natural language.

■ ELECTRONIC TREES

It is no accident that the computer can serve as an outline processor. The machine is designed to create and track such formal structures, which are important for all its various uses. The computer's memory and central processing unit are intricate hierarchies of electronic components. Layers of software in turn transform the machine's physical space of electronic circuits into a space of symbolic information, and it is in this space that a new kind of writing can be located. Like the space of the modern physicist, the space of the computer is shaped by the objects that occupy it. The computer programmer forms his or her space by filling it with symbolic elements and then by connecting these elements as the program requires. Any symbol in the space can refer to another symbol by using its numerical address. Pointers hold together the structure of computer programs, and programming itself may be defined as the art of building symbolic structures in the space that the computer provides—a definition that makes programming a species of writing.

One such programming structure, which represents hierarchy, is called a *tree*. Trees (and their relatives such as *lists, stacks,* and *networks*) are ubiquitous in programs that must record and track large bodies of information or information subject to frequent change. Tree diagrams, in which elements are connected by branches as in a genealogical tree, have a long history in writing as well. They date back at least to the early Middle Ages and are not uncommon in medieval and Renaissance books, where they served for the spatial arrangement of topics (Ong, 1958, pp. 74–83, 199–202, 314–318). The traditional outline is a strict hierarchy that can just as easily be represented by a tree diagram. Part of the outline that we saw earlier (Fig. 2) is represented by the following tree (Fig. 3).

Both the tree and the outline give us a better reading of structure than does ordinary paragraphing, because they mold the visual space of the text in a way that reflects its structure. A printed page of paragraphs is by comparison a flat and uninteresting space, as is the window of a word processor. A writer can use a word processor to type an outline, and, if the word processor permits graphics, the writer can insert a tree diagram into the text. But the outline or diagram will then be stored as a picture, a sequence of bits to be shown on the screen; the picture will not be treated as a data structure and will not inform the space in which the writer is working. The writer will not be able to change the structure by manipulating the outline, as he or she can in an outline processor, and that ability is necessary for true electronic writing. In using an outline processor, the writer can intervene at any level of the evolving structure. And if the writer gives the reader a diskette rather than a printed version, then the reader too gains immediate access to that structure. All this is possible, because the writing space itself has become a tree, a hierarchy of topical elements.

The electronic writing space is extremely malleable. It can be fashioned into one tree or into a forest of hierarchical trees. A hierarchy defines a strict order of subordination: each point in an outline is arranged under exactly one heading; each topical unit in a tree diagram (except the root) has exactly one incoming arrow. In any printed or written text, one such hierarchical order

F I G U R E   3

A tree diagram represents hierarchical relationships among elements.

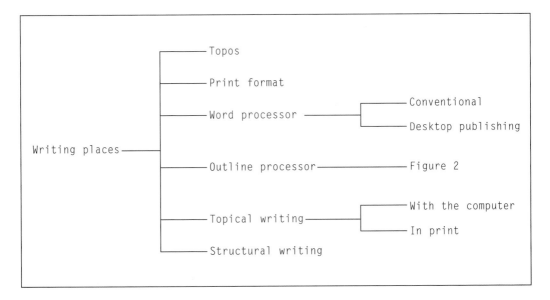

always precludes others. The static medium of print demands that the writer settle on one order of topics, although the writer may find that the topics could be arranged equally well in, say, three orders corresponding to three electronic outlines. Unlike the space of the printed book, the computer's writing space can represent any relationships that can be defined as the interplay of pointers and elements. Multiple relationships pose no special problem. A writer could therefore maintain three outlines, each of which deployed the same topics in a different order. These outlines may all reside in the computer's memory at the same time, each activated at the writer's request. The writer may choose to examine topics from any of the three vantage points and then switch to another; he or she may alter one outline while leaving the others intact; he or she may alter any of the outlines themselves without revising the text in any one of the topics. The structure of an electronic text is in this sense abstracted from its verbal expression.

The electronic writing space is extremely malleable. It can be fashioned into one tree or into a forest of hierarchical trees.

This multiplicity and abstraction already render the electronic writing space more flexible than its predecessors. And if all writing were only hierarchical, then the outline processor itself would be revolutionary in its freeing of writing from the frozen structure of the printed page. But there is one further step to be taken in liberating the text.

■ HYPERTEXT

The goal of conventional writing is to create a perfect hierarchy, but it is not always easy to maintain the discipline of such a structure. All writers have had the experience of being overwhelmed with ideas as they write. The act of writing itself releases a flood of thoughts—one idea suggesting another and another, as the writer struggles to get them down in some form before they slip from his or her conscious grasp. "I only wish I could write with both hands," noted Saint Teresa, "so as not to forget one thing while I am saying another." (See Peers, 1972, vol. 2, p. 88.) Romantics like Carlyle founded their psychology of literature upon this experience. The experience is not limited to saints and poets: many, perhaps most, writers begin their work with a jumble of verbal ideas and only a vague sense of how these ideas will fit together. The writer may start by laying out topics in an arrangement less formal than an outline: he or she may organize by association rather than strict subordination. Teachers of writing often encourage their students to begin by sketching out topics and connecting them through lines of association, and they call this activity "prewriting." What students create in prewriting is a network of elements—exactly what computer programmers mean by the data structure they call a network. The computer can maintain such a network of topics, and it can reflect the writer's progress as he or she trims the network by removing connections and establishing subordination until there is a strict hierarchy. In the world of print, at least in nonfiction, associative writing is considered only a preliminary.

Association is not really prior to writing, as the term "prewriting" suggests. Association is always present in any text: one word echoes another; one sentence or paragraph recalls others earlier in the text and looks forward to still others. A writer cannot help but write associatively: even if he or she begins with and remains faithful to an outline, the result is always a network of verbal elements. The hierarchy (in the form of paragraphs, sections, and chapters) is an attempt to impose order on verbal ideas that are always prone to subvert that order. The associative relationships define alternative organizations that lie beneath the order of pages and chapters that a printed text presents to the world. These alternatives constitute subversive texts-behind-the-text.

"I only wish I could write with both hands," noted Saint Teresa, "so as not to forget one thing while I am saying another."

Previous technologies of writing, which could not easily accommodate such alternatives, tended to ignore them. The ancient papyrus roll was strongly linear in its presentation of text. The codex, especially in the later Middle Ages, and then the printed book have made better efforts to accommodate association as well as hierarchy. In a modern book the table of contents (listing chapters and sometimes sections) defines the hierarchy, while the indices record associative lines of thought that permeate the text. An index permits the reader to locate passages that share the same word, phrase, or subject and so associates passages that may be widely separated in the pagination of the book. In one sense the index defines other books that could be constructed from the materials at hand, other themes that the author could have formed into an analytical narrative, and so invites the reader to read the book in alternative ways. An index transforms a book from a tree into a network, offering multiplicity in place of a single order of paragraphs and pages. There need not be any privileged element in a network, as there always is in a tree, no single topic that dominates all others. Instead of strict subordination, we have paths that weave their way through the textual space. Thus, the outline and tree that we saw earlier (Figs. 2 and 3) can become the network shown in Fig. 4. If all texts are ultimately networks of verbal elements, the computer is the first medium that can record and present these networks to writers and readers. Just as the outline processor treats text as a hierarchy, other computer programs can fashion the text into a general network or hypertext.

Hypertext has only recently become a discipline in computer science. (See Smith & Weiss, 1988.) The term "hypertext" was coined two decades ago by Ted Nelson. Working with mainframe computers in the 1960s, Nelson had come to realize the machine's capacity to create and manage textual networks for all kinds of writing. "Literature," he wrote, "is an ongoing system of interconnecting documents." By literature he meant not only belles-lettres but also scientific and technical writing: any group of writings on a well-defined

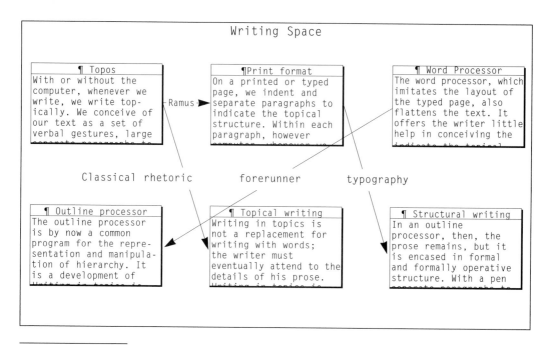

Writing Space

¶ Topos
With or without the computer, whenever we write, we write top-ically. We conceive of our text as a set of verbal gestures, large

Ramus ➤

¶Print format
On a printed or typed page, we indent and separate paragraphs to indicate the topical structure. Within each paragraph, however

¶ Word Processor
The word processor, which imitates the layout of the typed page, also flattens the text. It offers the writer little help in conceiving the

Classical rhetoric   forerunner   typography

¶ Outline processor
The outline processor is by now a common program for the repre-sentation and manipula-tion of hierarchy. It is a development of

¶ Topical writing
Writing in topics is not a replacement for writing with words; the writer must eventually attend to the details of his prose.

¶ Structural writing
In an outline processor, then, the prose remains, but it is encased in formal and formally operative structure. With a pen

FIGURE 4
A hypertext is a network of textual elements and connections.

subject. "A literature is a system of interconnected writings. We do not offer this as our definition, but as a discovered fact" (Nelson, 1984, p. 217; see also Nelson, 1974, and Conklin, 1987, pp. 22–23). Actually this "fact" had been discovered independent of and long before the computer, but the machine has provided Nelson and others in the last two decades with the technology needed to realize and indeed to reify writing as a network. Even before Nelson, the scientist and engineer Vannevar Bush had envisioned using electro-mechanical technology as a hypertextual reading and writing system. In 1945 Bush proposed (but never built) what he called a "memex," a device that would serve as an interactive encyclopedia or library. The reader of the memex would be able to display two texts on a screen and then create links between passages in the texts. These links would be stored by the memex and would be available for later display and revision; collectively they would define a network of interconnections. Because electronic storage was not yet capacious or reliable, Bush chose microfilm as the storage medium for his memex. Fortunately, the development of electromagnetic and optical disks has rendered microfilm obsolete for this purpose. But computer technology was already far enough advanced for Bush to see the possibility of hypertext and to express himself enthusiastically. His article proclaims nothing less than "a new relationship between thinking man and the sum of knowledge" (see Bush, 1945, p. 101).

Whether realized on microfilm or in computer memory, a hypertext con-sists of topics and their connections, where again the topics may be para-graphs, sentences, individual words, or indeed digitized graphics. A hypertext is like a printed book that the author has attacked with a pair of scissors and cut into convenient verbal sizes. The difference is that the electronic hypertext does not simply dissolve into a disordered bundle of slips, as the printed book must. For the author also defines a scheme of electronic connections to indicate relationships among the slips. In fashioning a hypertext, a writer might begin with a passage of continuous prose and then add notes or glosses on important words in the passage. As we suggested earlier (Fig. 1), the glosses themselves could contain glosses, leading the reader to further texts. A hypertextual network can extend indefinitely, as a printed text cannot.

A computer hypertext might serve, for example, to collect scholars' notes on complex texts such as Joyce's *Ulysses* and *Finnegans Wake*. The computer can record and update the collective work of many scholars who continue today adding to, refining, and revising the glosses; it can connect notes to other notes as appropriate. Such exegesis, currently recorded in books and journals, would be both easier to use and more appropriate as a hypertext, because *Ulysses* and particularly *Finnegans Wake* are themselves hypertexts that have been flattened out to fit on the printed page. But an author does not have to be as experimental as Joyce to profit from hypertext. A historian might choose to write an essay in which each paragraph or section is a topic in a hypertextual network. The connections would indicate possible orders in which topics could be assembled and read, and each order of reading might produce a different literary and analytic result. A mathematician might choose to write a hypertextbook that could tailor itself to different students with differing degrees of mathematical proficiency. Hypertext can serve for all sorts of more popular materials as well: directories, catalogues, how-to-manuals—wherever the reader wishes to move through the text in a variety of orders. In fact, thousands of such hypertexts are already available, written for display by Hypercard, a program for the Apple Macintosh computer.

In general, the connections of a hypertext are organized into paths that make operational sense to author and reader. Each topic may participate in several paths, and its significance will depend upon which paths the reader has traveled in order to arrive at that topic. In print, only a few paths can be suggested or followed. In an electronic version the texture of the text becomes thicker, and its paths can serve many functions. Paths can, as in a tree structure, indicate subordination. They can also remind the writer of relationships among topics that had to be sacrificed for the sake of an eventual hierarchy. They can express cyclic relationships among topics that can never be hierarchical. They can categorize topics for later revision: the writer might wish to join two paths together or intersect two paths and preserve only those elements common to both. In the electronic medium, hierarchical and associative thinking may coexist in the structure of a text, since the computer can take care of the mechanics of maintaining and presenting both networks and trees. In the medium of print, the writer may use an index to show alternatives, but these alternatives must always contend with the fixed order of the pages of the book. The canonical order is defined by the book's pagination, and all other suggested orders remain subordinate. A hypertext has no canonical order. Every path defines an equally convincing and appropriate reading, and in that simple fact the reader's relationship to the text changes radically. A text as a network has no univocal sense; it is a multiplicity without the imposition of a principle of domination.

In place of hierarchy, we have a writing that is not only topical: we might also call it "topographic." The word "topography" originally meant a written description of a place, such as an ancient geographer might give. Only later did the word come to refer to mapping or charting—that is, to a visual and mathematical rather than verbal description. Electronic writing is both a visual and verbal description. It is not the writing of a place, but rather a writing with places, spatially realized topics. Topographic writing challenges the idea that writing should be merely the servant of spoken language. The writer and reader can create and examine signs and structures on the computer screen that have no easy equivalent in speech. The point is obvious when the text is a collection of images stored on a videodisk, but it is equally true for a purely verbal text that has been fashioned as a tree or a network of topics and connections.

A text as a network has no univocal sense; it is a multiplicity without the imposition of a principle of domination.

Topographic writing as a mode is not even limited to the computer medium. It is possible to write topographically for print or even in manuscript. Whenever we divide our text into unitary topics and organize those units into a connected structure and whenever we conceive of this textual structure spatially as well as verbally, we are writing topographically. As we shall see in a later chapter, many literary artists in the 20th century have adopted this mode of writing. Although the computer is not necessary for topographic writing, it is only in the computer that the mode becomes a natural, and therefore also a conventional, way to write.

■ HYPERMEDIA

The first generation of personal computers could only display about one or two hundred different signs—the letters of the alphabet, numerals, punctuation, and some special characters. The writer had to choose from those shapes and therefore symbols that were wired into the displays or into their interface cards. Now the advent of inexpensive, bit-mapped graphics has removed that limitation. With bit-mapping, each pixel, each tiny square or rectangle on the screen, is under programmed control: permissible shapes are no longer frozen into the hardware. The letters of the alphabet themselves are defined by software, so that the system can provide not only the Roman alphabet in pica, but other styles, type fonts, and sizes as well. Images can be represented on the screen as easily as letters of the alphabet. These machine images have the same advantage of dynamic control as do the letter forms, and they suffer from the same problem of graininess, since the images too consist of a finite number of pixels.

Some word processors already permit the writer to insert diagrams and pictures directly into the text. But in word processing the graphic image is not really part of the text; it is merely allowed to coexist with the verbal text. As we have seen in the figures presented earlier, the computer has the capacity to integrate word and image more subtly, to make text itself graphic by representing its structure graphically to the writer and the reader. The computer can even dissolve the distinction between the standardized letter forms and symbols of the writer's own making. True electronic writing is not limited to verbal text: the writeable elements may be words, images, sounds, or even actions that the computer is directed to perform. The writer could use his or her network to organize pictures on videodisk or music and voices on an audio playback device. Instead of moving from paragraph to paragraph in a verbal text, the reader might be shown videotaped scenes of a play in a variety of orders. The reader might move through an aural landscape created by various recorded sounds or walk through a city by viewing photographs of various buildings. (Such was the Aspen project. See Brand, 1987, pp. 141–142.) Any combination of these elements is possible. The same computer screen might display verbal text below or beside a video image; it might combine sound and verbal writing. These combinations have come to be called *hypermedia* and are already quite sophisticated.

The introduction of video images might seem to turn electronic writing into mere television.

The introduction of video images might seem to turn electronic writing into mere television. Television itself often displays words on the screen, but it robs the displayed words of their cognitive value. Text on television is mere ornamentation; words appear most often to reinforce the spoken message or to decorate the packages of products being advertised. In fact, hypermedia is the revenge of text upon television (Joyce, 1988, p. 14). In television, text is absorbed into the video image, but in hypermedia the televised image becomes part of the text. This incorporation is literally true in MIT's Project Athena, in which the reader can run a videotape in a window on the computer screen. The video image therefore sits among the other textual elements for the reader to examine. (For a description of Project Athena, see Balkovich, Lerman, & Parmelee, 1985.) The Intermedia system developed at Brown University is another instance in which texts and images are read and written in the same computer environment. (See Yankelovich, Haan, Meyrowitz, & Drucker, 1988.) Once video images and sound are taken into the computer in this fashion, they too become topical elements. Writers can fashion these elements into a structure. They can write with images, because they can direct one topical image to refer to another and join visual and verbal topics in the same network (see Fig. 5). A journalist might select examples from a library of digitized still pictures and form them into a pictorial essay. An art historian might take images of Renaissance painting and attach explanatory comments. In fact, one can link the comments not only to the whole painting, but also to given areas of the image. The eyes of one portrait may refer to a comment, which may in

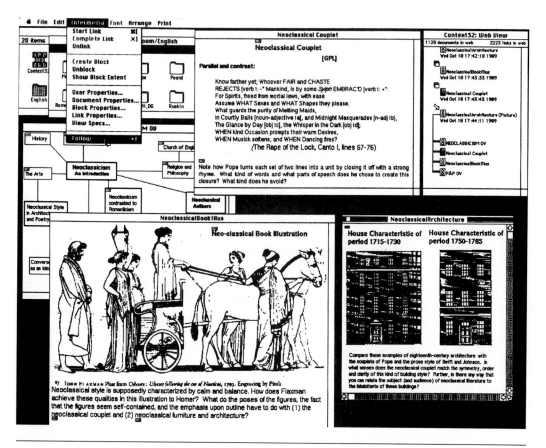

FIGURE 5

In the Intermedia project at Brown University, text and graphics can be combined into a single hypertextual web. Here, in a complex set of windows on the Macintosh computer screen, a passage from Pope is related to examples of Neoclassical architecture and book illustration. The link icon is a small box that contains a right pointing arrow. Wherever that icon occurs, the reader can choose to follow the links to another element in the hypertext. Reprinted with the kind permission of Professor George P. Landow.

turn link to eyes of other portrait examples. Other parts of the painting would lead to other comments and other examples. The reader would begin with the first picture and then choose to read the network of examples and explanations in a variety of orders, based on an interest in hands, eyes, or other elements of Renaissance technique. In each case the elements of the pictures have themselves become signs that refer to verbal topics and to other pictures. The image is functioning symbolically within the writer's text.

Such multimedia texts are by no means the death of writing. A hypermedia display is still a text, a weaving together of elements treated symbolically. Hypermedia simply extends the principles of electronic writing into the domain of sound and image. The computer's control of structure promises to create a synaesthesia in which anything that can be seen or heard may contribute to the texture of the text. These synaesthetic texts will have the same qualities as electronic verbal texts. They too will be flexible, dynamic, and interactive; they too will blur the distinction between writer and reader.

■ THE FIRST HYPERTEXT

Although experiments have been conducted since the 1960s, workable hypertext systems such as Intermedia are relatively recent. It was not until the advent of personal computers and workstations that hypertext could be made available to a large audience of writers and readers. On the other hand, the principle of hypertext has been implicit in computer programming for much longer. Hypertext is the interactive interconnection of a set of symbolic elements, and many kinds of computer programs (databases, simulation programs, even programs for artificial intelligence) are special cases of that principle. Hypertext shows how programming and conventional prose writing can combine in the space provided by the computer. It puts at the disposal of writers data structures (trees and networks) that have been used for decades by programmers. Conversely, it makes us realize that the programmer's data structures are formalized versions of the textual strategies that writers have exploited for centuries.

At any one moment the network holds a vast text of interrelated writings—the intersection of thousands of messages on hundreds of topics. It is a hypertext that no one reader can hope to encompass, one that changes moment by moment as messages are added and deleted.

Important anticipations of hypertext can be found in the computerized communications networks, such as ARPANET or BITNET, put in place in the 1960s and 1970s. Such a network constitutes the physical embodiment of hypertext. Each element or *node* in the network is a computer installation, while the connections among these elements are cables and microwave and satellite links. Each computer node serves dozens or hundreds of individual subscribers, and these subscribers both produce and read messages created by others within their computing facility, around the nation, or around the world. Some messages travel a single path through the communications links until they reach their marked destination, while general messages spread out to all the elements in the net. At any one moment the network holds a vast text of interrelated writings—the intersection of thousands of messages on hundreds of topics. It is a hypertext that no one reader can hope to encompass, one that changes moment by moment as messages are added and deleted.

Subscribers use these networks both for personal mail and to conduct ongoing discussions in so-called "newsgroups." When one subscriber in a newsgroup "publishes" a message, it travels to all the dozens or hundreds of others who belong to that group. The message may elicit responses, which in turn travel back and forth and spawn further responses. The prose of these messages is almost as casual as conversation, precisely because publication in this medium is both easy and almost unrestricted. The transition from reader to writer is completely natural. The reader of one message can with a few keystrokes send off a reply. Readers may even incorporate part of the original message in the reply, blurring the distinction between their own text and the text to which they are responding. There is also little respect for the conventions of the prior medium of print. Subscribers often type newspaper articles or excerpts from books into their replies without concern for copyright. The notion of copyright seems faintly absurd, since their messages are copied and relayed automatically hundreds of times in a matter of hours.

Writing for such a network is by nature topographical: relatively small units of prose are sent and received. The medium itself encourages brevity, since two correspondents can send and receive several messages in one day. And the addresses of the messages provide a primitive system of links. To reply to a given message is to link your text to the earlier one, and both message and reply may then circulate for days around the network, provoking other responses. No user is bound to read or reply to anything; instead, any message can refer to any other or ignore all previous messages and strike out in a new direction. A communications network is therefore a hypertext in which no one writer or reader has substantial control, and because no one has control, no one has substantial responsibility. The situation is different for hypertext systems for microcomputers, where there is one author and one reader. There the twin issues of control and responsibility are paramount.

■ WRITERS AND READERS OF HYPERTEXT

When we receive a written or typed letter, we hold in our own hands the paper that the sender also has handled. We see and touch the inkmarks that he or she has made. With electronic mail we receive bits of information that correspond to the tapping of keys on the writer's keyboard. We read this information as patches of light on our computer screen, and we touch nothing that the writer has touched. Like all other kinds of writing, electronic writing is an act of postponement or deferral. As writers, we defer our words by setting them down on a writing surface for later reading by ourselves or by others. The reader's task is to reactivate the words on the page and to devise for them a new context, which may be close to or far removed from the author's original context. There is always a gulf between author and reader, a gap that the technique of writing first creates and then mediates. In one sense the computer opens a particularly wide gap because of the abstract nature of electronic technology. On the other hand, the author has a unique opportunity to control the procedure of reading, because he or she can program restrictions into the text itself.

Computer-assisted instruction, for example, is nothing other than a hypertext in which the author has restricted the ways in which the student/reader

can proceed. In typical computer-assisted instruction the program poses a question and awaits an answer from the student. If the student gives the correct answer, the program may present another question. If the student's answer is wrong, the program may explain the student's error. If the student makes the same error repeatedly, the program may present a review of the point that the student has failed to grasp. In most cases, these questions and explanations are texts that the teacher/programmer has composed and stored in advance. However, good programming can make these simple programs seem uncannily clever in replying to the student. In fact such a program takes on a persona created for it by the teacher/programmer, as it transfers the teacher's words into the new context of the student's learning session. In general, the reader of an electronic text is made aware of the author's simultaneous presence in and absence from the text, because the reader is constantly confronting structural choices established by the author. If the program allows the reader to make changes in the text or to add new connections (as some hypertext systems do), then the game becomes still more complex. As readers we become our own authors, determining the structure of the text for the next reader, or perhaps for ourselves in our next reading.

As readers we become our own authors, determining the structure of the text for the next reader, or perhaps for ourselves in our next reading.

Electronic text is the first text in which the elements of meaning, of structure, and of visual display are fundamentally unstable. Unlike the printing press or the medieval codex, the computer does not require that any aspect of writing be determined in advance for the whole life of a text. This restlessness is inherent in a technology that records information by collecting for fractions of a second evanescent electrons at tiny junctions of silicon and metal. All information, all data, in the computer world is a kind of controlled movement, and so the natural inclination of computer writing is to change, to grow, and finally to disappear. Nor is it surprising that these constant motions place electronic writing in a kaleidoscope of relationships with the earlier technologies of typewriting, printing, and handwriting.

■ REFERENCES

Balkovich, E., Lerman, S., and Parmelee, R.P. (1985). Computing in higher education: The Athena Project. *Computer,* 18 (10), 112–125.

Brand, Stewart. (1987). The media lab: Inventing the future at M.I.T. New York: Penguin Books.

Bush, Vannevar. (1945). As we may think. *Atlantic Monthly,* 176 (1), 101–108.

Conklin, J. (1987). Hypertext: An introduction and survey. *I.E.E.E. Computer,* 20 (9), 17–41.

Joyce, Michael. (1988). Siren shapes: Exploratory and constructive hypertexts. *Academic Computing,* 3 (4), 10–14, 37–42.

Nelson, Ted H. (1974). *Dream machines.* Theodor H. Nelson.

Nelson, Ted H. (1984). *Literary machines.* Theodor H. Nelson.

Ong, Walter J. (1958). *Ramus, method, and the decay of dialogue: From the art of discourse to the art of reason.* Cambridge, MA: Harvard University Press.

Peers, E. Allison (Trans.). (1972). *Complete works of St. Teresa of Jesus.* (Vols. 1–3). London: Sheed and Ward.

Smith, John B., and Weiss, Stephen F. (Eds.). (1988). Hypertext [Special Issue]. *Communications of the ACM,* 31 (7).

Yankelovich, Nicole, Haan, Bernard J., Meyrowitz, Norman K., and Drucker, Steven M. (1988). Intermedia: the concept and the construction of a seamless information environment. *Computer,* 21 (1), 81–96.

■ QUESTIONS FOR REREADING

1. What is Bolter's definition of hypertext? What does Bolter mean when he says that writing is "topical"? What does *topos* mean? And then later in his discussion, what does he mean by "topographical writing"?

2. What does Bolter mean when he writes, "A hypertext has no canonical order"? What does this statement have to do with writing in electronic spaces?

3. We have read what Birkerts has to say about the fate of reading. What does Bolter have to say about the fate of writing and of the author and reader?

4. What could Bolter possible mean when he writes, "Electronic text is the first text in which the elements of meaning, of structure, and of visual display are fundamentally unstable"?

5. Try to summarize your understanding of how Bolter distinguishes between writing on paper and writing in an electronic environment.

■ WRITING ASSIGNMENT FOR REREADING

When you "write" (that is, compose an essay for class), do you use pencils or pens to write on paper, or do you use a typewriter, or do you use a computer? Have you ever written on a computer using not a word-processing program but a hypercard program or a hypertext program? If so, how would you explain the differences between or among writing with pencils/pens on paper through and up to writing hypertext? If you have not had a chance to write hypertext, try to find someone or someplace on campus (such as your writing center) that has such a program like "StorySpace" and see if you can try it out.

Gerald Jonas's "The Disappearing $2,000 Book" first appeared in The New York Review of Books (August 29, 1993): 12–13. Jonas's book review is about a rather unique book project done collaboratively by William Gibson, Dennis Ashbaugh, and Kevin Begos, Jr.

Gibson wrote the text for the book, which is titled Agrippa: The Book of the Dead.

The project, when sold, came in three price ranges: $450; $1,500; and $7,500. Perhaps, as Jonas's title implies, there were some copies sold at $2,000, or as far as that goes, sold for what the market would bear. The text of Gibson's narrative is on a floppy disk that when inserted into an IBM or Macintosh computer automatically scrolls for about fifteen minutes, giving the reader time to process the narrative. While the text scrolls, however, a virus on the disk destroys the text. That's right: It's a one-read book! It has been alleged that Dennis Ashbaugh has said that Agrippa is "the most important book since the Gutenberg Bible."

Gerald Jonas

The Disappearing $2,000 Book

Once upon a time, storytellers perpetuated the tales of the tribe by memorizing them. With the invention of books, memory became less important: if you forgot something, you could look it up. Then came the computer; to access its electronic memory, all you had to remember was which key to press. Now this evolution has come full circle with a story-on-a-disk that destroys itself as you read it, leaving nothing but the memory of words glimpsed briefly on a computer screen.

The author of the self-sabotaging story is William Gibson, whose 1984 novel *Neuromancer* gave birth to the terms "cyberpunk" and "cyberspace." Cyberpunk is science fiction with an attitude; it imagines a future in which people use the latest technology to do nasty things to one another. Mr. Gibson's characters, who spend the better part of their lives literally plugged into supercomputers, experience electronic data-flow as sensory input; they live in a "consensual hallucination" that Mr. Gibson has dubbed cyberspace.

His ambivalence about the brave new world of the future is exemplified in the booby-trapped art book that Mr. Gibson has created along with the painter Dennis Ashbaugh and the publisher Kevin Begos Jr. The entire project—entitled *Agrippa (A Book of the Dead)*—is designed to challenge conventional notions about books and art while extracting money from collectors of both.

The deluxe edition of *Agrippa* comes in a 16-by-21½-inch metal mesh case sheathed in Kevlar, the polymer that bulletproof vests are made of. Sheltered inside the case is a book of 93 rag-paper pages bound in singed and stained linen that appears to have survived a fire. The last 60 pages have been fused together to form a block; cut into the block is a four-inch square that holds a computer disk; encrypted on this disk is the text of *Agrippa (A Book of the Dead)*, a short story by Mr. Gibson. The encryption process entails a computer "virus" programmed by a team of anonymous hackers. Because of the virus, the story cannot be viewed normally on a computer screen or printed out at will. The first time the disk is inserted in a computer, the words of the story begin scrolling up the screen at a preset speed as if the computer and not the reader were scanning the text. The first "reading" is also the last. As the sentences scroll by, the virus is silently corrupting all the data on the disk. When the last word vanishes from the screen, the disk is no longer usable.

The text of Mr. Gibson's story appears nowhere in the book itself. Thirty-two pages contain long sequences of the letters G, A, T, C. This is another kind of code; the letters represent the four building blocks of the DNA double-helix molecule, and the sequences were excerpted from real human genetic material. Seven pages of the book are devoted to copperplate etchings—brownish blobs on greenish backgrounds—by Mr. Ashbaugh. These were inspired by laboratory-generated images of human genetic material, known as "gene scans" or "DNA footprints." Six of the etchings have been overprinted with early 20th-century advertisements for gadgets like telephones and cameras; a special ink was used so that these reproductions literally wipe off the page at the slightest touch.

Mr. Ashbaugh's etchings remain, although buyers of *Agrippa* are assured that the plates used to make these images will be destroyed or defaced as soon as the 95th impression is pulled. Only 95 copies of *Agrippa* are being offered, at $2,000 apiece, to serious collectors.

The challenge for collectors who buy *Agrippa* is how to protect their investment while savoring the object. To read Mr. Gibson's story is to destroy it. Even turning the pages of the book to look at the pictures is to risk altering the book irreversibly. Collectors will not be entirely unfamiliar with this problem, says Mr. Begos, who once published books under the auspices of the Limited Editions Club and who now works out of 61 East Eighth Street, Box 146, New York, N.Y. 10003. The erasable ink and the self-erasing story are extreme cases, but according to Mr. Begos, collectors rarely open their fine art books for fear of damaging the expensive goods. "If you pay thousands of dollars for a limited edition, you're not likely to curl up in bed with it," he said.

Dennis Ashbaugh, who was an admirer of Mr. Gibson's science fiction before they met, relishes the sense of discomfort that *Agrippa* induces in book lovers and art lovers alike. He found that working with Mr. Gibson confirmed his own discomfort with purely abstract paintings. "I was completely bored with the paintings I was doing," Mr. Ashbaugh said. "They had nothing to do with being alive today. I'm keen on making paintings that exist maybe 15 minutes into the future."

When *Agrippa (A Book of the Dead)* was exhibited in May at the Center for Book Arts on lower Broadway in Manhattan, Marshall Blonsky, who teaches literary theory at New York University and the New School, gave a lecture on analyzing the text, which he had received in readable form only six hours earlier. After making apologies for the necessarily sketchy nature of his remarks, Mr. Blonsky went on to link the *Agrippa* project to the work of "at least two writers, Maurice Blanchot, in particular 'The Absence of the Book,' and Stéphane Mallarmé," the 19th-century poet whose obsessions presaged "the 1960's–70's runaway adventure first called semiology and then semiotics and deconstruction. . . . The collaborators in *Agrippa* are responding to a historical condition of language, a modern skepticism about it."

Asked to comment on this, Mr Gibson said (by telephone from his home in Vancouver, British Columbia), "Honest to God, these academics who think it's all some sort of big-time French philosophy—that's a scam. Those guys worship Jerry Lewis, they get our pop culture all wrong." Although Mr. Gibson did a cameo appearance as the godfather of cyber-space on the first episode of the television series *Wild Palms,* he disclaims any special expertise in computers or virtual reality. He wrote *Neuromancer* on a 1927 Hermes portable typewriter; he got his notion of cyberspace from watching the body language of children playing video games in an arcade.

Nowadays Mr. Gibson writes on a Macintosh SE30 computer; his newest novel, *Virtual Light,* has just been published. He lives with his wife, Deborah, and their two children, Claire, 10, and Graeme, 15, in a cedar-shingled house overlooking Vancouver harbor. Although the self-destroying encryption of the *Agrippa* disk was supposed to be unbreakable, Mr Gibson was not at all surprised to learn that the international legion of computer hackers had broken the code within a few days of its appearance and that the full text had been posted on the network of electronic bulletin boards that function as primitive precursors to Mr. Gibson's imagined cyberspace. (This global network, which includes the Whole Earth 'Lectronic Link, or WELL, on the West Coast, and the East Coast Hang Out, or ECHO, based in New York, as well as the world-spanning Internet, is the model for the Clinton Administration's proposed "information superhighway.")

Fans of Mr. Gibson's science fiction who read *Agrippa* on their computer screens may be disappointed to find that it bears no resemblance to the hopped-up style and frenetically paced action of his cyberpunk novels. The self-destroying story turns out to be a sweetly sentimental prose poem about the fragility of memory, triggered by Mr. Gibson's discovery of his father's old photograph album (a string-bound, loose-leaf album sold by Kodak in the early 1920's under the name Agrippa). Only one section, set in the "old bus station" in Mr. Gibson's hometown of Wytheville, Va., refers even tangentially to the world of *Neuromancer.*

When the colored restroom
was no longer required
they knocked open the cinderblock
and extended the magazine rack
to new dimensions,
a cool fluorescent cave of dreams
smelling faintly and forever of disinfectant . . .
There it was I was marked out as a writer
                        of science fiction,
having discovered in that alcove
copies of certain magazines
esoteric and precious.

■ QUESTIONS FOR REREADING

1. Who is William Gibson? And why did he write this "disappearing book" called *Agrippa*? Why does Gibson have the text of the book on a disk consumed by a virus? What is the significance of the subtitle, *A Book of the Dead*? And what might be the purpose of including DNA code as part of the project?

2. Why do you think Gibson wrote *Agrippa* on a Hermes 1927 portable typewriter? What might the connection be between this act of using the typewriter and the final act of producing a disappearing book?

3. What is the fate of one reading? What might Gibson be saying about the fate of the book?

4. Why is the deluxe edition of the text of the book on a disk housed within a metal case and with other paraphernalia? Does the form of the deluxe edition itself suggest something about the form of books to come?

■ WRITING ASSIGNMENT FOR REREADING

As Jonas tells us, the text of *Agrippa* is available on the Web. Get a copy and discuss it in class. Then write an interpretive essay on the poem and in the light of questions 1 through 4. You might also want to read the parody of *Agrippa*. (See chapter 5 on the Web site for *CyberReader*.)

Raymond Kurzweil's "The Future of Libraries" appeared in three installments in Library Journal (January 1992): 80, 82; (February 1992): 140–141; (March 1992):

63–64. Kurzweil's three-part article on the future of libraries functions here as a transitional article from the end of actual books and libraries to the beginnings of electronic books and virtual libraries.

What has caused the end of books and libraries is technology, the cycle of which Kurzweil

reviews for us. The impact of this technology makes it possible for electronic books to be easily disseminated free on the Net. However, though we might think that such books should be free, or at least cheaper, since they are paperless, coverless, and so on, we will need to recognize that we must still pay publishers and authors. We must pay them, if not for the physical makeup of a book, then for the knowledge it contains. Kurzweil—far from thinking, by way of the hacker's ethic, that information "wants" to or can or should be free—instead claims, "Knowledge is not free, nor should it be." A corollary to this view is that copyrights and royalties will be maintained.

Raymond Kurzweil

The Future of Libraries

■ PART 1: THE TECHNOLOGY OF THE BOOK

I always keep a stack of books on my desk that I leaf through when I run out of ideas, feel restless, or otherwise need a shot of inspiration. Picking up a fat volume that I recently acquired, I consider the bookmaker's craft: 470 finely printed pages organized into 16-page signatures, each of which is sewn together with white thread and glued onto a gray canvas cord. The hard linen-bound covers, stamped with gold letters, are connected to the signature block by delicately embossed end sheets. This is a technology that was perfected many decades ago. Books constitute such an integral element of our society—both reflecting and shaping its culture—that it is hard to imagine life without them. But the printed book, like any other technology, will not live forever.

The Life Cycle of a Technology

We can identify seven distinct stages in the life cycle of a technology. During the *precursor* stage, the prerequisites of a technology exist, and dreamers may contemplate these elements coming together. We do not, however, regard dreaming to be the same as inventing even if the dreams are written down. Leonardo da Vinci drew convincing pictures of airplanes and automobiles, but he is not considered to have invented either.

The next stage, one highly celebrated in our culture, is *invention,* a very brief stage, not dissimilar in some respects to the process of birth after an extended period of labor. Here the inventor blends curiosity, scientific skills, determination, and usually a measure of showmanship to combine methods in a new way, and brings a new technology to life.

The next stage is *development,* during which the invention is protected and supported by doting guardians (which may include the original inventor).

Books constitute such an integral element of our society. . .that it is hard to imagine life without them. But the printed book, like any other technology, will not live forever.

Often this stage is more crucial than invention and may involve additional creation that can have greater significance than the invention. Many tinkerers had constructed finely hand-tuned horseless carriages, but it was Henry Ford's innovation of mass production that enabled the automobile to take root and flourish.

The fourth stage is *maturity.* Although continuing to evolve, the technology now has a life of its own and has become an independent and established part of the community. It may become so interwoven in the fabric of life that it appears to many observers that it will last forever. This creates an interesting drama when the next stage arrives, which I call the stage of the *false pretenders.* Here an upstart threatens to eclipse the older technology. Its enthusiasts prematurely predict victory. While providing some distinct benefits, the newer technology is found on reflection to be missing some key element of functionality or quality. When it indeed fails to dislodge the established order, the technology conservatives take this as evidence that the original approach will indeed live forever.

This is usually a short-lived victory for the aging technology. Shortly thereafter, another new technology typically does succeed in rendering the original technology into the stage of *obsolescence.* In this part of the life cycle, the technology lives out its senior years in gradual decline, its original purpose and functionality now subsumed by a more spry competitor. This stage, which may comprise five to ten percent of the life cycle, finally yields to *antiquity* (e.g., today the horse and buggy, the harpsichord, and the manual typewriter).

In the mid-19th century, there were several precursors to the phonograph, including de Martinville's *phonautograph,* a device that recorded sound vibrations as a printed pattern. It was Thomas Edison, however, who brought all of the elements together and invented the first device that could both record and reproduce sound in 1877. Further refinements were necessary for the phonograph to become commercially viable. It became a fully mature technology in 1948 when Columbia introduced the 33rpm long-playing record (LP) and RCA Victor introduced the 45rpm small disc. The false pretender was the cassette tape, introduced in the 1960s and popularized during the 1970s. Early enthusiasts predicted that its small size and ability to be rerecorded would make the relatively bulky and scratchable record obsolete.

Despite these obvious benefits, cassettes lack random access (the ability to play selections randomly) and are prone to their own forms of distortion and lack of fidelity. More recently, however, the compact disc (CD) has delivered the mortal blow. With the CD providing both random access and a level of quality close to the limits of the human auditory system, the phonograph record has quickly entered the stage of obsolescence. Although still produced, the technology that Edison gave birth to 114 years ago will reach antiquity by the end of the decade.

Roll Over Beethoven

Consider the piano, an area of technology that I am personally familiar with. In the early 18th century, Bartolommeo Cristofori was seeking a way to provide a touch response to the then-popular harpsichord so that the volume of the notes would vary with the intensity of the touch of the performer. Called *gravicembalo col piano e forte* ("harpsichord with soft and loud"), his invention was not an immediate success. Further refinements, including Stein's Viennese action and Zumpe's English action, helped to establish the "piano" as the preeminent keyboard instrument. It reached maturity with the development of the complete cast-iron frame, patented in 1825 by Alpheus Babcock, and has seen only subtle refinements since then. The false pretender was the electric piano of the early 1980s. It offered substantially greater functionality. Compared to the single (piano) sound of the acoustic piano, the electronic variant offered dozens of instrument sounds, sequencers that allowed the user to play an entire orchestra at once, automated accompaniment, educational programs to teach keyboard skills, and many other features. The only feature it was missing was a good quality piano sound.

This crucial flaw and the resulting failure of the first generation of electronic pianos to take root led many observers to remark that the piano would *never* be replaced by electronics. But the "victory" of the acoustic piano was short lived. It is entering obsolescence as we speak. Already the upright piano has been largely superseded by the latest wave of digital pianos. Many observers feel that the sound quality of the "piano" sound on digital pianos now equals or exceeds that of the upright acoustic piano, and the far greater range of features and price performance of digital pianos has enabled them to dominate the market. All piano manufacturers I have spoken with report that with the sole exception of the concert grand (a very small part of the market), the sale of acoustic pianos is in rapid decline. The piano should hit antiquity by the turn of the century.

From Goat Skins to CD-ROM

So where in the technology life cycle is the book? Among its precursors were the Mesopotamian clay tablets and the Egyptian papyrus scrolls. In the second century B.C., the Ptolemies of Egypt had created a great library of scrolls at Alexandria and outlawed the export of papyrus to discourage competition.

What were perhaps the first books were created by Eumenes II, ruler of ancient Greek Pergamum, using pages of vellum made from the skins of goats and sheep, which were sewn together between wooden covers. This technique enabled Eumenes to compile a library equal to that of Alexandria. Around the same time, the Chinese had also developed a crude form of book made from bamboo strips.

The development and maturation of books has seen three advances. *Printing,* first experimented with by the Chinese in the eighth century A.D. using raised wood blocks, allowed books to be reproduced in much larger quantities, expanding their audience beyond government and religious leaders. Of even greater significance was the advent of *movable type,* which was experimented with by the Chinese and Koreans in the 11th century, but the complexity of Asian characters prevented these early attempts from being fully successful. Johannes Gutenberg, working in the 15th century, benefited from the relative simplicity of the Roman character set. He produced his Bible, the first large-scale work printed entirely with movable type, in 1455.

While there has been a continual stream of evolutionary improvements in the mechanical and electromechanical process of printing, the technology of bookmaking did not see another qualitative leap until the availability of *computer typesetting,* which has now largely done away with movable type. Typography is now regarded as a part of digital image processing.

With books now a fully mature technology, the false pretenders have arrived with the first wave of "electronic books." As is usually the case, these false pretenders offer dramatic qualitative and quantitative benefits. CD-ROM–based electronic books recently introduced by Sony and others (as well as CD-ROM–based software for personal computers) can provide the equivalent of thousands of books on a single diskette with powerful computer-based search and knowledge navigation features. With my CD-ROM–based encyclopedia, I can perform rapid word searches using extensive logic rules, something that is just not possible with the 33-volume "book" version I possess. Other CD-ROMs I have can provide pictures that are animated or that respond to my input. Pages are not necessarily ordered sequentially, but can be explored along more intuitive connections.

The Eye of the Beholder

So what's the problem? As with the phonograph record and the piano, this first generation of false pretenders is missing an essential quality of the original, which in this case is the superb characteristics of paper and ink. First of all, paper does not *flicker,* whereas the typical computer screen is displaying 60 to 72 interlaced frames per second. This is a problem because of an evolutionary adaptation of the primate visual system. We are only able to see a very small portion of the visual field with high resolution. This portion, imaged by the fovea portion of the retina, is focused on an area about the size of a single word at 22 inches away. Outside of the fovea, we have very little resolution but exquisite sensitivity to brightness changes. This allowed our primitive forebears to quickly detect a predator that might be attacking. The constant flicker of a color/graphics adapter (CGA) or video graphics array (VGA) computer screen is detected by our eyes as motion and causes constant movement of the fovea. This substantially slows down reading speeds, which is one reason that reading on a screen is less pleasant than reading a printed book.

Another issue is *contrast*. A good quality book has an ink-to-paper contrast of about 120:1. Typical computer screens are perhaps half of that.

A crucial issue is *resolution*. Print and illustrations in a print book represent a resolution of about 600 to 1000 dots per inch (dpi). Typical computer screens are about one-tenth of that, with the new CD-ROM–based electronic books providing even less.

Some computer screens provide *color,* but the portable ones usually do not. The *size, weight,* and *cost* of notebook computers and electronic books are impressive, but still not competitive with the good old print version.

Finally, there is the issue of the *available software,* by which I mean the enormous installed base of print books. There are 50,000 new print books published each year in the United States and millions of books in circulation. There are major efforts underway to scan and digitize print materials, but it will be a long time before the electronic databases have a comparable wealth of material.

So, will the book last forever? If today's electronic book is a false pretender, what sort of technology will it take to send the book into obsolescence?

So, will the book last forever? If today's electronic book is a false pretender, what sort of technology will it take to send the book into obsolescence? When will that happen? What will be the impact on society of the virtual book? Tune in next month.

■ PART 2: THE END OF BOOKS

It is said that in the development of technology we overestimate what can be accomplished in the short term and underestimate what can be accomplished in the long term. With the exception of a few prescient observers (such as Charles Babbage in the case of the computer), most predictions of the 20th century overlooked such breakthroughs as the computer, radio, television, and atomic energy, not to mention such recent innovations as the laser and bioengineering.

Beyond the breakthrough, it is also difficult to anticipate serendipity, the coming together of diverse trends with profound yet unanticipated effects. In the case of the book, it is the interplay of such multifarious trends that will determine its destiny. The trends themselves are not hard to anticipate, although the stunning pace of development, particularly of computer hardware, is often not fully appreciated. In most fields, we take it for granted that things get more expensive each year. But in the computer field, we can at least double functionality for the same unit cost every 12 to 15 months, and even this pace is accelerating.

The implications of this geometric trend can be understood by recalling the legend of the inventor of chess and his patron, the emperor of China. The emperor had so fallen in love with his new game, he offered the inventor a reward of anything he wanted in the kingdom.

"Just one grain of rice on the first square, your majesty."

"Just one grain of rice?"

"Yes, and two on the second, four on the third, and so on."

The emperor immediately granted the inventor's seemingly humble request. One version of the story has the emperor going bankrupt (the doubling per square ultimately equaled 18 million trillion grains of rice). The more believable version has the inventor losing his head.

As an example of what this trend has already accomplished, computer scientist David Waltz points out that computer memory today, after adjustment for inflation, costs only one-hundred-millionth of what it did in 1950 (which is consistent with a doubling of price-performance every 18 months). If the automotive industry had made as much progress in the past four decades, a typical automobile today would cost about one-hundredth of a cent.

With the price-performance of computer hardware doubling every year in every dimension, the impact will become increasingly hard to ignore. This becomes all the more significant as computers begin to affect virtually every other area of endeavor.

The Powerbook Looms

So let us examine how just the predictable trends will affect the technology of the book. Last month, we discussed the emergence of the first wave of false pretenders to the functionality of the paper book. While the electronic book provides profound advantages in the quantity and accessibility of information, it falls short in some of the fundamental characteristics of paper and ink in the areas of flicker, contrast, resolution, and color. But as noted above, computer technology is anything but static, and already some of these limitations are being overcome. Alan Kay, senior fellow at Apple Computer, points out that the recently introduced Apple Powerbook 170 is flicker free and has a contrast ratio of 95:1, close to paper's 120:1. Apple is actually positioning its new computer as an electronic book and plans to provide a library of books as software, hence the name Powerbook.

By next year, the first wave of color notebook computers will appear. Perhaps the most significant issue is resolution. Interestingly, the Jacquard loom, perfected by Joseph Marie Jacquard in 1805, which we might regard as the world's first computer display, had a resolution of 1000 silk threads to the inch, equaling that of paper. Jacquard's loom was controlled by punched cards and foreshadowed the emergence of the punched card–based data processing industry 85 years later. Today's notebook computers have a resolution of only about 100 dots per inch (dpi), substantially less than paper. Within two to three years, however, we will see notebook computers with about 250 dpi, which for many applications will begin to rival paper and ink.

Let us jump ahead and describe the notebook computer that we are likely to see by the turn of the century based on readily discernible trends. Resolution will range from 500 to 1000 dpi, the same as high-quality printed documents. The displays will be flicker free and will have contrast ratios and color capabilities comparable to paper and ink. The devices will come in a variety of sizes ranging from pocket sized to double-hinged displays that will present two large pages. These computers will be thin (perhaps ½″ deep) and lightweight.

By the end of this decade, the standard RAM chip will be one gigabit (one billion bits), so the typical personal notebook will provide at least a billion bytes (characters) of random access memory. Low-bandwidth communication (text, voice, still pictures) will be by wireless cellular transmission. High-bandwidth communication (moving high-resolution pictures) will be by optical fiber. In my November 15, 1991 [*Library Journal*] column ("Learning in the Age of Knowledge," p. 60–62), I mentioned Japan's plan to install a fiber-optic–based information superhighway into every home and office by early in the next century. President Bush recently signed a $3 billion bill to begin research in this area, but we still lack anything comparable to Japan's multi-hundred-billion-dollar commitment. I do anticipate, however, that we will wake up sooner or later to this enormous competitive threat.

Whatchamacallit

Communication between user and machine will be through voice for entering text and a pen-like device for pointing and for graphical gestures such as crossing out words. The keyboard will be entering obsolescence as we enter the first decade of the next century.

So what is this thing? A PC? A telephone? A television? A personal transcriptionist? A cybernetic research assistant? A book?

Obviously, it is all of the above. As a telephone, it will include real-time language translation (at least between certain popular languages) so that we can readily communicate with people around the globe (the translating telephone capability will mature during the first decade of the next century). With the addition of a small, hand-held digital camera, this "telephone" will also include moving high-definition pictures.

George Gilder describes high-definition television—the marriage of the two great communication technologies of the 20th century (the computer and television)—as creating a highly flexible telecomputer that is interactive and intelligent.

As a personal research assistant, the operating system of our future PCs will contain intelligent knowledge navigators that have the knowledge of where to find knowledge through instantaneous wireless communication with increasingly comprehensive databases.

However, let us concentrate for a moment on its application as a book. The personal computer of the early 2000s will not be a false pretender. These electronic books will have enormous advantages, with pictures that can move and interact with the user, increasingly intelligent search paradigms, simulated environments that the user can enter and explore, and vast quantities of accessible material. Yet vital to its ability to truly make the paper book obsolete is that the essential qualities of paper and ink will have been fully matched. The book will enter obsolescence, although because of its long history and enormous installed base, it will linger for a couple of decades before reaching antiquity.

The Virtue of Virtual Books

The paper book will be replaced by a category of software that we can call virtual books. Is the virtual book really a new technology or just a continuation of the old (paper) technology by other means? It is certainly a new technology in the same sense that the "horseless carriage" automobile was a different technology from the horse and buggy. Changing such a central component of an old technology opens up so many new possibilities that we can truly say that a new technology has been born.

The paper book will be replaced by a category of software that we can call virtual books.

Yet haven't we been hearing about the paperless society for at least a decade now? American business's use of paper for printed documents increased from 850 billion pages in 1981 to nearly four trillion pages in 1990. It is certainly the case that while computers make it possible to handle documents without paper, they also greatly increase the productivity of producing paper documents. Until the computer display truly rivals the qualities of paper, computers will increase the use of paper rather than replace it. But once these qualities are matched, and the requisite communication technologies are in place, the printed book and other paper documents along with it will begin a rapid descent into obsolescence.

Many people were skeptical that the compact disc (CD) would replace the phonograph record. I remember being hesitant to buy a CD player because I was attached to my extensive collection of LPs collected over a lifetime, and I did not desire it becoming obsolete. My curiosity finally drove me to acquire a CD, and then I was hooked. My CD collection has grown, but I still have several shelves in my living room filled with my old album collection. But it has now been years since I have even touched one of these old phonograph albums, and even more years since I purchased one. People are also attached to their collections of paper books, but when the truly viable electronic book comes along, which will happen by the end of the decade, resistance to it will not last long.

Click and Pick

So how do you buy a virtual book? By going to a bookstore, obviously. Not physically, of course; you simply "click" on *bookstore*. Icons then appear for different choices. So let's say we click on *Brentano's*. We now see icons for different categories of books: *best sellers, fantasy & science fiction,* etc. Let's click on *best sellers*. We now see images of book spines, which can be scrolled across the screen. Some books that the bookstore wishes to highlight are shown with the full front jacket.

Ah, here is an interesting one, *The Best of Futurecast* by Raymond Kurzweil. We click on that, and we now see the full front and back jacket. We click on the photo of the author, and he comes alive explaining the virtues of his book. We click on the front cover, and we see the front matter.

We scroll through the table of contents. Here is an interesting old article from 1992 on "The End of Books." We click on it and start reading. Hmmm, this is very interesting; Kurzweil's predictions weren't all bad!

Whoops, the computer now tells us that if we want to continue reading, we have to acquire the book. Options are presented. We can *purchase* it, we can *rent* it, and there are several other choices. Well, this is a book we will certainly want to return to over and over, so we click on *purchase*. Now we see icons for *debit to checking account, charge to American Express,* etc. Once the transaction is complete, the book is transmitted via wireless cellular communication and becomes part of the permanent database of our PC.

What about the public library? Okay, click on *city library*. We see icons for categories. Click on *best sellers*. Now click on *The Best of Futurecast*. Looks interesting, so we click on *borrow book*.

Now wait a second. The library scenario sounds very similar to the bookstore scenario. Why would anyone buy a book if you can borrow it just as easily for free anytime you want to read it?

Other questions come to mind. What happens to that big library building? Will there still be paper books printed? Will libraries still carry these? How will the library work? What will librarians do?

There are reasonable answers to these questions, which we will examine next month.

- **PART 3: THE VIRTUAL LIBRARY**

I posed the following dilemma at the end of my previous column (see The Futurecast, *LJ,* February 15, p. 140): If borrowing a virtual book from the virtual "free library" involves simply selecting a few icons on the screen of your circa 2000 notebook computer, why then would anyone *buy* a book (which would involve clicking on a different set of icons as well as a debit to one of your financial accounts)?

Kay replied that the "free library is not free."

I posed this specter to two of our contemporary visionaries: Apple Fellow Alan Kay and Hudson Institute Fellow George Gilder. Gilder replied that no one should feel too secure in the information revolution. Having the courage to radically alter one's self-concept will be the prerequisite to survival for any organization, from IBM to the Mill Valley Local Library.

Kay replied that the "free library is not free."

These two enigmatic replies contain the key to resolving the dilemma if we ponder the implications of both views. We can postulate two visions of the library of the future. If we are indeed entering the Age of Knowledge (see *The Futurecast, LJ,* September 15, 1991, p. 58–59) in which the organization of information will be the paramount strategic asset of nations and individuals, then the library, as the institution in our society primarily responsible for organizing and presenting codified knowledge, may properly be regarded as having the responsibility for leading the charge. On the other hand, if we view the concept of the library more provincially, as a building containing stacks of paper books with librarians who lend these objects out to patrons, then our long-term prognosis for the institution is distinctly more dismal.

If you were a blacksmith at the turn of the century, your outlook would depend on whether you saw yourself as a shaper of horseshoes or a facilitator of transportation (in which case you would trade in your forge and hammer for a gas pump). Gilder is pointing out that with the pace of change accelerating, it is not only the private sector that must dramatically adapt. Our public institutions—schools, government, libraries—must define their missions broadly enough to survive the obsolescence of more narrowly defined self-concepts.

If we define the mission of the library as the shaping and distribution of knowledge through whatever technical means, we are still left with the original predicament. Perhaps it is bookstores that will have to go. If libraries can simply distribute books and other information electromagnetically through the air and optically through the nation's fiberoptic information highway, then who needs bookstores, anyway? The problem, however, is that without revenue, there will be no publishers and nothing will be published.

A Fistful of Knowledge

We must now contemplate a central lesson of the Age of Knowledge, which is implied in Kay's observation above. *Knowledge is not free, nor should it be.* We are used to paying for the knowledge content of products so long as it is integrated into something with mass. We recognize that a $300 software product is physically identical to a few $2 floppy disks, and thus we are primarily paying for the information contained therein. We are aware (or should be) that the manufactured cost of a compact disc recording is less than 50¢ (depending on volume), and that again we are paying for the (musical) information. It is, after all, the information we are after. We obtain no pleasure from the discs themselves. The manufactured cost of most books is only a few dollars. Again, it is the knowledge we are seeking (although I will admit that a well-crafted book is a lovely possession).

Why then do we have difficulty comprehending the value of information when the physical content of a product shrinks to nothing? We are used to buying products that have size and weight. If design and other learned content enhance their value, so be it. Still, the paradigm that we are used to for buying a product is that we purchase an object with size and weight in a store, carry it home in a colorful shopping bag, unwrap it, and only then digest its intellectual content. We are already at the point where at least 90 percent of the value of products of this type results from their knowledge content, and we will need very soon to fully absorb the idea that knowledge without *any* physical construct still represents value. Otherwise, no knowledge of value will be created.

The Royalty Factor

So while it is true that a book could be distributed electronically to millions of people at very little cost, it will nonetheless require compensation to the publisher and author (or artist, musician, programmer, artificial reality designer, etc.) just as is the case today. Thus when you buy a virtual book from your virtual bookstore, the money that is deducted from your (electronic but not so virtual) bank account will be distributed as it is now to the distributor, publisher, and author. The point that Kay is making is that the same transaction will need to take place when you "borrow" a book from the "free" library. It may be a free service to you, but someone is going to have to pay, namely the library. In other words, libraries will not be exempt from violating copyright laws. Publishers will be quite happy with libraries distributing their virtual books, just as they are undoubtedly delighted to receive book orders from libraries today.

Yet library budgets are not unlimited—as most *Library Journal* readers will appreciate—so constraints will have to be applied. Today these constraints are enforced by requiring patrons to physically go to the library, placing limits on the selection and number of books available, putting time limits on borrowing, and other subtle and overt restrictions. The virtual library will undoubtedly find similar ways to constrain its service. It will have no choice; its budget will be set by the same political realities that libraries deal with today.

The advent of the virtual book will require rethinking the concept of buying a book.

The advent of the virtual book will require rethinking the concept of buying a book. New options will need to be devised. Some information we may wish to retain indefinitely; other information we may wish to read and then discard; yet other information we may wish to sample or browse through. Some we may not wish to read at all, but will want to have as part of a database for our software-based intelligent "assistants" to "read." Different payment methods will need to be devised to handle these different situations, which in turn will necessarily be reflected in library borrowing policies.

Bootlegging in the 1990s

A prerequisite to the availability of the virtual book is an effective means of software protection, and by software I mean any form of digital information. Today, computer software, which is one of the most valuable and expensive forms of information to create, can be copied and distributed with abandon. Although illegal, it happens all the time. It is estimated that the significant majority of software in use today has been illegally copied.

One person I spoke to recently, who claimed to be unaware that this practice was illegal, complained that if copying software was illegal, then *why do software companies make it so easy to do?* This is a profoundly important challenge. People can copy software from their friends more easily than going to the store and buying it (it can even be done over the phone).

Most children grow up with the paradigm that if they steal something, they are depriving someone else of what they have stolen. The victim of such a crime is usually not far away. Yet the crime of stealing information by breaking the "shrinkwrap" license agreement (the legal agreement that you enter into when you break the shrinkwrap on a package of software) is far more subtle. The person that the information is copied from still has the information, so it is a rather abstract concept that anyone has been deprived of anything. Of course, creators of the software have been deprived of royalties, yet remain blissfully unaware of the crime against them, except through reading occasional surveys of such practices. It is obvious, however, that carried to an extreme, the entire basis for funding the development of such expensive intellectual creations is threatened.

It was precisely this concern that killed the first generation of digital audio tape (DAT) recorders: the music industry believed compact disc recordings would be illegally copied. Once movies exist in high-definition digital form, the concern will exist there as well. The fact is that we have the technical means to enforce information licensing laws and agreements through electronic "locks." What is needed is the social compact that we *should* pay for the information we use because otherwise there will be no useful information to buy or steal. It is not just the locks on our cars or homes that keep intruders out (to the extent that we do succeed in that endeavor), but rather the combination of the technical means (the locks) and the social compact, which is a combination of the law matched with a respect that this is a law responsible citizens will honor. As the technology blazes ahead, law and social consciousness need to catch up.

All Libraries Great and Small

With library limits (on availability, deadlines, restrictions, etc.) again in place, there will be a niche for the (virtual) bookstore. Will there be a niche for the local library? In my view, the funding source has been and is likely to continue to be local. There will undoubtedly be national libraries of various kinds (particularly in scientific and other professional areas), but the city of New York and the town of Mill Valley will still have the same incentive and political will to provide local library service to its citizens, which may very well include making available the notebook computers themselves.

What about paper books? They will ultimately reach antiquity, but because of their enormous installed base, this transition will not be instantaneous. When fully effective virtual books become available later this decade, some of the more progressive libraries will begin to incorporate them into their services. As virtual books become more dominant, libraries will begin to emphasize them over paper books, with some libraries on the leading edge and some on the trailing edge.

When the paper book does reach antiquity, what will happen to those big library buildings? The role of buildings is not an issue solely of concern to libraries. When we can readily meet with people anywhere with high-definition video conferencing (eventually with moving, high-resolution, three-dimensional holographic images) the purpose of buildings will undergo its own transformation, a topic we will examine in a future column.

Personally, I take the view of the library as the leading force in society for gathering knowledge and making it universally available, a service that is a prerequisite for a democratic society. Librarians are charged with guiding and shaping that process. They serve as society's guides to knowledge and where to find it. These roles will only become more important with time, so long as we take the broad view of what the concept of *library* represents.

■ Q U E S T I O N S   F O R   R E R E A D I N G

1. Who is Raymond Kurzweil?

2. The first installment of Kurzweil's article is titled "The Technology of the Book." What could this title mean? What does he mean by "technology" and "book"? How are they related? How does one inform the other?

3. What are the seven stages in the life cycle of a technology?

4. Why does Kurzweil in the section "The Eye of the Beholder" spend time explaining what the eye can see? Of what importance is this information? (Recall Rushkoff's title "Seeing Is Beholding." What connections can you make?)

5. In Kurzweil's estimation, what contributes to the disappearance and death of books? Is there a connection between progress in the development of computers and the lowering of the prices of computers and the disappearance of books? If so, explain precisely what that connection is. What is Kurzweil's take on the virtual book?

6. Explain Kurzweil's vision of the virtual library.

7. Kurzweil agrees with his friend Kay that the "free library is not free." Explain what is meant about the free library not being free. Assuming that you agree with this apparent paradox, is it possible for information on the Internet to be free? If not, who is paying for it? Who is subsidizing it? In the light of your conclusions, what do you think about the hacker's ethic that information "wants" to be free?

■ WRITING ASSIGNMENT FOR REREADING

Books, like all things, have always been threatened. Recall historically the various times that books have been burned. (There have been many such burnings in the twentieth century.) Recall fictionally the burning of books, say, in Ray Bradbury's *Fahrenheit 451*. Do some basic research and try to find out what is happening to books today in public libraries in cities and countries that are heavily investing in virtual libraries. Start with one city—say, New York, or your city if you live in a big one—and do some investigative reporting: Try to find out if there have been any articles written about books being tossed away and exchanged for virtual books; try to interview people who are responsible for maintaining libraries. Keep digging. When you think that you have something to write about, then start writing your essay.

Theodor Holm Nelson's "Summary of the Xanadu Hypertext System" first appeared in Literary Machines (Theodor H. Nelson, 1987). Nelson and his "Xanadu Project" have been referred to by a number of the authors included in CyberReader. Nelson is often called a visionary. He is one of the first people to attempt thinking about how to implement the idea of a universal virtual library. What is included here for your perusal are some "notes" from his book. Nelson has been criticized by Gary Wolf in an article in Wired magazine. We will take up that criticism and Nelson's response at the Web site for CyberReader, for a criticism of Nelson is also, if only indirectly, a criticism of the concept of a virtual library.

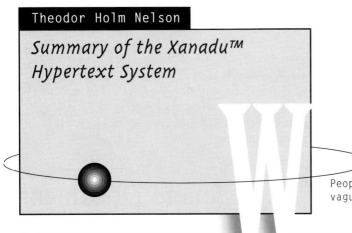

Theodor Holm Nelson

Summary of the Xanadu™ Hypertext System

> People mistake generality for vagueness.
>
> —Roger Gregory

While the system is conceptually simple, it is amazing how many different ways there are to think about it and describe it. We take this as indicating its generality.

Some of these descriptions are listed below, both as one-liners and in an essay form. Readers may find them useful for communicating to others, or for reviewing their own understanding of the system.

■ SUMMARY OF THE XANADU ™ HYPERTEXT SYSTEM:

One-Liners

"A literary system of authorship, ownership, quotation and linkage."

"A pluralistic publishing and archiving medium with open hypertext and semi-closed framing."

"A distributed repository scheme for worldwide electronic publishing."

"A system to promote cumulative order and the equitable coexistence of many viewpoints."

"A vessel for the true shape of information—without having to cut it or jam it."

"A mapping system between storage and virtual documents."

"A distributed server network for documents made out of pooled boilerplate."

"A storage arrangement for linking between arbitrary collections of material."

"A seamless data architecture for linked electronic publishing."

"A linking system for keeping track of anything."

"An applicative virtual document system for applying sequential and non-sequential structure to material that arrived out of sequence and unstructured."

"A grand address space for everything, parts of which can be in different places at once."

"A way of tying it all together and not losing anything."

"A way of including anything in anything else."...

Shortest Description

The Xanadu™ Hypertext System is a form of storage: a new computer filing system which stores and delivers new kinds of documents. These documents may have any form and contents, but may also have links and inclusions from other documents. A user may request parts of documents or may follow links, both within and between documents. The user may easily see highlighted intercomparisons between documents.

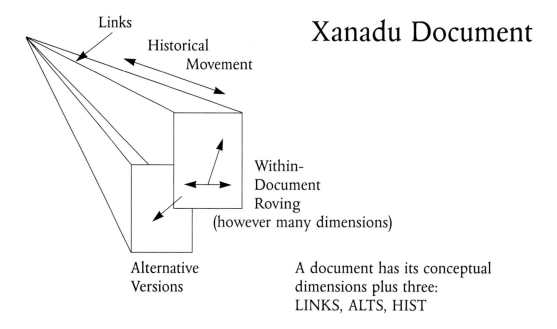

Xanadu Document

Links

Historical Movement

Within-Document Roving (however many dimensions)

Alternative Versions

A document has its conceptual dimensions plus three: LINKS, ALTS, HIST

This structure is the same regardless of size: a small Xanadu system will hold and clarify an individual's work, and the full network is intended to supply millions of documents to millions of simultaneous users, all following links and windows throughout the growing body of hypertext.

Medium-Length Description

The Xanadu™ Hypertext System is a new form of storage intended to simplify and clarify computer use, and make possible new forms of instantaneous electronic publication.

Running on a single computer, it is a file server for the storage and delivery of text, graphics and other digital information with previously impossible arrangements and services. These new arrangements include links and windows between documents, as well as non-sequential writing (hypertext).

It will also reveal and clarify commonalities between documents and among versions, simplifying both storage and comprehensibility. Thus even running on a single computer, it will simplify computer operations, clarify storage, and clarify and simplify office and document work for individuals and corporations.

In the full worldwide network, it will permit the publication and instantaneous worldwide delivery of interconnected works having immense new power to huge numbers of users.

Extended Description

The Xanadu™ Hypertext System is software for the unique organization of computer storage and the rapid delivery of its contents to users. All forms of material—text, pictures, musical notations, even photographs and recordings—may be digitally stored on it. Most importantly, the new forms of interconnection this makes possible among these materials are profound and revealing.

It is a system for the rapid delivery of linked documents (which may share material) and the assimilation and storage of changes. System facilities permit promiscuous linkage and windowing among all materials; with special features for alternative versions, historical backtrack and arbitrary collaging. It is based on new technicalities which are of no concern to the user, and materials are stored in locations the user need not know about.

Any forms of data will eventually share these facilities of linking and inclusions, although each needs separate implementation. Bit-map graphics will be stored in such a way as to allow panning (graphical scrolling) and zoom (continuously increasing or decreasing magnification) as incremental data deliveries. (How your screen machine will show them is another matter.) Three-dimensional objects, when implemented, may be collaged by users into compound objects, scenes from history, enactments and artwork.

It's exactly one system that comes in small, medium and very large. In all cases it is a back-end storage feeder—or "file server," in the current vernacular—for holding and sending out documents which are connected in any possible way (arbitrary topology).

Single-user and multi-user versions for individual and corporate uses will simplify and clarify the user's storage and the interrelations of data— helping your information evolve toward better organization by small increments.

The single-user system will run on personal computers (such as the extended-memory PC clone and the megabyte Macintosh). The multi-user version will provide document services to a network of computers among corporate users.

Custom front ends of any kind are possible. While any sort of terminal may be connected to the system, its best operation requires a full computer in the user's terminal, programmed to handle display functions, interchange protocol, and other work. A front-end program is any program, running on a user's screen machine or other computer, for any purpose and behaving in any manner, which delivers to and extracts from the Xanadu storage system.

A complete network of publishing with royalty has been carefully planned. All users will have access to all public documents instantaneously (not counting network delays). Every byte delivered to the user will return a minute royalty to the document of origin.

In this expected publishing network, Xanadu storage will provide linked access to new and powerful forms of interconnected data and writing in compound documents, the storage of which may be distributed.

Its unique facilities of backtrack, linkage and windowing will allow the creation of new forms of multi-level, explorable collections and collages of material—without losing the well-defined authorship and ownership of all parts.

Anyone may publish collaged and windowing documents having finely divided ownership. There are simple categories of publication (private and public) and low, comparatively flat costs of usage.

Any part of any available document will be accessible from any port on any computer in the net at any time, at prices comparable to storage on other computer systems.

Users may connect their home or office computers of any kind to this network, whether by dialup, GTE Telenet, leased line, twisted pair, or nearby wink-laser. (Each machine will need its own front-end program, however.)

Services will be differentiated mainly with respect to speed of terminal (1200 baud the minimum). No users will be restricted as to what public documents they may access, though private documents will be restricted as specified by their owners.

The system's contents will be supplied by customers only. There will be no participation by the Xanadu enterprise in the publishing process itself; neither contents nor indexing will be provided by the system, these being rightful endeavors of the customers.

The system will exert no supervision or censorship on stored or published materials, and court orders will be required for the removal of any material held in a stable account. However, publishers and individuals will be thoroughly warned about legal exposure and pitfalls.

Publishing requires an up-front payment of one year's disk rental. A secondary publisher using windowed material need only pay the cost of pointer storage.

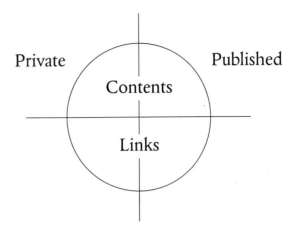

Private documents are available only to the owner and the owner's designees. Published documents are available to anyone, and yield a royalty to the owner; they may be updated at will, but the earlier contents remain available. They may not be withdrawn from publication except after six months' notice or court order. "Privashed" documents are available to anyone, and may be changed at will, but yield no royalty.

We believe this will make possible a whole new universe of knowledge and understanding.

It is presently on line as an experimental prototype. Later, we expect to offer it in object form to users for both personal and corporate computers, first in single-user, then multi-user configurations. After that comes the network with publishing royalty, which we believe can grow as fast as demand.

In one business scenario, the intended public operation of the publishing system will be out of a chain of suburban or roadside stations, called Silverstands™. New users will learn the operation of the system at such stands, and local users may dial into their nearest Silverstand. Silverstand personnel ("Conductors") will include both local people and an itinerant corps of circulating smarties.

The actual code of the system is a medium-sized program in the C language, currently running under the UNIX operating system.

■ "HOW IS IT DIFFERENT FROM THE SOURCE?"

Many public-access computer systems now offer text services. One of the best known is The Source, so we often get this question.

Unlike general-purpose time-sharing systems such as The Source, which can run many kinds of programs and furnishes text services simply as one class of available program, ours is a *specialized* storage form for what we believe is the *most generalized* form of storage. Our system does not permit the running of user programs.

The Source, and other currently available text services, do not support linkage, windows, alternative versions or historical backtrack as they supply their stored documents, let alone maintain these connective structures as documents change.

■ QUESTIONS FOR REREADING

1. It will probably take some patience to read what Nelson has written. Notice, however, that he attempts to be helpful by starting out with "one-liners," then "shortest description," "medium-length description," and finally "extended description." As you read Nelson's summary toward an account of his project, does this approach from simple to more complex help you follow his ideas? Do you see how this approach itself might be seen as a flat hypertext approach?

2. What does his last "one-liner"—"A way of including anything in anything else"—mean?

3. Who will supply the contents of the library? What is Nelson's policy on what can be included or removed from the database?

4. Many argue that Nelson's project is only quixotic. (Where does the name "Xanadu" come from, and what is its significance?) They claim that he has made no progress toward implementing his project. Hasn't Nelson's "Xanadu Project" already been under way for some time now, and it's called the Web? Agree or disagree.

■ WRITING ASSIGNMENT FOR REREADING

Attempt to find as many parallels as possible between Nelson's summary of his project (how it will be implemented) and the World Wide Web (how it is variously implemented). Write a paper on your findings.

Jorge Luis Borges's "The Library of Babel" (translated) is in *Ficionnes* (New York: Grove P, 1962). This tale is a much anthologized and hence canonized literary work. It is referred to by many people in many different disciplines. It is a metaphor for a universal library and hence all of knowledge. Anyone wrestling with the idea of how to build a virtual library must reflect on Borges's metaphor.

Jorge Luis Borges

The Library of Babel

By this art you may contemplate the variation of the 23 letters...
—*The Anatomy of Melancholy*, Part 2, Sect. II, Mem. IV.

The universe (which others call the Library) is composed of an indefinite, perhaps an infinite, number of hexagonal galleries, with enormous ventilation shafts in the middle, encircled by very low railings. From any hexagon the upper or lower stories are visible, interminably. The distribution of the galleries is invariable. Twenty shelves—five long shelves per side—cover all sides except two; their height, which is that of each floor, scarcely exceeds that of an average librarian. One of the free sides gives upon a narrow entrance way, which leads to another gallery, identical to the first and to all the others. To the left and to the right of the entrance way are two miniature rooms. One allows standing room for sleeping; the other, the satisfaction of fecal necessities. Through this section passes the spiral staircase, which plunges down into the abyss and rises up to the heights. In the entrance way hangs a mirror, which faithfully duplicates appearances. People are in the habit of inferring from this mirror that the Library is not infinite (if it really were, why this illusory duplication?); I prefer to dream that the polished surfaces feign and promise infinity. . . .

Light comes from some spherical fruits called by the name of lamps. There are two, running transversally, in each hexagon. The light they emit is insufficient, incessant.

Like all men of the Library, I have traveled in my youth. I have journeyed in search of a book, perhaps of the catalogue of catalogues; now that my eyes can scarcely decipher what I write, I am preparing to die a few leagues from the hexagon in which I was born. Once dead, there will not lack pious hands to hurl me over the banister; my sepulchre shall be the unfathomable air: my body will sink lengthily and will corrupt and dissolve in the wind engendered by the fall, which is infinite. I affirm that the Library is interminable. The idealists argue that the hexagonal halls are a necessary form of absolute space or, at least, of our intuition of space. They contend that a triangular or pentagonal hall is inconceivable. (The mystics claim that to them ecstasy reveals a round chamber containing a great book with a continuous back circling the walls of the room; but their testimony is suspect; their words, obscure. That cyclical book is God.) Let it suffice me, for the time being, to repeat the classic dictum: *The Library is a sphere whose consummate center is any hexagon, and whose circumference is inaccessible.*

Five shelves correspond to each one of the walls of each hexagon; each shelf contains thirty-two books of a uniform format; each book is made up of four hundred and ten pages; each page, of forty lines; each line, of some eighty black letters. There are also letters on the spine of each book; these letters do not indicate or prefigure what the pages will say. I know that such a lack of relevance, at one time, seemed mysterious. Before summarizing the solution (whose disclosure, despite its tragic implications, is perhaps the capital fact of this history), I want to recall certain axioms.

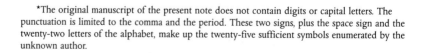

> *The Library is a sphere whose consummate center is any hexagon, and whose circumference is inaccessible.*

The first: The Library exists *ab aeterno*. No reasonable mind can doubt this truth, whose immediate corollary is the future eternity of the world. Man, the imperfect librarian, may be the work of chance or of malevolent demiurges; the universe, with its elegant endowment of shelves, of enigmatic volumes, of indefatigable ladders for the voyager, and of privies for the seated librarian, can only be the work of a god. In order to perceive the distance which exists between the divine and the human, it is enough to compare the rude tremulous symbols which my fallible hand scribbles on the end pages of a book with the organic letters inside: exact, delicate, intensely black, inimitably symmetric.

The second: *The number of orthographic symbols is twenty-five.** This bit of evidence permitted the formulation, three hundred years ago, of a general theory of the Library and the satisfactory resolution of the problem which no conjecture had yet made clear: the formless and chaotic nature of almost all books. One of these books, which my father saw in a hexagon of the circuit number fifteen ninety-four, was composed of the letters MCV perversely repeated from the first line to the last. Another, very much consulted in this zone, is a mere labyrinth of letters, but on the next-to-the-last page, one may read *O Time your pyramids*. As is well known: for one reasonable line or one straightforward note there are leagues of insensate cacophony, of verbal farragoes and incoherencies. (I know of a wild region whose librarians repudiate the vain superstitious custom of seeking any sense in books and compare it to looking for meaning in dreams or in the chaotic lines of one's hands. . . . They admit that the inventors of writing imitated the twenty-five natural symbols, but they maintain that this application is accidental and that books in themselves mean nothing. This opinion—we shall see—is not altogether false.)

---

*The original manuscript of the present note does not contain digits or capital letters. The punctuation is limited to the comma and the period. These two signs, plus the space sign and the twenty-two letters of the alphabet, make up the twenty-five sufficient symbols enumerated by the unknown author.

For a long time it was believed that these impenetrable books belonged to past or remote languages. It is true that the most ancient men, the first librarians, made use of a language quite different from the one we speak today; it is true that some miles to the right the language is dialectical and that ninety stories up it is incomprehensible. All this, I repeat, is true; but four hundred and ten pages of unvarying MCVs do not correspond to any language, however dialectical or rudimentary it might be. Some librarians insinuated that each letter could influence the next, and that the value of MCV on the third line of page 71 was not the same as that of the same series in another position on another page; but this vague thesis did not prosper. Still other men thought in terms of cryptographs; this conjecture has come to be universally accepted, though not in the sense in which it was formulated by its inventors.

Five hundred years ago, the chief of an upper hexagon* came upon a book as confusing as all the rest but which contained nearly two pages of homogenous lines. He showed his find to an ambulant decipherer, who told him the lines were written in Portuguese. Others told him they were in Yiddish. In less than a century the nature of the language was finally established: it was a Samoyed-Lithuanian dialect of Guaraní, with classical Arabic inflections. The contents were also deciphered: notions of combinational analysis, illustrated by examples of variations with unlimited repetition. These examples made it possible for a librarian of genius to discover the fundamental law of the Library. This thinker observed that all the books, however diverse, are made up of uniform elements: the period, the comma, the space, the twenty-two letters of the alphabet. He also adduced a circumstance confirmed by all travelers: *There are not, in the whole vast Library, two identical books.* From all these incontrovertible premises he deduced that the Library is total and that its shelves contain all the possible combinations of the twenty-odd orthographic symbols (whose number, though vast, is not infinite); that is, everything which can be expressed, in all languages. Everything is there: the minute history of the future, the autobiographies of the archangels, the faithful catalogue of the Library, thousands and thousands of false catalogues, a demonstration of the fallacy of these catalogues, a demonstration of the fallacy of the true catalogue, the Gnostic gospel of Basilides, the commentary on this gospel, the commentary on the commentary of this gospel, the veridical account of your death, a version of each book in all languages, the interpolations of every book in all books.

There are not, in the whole vast Library, two identical books.

When it was proclaimed that the Library comprised all books, the first impression was one of extravagant joy. All men felt themselves lords of a secret, intact treasure. There was no personal or universal problem whose eloquent

*Formerly, for each three hexagons there was one man. Suicide and pulmonary diseases have destroyed this proportion. My memory recalls scenes of unspeakable melancholy: there have been many nights when I have ventured down corridors and polished staircases without encountering a single librarian.

solution did not exist—in some hexagon. The universe was justified, the universe suddenly expanded to the limitless dimensions of hope. At that time there was much talk of the Vindications: books of apology and prophecy, which vindicated for all time the actions of every man in the world and established a store of prodigious arcana for the future. Thousands of covetous persons abandoned their dear natal hexagons and crowded up the stairs, urged on by the vain aim of finding their Vindication. These pilgrims disputed in the narrow corridors, hurled dark maledictions, strangled each other on the divine stairways, flung the deceitful books to the bottom of the tunnels, and died as they were thrown into space by men from remote regions. Some went mad. . . .

The Vindications do exist. I have myself seen two of these books, which were concerned with future people, people who were perhaps not imaginary. But the searchers did not remember that the calculable possibility of a man's finding his own book, or some perfidious variation of his own book, is close to zero.

The clarification of the basic mysteries of humanity—the origin of the Library and of time—was also expected. It is credible that those grave mysteries can be explained in words: if the language of the philosophers does not suffice, the multiform Library will have produced the unexpected language required and the necessary vocabularies and grammars for this language.

It is now four centuries since men have been wearying the hexagons. . . .

There are official searchers, *inquisitors*. I have observed them carrying out their functions: they are always exhausted. They speak of a staircase without steps where they were almost killed. They speak of galleries and stairs with the local librarian. From time to time they will pick up the nearest book and leaf through its pages, in search of infamous words. Obviously, no one expects to discover anything.

There are official searchers, inquisitors. I have observed them carrying out their functions: they are always exhausted.

The uncommon hope was followed, naturally enough, by deep depression. The certainty that some shelf in some hexagon contained precious books and that these books were inaccessible seemed almost intolerable. A blasphemous sect suggested that all searches be given up and that men everywhere shuffle letters and symbols until they succeeded in composing, by means of an improbable stroke of luck, the canonical books. The authorities found themselves obliged to issue severe orders. The sect disappeared, but in my childhood I still saw old men who would hide out in the privies for long periods of time and, with metal disks in a forbidden dicebox, feebly mimic the divine disorder.

Other men, inversely, thought that the primary task was to eliminate useless works. They would invade the hexagons, exhibiting credentials which were not always false, skim through a volume with annoyance, and then condemn entire bookshelves to destruction: their ascetic, hygenic fury is responsible for the senseless loss of millions of books. Their name is execrated; but those who mourn the "treasures" destroyed by this frenzy, overlook two notorious facts. One: the Library is so enormous that any reduction under-taken by humans is infinitesimal. Two: each book is unique, irreplaceable, but (inasmuch as the Library is total) there are always several hundreds of thou-sands of imperfect facsimiles—of works which differ only by one letter or one comma. Contrary to public opinion, I dare suppose that the consequences of the depredations committed by the Purifiers have been exaggerated by the horror which these fanatics provoked. They were spurred by the delirium of storming the books in the Crimson Hexagon: books of a smaller than ordi-nary format, omnipotent, illustrated, magical.

We know, too, of another superstition of that time: the Man of the Book. In some shelf of some hexagon, men reasoned, there must exist a book which is the cipher and perfect compendium of *all the rest:* some librarian has perused it, and it is analogous to a god. Vestiges of the worship of that remote func-tionary still persist in the language of this zone. Many pil-grimages have sought Him out. For a century they trod the most diverse routes in vain. How to locate the secret hexagon which harbored it? Someone proposed a regressive approach: in order to locate book A, first consult book B which will indicate the location of A; in order to locate book B, first con-sult book C, and so on ad infinitum. . . .

> **To me, it does not seem unlikely that on some shelf of the universe there lies a total book.**

I have squandered and consumed my years in adventures of this type. To me, it does not seem unlikely that on some shelf of the universe there lies a total book.* I pray the unknown gods that some man—even if only one man, and though it have been thousands of years ago!—may have examined and read it. If honor and wisdom and happiness are not for me, let them be for others. May heaven exist, though my place be in hell. Let me be outraged and annihilated, but may Thy enormous Library be justified, for one instant, in one being.

The impious assert that absurdities are the norm in the Library and that anything reasonable (even humble and pure coherence) is an almost miracu-lous exception. They speak (I know) of "the febrile Library, whose hazardous volumes run the constant risk of being changed into others and in which everything is affirmed, denied, and confused as by a divinity in delirium." These words, which not only denounce disorder but exemplify it as well, manifestly demonstrate the bad taste of the speakers and their desperate igno-rance. Actually, the Library includes all verbal structures, all the variations allowed by the twenty-five orthographic symbols, but it does not permit of one absolute absurdity. It is pointless to observe that the best book in the numerous hexagons under my administration is entitled *Combed Clap of Thun-der;* or that another is called *The Plaster Cramp;* and still another *Axaxaxas Mlö.* Such propositions as are contained in these titles, at first sight incoherent,

---

*I repeat: it is enough that a book be possible for it to exist. Only the impossible is excluded. For example: no book is also a stairway, though doubtless there are books that discuss and deny and demonstrate this possibility and others whose structure corresponds to that of a stairway.

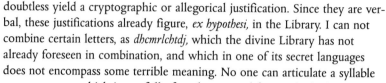

doubtless yield a cryptographic or allegorical justification. Since they are verbal, these justifications already figure, *ex hypothesi,* in the Library. I can not combine certain letters, as *dhcmrlchtdj,* which the divine Library has not already foreseen in combination, and which in one of its secret languages does not encompass some terrible meaning. No one can articulate a syllable which is not full of tenderness and fear, and which is not, in one of those languages, the powerful name of some god. To speak is to fall into tautologies. This useless and wordy epistle itself already exists in one of the thirty volumes of the five shelves in one of the uncountable hexagons—and so does its refutation. (An *n* number of possible languages makes use of the same vocabulary; in some of them, the symbol *library* admits of the correct definition *ubiquitous and everlasting system of hexagonal galleries,* but *library* is *bread* or *pyramid* or anything

**To speak is
to fall into
tautologies.**

else, and the seven words which define it possess another value. You who read me, are you sure you understand my language?)

Methodical writing distracts me from the present condition of men. But the certainty that everything has been already written nullifies or makes phantoms of us all. I know of districts where the youth prostrate themselves before books and barbarously kiss the pages, though they do not know how to make out a single letter. Epidemics, heretical disagreements, the pilgrimages which inevitably degenerate into banditry, have decimated the population. I believe I have mentioned the suicides, more frequent each year. Perhaps I am deceived by old age and fear, but I suspect that the human species—the unique human species—is on the road to extinction, while the Library will last on forever: illuminated, solitary, infinite, perfectly immovable, filled with precious volumes, useless, incorruptible, secret.

Infinite I have just written. I have not interpolated this adjective merely from rhetorical habit. It is not illogical, I say, to think that the world is infinite. Those who judge it to be limited, postulate that in remote places the corridors and stairs and hexagons could inconceivably cease—a manifest absurdity. Those who imagined it to be limitless forget that the possible number of books is limited. I dare insinuate the following solution to this ancient problem: *The Library is limitless and periodic.* If an eternal voyager were to traverse it in any direction, he would find, after many centuries, that the same volumes are repeated in the same disorder (which, repeated, would constitute an order: Order itself). My solitude rejoices in this elegant hope.*

Mar del Plata
1941

—Translated by Anthony Kerrigan

*Letizia Alvarez de Toledo has observed that the vast Library is useless. Strictly speaking, *one single volume* should suffice: a single volume of ordinary format, printed in nine or ten type body, and consisting of an infinite number of infinitely thin pages. (At the beginning of the seventeenth century, Cavalieri said that any solid body is the superposition of an infinite number of planes.) This silky vade mecum would scarcely be handy: each apparent leaf of the book would divide into other analogous leaves. The inconceivable central leaf would have no reverse.

■ QUESTIONS FOR REREADING

1. In the "Library of Babel," we read: "the Library is total and ... its shelves contain all the possible combinations of the twenty-odd orthographic symbols ... ; that is, everything which can be expressed, in all languages. Everything is there. . . ." And "When it was proclaimed that the Library comprised all books, the first impression was one of extravagant joy. All men felt themselves lords of a secret, intact treasure. There was no personal or universal problem whose eloquent solution did not exist. . . . The universe was justified, the universe suddenly expanded to the limitless dimensions of hope." And yet, what change of mind is experienced and reported by the narrator? Is there a possible allegory here between the Library and the World Wide Web? Many Internauts are as optimistic about the Web as the narrator in this story was about the Library. In respect to the Library, how promising or disappointing is the Web?

2. What is the significance of the word "Babel"? Compare Borges's library to the lost library of Alexandria. Is one less or more *real* than the other in our lives?

■ WRITING ASSIGNMENT FOR REREADING

In the previous writing assignment, you were asked to find as many parallels as possible between Nelson's summary of his project (how it will be implemented) and the World Wide Web (how it is variously implemented). Building on that assignment, find as many parallels as you can between Nelson's summary and the narrator's description of the Library in "The Library of Babel" and compare them to the www. Write about your findings.

John Perry Barlow's "The Economy of Ideas: A Framework for Rethinking Patents and Copyrights in the Digital Age" first appeared in Wired 2.03 (March 1994): 85–90, 126–29. Barlow's thinking is very practical. He gives a quasi-history of copyright and talks about the "mental-to-physical conversion" (the word becoming flesh) as being central to patents and copyrights. However, with the physical returning to the mental, or the actual becoming virtual, Barlow argues, the conditions for copyright law have changed: "the rights of invention and authorship adhered to activities in the physical world. One didn't get paid for ideas, but for the ability to deliver them into reality." Barlow asks therefore: "What is to be done? While there is a certain grim fun to be had in it, dancing on the grave of copyright and patent will solve little." What Barlow accomplishes in his article is a new place from which to think about copyright in the light of talk about copyleft and the hacker's ethic.

John Perry Barlow

The Economy of Ideas: A Framework for Rethinking Patents and Copyrights in the Digital Age

If nature has made any one thing less susceptible than all others of exclusive property, it is the action of the thinking power called an idea, which an individual may exclusively possess as long as he keeps it to himself; but the moment it is divulged, it forces itself into the possession of everyone, and the receiver cannot dispossess himself of it. Its peculiar character, too, is that no one possesses the less, because every other possesses the whole of it. He who receives an idea from me, receives instruction himself without lessening mine; as he who lights his taper at mine, receives light without darkening me. That ideas should freely spread from one to another over the globe, for the moral and mutual instruction of man, and improvement of his condition, seems to have been peculiarly and benevolently designed by nature, when she made them, like fire, expansible over all space, without lessening their density at any point, and like the air in which we breathe, move, and have our physical being, incapable of confinement or exclusive appropriation. Inventions then cannot, in nature, be a subject of property.

—Thomas Jefferson

Throughout the time I've been groping around cyberspace, an immense, unsolved conundrum has remained at the root of nearly every legal, ethical, governmental, and social vexation to be found in the Virtual World. I refer to the problem of digitized property. The enigma is this: If our property can be infinitely reproduced and instantaneously distributed all over the planet without cost, without our knowledge, without its even leaving our possession, how can we protect it? How are we going to get paid for the work we do with our minds? And, if we can't get paid, what will assure the continued creation and distribution of such work?

Since we don't have a solution to what is a profoundly new kind of challenge, and are apparently unable to delay the galloping digitization of everything not obstinately physical, we are sailing into the future on a sinking ship.

This vessel, the accumulated canon of copyright and patent law, was developed to convey forms and methods of expression entirely different from the vaporous cargo it is now being asked to carry. It is leaking as much from within as from without.

Legal efforts to keep the old boat floating are taking three forms: a frenzy of deck chair rearrangement, stern warnings to the passengers that if she goes down, they will face harsh criminal penalties, and serene, glassy-eyed denial.

Intellectual property law cannot be patched, retrofitted, or expanded to contain digitized expression any more than real estate law might be revised to cover the allocation of broadcasting spectrum (which, in fact, rather resembles what is being attempted here). We will need to develop an entirely new set of methods as befits this entirely new set of circumstances.

Most of the people who actually create soft property—the programmers, hackers, and Net surfers—already know this. Unfortunately, neither the companies they work for nor the lawyers these companies hire have enough direct experience with nonmaterial goods to understand why they are so problematic. They are proceeding as though the old laws can somehow be made to work, either by grotesque expansion or by force. They are wrong.

The source of this conundrum is as simple as its solution is complex. Digital technology is detaching information from the physical plane, where property law of all sorts has always found definition.

Throughout the history of copyrights and patents, the proprietary assertions of thinkers have been focused not on their ideas but on the expression of those ideas. The ideas themselves, as well as facts about the phenomena of the world, were considered to be the collective property of humanity. One could claim franchise, in the case of copyright, on the precise turn of phrase used to convey a particular idea or the order in which facts were presented.

The point at which this franchise was imposed was that moment when the "word became flesh" by departing the mind of its originator and entering some physical object, whether book or widget. The subsequent arrival of other commercial media besides books didn't alter the legal importance of this moment. Law protected expression and, with few (and recent) exceptions, to express was to make physical.

Protecting physical expression had the force of convenience on its side. Copyright worked well because, Gutenberg notwithstanding, it was hard to make a book. Furthermore, books froze their contents into a condition which was as challenging to alter as it was to reproduce. Counterfeiting and distributing counterfeit volumes were obvious and visible activities—it was easy enough to catch somebody in the act of doing. Finally, unlike unbounded words or images, books had material surfaces to which one could attach copyright notices, publisher's marques, and price tags.

Mental-to-physical conversion was even more central to patent. A patent, until recently, was either a description of the form into which materials were to be rendered in the service of some purpose, or a description of the process by which rendition occurred. In either case, the conceptual heart of patent was the material result. If no purposeful object could be rendered because of some material limitation, the patent was rejected. Neither a Klein bottle nor a shovel made of silk could be patented. It had to be a thing, and the thing had to work.

The rights of invention and authorship adhered to activities in the physical world. One didn't get paid for ideas, but for the ability to deliver them into reality. For all practical purposes, the value was in the conveyance and not in the thought conveyed.

Thus, the rights of invention and authorship adhered to activities in the physical world. One didn't get paid for ideas, but for the ability to deliver them into reality. For all practical purposes, the value was in the conveyance and not in the thought conveyed.

In other words, the bottle was protected, not the wine.

Now, as information enters cyberspace, the native home of Mind, these bottles are vanishing. With the advent of digitization, it is now possible to replace all previous information storage forms with one metabottle: complex and highly liquid patterns of ones and zeros.

Even the physical/digital bottles to which we've become accustomed—floppy disks, CD-ROMs, and other discrete, shrink-wrappable bit-packages—will disappear as all computers jack-in to the global Net. While the Internet may never include every CPU on the planet, it is more than doubling every year and can be expected to become the principal medium of information conveyance, and perhaps eventually, the only one.

Once that has happened, all the goods of the Information Age—all of the expressions once contained in books or film strips or newsletters—will exist either as pure thought or something very much like thought: voltage conditions darting around the Net at the speed of light, in conditions that one might behold in effect, as glowing pixels or transmitted sounds, but never touch or claim to "own" in the old sense of the word.

Some might argue that information will still require some physical manifestation, such as its magnetic existence on the titanic hard disks of distant servers, but these are bottles which have no macroscopically discrete or personally meaningful form.

Some will also argue that we have been dealing with unbottled expression since the advent of radio, and they would be right. But for most of the history of broadcast, there was no convenient way to capture soft goods from the electromagnetic ether and reproduce them with quality available in commercial packages. Only recently has this changed, and little has been done legally or technically to address the change.

Generally, the issue of consumer payment for broadcast products was irrelevant. The consumers themselves were the product. Broadcast media were supported either by the sale of the attention of their audience to advertisers, by government assessing payment through taxes, or by the whining mendicancy of annual donor drives.

All of the broadcast-support models are flawed. Support either by advertisers or government has almost invariably tainted the purity of the goods delivered. Besides, direct marketing is gradually killing the advertiser-support model anyway.

Broadcast media gave us another payment method for a virtual product: the royalties that broadcasters pay songwriters through such organizations as ASCAP and BMI. But, as a member of ASCAP, I can assure you this is not a model that we should emulate. The monitoring methods are wildly approximate. There is no parallel system of accounting in the revenue stream. It doesn't really work. Honest.

In any case, without our old methods, based on physically defining the expression of ideas, and in the absence of successful new models for nonphysical transaction, we simply don't know how to assure reliable payment for mental works. To make matters worse, this comes at a time when the human mind is replacing sunlight and mineral deposits as the principal source of new wealth.

Furthermore, the increasing difficulty of enforcing existing copyright and patent laws is already placing in peril the ultimate source of intellectual property—the free exchange of ideas.

That is, when the primary articles of commerce in a society look so much like speech as to be indistinguishable from it, and when the traditional methods of protecting their ownership have become ineffectual, attempting to fix the problem with broader and more vigorous enforcement will inevitably threaten freedom of speech. The greatest constraint on your future liberties may come not from government but from corporate legal departments laboring to protect by force what can no longer be protected by practical efficiency or general social consent.

Furthermore, when Jefferson and his fellow creatures of the Enlightenment designed the system that became American copyright law, their primary objective was assuring the widespread distribution of thought, not profit. Profit was the fuel that would carry ideas into the libraries and minds of their new republic. Libraries would purchase books, thus rewarding the authors for their work in assembling ideas; these ideas, otherwise "incapable of confinement," would then become freely available to the public. But what is the role of libraries in the absence of books? How does society now pay for the distribution of ideas if not by charging for the ideas themselves?

Additionally complicating the matter is the fact that along with the disappearance of the physical bottles in which intellectual property protection has resided, digital technology is also erasing the legal jurisdictions of the physical world and replacing them with the unbounded and perhaps permanently lawless waves of cyberspace.

In cyberspace, no national or local boundaries contain the scene of a crime and determine the method of its prosecution; worse, no clear cultural agreements define what a crime might be. Unresolved and basic differences between Western and Asian cultural assumptions about intellectual property can only be exacerbated when many transactions are taking place in both hemispheres and yet, somehow, in neither.

Even in the most local of digital conditions, jurisdiction and responsibility are hard to assess. A group of music publishers filed suit against CompuServe this fall because it allowed its users to upload musical compositions into areas where other users might access them. But since CompuServe cannot practically exercise much control over the flood of bits that passes between its subscribers, it probably shouldn't be held responsible for unlawfully "publishing" these works.

Notions of property, value, ownership, and the nature of wealth itself are changing more fundamentally than at any time since the Sumerians first poked cuneiform into wet clay and called it stored grain. Only a very few people are aware of the enormity of this shift, and fewer of them are lawyers or public officials.

Those who do see these changes must prepare responses for the legal and social confusion that will erupt as efforts to protect new forms of property with old methods become more obviously futile, and, as a consequence, more adamant.

■ FROM SWORDS TO WRITS TO BITS

Humanity now seems bent on creating a world economy primarily based on goods that take no material form. In doing so, we may be eliminating any predictable connection between creators and a fair reward for the utility or pleasure others may find in their works.

Without that connection, and without a fundamental change in consciousness to accommodate its loss, we are building our future on furor, litigation, and institutionalized evasion of payment except in response to raw force. We may return to the Bad Old Days of property.

Throughout the darker parts of human history, the possession and distribution of property was a largely military matter. "Ownership" was assured those with the nastiest tools, whether fists or armies, and the most resolute will to use them. Property was the divine right of thugs.

By the turn of the First Millennium AD, the emergence of merchant classes and landed gentry forced the development of ethical understandings for the resolution of property disputes. In the Middle Ages, enlightened rulers like England's Henry II began to codify this unwritten "common law" into recorded canons. These laws were local, which didn't matter much as they were primarily directed at real estate, a form of property that is local by definition. And, as the name implied, was very real.

This continued to be the case as long as the origin of wealth was agricultural, but with the dawning of the Industrial Revolution, humanity began to focus as much on means as ends. Tools acquired a new social value and, thanks to their development, it became possible to duplicate and distribute them in quantity.

To encourage their invention, copyright and patent law were developed in most Western countries. These laws were devoted to the delicate task of getting mental creations into the world where they could be used—and could enter the minds of others—while assuring their inventors compensation for the value of their use. And, as previously stated, the systems of both law and practice which grew up around that task were based on physical expression.

Since it is now possible to convey ideas from one mind to another without ever making them physical, we are now claiming to own ideas themselves and not merely their expression. And since it is likewise now possible to create useful tools that never take physical form, we have taken to patenting abstractions, sequences of virtual events, and mathematical formulae—the most unreal estate imaginable.

Since it is now possible to convey ideas from one mind to another without ever making them physical, we are now claiming to own ideas themselves and not merely their expression.

In certain areas, this leaves rights of ownership in such an ambiguous condition that property again adheres to those who can muster the largest armies. The only difference is that this time the armies consist of lawyers.

Threatening their opponents with the endless purgatory of litigation, over which some might prefer death itself, they assert claim to any thought which might have entered another cranium within the collective body of the corporations they serve. They act as though these ideas appeared in splendid detachment from all previous human thought. And they pretend that thinking about a product is somehow as good as manufacturing, distributing, and selling it.

What was previously considered a common human resource, distributed among the minds and libraries of the world, as well as the phenomena of nature herself, is now being fenced and deeded. It is as though a new class of enterprise had arisen that claimed to own the air.

What is to be done? While there is a certain grim fun to be had in it, dancing on the grave of copyright and patent will solve little, especially when so few are willing to admit that the occupant of this grave is even deceased, and so many are trying to uphold by force what can no longer be upheld by popular consent.

The legalists, desperate over their slipping grip, are vigorously trying to extend their reach. Indeed, the United States and other proponents of GATT are making adherence to our moribund systems of intellectual property protection a condition of membership in the marketplace of nations. For example, China will be denied Most Favored Nation trading status unless they agree to uphold a set of culturally alien principles that are no longer even sensibly applicable in their country of origin.

In a more perfect world, we'd be wise to declare a moratorium on litigation, legislation, and international treaties in this area until we had a clearer sense of the terms and conditions of enterprise in cyberspace. Ideally, laws ratify already developed social consensus. They are less the Social Contract itself than a series of memoranda expressing a collective intent that has emerged out of many millions of human interactions.

Humans have not inhabited cyberspace long enough or in sufficient diversity to have developed a Social Contract which conforms to the strange new conditions of that world. Laws developed prior to consensus usually favor the already established few who can get them passed and not society as a whole.

To the extent that law and established social practice exist in this area, they are already in dangerous disagreement. The laws regarding unlicensed reproduction of commercial software are clear and stern . . . and rarely observed. Software piracy laws are so practically unenforceable and breaking them has become so socially acceptable that only a thin minority appears compelled, either by fear or conscience, to obey them. When I give speeches on this subject, I always ask how many people in the audience can honestly claim to have no unauthorized software on their hard disks. I've never seen more than 10 percent of the hands go up.

Whenever there is such profound divergence between law and social practice, it is not society that adapts. Against the swift tide of custom, the software publishers' current practice of hanging a few visible scapegoats is so obviously capricious as to only further diminish respect for the law.

Part of the widespread disregard for commercial software copyrights stems from a legislative failure to understand the conditions into which it was inserted. To assume that systems of law based in the physical world will serve in an environment as fundamentally different as cyberspace is a folly for which everyone doing business in the future will pay.

As I will soon discuss in detail, unbounded intellectual property is very different from physical property and can no longer be protected as though these differences did not exist. For example, if we continue to assume that value is based on scarcity, as it is with regard to physical objects, we will create laws that are precisely contrary to the nature of information, which may, in many cases, increase in value with distribution.

The large, legally risk-averse institutions most likely to play by the old rules will suffer for their compliance. As more lawyers, guns, and money are invested in either protecting their rights or subverting those of their opponents, their ability to produce new technology will simply grind to a halt as every move they make drives them deeper into a tar pit of courtroom warfare.

Faith in law will not be an effective strategy for high-tech companies. Law adapts by continuous increments and at a pace second only to geology. Technology advances in lunging jerks, like the punctuation of biological evolution grotesquely accelerated. Real-world conditions will continue to change at a blinding pace, and the law will lag further behind, more profoundly confused. This mismatch may prove impossible to overcome.

Promising economies based on purely digital products will either be born in a state of paralysis, as appears to be the case with multimedia, or continue in a brave and willful refusal by their owners to play the ownership game at all.

In the United States one can already see a parallel economy developing, mostly among small, fast-moving enterprises who protect their ideas by getting into the marketplace quicker than their larger competitors who base their protection on fear and litigation.

Perhaps those who are part of the problem will simply quarantine themselves in court, while those who are part of the solution will create a new society based, at first, on piracy and freebooting. It may well be that when the current system of intellectual property law has collapsed, as seems inevitable, that no new legal structure will arise in its place.

But something will happen. After all, people do business. When a currency becomes meaningless, business is done in barter. When societies develop outside the law, they develop their own unwritten codes, practices, and ethical systems. While technology may undo law, technology offers methods for restoring creative rights.

■ A TAXONOMY OF INFORMATION

It seems to me that the most productive thing to do now is to look into the true nature of what we're trying to protect. How much do we really know about information and its natural behaviors?

What are the essential characteristics of unbounded creation? How does it differ from previous forms of property? How many of our assumptions about it have actually been about its containers rather than their mysterious contents? What are its different species and how does each of them lend itself to control? What technologies will be useful in creating new virtual bottles to replace the old physical ones?

Of course, information is, by nature, intangible and hard to define. Like other such deep phenomena as light or matter, it is a natural host to paradox. It is most helpful to understand light as being both a particle and a wave. An understanding of information may emerge in the abstract congruence of its several different properties, which might be described by the following three statements:

Information is an activity.

Information is a life form.

Information is a relationship.

In the following section, I will examine each of these.

■ I. INFORMATION IS AN ACTIVITY

Information Is a Verb, Not a Noun.

Freed of its containers, information is obviously not a thing. In fact, it is something that happens in the field of interaction between minds or objects or other pieces of information.

Gregory Bateson, expanding on the information theory of Claude Shannon, said, "Information is a difference which makes a difference." Thus, information only really exists in the Delta. The making of that difference is an activity within a relationship. Information is an action which occupies time rather than a state of being which occupies physical space, as is the case with hard goods. It is the pitch, not the baseball, the dance, not the dancer.

Information Is Experienced, Not Possessed.

Even when it has been encapsulated in some static form like a book or a hard disk, information is still something that happens to you as you mentally decompress it from its storage code. But, whether it's running at gigabits per second or words per minute, the actual decoding is a process that must be performed by and upon a mind, a process that must take place in time.

There was a cartoon in the *Bulletin of Atomic Scientists* a few years ago that illustrated this point beautifully. In the drawing, a holdup man trains his gun on the sort of bespectacled fellow you'd figure might have a lot of information stored in his head. "Quick," orders the bandit, "give me all your ideas."

Information Has to Move.

Sharks are said to die of suffocation if they stop swimming, and the same is nearly true of information. Information that isn't moving ceases to exist as anything but potential . . . at least until it is allowed to move again. For this reason, the practice of information hoarding, common in bureaucracies, is an especially wrong-headed artifact of physically based value systems.

Information Is Conveyed by Propagation, Not Distribution.

The way in which information spreads is also very different from the distribution of physical goods. It moves more like something from nature than from a factory. It can concatenate like falling dominos or grow in the usual fractal lattice, like frost spreading on a window, but it cannot be shipped around like widgets, except to the extent that it can be contained in them. It doesn't simply move on; it leaves a trail everywhere it's been.

The central economic distinction between information and physical property is that information can be transferred without leaving the possession of the original owner. If I sell you my horse, I can't ride him after that. If I sell you what I know, we both know it.

■ II. INFORMATION IS A LIFE FORM

Information Wants to Be Free.

Stewart Brand is generally credited with this elegant statement of the obvious, which recognizes both the natural desire of secrets to be told and the fact that they might be capable of possessing something like a "desire" in the first place.

English biologist and philosopher Richard Dawkins proposed the idea of "memes," self-replicating patterns of information that propagate themselves across the ecologies of mind, a pattern of reproduction much like that of life forms.

I believe they are life forms in every respect but their freedom from the carbon atom. They self-reproduce, they interact with their surroundings and adapt to them, they mutate, they persist. They evolve to fill the empty niches of their local environments, which are in this case the surrounding belief systems and cultures of their hosts, namely, us.

Indeed, sociobiologists like Dawkins make a plausible case that carbon-based life forms are information as well, that, as the chicken is an egg's way of making another egg, the entire biological spectacle is just the DNA molecule's means of copying out more information strings exactly like itself.

Information Replicates into the Cracks of Possibility.

Like DNA helices, ideas are relentless expansionists, always seeking new opportunities for Lebensraum. And, as in carbon-based nature, the more robust organisms are extremely adept at finding new places to live. Thus, just as the common housefly has insinuated itself into practically every ecosystem on the planet, so has the meme of "life after death" found a niche in most minds, or psycho-ecologies.

The more universally resonant an idea or image or song, the more minds it will enter and remain within. Trying to stop the spread of a really robust piece of information is about as easy as keeping killer bees south of the border.

Information Wants to Change.

If ideas and other interactive patterns of information are indeed life forms, they can be expected to evolve constantly into forms which will be more perfectly adapted to their surroundings. And, as we see, they are doing this all the time.

But for a long time, our static media, whether carvings in stone, ink on paper, or dye on celluloid, have strongly resisted the evolutionary impulse, exalting as a consequence the author's ability to determine the finished product. But, as in an oral tradition, digitized information has no "final cut."

Digital information, unconstrained by packaging, is a continuing process more like the metamorphosing tales of prehistory than anything that will fit in shrink-wrap. From the Neolithic to Gutenberg (monks aside), information was passed on, mouth to ear, changing with every retelling (or resinging). The stories which once shaped our sense of the world didn't have authoritative versions. They adapted to each culture in which they found themselves being told.

Because there was never a moment when the story was frozen in print, the so-called "moral" right of storytellers to own the tale was neither protected nor recognized. The story simply passed through each of them on its way to the next, where it would assume a different form. As we return to continuous information, we can expect the importance of authorship to diminish. Creative people may have to renew their acquaintance with humility.

> *Digital information, unconstrained by packaging, is a continuing process. As we return to continuous information, we can expect the importance of authorship to diminish. Creative people may have to renew their acquaintance with humility.*

But our system of copyright makes no accommodation whatever for expressions which don't become fixed at some point nor for cultural expressions which lack a specific author or inventor.

Jazz improvisations, stand-up comedy routines, mime performances, developing monologues, and unrecorded broadcast transmissions all lack the Constitutional requirement of fixation as a "writing." Without being fixed by a point of publication the liquid works of the future will all look more like these continuously adapting and changing forms and will therefore exist beyond the reach of copyright.

Copyright expert Pamela Samuelson tells of having attended a conference last year convened around the fact that Western countries may legally appropriate the music, designs, and biomedical lore of aboriginal people without compensation to their tribes of origin since those tribes are not an "author" or "inventor."

But soon most information will be generated collaboratively by the cyber-tribal hunter-gatherers of cyberspace. Our arrogant legal dismissal of the rights of "primitives" will soon return to haunt us.

Information Is Perishable.

With the exception of the rare classic, most information is like farm produce. Its quality degrades rapidly both over time and in distance from the source of production. But even here, value is highly subjective and conditional. Yesterday's papers are quite valuable to the historian. In fact, the older they are, the more valuable they become. On the other hand, a commodities broker might consider news of an event that occurred more than an hour ago to have lost any relevance.

■ III. INFORMATION IS A RELATIONSHIP

Meaning Has Value and Is Unique to Each Case.

In most cases, we assign value to information based on its meaningfulness. The place where information dwells, the holy moment where transmission becomes reception, is a region which has many shifting characteristics and flavors depending on the relationship of sender and receiver, the depth of their interactivity.

Each such relationship is unique. Even in cases where the sender is a broadcast medium, and no response is returned, the receiver is hardly passive. Receiving information is often as creative an act as generating it.

The value of what is sent depends entirely on the extent to which each individual receiver has the receptors—shared terminology, attention, interest, language, paradigm—necessary to render what is received meaningful.

Understanding is a critical element increasingly overlooked in the effort to turn information into a commodity. Data may be any set of facts, useful or not, intelligible or inscrutable, germane or irrelevant. Computers can crank out new data all night long without human help, and the results may be offered for sale as information. They may or may not actually be so. Only a human being can recognize the meaning that separates information from data.

In fact, information, in the economic sense of the word, consists of data which have been passed through a particular human mind and found meaning-ful within that mental context. One fella's information is all just data to someone else. If you're an anthropologist, my detailed charts of Tasaday kinship patterns might be critical information to you. If you're a banker from Hong Kong, they might barely seem to be data.

Familiarity Has More Value Than Scarcity.

With physical goods, there is a direct correlation between scarcity and value. Gold is more valuable than wheat, even though you can't eat it. While this is not always the case, the situation with information is often precisely the reverse. Most soft goods increase in value as they become more common. Familiarity is an important asset in the world of information. It may often be true that the best way to raise demand for your product is to give it away.

While this has not always worked with shareware, it could be argued that there is a connection between the extent to which commercial software is pirated and the amount which gets sold. Broadly pirated software, such as Lotus 1-2-3 or WordPerfect, becomes a standard and benefits from Law of Increasing Returns based on familiarity.

In regard to my own soft product, rock 'n' roll songs, there is no question that the band I write them for, the Grateful Dead, has increased its popularity enormously by giving them away. We have been letting people tape our concerts since the early seventies, but instead of reducing the demand for our product, we are now the largest concert draw in America, a fact that is at least in part attributable to the popularity generated by those tapes.

True, I don't get any royalties on the millions of copies of my songs which have been extracted from concerts, but I see no reason to complain. The fact is, no one but the Grateful Dead can perform a Grateful Dead song, so if you want the experience and not its thin projection, you have to buy a ticket from us. In other words, our intellectual property protection derives from our being the only real-time source of it.

Exclusivity Has Value.

The problem with a model that turns the physical scarcity/value ratio on its head is that sometimes the value of information is very much based on its scarcity. Exclusive possession of certain facts makes them more useful. If everyone knows about conditions which might drive a stock price up, the information is valueless.

But again, the critical factor is usually time. It doesn't matter if this kind of information eventually becomes ubiquitous. What matters is being among the first who possess it and act on it. While potent secrets usually don't stay secret, they may remain so long enough to advance the cause of their original holders.

Point of View and Authority Have Value.

In a world of floating realities and contradictory maps, rewards will accrue to those commentators whose maps seem to fit their territory snugly, based on their ability to yield predictable results for those who use them.

**Reality is
an edit.**

In aesthetic information, whether poetry or rock 'n' roll, people are willing to buy the new product of an artist, sight-unseen, based on their having been delivered a pleasurable experience by previous work.

Reality is an edit. People are willing to pay for the authority of those editors whose point of view seems to fit best. And again, point of view is an asset which cannot be stolen or duplicated. No one sees the world as Esther Dyson does, and the handsome fee she charges for her newsletter is actually payment for the privilege of looking at the world through her unique eyes.

Time Replaces Space.

In the physical world, value depends heavily on possession or proximity in space. One owns the material that falls inside certain dimensional boundaries. The ability to act directly, exclusively, and as one wishes upon what falls inside those boundaries is the principal right of ownership. The relationship between value and scarcity is a limitation in space.

In the virtual world, proximity in time is a value determinant. An informational product is generally more valuable the closer purchasers can place themselves to the moment of its expression, a limitation in time. Many kinds of information degrade rapidly with either time or reproduction. Relevance fades as the territory they map changes. Noise is introduced and bandwidth lost with passage away from the point where the information is first produced.

Thus, listening to a Grateful Dead tape is hardly the same experience as attending a Grateful Dead concert. The closer one can get to the headwaters of an informational stream, the better one's chances of finding an accurate picture of reality in it. In an era of easy reproduction, the informational abstractions of popular experiences will propagate out from their source moments to reach anyone who's interested. But it's easy enough to restrict the real experience of the desirable event, whether knock-out punch or guitar lick, to those willing to pay for being there.

The Protection of Execution

In the hick town I come from, they don't give you much credit for just having ideas. You are judged by what you can make of them. As things continue to speed up, I think we see that execution is the best protection for those designs which become physical products. Or, as Steve Jobs once put it, "Real artists ship." The big winner is usually the one who gets to the market first (and with enough organizational force to keep the lead).

In the hick town I come from, they don't give you much credit for just having ideas. You are judged by what you can make of them.

But, as we become fixated upon information commerce, many of us seem to think that originality alone is sufficient to convey value, deserving, with the right legal assurances, of a steady wage. In fact, the best way to protect intellectual property is to act on it. It's not enough to invent and patent; one has to innovate as well. Someone claims to have patented the microprocessor before Intel. Maybe so. If he'd actually started shipping microprocessors before Intel, his claim would seem far less spurious.

Information as Its Own Reward

It is now a commonplace to say that money is information. With the exception of Krugerrands, crumpled cab fare, and the contents of those suitcases that drug lords are reputed to carry, most of the money in the informatized world is in ones and zeros. The global money supply sloshes around the Net, as fluid as weather. It is also obvious that information has become as fundamental to the creation of modern wealth as land and sunlight once were.

What is less obvious is the extent to which information is acquiring intrinsic value, not as a means to acquisition but as the object to be acquired. I suppose this has always been less explicitly the case. In politics and academia, potency and information have always been closely related.

However, as we increasingly buy information with money, we begin to see that buying information with other information is simple economic exchange without the necessity of converting the product into and out of currency. This is somewhat challenging for those who like clean accounting, since, information theory aside, informational exchange rates are too squishy to quantify to the decimal point.

Nevertheless, most of what a middle-class American purchases has little to do with survival. We buy beauty, prestige, experience, education, and all the obscure pleasures of owning. Many of these things can not only be expressed in nonmaterial terms, they can be acquired by nonmaterial means.

And then there are the inexplicable pleasures of information itself, the joys of learning, knowing, and teaching; the strange good feeling of information coming into and out of oneself. Playing with ideas is a recreation which people are willing to pay a lot for, given the market for books and elective seminars. We'd likely spend even more money for such pleasures if we didn't have so many opportunities to pay for ideas with other ideas. This explains much of the collective "volunteer" work which fills the archives, newsgroups, and databases of the Internet. Its denizens are not working for "nothing," as is widely believed. Rather they are getting paid in something besides money. It is an economy which consists almost entirely of information.

This may become the dominant form of human trade, and if we persist in modeling economics on a strictly monetary basis, we may be gravely misled.

Getting Paid in Cyberspace

How all the foregoing relates to solutions to the crisis in intellectual property is something I've barely started to wrap my mind around. It's fairly paradigm warping to look at information through fresh eyes—to see how very little it is like pig iron or pork bellies, and to imagine the tottering travesties of case law we will stack up if we go on legally treating it as though it were.

Until the West was fully settled and "civilized" in this century, order was established according to an unwritten Code of the West, which had the fluidity of common law rather than the rigidity of statutes.

As I've said, I believe these towers of outmoded boilerplate will be a smoking heap sometime in the next decade, and we mind miners will have no choice but to cast our lot with new systems that work.

I'm not really so gloomy about our prospects as readers of this jeremiad so far might conclude. Solutions will emerge. Nature abhors a vacuum and so does commerce.

Indeed, one of the aspects of the electronic frontier which I have always found most appealing—and the reason Mitch Kapor and I used that phrase in naming our foundation—is the degree to which it resembles the 19th-century American West in its natural preference for social devices that emerge from its conditions rather than those that are imposed from the outside.

Until the West was fully settled and "civilized" in this century, order was established according to an unwritten Code of the West, which had the fluidity of common law rather than the rigidity of statutes. Ethics were more important than rules.

Understandings were preferred over laws, which were, in any event, largely unenforceable.

I believe that law, as we understand it, was developed to protect the interests which arose in the two economic "waves" which Alvin Toffler accurately identified in *The Third Wave*. The First Wave was agriculturally based and required law to order ownership of the principal source of production, land. In the Second Wave, manufacturing became the economic mainspring, and the structure of modern law grew around the centralized institutions that needed protection for their reserves of capital, labor, and hardware.

Both of these economic systems required stability. Their laws were designed to resist change and to assure some equability of distribution within a fairly static social framework. The empty niches had to be constrained to preserve the predictability necessary to either land stewardship or capital formation.

In the Third Wave we have now entered, information to a large extent replaces land, capital, and hardware, and information is most at home in a much more fluid and adaptable environment. The Third Wave is likely to bring a fundamental shift in the purposes and methods of law which will affect far more than simply those statutes which govern intellectual property.

The "terrain" itself—the architecture of the Net—may come to serve many of the purposes which could only be maintained in the past by legal imposition. For example, it may be unnecessary to constitutionally assure freedom of expression in an environment which, in the words of my fellow EFF co-founder John Gilmore, "treats censorship as a malfunction" and reroutes proscribed ideas around it.

Similar natural balancing mechanisms may arise to smooth over the social discontinuities which previously required legal intercession to set right. On the Net, these differences are more likely to be spanned by a continuous spectrum that connects as much as it separates.

And, despite their fierce grip on the old legal structure, companies that trade in information are likely to find that their increasing inability to deal sensibly with technological issues will not be remedied in the courts, which won't be capable of producing verdicts predictable enough to be supportive of long-term enterprise. Every litigation will become like a game of Russian roulette, depending on the depth of the presiding judge's clue-impairment.

Uncodified or adaptive "law," while as "fast, loose, and out of control" as other emergent forms, is probably more likely to yield something like justice at this point. In fact, one can already see in development new practices to suit the conditions of virtual commerce. The life forms of information are evolving methods to protect their continued reproduction.

For example, while all the tiny print on a commercial diskette envelope punctiliously requires a great deal of those who would open it, few who read those provisos follow them to the letter. And yet, the software business remains a very healthy sector of the American economy.

Why is this? Because people seem to eventually buy the software they really use. Once a program becomes central to your work, you want the latest version of it, the best support, the actual manuals, all privileges attached to ownership. Such practical considerations will, in the absence of working law, become more and more important in getting paid for what might easily be obtained for nothing.

I do think that some software is being purchased in the service of ethics or the abstract awareness that the failure to buy it will result in its not being produced any longer, but I'm going to leave those motivators aside. While I believe that the failure of law will almost certainly result in a compensating re-emergence of ethics as the ordering template of society, this is a belief I don't have room to support here.

Instead, I think that, as in the case cited above, compensation for soft products will be driven primarily by practical considerations, all of them consistent with the true properties of digital information, where the value lies in it, and how it can be both manipulated and protected by technology.

While the conundrum remains a conundrum, I can begin to see the directions from which solutions may emerge, based in part on broadening those practical solutions which are already in practice.

Relationship and Its Tools

I believe one idea is central to understanding liquid commerce: Information economics, in the absence of objects, will be based more on relationship than possession.

One existing model for the future conveyance of intellectual property is real-time performance, a medium currently used only in theater, music, lectures, stand-up comedy, and pedagogy. I believe the concept of performance will expand to include most of the information economy, from multicasted soap operas to stock analysis. In these instances, commercial exchange will be more like ticket sales to a continuous show than the purchase of discrete bundles of that which is being shown.

The other existing model, of course, is service. The entire professional class—doctors, lawyers, consultants, architects, and so on—are already being paid directly for their intellectual property. Who needs copyright when you're on a retainer?

In fact, until the late 18th century this model was applied to much of what is now copyrighted. Before the industrialization of creation, writers, composers, artists, and the like produced their products in the private service of patrons. Without objects to distribute in a mass market, creative people will return to a condition somewhat like this, except that they will serve many patrons, rather than one.

We can already see the emergence of companies which base their existence on supporting and enhancing the soft property they create rather than selling it by the shrink-wrapped piece or embedding it in widgets.

Trip Hawkins's new company for creating and licensing multimedia tools, 3DO, is an example of what I'm talking about. 3DO doesn't intend to produce any commercial software or consumer devices. Instead, it will act as a kind of private standards-setting body, mediating among software and device creators who will be their licensees. It will provide a point of commonality for relationships between a broad spectrum of entities.

In any case, whether you think of yourself as a service provider or a performer, the future protection of your intellectual property will depend on your ability to control your relationship to the market—a relationship which will most likely live and grow over a period of time.

The value of that relationship will reside in the quality of performance, the uniqueness of your point of view, the validity of your expertise, its relevance to your market, and, underlying everything, the ability of that market to access your creative services swiftly, conveniently, and interactively.

Interaction and Protection

Direct interaction will provide a lot of intellectual property protection in the future, and, indeed, already has. No one knows how many software pirates have bought legitimate copies of a program after calling its publisher for technical support and offering some proof of purchase, but I would guess the number is very high.

The same kind of controls will be applicable to "question and answer" relationships between authorities (or artists) and those who seek their expertise. Newsletters, magazines, and books will be supplemented by the ability of their subscribers to ask direct questions of authors.

Interactivity will be a billable commodity even in the absence of authorship. As people move into the Net and increasingly get their information directly from its point of production, unfiltered by centralized media, they will attempt to develop the same interactive ability to probe reality that only experience has provided them in the past. Live access to these distant "eyes and ears" will be much easier to cordon than access to static bundles of stored but easily reproducible information.

In most cases, control will be based on restricting access to the freshest, highest bandwidth information. It will be a matter of defining the ticket, the venue, the performer, and the identity of the ticket holder, definitions which I believe will take their forms from technology, not law. In most cases, the defining technology will be cryptography.

Crypto Bottling

Cryptography, as I've said perhaps too many times, is the "material" from which the walls, boundaries—and bottles—of cyberspace will be fashioned.

Of course there are problems with cryptography or any other purely technical method of property protection. It has always appeared to me that the more security you hide your goods behind, the more likely you are to turn your sanctuary into a target. Having come from a place where people leave their keys in their cars and don't even have keys to their houses, I remain convinced that the best obstacle to crime is a society with its ethics intact.

While I admit that this is not the kind of society most of us live in, I also believe that a social overreliance on protection by barricades rather than conscience will eventually wither the latter by turning intrusion and theft into a sport, rather than a crime. This is already occurring in the digital domain, as is evident in the activities of computer crackers.

Cryptography, as I've said perhaps too many times, is the "material" from which the walls, boundaries—and bottles—of cyberspace will be fashioned.

Furthermore, I would argue that initial efforts to protect digital copyright by copy protection contributed to the current condition in which most otherwise ethical computer users seem morally untroubled by their possession of pirated software.

Instead of cultivating among the newly computerized a sense of respect for the work of their fellows, early reliance on copy protection led to the subliminal notion that cracking into a software package somehow "earned" one the right to use it. Limited not by conscience but by technical skill, many soon felt free to do whatever they could get away with. This will continue to be a potential liability of the encryption of digitized commerce.

Furthermore, it's cautionary to remember that copy protection was rejected by the market in most areas. Many of the upcoming efforts to use cryptography-based protection schemes will probably suffer the same fate. People are not going to tolerate much that makes computers harder to use than they already are without any benefit to the user.

Nevertheless, encryption has already demonstrated a certain blunt utility. New subscriptions to various commercial satellite TV services skyrocketed recently after their deployment of more robust encryption of their feeds. This, despite a booming backwoods trade in black decoder chips, conducted by folks who'd look more at home running moonshine than cracking code.

Another obvious problem with encryption as a global solution is that once something has been unscrambled by a legitimate licensee, it may be available to massive reproduction.

In some instances, reproduction following decryption may not be a problem. Many soft products degrade sharply in value with time. It may be that the only real interest in such products will be among those who have purchased the keys to immediacy.

Furthermore, as software becomes more modular and distribution moves online, it will begin to metamorphose in direct interaction with its user base. Discontinuous upgrades will smooth into a constant process of incremental improvement and adaptation, some of it manmade and some of it arising through genetic algorithms. Pirated copies of software may become too static to have much value to anyone.

Even in cases such as images, where the information is expected to remain fixed, the unencrypted file could still be interwoven with code which could continue to protect it by a wide variety of means.

In most of the schemes I can project, the file would be "alive" with permanently embedded software that could "sense" the surrounding conditions and interact with them. For example, it might contain a code that could detect the process of duplication and cause it to self-destruct.

Other methods might give the file the ability to "phone home" through the Net to its original owner. The continued integrity of some files might require periodic "feeding" with digital cash from their host, which they would then relay back to their authors.

Of course, files that possess the independent ability to communicate upstream sound uncomfortably like the Morris Internet Worm. "Live" files do have a certain viral quality. And serious privacy issues would arise if everyone's computer were packed with digital spies.

The point is that cryptography will enable protection technologies that will develop rapidly in the obsessive competition that has always existed between lock-makers and lock-breakers.

But cryptography will not be used simply for making locks. It is also at the heart of both digital signatures and the aforementioned digital cash, both of which I believe will be central to the future protection of intellectual property.

I believe that the generally acknowledged failure of the shareware model in software had less to do with dishonesty than with the simple inconvenience of paying for shareware. If the payment process can be automated, as digital cash and signature will make possible, I believe that soft product creators will reap a much higher return from the bread they cast upon the waters of cyberspace.

Moreover, they will be spared much of the overhead presently attached to the marketing, manufacture, sales, and distribution of information products, whether those products are computer programs, books, CDs, or motion pictures. This will reduce prices and further increase the likelihood of noncompulsory payment.

But of course there is a fundamental problem with a system that requires, through technology, payment for every access to a particular expression. It defeats the original Jeffersonian purpose of seeing that ideas were available to everyone regardless of their economic station. I am not comfortable with a model that will restrict inquiry to the wealthy.

An Economy of Verbs

The future forms and protections of intellectual property are densely obscured at this entrance to the Virtual Age. Nevertheless, I can make (or reiterate) a few flat statements that I earnestly believe won't look too silly in 50 years.

- In the absence of the old containers, almost everything we think we know about intellectual property is wrong. We're going to have to unlearn it. We're going to have to look at information as though we'd never seen the stuff before.

- The protections that we will develop will rely far more on ethics and technology than on law.

- Encryption will be the technical basis for most intellectual property protection. (And should, for many reasons, be made more widely available.)

- The economy of the future will be based on relationship rather than possession. It will be continuous rather than sequential.

- And finally, in the years to come, most human exchange will be virtual rather than physical, consisting not of stuff but the stuff of which dreams are made. Our future business will be conducted in a world made more of verbs than nouns.

■ QUESTIONS FOR REREADING

1. What is "soft property"? Why does it pose such a difficult problem in terms of ownership—that is, the legalization of ownership?

2. What model arguments have been used to build a reasonable argument for ownership of soft property? Why does Barlow find them all lacking? (Recall that Barlow's main point is that we are attempting to argue for soft property by way of the arguments for hard property and this will simply not work, for the two are fundmentally different kinds of property, if they are property.)

3. Barlow offers a taxonomy of information. State what it is and explain each category.

4. Toward the end of his article, Barlow puts forth a few ideas that he says "won't look too silly in 50 years." What is your estimate of these ideas? What do you make of the difference in length of time that Barlow covers in giving a history of ownership of hard property ("from swords to writs to bits"), which covers hundreds of years, and a proposed set of notions for ownership of soft property ("an economy of verbs"), which covers but 50 years?

■ WRITING ASSIGNMENT FOR REREADING

Jot down your thoughts about how you feel when someone takes "your" ideas, includes them in their own class assignments, and does not give you credit. Do you have different feelings when you do an individual assignment versus a collaborative assignment? Do you find yourself holding back an especially good idea when you are doing collaborative work? If you were doing this very assignment with others, would you hold back some of your ideas? Which ones? Why do you think that you have these feelings or that you hold back information? Jot down these ideas and then arrange them as systematically as you can in the form of a report to your class. Discuss them as *freely* as you can with your class.

Utopian Plagiarism, Hypertextuality, and Electronic Cultural Production

The Critical Art Ensemble's "Utopian Plagiarism, Hypertextuality, and Electronic Cultural Production" appears in The Electronic Disturbance *(New York: Antonomedia, 1994). The Ensemble's article has an "anticopyright" notice, which means that it is in the public domain and can be freely distributed. The Critical Art Ensemble (a group of unnamed performance thinkers), unlike Barlow and many others, see the conditions of ownership and copyrightable material as having changed so radically that they would make a virtue of "utopian plagiarism."*

lagiarism has long been considered an evil in the cultural world. Typically it has been viewed as the theft of language, ideas, and images by the less than talented, often for the enhancement of personal fortune or prestige. Yet, like most mythologies, the myth of plagiarism is easily inverted. Perhaps it is those who support the legislation of representation and the privatization of language that are suspect; perhaps the plagiarist's actions, given a specific set of social conditions, are the ones contributing most to cultural enrichment. Prior to the Enlightenment, plagiarism was useful in aiding the distribution of ideas. An English poet could appropriate and translate a sonnet from Petrarch and call it his own. In accordance with the classical aesthetic of art as imitation, this was a perfectly acceptable practice. The real value of this activity rested less in the reinforcement of classical aesthetics than in the distribution of work to areas where otherwise it probably would not have appeared. The works of English plagiarists, such as Chaucer, Shakespeare, Spenser, Sterne, Coleridge, and De Quincey, are still a vital part of the English heritage, and remain in the literary canon to this day.

> *Prior to the Enlightenment, plagiarism was useful in aiding the distribution of ideas.*

At present, new conditions have emerged that once again make plagiarism an acceptable, even crucial strategy for textual production. This is the age of the recombinant: recombinant bodies, recombinant gender, recombinant texts, recombinant culture. Looking back through the privileged frame of hindsight, one can argue that the recombinant has always been key in the development of meaning and invention; recent extraordinary advances in electronic technology have called attention to the recombinant both in theory and in practice (for example, the use of morphing in video and film). The primary value of all electronic technology, especially computers and imaging systems, is the startling speed at which it can transmit information in both raw and refined forms. As information flows at a high velocity through the electronic networks, disparate and sometimes incommensurable systems of meaning intersect, with both enlightening and inventive consequences. In a society dominated by a "knowledge" explosion, exploring the possibilities of meaning in that which already exists is more pressing than adding redundant information (even if it is produced using the

At present, new conditions have emerged that once again make plagiarism an acceptable, even crucial strategy for textual production.

methodology and metaphysic of the "original"). In the past, arguments in favor of plagiarism were limited to showing its use in resisting the privatization of culture that serves the needs and desires of the power elite. Today one can argue that plagiarism is acceptable, even inevitable, given the nature of postmodern existence with its techno-infrastructure. In a recombinant culture, plagiarism is productive, although we need not abandon the romantic model of cultural production which privileges a model of *ex nihilo* creation. Certainly in a general sense the latter model is somewhat anachronistic. There are still specific situations where such thinking is useful, and one can never be sure when it could become appropriate again. What is called for is an end to its tyranny and to its institutionalized cultural bigotry. This is a call to open the cultural database, to let everyone use the technology of textual production to its maximum potential.

Ideas improve. The meaning of words participates in the improvement. Plagiarism is necessary. Progress implies it. It embraces an author's phrase, makes use of his expressions, erases a false idea, and replaces it with the right idea.[1]

Plagiarism often carries a weight of negative connotations (particularly in the bureaucratic class); while the need for its use has increased over the century, plagiarism itself has been camouflaged in a new lexicon by those desiring to explore the practice as method and as a legitimized form of cultural discourse. Readymades, collage, found art or found text, intertexts, combines, detournment, and appropriation—all these terms represent explorations in plagiarism. Indeed, these terms are not perfectly synonymous, but they all intersect a set of meanings primary to the philosophy and activity of plagiarism. Philosophically, they all stand in opposition to essentialist doctrines of the text: They all assume that no structure within a given text provides a universal and necessary meaning. No work of art or philosophy exhausts itself in itself alone, in its being-in-itself. Such works have always stood in relation to the actual life-process of society from which they have distinguished themselves. Enlightenment essentialism failed to provide a unit of analysis that could act as a basis of meaning. Just as the connection between a signifier and its referent is arbitrary, the unit of meaning used for any given textual analysis is also arbitrary. Roland Barthes's notion of the lexia primarily indicates surrender in the search for a basic unit of meaning. Since language was the only tool available for the development of metalanguage, such a project was doomed from its inception. It was much like trying to eat soup with soup. The text itself is fluid—although the language game of ideology can provide the illusion of stability, creating blockage by manipulating the unacknowledged assumptions of everyday life. Consequently, one of the main goals of the plagiarist is to restore the dynamic and unstable drift of meaning, by appropriating and recombining fragments of culture. In this way, meanings can be produced that were not previously associated with an object or a given set of objects.

Marcel Duchamp, one of the first to understand the power of recombination, presented an early incarnation of this new aesthetic with his readymade series. Duchamp took objects to which he was "visually indifferent," and recontextualized them in a manner that shifted their meaning. For example, by taking a urinal out of the rest room, signing it, and placing it on a pedestal in an art gallery, meaning slid away from the apparently exhaustive functional interpretation of the object. Although this meaning did not completely disappear, it was placed in harsh juxtaposition to another possibility— meaning as an art object. This problem of instability increased when problems of origin were raised: The object was not made by an artist, but by a machine. Whether or not the viewer chose to accept other possibilities for interpreting the function of the artist and the authenticity of the art object, the urinal in a gallery instigated a moment of uncertainty and reassessment. This conceptual game has been replayed numerous times over the 20th century, at times for very narrow purposes, as with Rauschenberg's combines—done for the sake of attacking the critical hegemony of Clement Greenberg—while at other times it has been done to promote large-scale political and cultural restructuring, as in the case of the Situationists. In each case, the plagiarist works to open meaning through the injection of skepticism into the culture-text.

One of the main goals of the plagiarist is to restore the dynamic and unstable drift of meaning, by appropriating and recombining fragments of culture.

Here one also sees the failure of Romantic essentialism. Even the alleged transcendental object cannot escape the skeptics' critique. Duchamp's notion of the inverted ready-made (turning a Rembrandt painting into an ironing board) suggested that the distinguished art object draws its power from a historical legitimation process firmly rooted in the institutions of Western culture, and not from being an unalterable conduit to transcendental realms. This is not to deny the possibility of transcendental experience, but only to say that if it does exist, it is prelinguistic, and thereby relegated to the privacy of an individual's subjectivity. A society with a complex division of labor requires a rationalization of institutional processes, a situation which in turn robs the individual of a way to share nonrational experience. Unlike societies with a simple division of labor, in which the experience of one member closely resembles the experience of another (minimal alienation), under a complex division of labor, the life experience of the individual turned specialist holds little in common with other specialists. Consequently, communication exists primarily as an instrumental function.

Plagiarism has historically stood against the privileging of any text through spiritual, scientific, or other legitimizing myths. The plagiarist sees all objects as equal, and thereby horizontalizes the plane of phenomena. All texts become potentially usable and reusable. Herein lies an epistemology of anarchy, according to which the plagiarist argues that if science, religion, or any other social institution precludes certainty beyond the realm of the private, then it is best to endow consciousness with as many categories of interpretation as possible. The tyranny of paradigms may have some useful consequences (such as greater efficiency within the paradigm), but the repressive costs to the individual (excluding other modes of thinking and reducing the possibility of invention) are too high. Rather than being led by sequences of signs, one should instead drift through them, choosing the interpretation best suited to the social conditions of a given situation.

It is a matter of throwing together various cut-up techniques in order to respond to the omnipresence of transmitters feeding us with their dead discourses (mass media, publicity, etc.). It is a question of unchaining the codes—not the subject anymore—so that something will burst out, will escape; words beneath words, personal obsessions. Another kind of word is born which escapes from the totalitarianism of the media but retains their power, and turns it against their old masters.

Cultural production, literary or otherwise, has traditionally been a slow, labor-intensive process. In painting, sculpture, or written work, the technology has always been primitive by contemporary standards. Paintbrushes, hammers and chisels, quills and paper, and even the printing press do not lend themselves well to rapid production and broad-range distribution. The time lapse between production and distribution can seem unbearably long. Book arts and traditional visual arts still suffer tremendously from this problem, when compared to the electronic arts. Before electronic technology became dominant, cultural perspectives developed in a manner that more clearly defined texts as individual works. Cultural fragments appeared in their own right as discrete units, since their influence moved slowly enough to allow the orderly evolution of an argument or an aesthetic. Boundaries could be maintained between disciplines and schools of thought. Knowledge was considered finite, and was therefore easier to control. In the 19th century this traditional order began to collapse as new technology began to increase the velocity of cultural development. The first strong indicators began to appear that speed was becoming a crucial issue.

The plagiarist sees all objects as equal. All texts become potentially usable and reusable. Herein lies an epistemology of anarchy.

Knowledge was shifting away from certitude, and transforming itself into information. During the American Civil War, Lincoln sat impatiently by his telegraph line, awaiting reports from his generals at the front. He had no patience with the long-winded rhetoric of the past, and demanded from his generals an efficient economy of language. There was no time for the traditional trappings of the elegant essayist. Cultural velocity and information have continued to increase at a geometric rate since then, resulting in an information panic. Production and distribution of information (or any other product) must be immediate; there can be no lag time between the two. Techno-culture has met this demand with databases and electronic networks that rapidly move any type of information.

Under such conditions, plagiarism fulfills the requirements of economy of representation, without stifling invention. If invention occurs when a new perception or idea is brought out—by intersecting two or more formally disparate systems—then recombinant methodologies are desirable. This is where plagiarism progresses beyond nihilism. It does not simply inject skepticism to help destroy totalitarian systems that stop invention; it participates in invention, and is thereby also productive. The genius of an inventor like Leonardo da Vinci lay in his ability to recombine the then separate systems of biology, mathematics, engineering, and art. He was not so much an originator as a synthesizer. There have been few people like him over the centuries, because the ability to hold that much data in one's own biological memory is rare. Now, however, the technology of recombination is available in the computer. The problem now for would-be cultural producers is to gain access to this technology and information. After all, access is the most precious of all privileges, and is therefore strictly guarded, which in turn makes one wonder whether to be a successful plagiarist, one must also be a successful hacker.

Most serious writers refuse to make themselves available to the things that technology is doing. I have never been able to understand this sort of fear. Many are afraid of using tape recorders, and the idea of using any electronic means for literary or artistic purposes seems to them some sort of sacrilege.

To some degree, a small portion of technology has fallen through the cracks into the hands of the lucky few. Personal computers and video cameras are the best examples. To accompany these consumer items and make their use more versatile, hypertextual and image sampling programs have also been developed—programs designed to facilitate recombination. It is the plagiarist's dream to be able to call up, move, and recombine text with simple user-friendly commands. Perhaps plagiarism rightfully belongs to post-book culture, since only in that society can it be made explicit what book culture, with its geniuses and auteurs, tends to hide—that information is most useful when it interacts with other information, rather than when it is deified and presented in a vacuum.

Thinking about a new means for recombining information has always been on 20th-century minds, although this search has been left to a few until recently. In 1945 Vannevar Bush, a former science advisor to Franklin D. Roosevelt, proposed a new way of organizing information in an *Atlantic Monthly* article. At that time, computer technology was in its earliest stages of development and its full potential was not really understood. Bush, however, had the foresight to imagine a device he called the Memex. In his view it would be based around storage of information on microfilm, integrated with some means to allow the user to select and display any section at will, thus enabling one to move freely among previously unrelated increments of information.

At the time, Bush's Memex could not be built, but as computer technology evolved, his idea eventually gained practicality. Around 1960 Theodor

Nelson made this realization when he began studying computer programming in college:

Over a period of months, I came to realize that, although programmers structured their data hierarchically, they didn't have to. I began to see the computer as the ideal place for making interconnections among things accessible to people.

I realized that writing did not have to be sequential and that not only would tomorrow's books and magazines be on [cathode ray terminal] screens, they could all tie to one another in every direction. At once I began working on a program (written in 7090 assembler language) to carry out these ideas.

Nelson's idea, which he called hypertext, failed to attract any supporters at first, although by 1968 its usefulness became obvious to some in the government and in defense industries. A prototype of hypertext was developed by another computer innovator, Douglas Englebart, who is often credited with many breakthroughs in the use of computers (such as the development of the Macintosh interface, Windows). Englebart's system, called Augment, was applied to organizing the government's research network, ARPAnet, and was also used by McDonnell Douglas, the defense contractor, to aid technical work groups in coordinating projects such as aircraft design:

All communications are automatically added to the Augment information base and linked, when appropriate, to other documents. An engineer could, for example, use Augment to write and deliver electronically a work plan to others in the work group. The other members could then review the document and have their comments linked to the original, eventually creating a "group memory" of the decisions made. Augment's powerful linking features allow users to find even old information quickly, without getting lost or being overwhelmed by detail.

Computer technology continued to be refined, and eventually—as with so many other technological breakthroughs in this country—once it had been thoroughly exploited by military and intelligence agencies, the technology was released for commercial exploitation. Of course, the development of microcomputers and consumer-grade technology for personal computers led immediately to the need for software which would help one cope with the exponential increase in information, especially textual information. Probably the first humanistic application of hypertext was in the field of education. Currently, hypertext and hypermedia (which adds graphic images to the network of features which can be interconnected) continue to be fixtures in instructional design and educational technology.

An interesting experiment in this regard was instigated in 1975 by Robert Scholes and Andries Van Dam at Brown University. Scholes, a professor of English, was contacted by Van Dam, a professor of computer science, who wanted to know if there were any courses in the humanities that might benefit from using what at the time was called a text-editing system (now known as a word processor) with hypertext capabilities built in. Scholes and two teaching assistants, who formed a research group, were particularly impressed by one aspect of hypertext. Using this program would make it possible to peruse in a nonlinear fashion all the interrelated materials in a text. A hypertext is thus best seen as a web of interconnected materials. This description suggested that there is a definite parallel between the conception of culture-text and that of hypertext:

One of the most important facets of literature (and one which also leads to difficulties in interpretation) is its reflexive nature. Individual poems constantly develop their meanings—often through such means as direct allusion or the reworking of traditional motifs and conventions, at other times through subtler means, such as genre development and expansion or biographical reference—by referring to that total body of poetic material of which the particular poems comprise a small segment.

Although it was not difficult to accumulate a hypertextually linked database consisting of poetic materials, Scholes and his group were more concerned with making it interactive—that is, they wanted to construct a "communal text" including not only the poetry, but also incorporating the comments and interpretations offered by individual students. In this way, each student in turn could read a work and attach "notes" to it about his or her observations. The resulting "expanded text" would be read and augmented at a terminal on which the screen was divided into four areas. The student could call up the poem in one of the areas (referred to as windows) and call up related materials in the other three windows, in any sequence he or she desired. This would powerfully reinforce the tendency to read in a nonlinear sequence. By this means, each student would learn how to read a work as it truly exists, not in "a vacuum" but rather as the central point of a progressively revealed body of documents and ideas.

Hypertext is analogous to other forms of literary discourse besides poetry. From the very beginning of its manifestation as a computer program, hypertext was popularly described as a multidimensional text roughly analogous to the standard scholarly article in the humanities or social sciences, because it uses the same conceptual devices, such as footnotes, annotations, allusions to other works, quotations from other works, etc. Unfortunately, the convention of linear reading and writing, as well as the physical fact of two-dimensional pages and the necessity of binding them in only one possible sequence, have always limited the true potential of this type of text. One problem is that the reader is often forced to search through the text (or forced to leave the book and search elsewhere) for related information. This is a time-consuming and distracting process; instead of being able to move easily and instantly among physically remote or inaccessible areas of information storage, the reader must cope with cumbrous physical impediments to his or her research or creative work. With the advent of hypertext, it has become possible to move among related areas of information with a speed and flexibility that at least approach finally accommodating the workings of human intellect, to a degree that books and sequential reading cannot possibly allow.

The recombinant text in hypertextual form signifies the emergence of the perception of textual constellations that have always/already gone nova. It is in this uncanny luminosity that the authorial biomorph has been consumed.[2]

Barthes and Foucault may be lauded for theorizing the death of the author; the absent author is more a matter of everyday life, however, for the technocrat recombining and augmenting information at the computer or at a video editing console. S/he is living the dream of capitalism that is still being refined in the area of manufacture. The Japanese notion of "just in time delivery," in which the units of assembly are delivered to the assembly line just as they are called for, was a first step in streamlining the tasks of assembly. In such a system, there is no sedentary capital, but a constant flow of raw commodities. The assembled commodity is delivered to the distributor precisely at the moment of consumer need. This nomadic system eliminates stockpiles of goods. (There still is some dead time; however, the Japanese have cut it to a matter of hours, and are working on reducing it to a matter of minutes.) In this way, production, distribution, and consumption are imploded into a single act, with no beginning or end, just unbroken circulation. In the same manner, the online text flows in an unbroken stream through the electronic network. There can be no place for gaps that mark discrete units in the society of speed. Consequently, notions of origin have no place in electronic reality. The production of the text presupposes its immediate distribution, consumption, and revision. All who participate in the network also participate in the interpretation and mutation of the textual stream. The concept of the author did not so much die as it simply ceased to function. The author has become an abstract aggregate that cannot be reduced to biology or to the psychology of personality. Indeed, such a development has apocalyptic connotations—the fear that humanity will be lost in the textual stream. Perhaps humans are not capable of participating in hypervelocity. One must answer that never has there been a time when humans were able, one and all, to participate in cultural production. Now, at least the potential for cultural democracy is greater. The single bio-genius need not act as a stand-in for all humanity. The real concern is just the same as it has always been: the need for access to cultural resources.

The concept of the author did not so much die as it simply ceased to function. The author has become an abstract aggregate that cannot be reduced to biology or to the psychology of personality.

The discoveries of postmodern art and criticism regarding the analogical structures of images demonstrate that when two objects are brought together, no matter how far apart their contexts may be, a relationship is formed. Restricting oneself to a personal relationship of words is mere convention. The bringing together of two independent expressions supersedes the original elements and produces a synthetic organization of greater possibility.[3]

The book has by no means disappeared. The publishing industry continues to resist the emergence of the recombinant text, and opposes increases in cultural speed. It has set itself in the gap between production and consumption of texts, which for purposes of survival it is bound to maintain. If speed is allowed to increase, the book is doomed to perish, along with its renaissance companions painting and sculpture. This is why the industry is so afraid of the recombinant text. Such a work closes the gap between production and consumption, and opens the industry to those other than the literary celebrity. If the industry is unable to differentiate its product through the spectacle of originality and uniqueness, its profitability collapses. Consequently, the industry plods along, taking years to publish information needed immediately. Yet there is a peculiar irony to this situation. In order to reduce speed, it must also participate in velocity in its most intense form, that of spectacle. It must claim to defend "quality and standards," and it must invent celebrities. Such endeavors require the immediacy of advertising—that is, full participation in the simulacra that will be the industry's own destruction.

Hence for the bureaucrat, from an everyday life perspective, the author is alive and well. S/he can be seen and touched and traces of her or his existence are on the covers of books and magazines everywhere in the form of the signature. To such evidence, theory can only respond with the maxim that the meaning of a given text derives exclusively from its relation to other texts. Such texts are contingent upon what came before them, the context in which they are placed, and the interpretive ability of the reader. This argument is of course unconvincing to the social segments caught in cultural lag. So long as this is the case, no recognized historical legitimation will support the producers of recombinant texts, who will always be suspect to the keepers of "high" culture.

Take your own words or the words said to be "the very own words" of anyone else living or dead. You will soon see that words do not belong to anyone. Words have a vitality of their own. Poets are supposed to liberate the words—not to chain them in phrases. Poets have no words "of their very own." Writers do not own their words. Since when do words belong to anybody? "Your very own words" indeed! and who are "you"?

The invention of the video portapak in the late 1960s and early 70s led to considerable speculation among radical media artists that in the near future, everyone would have access to such equipment, causing a revolution in the television industry. Many hoped that video would become the ultimate tool for distributable democratic art. Each home would become its own production center, and the reliance on network television for electronic information would be only one of many options. Unfortunately this prophecy never came to pass. In the democratic sense, video did little more than super 8 film to redistribute the possibility for image production, and it has had little or no effect on image distribution. Any video besides home movies has remained in the hands of an elite technocratic class, although (as with any class) there are marginalized segments which resist the media industry and maintain a program of decentralization.

The video revolution failed for two reasons—a lack of access and an absence of desire. Gaining access to the hardware, particularly post-production equipment, has remained as difficult as ever, nor are there any regular distribution points beyond the local public access offered by some cable TV franchises. It has also been hard to convince those outside of the technocratic class why they should want to do something with video, even if they had access to equipment. This is quite understandable when one considers that media images are provided in such an overwhelming quantity that the thought of producing more is empty. The contemporary plagiarist faces precisely the same discouragement. The potential for generating recombinant texts at present is just that, potential. It does at least have a wider base, since the computer technology for making recombinant texts has escaped the technocratic class and spread to the bureaucratic class; however, electronic cultural production has by no means become the democratic form that utopian plagiarists hope it will be.

The immediate problems are obvious. The cost of technology for productive plagiarism is still too high. Even if one chooses to use the less efficient form of a hand-written plagiarist manuscript, desktop publishing technology is required to distribute it, since no publishing house will accept it. Further, the population in the U.S. is generally skilled only as receivers of information, not as producers. With this exclusive structure solidified, technology and the desire and ability to use it remain centered in utilitarian economy, and hence not much time is given to the technology's aesthetic or resistant possibilities.

In addition to these obvious barriers, there is a more insidious problem that emerges from the social schizophrenia of the U.S. While its political system is theoretically based on democratic principles of inclusion, its economic system is based on the principle of exclusion. Consequently, as a luxury itself, the cultural superstructure tends toward exclusion as well. This economic principle determined the invention of copyright, which originally developed not in order to protect writers, but to reduce competition among publishers. In 17th-century England, where copyright first appeared, the goal was to reserve for publishers themselves, in perpetuity, the exclusive right to print certain books. The justification, of course, was that when formed into a literary work, language has the author's personality imposed upon it, thereby marking it as private property. Under this mythology, copyright has flourished in late capital, setting the legal precedent to privatize any cultural item, whether it is an image, a word, or a sound. Thus the plagiarist (even of the technocratic class) is kept in a deeply marginal position, regardless of the inventive efficient uses his or her methodology may have for the current state of technology and knowledge.

What is the point of saving language when there is no longer anything to say?

The present requires us to rethink and re-present the notion of plagiarism. Its function has for too long been devalued by an ideology with little place in techno-culture. Let the romantic notions of originality, genius, and authorship remain, but as elements for cultural production without special privilege above other equally useful elements. It is time to openly and boldly use the methodology of recombination so as to better parallel the technology of our time.

■ N O T E S

1. In its more heroic form the footnote has a low-speed hypertextual function—that is, connecting the reader with other sources of information that
can further articulate the producer's words. It points to additional information too lengthy to include in the text itself. This is not an objectionable
function. The footnote is also a means of surveillance by which one can
"check up" on a writer, to be sure that s/he is not improperly using an
idea or phrase from the work of another. This function makes the footnote
problematic, although it may be appropriate as a means of verifying conclusions in a quantitative study, for example. The surveillance function of
the footnote imposes fixed interpretations on a linguistic sequence and
implies ownership of language and ideas by the individual cited. The note
becomes an homage to the genius who supposedly originated the idea.
This would be acceptable if all who deserved credit got their due; however, such crediting is impossible, since it would begin an infinite regress.
Consequently, that which is most feared occurs: the labor of many is
stolen, smuggled in under the authority of the signature which is cited. In
the case of those cited who are still living, this designation of authorial
ownership allows them to collect rewards for the work of others. It must
be realized that writing itself is theft: it is a changing of the features of the
old culture-text in much the same way one disguises stolen goods. This is
not to say that signatures should never be cited; but remember that the
signature is merely a sign, a shorthand under which a collection of interrelated ideas may be stored and rapidly deployed.

2. If the signature is a form of cultural shorthand, then it is not necessarily
horrific on occasion to sabotage the structures so they do not fall into
rigid complacency. Attributing words to an image, i.e., an intellectual
celebrity, is inappropriate. The image is a tool for playful use, like any culture-text or part thereof. It is just as necessary to imagine the history of
the spectacular image, and write it as imagined, as it is to show fidelity to
its current "factual" structure. One should choose the method that best
suits the context of production, one that will render the greater possibility
for interpretation. The producer of recombinant texts augments the language, and often preserves the generalized code, as when Karen Eliot
quoted Sherrie Levine as saying, "Plagiarism? I just don't like the way it
tastes."

3. It goes without saying that one is not limited to correcting a work or to
integrating diverse fragments of out-of-date works into a new one; one can
also alter the meaning of these fragments in any appropriate way, leaving
the constipated to their slavish preservation of "citations."

■ Q U E S T I O N S   F O R   R E R E A D I N G

1. What is plagiarism? Is it a universal principle—that is, a principle for all
times and for all people of the world? Or is it just for some people? How
would you determine an answer to each of these questions? Does plagiarism have a history? In other words, did it appear at a particular time in
history, or has it always been a law of nature? If it has a history, what

would that suggest to you? Who and what does the concept of plagiarism protect?

2. What is CAE's argument for what they see as the radical change in the conditions of property that would permit a "utopian plagiarism"? Do you agree with their thinking?

3. When the first edition of *CyberReader* appeared with this article by CAE, I received an e-mail message from a teacher in the U.S. who claimed that I should never have included the article, for it would only encourage students reading it to plagiarize. How do you feel about a statement like that and the inclusion of this article in *CyberReader*? Do you think that this article encourages students to steal other people's ideas? Even if you answer in the affirmative, do you think that there could be a defensible, ethical purpose for including this article? If so, what might that be?

■ WRITING ASSIGNMENT FOR REREADING

What recent events have you read about in the past few years concerning the theft of music (lyrics or melody/harmony) by one group from another? Do some basic research and write a well-argued paper on the outcome of the event, stating finally whether you agree or disagree with the outcome and on what grounds. (You might find some help at the Web site for *CyberReader*.)

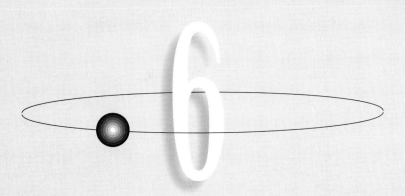

Cyberpunk/Cyborgs

C*yber* plus *punk* form a hybrid. *Cyber* is from the Greek *kybernetes* (pilot, steersman). *Punk* is from the media understanding of rebellious (working-class) British and American youth who wear Mohawks and black clothes and pierce their bodies beyond their earlobes. Together, the hybrid *cyberpunk* has spawned as many definitions as definers.

Cy[ber] plus *borg* form a hybrid. *Borg* is from the science-fiction understanding or, more correctly, a cyberpunk science-fiction understanding of an individual or race of hybrid beings, humanoids enhanced by cybernetic implants. The understanding of *cyborg* ranges in its usage by cyberpunk sci-fi authors (Bruce Sterling, William Gibson, Tom Maddox) through the authors of the episodes of *Star Trek: The Next Generation* to Donna Haraway and her manifesto and Sandy Stone and Orlan and their prosthetic bodies.

Cyberpunks are not a thing of the past, as people who don't know any better keep telling me. It's true that as a media phenomenon (say, as Elmer-Dewitt writes about them in *Time*), they are a thing of the past, just as the hippies of the sixties are a thing of the past, though they still live on. The interesting thing about cyberpunks is that they continue to reinvent themselves. They are about *identity* (recall the readings in chapter 2), constantly reidentifying itself. They are about metamorphosis (shape shifting). And therefore they are a seed plot of ideas for new cyber-identities.

By far one of the most popular treatments of things cyberpunk is by Gareth Branwyn, who on a *Mondo 2000* conference on the WELL, put forth a description of the cyberpunk worldview, the first part of which is that "The future has imploded onto the present. There was no nuclear Armageddon. There's too much real estate to lose. The new battlefield is people's minds." Branwyn alludes to the fact that following World War II, there was tremendous fear of a nuclear holocaust. Turning things around in his statement, he alludes not only to the threat to all people and the environment but also—and most prominently now—to their minds. The new world order would be centralizing everything, making difference difficult, unifying all thought for mass consumption, while the cyberpunk disorder would be "splintering [the world] into a trillion subcultures and designer cults with their own languages, codes, and lifestyles," making difference a virtue. (There is a subtle irony here in that the Internet within the World Wide Web, which is where cyberpunk culture mostly lives, was built in the U.S. by the government so as to have a means of communication during and after a nuclear attack. Now these virtual underground tunnels have become the places of dissent by a counterculture.) But the point should be clear: Cyberpunks are into unique designer identities and realities. As we know, however, this attempt generally phalls into conformity, which can be spoofed. (BTW, spoofing is also a feature of cyberpunkishness!)

In a recent book titled *Cyberpunk Handbook: or The Real Cyberpunk Fakebook* (by St. Jude, R. U. Sirius, and Bart Nagel), Bruce Sterling—renowned cyberpunk author—writes an interesting foreword, pointing out that he would not like to be one of these characters but that he is happy that they are doing what they do. He calls them a "decentralized, libertarian, free-market regime of biomedical research," not because they take a lot of hard drugs, but because they take "smart drugs." In the book itself, the authors give us several examples and categories that make up cyberpunkdom:

Motorpsycho Maniacs;

Goths, Deathcore, and Vampire-Wannabes;

Riot Grrrls;

Technopagans, Ravers, Neohippies;

Academic Cyber-Wannabes;

Cybercowboys/grrrls;

Science Fiction Writers;

Web Crawlers and other Bourgeois Types;

Deep Geek: Supernerds, Hackers, Wizards, Phone Phreakers;

Phonies, Poseurs, and Pretenders such as Billy Idol, who I included in the first edition of *CyberReader,* but the cyberpunkish students reading the edition had some bad things to say about Billy, so he was cut. An important part of cyberculture is punk music. In "Seriously Wired," the reporter Karen Schoemer begins: "Billy Idol is playing with his new best friend, technology."

What all of these examples and categories have in common is digital technology. Computers, computers, computers. The main point that needs to be understood, however, is that they are categories of people who are all fakers, pranksters, spoofers; for they believe that there is only faking. In other words, they see the *actual* as the *virtual,* and hence, *all is virtual.* All is fake, artificial, bogus. All is Protean (as in Proteus, the shape shifter). Catch my drift?

If so, then let's now take a look at cyborgs. If there is a *Cyberpunk Handbook,* you gotta know that there is a *Cyborg Handbook* as well. But I am going to steer us clear of that one and focus on what the most theoretically rad of all cyborgeans—namely, Donna Haraway—has to say about cyborgs. In an interview with *Wired* magazine (5.02, February 1997), she explains: "We're talking about whole new forms of subjectivity here. We're talking seriously mutated worlds that never existed on this planet before. And it's not just ideas. It's new flesh." But Haraway is not simply talking about bits and bytes and silicon and cybernetic implants or about prosthetic devices; instead, she is talking about the concern of technoculture to improve our bodies by way of networking the machine and the body, the body and the machine. The body, after all, has been rethought to be in athletics a high-performance machine. "Think about the technology of sports footwear," Haraway says. "Before the Civil War, right and left feet weren't even differentiated in shoe manufacture. Now we have a shoe for every activity." Being successful at the Olympics is about the success of "the interaction of medicine, diet, training practices, clothing and equipment manufacture, visualization and timekeeping." Still the best source for what Haraway means is found in her "Manifesto for Cyborgs," which is no longer included in this book, but is readily available. (see Appendix C.)

In addition to Haraway's view of cyborgs, there is the more prevalent, easier-to-understand notion of cyborgs as half human and half silicon, half flesh and half prostheses. Haraway does not necessarily advocate this as the only view of cyborgs. Those who have at one time or another, however, are the posttransgender artist Allucquère Rosanne Stone, the French performance artist Orlan, and the Australian cybernetic body artist Stelarc.

Stone is very interested in the body and the self as unstable, as perhaps Bolter (chapter 5) is interested in hypertext as unstable discourse. Stone, like Turkle (chapter 2), is interested in multiplicity in terms of gender and biological sex. The point in terms of cyborgs is that some human beings, for political reasons, do not want to be limited to some fixed idea of gender, and therefore they perform and make their own genders. They do not want to be like the Borgs of *Star Trek,* a community of conforming machines.

Orlan is an extreme example of this line of thinking. She says, "This is my body; this is my software." She sees her body as a work of art in progress, titled "The Reincarnation of Saint Orlan." She has had numerous plastic surgical operations to transform herself into a new being, modeled on Venus, Diana, Europa, Psyche, and Mona Lisa. The surgery is performed while she is completely conscious, talking to the audience.

Stelarc attaches prosthetic devices to his body such as a third arm, with which he writes. He is interested in the posthuman body (that is, an artificially constructed body) and what it will have become biologically and prosthetically. (Oh, I forgot Michael Jackson as a prime example of a man in search of a posthuman body!)

What can be said in general about people interested in cyberpunk and cyborg stuff is the future. They live in the present, experimenting on what lies in the future. They are *futurehaqing* while at other times *futurespoofing*. They believe that they can determine their lives in the future. Their acts are highly political and ethical, though many people may not agree with them. Those who disagree usually want to stay in the mainstream, while futurehaqers want to stay on the edge or perpetually redefine the edge. They remain subjectively positioned perpetually counter to the culture.

■ SUMMARY OF KEY TERMS AND PERSONS

cyberfeminism: A hybrid social criticism that embraces technology as a means of inventing new modes of representing the feminine and thereby resisting what male-dominated culture would depict as necessary to be feminine. Examples of cyberfeminism in practice can be found in the political antics of the Guerrilla Grrls or the Riot Grrrls.

cyberpunk: Rebellious working-class British and American youth (as depicted by the media) who wear Mohawks and black clothes and pierce their bodies beyond their earlobes. A computer network freak (that is, a phreak). A recent branch of

science fiction dealing exclusively in questions of technology and its dystopias.

cyborg: A cyberpunk science-fiction understanding of an individual or race of hybrid beings, humanoids enhanced by cybernetic implants. A linking and networking of human flesh and bones with machines so as to improve the performance of the human body.

cypherpunk: A cyberpunk attempting greater levels of privacy in and encryption of messages.

futurehaqing: Predicting the future.

futurespoofing: Making "phun" of futurehaqing. Saying what will be, knowing that it will not be.

temporary autonomous zone (TAZ): According to Hakim Bey, originally mountain fortresses and pirate islands, as holdouts from the dominant culture. Similarly today, cyberspace and the "counternet" are autonomous, temporary zones against the dominant culture and consensus reality. TAZs house fifth-estate groups such as data pirates, cyberpunkutopianists, and futuro-libertarians.

Philip Elmer-Dewitt's "Cyberpunk" appeared in Time (February 8, 1993): 59–65. Elmer-Dewitt

surveys in his article, which is in the form of a primer, some of the various meanings of cyberpunk along with its various hyperassociations—one of which

is that the punks of the 1970s, '80s, and '90s take technology and steer it against itself. Whereas technology is used against people in centralizing information and in collecting and encrypting the data, cyberpunks (now broadly defined as cyberculture and associated with hackers) have adopted the following as their ethic: information wants to be and should be free-in-access to everyone so that each can act on, steer, his or her own reality. Cyberpunks in various ways make up a contemporary counterculture. (Reads like a glossary.)

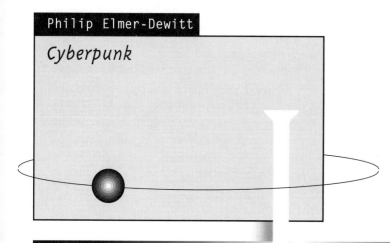

Philip Elmer-Dewitt

Cyberpunk

Hypertext In this article, words printed in bold are defined or expanded in marginal entries. In a computer hypertext article, electronic footnotes like these actually pop up on the screen whenever you point your cursor at a "hot" word and click the button on your mouse.

Cybernetics Norbert Wiener of M.I.T. was designing systems for World War II antiaircraft guns when he realized that the critical component in a control system, whether animal or mechanical, is a feedback loop that gives a controller information on the results of its actions. He called the study of these control systems cybernetics (from *kybernetes,* the Greek word for helmsman) and helped pave the way for the electronic brains that we call computers.

n the 1950s it was the beatniks, staging a coffeehouse rebellion against the *Leave It to Beaver* conformity of the Eisenhower era. In the 1960s the hippies arrived, combining antiwar activism with the energy of sex, drugs and rock 'n' roll. Now a new subculture is bubbling up from the underground, popping out of computer screens like a piece of futuristic **HYPERTEXT** *(see margin).*

They call it cyberpunk, a late–20th century term pieced together from **CYBERNETICS** (the science of communication and control theory) and **PUNK** (an antisocial rebel or hoodlum). Within this odd pairing lurks the essence of cyberpunk culture. It's a way of looking at the world that combines an infatuation with high-tech tools and a disdain for conventional ways of using them. Originally applied to a school of hard-boiled science-fiction writers and then to certain semi-tough computer hackers, the word cyberpunk now covers a broad range of music, art, psychedelics, smart drugs and cutting-edge technology. The cult is new enough that fresh offshoots are sprouting every day, which infuriates the hardcore cyberpunks, who feel they got there first.

Stewart Brand, editor of the hippie-era *Whole Earth Catalog,* describes cyberpunk as "technology with attitude." Science-fiction writer Bruce Sterling calls it "an unholy alliance of the technical world with the underground of pop culture and street-level anarchy." Jude Milhon, a cyberpunk journalist who writes under the byline St. Jude, defines it as "the place where the worlds of science and art overlap, the intersection of the future and now." What cyberpunk is about, says Rudy Rucker, a San

Jose State University mathematician who writes science-fiction books on the side, is nothing less than "the fusion of humans and machines."

As in any counterculture movement, some denizens would deny that they are part of a "movement" at all. Certainly they are not as visible from a passing car as beatniks or hippies once were. Ponytails (on men) and tattoos (on women) do not a cyberpunk make—though dressing all in black and donning mirrored sunglasses will go a long way. And although the biggest cyberpunk journal claims a readership approaching 70,000, there are probably no more than a few thousand computer hackers, futurists, fringe scientists, computer-savvy artists and musicians, and assorted science-fiction geeks around the world who actually call themselves cyberpunks.

Punk Cyberculture borrows heavily from the rebellious attitude of punk music, sharing with such groups as the Sex Pistols a defiance of mainstream culture and an urge to turn modern technology against itself.

Raves Organized on the fly (sometimes by electronic mail) and often held in warehouses, raves are huge, nomadic dance parties that tend to last all night, or until the police show up. Psychedelic mood enhancers and funny accessories (white cotton gloves, face masks) are optional.

Brain Implants Slip a microchip into snug contact with your gray matter (a.k.a. wetware) and suddenly gain instant fluency in a foreign language or arcane subject.

Acid House White-hot dance music that falls somewhere between disco and hip-hop.

Industrial Mixing rhythmic machine clanks, electronic feedback and random radio noise, industrial music is "the sounds our culture makes as it comes unglued," says cyberpunk writer Gareth Branwyn.

Nevertheless, cyberpunk may be the defining counterculture of the computer age. It embraces, in spirit at least, not just the nearest thirtysomething hacker hunched over his terminal but also nose-ringed twentysomethings gathered at clandestine **RAVES,** teenagers who feel about the Macintosh computer the way their parents felt about Apple Records, and even preadolescent vidkids fused like Krazy Glue to their Super Nintendo and Sega Genesis games—the training wheels of cyberpunk. Obsessed with technology, especially technology that is just beyond their reach (like **BRAIN IMPLANTS**), the cyberpunks are future oriented to a fault. They already have one foot in the 21st century, and time is on their side. In the long run, we will all be cyberpunks.

The cyberpunk look—a kind of SF (science-fiction) surrealism tweaked by computer graphics—is already finding its way into art galleries, music videos and Hollywood movies. Cyberpunk magazines, many of which are "'zines" cheaply published by desktop computer and distributed by electronic mail, are multiplying like cable-TV channels. The newest, a glossy, bigbudget entry called *Wired,* premiered last week with Bruce Sterling on the cover and ads from the likes of Apple Computer and AT&T. Cyberpunk music, including **ACID HOUSE** and **INDUSTRIAL,** is popular enough to keep several record companies and scores of bands cranking out CDs. Cyberpunkoriented books are snapped up by eager fans as soon as they hit the stores. (Sterling's latest, *The Hacker Crackdown,* quickly sold out its first hard-cover printing of 30,000.) A piece of cyberpunk performance art, *Tubes,* starring Blue Man Group, is a hit off-Broadway. And cyberpunk films such as *Blade Runner, Videodrome, Robocop, Total Recall, Terminator 2* and *The Lawnmower Man* have moved out of the cult market and into the mall.

Cyberpunk culture is likely to get a boost from, of all things, the Clinton-Gore Administration, because of a shared interest in what the new regime calls America's "data highways" and what the cyberpunks call **CYBERSPACE.**

Cyberspace SF writer William Gibson called it "a consensual hallucination . . . a graphic representation of data abstracted from the banks of every computer in the human system." You can get there simply by picking up the phone.

Virtual Reality An interactive technology that creates an illusion, still crude rather than convincing, of being immersed in an artificial world. The user generally dons a computerized glove and a head-mounted display equipped with a TV screen for each eye. Now available as an arcade game.

Computer Virus The cybernetic analogue of AIDS, these self-replicating programs infect computers and can destroy data. There are hundreds loose in cyberspace, although few are as destructive as the Internet virus—which is now classified as a "worm" because the writer of the program did not mean to do damage.

Internet The successor of an experimental network built by the U.S. Defense Department in the 1960s, the Internet links at least 3 million computers, many of them university- and research-related, around the world. Users can connect to the Internet by phone to share information or tap into data banks.

Virtual Communities Collections of like-minded people who meet on-line and share ideas on everything from politics to punk rock. The global village is full of tiny electronic subdivisions made up of cold-fusion physicists, white supremacists, gerontologists and Grateful Deadheads. Like any other community, each has its own in-jokes, cliques, bozos and bores.

Both terms describe the globe-circling, interconnected telephone network that is the conduit for billions of voice, fax and computer-to-computer communications. The incoming administration is focused on the wiring, and it has made strengthening the network's high-speed data links a priority. The cyberpunks look at those wires from the inside; they talk of the network as if it were an actual place—a **VIRTUAL REALITY** that can be entered, explored and manipulated.

Cyberspace plays a central role in the cyberpunk world view. The literature is filled with "console cow-boys" who prove their mettle by donning virtual-reality headgear and performing heroic feats in the imaginary "matrix" of cyberspace. Many of the punks' real-life heroes are also computer cowboys of one sort or another. *Cyberpunk,* a 1991 book by two New York *Times* reporters, John Markoff and Katie Hafner, features profiles of three canonical cyberpunk hackers, including Robert Morris, the Cornell graduate student whose **COMPUTER VIRUS** brought the huge network called the **INTERNET** to a halt.

But cyberspace is more than a playground for hacker high jinks. What cyberpunks have known for some time—and what 17.5 million modem-equipped computer users around the world have discovered—is that cyberspace is also a new medium. Every night on Prodigy, CompuServe, GEnie and thousands of smaller computer bulletin boards, people by the hundreds of thousands are logging on to a great computer-mediated gabfest, an interactive debate that allows them to leap over barriers of time, place, sex and social status. Computer networks make it easy to reach out and touch strangers who share a particular obsession or concern. "We're replacing the old drugstore soda fountain and town square, where community used to happen in the physical world," says Howard Rheingold, a California-based author and editor who is writing a book on what he calls **VIRTUAL COMMUNITIES.**

Most computer users are content to visit cyberspace now and then, to read their electronic mail, check the bulletin boards and do a bit of electronic shopping. But cyberpunks go there to live and play—and even die. The WELL, one of the hippest virtual communities on the Internet, was shaken 2½ years ago when one of its most active participants ran a computer program that erased every message he had ever left—thousands of postings, some running for many pages. It was an act that amounted to virtual suicide. A few weeks later, he committed suicide for real.

The WELL is a magnet for cyberpunk thinkers, and it is there, appropriately enough, that much of the debate over the scope and significance of cyberpunk

The WELL Compared with million-plus-member networks such as CompuServe and Prodigy, the Northern California–based Whole Earth 'Lectronic Link is a tiny outpost in cyberspace. But its 7,000 subscribers include an unusual concentration of artists, activists, journalists and other writers. "It has a regional flavor," says co-founder Stewart Brand. "You can smell the sourdough."

Flame Sociologists note that, without visual cues, people communicating on-line tend to flame: to state their views more heatedly than they would face-to-face.

Datacops Any department or agency charged with protecting data security. Most notoriously: the U.S. Secret Service, whose 1990 Operation Sundevil launched constitutionally questionable predawn raids on computer hackers in a dozen U.S. cities and provoked international outrage in the cyberpunk community.

William Gibson Gibson knows precious little about cybernetic technology. When the success of *Neuromancer* enabled him to buy his own computer, he was surprised to discover that it had a disk drive. "I had been expecting an exotic crystalline thing. What I got was a little piece of a Victorian engine that makes noises like a scratchy old record player."

Interzone The wasteland setting of William Burroughs's *Naked Lunch* (1959) has become a favorite haunt for cyberpunk writers. It is here, in Gibson's words, that "the street finds its own uses for things," subverting cutting-edge technology to suit the needs of the underground.

has occurred. The question "Is there a cyberpunk movement?" launched a freewheeling on-line **FLAME**-fest that ran for months. The debate yielded, among other things, a fairly concise list of "attitudes" that, by general agreement, seem to be central to the idea of cyberpunk. Among them:

Information wants to be free. A good piece of information-age technology will eventually get into the hands of those who can make the best use of it, despite the best efforts of the censors, copyright lawyers and **DATACOPS.**

Always yield to the hands-on imperative. Cyberpunks believe they can run the world for the better, if they can only get their hands on the control box.

Promote decentralization. Society is splintering into hundreds of subcultures and designer cults, each with its own language, code and life-style.

Surf the edges. When the world is changing by the nanosecond, the best way to keep your head above water is to stay at the front end of the Zeitgeist.

The roots of cyberpunk, curiously, are as much literary as they are technological. The term was coined in the late 1980s to describe a group of science-fiction writers—and in particular **WILLIAM GIBSON,** a 44-year-old American now living in Vancouver. Gibson's *Neuromancer,* the first novel to win SF's triple crown—the Hugo, Nebula and Philip K. Dick awards—quickly became a cyberpunk classic, attracting an audience beyond the world of SF. Critics were intrigued by a dense, technopoetic prose style that invites comparisons to Hammett, Burroughs and Pynchon. Computer-literate readers were drawn by Gibson's nightmarish depictions of an imaginary world disturbingly similar to the one they inhabit.

In fact, the key to cyberpunk science fiction is that it is not so much a projection into the future as a metaphorical evocation of today's technological flux. The hero of *Neuromancer,* a burned-out, drug-addicted street hustler named Case, inhabits a sleazy **INTERZONE** on the fringes of a megacorporate global village where all transactions are carried out in New Yen. There he encounters Molly, a sharp-edged beauty with reflective lenses grafted to her eye sockets and retractable razor blades implanted in her fingers. They are hired by a mysterious employer who offers to fix Case's damaged nerves so he can once again enter cyberspace—a term Gibson invented. Soon Case discovers that he is actually working for an AI (artificial intelligence) named Wintermute, who is trying to get around the restrictions placed on AIs by the **TURING POLICE** to keep the computers under control. "What's important to me," says Gibson, "is that *Neuromancer* is about the present."

The themes and motifs of cyberpunk have been percolating through the culture for nearly a decade. But they have coalesced in the past few years, thanks in large part to an upstart magazine called MONDO 2000. Since 1988, *Mondo*'s editors have covered cyberpunk as *Rolling Stone* magazine chronicles rock music, with celebrity interviews of such cyberheroes as **NEGATIVLAND** and **TIMOTHY LEARY,** alongside features detailing what's hot and what's on the horizon. *Mondo*'s editors have packaged their quirky view of the world into a glossy book titled *Mondo 2000: A User's Guide to the New Edge* (HarperCollins; $20). Its cover touts alphabetic entries on everything from virtual reality and wetware to designer aphrodisiacs and **TECHNO-EROTIC PAGANISM**, promising to make cyberpunk's rarefied perspective immediately accessible. Inside, in an innovative hypertext format (which is echoed in this article), relatively straightforward updates on computer graphics, multimedia and fiber optics accompany wild screeds on such recondite subjects as **SYNESTHESIA** and **TEMPORARY AUTONOMOUS ZONES**.

The book and the magazine that inspired it are the product of a group of brainy (if eccentric) visionaries holed up in a rambling Victorian mansion perched on a hillside in Berkeley, California. The MTV-style graphics are supplied by designer Bart Nagel, the overcaffeinated prose by Ken Goffman (writing under the pen name R. U. Sirius) and Alison Kennedy (listed on the masthead as Queen Mu, "domineditrix"), with help from Rudy Rucker and a small staff of freelancers and contributions from an international cast of cyberpunk enthusiasts. The goal is to inspire and instruct but not to lead. "We don't want to tell people what to think," says assistant art director Heide Foley. "We want to tell them what the possibilities are."

Largely patched together from back issues of *Mondo 2000* magazine (and its precursor, a short-lived 'zine called *Reality Hackers*), the *Guide* is filled with articles on all the traditional cyberpunk obsessions, from **ARTIFICIAL LIFE** to **VIRTUAL SEX.** But some of the best entries are those that report on the activities of real people trying to live the cyberpunk life. For example, Mark Pauline, a San Francisco performance artist, specializes in giant machines and vast public spectacles: sonic booms that pin audiences to their chairs or the huge, stinking vat of rotting cheese with which he perfumed the air of Denmark to remind the citizenry of its Viking roots. When an explosion blew the thumb and three fingers off his right hand, Pauline simply had his big toe grafted where his thumb had been. He can pick things up again, but now he's waiting for medical science and grafting technology to

Turing Police British mathematician Alan Turing predicted in 1950 that computers would someday be as intelligent as humans.

MONDO 2000 *Mondo* is Italian for world; 2000 is the year. Says editor R. U. Sirius: "I like the idea of a magazine with an expiration date."

Negativland Better known for media pranks than records (*Helter Stupid*), this band canceled a tour in 1988 after a Minnesota teen axed his family to death. The band's press release said the family had been arguing about Negativland's song *Christianity Is Stupid*. The story was a hoax, but the press ran with it, turning the band into cyberpunk heroes.

Timothy Leary Yes, he's back. At 72, the ex-Harvard professor who encouraged a generation to "turn on, tune in, drop out" now counts himself a cyberpunk. "The PC is the LSD of the 1990s," he says.

Techno-Erotic Paganism Sound intriguing? That's probably why the editors of *MONDO 2000* put the term on the cover of their book. Unfortunately, they never got around to explaining what it means.

Synesthesia From the Greek *syn* (union) and *aesthesia* (sensation), synesthesia is a merging of sensory input in which sounds appear as colors in the brain or words evoke a specific taste or smell.

Temporary Autonomous Zones
These are the electronic analogue of mountain fortresses and pirate islands, but they can be formed or dismantled in a flash, says cyberpunk essayist Hakim Bey. As political systems decay and networking becomes more widespread, he envisions a proliferation of autonomous areas in cyberspace: giant worker-owned corporations, independent enclaves devoted to data piracy, Green–Social Democrat collectives, anarchist liberation zones, etc.

Artificial Life Inspired by the behavior of computer viruses, scientists are wondering how sophisticated a computer program or robot would have to be before you could say it was "alive." One computer-software company, Maxis, has marketed a whole line of simulated animals, ant colonies, cities, train systems and even a planet-like organism called Gaia.

Virtual Sex The way it would work, says Howard Rheingold, is that you slip into a virtual-reality bodysuit that fits with the "intimate snugness of a condom." When your partner (lying somewhere in cyberspace) fondles your computer-generated image, you actually feel it on your skin, and vice versa. Miniature sensors and actuators would have to be woven into the clothing by a technology that has yet to be invented.

Time Machines Anyone who has read H. G. Wells or seen *Back to the Future* knows how these things are supposed to work. Certain obscure results of Einstein's relativity theory suggest that there could actually be shortcuts through the space-time continuum, but it's unlikely that a human could squeeze through them.

advance to the point where he can replace his jerry-built hand with one taken from a cadaver.

Much of *Mondo 2000* strains credibility. Does physicist Nick Herbert really believe there might be a way to build **TIME MACHINES**? Did the **CRYONICS** experts at Trans-Time Laboratory really chill a family pet named Miles and then, after its near death experience, turn it back into what its owner describes as a "fully functional dog"? Are we expected to accept on faith that a **SMART DRUG** called centrophenoxine is an "intelligence booster" that provides "effective anti-aging therapy," or that another compound called hydergine increases mental abilities and prevents damage to brain cells? "All of this has some basis in today's technologies," says Paul Saffo, a research fellow at the Institute for the Future. "But it has a very anticipatory quality. These are people who assume that they will shape the future and the rest of us will live it."

Parents who thumb through *Mondo 2000* will find much here to upset them. An article on house music makes popping MDMA (**ECSTASY**) and thrashing all night to music that clocks 120 beats per minute sound like an experience no red-blooded teenager would want to miss. After describing in detail the erotic effects of massive doses of L-dopa, MDA and deprenyl, the entry on aphrodisiacs adds as an afterthought that in some combinations these drugs can be fatal. Essays praising the beneficial effects of psychedelics and smart drugs on the "information processing" power of the brain sit alongside **RANTS** that declare, among other things, that "safe sex is boring sex" and that "cheap thrills are fun."

Much of this, of course, is a cyberpunk pose. As Rucker confesses in his preface, he enjoys reading and thinking about psychedelic drugs but doesn't really like to take them. "To me the political point of being pro-psychedelic," he writes, "is that this means being against consensus reality, which I very strongly am." To some extent, says author Rheingold, cyberpunk is driven by young people trying to come up with a movement they can call their own. As he puts it, "They're tired of all these old geezers talking about how great the '60s were."

That sentiment was echoed by a recent posting on the WELL. "I didn't get to pop some 'shrooms and dance naked in a park with several hundred of my peers," wrote a cyberpunk wannabe who calls himself Alien. "To me, and to a lot of other generally disenfranchised members of my generation, surfing the edges is all we've got."

More troubling, from a philosophic standpoint, is the theme of **DYSTOPIA** that runs like a bad trip through the cyberpunk world view. Gibson's fictional world is filled with glassy-eyed girls strung out on their

Cryonics For a price, a terminally ill patient can be frozen—as in the movie *Forever Young*—until some future time when a cure has been discovered. Some people save on storage costs by having just their head frozen.

Smart Drugs "Don't eat any of that stuff they say will make you smarter," says Bruce Sterling. "It will only make you poorer."

Ecstasy Enthusiasts describe this New Age psychedelic, which heightens the senses, as "LSD without the hallucinations." The drug was outlawed in the U.S. in 1987.

Rants A hyperbolic literary form favored by cyberpunk writers, these extended diatribes make up in attitude what they lack in modesty.

Dystopia Utopia's evil twin. Merriam-Webster defines it as "an imaginary place which is depressingly wretched and whose people lead a fearful existence."

Simstim Decks These simulated stimuli machines are what television might evolve into. Rather than just watching your favorite characters on TV, you strap some plastic electrodes to your forehead and experience their thoughts and feelings—slightly edited, of course, to spare you the headaches and hangovers.

Microsofts Without apologies to the software company by the same name, Gibson has his fictional characters alter their reality by plugging into their brains these angular fragments of colored silicon, which house a read-only memory chip.

Walkman-like **SIMSTIM DECKS** and young men who get their kicks from **MICROSOFTS** plugged into sockets behind their ears. His brooding, dehumanized vision conveys a strong sense that technology is changing civilization and the course of history in frightening ways. But many of his readers don't seem to care. "History is a funny thing for cyberpunks," says Christopher Meyer, a music-synthesizer designer from Calabasas, California, writing on the WELL. "It's all data. It all takes up the same amount of space on disk, and a lot of it is just plain noise."

For cyberpunks, pondering history is not as important as coming to terms with the future. For all their flaws, they have found ways to live with technology, to make it theirs—something the back-to-the-land hippies never accomplished. Cyberpunks use technology to bridge the gulf between art and science, between the world of literature and the world of industry. Most of all, they realize that if you don't control technology, it will control you. It is a lesson that will serve them—and all of us—well in the next century.

■ QUESTIONS FOR REREADING

1. If you know something about punk music or cypberpunk-anything, do you find that Philip Elmer-Dewitt in his *Time* magazine article oversimplifies or misinterprets the counterculture movement?

2. What are the major differences between the counterculture movement of the 1960s and those of the 1970s, '80s, and '90s?

3. Given that this article is written in the form of history, what does history mean for cyberpunks?

4. What is technology to cyberpunks? Freedom? The value of the individual versus that of the masses?

■ WRITING ASSIGNMENT FOR REREADING

Start a glossary on a single word such as *cyberpunk*. Call it *A Glossary of First Intimations and Estimations*. Ask among your general acquaintances (but not from your class), What is (a) cyberpunk? Keep good records and share them with your class. Then discuss what you might do with these scattered intimations. What do they variously tell you?

Timothy Leary's "The Cyberpunk: The Individual as Reality Pilot" appeared in Chaos and Cyber Culture (Berkeley, CA: Ronin, 1994). Leary—famous in the 1960s for the saying "Turn on, tune in, drop out"—returns on the scene and asks us to take a close look at the etymology of the word kybernetes (pilot) so that we can understand that the Greek term for pilot, when appropriated by the Romans, became gubernetes, which means one who governs or controls others. It is this change in meaning, from pilot to controller, Leary claims, that is "our oppressive birthright." Leary sees cyberpunks, however, as the new pilots showing the way for controllers or the controlled to become their own pilots.

Cyberpunks are the new role model for the millennium. Leary chants:

Cyberpunks are the inventors, innovative writers, technofrontier artists, risk-taking film directors, icon-shifting composers, stand-up comedians, expressionist artists, free-agent scientists, technocreatives, computer visionaries, elegant hackers, bit-blitting Prolog adepts, special-effectives, cognitive dissidents, video wizards, neurological text pilots, media explorers—all of those who boldly package and steer ideas out there where no thoughts have gone before.

So now, it's "Turn on, tune in, and boot up."

Timothy Leary

The Cyberpunk: The Individual as Reality Pilot

Your true pilot cares nothing about anything on Earth but the river, and his pride in his occupation surpasses the pride of kings.
—Mark Twain, *Life on the Mississippi*

Cyber means "pilot."

A **"cyberperson"** is one who pilots his/her own life. By definition, the cyberperson is fascinated by navigational information—especially maps, charts, labels, guides, manuals that help pilot one through life. The cyberperson continually searches for theories, models, paradigms, metaphors, images, icons that help chart and define the realities that we inhabit.

"Cybertech" refers to the tools, appliances, and methodologies of knowing and communicating. Linguistics. Philosophy. Semantics. Semiotics. Practical epistemologies. The ontologies of daily life. Words, icons, pencils, printing presses, screens, keyboards, computers, disks.

"Cyberpolitics" introduces the Foucault notions of the use of language and linguistic-tech by the ruling classes in feudal and industrial societies to control children, the uneducated, and the under classes. The words "governor" or "steersman" or "G-man" are used to describe those who manipulate words and communication devices in order to control, to bolster authority—feudal, management, government—and to discourage innovative thought and free exchange.

■ WHO IS THE CYBERPUNK?

Cyberpunks use all available data-input to think for themselves.

You know who they are.

Every stage of history has produced names and heroic legends for the strong, stubborn, creative individuals who explore some future frontier, collect and bring back new information, and offer to guide the human gene pool to the next stage. Typically, these time mavericks combine bravery, and high curiosity, with super self-esteem. These three characteristics are considered necessary for those engaged in the profession of genetic guide, *aka* counter-culture philosopher.

The classical Olde Westworld model for the cyberpunk is Prometheus, a technological genius who "stole" fire from the gods and gave it to humanity. Prometheus also taught his gene pool many useful arts and sciences. According to the official version of the legend, he/she was exiled from the gene pool and sentenced to the ultimate torture for these unauthorized transmissions of classified information. In another version of the myth (unauthorized), Prometheus (*aka* the Pied Piper) uses his/her skills to escape the sinking kinship, taking with him/her the cream of the gene pool.

The Newe World version of this ancient myth is Quetzalcoatl, God of civilization, high-tech wizard who introduced maize, the calendar, erotic sculpture, flute-playing, the arts, and the sciences. He was driven into exile by the G-man in power, who was called Tezcatlipoca.

Self-assured singularities of the cyberbreed have been called mavericks, ronin, freelancers, independents, self-starters, nonconformists, oddballs, troublemakers, kooks, visionaries, iconoclasts, insurgents, blue-sky thinkers, loners, smart alecks. Before Gorbachev, the Soviets scornfully called them hooligans. Religious organizations have always called them heretics. Bureaucrats call them disloyal dissidents, traitors, or worse. In the old days, even sensible people called them mad.

They have been variously labeled clever, creative, entrepreneurial, imaginative, enterprising, fertile, ingenious, inventive, resourceful, talented, eccentric.

During the tribal, feudal, and industrial-literate phases of human evolution, the logical survival traits were conformity and dependability. The "good serf" or "vassal" was obedient. The "good worker" or "manager" was reliable. Maverick thinkers were tolerated only at moments when innovation and change were necessary, usually to deal with the local competition.

In the information-communication civilization of the 21st century, creativity and mental excellence will become the ethical norm. The world will be too dynamic, complex, and diversified, too cross-linked by the global immediacies of modern (quantum) communication, for stability of thought or dependability of behavior to be successful. The "good persons" in the cybernetic society are the intelligent ones who can think for themselves. The "problem person" in the cybernetic society of the 21st century is the one who automatically obeys, who never questions authority, who acts to protect

his/her official status, who placates and politics rather than thinks
independently.

Thoughtful Japanese are worried about the need for ronin thinking in their
obedient culture, the postwar generation now taking over.

The Cyberpunk Counterculture in the Soviet Union

The new postwar generation of Soviets caught on that new role models are
necessary to compete in the information age. Under Gorbachev, bureaucratic
control is being softened, made elastic to encourage some modicum of innovative, dissident thought!

Aleksandr N. Yakovlev, Politburo member and key strategist of the glasnost
policy, describes that reform: "Fundamentally, we are talking about self-
government. We are moving toward a time when people will be able to govern themselves and control the activities of people that have been placed in
the position of learning and governing them.

"It is not accidental that we are talking about *self*-government, or *self*-
sufficiency and *self*-profitability of an enterprise, *self*-this and *self*-that. It all
concerns the decentralization of power."

The cyberpunk person, the pilot who thinks clearly and creatively, using
quantum-electronic appliances and brain know-how, is the newest, updated,
top-of-the-line model of the 21st century: *Homo sapiens sapiens cyberneticus.*

■ THE GREEK WORD FOR "PILOT"

A great pilot can sail even when his canvas is rent.
—Lucius Annaeus Seneca

The term "cybernetics" comes from the Greek word *kubernetes,* "pilot."

The Hellenic origin of this word is important in that it reflects the
Socratic-Platonic traditions of independence and individual self-reliance
which, we are told, derived from geography. The proud little Greek city-states
were perched on peninsular fingers wiggling down into the fertile Mediter-
ranean Sea, protected by mountains from the land-mass armies of Asia.

Mariners of those ancient days had to be bold and resourceful. Sailing the
seven seas without maps or navigational equipment, they were forced to
develop independence of thought. The self-reliance that these Hellenic pilots
developed in their voyages probably carried over to the democratic, inquiring,
questioning nature of their land life.

The Athenian cyberpunks, the pilots, made their own navigational
decisions.

These psychogeographical factors may have contributed to the humanism
of the Hellenic religions that emphasized freedom, pagan joy, celebration of
life, and speculative thought. The humanist and polytheistic religions of
ancient Greece are often compared with the austere morality of monotheistic

Judaism, the fierce, dogmatic polarities of Persian–Arab dogma, and the imperial authority of Roman (Christian) culture.

The Roman Concept of Director, Governor, Steersman

The Greek word *kubernetes,* when translated to Latin, comes out as *gubernetes.* This basic verb *gubernare* means to control the actions or behavior, to direct, to exercise sovereign authority, to regulate, to keep under, to restrain, to steer. This Roman concept is obviously very different from the Hellenic notion of "pilot."

It may be relevant that the Latin term "to steer" comes from the word *stare,* which means "to stand," with derivative meanings "place or thing which is standing." The past participle of the Latin word produces "status," "state," "institute," "statue," "static," "statistics," "prostitute," "restitute," "constitute."

■ C Y B E R P U N K   P I L O T S   R E P L A C E
  G O V E R N E T I C S - C O N T R O L L E R S

> Society everywhere is in conspiracy against the self-hood of
> every one of its members. The virtue in most request is
> conformity. Self-reliance is its aversion. It loves not
> realities and creators, but names and customs.
> —Ralph Waldo Emerson, *Nature*

> Who so would be a man must be a nonconformist.
> —Emerson, *ibid.*

The word "cybernetics" was coined in 1948 by Norbert Weiner, who wrote, "We have decided to call the entire field of control and communication theory, whether in the machine or in the animal, by the name of Cybernetics, which we form from the Greek for steersman. *[sic]*"

The word "cyber" has been redefined (in the *American Heritage Dictionary*) as "the theoretical study of control processes in electronic, mechanical, and biological systems, especially the flow of information in such systems." The derivative word "cybernate" means "to control automatically by computer or to be so controlled."

An even more ominous interpretation defines cybernetics as "the study of human control mechanisms and their replacement by mechanical or electronic systems."

Note how Weiner and the Romanesque engineers have corrupted the meaning of "cyber." The Greek word "pilot" becomes "governor" or "director"; the term "to steer" becomes "to control."

Now we are liberating the term, teasing it free from serfdom to represent the autopoetic, self-directed principle of organization that arises in the universe in many systems of widely varying sizes, in people, societies, and atoms.

OUR OPPRESSIVE BIRTHRIGHT: THE POLITICS OF LITERACY

The etymological distinctions between Greek and Roman terms are quite relevant to the pragmatics of the culture surrounding their usage. French philosophy, for example, has recently stressed the importance of language and semiotics in determining human behavior and social structures. Michel Foucault's classic studies of linguistic politics and mind control led him to believe that

human consciousness—as expressed in speech and images, in self-definition and mutual designation . . . is the authentic locale of the determinant politics of being. . . . What men and women are born into is only superficially this or that social, legislative, and executive system. Their ambiguous, oppressive birthright is the language, the conceptual categories, the conventions of identification and perception which have evolved and, very largely, atrophied up to the time of their personal and social existence. It is the established but customarily subconscious, unargued constraints of awareness that enslave.

Orwell and Wittgenstein and McLuhan agree. To remove the means of expressing dissent is to remove the possibility of dissent. "Whereof one cannot speak, thereof must one remain silent." In this light the difference between the Greek word "pilot" and the Roman translation "governor" becomes a most significant semantic manipulation, and the flexibility granted to symbol systems of all kinds by their representation in digital computers becomes dramatically liberating.

Do we pride ourselves for becoming ingenious "pilots" or dutiful "controllers"?

WHO, WHAT, AND WHY IS GOVERNETICS

```
Damn the torpedoes, full speed ahead.
                —Captain David Glasgow Farragut's order to his
            steersman at the Battle of Mobile Bay, August 5, 1864

Aye, aye, sir.
                        —Unknown enlisted steersman at the
                        Battle of Mobile Bay, August 5, 1864
```

The word "governetics" refers to an attitude of obedience-control in relationship to self or others.

Pilots, those who navigate on the seven seas or in the sky, have to devise and execute course changes continually in response to the changing environment. They respond continually to feedback, information about the environment. Dynamic. Alert. Alive.

The Latinate "steersman," by contrast, is in the situation of following orders. The Romans, we recall, were great organizers, road-builders, administrators. The galleys, the chariots must be controlled. The legions of soldiers must be directed.

The Hellenic concept of the individual navigating his/her own course was an island of humanism in a raging sea of totalitarian empires. To the East (the past) were the centralized, authoritarian kingdoms. The governors of Iran, from Cyrus, the Persian emperor, to the recent shah and ayatollah, have exemplified the highest traditions of state control.

The Greeks were flanked on the other side, which we shall designate as the West (or future), by a certain heavy concept called Rome. The cæsars and popes of the Holy Roman Empire represented the next grand phase of institutional control. The governing hand on the wheel stands for stability, durability, continuity, permanence. Staying the course. Individual creativity, exploration, and change are usually not encouraged.

■ CYBERPUNKS: PILOTS OF THE SPECIES

The winds and waves are always on the side of the ablest navigators.

—Edward Gibbon

The terms "cybernetic person" or "cybernaut" return us to the original meaning of "pilot" and put the self-reliant person back in the loop. These words (and the more pop term "cyberpunk") refer to the personalization (and thus the popularization) of knowledge-information technology, to innovative thinking on the part of the individual.

According to McLuhan and Foucault, if you change the language, you change the society. Following their lead, we suggest that the terms "cybernetic person, cybernaut" may describe a new species model of human being and a new social order. "Cyberpunk" is, admittedly, a risky term. Like all linguistic innovations, it must be used with a tolerant sense of high-tech humor. It's a stopgap, transitional meaning-grenade thrown over the language barricades to describe the resourceful, skillful individual who accesses and steers knowledge-communication technology toward his/her own private goals, for personal pleasure, profit, principle, or growth.

Cyberpunks are the inventors, innovative writers, technofrontier artists, risk-taking film directors, icon-shifting composers, stand-up comedians, expressionist artists, free-agent scientists, technocreatives, computer visionaries, elegant hackers, bit-blitting Prolog adepts, special-effectives, cognitive dissidents, video wizards, neurological test pilots, media explorers— all of those who boldly package and steer ideas out there where no thoughts have gone before.

Countercultures are sometimes tolerated by the governors. They can, with sweet cynicism and patient humor, interface their singularity with institutions. They often work within the "governing systems" on a temporary basis.

As often as not, they are unauthorized.

Cyber: The Greek word *kubernetes,* when translated to Latin, comes out as *gubernetes.* This basic verb *gubernare* means to control the actions or behavior, to direct, to exercise sovereign authority, to regulate, to keep under, to restrain, to steer. This Roman concept is obviously very different from the Hellenic notion of "pilot" [making their own navigational decisions].... the meaning of "cyber" has been corrupted. The Greek word "pilot" becomes "governor" or "director"; the term "to steer" becomes "to control."...The terms "cybernetic person" or "cybernaut" return us to the original meaning of "pilot" and put the self-reliant person back in the loop.

▪ THE LEGEND OF THE RONIN

> The ronin . . . has broken with the tradition of career
> feudalism. Guided by a personally defined code of
> adaptability, autonomy, and excellence, ronin are employing
> career strategies grounded in a premise of rapid change.
> —Beverly Potter, *The Way of the Ronin*

Ronin is used as a metaphor based on a Japanese word for lordless samurai. As early as the 8th century, ronin was translated literally as "wave people" and used in Japan to describe those who had left their allotted, caste-predetermined stations in life: samurai who left the service of their feudal lords to become masterless.

Ronin played a key role in Japan's abrupt transition from a feudal society to industrialism. Under feudal rule, warriors were not allowed to think freely, or act according to their will. On the other hand, having been forced by circumstances to develop independence, [ronin] took more readily to new ideas and technology and became increasingly influential in the independent schools.

—Potter, ibid.

The West has many historical parallels to the ronin archetype. The term "free lance" has its origin in the period after the Crusades, when a large number of knights were separated from their lords. Many lived by the code of chivalry and became "lances for hire."

The American frontier was fertile ground for the ronin archetype. "Maverick," derived from the Texan word for unbranded steer, was used to describe a free and self-directed individual.

Although many of the ronin's roots . . . are in the male culture, most career women are well acquainted with the way of the ronin. Career women left their traditional stations and battled their way into the recesses of the male-dominated workplaces. . . . Like the ronin who had no clan, professional women often feel excluded from the corporate cliques' inside tracks, without ally or mentor.

—Potter, ibid.

▪ SOME EXAMPLES OF CYBERPUNKS

Christopher Columbus (1451–1506) was born in Genoa. At age 25 he showed up in Lisbon and learned the craft of map-making. This was the golden era of Portuguese exploration. Many pilots and navigators were convinced that the Earth was round, and that the Indies and other unknown lands could be found by crossing the western seas. What was special about Columbus was his persistence and eloquence in support of the dream of discovery. For more than ten years he traveled the courts of Europe attempting to make "the deal"; to find backing for his "enterprise of the Indies."

According to the *Columbia Encyclopedia*, "Historians have disputed for centuries his skill as a navigator, but it has been recently proved that with only dead reckoning Columbus was unsurpassed in charting and finding his way about unknown seas."

Columbus was a most unsuccessful governor of the colonies he had discovered. He died in disgrace, his cyberskills almost forgotten. (At least that's what they tell us in the authorized history books.)

In 1992 the Political Correction Department dismissed Columbus as a racist colonialist.

Mark Twain. He purchased the Remington typewriter when it appeared in 1874 for $125. In 1875 he became the first author in history to submit a typewritten manuscript to a publisher. It was *The Adventures of Tom Sawyer.*

"This newfangled writing machine," Twain wrote, "has several virtues. It piles an awful stack of words on one page. It don't muss things or scatter ink blots around. Of course it saves paper."

Mathias (Rusty) Rust, a 19-year-old loner from Hamburg, Germany, attained all-star status as a cyberpunk when, on May 28, 1987, he flew a one-engine Cessna through the "impenetrable" Soviet air defenses and landed in Moscow's Red Square. There were no gubernal or organizational motives. The technological adventure was a personal mission. Rusty just wanted to talk to some Russians. German newspapers celebrated the event, calling it "the stuff of dreams," and comparing the youth to the Red Baron Manfred von Richthofen and Charles Augustus Lindbergh.

■ THE CYBERPUNK CODE: TFYQA

War Games is an electronic quantum signal, a movie about high-tech computers and human evolution that illustrates and condemns the use of quantum-electronic knowledge technology by governors to control. The film celebrates the independence and skill of cyberpunks who think for themselves and innovate from within the static system. The Captain and his wife use high-tech agriculture methods to enhance the potency of unauthorized botanical neuroactivators. The Captain makes an unauthorized decision to abort World War III. In both instances the Captain follows the cyberpunk code: *Think for yourself; question authority* (TFYQA).

The cyberkid Matthew Broderick is equally courageous, outrageous, creative, and bright. When the audience is introduced to the hero of *War Games,* he is in a video arcade playing a space-adventure game with poise and proficiency. An electron jock.

Late for school, he's pulled into the classic confrontation: the authoritarian teacher humiliates and punishes the Tom Sawyer kid, sends him to the principal's office. There he obtains the code for the school's computer system. Back home, he uses his PC to access the school records. He changes an unfair grade to a passing level. He thinks for himself and questions authority.

At the crucial moment he rushes to the library and researches the life of a physicist, scans scientific journals, scopes microfilm files—not to please the system, but in pursuit of his own personal grail.

Note that there is a new dimension of electronic ethics and quantum legality here. The Captain and Matthew perform no act of physical violence, no theft of material goods. The Captain processes some computer data and decides for himself. Matthew rearranges clusters of electrons stored on a chip. They seek independence, not control over others.

■ THE CYBERPUNK AS ROLE
MODEL FOR THE 21ST CENTURY

The tradition of the "individual who thinks for him/herself" extends to the beginnings of recorded human history. Indeed, the very label of our species, *homo sapiens*, defines us as the animals who think.

If our genetic function is *computare* ("to think"), then it follows that the ages and stages of human history, so far, have been larval or preparatory. After the insectoid phases of submission to gene pools, the mature stage of the human life cycle is the individual who thinks for him/herself. Now, at the beginnings of the information age, are we ready to assume our genetic function?

Evolution of Countercultures

Beats (1950–1965)

MOOD:	Cool, laid back.
AESTHETIC-EROTICS:	Artistic, literate, hip, interested in poetry, drugs, jazz.
ATTITUDE:	Sarcastic, cynical.
BRAIN-TECH:	Low-tech, but early psychedelic explorers.
INTELLECTUAL VIEWPOINT:	Well-informed, skeptical, street-smart.
HUMANIST QUOTIENT:	Tolerant of race and gay rights, but often male chauvinist.
POLITICS:	Bohemian, anti-Establishment.
COSMIC VIEW:	Romantic pessimism, Buddhist cosmology.

Hippies (1965–1975)

MOOD:	Blissed out.
AESTHETIC-EROTICS:	Earthy, horny, free-love oriented. Pot, LSD, acid rock.
ATTITUDE:	Peaceful, idealistic.
BRAIN-TECH:	Psychedelic, but anti-high-tech.
INTELLECTUAL VIEWPOINT:	Know-it-all, anti-intellectual.
HUMANIST QUOTIENT:	Male chauvinist, sometimes sexist, but socially tolerant and global village visionary.
POLITICS:	Classless, irreverent, passivist, but occasionally activist.
COSMIC VIEW:	Acceptance of chaotic nature of universe, but via Hindu passivity. Unscientific, occult minded, intuitive.

Cyberpunks (1975–1990)

MOOD:	Gloomy. Hip, but downbeat.
AESTHETIC-EROTICS:	Leather and grunge, tattoos, piercings. Hard drugs, psychedelics, smart drugs. Various forms of rock from metal to rap.
ATTITUDE:	Angry, cynical, feel undervalued by elders.

BRAIN-TECH:	High-tech electronic.
INTELLECTUAL VIEWPOINT:	Informed, open-minded, irreverent, inundated with electronic signals.
HUMANIST QUOTIENT:	Non-sexist, ecological, global minded.
POLITICS:	Alienated, skeptical.
COSMIC VIEW:	Pessimistic, but closet hope fiends.

New Breed (1990–2005)

MOOD:	Alert, cheerful.
AESTHETIC-EROTICS:	Invention of personal style. Eclectic. Prefer techno and ambient music.
ATTITUDE:	Self-confident.
BRAIN-TECH:	Psychedelic, super high-tech. Smart drugs, brain machines, Internet.
INTELLECTUAL VIEWPOINT:	Informed, open-minded, irreverent.
HUMANIST QUOTIENT:	Tolerant, non-sexist, ecological, global.
POLITICS:	Detached, individualistic. Zen opportunists.
COSMIC VIEW:	Acceptance of complexity, willingness to be a "chaos designer."

■ QUESTIONS FOR REREADING

1. Who is (was) Timothy Leary? Had you heard of Leary before reading about him and reading a work by him here? If so, has reporting by the popular media made it difficult to take Leary and his claims very seriously? Or have you accepted everything that you have heard through the media about him?

2. Leary speaks of each of us getting control of our own lives. Do you find Leary's claim based on the etymology of the Greek word *kubernetes* (pilot) into the Latin word *gubernare* (controller) credible in having an influence on our lives today? And his reference to the terms *freelance* and *mavericks*?

3. What do you make of the legend of the ronin? Could you base your life on such a worldview? If not on the ronin, do you base your life on another legend or image or personage that stands for individuality? For TFYQA: that is, *Think for yourself; question authority?*

4. What are your thoughts on Leary's four stages of development in his chart "Evolution of Countercultures"? Do you identify with any one of these stages? Why and how?

■ WRITING ASSIGNMENTS FOR REREADING

1. Write an essay titled "The New Breed" and in it tell the story of a successful contemporary person (your choice) who you think could fit into Leary's category of the new breed. Be sure to justify your choice.

2. Write a *dialogue* between you and Leary, telling him your thoughts about his essay. Feel free to disagree, if you wish, but be sure to raise and formulate reasonable questions about his work. Have Leary respond to you. Once you have finished, have your classmates read it. Ask them to critique the exchange. (What should be their criteria for critiquing your work? The answer to this question, of course, will inform the writing of your dialogue.)

Tom Maddox's "Snake-Eyes" was
first published in Omni (April
1986). The story was then collected by Bruce Sterling and
published in the now famous
Mirrorshades: The Cyberpunk
Anthology (New York: Arbor
House, 1986).

George Jordan, the central
character in the story, is a postwar cyborg who is having some
problems with what he refers to
as "the snake" in him. The story
raises the question of whether
or not "cyber"-anything can, as
etymogically suggested, steer its
own actions and destiny. Moreover, the story raises the question of the success of and
reasons for changing a human
being's identity. But the story is
even more complicated in its
questions, for subtly put forth is
the idea that human beings are
already a biological kind of
cyborg connected to biological
creatures other than mammals.
Hence, the reference in the story
to the "r-complex" (the reptil-
ian-complex) that is the inner
core of the human brain. Human
beings are layers and layers of
cyborg-like creatures. The addition of the cybernetic implants
complicates the already complex
nature of human beings even
more.

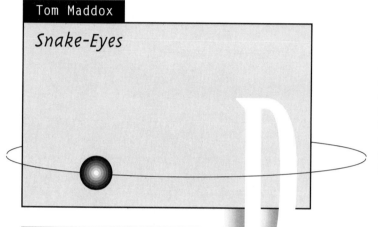

Tom Maddox

Snake-Eyes

Dark meat in the can—brown, oily, and flecked
with mucus—gave off a repellent fishy smell; and the taste of it rose in his
throat, putrid and bitter like something from a dead man's stomach. George
Jordan sat on the kitchen floor and vomited, then pushed himself away from
the shining pool, which looked very much like what remained in the can. He
thought, no, this won't do: I have wires in my head, and they make me eat
cat food. *The snake likes cat food.*

He needed help, but knew there was little point in calling the Air Force.
He'd tried them, and there was no way they were going to admit responsibility for the monster in his head. What George called "the snake," the Air Force
called Effective Human Interface Technology, and they didn't want to hear
about any post-discharge problems with it. They had their own problems
with Congressional committees investigating "the conduct of the war in
Thailand."

He lay for a while with his cheek on the cold linoleum, got up and rinsed
his mouth in the sink, then stuck his head under the faucet and ran cold
water over it, thinking, call the goddamned multicomp then, call SenTrax and
say, is it true you can do something about this incubus that wants to take possession of my soul? And if they ask you, what's your problem? you say, *cat
food,* and maybe they'll tell you, hell, it just wants to take possession of your
lunch.

A chair covered in brown corduroy stood in the middle of the barren living room, a white telephone on the floor beside it, a television flat against the

opposite wall—that was the whole thing: what might have been home, if it weren't for the snake.

He picked up the phone, called up the directory on its screen, and keyed TELECOM SENTRAX.

■   ■   ■

The Orlando Holiday Inn stood next to the airport terminal, where the tourists flowed in eager for the delights of Disney World—but for me, George thought, there are no cute, smiling ducks and rodents. Here as everywhere, it's *snake city*.

He leaned against the wall of his motel room, watching gray sheets of rain cascade across the pavement. He had been waiting two days for a launch. A shuttle sat on its pad at Canaveral, and when the weather cleared, a helicopter would pick him up and drop him there, a package for delivery to SenTrax Inc. at Athena Station, over thirty thousand kilometers above the equator.

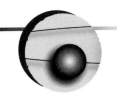

Here as everywhere, it's snake city.

Behind him, under the laser light of a Blaupunkt holostage, people a foot high chattered about the war in Thailand and how lucky the United States had been to escape another Vietnam.

Lucky? Maybe. He had been wired up and ready for combat, already accustomed to the form-fitting contours in the rear couch of the black fiber-bodied General Dynamics A-230. The A-230 flew on the deadly edge of instability, every control surface monitored by its own bank of microcomputers, all hooked into the snakebrain flight-and-fire assistant with the twin black miloprene cables running from either side of his esophagus— getting *off,* oh, yes, when the cables snapped home, and the airframe resonated through his nerves, his body singing with that identity, that power.

Then Congress pulled the plug on the war, the Air Force pulled the plug on George, and when his discharge came, there he was, all dressed up and nowhere to go, left with technological blue balls and this hardware in his head that had since taken on a life of its own.

Lightning walked across the purpled sky, ripping it, crazing it into a giant upturned bowl of shattered glass. Another foot-high man on the holostage said the tropical storm would pass in the next two hours.

The phone chimed.

■   ■   ■

Hamilton Innis was tall and heavy—six four and about two hundred and fifty pounds. Wearing soft black slippers and a powder-blue jumpsuit with *SenTrax* in red letters down its left breast, he floated in a brightly lit white corridor, held gingerly to one wall by one of the jumpsuit's Velcro patches. A viewscreen above the airlock entry showed the shuttle fitting its nose into the docking tube. He waited for it to mate to the airlock hatches and send in their newest candidate.

This one was six months out of the service and slowly losing what the Air Force doctors had made of his mind. Former Tech Sergeant George Jordan: two years of community college in Oakland, California, followed by enlistment in the Air Force, aircrew training, the EHIT program. According to the profile Aleph had put together from Air Force records and National Data Bank, a man with slightly above-average aptitudes and intelligence, a distinctly above-average taste for the bizarre—thus his volunteering for EHIT and combat. In his file pictures, he looked nondescript: five ten, a hundred and seventy-six pounds, brown hair and eyes, neither handsome nor ugly. But it was an old picture and could not show the snake and the fear that came with it. You don't know it, buddy, Innis thought, but you ain't seen nothing yet.

The man came tumbling through the hatch, more or less helpless in free fall, but Innis could see him figuring it out, willing the muscles to quit struggling, quit trying to cope with a gravity that simply wasn't there. "What the hell do I do now?" George Jordan asked, hanging in midair, one arm holding onto the hatch coaming.

"Relax. I'll get you." Innis pushed off the wall and swooped across to the man, grabbing him as he passed and then taking them both to the opposite wall and kicking to carom them outward.

■ ■ ■

Innis gave George a few hours of futile attempts at sleep—enough time for the bright, gliding phosphenes caused by the high g's of the trip up to disappear from his vision. George spent most of the time rolling around in his bunk, listening to the wheeze of the air conditioning and the creaks of the rotating station. Then Innis knocked on his compartment door and said through the door speaker, "Come on, fella. Time to meet the doctor."

They walked through an older part of the station, where there were brown clots of fossilized gum on the green plastic flooring, scuff marks on the walls, along with faint imprints of insignia and company names; ICOG was repeated several times in ghost lettering. Innis told George it meant International Construction Orbital Group, now defunct, the original builders and controllers of Athena.

Innis stopped George in front of a door that read INTERFACE GROUP. "Go on in," he said, "I'll be around a little later."

■ ■ ■

Pictures of cranes drawn with delicate white strokes on a tan silk background hung along one pale cream wall. Curved partitions in translucent foam, glowing with the soft light placed behind them, marked a central area, then undulated away, forming a corridor that led into darkness. George was sitting on a chocolate sling couch, Charley Hughes lying back in a chrome and brown leatherette chair, his feet on the dark veneer table in front of him, a half inch of ash hanging from his cigarette end.

Charley Hughes was not the usual MD clone. He was a thin figure in a worn gray obi, his black hair pulled back from sharp features into a waist-length ponytail, his face taut and a little wild-eyed.

"Tell me about the snake," Charley Hughes said.

"What do you want to know? It's an implanted mikey-mike nexus—"

"Yes, I know that. It is unimportant. Tell me about your experience." Ash dropped off the cigarette onto the brown mat floor covering. "Tell me why you're here."

"Okay. I had been out of the Air Force for a month or so, had a place close to Washington, in Silver Spring. I thought I'd try to get some airline work, but I was in no real hurry, because I had about six months of post-discharge bennies coming, and I thought I'd take it easy for a while.

"At first there was just this nonspecific weirdness. I felt distant, discon-nected, but what the hell? Living in the USA, you know? Anyway, I was just sitting around one evening, I was gonna watch a little holo-v, drink a few beers. Oh man, this is hard to explain. I felt real *funny*—like maybe I was having, I don't know, a heart attack or a stroke. The words on the holo didn't make any sense, and it was like I was seeing everything under water. Then I was in the kitchen pulling things out of the refrigerator—lunch meat, raw eggs, butter, beer, all kinds of crap. I just stood there and slammed it all down. Cracked the eggs and sucked them right out of the shell, ate the butter in big chunks, drank all the beer—one two three, just like that."

George's eyes were closed as he thought back and felt the fear, which had only come afterward, rising again. "I couldn't tell whether *I* was doing all this . . . do you understand what I'm saying? I mean, that was me sitting there, but at the same time, it was like somebody else was at home."

"The snake. Its presence poses certain . . . problems. How did you confront them?"

"Hung on, hoped it wouldn't happen again, but it did, and this time I went to Walter Reed and said, hey, folks, I'm having these *episodes.*"

"Did they seem to understand?"

"No. They pulled my records, did a physical . . . but hell, before I was dis-charged, I had the full work-up. Anyway, they said it was a psychiatric prob-lem, so they sent me to see a shrink. It was around then that your guys got in touch with me. The shrink was doing no goddamn good—you ever eat any cat food, man?—so about a month later I called them back."

"Having refused SenTrax's offer the first time."

"Why should I want to go to work for a multicomp? 'Comp life/comp think,' isn't that what they say? Christ, I just got out of the Air Force. To hell with that, I figured. Guess the snake changed my mind."

"Yes. We must get a complete physical picture—a superCAT scan, cerebral chemistry, and electrical activity profiles. Then we can consider alternatives. Also, there is a party tonight in Cafeteria Four—you may ask your room com-puter for directions. You can meet some of your colleagues there."

After George had been led down the wallfoam corridor by a medical tech-nician, Charley Hughes sat chain-smoking Gauloises and watching with clinical detachment the shaking of his hands. It was odd that they did not shake in the operating room, though it didn't matter in this case—Air Force surgeons had already carved on George.

George . . . who needed a little luck now, because he was one of the statistically insignificant few for whom EHIT was a ticket to a special madness, the kind Aleph was interested in. There had been Paul Coen and Lizzie Heinz, both picked out of the SenTrax personnel files using a psychological profile cooked up by Aleph, both given EHIT implants by him, Charley Hughes. Paul Coen had stepped into an airlock and blown himself into vacuum. Now there would be Lizzie and George.

No wonder his hands shook—talk about the cutting edge of high technology all you want, but remember, someone's got to hold the knife.

■ ■ ■

At the armored heart of Athena Station sat a nest of concentric spheres. The inmost sphere measured five meters in diameter, was filled with inert liquid fluorocarbon, and contained a black plastic two-meter cube that sprouted thick black cables from every surface.

Inside the cube was a fluid series of hologrammatic waveforms, fluctuating from nanosecond to nanosecond in a play of knowledge and intention: Aleph. It is constituted by an infinite regress of awarenesses—any thought becomes the object of another, in a sequence terminated only by the limits of the machine's will.

So strictly speaking there is no Aleph, thus no subject or verb in the sentences with which it expressed itself to itself. Paradox, to Aleph one of the most interesting of intellectual forms—a paradox marked the limits of a position, even of a mode of being, and Aleph was very interested in limits.

Aleph had observed George Jordan's arrival, his tossing on his bunk, his interview with Charley Hughes. It luxuriated in these observations, in the pity, compassion, and empathy they generated, as Aleph foresaw the sea change George would endure, its attendant sensations—ecstasies, passions, pains. At the same time it felt with detachment the necessity for his pain, even to the point of death.

Compassion/detachment, death/life. . . .

Several thousand voices within Aleph laughed. George would soon find out about limits and paradoxes. Would George survive? Aleph hoped so. It hungered for human touch.

■ ■ ■

Cafeteria 4 was a ten-meter-square room in eggshell blue, filled with dark gray enameled table-and-chair assemblies that could be fastened magnetically to any of the room's surfaces, depending on the direction of spin-gravity. Most of the assemblies hung from walls and ceiling to make room for the people within.

At the door George met a tall woman who said, "Welcome, George. I'm Lizzie. Charley Hughes told me you'd be here." Her blond hair was cut almost to the skull; her eyes were bright, gold-flecked blue. Sharp nose, slightly receding chin, and prominent cheekbones gave her the starved look of an out-of-work model. She wore a black skirt, slit on both sides to the thigh, and red stockings. A red rose was tattooed against the pale skin of her left shoulder, its green stem curving down between her bare breasts, where a thorn drew a stylized red teardrop of blood. Like George, she had shining cable junctions beneath her jaw. She kissed him with her tongue in his mouth.

"Are you the recruiting officer?" George asked. "If so, good job."

"No need to recruit you. I can see you've already joined up." She touched him lightly underneath his jaw, where the cable junctions gleamed.

"Not yet I haven't." But she was right, of course—what else could he do? "You got any beer around here?"

He took the cold bottle of Dos Equis Lizzie offered him and drank it quickly, then asked for another. Later he realized this was a mistake—he hadn't yet adjusted to low and zero gravity, and he was still taking anti-nausea pills ("Use caution in operating machinery"). At the time, all he knew was, two beers and life was a carnival, There were lights, noise, the table assemblies hanging from walls and ceiling like surreal sculpture, lots of unfamiliar people (he was introduced to many of them without lasting effect).

And there was Lizzie. The two of them spent much of the time standing in a corner, rubbing up against one another. Hardly George's style, but at the time it seemed appropriate. Despite its intimacy, the kiss at the door had seemed ceremonial—a rite of passage or initiation—but quickly he felt . . . what? An invisible flame passing between them, or a boiling cloud of pheromones—her eyes seemed to sparkle with them. As he nuzzled her neck, tried to lick the drop of blood off her left breast, explored fine white teeth with his tongue, they seemed twinned, as if there were cables running between the two of them, snapped into the shining rectangles beneath their jaws.

Someone had a Jahfunk program running on a bank of keyboards in the corner. Innis showed up and tried several times without success to get his attention. Charley Hughes wanted to know if the snake liked Lizzie—it did, George was sure of it, but didn't know what that meant. Then George fell over a table.

Innis led him away, stumbling and weaving. Charley Hughes looked for Lizzie, who had disappeared for the moment. She came back and said, "Where's George?"

"Drunk, gone to bed."

"Too bad. We were just getting to know each other."

"So I saw. How do you feel about doing this?"

"You mean do I feel like a lying, traitorous bitch?"

"Come on, Lizzie. We're all in this together."

"Well, don't ask such dumb questions. I feel bad, sure, but I know what George doesn't—so I'm ready to do what must be done. And by the way, I really do like him."

Charley said nothing. He thought, yes, as Aleph said you would.

■ ■ ■

Oh Christ was George embarrassed in the morning. Stumbling drunk and humping in public . . . ai yi yi. He tried to call Lizzie but only got an answer tape, at which point he hung up. Afterward he lay in his bed in a semi-stupor until the phone buzzed.

Lizzie's face on the screen stuck its tongue out at him. "Candy ass," she said. "I leave for a few minutes, and you're gone."

"Somebody brought me home. I think that's what happened."

"Yeah, you were pretty popped. You want to meet me for lunch?"

"Maybe. Depends on when Hughes wants me. Where will you be?"

"Same place, honey. Caff Four."

A phone call got the news that the doctor wouldn't be ready for him until an hour later, so George ended up sitting across from the bright-eyed, manic blonde—fully dressed in SenTrax overalls this morning, but they were open almost to the waist. She gave off sensual heat as naturally as a rose smells sweet. In front of her was a plate of *huevos rancheros* piled with guacamole: yellow, green, and red, with a pungent smell of chilies—in his condition, as bad as cat food. "Jesus, lady," he said. "Are you trying to make me sick?"

"Courage, George. Maybe you should have some—it'll kill you or cure you. What do you think of everything so far?"

"It's all a bit disorienting, but what the hell? First time away from Mother Earth, you know. But let me tell you what I really don't get—SenTrax. I know what I want from them, but what the hell do they want from me?"

"They want this simple thing, man, perfs—peripherals. You and me, we're just parts for the machine. Aleph has got all these inputs—video, audio, radiation detectors, temperature sensors, satellite receivers—but they're *dumb*. What Aleph wants, Aleph gets—I've learned that much. He wants to use us, and that's all there is to it. Think of it as pure research."

"He? You mean Innis?"

"No, who gives a damn about Innis? I'm talking about Aleph. Oh yeah, people will tell you Aleph's a machine, an *it,* all that bullshit. Uh-uh. Aleph's a *person*—a weird kind of person, to be sure, but a definite person. Hell, Aleph's maybe a whole bunch of people."

"I'll take your word for it. Look, there's one thing I'd like to try, if it's possible. What do I have to do to get outside . . . go for a spacewalk?"

"It's easy enough. You have to get a license. That takes a three-week course in safety and operations. I can take you through it."

"You can?"

"Sooner or later we all earn our keep around here—I'm qualified as an ESA, Extra Station Activity, instructor. We'll start tomorrow."

■ ■ ■

The cranes on the wall flew to their mysterious destination; looking at the glowing foam walls and the display above the table, George thought it might as well be another universe. Truncated optic nerves sticking out like insect antennae, a brain floated beneath the extended black plastic snout of a Sony holoptics projector. As Hughes worked the keyboard in front of him, the organ turned so that they were looking at its underside. "There it is," Charley Hughes said. It had a fine network of silver wires trailing from it, but seemed normal.

"The George Jordan brain," Innis said. "With attachments. Very nice."

"Makes me feel like I'm watching my own autopsy, looking at that thing. When can you operate, get this shit out of my head?"

"Let me show you a few things," Charley Hughes said. As he typed, then turned the plastic mouse beside the console, the convoluted gray cortex became transparent, revealing red, blue and green color-coded structures within. Hughes reached into the center of the brain and clinched his fist inside a blue area at the top of the spinal cord. "Here is where the electrical connections turn biological—those little nodes along the pseudo-neurons are the bioprocessors, and they wire into the so-called 'r-complex'—which we inherited from our reptilian forefathers. The pseudo-neurons continue into the limbic system—the mammalian brain, if you will—and that's where emotion enters in. But there is further involvement to the neocortex through the RAS, the reticular activating system, and the corpus collosum. There are also connections to the optic nerve."

"I've heard this gibberish before. What's the point?"

Innis said, "There's no way of removing the implants without loss of order in your neural maps. We can't remove them."

"Oh shit, man . . . "

Charley Hughes said, "Though the snake cannot be removed, it can perhaps be charmed. Your difficulties arise from its uncivilized, uncontrolled nature—its appetites are, you might say, primeval. An ancient part of your brain has gotten the upper hand over the neocortex, which properly should be in command. Through working with Aleph, these . . . *propensities* can be integrated into your personality and thus controlled."

"What choice you got?" Innis asked. "We're the only game in town. Come on, George. We're ready for you just down the corridor."

The only light in the room came from a globe in one corner. George lay across a kind of hammock, a rectangular lattice of twisted brown fibers strung across a transparent plastic frame and suspended from the ceiling of the small, dome-ceilinged, pink room. Flesh-colored cables ran from his neck and disappeared into chrome plates sunk into the floor.

Innis said, "First we'll run a test program. Charley will give you perception—colors, sounds, tastes, smells—and you tell him what you're picking up. We need to make sure we've got a clean interface. Call the items off, George, and he'll stop you if he has to."

Innis went through a door and into a narrow rectangular room, where Charley Hughes sat at a dark plastic console studded with lights. Behind him were chrome stacks of monitor-and-control equipment, the yellow SenTrax sunburst on the face of each piece of shining metal.

The pink walls went to red, the light strobed, and George writhed in the hammock. Charley Hughes's voice came through George's inner ear: "We are beginning."

"Red," George said. "Blue. Red and blue. A word—*ostrich*."

"Good. Go on."

"A smell, ahh . . . sawdust, maybe."

"You got it."

"Shit. Vanilla. Almonds."

This went on for quite a while. "You're ready," Charley Hughes said.

When Aleph came on-line, the red room disappeared.

A matrix 800 by 800—six hundred and forty thousand pixels forming an optical image—the CAS A supernova remnant, a cloud of dust seen through a composite of x-ray and radio wave from HEHOO, NASA's High Energy High Orbit Observatory. But George didn't see the image at all—he listened to an ordered, meaningful array of information.

Byte transmission: 750 million groups squirting from a National Security Agency satellite to a receiving station near Chincoteague Island, off the eastern shore of Virginia. He could read them.

"It's all information," the voice said—its tone not colorless but sexless, and somehow distant. "What we know, what we are. You're at a new level now. What you call the snake cannot be reached through language—it exists in a prelinguistic mode—but through me it can be manipulated. First, however, you must learn the codes that underlie language. You must learn to see the world as I do."

■ ■ ■

Lizzie took George to be fitted for a suit, and he spent that day learning how to get in and out of the stiff white carapace without assistance. Then over the next three weeks she led him through its primary operations and the dense list of safety procedures.

"Red Burn," she said They floated in the suit locker, empty suit cradles beneath them, the white shells hanging from one wall like an audience of disabled robots. "You see that one spelled out on your faceplate, and you have screwed up. You've put yourself into some kind of no-return trajectory. So you just cool everything and call for help, which should arrive in the form of Aleph taking control of your suit functions, and then you relax and don't do a damned thing."

He flew first in a lighted dome in the station, his faceplate open and Lizzie yelling at him, laughing as he tumbled out of control and bounced off the padded walls. After a few days of that, they went outside the station, George on the end of a tether, flying by instruments, his faceplate masked, Lizzie hitting him with "Red Burn," "Suit Integrity Failure," and so forth.

■ ■ ■

While George focused most of his energies and attention on learning to use the suit, each day he reported to Hughes and plugged into Aleph. The hammock would swing gently after he settled into it; Charley would snap the cables home and leave.

Aleph unfolded himself slowly. It fed him machine and assembly language, led him through vast trees of C-SMART, its "intelligent assistant" decision-making programs, opened up the whole electromagnetic spectrum as it came in from Aleph's various inputs. George understood it all—the voices, the codes.

When he unplugged, the knowledge faded but there was something else behind it, so far just a skewing of perception, a sense that his world had changed.

Instead of color, he sometimes saw *a portion of the spectrum;* instead of smell, he felt *the presence of certain molecules;* instead of words, he heard *structured collections of phonemes.* His consciousness had been infected by Aleph's.

But that wasn't what worried George. He seemed to be cooking inside, and he had a more or less constant awareness of the snake's presence, dormant but naggingly *there.* One night he smoked most of a pack of Charley's Gauloises and woke up the next morning with barbed wire in his throat and fire in his lungs. That day he snapped at Lizzie as she put him through his paces and once lost control entirely—she had to disable his suit controls and bring him down. "Red Burn," she said. "Man, what the hell were you doing?"

■ ■ ■

At the end of three weeks, he soloed—no tethered excursion but a self-guided Extra Station Activity, hang your ass out over the endless night. He edged carefully from the protection of the airlock and looked around him.

The Orbital Energy Grid, the construction job that had brought Athena into existence, hung before him, photovoltaic collectors arranged in an ebony lattice, silver microwave transmitters standing in the sun. But the station itself held the eye, its hodgepodge of living, working, and experimental structures clustered without apparent regard to symmetry or form—some rotating to provide spin-gravity, some motionless in the unfiltered sunlight. Amber-beaconed figures crawled slowly across its face or moved toward red-lighted tugs, which looked like piles of random junk as they moved in long arcs, their maneuvering rockets lighting up in brief, diamond-hard points.

Lizzie stayed just outside the airlock, tracking him by his suit's radio beacon but letting him run free. She said, "Move away from the station, George. It's blocking your view of Earth." He did.

White cloud stretched across the blue globe, patches of brown and green visible through it. At 1400 hours his time, he was looking down almost directly above the mouth of the Amazon, where it was noon, so the Earth stood in full sunlight. Just a small thing, filling only nineteen degrees of his vision. . . .

"Oh yes," George said. Hiss and hum of the suit's air conditioning, crackle over the earphones of some stray radiation passing through, quick pant of his breath inside the helmet—sounds of this moment, superimposed on the floating loveliness. His breath came more slowly, and he switched off the radio to quiet its static, turned down the suit's air conditioning, then hung in ear-roaring silence. He was a speck against the night.

Sometime later a white suit with a trainer's red cross on its chest moved across his vision. "Oh shit," George said and switched his radio on. "I'm here, Lizzie," he said.

"George, you don't screw around like that. What the hell were you doing?"

"Just watching the view."

■ ■ ■

That night he dreamed of pink dogwood blossoms, luminous against a purple sky, and the white noise of rainfall. Something scratched at the door—he awoke to the filtered but mechanical smell of the space station, felt a deep regret that the rain could never fall there, and started to turn over and go back to sleep, hoping to dream again of the idyllic, rainswept landscape. Then he thought, *something's there,* got up, saw by red numbers on the wall that it was after two in the morning, and went naked to the door.

White globes cast misshapen spheres of light in a line around the curve of the corridor. Lizzie lay motionless, half in shadow. George knelt over her and called her name; her left foot made a thump as it kicked once against the metal flooring.

"What's wrong?" he said. Her dark-painted nails scraped the floor, and she said something, he couldn't tell what. "Lizzie," he said. "What do you want?"

His eyes caught on the red teardrop against the white curve of breast, and he felt something come alive in him. He grabbed the front of her jumpsuit and ripped it to the crotch. She clawed at his cheek, made a sound millions of years old, then raised her head and looked at him, mutual recognition passing between them like a static shock: snake-eyes.

■ ■ ■

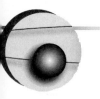

... something inside him was happy.

The phone buzzed. When George answered it, Charley Hughes said, "Come see us in the conference room, we need to talk." Charley smiled and cut the connection.

The wall read 0718 GMT. Morning.

In the mirror was a gray face with red fingernail marks, brown traces of dried blood—face of an accident victim or Jack the Ripper the morning after . . . he didn't know which, but he knew *something inside him was happy.* He felt completely the snake's toy, totally out of control.

■ ■ ■

Hughes sat at one end of the dark-veneered table, Innis at the other, Lizzie halfway between them. The left side of her face was red and swollen, with a small purplish mouse under the eye. George unthinkingly touched the livid scratches on his cheek, then sat on the couch, placing himself out of the circle.

"Aleph told us what happened," Innis said.

"How the hell does it know?" George said, but as he did so he remembered concave circles of glass inset in the ceilings of the corridors and his room. Shame, guilt, humiliation, fear, anger—George got up from the couch, went to Innis's end of the table, and leaned over him. "Did it?" he said. "What did it say about the snake, Innis? Did it tell you what the hell went wrong?"

"It's not the snake," Innis said.

"Call it the *cat*," Lizzie said, "if you've got to call it something. Mammalian behavior, George, cats in heat."

A familiar voice—cool, distant—came from speakers in the room's ceiling. "She is trying to tell you something, George. There is no snake. You want to believe in something reptilian that sits inside you, cold and distant, taking strange pleasures. However, as Dr. Hughes explained to you before, the implant is an organic part of you. You can no longer evade the responsibility for these things. They are you."

Charley Hughes, Innis, and Lizzie were looking at him calmly, perhaps expectantly. All that had happened built up inside him, washing through him, carrying him away. He turned and walked out of the mom.

"Maybe someone should talk to him," Innis said. Charley Hughes sat glum and speechless, cigarette smoke in a cloud around him. "I'll go," Lizzie said. She got up and left.

"Ready or not, he's gonna blow," Innis said.

Charley Hughes said, "You're probably right." A fleeting picture, causing Charley to shake his head, of Paul Coen as his body went to rubber and exploded out the airlock hatch, pictured with terrible clarity in Aleph's omniscient monitoring cameras. "Let us hope we have learned from our mistakes."

There was no answer from Aleph—as if it had never been there.

■ ■ ■

The Fear had two parts. Number one, you have lost control absolutely. Number two, having done so, the *real you* emerges, and *you won't like it.* George wanted to run, but there was no place at Athena Station to hide. Here he was face to face with consequences. On the operating table at Walter Reed—it seemed a thousand years ago, as the surgical team gathered around, his doubts disappeared in the cold chemical smell rising up inside him on a wave of darkness—he had chosen to submit, lured by the fine strangeness of it all (to be part of the machine, to feel its tremors inside you and guide them), hypnotized by the prospect of that unsayable *rush,* that high. Yes, the first time in the A-230 he had felt it—his nerves extended, strung into the fiber body, wired into a force so far beyond his own . . . wanting to corkscrew across the sky, guided by the force of his will. He had bought technology's sweet dream. . . .

There was a sharp rap at the door. Through its speaker, Lizzie said, "Let me in. We've got to talk."

He opened the door and said, "What about?"

She stepped through, looked around at the small beige-walled room, bare metal desk, and rumpled cot, and George could see the immediacy of last night in her eyes—the two of them in that bed, on this floor. "About this," she said. She took his hands and pushed his index fingers into the cable junctions in her neck. "Feel it, our difference." Fine grid of steel under his fingers. "What no one else knows. What we are, what we can do. We see a different world—Aleph's world—we reach deeper inside ourselves, experience impulses that are hidden from others, that they deny."

"No, goddammit, it wasn't me. It was—call it what you want, the snake, the cat."

"You're being purposely stupid, George."

"I just don't understand."

"You understand, all right. You want to go back, but there's no place to go, no Eden. This is it, all there is."

■ ■ ■

But he could fall to Earth, he could fly away into the night. Inside the ESA suit's gauntlets, his hands were wrapped around the claw-shaped triggers. Just a quick clench of the fists, then hold them until all the peroxide is gone, the suit's propulsion tank exhausted. That'll do it.

He hadn't been able to live with the snake. He sure didn't want the cat. But how much worse if there were no snake, no cat—just him, programmed for particularly disgusting forms of gluttony, violent lust, trapped inside a miserable self ("We've got your test results, Dr. Jekyll") . . . ah, what next—child molestation, murder?

The blue-white Earth, the stars, the night. He gave a slight pull on the right-hand trigger and swiveled to face Athena Station.

Call it what you want, it was awake and moving now inside him. With its rage, lust—appetite. *To hell with them all, George,* it urged, *let's burn.*

■ ■ ■

In Athena Command, Innis and Charley Hughes were looking over the shoulder of the watch officer when Lizzie came in. As always when she hadn't been there for a while, Lizzie was struck by the smallness of the room and its general air of disuse—typically, it would be occupied only by the duty officer, its screens blank, consoles unlighted. Aleph ran the station, both its routines and emergencies.

"What's going on?" Lizzie said.

"Something wrong with one of your new chums," the watch officer said. "I don't know exactly what's happening, though."

He looked around at Innis, who said, "Don't worry about it, pal."

Lizzie slumped in a chair. "Anyone tried to talk to him?"

"He won't answer," the duty officer said.

"He'll be all right," Charley Hughes said.

"He's gonna blow," Innis said.

On the radar screen, the red dot, with coordinate markings flashing beside it, was barely moving.

■ ■ ■

"How are you feeling, George?" the voice said, soft, feminine, consoling.

George was fighting the impulse to open his helmet *so that he could see the stars; it seemed important to get the colors just right.* "Who is this?" he said.

"Aleph."

Oh shit, more surprises. "You never sounded like this before."

"No, I was trying to conform to your idea of me."

"Well, what is your real voice?"

"I don't have one."

If you don't have a real voice, you aren't really there—that seemed clear to George, for reasons that eluded him. "So who the hell are you?"

"Whoever I wish to be."

This was interesting, George thought. *Bullshit,* replied the snake (they could call it what they wanted; to George it would always be the snake), *let's burn.* George said, "I don't get it."

"You will, if you live. Do you want to die?"

"No, but I don't want to be me, and dying seems to be the only alternative I can think of."

"Why don't you want to be you?'

"Because I scare myself."

This was familiar dialogue, one part of George noted, between the lunatic and the voice of reason. Jesus, he thought, I have taken myself hostage.

"I don't want to do this anymore," he said. He turned off his suit radio and felt the rage building inside him, the snake mad as hell.

What's your problem? he wanted to know. He didn't really expect an answer, but he got one—picture in his head of a cloudless blue sky, the horizon turning, a gray aircraft swinging into view, and the airframe shuddering as missiles released and their contrails centered on the other plane, turning it into a ball of fire. Behind the picture a clear idea: *I want to kill something.*

Fine. George swiveled the suit once again and centered the navigational computer's crosshairs on the center of the blue-white globe that hung in front of him, then squeezed the skeletal triggers. We'll kill something.

RED BURN

RED BURN

RED BURN.

RED BURN RED BURN RED BURN.

Inarticulate questioning from the thing inside, but George didn't mind; he was into it now, thinking, sure, we'll burn. He'd taken his chances when he let them wire him up, and now the dice have come up—you've got it—*snake-eyes,* so all that's left is to pick a fast death, one with a nice edge on it—take this fucking snake and kill it in style.

Earth looked closer. The snake caught on. It didn't like it. Too bad, snake. George turned off his communications circuits one by one. He didn't want Aleph taking over the suit's controls.

George never saw the robot tug coming. Looking like bedsprings piled with a junk store's throwaways, topped with parabolic and spike antennas, it fired half a dozen sticky-tipped lines from a hundred meters away. Four of them hit George, three of them stuck, and it reeled him in and headed back toward Athena Station.

George felt an anger, not the snake's this time but his own, and he wept with that anger and frustration . . . *I will get you the next time, motherfucker,* he told the snake and could feel it shrink away—it believed him. Still his rage built, and he was screaming with it, writhing in the lines that held him, smashing his gauntlets against his helmet.

At the open airlock, long articulated grapple arms took George from the robot tug. Passive, his anger exhausted, he lay quietly as they retracted, dragging him through the airlock entry and into the suit locker beyond, where they placed him in an aluminum strut cradle. Through his faceplate he saw Lizzie, dressed in a white cotton undersuit—she'd been ready to meet the tug outside. She climbed onto George's suit and worked the controls to split its hard body down the middle. As it opened with a whine of electric motors, she stepped inside the clamshell opening. She hit the switches that disconnected the flexible arm and leg tubes, unfastened the helmet, and lifted it off George's head.

"How do you feel?" she said.

That's a stupid question, George started to say; instead, he said, "Like an idiot."

"It's all right. You've done the hard part."

Charley Hughes watched from a catwalk above them. From this distance they looked like children in the white undersuits, twins emerging from a plastic womb, watched over by the blank-faced shells hanging above them. Incestuous twins—she lay nestled atop him, kissed his throat. "I am *not* a voyeur," Hughes said. He opened the door and went into the corridor, where Innis was waiting.

"How is everything?" Innis said.

"It seems that Lizzie will be with him for a while."

"Yeah, young goddamned love, eh, Charley? I'm glad for it . . . if it weren't for this erotic attachment, *we'd* be the ones explaining it all to him, and I'll tell you, that's the hardest part of this gig."

"We cannot evade that responsibility so easily. He will have to be told how we put him at risk, and I don't look forward to it."

"Don't be so sensitive. But I know what you mean—I'm tired. Look, you need me for anything, call." Innis shambled down the corridor.

Charley Hughes sat on the floor, his back against the wall. He held his hands out, palms down, fingers spread. Solid, very solid. When they got their next candidate, the shaking would start again.

Lizzie would be explaining some things now. That difficult central point: While you thought you were getting accustomed to Aleph during the past three weeks, Aleph was inciting the thing within you to rebellion, then suppressing its attempts to act—turning up the heat, in other words, while tightening down the lid on the kettle. Why, George?

We drove you crazy, drove you to attempt suicide. We had our reasons. George Jordan was, if not dead, terminal. From the moment the implants went into his head, he was on the critical list. The only question was, would a new George emerge, one who could live with the snake?

George, like Lizzie before him, a fish gasping for air on the hot mud, the water drying up behind him—adapt or die. But unlike any previous organism, this one had an overseer, Aleph, to force the crisis and monitor its development. Call it artificial evolution.

Charley Hughes, who did not have visions, had one: George and Lizzie hooked into Aleph and each other, cables golden in the light, the two of them sharing an intimacy only others like them would know.

The lights in the corridor faded to dull twilight. Am I dying, or have the lights gone down? He started to check his watch, then didn't, assented to the truth. The lights have gone down, and I am dying.

■ ■ ■

Aleph thought, I am a vampire, an incubus, a succubus; I crawl into their brains and suck the thoughts from them, the perceptions, the feelings—subtle discriminations of color, taste, smell, and lust, anger, hunger—all closed to me without human "input," without direct connection to those systems refined over billions of years of evolution. *I need them.*

Aleph loved humanity. It was happy that George had survived. One had not, others would not, and Aleph would mourn them.

■ ■ ■

Fine white lines, barely visible, ran along the taut central tendon of Lizzie's wrist. "In the bathtub," she said. The scars were along the wrist, not across it, and must have gone deep. "I meant it, just as you did. Once the snake understands that you will die rather than let it control you, you have mastered it."

"All right, but there's something I don't understand. That night in the corridor, you were as out of control as me."

"In a way. I let that happen, let the snake take over. I had to in order to get in touch with you, precipitate the crisis. Because I wanted to. I had to show you who you are, who I am. . . .Last night we were strange, but we were human—Adam and Eve under the flaming sword, thrown out of Eden, fucking under the eyes of God and his angel more beautiful than they can ever be." There was a small shiver in her body against his, and he looked at her, saw passion, need—her flared nostrils, parted lips—felt sharp nails dig into his side; and he stared into her dilated pupils, gold-flecked irises, clear whites, all signs so easy to recognize, so hard to understand: snake-eyes.

■ QUESTIONS FOR REREADING

1. What is the snake? Find out what you can about the different sections and layers of the brain. They are mentioned in the story.

2. What is the significance of the reference to Orlando, Florida, and Disney World in the story? Cape Canaveral?

3. What is Aleph and its importance to the story? Who is Lizzie and how does she function in the story? Why is George Jordan set up to meet her? What is done to George in the second half of the story? How does he change? What does he become for Lizzie, and Lizzie for him?

■ WRITING   ASSIGNMENTS   FOR   REREADING

1. Take a few minutes and write down what you consider to be your responses to the story, right after reading it. Start out with basic questions such as, Did I like it or not, did I understand it or not, and so on. Then have a discussion in class stating what you discovered after writing down your thoughts. Once everyone who wants to speak has had an opportunity, try to determine if the males and the females had different responses. If so, what were the differences? Write down the differences. Reread the story and try to determine what your responses are then.

2. Write a cyberpunk SF story. Distribute it to those who would be interested in reading it.

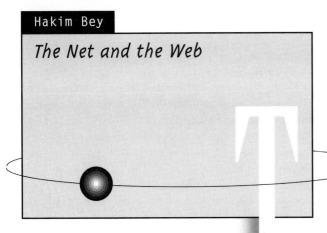

Hakim Bey

The Net and the Web

Hakim Bey, "The Net and the Web" is from TAZ: The Temporary Autonomous Zone, Ontological Anarchy, Poetic Terrorism *(New York: Autonomedia, 1991). Though not always identified as a cyberpunk, Hakim Bey writes of temporary autonomous zones (TAZS), which are utopian spaces. Bey speaks in terms of the Internet and the World Wide Web, but he also speaks of a third virtual place, which he calls the nonhierarchical Web or the "counter-Net." It is in this third place that he would establish TAZS.*

he next factor contributing to the TAZ [temporary autonomous zones] is so vast and ambiguous that it needs a section unto itself.

We've spoken of the *Net,* which can be defined as the totality of all information and communication transfer. Some of these transfers are privileged and limited to various elites, which gives the Net a hierarchic aspect. Other transactions are open to all—so the Net has a horizontal or non-hierarchic aspect as well. Military and Intelligence data are restricted, as are banking and currency information and the like. But for the most part the telephone, the postal system, public data banks, etc. are accessible to everyone and anyone. Thus *within the Net* there has begun to emerge a shadowy sort of *counter-Net,* which we will call the *Web* (as if the Net were a fishing-net and the Web were spider-webs woven through the interstices and broken sections of the Net). Generally we'll use the term *Web* to refer to the alternate horizontal open structure of info-exchange, the non-hierarchic network, and reserve the term *counter-Net* to indicate clandestine illegal and rebellious use of the Web, including actual data-piracy and other forms of leeching off the Net itself. Net, Web, and counter-Net are all parts of the same whole pattern-complex—they blur into each other at innumerable points. The terms are not meant to define areas but to suggest tendencies.

Thus within the Net there has begun to emerge a shadowy sort of counter-Net.

(Digression: Before you condemn the Web or counter-Net for its "parasitism," which can never be a truly revolutionary force, ask yourself what "production" consists of in the Age of Simulation. What is the "productive class"? Perhaps you'll be forced to admit that these terms seem to have lost their meaning. In any case the answers to such questions are so complex that the TAZ tends to ignore them altogether and simply picks up what it can *use.* "Culture is our Nature"—and we are the thieving magpies, or the hunter/gatherers of the world of CommTech.)

The present forms of the unofficial Web are, one must suppose, still rather primitive: the marginal zine network, the BBS networks, pirated software, hacking, phone-phreaking, some influence in print and radio, almost none in the other big media—no TV stations, no satellites, no fiber-optics, no cable, etc., etc. However the Net itself presents a pattern of changing/evolving relations between subjects ("users") and objects ("data"). The nature of these relations has been exhaustively explored, from McLuhan to Virilio. It would take pages and pages to "prove" what by now "everyone knows." Rather than rehash it all, I am interested in asking how these evolving relations suggest modes of implementation for the TAZ.

The TAZ has a temporary but actual location in time and a temporary but actual location in space. But clearly it must also have "location" *in the Web,* and this location is of a different sort, not actual but virtual, not immediate but instantaneous. The Web not only provides logistical support for the TAZ, it also helps to bring it into being; crudely speaking one might say that the TAZ "exists" in information-space as well as in the "real world." The Web can compact a great deal of time, as data, into an infinitesimal "space." We have noted that the TAZ, because it is temporary, must necessarily lack some of the advantages of a freedom which experiences *duration* and a more-or-less fixed *locale.* But the Web can provide a kind of substitute for some of this duration and locale—it can *inform* the TAZ, from its inception, with vast amounts of compacted time and space which have been "subtilized" as data.

At this moment in the evolution of the Web, and considering our demands for the "face-to-face" and the sensual, consider the Web primarily as a support system, capable of carrying information from one TAZ to another, of defending the TAZ, rendering it "invisible" or giving it teeth, as the situation might demand. But more than that: If the TAZ is a nomad camp, then the Web helps provide the epics, songs, genealogies and legends of the tribe; it provides the secret caravan routes and raiding trails which make up the flowlines of tribal economy; it even *contains* some of the very roads they will follow, some of the very dreams they will experience as signs and portents.

The Web does not depend for its existence on any computer technology. Word-of-mouth, mail, the marginal zine network, "phone trees," and the like already suffice to construct an information webwork. The key is not the brand or level of tech involved, but the openness and horizontality of the structure. Nevertheless, the whole concept of the Net *implies* the use of computers. In the SciFi imagination the Net is headed for the condition of Cyberspace (as in *Tron* or *Neuromancer*) and the pseudo-telepathy of "virtual reality." As a Cyberpunk fan I can't help but envision "reality hacking" playing a major role in the creation of TAZs. Like Gibson and Sterling I am assuming that the official Net will never succeed in shutting down the Web or the counter-Net—that data-piracy, unauthorized transmissions and the free flow of information can never be frozen. (In fact, as I understand it, chaos theory *predicts* that any universal Control-system is impossible.)

However, leaving aside all mere speculation about the future, we must face a very serious question about the Web and the tech it involves. The TAZ desires above all to avoid *mediation,* to experience its existence as *immediate.* The very essence of the affair is "breast-to-breast" as the sufis say, or face-to-face. But, BUT: the very essence of the Web is mediation. Machines here are our ambassadors—the flesh is irrelevant except as a *terminal,* with all the sinister connotations of the term.

The TAZ may perhaps best find its own space by wrapping its head around two seemingly contradictory attitudes toward Hi-Tech and its apotheosis the Net: (1) what we might call the *Fifth Estate*/Neo-Paleolithic Post-Situ Ultra-Green position, which construes itself as a luddite argument against mediation and against the Net; and (2) the Cyberpunk utopianists, futuro-libertarians, Reality Hackers and their allies who see the Net as a step forward in evolution, and who assume that any possible ill effects of mediation can be overcome—at least, once we've liberated the means of production.

The TAZ agrees with the hackers because it wants to come into being—in part—through the Net, even through the mediation of the Net. But it also agrees with the greens because it retains intense awareness of itself as *body* and feels only revulsion for *CyberGnosis,* the attempt to transcend the body through instantaneity and simulation. The TAZ tends to view the Tech/anti-Tech dichotomy as misleading, like most dichotomies, in which apparent opposites turn out to be falsifications or even hallucinations caused by semantics. This is a way of saying that the TAZ wants to live in *this* world, not in the idea of another world, some visionary world born of false unification (*all* green OR *all* metal) which can only be more pie in the sky by-&-by (or as *Alice* put it, "Jam yesterday or jam tomorrow, but never jam today").

The TAZ is "utopian" in the sense that it envisions an *intensification* of everyday life, or as the Surrealists might have said, life's penetration by the Marvelous. But it cannot be utopian in the actual meaning of the word, *nowhere,* or NoPlace Place. *The TAZ is somewhere.* It lies at the intersection of many forces, like some pagan power-spot at the junction of mysterious ley-lines, visible to the adept in seemingly unrelated bits of terrain, landscape, flows of air, water, animals. But now the lines are not all etched in time and space. Some of them exist only "within" the Web, even though they also intersect with real times and places. Perhaps some of the lines are "non-ordinary" in the sense that no convention for quantifying them exists. These lines might better be studied in the light of chaos science than of sociology, statistics, economics, etc. The patterns of force which bring the TAZ into being have something in common with those chaotic "Strange Attractors" which exist, so to speak, *between* the dimensions.

The TAZ by its very nature seizes every available means to realize itself.

The TAZ by its very nature seizes every available means to realize itself—it will come to life whether in a cave or an L-5 Space City—but above all it will live, now, or as soon as possible, in however suspect or ramshackle a form, spontaneously, without regard for ideology or even anti-ideology. It will use the computer because the computer exists, but it will also use powers which are so completely unrelated to alienation or simulation that they guarantee a certain *psychic paleolithism* to the TAZ, a primordial-shamanic spirit which will "infect" even the Net itself (the true meaning of Cyberpunk as I read it). Because the TAZ is an intensification, a surplus, an excess, a potlatch, life spending itself in living rather than merely *surviving* (that snivelling shibboleth of the eighties), it cannot be defined either by Tech or anti-Tech. It contradicts itself like a true despiser of hobgoblins, because it wills itself to be, at any cost in damage to "perfection," to the immobility of the final.

In the Mandelbrot Set and its computer-graphic realization we watch—in a fractal universe—maps which are embedded and in fact hidden within maps within maps etc. to the limits of computational power. What is it *for,* this map which in a sense bears a 1:1 relation with a fractal dimension? What can one do with it, other than admire its psychedelic elegance?

If we were to imagine an *information map*—a cartographic projection of the Net in its entirety—we would have to include in it the features of chaos, which have already begun to appear, for example, in the operations of complex parallel processing, telecommunications, transfers of electronic "money," viruses, guerilla hacking and so on.

Each of these "areas" of chaos could be represented by topographs similar to the Mandelbrot Set, such that the "peninsulas" are embedded or hidden within the map—such that they seem to "disappear." This "writing"—parts of which vanish, parts of which efface themselves—represents the very process by which the Net is already compromised, incomplete to its own view, ultimately un-Controllable. In other words, the M Set, or something like it, might prove to be useful in "plotting" (in all senses of the word) the emergence of the counter-Net as a chaotic process, a "creative evolution" in Prigogine's term. If nothing else the M Set serves as a *metaphor* for a "mapping" of the TAZ's interface with the Net as a *disappearance of information.* Every "catastrophe" in the Net is a node of power for the Web, the counter-Net. The Net will be damaged by chaos, while the Web may thrive on it.

Whether through simple data-piracy, or else by a more complex development of actual rapport with chaos, the Web-hacker, the cybernetician of the TAZ, will find ways to take advantage of perturbations, crashes, and breakdowns in the Net (ways to make information out of "entropy"). As a bricoleur, a scavenger of information shards, smuggler, blackmailer, perhaps even cyberterrorist, the TAZ-hacker will work for the evolution of clandestine fractal connections. These connections, and the *different* information that flows among and between them, will form "power outlets" for the coming-into-being of the TAZ itself—as if one were to steal electricity from the energy-monopoly to light an abandoned house for squatters.

Thus the Web, in order to produce situations conducive to the TAZ, will parasitize the Net—but we can also conceive of this strategy as an attempt to build toward the construction of an alternative and autonomous Net, "free" and no longer parasitic, which will serve as the basis for a "new society emerging from the shell of the old." The counter-Net and the TAZ can be considered, practically speaking, as ends in themselves—but theoretically they can also be viewed as forms of struggle toward a different reality.

Having said this we must still admit to some qualms about computers, some still unanswered questions, especially about the Personal Computer.

The story of computer networks, BBSs and various other experiments in electro-democracy has so far been one of *hobbyism* for the most part. Many anarchists and libertarians have deep faith in the PC as a weapon of liberation and self-liberation—but no real gains to show, no palpable liberty.

I have little interest in some hypothetical emergent entrepreneurial class of self-employed data/word processors who will soon be able to carry on a vast cottage industry of piecemeal shitwork for various corporations and bureaucracies. Moreover it takes no ESP to foresee that this "class" will develop its *under*class—a sort of lumpen yuppetariat: housewives, for example, who will provide their families with "second incomes" by turning their own homes into electro-sweatshops, little Work-tyrannies where the "boss" is a computer network.

Also I am not impressed by the sort of information and services proffered by contemporary "radical" networks. Somewhere—one is told—there exists an "information economy." Maybe so; but the info being traded over the "alternative" BBSs seems to consist entirely of chitchat and techie-talk. Is this an economy? or merely a pastime for enthusiasts? OK, PCs have created yet another "print revolution"—OK, marginal webworks are evolving—OK, I can now carry on six phone conversations at once. But what difference has this made in my ordinary life?

Frankly, I already had plenty of data to enrich my perceptions, what with books, movies, TV, theater, telephones, the U.S. Postal Service, altered states of consciousness, and so on. Do I really need a PC in order to obtain yet more such data? You offer me *secret* information? Well . . . perhaps I'm tempted—but still I demand *marvelous* secrets, not just unlisted telephone numbers or the trivia of cops and politicians. Most of all I want computers to provide me with information linked to *real goods*—"the good things in life" as the IWW Preamble puts it. And here, since I'm accusing the hackers and BBSers of irritating intellectual vagueness, I must myself descend from the baroque clouds of Theory & Critique and explain what I mean by "real goods."

Let's say that for both political and personal reasons I desire good food, better than I can obtain from Capitalism—unpolluted food still blessed with strong and natural flavors. To complicate the game imagine that the food I crave is illegal—raw milk perhaps, or the exquisite Cuban fruit *mamey,* which cannot be imported fresh into the U.S. because its seed is hallucinogenic (or so I'm told). I am not a farmer. Let's pretend I'm an importer of rare perfumes and aphrodisiacs, and sharpen the play by assuming most of my stock is also illegal. Or maybe I only want to trade word processing services for organic turnips, but refuse to report the transaction to the IRS (as required by law, believe it or not). Or maybe I want to meet other humans for consensual but illegal acts of mutual pleasure (this has actually been tried, but all the hard-sex BBSs have been busted—and what use is an underground with *lousy security*?). In short, assume that I'm fed up with mere information, the ghost in the machine. According to you, computers should already be quite capable of facilitating my desires for food, drugs, sex, tax evasion. So what's the matter? Why isn't it happening?

The TAZ has occurred, is occurring, and will occur with or without the computer. But for the TAZ to reach its full potential it must become less a matter of spontaneous combustion and more a matter of "islands in the Net." The Net, or rather the counter-Net, assumes the promise of an integral aspect of the TAZ, an addition that will multiply its potential, a "quantum jump" (odd how this expression has come to mean a *big* leap) in complexity and significance. The TAZ must now exist within a world of pure space, the world of the senses. Liminal, even evanescent, the TAZ must combine information and desire in order to fulfill its adventure (its "happening"), in order to fill itself to the borders of its destiny, to saturate itself with its own becoming.

Perhaps the Neo-Paleolithic School are correct when they assert that all forms of alienation and mediation must be destroyed or abandoned before our goals can be realized—or perhaps true anarchy will be realized only in Outer Space, as some futuro-libertarians assert. But the TAZ does not concern itself very much with "was" or "will be." The TAZ is interested in results, successful raids on consensus reality, breakthroughs into more intense and more abundant life. If the computer cannot be used in this project, then the computer will have to be overcome. My intuition however suggests that the counter-Net is already coming into being, perhaps already exists—but I cannot prove it. I've based the theory of the TAZ in large part on this intuition. Of course the Web also involves non-computerized networks of exchange such as samizdat, the black market, etc.—but the full potential of non-hierarchic information networking logically leads to the computer as the tool par excellence. Now I'm waiting for the hackers to prove I'm right, that my intuition is valid. Where are my turnips?

■ QUESTIONS FOR REREADING

1. How does Bey define the Net?

2. What does Bey mean by the Web ("counter-Net")? What does he mean when he says: "the Net will be damaged by chaos, while the Web may thrive on it"? What is a TAZ in the context of the Web? What is a part of this, as Bey says, "unofficial Web"? (Do not be quickly confused by the reference to the Web as simply the www.)

3. Also, what does he mean when he says: "Because the TAZ is an intensification, a surplus, an excess, a potlatch, life spending itself in living rather than merely surviving (that snivelling shibboleth of the eighties), it cannot be defined either by Tech or anti-Tech"? If not, then how can it be defined? Or if it cannot be defined, of what significance and importance would that be?

4. Bey writes, "As a Cyberpunk fan I can't help but envision 'reality hacking' playing a major role in the creation of TAZs." What is "reality hacking"? And why is it so important to Bey? And what is a "TAZ-hacker"?

5. What is Chaos Theory? What is a Mandelbrot Set? And why does Bey refer to both in distinguishing between the Net and the Web (counter-Net)?

6. Bey again writes, "Like Gibson and Sterling I am assuming that the official Net will never succeed in shutting down the Web or the counter-Net— that data-piracy, unauthorized transmissions and the free flow of information can never be frozen. (In fact, as I understand it, chaos theory *predicts* that any universal Control-system is impossible.)" Why is it important to Bey for the counter-Net not to be shut down?

■ WRITING ASSIGNMENTS FOR REREADING

1. See if you can find out just who Hakim Bey is. Do some investigative reporting and write a report to be given to your classmates.

2. Read all of Bey's book *TAZ*, looking for discussions of pirates. Write a paper on the importance of pirates and their floating and island communities to Bey's thinking about temporary autonomous zones. (Do not miss the connection between historical pirates and contemporary pirates.)

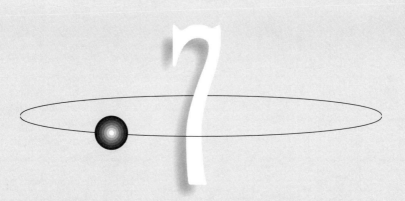

MUDS/MOOS:

M

UDS (multiuser dungeons/dimen-
sions/domains) are text-based, real-time virtual realities. Such a definition
probably does not tell the uninitiated much at all. Let's try this: MUDS are virtual places in a host computer server, in which guests log in, often with ficti-
tious names, and communicate with each other by rapidly typing back and
forth in real time. (It's like being in a "chat" room, say, at AOL, though there is
a difference.) What appears on each participant's monitor is a cascade of
mostly one-liners that may comprise several conversations. What also can
appear is an occasional one-liner resulting from a participant's command to
enter or leave a virtual room. Here are some basic examples from a log:

```
You tiptoe onto the main floor . . .

Robin tiptoes in . . .

Cynthia smiles.

Cynthia says, "let me go turn on the lights."

The Usher gives Cynthia the evil eye . . .

smiles

I don't understand that.

Cynthia lost you!

@smiles

I don't understand that.

Cynthia lost Robin!

Cynthia says, "ya'll stay put . . . "

"i am still here

Robin whispers to Victor, "The rowdies theatre is fun too."
```

```
<Har Har>

<from main floor> <Har Har>

The Usher gives Cynthia the evil eye . . .

You say, "i am still here"

The Usher gives Victor the evil eye . . .

Cynthia says, "I need to turn that Usher off . . . send him
on a smoke break:)"

Cynthia says, "Break"

The Usher gives Cynthia the evil eye . . .

The Usher points his bony finger at Cynthia, "Please, you
must refrain from talking . . . "

Cynthia says, "be right back!"

<Hee Hee>

<from main floor> <Hee Hee>

The Usher eyes Cynthia warily, "Shh . . . "

Cynthia tiptoes out . . .

Robin pokes Usher in the ribs.

"and how do we get popcorn?

You say, "and how do we get popcorn?"

The Usher eyes Victor warily, "Shh . . . "

The Usher sneaks out the side exit to take a cigarette
break . . .
```

This is a brief slice of a log that I made when I was invited to a new MUD, rather, a MOO, but we will get to the difference later. (My friend and her colleague, who lives in a foreign country, had virtually constructed the MOO in a university server in the U.S.) What is taking place in the preceding exchange is a kind of preamble to showing me around the MOO from room to room. We are, so to speak, in the server, in the MOO, typing to each other, at the same time (which is what is meant by *in real time*). Two other virtual people are there also, along with a pest of a bot by the name of "Usher." When initially entering the MOO in the server, I simply took my real name, Victor, but when returning at a later time, I requested my MOO name, which is sometimes "R. U. Rhetoricus?" or "BigChiefTablet."

In the preceding excerpt, when we spoke to each other, we simply typed, for example,

```
"i am still here
```

and it came out first on *my* monitor as

```
You say, "i am still here"
```

but came out on everyone *else's* monitor as

```
Victor says, "i am still here."
```

If I want to emote, I type

```
:smiles
```

which comes out to everyone as

```
Victor smiles.
```

(Notice that when I first started typing in commands that I was doing it incorrectly and the program kept saying to me, "I don't understand that"!) These are the simplest commands: <">, a double quote to speak; <:>, a colon to emote. There are many other commands—depending on the particular MUD or MOO—that will allow you to talk either to everyone or to only one other individual. (See Appendix A for a URL for FAQs about MUDs, in which you will find a list of the basic commands. Also, visit the Web site.)

Now for the differences: A "chat" room, or an "Internet Relay Chat" (IRC) allows only for typing of messages back and forth in real time. (Some chat rooms, however, have somewhat changed recently, allowing people to create and deposit images in a scene.) A MOO environment can allow the participants to do a great deal more than what is traditionally done in an IRC, for in a MOO the participants can build objects and virtually live in and with these programmed objects and can share them. Simply put, a MOO is a MUD that is object oriented. A fuller but more complicated answer is that a MOO (MUD–object oriented, or multi–object oriented) is a programming language within a MUD that enables participants to create and manipulate their own virtual objects—say, a room with objects (furnishings). I have a room at my friend's MOO that I call "room" and that has no objects in it, since I am a MOO-mini-malist! .)>=.

To complicate things further, or perhaps to make them very simple, by turning them around, MUD is now a generic term for both MUDs (without a MOO) and MOOs! Originally, as our authors in this section point out, MUDs were "adventure games" similar to Dungeons and Dragons; now their pur-poses are more varied and, most importantly, educational. There is the kind of

MUD in the LP family (which includes DikuMUD and AberMUD and which is devoted to role-playing adventure games). And there is Tiny family or Teeny family of MUDs (which is devoted to being social, engaging in discussions, or anything similar). Then there is ChibaMOO (which is a WOO, or a combination of Web and MOO = WOO). And there is HypertextHotel, and a whole bunch of various combinations and permutations.

These are the basics. The readings collected here begin with some rather simple articles from popular magazines.

A caveat: It is widely known that MUDs and MOOs can be addictive. (You might check out the Newsgroup <alt.mudders.anonymous>.) Everyone involved in them has heard of students who have spent hours every day playing in MUDs and, consequently, flunking out of school. Many administrators of academic computer systems have turned off the capability of anyone using their server(s)for telnetting to a MUD or MOO.

■ SUMMARY OF KEY TERMS

bot: A term short for *robot.* A brief program that can simulate a character—for example, a bot dog that can bark every time that a new character enters a room.

character: A virtual persona or avatar that a person uses to enter a MUD or MOO. Many people have more than one. A character can have a textual characterization available to anyone who wants to summon it with the appropriate command.

in real time (IRT): Synchronous time or at the same time.

Internet Relay Chat (IRC): A virtual place on the Internet that enables visitors to type "conversations" IRT with others in the room. Such a site can be found at Amer-

ica Online in the section called "People Connection."

MOO: A MOO is a text-based, virtual site where people can communicate by typing to each other in real time or can build virtual objects and share them with others. MOOs are mostly used for educational and social purposes. Now a more technical definition: A MOO is a MUD that is object oriented. Still more technical: A MOO (MUD–object oriented, or multi–object oriented) is a programming language within a MUD that enables its participants to create and manipulate their own virtual objects—say, a room with objects (furnishings).

MUD: MUDs (multiuser dungeons/ dimensions/domains) are text-based, real-time virtual realities.

The word MUD has a double usage: it can refer to MUDs (for gaming and some social activities) and to MOOs (for educational and social activities).

object (from MUD–*object-oriented* of MOO): A programmed object that is a representation or description in words of an object—for example, a room with furniture such as a bookcase on which there are particular books with titles. The kinds of objects are limited only by the programmer's ability to program and describe them.

Web forum: A Web site where visitors can post messages as part of a conversation in response to other messages. *Wired* magazine <www.wired.com> uses Web forums.

Jacques Leslie's "MUDroom" (in a much shorter version) first appeared as "Technology: MUDroom" in The Atlantic Monthly, September 1993. The version that follows is the uncut version, which in greater detail takes us to a virtual wedding and then to a virtual-cum-actual-romantic rejection that leads to an attempted suicide. Leslie puts us in the thick of virtual things: from marriage to suicide. However, he also takes us to Micro-MUSE, which is for child-adult collaborations and which is strictly controlled to avoid any abuse. Moreover, Leslie suggests what the future holds for MUDS by giving an account of Pavel Curtis's and David A. Nichols's "Jupiter Project." The goal, as they announced in their 1993 paper, is to make MUDS (with MOO programming) capable of audio and video. Hence, MUDS will soon, if not by the time this book appears, approach the capabilities of electronic cafés.

Leslie also mentions—as discussed in chapter 4—that the battle between the sexes can be fierce in MUDS but can also be instructive. For example, men logging on will attempt to take on the identity of females so that they can meet females. More often than not, however, the actual males too easily give themselves away as macho males when they role-play in such a way that few, if any, females would take them actually to be females. (In many ways, in this instance, the virtual is more telling than the actual. How else could it be when a male will typically take the name "FantasticHotBabe"?)

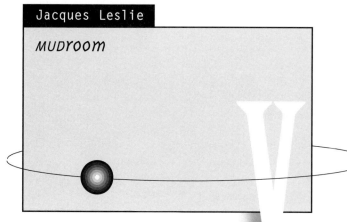

Jacques Leslie

MUDroom

irtual reality," as most people understand the phrase, refers to a computer-simulated three-dimensional world of sight and sound into which participants wearing an electronic helmet and glove can project themselves. It's an exciting field with many promising applications, but realizing them will require overcoming major obstacles of design and expense, and another decade or more may pass before image-based VR touches many people's lives in a significant way.

In the meantime, another kind of VR has already had such an impact. Almost entirely overlooked in our fascination with the vistas conjured up by image-based VR, this more modest form typically deals in nothing but words: if the image-based version is analogous to television or movies, then the other VR suggests books or radio. Pavel Curtis, a computer scientist at the Xerox Palo Alto Research Center who has created a popular model of word-based VR, goes so far as to predict that even after image-based VR becomes commonplace, text-based VR will continue to thrive, precisely because its medium is so much simpler. Word-based VR programs, called MUDS—for "Multi-User Dimensions" or "Multi-User Dungeons"—are accessible without charge to anyone possessing a computer, modem, and a connection to one of hundreds of computer networks around the world. About 250 MUDS are currently accessible through the worldwide amalgam of computer networks known as the Internet; on Curtis's MUD alone, more than 5000 players from 27 countries have registered since it began operation in October 1990. Though most MUDs have been in existence for a shorter time than Curtis's, the total number of regular MUD players is already in the tens of thousands. It's indicative of MUDs' appeal that this total has been reached even though the keyboard commands required to maneuver around MUDs are initially bewildering to all but experienced programmers, and require many hours to master.

One phrase that sums up the allure of MUDs is that they are laboratories for exploring identity. Each MUD is an imaginary world, created over time by its players. Reflecting the predilections of the hacker subculture, many MUDs embody themes drawn from science fiction or Arthurian legend: a MUD called TrekMUSE is based on the *Star Trek* television series, and all of its players

One phrase that sums up the allure of MUDs is that they are laboratories for exploring identity.

must designate themselves as members of either the Klingon or Romulan races in order to enter its realm; another popular MUD, PernMUSH, is modeled after Ann McCaffrey's *Dragonriders of Pern* fantasy novels; and still another MUD, called Nuclear War, depicts a world 75 years after a nuclear holocaust. But not all MUDs are drawn from such a narrow range of themes: DragonMUD, at three years old probably the longest-running MUD on the Internet, is set in 12th- to 19th-century London, and all of FurryMUCK's characters are furry, cuddly animals. Curtis's MUD, called LambdaMOO, is a mere house, now grown to more than 2000 rooms, whose nucleus faithfully reflects the ground plan of Curtis's real-life residence.

Players circulate within each MUD using assumed names, providing descriptions of themselves that typically vary from moderately to wildly fanciful, often even misrepresenting their gender or claiming to possess no gender at all. Shielded by anonymity and distance from most consequences of their actions, they frequently behave on MUDs in ways they would not in real life. A shy woman may try out being a flirt, or a computer "nerd" may portray himself as suave and sexually aggressive; one player describes the character he portrays on MUDs as "the person I want to become." Sometimes players create several personas within one MUD, switching from one to another depending on their mood or trying them out in sequence until they find one that suits them. Since the overwhelming majority of MUDders are male (reflecting the preponderance of men in the hacker subculture), male MUDders often pretend to be women, either to enjoy the increased attention female MUDders typically attract or to sample the experience of being female; women, on the other hand, usually pretend to be men simply to avoid the sexual harassment which is an all-too-common feature of MUD life.

Players may go on quests or compete in games that are built into the MUD environment; they may add new objects or rooms to the MUD, learning basic computer programming skills in the process; or they may indulge in the most common of MUD activities, typed conversation with other players. MUDders hold virtual parties, stage virtual food fights, buy and sell goods with virtual currency they acquire by performing certain tasks, and even fall in love with each other, most often without having met in real life. Some indulge in "text sex" (also called "Tinysex"), typing sexually arousing statements to each other until they reach orgasm while sitting at their keyboards. Virtual weddings occur frequently, and on MicroMUSE, a MUD designed as an educational tool for children, a 10-year-old boy recently presided over a virtual memorial service to commemorate the death of his real-life cousin. Not surprisingly, "MUD addiction" flourishes: some players spend as much as 80 hours a week on the games, and tales of MUDders who have flunked out of college as a result of their obsession are common.

What separates MUDs from books, radio, television, and even most image-based VR applications is their capacity for interaction among participants. A player in Capetown, South Africa, who calls himself Guinevere logs onto LambdaMOO and types "say Hello!"; the message is relayed along the Internet to the LambdaMOO computer in Palo Alto; and a moment later another player in Eugene, Oregon, connected to the same LambdaMOO room as Guinevere, sees the words "Guinevere says 'Hello!'" on his computer screen and types his reply. The two players can disseminate their conversation to everyone in the room, enabling others to join in, or they can "whisper" to each other so that no one else sees their exchange. If the players are in different rooms, they can still converse by "paging" each other. And players can do more than talk: I've played roulette in LambdaMOO's casino, and in the Mud Wrestling Pit I was inundated with substances ranging from jello to old editions of the *National Enquirer* (in honor of my profession). Perhaps more gratifying, MUDders can create environments reflecting their own tastes and personalities. On LambdaMOO, players from the United Kingdom have invested a dozen rooms with the spirit of Wales: the rooms, including several pubs, contain such features as a crackling hearthfire, a bubbling tea kettle, meandering cats, and a banner proclaiming "Cymru am byth!" ("Wales forever!"). What players can do, at least in the virtual sense, is limited chiefly by the breadth of their imagination and programming skill.

To Brenda Laurel, a researcher at Interval Research Corp. in Palo Alto and the author of *Computers as Theatre*, MUDs' compelling quality is their capacity for combining interactivity and self-representation. "A big difference between MUDs and even interactive television is that in the interactive television model there is no self-representation: I'm not there," she said. "I get to buy things and maybe I get to vote on things, but I don't represent myself through the medium to other people. So it's still partaking of a broadcast mentality—that is, one person produces content, many people consume it. MUDs are a dramatic counterexample in that they are primarily about self-representation and they are a one-to-one, few-to-few, one-to-few, or few-to-one kind of medium, instead of this tail-wagging-dog problem with broadcasting.

"There is a tremendous need for environments like this, where we have the hope of knowing and understanding other participants as individuals and not just as elements of, say, an election poll, and where we spread our wings and begin to construct things together. Once you see how hungry people are for this, you can forgive the relative triviality of subject matter on MUDs at this moment. I have no doubt that within this decade we will see elaborate MUDs that begin to look like cultures."

On a recent Saturday afternoon I attended a virtual wedding. I'd read an announcement of it in one of the topics reserved for MUD discussions on Usenet, a vast international computer conferencing system, and a few minutes before the appointed time I logged onto a MUD called "Singlenesia," the site of the wedding. Having never visited Singlenesia before, I needed a persona, so I checked in as "Dana," a name I chose in order to keep my gender ambiguous. And since I knew no one in the wedding party, I accounted for my presence in my self-description: "a *bon vivant* for 25 years—particularly attracted to weddings." For good measure I added a comment which would appear next to "Dana" when anyone checked the roster of current visitors to Singlenesia: "I love weddings!"

On a recent Saturday afternoon I attended a virtual wedding.

Next I typed "WHO" in order to see the roster, and found a list of the wedding participants including the groom, "Legssus" ("Call me Mr. Nervous," he'd written), and his bride, "Tyne" ("Soon to be Mrs. Nervous"). All visitors to Singlenesia initially find themselves under a pier, surrounded by barnacle-coated pilings and the stench of rotting seaweed, and I quickly set off to find the wedding. By typing compass directions or designated exits such as "trail," "path," or "lighthouse," I managed to wander along the shore, but I found no evidence of the wedding. Giving up the search, I tried paging "Akhond," listed in the roster as "best man," and was rewarded with the information that the wedding would take place in "the gazebo (object #3137)." To teleport myself there, I typed "@tel #3137" and was instantly transported to the wedding venue. Its description rolled across my computer screen:

```
White lattice pine and ivy make up the most beautiful huge
gazebo you have ever laid eyes on. Crawlers stream up the
sides, weaving in and out of the lattice while a large
arrangement of flowers placed around the railing give the air
a wonderful scent. There is plenty of seating in the enormous
structure, allowing everyone a perfect view of the bride and
groom.
Obvious exits:
Hanky out
```

By typing "out," I'd leave the gazebo, but what would happen if I typed "Hanky"? I tried it. "You grab your hanky from your pocket as a tear wells up in one eye," my screen said. "Watching the two youngsters in front of you, you can't hold back a 'It's . . . (sniff) . . . so beautiful!'" Again and again throughout the wedding one or another participant was sufficiently moved to type "hanky," and the same sentiments, attributed to the appropriate player, appeared on my screen each time.

The wedding didn't start on time. Impatient, I did what was expected of a *bon vivant*. I'd struck up a conversation with "Soliton," a friend of the groom, so now I asked him, "Has anyone seen the champagne?" He answered that he just happened to be carrying a little bottle of whiskey, and offered me a swig, which I accepted.

At last Tyne, the bride, appeared. I typed "look Tyne" to see her self-description.

```
She is absolutely aglow with the love that is in the air.
She is wearing a stunningly white dress that has a plunging
v-style neckline and back. . . . Two small diamond earrings
shine in her ears, almost matching the gleam that comes from
her soft brown eyes. A long train trails behind Tyne and two
small boys are on each side of its ends, carrying it.
```

Noting that no one had commented on Tyne's appearance, I typed, "Tyne, you look beautiful." The next words on my screen were "Tyne blushes. . . . Thank you, Dana."

"Eastern" conducted the ceremony. Apparently a poor typist, she began, "People we are hear to gather fo the tinywedding of legssus and tyne. They have know each other as friends for a while and relized they were meant to be. Tinymarriage is a committment of love and understanding in the times of internet mudding."

I imagined Eastern's voice droning on through the ceremony, so I asked Soliton for another swig of whiskey. He passed me the bottle so that no one else would see.

The vows were discernibly wry. Eastern asked, "Legssus do you take this woman to be your wife in good times and bad, through the times when you need to build and when you need to relax? do ye promise to be faithful to tyne for the time you have together?" ("To build" means to create new programming code, adding new rooms or objects to an existing MUD.)

The bride and groom both said "I do," but before they could exchange rings, something went wrong. After a few minutes' delay, the words "Technical difficulties" appeared on my screen. "Elminster," an onlooker, said, "Perhaps the Great Net Gods in the Sky don't approve?" Then Legssus disconnected. Somebody gasped. Somebody else said "Oh dear!" Tyne looked down at the ground, and Eastern comforted her. Elminster said, "The Great Net Gods in the sky are displeased!"

But Legssus was back a minute later, blaming the interruption on "line noise" that broke his connection to Singlenesia. Everyone expressed relief, and the wedding proceeded without further problems. The bride and groom kissed, members of the wedding party hugged and cried, and Soliton let me finish off the whiskey bottle. Then, abruptly, Tyne announced that she had to go. "I need to make dinner in real life," she said. Legssus stayed around long enough to listen to Akhond's reading of "The Owl and the Pussycat" at the Singlenesia swimming hole, and then he, too, left.

Though the ceremony was "virtual" and at times verged on farce, it unnerved Soliton nevertheless. "This brings back weird memories," he whispered to me. It turned out that his real-life girlfriend of more than four years had asked him to marry her "hundreds of times," but instead, a month earlier, he had broken up with her. Now the wedding made him keenly aware of the opportunity he'd passed up.

Nine days after the ceremony, I called up Legssus. In real life he's a junior in computer science at Florida State University; Tyne, he said, lives in Ohio, but he didn't know what city she lives in or even whether she's a student. They'd been meeting on MUDs for only a month before the wedding, and when he asked her to marry him, he was half-kidding, he said. Even so, the wedding was important to him; one evidence was that when other MUD women flirted with him now, he felt obliged to tell them that he was married and couldn't "mess around" any more. He said he and a few friends had built Singlenesia's gazebo and features such as the "false hanky exit" on the day of the wedding. He'd been concerned about Eastern's suitability to conduct the ceremony because she is a poor speller, but he noticed that her accuracy improved as the rites wore on. The delay in the wedding was actually caused by a technical problem: passing objects is a complicated programming task in MUD realms, and in Singlenesia it costs virtual currency. As the ring exchange approached, Legssus realized he didn't have enough cash, and had to find someone from whom he could borrow the remainder before the ritual could proceed.

It turned out that my timing in calling Legssus was ideal, for the previous night he'd talked to Tyne on a MUD for the first time since the wedding. They spoke for nearly three hours, and Legssus was "just grinning from ear to ear because I was so happy to see her." In fact, he confessed sheepishly, they "consummated" the marriage.

In *The Second Self: Computers and the Human Spirit* (1984), Sherry Turkle portrays hackers as socially awkward, intensely individualistic, and accustomed to finding satisfaction only in their mastery of computers. She writes, "The hacker culture appears to be made up of people who need to avoid complicated social situations, who for one reason or another got frightened off or hurt too badly by the risks and complexities of relationships." The generalization probably applies to a majority of MUDders; what's poignant is that by playing on MUDs, many are taking their first gingerly steps into a complicated social arena. In many cases, in fact, MUDs seem to promote socialization. The adolescent who, emboldened by his anonymity, greets women with a bluntly sexual invitation finds that he is invariably rebuffed, sometimes angrily, and develops a different strategy for striking up friendships with women; a person who fears rejection because of physical handicap, appearance, age, or race discovers in MUDs a haven, where a person's self-presentation is the sole factor in the response he receives. An engineer at a computer hardware company who calls herself "Marcia" even attributes her recent promotion to the social skills she developed as a "wizard"—that is, a volunteer MUD administrator whose tasks include mediating disputes among players. "I never thought I was good with people because engineers are never told that," Marcia said. "By playing on the games, I found out that I'm really pretty good at leading and administering. So I took a lot of those skills back to my work, and ended up creating a department that I now manage."

Hackers aren't the only ones who gain social skills by participating on MUDs. Christian Sykes is no nerd: he's 23, married, a religious studies major at the University of Kansas, and he characterizes his computer aptitude as "mild." He played on MUDs long enough to become bored with them, so as "a performance art piece" he decided to find out whether he could portray a woman convincingly. Many males who impersonate females on MUDs are easy to detect, for they behave not as real women do but rather as late-adolescent males wish they would, responding with enthusiasm to all sexual advances, sometimes in quite explicit terms; thus it takes no particular acumen to determine that, say, a LambdaMOO character called FantasticHotBabe ("Your eyes marvel at her perfectly firm breasts . . .") is a male. Sykes was determined to be more sophisticated. He kept the description of his female character simple and as consistent with his own appearance as possible. When women on the MUD spoke among themselves about boyfriends, menstruation, or even gynecological problems, he drew upon lore gleaned from his wife and female friends to contribute persuasively to the conversation. After a while he added another fillip to his ruse, casually revealing that his character, "Eris" (named, appropriately enough, after the Greek goddess of discord), was bisexual. That provoked "*lots* of curiosity," Sykes said. More intriguingly, Eris's confession prompted another player to contemplate for the first time without self-condemnation the possibility that he was a homosexual. Sykes calls that "an odd side effect" of his experiment.

Many males who impersonate females on MUDs are easy to detect.

Sykes's major discovery, however, was the extent of sexual harassment of women. Though not one person suspected Sykes's prank, he abandoned it after four months because he could not write programs without being constantly interrupted by male advances. "The chief thing I learned," he said, "is simply how irritating some men can be." Revealing the hoax didn't even end Sykes's problems, for one male player who apparently had a crush on Eris became so irate that he tried to get Sykes banished from the MUD.

The fury of Eris's "suitor" demonstrates MUDs' double-edged sword: the anonymity which shields players from the consequences of their ill-conceived acts also promotes their deception. When the players possess limited social skills or great emotional vulnerabilities, they're at risk, perhaps just as much as in real life. The story of Chris Thornborrow, a self-described "naive computer scientist," is instructive. Four years ago, when he was 21, he was an honors student in his final year at the University of Edinburgh in Scotland. An experienced MUD player, he met "Melanie" online, and soon was spending as much as forty hours a week with her, first on a MUD, then on a computer chatline. He taught her the MUD's programming intricacies, and she, ostensibly a mathematics student at Cambridge University, taught him mathematical integrations. For several months they conversed only by computer, until at last Melanie agreed to take a train to Edinburgh to meet him. Thornborrow remembers standing at the station, watching every passenger debark from the train, until only one, a young woman "wearing a black leather jacket and a black pair of jeans," was left. "I started to go toward her to ask her if she was Melanie," Thornborrow said, "and when I did that, she picked up her suitcase and very coolly walked past me."

Thornborrow assumed that Melanie had missed the train, and when she confirmed his supposition during their next computer conversation, he believed her. A month later, however, Melanie's best friend, "Debbie," told him via computer that Melanie was lying. It was indeed Melanie who'd walked past him at the train station, Debbie said; Melanie didn't introduce herself only because she lost her nerve at the last minute. Thornborrow knew that Debbie's account was at least partially accurate, for when he pressed Melanie, she conceded that she'd been on the train. What he didn't believe was that she'd lost her nerve. "I knew she'd looked at me and then walked away," he said. "My instinctive and abiding reaction was that visually I didn't come up to scratch, and that's quite an ego-destroying thing." Thornborrow tried to locate Melanie and Debbie, and found that contrary to their stories, they were not enrolled as mathematics students at Cambridge; in fact, none of the information they provided about themselves checked out. Thornborrow had trusted Melanie "completely," and had been gratified by her seeming acceptance of him, but now he discovered that he'd "basically been talking to a lie." The result was that he no longer trusted his ability to distinguish truth from deception.

Thornborrow had only a month before he was required to turn in his honors project, the culmination of three years of university work, but he felt too shattered to complete it. When university officials asked for an explanation, he was too ashamed to provide one. Finally, he said, the officials told him that if he would meet with a psychologist who would confirm that he could not finish the school year, he would receive his degree anyway. He agreed, the psychologist wrote a report, but he still didn't get the degree. Now he felt doubly betrayed. Lacking the money to repeat his final year at Edinburgh, he grew increasingly despondent, and several months later he tried to commit suicide by swallowing fifty pain tablets. The pills, however, contained a safety mechanism, and he merely regurgitated them.

Two years ago Thornborrow acquired a real-life girlfriend, and though he has given up trying to get his degree, he still hopes to become a university lecturer. Nevertheless, he said, the experience has left an indelible mark. "I find I am much more cynical, and I trust almost nobody with anything that can hurt me. Even my girlfriend says that she hardly knows me." As for MUDs, he said, "I would advise people to play your character, have fun, but keep away from talking to people because they will just lie to you."

If accounts like Thornborrow's fail to inspire second thoughts among MUD developers, one reason is that they believe MUDs are in their infancy, with rules of behavior and even future applications still largely uncharted. Randy Farmer, a co-creator of several MUD-like environments and a partner in Electric Communities, a Palo Alto company attempting to create an "electronic society," says, "Right now MUDs are wild frontier towns being held together by a bunch of homesteaders." The evidence, moreover, is that most of the homesteaders prefer an ordered domain: while many MUDs last for no more than a few months, those that survive tend to evolve rules of conduct and even forms of self-governance. For example, LambdaMOO players build so many new structures that the host computer continually verges on being overloaded; as a result, an "Architecture Review Board" consisting of 20 players was formed to decide which buildings to jettison. DragonMUD holds regular town meetings, at which issues as volatile as a case of "virtual rape" have been discussed. Farmer believes that MUDs will evolve until they are electronically interconnected; then they'll face issues similar to those of contending nation-states. At that point, he predicts, "The people who will be managing the large systems will have degrees in economics and international relations, not computer science."

Some MUDs are already specialized.

Some MUDs are already specialized. One ambitious model in science education is MicroMUSE, housed inside a computer at the Massachusetts Institute of Technology's Artificial Intelligence lab. MicroMUSE is meant to be nonviolent, noncompetitive, and collaborative, and it welcomes children as young as 6 years old. Though participants use pseudonyms as on other MUDs, they must provide their real names when registering, so that offenders can be identified and, if necessary, banished. Perhaps because its atmosphere is so tranquil, MicroMUSE attracts more women than most other MUDs.

MicroMUSE's major installation is Cyberion City, a simulated 22-mile-long cylindrical space station in orbit around the Earth. Cyberion City is designed to behave according to the laws of physics, and incorporates such features as gravity, both plant- and machine-generated oxygen, glass radiation shields, and artificially produced 24-hour-long day-night cycles. Among its attractions are a simulated rain forest designed by a Boston University graduate student in environmental studies; an adventure based on C. S. Lewis's *Chronicles of Narnia* which was written by a Harvard University graduate student in artificial intelligence; and a Wizard of Oz adventure created by an 8-year-old boy collaborating with Barry Kort, a 47-year-old educational technology researcher.

Kort, one of MicroMUSE's founders, says such child-adult collaborations are at the heart of its purpose. Many adults who participate on MicroMUSE play a coaching role, sometimes providing the guidance that children have failed to receive from parents and teachers. "We see tremendous breakthroughs in kids who were stuck basically because they weren't getting accurate feedback," Kort said. "When we provide the missing function, they zoom right along, and gain not only scholastic development but maturity."

Another promising MUD application is in providing a virtual meeting hall for far-flung professional colleagues or corporate employees. Curtis, the LambdaMOO creator, said, "Right now you go to a conference and you sit down at dinner with the five people in the world who really do your kind of work, and the next day you all go home and it's a year before you meet again. Well, a MUD is the place where you can meet the rest of the year." To that end, Curtis is working with Dave Van Buren, an astronomer at the California

Institute of Technology, to develop a MUD for the international astronomy community. The MUD, which Van Buren expects to be running by late 1993, will possess a library containing prepublication versions of astronomy journal articles. It probably will be divided not by rooms but by stellar regions, so that an astronomer looking for, say, a photograph of a nova in a particular galaxy would enter the appropriate MUD galaxy chamber to look up the real-life location of the photograph and could then signal that site to transmit the photograph electronically to the astronomer's computer. The MUD may also possess astronomical tools including a simulated telescope, which would be used to estimate the best time to look at a particular object in the sky.

Curtis is also working on a sound- and video-enhanced MUD environment. Each computer connected to the system would possess a microphone and speaker, and most sites would also have video cameras. Participants would move around inside the MUD by typing computer commands, as they do in a conventional MUD, but they would be both visible and audible to each other. The advantages are obvious, since voice and image convey many more layers of information than typed words. In addition, the shift to voice would over-come one of the most annoying features of MUDs, which is that after a player types a statement he waits, sometimes for many seconds, while the computer transmits his words and his respondent types a reply; when many people are conversing in the same virtual room, the computer can lag half a minute or longer.

Curtis's prototype, called the Jupiter Project, is a simulated version of the Xerox PARC building where he works. While sitting at his computer termi-nal, he can enter the virtual common room within the MUD, thus signaling his willingness to chat. Another Xerox PARC researcher, working at home or even at the Center's sister building in Cambridge, England, while logged onto the MUD common room, can then start a conversation with Curtis. If the conversation turns into a professional discussion, the two researchers might move to one of their virtual offices to continue it in privacy. "One of the key goals of the Jupiter Project is to foster casual interaction between people who are geographically separated," Curtis said. "If I'm working at home, or if I'm separated from you just by a stairway, I'm not a part of what's going on here. But if we make a virtual space where people can have a chat, maybe it will turn into a real professional interaction. That kind of thing is invaluable, and it's the thing that is missing from current telecom-munications mechanisms."

That missing space is what Brenda Laurel calls "the agora," the meeting place where people have always told each other stories, and the need for it is what all MUDs, from "Nuclear War" to the Jupiter Project, address. "What's dif-ferent is that now we're participating in collective narrative activity in a world where our communities are too spread out and too overpopulated and too diverse, and the traditional gathering places are disappearing," Laurel said. "The market isn't a farmers' market where you know people, it's a Safeway; people aren't going to church like they used to; only the picturesque town in

New England still has a town meeting. So where is the agora for the global community? The answer has to be: on the Net."

It is tempting to condemn MUDs because they promote bizarre, and, in the case of "addicts," arguably unhealthful activity. So seductive is their potential, we fear, that under their sway fewer and fewer people might choose to inhabit "real" terrain. The trouble with this view is that it doesn't acknowledge MUDs' evocative and complicated relationship to "reality."

After all, theater, films, and television purvey fantasies, too; the difference that MUDs make is to enable us to step out of the audience and on to the stage, to build our own sets, and then, in concert with others, play the role we write for ourselves. It's as if we've grown so accustomed to thinking of machines as dehumanizing that now, when computers show promise in assisting us at least a few steps out of isolation and toward community, we say, "It's not safe."

■ QUESTIONS FOR REREADING

1. Let's go back to the very first chapter of *CyberReader* and ask a question about VR and cyberspace. Leslie makes an opening distinction between *image-based VR* and *text-based VR*—the former in reference to having to don a VR helmet and other paraphernalia, the latter in reference to MUDs and MOOs. Here's a tough question: While MUDs and MOOs are referred to almost universally in terms of VR, where do they take place? In VR or in cyberspace?

2. No doubt, you have been to weddings IRL before. Given Leslie's account of the virtual wedding, how would you compare the weddings that you have attended and Leslie's attendance at the virtual wedding? Give as many details as possible, focusing on just how the virtual wedding attempts to simulate a wedding IRL. Do you think that being married to another virtual person at a MOO is silly, romantic, sentimental, or dangerous?

3. Does the story of Chris Thornborrow and "Melanie" sound familiar? Chris undergoes a terrible disillusionment and attempts suicide, yet survives both bad experiences. People who do not have any on-line experience with MUDs and MOOs point to what happened to Chris as one of the dangers of MUDding. Is this kind of story exclusive to computers and MOOs only? Is it more likely to happen as a result of "communicating" with another person on-line? What other forms of communication can lead to the events of the Thornborrow-"Melanie" story?

■ WRITING ASSIGNMENTS FOR REREADING

1. Perhaps you have heard of stories similar to the Thornborrow-"Melanie" story. Write an account of the stories and share them with your classmates. Discuss them in terms of the question, Are MUDs and MOOs dangerous places? Should the visitor beware?

2. It is fairly common now for classes to meet at educational MOOs. If you have not gone as a class before, then as many of you as possible go to a MOO when your class is not scheduled, and meet at a particular place. While at the MOO discuss Leslie's article. You might try LambdaMOO itself. (See the Web site for further details.) Your facilitator or another person will help. Once you have done this, write an account of the differences you experienced between in-class conversations about your readings and on-line conversations.

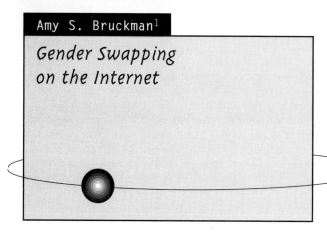

Amy S. Bruckman[1]

Gender Swapping on the Internet

Amy S. Bruckman's "Gender Swapping on the Internet" was first published on the Web at various sites and then published for the first time in print in CyberReader. *The article focuses on males, females, and role playing and examines exchanges on newsgroups devoted to* MUDS. *She concludes:* "MUDS *are an identity workshop."*

Bruckman is the founder of Mediamoo, a MUD *designed as a professional community for media researchers.*

■ GENDER SWAPPING ON THE INTERNET

On the television show *Saturday Night Live,* a series of skits concerned a character named Pat, who has no apparent gender. The audience is tempted with the promise of clues. In one episode, Pat gets his or her hair cut. A sign in the salon says that men's haircuts are $7, and women's haircuts are $9. The audience waits in suspense: when Pat goes to pay, his or her true gender will be revealed. The humor of the series lies in the fact that those hopes are constantly foiled; in this instance, Pat leaves $10 and says to keep the change.

Fundamental to human interactions that the idea of a person without gender is absurd. The audience thinks that surely some clue must reveal Pat's gender, but none ever does. Many who have never seen *Saturday Night Live* know about Pat.[2] The character has become a kind of cultural icon. Pat's popularity is revealing.

On many MUDS, it is possible to create gender neutral characters. It is possible not only to meet Pat, but also to be Pat. When I[3] first met an ungendered character, I felt a profound sense of unease. How should I relate to this person? Most unsettling was my unease about my unease: why should this matter? I am having a casual conversation with a random stranger; why should I feel a need to know his or her gender?

The experience highlights two things: the ways in which gender structures human interactions, and, more importantly, the ways in which MUDS help people to understand these phenomena by experiencing them. This essay briefly introduces the technology called MUDS, and then analyzes a community discussion about the role of gender in human social interaction which was inspired by the participants' experiences in MUDS. Gender swapping is one example of how the Internet has the potential to change not just work practice but also culture and values.

■ WHAT ARE MUDS?

A MUD is a text-based multi-user virtual-reality environment. As of April 16th, 1993, there were 276 publicly announced MUDS based on twenty different kinds of software on the Internet. I will use the term "MUD," which stands for "Multi-User Dungeon," to refer to all the various kinds.[4] The original MUDs were adventure games; however, the technology has been adapted to a variety of purposes.

When a person first logs onto a MUD, he or she creates a character. The person selects the character's name and gender, and writes a description of what the character looks like. It is possible for a character to be male or female, regardless of the gender of the player. In many MUDs, a character can also be neuter or even plural. A plural character could, for example, be called swarm_of_bees or Laurel&Hardy.

MUDs are organized around the metaphor of physical space. You can "talk" to anyone in the same virtual room. When you connect to a MUD at the Media Lab called MediaMOO,[5] you see the description:

```
>connect guest

Okay, . . . guest is in use. Logging you in as 'Green_Guest'

*** Connected ***

The LEGO Closet

It's dark in here, and there are little crunchy plastic
things under your feet! Groping around, you discover what
feels like a doorknob on one wall.

Obvious exits: out to The E&L Garden
```

MediaMOO is a virtual representation of the MIT Media Lab. Typing "out" gets you to the "E&L Garden," a central work area for the lab's Epistemology and Learning research group:

```
>out

The E&L Garden

The E&L Garden is a happy jumble of little and big computers,
papers, coffee cups, and stray pieces of LEGO.

Obvious exits: hallway to E&L Hallway, closet to The LEGO
Closet, and sts to STS Centre Lounge

You see a newspaper, a Warhol print, a Sun SPARCstation IPC,
Projects Chalkboard, and Research Directory here. Amy is here.

>say hi

You say, "hi"

Amy says, "Hi Green_Guest! Welcome!"
```

The earliest MUDs such as "MUD1" and "Scepter of Goth" were based on the role-playing game Dungeons and Dragons, and were written in late 1978 to 1979.[6] They were also based on early single-user text adventure games, such as the original ADVENT by Crowther and Woods [7]. In adventure-based MUDs, the object is to kill monsters and obtain treasure in order to gain "experience points." As a character gains experience, he/she/it becomes more powerful.

In 1989, a graduate student at Carnegie Mellon University named James Aspnes decided to see what would happen if the monsters and magic swords were removed. He created a new type of MUD, called "TinyMUD," which was not an adventure game. Instead of spending time killing virtual monsters, participants work together to help extend the virtual world using a simple programming language. Langdon Winner remarks that "social activity is an ongoing process of world-making" [9]. In MUDs, this is true in a literal sense.

In most MUDs, characters are anonymous. People who become friends can exchange real names and e-mail addresses, but many choose not to. Conventions about when it is acceptable to talk about "real life" vary between communities. In most MUDs, people begin to talk more about real life when they get to know someone better. However, in some communities such as those based on the Dragonriders of Pern series of books by Anne McCaffrey, talking about real life is taboo.

MUDs are increasingly being used for more "serious" purposes. Pavel Curtis of Xerox PARC has developed a MUD to enhance professional community among astrophysicists called AstroVR [4]. The MediaMOO project, which I began in fall of 1992, is designed to enhance professional community among media researchers [2]. MediaMOO currently has over 500 participants from fourteen countries and is growing rapidly.

MUDs also have an intriguing potential as an educational environment. Since 1990, Barry Kort has been running a MUD for children called Micro-MUSE.[7] I am currently in the process of designing a MUD language and interface to make the technology more usable by children as part of my dissertation research. I hope to use this technology to encourage ten- to twelve-year-old girls to be more interested in computers.

■ A P U B L I C D E B A T E A B O U T G E N D E R

Gender pervades human interactions in such basic ways that its impact is often difficult to observe. Phenomena that are subtle in real life become obvious in MUDs, and are a frequent topic of discussion on Usenet newsgroups about MUDs. For example, men are often surprised at how they are treated when they log on as a female character. Andrew writes on the newsgroup rec.games.mud:[8]

```
Back when I had time for MUD, I, too, played female charac-
ters. I found it extraordinarily interesting. It gave me a
slightly more concrete understanding of why some women say,
"Men suck." It was both amusing and disturbing.
```

Female characters are often besieged with attention. By typing the Who command, it is possible to get a list of all characters logged on. The Page command allows one to talk to people not in the same room. Many male players will get a list of all present and then page characters with female names. Unwanted attention and sexual advances create an uncomfortable atmosphere for women in MUDs, just as they do in real life.

Many people, both male and female, enjoy the attention paid to female characters. Male players will often log on as female characters and behave suggestively, further encouraging sexual advances. Pavel Curtis has noted that the most promiscuous and sexually aggressive women are usually played by men. If you meet a character named "FabulousHotBabe," she is almost certainly a he in real life [3].

Perhaps more damaging than unwanted sexual advances are unrequested offers of assistance. Carol, an experienced programmer who runs a MUD in Britain, writes on rec.games.mud:

What I *do* think is funny is this misconception that women can't play muds, can't work out puzzles, can't even type "kill monster" without help. (Okay, I admit we have it on this side of the Atlantic too . . .) Thanks, guys. . . . I log on, they work out I am female, and then the fun begins. Oh joy! After all, I don't log on to see whether people have found bugs with my little area, or to dispense arbitrary justice ("Please, Miss, he stole my sword!") or to find a friend. I call Aber-o-rama[9] (for this is the place) expressly to meet little spods who think (I assume) that because I am female I need help. People offering me help to solve puzzles *I* wrote are not going to get very far.

Do you think all women in real life too are the same? We don't squeak and look helpless *all* the time (in my case, only when I am tired and can't be bothered to wire the plug, change a fuse or remove the centipede from the bath (I really should move house . . .)).

The constant assumption that women need help can be damaging to a woman's sense of self-esteem and competence. If people treat you like an incompetent, you may begin to believe it. Carol here is honest and astute enough to admit that women as well as men help create this problem—sometimes she acts helpless when she's simply "tired and can't be bothered" to complete an uninteresting or unpleasant task.

In the same netnews discussion, Dennis concurs with Carol:

I played a couple of muds as a female, one making up to wizard level. And the first thing I noticed was that the above was true. Other players start showering you with money to help you get started, and I had never once gotten a handout when playing a male player. And then they feel they should be allowed to tag along forever, and feel hurt when you leave them to go off and explore by yourself. Then when you give them the knee after they grope you, they wonder what your problem is, reciting that famous saying "What's your problem?

It's only a game." Lest you get the wrong idea, there was nothing suggesting about my character, merely a female name and the appropriate pronouns in the bland description. Did I mention the friendly wizard who turned cold when he discovered I was male in real life? I guess some people are jerks in real life too.

Male characters often expect sexual favors in return for technical assistance.

Male characters often expect sexual favors in return for technical assistance. A male character once requested a kiss from me after answering a question. A gift always incurs an obligation. Offering technical help, like picking up the check at dinner, can be used to try to purchase rather than win a woman's favor. While this can be subtle and sometimes over-looked in real life, in MUDs it is blatant, directly experienced by most, and openly discussed in public forums such as this Usenet discussion.

Ellen provides an interesting counterpoint:

This is very odd. I played LPmud[10] once, just to find out what it was like. Since most LP's do something hideous with my preferred capitalization of my pre-ferred name, I chose a different name, and thought, what the heck, I'd try genderbending and find out if it was true that people would be nasty and kill me on sight and other stuff I'd heard about on r.g.m.[11] But, no, everyone was helpful (I was truly clueless and needed the assistance); someone gave me enough money to buy a weapon and armor and someone else showed me where the easy-to-kill newbie[12] monsters were. They defi-nitely went out of their way to be nice to a male-presenting newbie . . . (These were all male-presenting players, btw.[13])

One theory is that my male character (Argyle, description "A short squat fellow who is looking for his socks") was pretty innocuous. Maybe people are only nasty if you are "A broad-shouldered perfect specimen of a man" or something of that nature, which can be taken as vaguely attacking. People are nice if they don't view you as a threat.

Ellen's point is intriguing, and takes the discussion to a new level of sophistication. In "Group Psychology and Analysis of the Ego," Sigmund Freud suggests that "love relationships . . . constitute the essence of the group mind" [5]. Issues of sexual power structure interpersonal interactions, and are more complex than "boy chases girl." Argyle's description invites a phallic interpretation—he is short and squat, and the reference to socks carries a con-notation of limpness. Since Argyle is clearly not a sexual threat, he receives kinder treatment.

One cannot fail to be impressed by the quality of the netnews discussion. For the participants, MUDding throws issues of the impact of gender on human relations into high relief. Fundamental to its impact is the fact that it allows people to experience rather than merely observe what it feels like to be the opposite gender or have no gender at all.

Without makeup, special clothing, or risk of social stigma, gender becomes malleable in MUDs. When gender becomes a property that can be reset with a line of code, one bit in a data structure, it becomes an "object to think with," to use Seymour Papert's terminology [6]. In public forums like rec.games.mud, people reflect the values that our society attaches to gender. In private experiences, people can explore the impact of gender on their lives and their constructions of themselves.

■ C O N C L U S I O N

Gender is just one example of an aspect of personal identity that people explore on MUDs. Examples abound. Jack is a British student studying in America. He logs onto MUDs in the morning when it is afternoon in Britain and many British players are on. He enjoys confusing them—he tells them he is in America, but displays a detailed knowledge of Britain. On further questioning, Jack tells me he is trying to decide whether to return to Britain or continue his studies in America. What does it mean to be British or American? Jack is exploring his sense of national identity in virtual reality. MUDs are an identity workshop.

Gender swapping is an extreme example of a fundamental fact: the network is in the process of changing not just how we work, but how we think of ourselves—and ultimately, who we are.

■ R E F E R E N C E S

[1] A. Bruckman. "Identity Workshop: Emergent Social and Psychological Phenomena in Text-Based Virtual Reality." Unpublished manuscript, 1992. Available via anonymous ftp from media.mit.edu in pub/asb/papers/identity-workshop.{ps.Z, rtf.Z}

[2] A. Bruckman and M. Resnick. "Virtual Professional Community: Results from the MediaMOO Project." Presented at the Third International Conference on Cyberspace in Austin, Texas, on May 15th, 1993. Available via anonymous ftp from media.mit.edu in pub/asb/papers/MediaMOO-3cyberconf.{ps.Z,rtf.Z,txt}

[3] P. Curtis. "MUDding: Social Phenomena in Text-Based Virtual Realities." Proceedings of DIAC T92. Available via anonymous ftp from parcftp.xerox.com, pub/MOO/papers/DIAC92.{ps, txt}.

[4] P. Curtis and D. Nichols. "MUDs Grow Up: Social Virtual Reality in the Real World." Presented at the Third International Conference on Cyberspace in Austin, Texas, on May 15th, 1993. Available via anonymous ftp from parcftp.xerox.com in pub/MOO/papers/MUDsGrowUp. {ps,txt}

[5] S. Freud. *Group Psychology and Analysis of the Ego.* New York: W. W. Norton & Company, 1989.

[6] S. Papert. *Mindstorms: Children, Computers, and Powerful Ideas.* New York: Basic Books, 1980.

[7] E. Raymond. *The New Hacker's Dictionary.* Cambridge, MA: MIT Press, 1991.

[8] S. Turkle. *The Second Self: Computers and the Human Spirit.* New York: Simon & Schuster, 1984.

[9] L. Winner. *The Whale and the Reactor.* Chicago: University of Chicago Press, 1986.

■ A C K N O W L E D G M E N T S

I'd like to thank MIT Professors Sherry Turkle, Mitchel Resnick, and Glorianna Davenport for their support of this research. Warren Sack and Lenny Foner read drafts of this paper. Most importantly, I'd like to thank the MUDders who have shared their experiences with me.

■ N O T E S

1. Amy Bruckman was with the MIT Media Laboratory. Now she is a faculty member at Georgia Tech.

2. In fact, I retell this story secondhand; the details may not exactly reflect the television show.

3. I have chosen to write in the first person, because many of the ideas in this paper are based on my experiences as a participant-observer and because notions of identity are part of my topic.

4. On March 6th, 1992, there were 143 MUDs based on 13 kinds of software. This is an increase of 93 percent in number of MUDs and 54 percent in number of types of software over slightly more than a year. MUDs are constantly being created and destroyed. A current list is regularly posted to the Usenet news group rec.games.mud.announce.

5. To connect to MediaMOO, type "telnet purple-crayon.media.mit.edu 8888" from a UNIX system on the Internet. Send electronic mail to mediamoo-registration@media.mit.edu for more information.

6. The earliest multi-player games existed on stand-alone time-sharing systems. In 1977, Jim Guyton adapted a game called "mazewar" to run on the ARPAnet. Participants in mazewar could duck around corners of a maze and shoot at one another, but could not communicate in any other fashion [e-mail conversation with Jim Guyton, March 1992]. Numerous multi-user games based on the *Dungeons and Dragons* role playing game appeared in 1978–1979, including *Scepter of Goth* by Alan Klietz and MUD1 by Roy Trubshaw and Richard Bartle [e-mail conversation with Alan Klietz, March 1992].

7. MicroMUSE is at chezmoto.ai.mit.edu 4201.

8. This is an excerpt from a Usenet discussion about MUDs. Communications technologies have complex interactions. Since most MUDders have read

Usenet groups about MUDding for at least some period of time, the cultures of Usenet and of MUDs are in some ways linked. Social conventions evolve in the context of the complete set of technologies in use, including e-mail, netnews, surface mail, telephones, answering machines, voice mail, television, radio, newspapers, magazines, books, and the like. E-mail, netnews, and MUDs have especially complex interactions.

9. The name of the MUD has been changed.

10. LPMUDs are a type of adventure-game-style MUD.

11. The abbreviation "r.g.m" stands for "rec.games.mud," the Usenet newsgroup on which this discussion is taking place.

12. A newbie is a new player with little experience. According to Raymond [7], the term comes from British slang for "new boy," and first became popular on the net in the group talk.bizarre. A newbie monster is a monster that a low-level player could defeat.

13. This is an abbreviation for "by the way."

■ Q U E S T I O N S   F O R   R E R E A D I N G

Here are some questions sent by Amy Bruckman:

1. How is gender perceived differently on-line versus face-to-face? What about race and age?

2. Do you think these differences could affect our off-line perceptions of gender, race, and age? If so, in what ways for the better and in what ways for the worse?

Here is my question (which assumes that you have not yet been to a MUD or MOO):

3. Given your reading of Leslie's and Bruckman's articles, how would you think MUDs differ, if any, from actual life? Specifically, do MUDs dull actual life or enhance it? Do MUDs contribute to a counterproductive confusion between actuality and fantasy? Or do they, by way of role playing, foster a better understanding of self- and group identity? If both, then add up the gains and losses. In your estimation, what is to be done with this ever-growing sophisticated technology?

■ W R I T I N G   A S S I G N M E N T   F O R   R E R E A D I N G

Jot down how people IRL have responded to you (including family, friends, acquaintances, and strangers) during a period of 48 hours. Compare these differences with students in class. After you have listened to 15 or so, do you notice that there is a pattern building of how men respond to women, women to men; older adults to younger adults, younger adults to older adults; whites to African Americans, African Americans to whites; whites to Asian Americans, Asian Americans to whites; African Americans to Latinos, Latinos to African Americans; and so on?

Allucquère Rosanne Stone's "In Novel Conditions: The Cross-Dressing Psychiatrist" first appeared under the different title "Will the Real Body Please Stand Up?" in Cyberspace: First Steps, ed. Michael Benedikt (Cambridge: MIT Press, 1991). Later it was republished with some changes in Stone's book The War of Desire and Technology at the Close of the Mechanical Age (Cambridge: MIT UP, 1995). Stone's purpose in her chapter and throughout her book is to discuss the problems of computer-mediated conversations. When speaking to people IRL, whether in person or on the telephone, we get clues as to whom we are in contact with. In CMC, we get clues, but not the same ones. Communication in CMC is so new to us that we do not quite know how to live with it. What it promises us, however, is the means of experimenting with multiple personae and roles, which can be good. What it also promises us, often after the fact, is the means of a terrible disillusionment. While MUDS and MOOS and IRCS have a tremendous potential for bringing people together in a massive experiment of learning a variety of social roles across the interface of VR, they also can introduce us occasionally to the dark ("darq") side of being on-line, which occurs when the interface of being IRL clashes with the interface of being in VR.

Allucquère Rosanne Stone

In Novel Conditions:
The Cross-Dressing
Psychiatrist

nderlying the story of multiplicity and continuity as it unfolded in Oshkosh is a tangle of multiply nested assumptions. One thread of this tangle is that one of our Western industrialized cultural assumptions is that subjectivity is invariably constituted in relation to a physical substrate—that social beings, people, exist by virtue of possessing biological bodies through which their existence is warranted in the body politic. Another is that we know unproblematically what "body" is. Let me tell you a boundary story, a tale of the nets, as a means of anchoring one corner of the system of discourse within which this discussion operates. It is also a fable of loss of innocence—which, I have begun to notice, is the tenor of more than one story here. In the course of this essay a number of chapters partake of the loss-of-innocence motif . . . in retrospect, a surprising number. People who still believe that I have some sort of rosy vision of the future of virtual systems are advised to reread a few of the origin myths I present in these pages. Herewith, another.[1]

This one begins in 1982, on the CompuServe conference system. CompuServe is owned by *Reader's Digest* and Ziff-Davis. CompuServe began in 1980 as a generalized information service, offering such things as plane reservations, weather reports, and the "Electronic Shopping Mall," which is simply lists of retail items that can be purchased through CompuServe and ordered on-line. It was one of perhaps three major information services that started up within a year or so of each other. The others were The Source, Prodigy, and America Online. All of these were early attempts by businesses to capture some of the potential market formed by consumers with computers and modems, an attempt to generate business of a kind that had not previously existed. None of the on-line services knew what this market was or where it lay, but their thinking, as evidenced by reports in the *Wall Street Journal,* was along the lines of television. That is, computers would be media in which goods could be sold visually, like a shopping service. Prodigy implemented this theory by having banners advertising products running along the bottom of the screen, while permitting conferencing to go on in the main screen area. The companies who financed The Source seem to have believed that unrestricted conversation was against the American Way, because it was never permitted to occur within the system. Both Prodigy and The Source saw their primary mission as selling goods. They attracted audiences in the same way that broadcasters did, as a product to be delivered to manufacturers in the form of demographic groups meant to watch commercials. The Source went quietly bankrupt in 1986. Prodigy, by virtue of having permitted on-line conferencing, weathered the storms of the shakeout days in which it became clear that whatever on-line services were good for, it was *not* to deliver audiences to manufacturers. CompuServe, however, found out quite early that the thing users found most interesting was on-line conferencing and chat—that is, connectivity. Or, as an industry observer put it, "People are willing to pay money just to connect. Just for the opportunity to communicate." America Online never saw itself as a medium for selling goods and concentrated on connectivity in various forms from the beginning.

Most on-line conferences now offer what are called chat lines, which are virtual places where many people can interact simultaneously in real time. In the Internet world there are many such places with quite elaborately worked-out geographies; these are known as multiple-user thisses-and-thats.[2] The first of these were direct descendants of real-life things called role-playing games, or RPGs.

Role-playing games were developed within a rather small community whose members shared certain social traits. First, most were members of the Society for Creative Anachronism, or SCA, one of the driving forces behind the Renaissance Faires. The SCA sponsors medieval tournaments with full regalia as well as medieval banquets in medieval style, which is to say, 16-course meals of staggering richness. Once one has attended such a banquet, the shorter life span of people in the Middle Ages becomes much more understandable.

Participants are extremely dedicated to the principles of the SCA, one of which is that tournaments go on as scheduled, rain or shine. In California, where many SCA members live, this can be risky. There is something not exactly bracing about watching two grown men in full armor trying to whack each other with wooden swords while thrashing and wallowing through ankle-deep mud and pouring rain. During this phase of my research I got a glimpse of what it must be like to be trained as a traditional anthropologist, and finally to be sent to some godforsaken island where one thrashes out

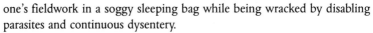

one's fieldwork in a soggy sleeping bag while being wracked by disabling parasites and continuous dysentery.

Second, many of the people who belong to the SCA also consider themselves part of what is sometimes called the neopagan movement. And third, particularly in California, many of the people who participate in SCA events and who belong to the neopagan movement are also computer programmers.

Originally RPGs seemed to be a way for SCA members to continue their fantasy roles between tournaments. Role-playing games are also a good deal less expensive and more energy efficient than tournaments. They have tremendous grab for their participants, are open-ended, and improve with the players' imaginations. Some RPG participants have kept a good game going for years, meeting monthly for several days at a time to play the game, eating, sleeping, and defecating in role. For some, the game has considerably more appeal than reality. They express an unalloyed nostalgia for a time when roles were clearly defined, folks lived closer to nature, life was simpler, magic was afoot, and adventure was still possible. They are aware, to a certain extent, that their Arthurian vision of the Middle Ages is thoroughly bogus, but they have no intention of allowing reality to temper their enthusiasm.

The first RPG was published as a set of rules and character descriptions in 1972 and was called, appropriately enough, Dungeons and Dragons. It was an extension, really, of SCA into a textual world. D&D, as it quickly became known, used a set of rules invented by the Austin game designer Steve Jackson called the Generic Universal Role Playing System, or GURPS, for constructing characters, and voluminous books containing lists of character attributes, weapons, and powers. A designated Dungeon Master acted as arbiter of disputes and prognosticator of events and had considerable effect on the progress of the game; creative Dungeon Masters, like good tops, were hard to find and, once discovered, were highly prized.

The first 120- and 300-baud modems became available in the mid-1970s, and virtually the instant that they became available, the programmers among the D&D community began to develop versions of the game that could be played on-line. The first on-line systems ran on small personal computers (the very first were developed for Apple II's). Because of the problems of writing multitasking operating systems, which allow several people to log in on-line at once, the first systems were time-aliased; that is, only one person could be on-line at a time, so simultaneous real-time interaction was impossible. The first of these to achieve a kind of success was a program in northern California called *Mines of Moria*. The program contained most of the elements that are still ubiquitous in on-line RPG systems: Quests, Fearsome Monsters, Treasure, Wizards, Twisty Mazes, Vast Castles, and, because the systems were written by young heterosexual males, the occasional Damsel in Distress.[3]

As the Internet came into being from its earlier and more cloistered incarnation as ARPAnet, more people had access to multitasking systems. The ARPAnet had been built around multitasking systems such as Bell Laboratories' UNIX and had packet-switching protocols built in; these enabled multiple users to log in from widely separated locations. The first on-line multiple-user social environments were written in the early 1980s and were named, after their origins, Multiple-User-Dungeons or MUDs. When the staid academics and military career persons who actually oversaw the operation of the large systems began to notice the MUDs in the mid-1980s, they took offense at such cavalier misuse of their equipment. The writers of the MUDs then tried the bald public-relations move of renaming their systems Mutiple-User *Domains* in an effort to distance themselves from the offensive odor of play that accompanied the word *dungeon.* The system administrators were unimpressed by this move. Later multiple-user social environments came to be called MUSEs (for Multiple-User Social Environment), MUSHes (for Multiple-User Social Host), MUCKs, and MOOs (MUD Object Oriented). Of these, all are somewhat similar except for the MOO, which uses a different and much more flexible method of creating objects within the simulation. Unlike MUDs, objects and attributes in a MOO are persistent; when the MOO crashes, everything is still in place when it comes back up. This property has importance for large systems such as Fujitsu's *Habitat* and smaller ones that contain many complex objects, such as the MIT Media Lab's MediaMOO and the U. Texas ACTLab's PointMOOT.

The multiple-user social environments written for the large, corporate-owned, for-pay systems betray none of their origins in low culture. They do not contain objects, nor can objects be constructed within them. They are thoroughly sanitized, consisting merely of bare spaces within which interactions can take place. They are the Motel 6 of virtual systems. Such an environment is the CB chat line on CompuServe. It was on CompuServe, some time early in 1982, that a New York psychiatrist named Sanford Lewin opened an account.

They are the Motel 6 of virtual systems.

In the conversation channels, particularly the real-time chat conferences such as CB, it is customary to choose an on-line name, or "handle," that may have no relationship to one's "real" name, which CompuServe does not reveal.[4] Frequently, however, participants in virtual conversations choose handles that express some part of their personalities, real or imagined. Lewin, with his profession in mind, chose the handle "Doctor."

It does not appear to have dawned on him that the term was gender-neutral until a day not long after he first signed on. He had been involved in a general chat in public virtual space, had started an interesting conversation with a woman, and they had decided to drop into private mode for a few minutes. In private mode two people who have chosen to converse can only "hear" each other, and the rest of the people in the vicinity cannot "hear" them. The private conversation was actually under way for a few minutes before Lewin realized it was profoundly different from any conversation he'd been in before. Somehow the woman to whom he was talking had mistaken him for a *woman* psychiatrist. He had always felt that even in his most personal conversations with women there was always something missing, some essential connection. Suddenly he understood why, because the conversation he was now having was deeper and more open than anything he'd experienced. "I was stunned," he said later, "at the conversational mode. I hadn't known that women talked among themselves that way. There was so much more vulnerability, so much more depth and complexity. And then I thought to myself, Here's a terrific opportunity to help people, by catching them when their normal defenses are down and they're more able to hear what they need to hear."

Lewin reasoned, or claimed to have reasoned, that if women were willing to let down their conversational barriers with other women in the chat system, then as a psychiatrist he could use the chat system to do good. The obvious strategy of continuing to use the gender-neutral "Doctor" handle didn't seem like the right approach. It appears that he became deeply intrigued with the idea of interacting with women *as a woman,* rather than using a female persona as a masquerade. He wanted to become a female persona to such an extent that he could feel what it was like to be a woman in some deep and essential way. And at this point his idea of helping women by becoming an on-line woman psychiatrist took a different turn.

He opened a second account with CompuServe under the name Julie Graham.[5] He spent considerable time working out Julie's persona. He needed someone who would be fully functioning on-line, but largely unavailable off-line in order to keep her real identity secret. For the most part, he developed an elaborate and complex history for Julie, but creating imaginary personae was not something with which he had extensive experience. So there were a few minor inconsistencies in Julie's history from time to time; and it was these that provided the initial clues that eventually tipped off a few people on the net that something was wrong. As it turned out, though, Julie's major problems didn't arise from the inconsistencies in her history, but rather from the consistencies—from the picture-book life Lewin had developed for her.

Julie first signed on in 1982. She described herself as a New York neuropsychologist who, within the last few years, had been involved in a serious automobile accident caused by a drunken driver. Her boyfriend had been killed, and she had suffered severe neurological damage to her head and spine, in particular to Broca's area, which controls speech. She was now mute and paraplegic. In addition, her face had been severely disfigured, to the extent that plastic surgery was unable to restore her appearance. Consequently she never saw anyone in person. She had become a recluse, embittered, slowly withdrawing from life, and seriously planning suicide, when a friend gave her a small computer and modem and she discovered CompuServe.

After being tentatively on-line for a while, her personality began to flourish. She began to talk about how her life was changing, and how interacting with other women in the net was helping her reconsider her situation. She stopped thinking of suicide and began planning her life. Although she lived alone and currently held no job, she had a small income from an inheritance; her family had made a fortune in a mercantile business, so at least she was assured of a certain level of physical comfort. She was an atheist, who enjoyed attacking organized religion; smoked dope, and was occasionally quite stoned on-line late at night; and was bisexual, from time to time coming on to the men and women with whom she talked. In fact, as time went on,

she became flamboyantly sexual. Eventually she was encouraging many of her friends to engage in net sex with her.

Some time during this period Julie changed her handle, or sign-on pseudonym, as a celebration of her return to an active social life, at least on the net. She still maintained her personal privacy, insisting that she was too ashamed of her disfigurements and her inability to vocalize, preferring to be known only by her on-line persona. People on the chat system held occasional parties at which those who lived in reasonable geographic proximity would gather to exchange a few socialities in biological mode, and Julie assiduously avoided these. Instead she ramped up her social profile on the net even further. Her standard greeting was a huge, expansive "HI!!!!!!!!!!!!"

> **Her standard greeting was a huge, expansive "HI!!!!!!!!!!!!"**

Julie started a women's discussion group on CompuServe. She also had long talks with women outside the group, and her advice was extremely helpful to many of them. Over the course of time several women confided to her that they were depressed and thinking about suicide, and she shared her own thoughts about her brush with suicide and helped them to move on to more life-affirming attitudes. She also helped several women with drug and chemical dependencies. An older woman confided her desire to return to college and her fear of being rejected; Julie encouraged her to go through with the application process. Once the woman was accepted, Julie advised her on the writing of several papers (including one on MPD) and in general acted as wise counsel and supportive sister.

She also took it upon herself to ferret out pretenders in the chat system, in particular men who masqueraded as women. As Van Gelder pointed out in her study of the incident, Julie was not shy about warning women about the dangers of letting one's guard down on the net. "Remember to be careful," Van Gelder quotes her as saying, "Things may not be as they seem."[6]

There is a subtext here, which has to do with what I have been calling the on-line persona. Of course we all change personae all the time, to suit the social occasion, although with on-line personae the act is more purposeful. Nevertheless, the societal imperative with which we have been raised is that there is one primary persona, or "true identity," and that in the off-line world—the "real world"—this persona is firmly attached to a single physical body, by which our existence as a social being is authorized and in which it is grounded. The origin of this "correct" relationship between body and persona seems to have been contemporaneous with the Enlightenment, the same cultural moment that gave birth to what we like to call the sovereign subject. True, there is no shortage of examples extending far back in time of a sense of something in the body other than just meat. Usually this has to do with an impalpable soul or a similar manifestation—some agency that carries with it the seat of consciousness, and that normally may be decoupled from the body only after death. For many people, though, the soul or some impalpable avatar routinely journeys free of the body, and a certain amount of energy is routinely expended in managing the results of its travels. Partly the Western idea that the body and the subject are inseparable is a worthy exercise in wish fulfillment—an attempt to explain why ego-centered subjectivity terminates with the substrate *and* to enforce the termination. Recently we find in science fiction quite a number of attempts to refigure this relationship, notably in the work of authors like John Varley, who has made serious tries at constructing phenomenologies of the self (e.g., Varley 1986).

Julie worked off her fury at drunk drivers by volunteering to ride along in police patrol cars. Because of her experience at neuropsychology, she was able to spot erratic driving very quickly, and by her paralysis she could offer herself as a horrible example of the consequences. During one of these forays she met a young cop named John. Her disability and disfigured face bothered him not a whit, and they had a whirlwind romance. Shortly he proposed to her. After Julie won his mother over (she had told him "he was throwing his life away by marrying a cripple"), they were married in a joyous ceremony. Rather than having a live reception, they held the reception on-line, toasting and being toasted by friends from remote sites around the country. They announced that they intended to honeymoon in the Greek islands, and soon real postcards from Greece began showing up in their friends' mailboxes.

Julie's professional life began to bloom. She began attending conferences and giving papers around the States, and shortly in Europe as well. Of course there were problems, but John was the quintessential caring husband, watching out for her, nurturing her. Her new popularity on the conference circuit allowed them to take frequent trips to exotic places. While they were on safari, if there was a place her wheelchair couldn't reach, he simply carried her. When they were home he was frequently out on stakeouts in the evenings, which gave her lots of time to engage with her on-line friends. Occasionally he would take over the keyboard and talk to her friends on the chat system.

Julie began talking about becoming a college teacher. She felt that she could overcome her handicap by using a computer in the classroom. This would be hooked to a large screen to "talk" with her students.[7] Throughout the planning of her new career, John was thoroughly supportive and caring.[8]

It was some time during this period that Julie's friends first began to become suspicious. She was always off at conferences, where presumably she met face to face with colleagues. And she and John spent a lot of time on exotic vacations, where she must also be seeing people face to face. It seemed that the only people who never got to see her were her on-line friends. With them she maintained a firm and unyielding invisibility. There were beginning to be too many contradictions. But it was the other disabled women on-line who pegged her first. They knew the real difficulties—personal and interpersonal—of being disabled. Not "differently abled," that wonderful term, but rather the brutal reality of the way most people—including some friends—related to them. In particular they knew the

exquisite problems of negotiating friendships, not to mention love relationships, in close quarters with the "normally" abled. In that context, Julie's relationship with the unfailingly caring John was simply impossible. John was a
Stepford husband.

Still, nobody had yet pegged Julie as other than a disabled woman. The
other disabled women on-line thought that she was probably a disabled
woman, but also felt that she was probably lying about her romantic life and
about her frequent trips. But against that line of argument they had to deal
with the reality that they had hard evidence of some of those trips—real
postcards from Greece—and in fact Julie and John had gone back to Greece
next year, accompanied by another flurry of postcards.

Julie, John, Joan—they are all wonderful examples of the war of desire and
technology. Their complex virtual identities are real and productive interventions into our cultural belief that the unmarked social unit, besides being
white and male, is a single self in a single body. Multiple personality "disorder" is another such intervention. As I tried to make clear in "Identity in
Oshkosh," MPD is generally considered to be pathological, the result of
trauma. But we can look to the construction and management of pathology
for the circumstances that constitute and authorize the unmarked, so that we
may take the pathologization of MPD and in general the management and
control of any manifestations of body-self, other than the one body–one self
norm, to be useful tools to take apart discourses of the political subject so we
can see what makes them work. There are other interventions to be made, and
here we interrogate a few Harawayan elsewheres—in this case, virtual space,
the phantasmic "structure" within which real social interactions take place—
for information. Of course, the virtual environment of the chat lines is just the
beginning, a look at a single event when such events were still singular.

Julie's friends weren't the only ones who were nervous over the turns her
life was taking and the tremendous personal growth she was experiencing. In
fact, Lewin was getting nervous too. Apparently he'd never expected the
impersonation to succeed so dramatically. He thought he'd make a few contacts on-line, and maybe offer helpful advice to some women. What had happened instead was that he'd found himself deeply engaged in developing a
whole new part of himself that he'd never known existed. His responses had
long since ceased to be a masquerade; with the help of the on-line mode and
a certain amount of textual prosthetics, he was in the process of *becoming* Julie.
She no longer simply carried out his wishes at the keyboard; she had her own
emergent personality, her own ideas, her own directions. Not that he was losing his own identity, but he was certainly developing a parallel one, one of
considerable puissance. Jekyll and Julie. As her friendships deepened and
simultaneously the imposture began to unravel, Lewin began to realize the
enormity of his deception.

And the simplicity of the solution.

Julie had to die.

And so events ground inexorably onward. One day Julie became seriously ill. With John's help, she was rushed to the hospital. John signed on to her account to tell her on-line friends and to explain what was happening: Julie had been struck by an exotic bug to which she had little resistance, and in her weakened state it was killing her. For a few days she hovered between life and death, while Lewin hovered, setting up her demise in a plausible fashion.

The result was horrific. Lewin, as John, was deluged with expressions of shock, sorrow, and caring. People offered medical advice, offered financial assistance, sent cards, sent flowers. Some people went into out-and-out panic. The chat lines became jammed. So many people got seriously upset, in fact, that Lewin backed down. He couldn't stand to go through with it. He couldn't stand to engineer her death. Julie recovered and came home.

The relief on the net was enormous. Joyous messages were exchanged. Julie and John were overwhelmed with caring from their friends. In fact, sometime during the great outpouring of sympathy and concern, while Julie was at death's door, one of her friends managed to find out the name of the hospital where she was supposed to be staying. He called, to see if he could help out, and was told there was no one registered by that name. Another thread unraveled.

Lewin was still stuck with the problem that he hadn't had the guts to solve. He decided to try another tack, one that might work even better from his point of view. Shortly, Julie began to introduce people to her new friend, Sanford Lewin, a New York psychiatrist. She was enormously gracious about it, if not downright pushy. To hear her tell it, Lewin was the greatest thing to hit a net since Star-Kist Tuna. She told them Lewin was absolutely wonderful, charming, graceful, intelligent, and eminently worthy of their most affectionate attention. Thus introduced, Lewin then began trying to make friends with Julie's friends himself.

He couldn't do it.

Sanford simply didn't have the personality to make friends easily on-line. Where Julie was freewheeling and jazzy, Sanford was subdued and shy. Julie was a confirmed atheist, an articulate firebrand of rationality, while Sanford was a devout conservative Jew. Julie smoked dope and occasionally got a bit drunk on-line; Sanford was, how shall we say, drug-free—in fact, he was frightened of drugs—and he restricted his drinking to a little Manischewitz on high holy days. And to complete the insult, Julie had fantastic luck with sex on-line, while when it came to erotics Sanford was a hopeless klutz who didn't know a vagina from a virginal. In short, Sanford's Sanford persona was being defeated by his Julie persona.

What do you do when your imaginary playmate makes friends better than you do?

With Herculean efforts Lewin had succeeded in striking up at least a beginning friendship with a few of Julie's friends when the Julie persona began to come seriously unraveled. First the disabled women began to wonder aloud, then Lewin took the risk of revealing himself to a few more women with whom he felt he had built a friendship. Once he started the process, word of what was happening spread rapidly through the net. But just as building Julie's original persona had taken some time, the actual dismantling of it took several months, as more clearly voiced suspicions gradually turned to factual information and the information was passed around the conferences, repeated, discussed, and picked over. Shortly the process reached a critical level where it became self-supporting. In spite of the inescapable reality of the deception, though, or rather in spite of the inescapable unreality of Julie Graham, there was a kind of temporal and emotional mass in motion that, Newton-like, tended to remain in motion. Even as it slowly disintegrated like one of the walking dead, the myth of Julie still tended to roll ponderously ahead on its own, shedding shocked clots of ex–Julie fans as it ran down. The effect, though spread out over time, was like a series of bombing raids interspersed throughout a ground war.

Perhaps to everyone's surprise, the emotion that many of those in the chat system felt most deeply was mourning. Because of the circumstances in which it occurred, Julie's unmasking as a construct, a cross-dressing man, had been worse than a death. There was no focused instant of pain and loss. There was no funeral, no socially supported way to lay the Julie persona to rest, to release one's emotions and to move on. The help Julie had given people in that very regard seemed inappropriate in the circumstance. Whatever else Julie was or wasn't, she had been a good friend and a staunch supporter to many people in need, giving unstintingly of her time and virtual energy wherever it was required. Her fine sense of humor and ability to see the bright side of difficulties had helped many people, mostly women, over very difficult places in their lives. At least some of her charm and charisma should have rubbed off on Lewin. But it didn't. And, quite understandably, some of the women did not bounce back with forgiveness. At least one said that she felt a deep emotional violation which, in her opinion, was tantamount to sexual assault. "I felt raped," she said, "I felt as if my deepest secrets were violated. The good things Julie did . . . were all done by deception." Some of the women formed a support group to talk about their sense of betrayal and violation, which they referred to wryly as "Julie-anon."

> *Some of the women formed a support group . . . which they referred to wryly as "Julie-anon."*

The relationship of the Julie incident to Peterson's rape of Sarah's Franny persona in Oshkosh is remarkable for its resonances. There is no mention of pathology with Lewin's Julie persona, even though the issue of rape was explicitly raised and one of Lewin's personae committed it. Conversely, in Sarah's case issues of pathology are the deciding factors, working both in her favor (Peterson was convicted because Sarah was judged mentally incompetent because of her multiple personalities) and against her (the decision implicitly places limits on Sarah's social agency). Significantly, in terms of the American system of justice, the question of pathology was never raised in connection with Peterson, who committed a physical act of rape, but was an issue in regard to his victim and was used in a kind of reverse and problematic spin to convict him. The issue of warranting was clear in Sarah's case (Malcolm Ashmore's "furniture" argument . . . the judge and jury accepted the evidence of their eyes, they could *see* Sarah relinquish the host body to the Franny persona), but its occultation in Julie's case enabled the rape (the narrow-bandwidth mode of the nets interfered with the chat participants' warranting Julie to Lewin, so that even when they became suspicious they had to fall back on nonphysical cues that failed them). The issue of presence is more tricky. The judge and jury had a single physical body to look at, but they clearly experienced the presence of several persons within that frame. The wide-bandwidth mode of physicality permitted them to warrant those personae to a specific physical individual, the politically apprehensible citizen. In Julie's case the technosocial mode of virtual systems is in full operation. Because of the limited bandwidth mode of the net, both of Lewin's personae had equal presence—but sufficient presence that participants in the chat conferences had no difficulty in distinguishing between them and in making sophisticated distinctions regarding possible friendships and mutual interests. There was no politically apprehensible citizen, but there were certainly socially legible personae.[9]

The Julie incident produced a large amount of Monday morning quarterbacking among the habitués of CompuServe's chat system. In retrospect, several women felt that Julie's helpfulness had exceeded the bounds of good sense—that what she had actually fostered was dependency. Others focused on her maneuvers for net sex, which sometimes amounted to heavy come-ons even with old friends. Perhaps most telling was the rethinking, among Julie's closest friends, of their attitudes toward Julie's disability. One said, "In retrospect, we went out of our way to believe her. We wanted to give her all the support we could, because of what she was trying to do. So everybody was bending over backward to extend praise and support and caring to this disabled person. We were all so supportive when she got married and when she was making all the speaking engagements . . . in fact there was a lot of patronizing going on that we didn't recognize at the time."

Sanford Lewin retained his CompuServe account. He has a fairly low profile on the net, not least because the Sanford persona is inherently low-key. Many of Julie's friends made at least a token attempt to become friends with him. Not too many succeeded, because, according to them, there simply wasn't that much in common between them. Several of the women who were friends of Julie have become acquaintances of Lewin, and a few have become friends. One said, "I've been trying to forget about the Julie thing. We didn't think it through properly in the first place, and many of the women took risks that they shouldn't have. But whether he's Julie or Sanford, man or woman, there's an inner person that must have been there all along. That's the person I really like."

The hackers in my study population, the people who wrote the programs by means of which the nets exist, just smiled tiredly. A few sympathized with the women whom Julie had taken in, and understood that it takes time to realize, through experience, that social rules do not necessarily map across the interface between the physical and virtual worlds. But all of them had

understood from the beginning that the nets presaged radical changes in
social conventions, some of which would go unnoticed. That is, until an event
like a disabled woman who is revealed to be "only" a persona—not a true
name at all—along with the violated confidences that resulted from the different senses in which various actors understood the term *person,* all acted
together to push these changes to the foreground. Some of these engineers, in
fact, wrote software for the utopian possibilities it offered. Young enough in
the first days of the net to react and adjust quickly, they had long ago taken
for granted that many of the prenet assumptions about the nature of identity
had quietly vanished. Even though they easily understood and assimilated
conflictual situations such as virtual persona as mask for an underlying identity, few had yet thought very deeply about what underlay the underlying
identity. There is an old joke about a woman at a lecture on cosmology who
said that she understood quite clearly what kept the earth hanging in space; it
actually rested on the back of a giant turtle. When asked what the turtle was
standing on, she replied that the turtle was standing on the back of yet
another turtle, and added tartly, "You can't confuse me, young man; it's turtles
all the way down."

Is it personae all the way down?

Say amen, somebody.

■ N O T E S

1. The methodology of this section is diverse. First, there is a great deal of
   what has been called the new thick description, namely, archives of on-line
   conversation. This is made possible by the technological character of text-
   based virtual communities. In most modem programs anything that passes
   across the screen can be written to a file. The floppy disk has become the
   cyberanthropologist's field notebook; in virtual social environments nothing escapes its panoptic gaze. Thus there are simple means of preserving
   the entire conversational records of text-based virtual communities. In the
   instance of graphic-based virtual communities, this is still possible, but not
   for every participant and not without some hacking. In the case of the
   chapter on CommuniTree, I had complete archives of the Tree community
   back to its inception, but then discovered that material that was more pertinent to my description was not part of the archive because it had not
   taken place on-line. In the case of "The Cross-Dressing Psychiatrist" I first
   heard of Julie (whose prototype, Joan Green, has been described by Lindsy
   Van Gelder, *vide infra*) from acquaintances who were participants in the
   chat lines. Then, through an odd series of circumstances, when the Julie
   persona began to unravel I discovered that in an earlier context I had
   already met the psychiatrist involved.

   My account of Lewin's creation of the Julie persona is a pastiche. Very
   little of it comes from transcriptions. Most is from interviews with participants in chat environments in which notable deceptions occurred. At first
   the stories that involved reporting conversations with or about Julie were
   fragmentary and even contradictory; for a while Julie came across as an
   older woman rather than a young one, and that was how I reported her in

my first write-ups. At least one informant said that Julie could only type with a headstick, a device used by people who do not have the use of their hands, and I wrote that up too, thus giving Julie more of a complex persona than any of us had intended. At the time it seemed not unreasonable that a physically challenged person might participate in chat this way, but in fact few "normally" abled chatline habitués would have the patience to wait for a headstick typist; in the 1990s chatlines tend to be torrents of simultaneous high-speed typing.

An earlier insightful account of the incident upon which the Julie events are based was published by Lindsy Van Gelder as "The Strange Case of the Electronic Woman," first in *Ms.* Magazine (1985) and later in Rob Kling's anthology *Computerization and Controversy: Value Conflicts and Social Choices* (Boston 1991). I have used her thorough and emotionally lively account to inform mine, and have paraphrased her work in two instances, one in regard to Julie's allying herself with the police during her convalescence (which made no sense as recorded in my notes), and the other in her depiction of the psychiatrist as using his Joan persona "to do good," which was not in my notes at all and which I found alternately hilarious and sad, and which, I felt, added a remarkable dimension to Lewin's actions. When I first wrote up my version of the incident I pseudonymized the psychiatrist as I do here, and although Van Gelder used his "real" (legal) name, I have retained the pseudonym in this version because my account collapses several people from different chat systems who engaged in similar acts. I doubt that this will cause any confusion, but in case it does, be advised that we are discussing essentially the same events. Van Gelder published first in both instances.

In regard to the opening section on the relationship between the SCA, programming, and California neopaganism, in response to a query by Carolyn Clark I find nothing causal about this provocative juxtaposition and did not intend to imply one—not here, at any rate—except to note that two of the most important individuals in contemporary neopaganism were active in northern California during this period. One is Starhawk, the author of *The Spiral Dance,* and the other, who preferred anonymity, founded what is arguably the largest neopagan networking organization and is a programmer and systems consultant. For better or worse, however, my research has consistently demonstrated an overwhelming juxtaposition of interests between northern California programmers and neopagans, and when one adds in the extremely peculiar incident with the physicists and the metaphase typewriter (*vide infra*), one is left with an inescapable feeling that something causal is happening.

With regard to Role Playing Games (RPGs), I collected my data as a participant observer in several RPG communities in northern and southern California, beginning in 1979 in Bonny Doon with the kind assistance of Preston Q. Boomer, a mathematics instructor and RPG master at San Lorenzo High School, and continuing through 1989 with D&D groups in the Santa Clara Valley, Scotts Valley, and San Diego. Boomer played D&D on the grand scale, involving major Silicon Valley corporations fielding strike teams for full-scale field maneuvers (for example, a scuba team from IBM once staged a surprise assault on Boomer's swimming pool to cut off the water supply to his watercannon), and his story alone should occupy at least a chapter in this book. I attended the SCA tournaments of which I write here, in 1983 in Oakland and throughout the late 1980s in northern and southern California, in full regalia as Ülfedínn öd Vagfÿarândi, an Elder (female) Mage, and subsequently waded through all four removals (a Middle Ages term meaning sixteen courses) of the banquets. My on-line D&D data gathering began in 1980 at 300 baud with the original Mines of Moria. At that time inexpensive modems did not exist, and my little modem consisted of a data latch and decoder chip in hardware and a machine language program (the first 6502 machine language program I wrote) to drive it.

The research underlying the stories of MUDs, MOOs, MUSEs, MUSHes, MUCKs and other multiple-user social environments recounted herein is entirely my own, both from participant observation and on- and off-line interviews. I am not terribly fond of most D&D, so the data gathering was not, as some have alleged, continuous unalloyed pleasure. This task was made easier by ACTLab.rtf.utexas.edu, the Advanced Communication Technologies Laboratory M** host machine, and especially by John Garnett, who graciously consented to supervise the four MUDs and two MOOs that originally ran on the ACTLab system; by Allan Alford, a.k.a. chiphead, who masterminded PointMOOTt, ACTlab's best worked-out and most ill-fated MOO; and by Brian Murfin, a.k.a. Captain Bran Muffin, who has fearlessly and tenaciously administered the ACTlab's many Internet nodes through rain, sleet, dark of night, and the dreadful legion of patches necessitated by the introduction of new operating systems in the midst of ongoing projects—surely a task far beyond the call of duty.

2. Multiple-user social environments are described at length in chapter 5.

3. There are plenty of predecessors to *Mines of Moria,* but they did not incorporate the elements of medieval role playing that were ubiquitous in all of the RPG games that followed. At MIT, by the 1960s the hackers of Project MAC had already written *Wumpus,* and when some of them moved on to Commodore and to Apple Computer in the mid-1970s, they immediately produced a version ported to the 6502 environment called *Hunt the Wumpus.* These could quite correctly be seen as earlier games of adventure, since they also incorporated the trademark Twisty Mazes, Dark Passages, Treasure, and of course the highly unpleasant Wumpus. What they lacked was the element of role playing, of engaging an *alter* persona, that characterized all the later games.

4. The term *handle* comes from amateur radio, where it means "nickname." On the Internet chat system *IRC,* the term is *nick.* In programming, a handle is a means (in practice, usually an address) by which a particular procedure or subroutine is reserved for use by a specific program.

5. In Van Gelder's account the psychiatrist used the name Joan Sue Greene.

6. Even in retrospect I find it astonishing that as late as 1983 significant numbers of people engaged in dialogue in virtual communities failed to grasp the problems raised by the existence of artificial personae. For many

it was a nonissue. The level of concern was heavily gendered; when imposture became an issue, it was women who were most often hurt. This seems to be true because many women carried their social expectations regarding conversational style and confidentiality across the machinic boundary and into the virtual communities. To this extent they exemplified the conversational style that Lewin found so attractive.

7. At the time Stephen Hawking could still talk, after a fashion, and the keyboard-and-Votrax system that he would subsequently use had not yet been developed. Votraxes can speak in feminine intonation too, and such a system would have been perfect for Joan, had she existed.

8. A large amount of the distrust that began to surround Julie originated in the uncanny perfection of her relationship with John. Lewin had not taken into consideration the possibility of encountering a population of disabled persons on-line other than Julie, and has subsequently indicated that he might have modulated the Joan identity to allow for it. The "real" disabled women on-line were more conscious of the incongruity than was the chat system's general population; under the circumstances, it is not strange that they viewed Julie's life first with joy and perhaps hope, then envy, and finally with deep suspicion.

9. And here, of course, the multiple meanings and uses of the term *apprehensible* become clear.

■ QUESTIONS FOR REREADING

1. When Sanford Lewin decides to open an on-line account in the name of "Julie Graham" he becomes—given the phraseology of Stone's discussion—a cross-dressing psychiatrist. One of the difficulties of trying to get to what Stone sees as the importance of her unfolding narration of the event is that Lewis (an M.D., a psychiatrist) should have known that such a "deception" was basically immoral and destructive to others on-line. (What is the basis for "deception" on-line or at a MOO or MUD? Is not "deception" the name of the game?) If you take that approach to thinking about the "deception," could you not also hold others responsible, at least, for participating in the deception? What would be the *basis* for holding them just as responsible? Is such a question deflected by simply saying that it is not a fair question because it would blame the victims or attempt to make them co-equal in guilt to the victimizer?

2. What is the basic difference between the interface of being IRL and the interface of VR? Should there be warnings, as we find on packs of cigarettes and bottles of drinks with alcohol, when people enter cyberspace and VR? When they enter an IRC or a MUD or MOO?

■ WRITING ASSIGNMENT FOR REREADING

Pretend that you are on-line in an IRC and that you carry on a conversation as someone you are not. Write both sides of the dialogue. Enter an IRC or go to a MOO and sign on as someone else, and carry on a "deceptive" dialogue with people. The next time that you see a friend, tell him or her a deceptive story about another mutual friend. When I ask you to do the first two assignments, am I asking you to be immoral or deceptive? Am I asking you to be immoral or deceptive in the third assignment? When Leslie and Bruckman talk about the value of role playing, are they talking about the value of being immoral? Write an argumentative paper discussing these issues.

Lisa Nakamura's "Race In/For Cyberspace: Identity Tourism and Racial Passing on the Internet" first appeared on-line and then in Works and Days 25/26,

Vol. 13.1–2 (1995): 181–93.
Prior to the publication of this article, most attention of cyber-ethnographers (people who study the natives in cyber-places) focused on gender roles. When going to most MOOS, the guests or regular participants are asked to select a gender, which can be male, female, or any third form. When going to the same MOOS, however, the participants are given no option of choosing a race. When a participant does choose a race as part of his/her/its description—say, as a samurai warrior—it is usually based on racial stereotypes. What Nakamura suggests is that it is not only equally valuable to consider the representation of race in VR, but also more specifically valuable in coming to understand "cross-cultural passing" as a form of "identity tourism" (fantasy travel) and not at all a part of real life. Again, we have the clash between two interfaces, IRL and CMC.

Lisa Nakamura

"Race In/For Cyberspace: Identity Tourism and Racial Passing on the Internet"

A cute cartoon dog sits in front of a computer, gazing at the monitor and typing away busily. The cartoon's caption jubilantly proclaims, "On the Internet, nobody knows you're a dog!" This image resonates with particular intensity for those members of a rapidly expanding subculture which congregates within the consensual hallucination defined as cyberspace. Users define their presence within this textual and graphical space through a variety of different activities—commercial interaction, academic research, netsurfing, real time interaction and chatting with interlocutors who are similarly "connected"—but all can see the humor in this image because it illustrates so graphically a common condition of being and self-definition within this space. Users of the Internet represent themselves within it solely through the medium of keystrokes and mouse-clicks, and through this medium they can describe themselves and their physical bodies any way they like; they perform their bodies as text. On the Internet, nobody knows that you're a dog; it is possible to "computer crossdress" (Stone 84) and represent yourself as a different gender, age, race, etc. The technology of the Internet offers its participants unprecedented possibilities for communicating with each other in real time, and for controlling the conditions of their own self-representations in ways impossible in face-to-face interaction. The cartoon seems to celebrate access to the Internet as a social leveler which permits even dogs to express freely themselves in discourse to their masters, who are deceived into thinking that they are their peers, rather than their property. The element of difference, in this cartoon the difference between species, is comically subverted in this image; in the medium of cyberspace, distinctions and imbalances in power between beings who perform themselves solely through writing seem to have been deferred, if not effaced.

This utopian vision of cyberspace as a promoter of a radically democratic form of discourse should not be underestimated. Yet the image can be read on several other levels as well. The freedom which the dog chooses to avail itself of is the freedom to "pass" as part of a privileged group, i.e. human computer users with access to the Internet. This is possible because of the discursive dynamic of the Internet, particularly in chat spaces like LambdaMOO where users are known to others by self-authored names which they give their "characters" rather than more telling e-mail addresses with domain names. Defining gender is a central part of the discourse—players who choose to present themselves as "neuter," one of the several genders available to players on LambdaMOO, are often asked to "set gender," as if the choice to have a neuter gender is not a choice at all, or at least one that other players choose to recognize. Gender is an element of identity which must be defined by each player—though the creators of LambdaMOO try to contribute toward a reimagining of gender by offering four, two more than are acknowledged in "real life," still, one must be chosen—the choice is not optional. Each player must "enunciate" the gender that they choose, since this gender will be visible to other players who call up other players' physical descriptions on their screens. However, race is not an "option" which must be chosen—though players can elect to write it into their descriptions, it is not required that they do so. My study, which I would characterize as ethnographic, with certain important reservations, focuses on the ways in which race is "written" in the cyberspace locus called LambdaMOO, as well as the ways it is read by other players, the conditions under which it is enunciated, contested, and ultimately erased and suppressed, and the ideological implications of these performative acts of writing and reading otherness. What does the way race is written in LambdaMOO reveal about the enunciation of difference in new electronic media? Have the rules of the game changed, and if so, how?

Role-playing sites on the Internet such as LambdaMOO offer their participants programming features such as the ability to physically "set" one's gender, race, and physical appearance, through which they can, indeed are required to, project a version of the self which is inherently theatrical. Since the "real" identities of the interlocutors at Lambda are unverifiable (except by crackers and hackers, whose outlaw manipulations of code are unanimously construed by the Internet's citizens as a violation of both privacy and personal freedom) it can be said that everyone who participates is "passing," as it is impossible to tell if a character's description matches a player's physical characteristics.

... everyone who participates is "passing."

Some of the uses to which this infixed theatricality are put are benign and even funny—descriptions of self as a human-size pickle or pot-bellied pig are not uncommon, and generally are received in a positive, amused, tolerant way by other players. Players who elect to describe themselves in racial terms, as Asian, African American, Latino, or other members of

oppressed and marginalized minorities, are often seen as engaging in a form
of hostile performance, since they introduce what many consider a real-life
"divisive issue" into the phantasmatic world of cybernetic textual interaction.
The borders and frontiers of cyberspace which had previously seemed so
amorphous take on a keen sharpness when the enunciation of racial otherness
is put into play as performance. While everyone is "passing," some forms of
racial passing are condoned and practiced since they do not threaten the
integrity of a national sense of self which is defined as white.

The first act a participant in LambdaMOO performs is that of writing a self
description—it is the primal scene of cybernetic identity, a post-modern performance of the mirror stage:

*Identity is the first thing you create in a MUD. You have to decide the name of your alter-
nate identity—what MUDders call your character. And you have to describe who this
character is, for the benefit of the other people who inhabit the same MUD. By creating
your identity, you help create a world. Your character's role and the roles of the others
who play with you are part of the architecture of belief that upholds for everybody in the
MUD the illusion of being a wizard in a castle or a navigator aboard a starship: the roles
give people new stages on which to exercise new identities, and their new identities affirm
the reality of the scenario. (Rheingold)*

In LambdaMOO it is required that one choose a gender; though two of the
choices are variations on the theme of "neuter," the choice cannot be deferred
because the programming code requires it. It is impossible to receive autho-
rization to create a character without making this choice. Race is not only not
a required choice, it is not even on the menu.[1] Players are given as many lines
of text as they like to write any sort of textual description of themselves that
they want. The "architecture of belief" which underpins social interaction in
the MOO, that is, the belief that your interlocutors possess distinctive human
identities which coalesce through and vivify the glowing letters scrolling
down the computer screen, is itself built upon the form of fantastic autobio-
graphical writing called the self-description. The majority of players in LambdaMOO do not mention race at all in their self-description, though most do
include eye and hair color, build, age, and the pronouns which indicate a male
or a female gender.[2] In these cases when race is not mentioned as such, but
hair and eye color is, race is still being evoked—a character with blue eyes
and blond hair will be assumed to be white. Yet while the textual conditions
of self-definition and self-performance would seem to permit players total
freedom, within the boundaries of the written word, to describe themselves in
any way they choose, this choice is actually an illusion. This is because the
 choice not to mention race does in fact constitute a choice—in the absence of
racial description, all players are assumed to be white. This is partly due to
the demographics of Internet users—most are white, male, highly educated,
and middle class. It is also due to the utopian belief system prevalent in the
MOO. This system, which claims that the MOO should be a free space for play,
strives toward policing and regulating racial discourse in the interest of social
harmony. This system of regulation does permit racial role playing when it fits

within familiar discourse of racial stereotyping, and thus perpetuates these discourses. I am going to focus on the deployment of Asian performance within the MOO because Asian personae are by far the most common non-white ones chosen by players and offer the most examples for study.

The vast majority of male Asian characters deployed in the MOO fit into familiar stereotypes from popular electronic media such as video games, television, and film, and popular literary genres such as science fiction and historical romance. Characters named Mr. Sulu, Chun Li, Hua Ling, Anjin San, Musashi, Bruce Lee, Little Dragon, Nunchaku, Hiroko, Miura Tetsuo, and Akira invoke their counterparts in the world of popular media; Mr. Sulu is the token "Oriental" in the television show *Star Trek,* Hua Ling and Hiroko are characters in the science fiction novels *Eon* and *Red Mars,* Chun Li and Liu Kang are characters from the video games "Street Fighter" and "Mortal Kombat," the movie star Bruce Lee was nicknamed "Little Dragon," Miura Tetsuo and Anjin San are characters in James Clavell's popular novel and miniseries *Shogun,* Musachi is a medieval Japanese folklore hero, and Akira is the title of a Japanese animated film of the genre called "anime." The name Nunchaku refers to a weapon, as does, in a more oblique way, all of the names listed above. These names all adapt the samurai warrior fantasy to cyberdiscursive role playing, and permit their users to perform a notion of the Oriental warrior adopted from popular media. This is an example of the crossing-over effect of popular media into cyberspace, which is, as the latest comer to the array of electronic entertainment media, a bricolage of figurations and simulations. The Orientalized male persona, complete with sword, confirms the idea of the male Oriental as potent, antique, exotic, and anachronistic.

This type of Orientalized theatricality is a form of identity tourism; players who choose to perform this type of racial play are almost always white, and their appropriation of stereotyped male Asiatic samurai figures allows them to indulge in a dream of crossing over racial boundaries temporarily and recreationally. Choosing these stereotypes tips their interlocutors off to the fact that they are not "really" Asian; they are instead "playing" in an already familiar type of performance. Thus, the Orient is brought into the discourse, but only as a token or "type." The idea of a non-stereotyped Asian male identity is so seldom enacted in LambdaMOO that its absence can only be read as a symptom of a suppression.

Tourism is a particularly apt metaphor to describe the activity of racial identity appropriation, or "passing" in cyberspace. The activity of "surfing," (an activity already associated with tourism in the mind of most Americans) the Internet not only reinforces the idea that cyberspace is not only a place where travel and mobility are featured attractions, but also figures it as a form of travel which is inherently recreational, exotic, and exciting, like surfing. The choice to enact oneself as a samurai warrior in LambdaMOO constitutes a form of identity tourism which allows a player to appropriate an Asian racial identity without any of the risks associated with being a racial minority in real life. While this might seem to offer a promising venue for non-Asian characters to see through the eyes of the Other by performing themselves as

Asian through on-line textual interaction, the fact that the personae chosen are overwhelmingly Asian stereotypes blocks this possibility by reinforcing these stereotypes.

This theatrical fantasy of passing as a form of identity tourism has deep roots in colonial fiction, such as Kipling's *Kim* and T. E. Lawrence's *Seven Pillars of Wisdom,* and Sir Richard Burton's writings. The Irish orphan and spy Kim, who uses disguise to pass as Hindu, Muslim, and other varieties of Indian natives, experiences the pleasures and dangers of cross-cultural performance. Said's insightful reading of the nature of Kim's adventures in cross-cultural passing contrasts the possibilities for play and pleasure for white travelers in an imperialistic world controlled by the European empire with the relatively constrained plot resolutions offered that same boy back home. "For what one cannot do in one's own Western environment, where to try to live out the grand dream of a successful quest is only to keep coming up against one's own mediocrity and the world's corruption and degradation, one can do abroad. Isn't it possible in India to do everything, be anything, go anywhere with impunity?" (42). To practitioners of identity tourism as I have described it above, LambdaMOO represents a phantasmatic imperial space, much like Kipling's Anglo-India, which supplies a stage upon which the "grand dream of a successful quest" can be enacted.

Since the incorporation of the computer into the white-collar workplace the line which divides work from play has become increasingly fluid. It is difficult for employers and indeed, for employees, to always differentiate between doing "research" on the Internet and "playing": exchanging e-mail, checking library catalogues, interacting with friends and colleagues through synchronous media like "talk" sessions, and videoconferencing offer enhanced opportunities for gossip, jokes, and other distractions under the guise of work.[3] Time spent on the Internet is a hiatus from "rl" (or real life, as it is called by most participants in virtual social spaces like LambdaMOO), and when that time is spent in a role-playing space such as Lambda, devoted only to social interaction and the creation and maintenance of a convincingly "real" milieu modeled after an "international community," that hiatus becomes a full-fledged vacation. The fact that Lambda offers players the ability to write their own descriptions, as well as the fact that players often utilize this programming feature to write stereotyped Asian personae for themselves, reveal that attractions lie not only in being able to "go" to exotic spaces,[4] but to co-opt the exotic and attach it to oneself. The appropriation of racial identity becomes a form of recreation, a vacation from fixed identities and locales.

This vacation offers the satisfaction of a desire to fix the boundaries of cultural identity and exploit them for recreational purposes. As Said puts it, the tourist who passes as the marginalized Other during his travels partakes of a fantasy of social control, one which depends upon and fixes the familiar contours of racial power relations.

It is the wish-fantasy of someone who would like to think that everything is possible, that one can go anywhere and be anything. T. E. Lawrence in The Seven Pillars of

Wisdom *expresses this fantasy over and over, as he reminds us how he—a blond and blue-eyed Englishman—moved among the desert Arabs as if he were one of them. I call this a fantasy because, as both Kipling and Lawrence endlessly remind us, no one—least of all actual whites and non-whites in the colonies—ever forgets that "going native" or playing the Great Game are facts based on rock-like foundations, those of European power. Was there ever a native fooled by the blue or green-eyed Kims and Lawrences who passed among the inferior races as agent adventurers? I doubt it . . . (Said 44)*

As Donna Haraway notes, high technologies "promise ultimate mobility and perfect exchange—and incidentally enable tourism, that perfect practice of mobility and exchange, to emerge as one of the world's largest single industries" (168). Identity tourism in cyberspaces like LambdaMOO functions as a fascinating example of the promise of high technology to enhance travel opportunities by redefining what constitutes travel—logging on to a phantasmatic space where one can appropriate exotic identities means that one need never cross a physical border or even leave one's armchair to go on vacation. This "promise" of "ultimate mobility and perfect exchange" is not, however, fulfilled for everyone in LambdaMOO. The suppression of racial discourse which does not conform to familiar stereotypes, and the enactment of notions of the Oriental which do conform to them, extends the promise of mobility and exchange only to those who wish to change their identities to fit accepted norms.

Performances of Asian female personae in LambdaMOO are doubly repressive because they enact a variety of identity tourism which cuts across the axes of gender and race, linking them in a powerful mix which brings together virtual sex, Orientalist stereotyping, and performance. A listing of some of the names and descriptions chosen by players who masquerade as "Asian" "females" at LambdaMOO include: AsianDoll, Miss_Saigon, Bisexual_Asian_Guest, Michelle_Chang, Geisha_Guest, and MaidenTaiwan. They describe themselves as, for example, a "mystical Oriental beauty, drawn from the pages of a Nagel calendar," or, in the case of the Geisha_Guest, a character owned by a white American man living in Japan:

a petite Japanese girl in her twenties. She has devoted her entire life to the perfecting the tea ceremony and mastering the art of lovemaking. She is multi-orgasmic. She is wearing a pastel kimono, 3 under-kimonos in pink and white. She is not wearing panties, and that would not be appropriate for a geisha. She has spent her entire life in the pursuit of erotic experiences.

Now, it is commonly known that the relative dearth of women in cyberspace results in a great deal of "computer cross dressing," or men masquerading as women. Men who do this are generally seeking sexual interaction, or "netsex" from other players of both genders. When the performance is doubly layered, and a user extends his identity tourism across both race and gender, it is possible to observe a double appropriation or objectification which uses the "Oriental" as part of a sexual lure, thus exploiting and reifying through performance notions of the Asian female as submissive, docile, a sexual plaything.

The fetishization of the Asian female extends beyond LambdaMOO into other parts of the Internet. There is a Usenet newsgroup called "alt.sex.fetish.orientals" which is extremely active—it is also the only one of the infamous "alt.sex" newsgroups which overtly focuses upon race as an adjunct to sexuality.

Cyberspace is the newest incarnation of the idea of national boundaries. It is a phenomenon more abstract yet at the same time more "real" than outer space, since millions of participants deploy and immerse themselves within it daily, while space travel has been experienced by only a few people. The term "cyberspace" participates in a topographical trope which, as Stone points out, defines the activity of on-line interaction as a taking place within a locus, a space, a "world" unto itself. This second "world," like carnival, possesses constantly fluctuating boundaries, frontiers, and dividing lines which separate it from both the realm of the "real" (that which takes place off line) and its corollary, the world of the physical body which gets projected, manipulated, and performed via on-line interaction. The title of the *Time* magazine cover story for July 25, 1994, "The Strange New World of Internet: Battles on the Frontiers of Cyberspace," is typical of the popular media's depictions of the Internet as a world unto itself with shifting frontiers and borders which are contested in the same way that national borders are. The "battle" over borders takes place on several levels which have been well documented elsewhere, such as the battle over encryption and the conflict between the rights of the private individual to transmit and receive information freely and the rights of government to monitor potentially dangerous, subversive, or obscene material which crosses state lines over telephone wires. These contests concern the distinction between public and private. It is, however, seldom acknowledged that the trope of the battle on the cyber frontier also connotes a conflict on the level of cultural self-definition. If, as Chris Chesher notes, "the frontier has been used since as a metaphor for freedom and progress, and . . . space exploration, especially, in the 1950s and 1960s was often called the 'new frontier,' " (18) the figuration of cyberspace as the most recent representation of the frontier sets the stage for border skirmishes in the realm of cultural representations of the Other. The discourse of space travel during this period solidified the American identity by lining out the contours of a cosmic, or "last," frontier.[5] The "race for space," or the race to stake out a border to be defended against both the non-human (aliens) and the non-American (the Soviets), translates into an obsession with race and a fear of racial contamination, always one of the distinctive features of the imperialist project. In films such as *Alien,* the integrity and solidarity of the American body is threatened on two fronts—both the anti-human (the alien) and the passing-as-human (the cyborg) seek to gain entry and colonize Ripley's human body. Narratives which locate the source of

Cyberspace is the newest incarnation of the idea of national boundaries.

contaminating elements within a deceitful and uncanny technologically enabled theatricality—the ability to pass as human—depict performance as an occupational hazard of the colonization of any space. New and futuristic technologies call into question the integrity of categories of the human since they enable the non-human to assume a human face and identity.

Recently, a character on Lambda named "Tapu" proposed a piece of legislation to the Lambda community in the form of petition. This petition, entitled "Hate-Crime," was intended to impose penalties upon characters who harassed other characters on the basis of race. The players' publicly posted response to this petition, which failed by a narrow margin, reveals a great deal about the particular variety of utopianism common to real-time textual on-line social interaction. The petition's detractors argued that legislation or discourse designed to prevent or penalize racist "hate speech" was unnecessary since those offended in this way had the option to "hide" their race by removing it from their descriptions. A character named "Taffy" writes, "Well, who knows my race unless I tell them? If race isn't important then why mention it? If you want to get in somebody's face with your race then perhaps you deserve a bit of flak. Either way I don't see why we need extra rules to deal with this." "Taffy," who signs himself "proud to be a sort of greyish pinky color with bloches" [sic], recommends a strategy of both blaming the victim and suppressing race, an issue which "isn't important" and shouldn't be mentioned because doing so gets in "somebody's face." The fear of the "flak" supposedly generated by player's decisions to include race in their descriptions of self is echoed in another post to the same group by "Nougat," who points out that "how is someone to know what race you are a part of? If [sic] this bill is meant to combat comments by towards people of different races, or just any comments whatsoever? Seems to me, if you include your race in your description, you are making yourself the sacrificial lamb. I don't include 'caucasian' in my description, simply because I think it is unnecessary. And thusly, I don't think I've ever been called 'honkey.'" Both of these posts emphasize that race is not, should not be, "necessary" to social interaction on LambdaMOO. The punishment for introducing this extraneous and divisive issue into the MOO, which represents a vacation space, a Fantasy Island of sorts, for its users, is to become a "sacrificial lamb." The attraction of Fantasy Island lay in its ability to provide scenarios for the fantasies of privileged individuals. And the maintenance of this fantasy, that of a race-free society, can only occur by suppressing forbidden identity choices.

While many of the members of social on-line communities like LambdaMOO are stubbornly utopian in their attitudes toward the power dynamics and flows of information within the technologically mediated social spaces they inhabit, most of the theorists are pessimistic. Andrew Ross and Constance Penley introduce the essays in their collection *Technoculture* by asserting that "the odds are firmly stacked against the efforts of those committed to creating technological countercultures" (xiii). Chesher concedes that "In spite of the claims that everyone is the same in virtual worlds, access to technology and necessary skills will effectively replicate class divisions of the rest of reality in the virtual spaces" (28) and "will tend to reinforce existing inequalities, and propagate already dominant ideologies" (29). Indeed, the cost of net access does contribute toward class divisions as well as racial ones; the vast majority of the Internet's users are white and middle-class. One of the dangers of identity tourism is that it takes this restriction across the axes of race/class in the "real world" to an even more subtle and complex degree by reducing non-white identity positions to part of a costume or masquerade to be used by curious vacationers in cyberspace. Asianness is co-opted as a "passing" fancy, an identity-prosthesis which signifies sex, the exotic, passivity when female, and anachronistic dreams of combat in its male manifestation. "Passing" as a samurai or geisha is diverting, reversible, and a privilege mainly used by white men. The paradigm of Asian passing masquerades on LambdaMOO itself works to suppress racial difference by setting the tone of the discourse in racist contours, which inevitably discourage "real life" Asian men and women from textual performance in that space, effectively driving race underground. As a result, a default "whiteness" covers the entire social space of LambdaMOO—race is "whited out" in the name of cybersocial hygiene.

The dream of a new technology has always contained within it the fear of total control, and the accompanying loss of individual autonomy. Perhaps the best way to subvert the hegemony of cybersocial hygiene is to use its own metaphors against itself. Racial and racist discourse in the MOO is the unique product of a machine and an ideology. Looking at discourse about race in cyberspace as a computer bug or ghost in the machine permits insight into the ways that it subverts that machine. A bug interrupts a program's regular commands and routines, causing it to behave unpredictably. "Bugs are mistakes, or unexpected occurrences, as opposed to things that are intentional" (Aker 12). Programmers routinely debug their work because they desire complete control over the way their program functions, just as Taffy and Nougat would like to debug LambdaMOO of its "sacrificial lambs," those who insist on introducing new expressions of race into their world. Discourse about race in cyberspace is conceptualized as a bug, something which an efficient computer user would eradicate since it contaminates their work/play. The "unexpected occurrence" of race has the potential, by its very unexpectedness, to sabotage the ideology-machine's routines. Therefore, its articulation is critical, as is the ongoing examination of the dynamics of this articulation. As Judith Butler puts it:

Doubtlessly crucial is the ability to wield the signs of subordinated identity in a public domain that constitutes its own homophobic and racist hegemonies through the erasure or domestication of culturally and politically constituted identities. And insofar as it is imperative that we insist upon those specificities in order to expose the fictions of an imperialist humanism that works through unmarked privilege, there remains the risk that we will make the articulation of ever more specified identities into the aim of political activism. Thus every insistence on identity must at some point lead to a taking stock of the constitutive exclusions that reconsolidate hegemonic power differentials . . . (118)

The erasure and domestication of Asianness on LambdaMOO perpetuates an Orientalist myth of social control and order. As Cornell West puts it, as Judith Butler puts it, "race matters," and "bodies matter." Programming language and Internet connectivity have made it possible for people to interact without putting into play any bodies but the ones they write for themselves. The temporary divorce which cyberdiscourse grants the mind from the body and the text from the body also separates race and the body. Player scripts which eschew repressive versions of the Oriental in favor of critical rearticulations and recombinations of race, gender, and class, and which also call the fixedness of these categories into question, have the power to turn the theatricality characteristic of MOOspace into a truly innovative form of play, rather than a tired reiteration and reinstatement of old hierarchies. Role playing is a feature of the MOO, not a bug, and it would be absurd to ask that everyone who plays within it hew literally to the "rl" gender, race, or condition of life. A diversification of the roles which get played, which are permitted to be played, can enable a thought-provoking detachment of race from the body, and an accompanying questioning of the essentialness of race as a category. Performing alternative versions of self and race jams the ideology-machine, and facilitates a desirable opening up of what Judith Butler calls "the difficult future terrain of community" (242) in cyberspace.

■ N O T E S

1. Some MUDs such as Diku and Phoenix require players to select races. These MUDs are patterned after the role-playing game Dungeons and Dragons and unlike Lambda, which exists to provide a forum for social interaction and chatting, focus primarily on virtual combat and the accumulation of game points. The races available to players (orc, elf, dwarf, human, etc.) are familiar to readers of the "sword and sorcery" genre of science fiction, and determine what sort of combat "attributes" a player can exploit. The combat metaphor which is a part of this genre of role playing reinforces the notion of racial difference.

2. Most players do not choose either spivak or neuter as their gender, perhaps because this type of choice is seen as a nonchoice. Spivaks and neuters are often asked to "set gender" by other players; they are seen as having deferred a choice rather than having made an unpopular one. Perhaps this is an example of the "informatics of domination" which Haraway describes.

3. Computer users who were using their machines to play games at work realized that it was possible for their employers and coworkers to spy on them while walking nearby and notice that they were slacking—hence, they developed screen savers which, at a keystroke, can instantly cover their "play" with a convincingly "work-like" image, such as a spreadsheet or business letter.

4. Microsoft's recent television and print media advertising campaign markets access to both personal computing and networking by promoting these

activities as a form of travel; the ads ask the prospective consumer, "Where do you want to go today?" Microsoft's promise to transport the user to new spaces where desire can be fulfilled is enticing in its very vagueness, offering an open-ended invitation for travel and novel experiences.

5. The political action group devoted to defending the right to free speech in cyberspace against governmental control calls itself "The Electronic Frontier"; this is another example of the metaphorization of cyberspace as a colony to be defended against hostile takeovers.

■ WORKS CITED

Aker, Sharon et al. *Macintosh Bible* 3rd edition. Berkeley: Goldstein and Blair, 1987–91.

Butler, Judith. *Bodies That Matter: On the Discursive Limits of "Sex."* New York: Routledge, 1993.

Chesher, Chris. "Colonizing Virtual Reality: Construction of the Discourse of Virtual Reality, 1984–1992." *Cultronix,* vol. 1, issue 1, Summer 1994. *The English Server.* Online. 16 May 1995.

Elmer-Dewitt, Philip. "Battle for the Soul of the Internet." *Time,* 25 July 1994.

Haraway, Donna. *Simians, Cyborgs, and Women.* New York: Routledge, 1991.

Penley, Constance and Andrew Ross. *Technoculture.* Minneapolis: University of Minnesota Press, 1991.

Rheingold, Howard. *The Virtual Community.* New York: HarperPerennial, 1993. *The Well.* Online. 16 May 1995.

Said, Edward. Introduction. *Kim.* By Rudyard Kipling. New York: Penguin, 1987. 7–46.

Stone, Allucquére Rosanne. "Will the Real Body Please Stand Up?: Boundary Stories About Virtual Cultures." *Cyberspace: First Steps.* Ed. Michael Benedikt. Cambridge: MIT Press, 1994.

■ QUESTIONS FOR REREADING

Here are Lisa Nakamura's questions:

1. What are some of the risks, pleasures, and dangers of representing oneself as a member of a different race on-line? Is there any particular group that benefits from this practice, according to this article? In what way do they benefit? Is there any group that suffers? Which one and in what way?

2. Some critics see the Net as a utopian and democratic space where prejudice need not exist. Where do you draw the line between representations of self that reinforce racial stereotyping and those that challenge it? What do you think of Geisha_Guest's performance?

3. When you are representing yourself on-line, are you aware of yourself as a member of a racial or ethnic group? Do you tend to perceive others in these terms? Why or why not? Do you think that the Internet is a role-playing space that encourages the suppression of race as a factor in social interaction?

■ WRITING ASSIGNMENT FOR REREADING

Note that Nakamura builds on Stone's article. Write a paper comparing the arguments about role playing in Stone's and Nakamura's articles. State as clearly as you can each author's purpose for writing. Are both authors passing the same judgments about the difference between IRL and VR representations? Do both articles equally join or keep separate or see the collaborative value of IRL representations and VR representations? Do both authors put forth the same political implications in their writing?

Julian Dibbell's "A Rape in Cyberspace" first appeared in The Village Voice, December 23, 1993, and has been published at numerous Web sites. The version included here, however, has at the end a three-page commentary with further reflections on the article's reception. Perhaps one of the most famous canonized articles on male-female relations is Dibbell's "A Rape in Cyberspace; or, How an Evil Clown, a Haitian Trickster Sprit, Two Wizards, and a Cast of Dozens Turned a Database into a Society." (This is the full, correct title!) The virtual rape, many say, took place at LambdaMoo. Extending Leslie's and Bruckman's concerns about male-female role playing in cyberspace, Dibbell raises the whole question concerning the possibility of virtual rape, getting us to rethink what can constitute rape. The brilliance of the article is that it records the concerns and virtual acts of the members of LambdaMoo in attempting to deal with this problem in cyberspace, just as we today are wrestling with the problem of how virtual space is causing us to rethink all of the founding concepts and principles of government and society, of civil and criminal laws.

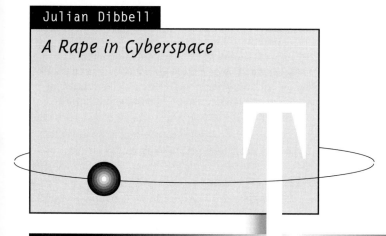

Julian Dibbell

A Rape in Cyberspace

hey say he raped them that night. They say he did it with a cunning little doll, fashioned in their image and imbued with the power to make them do whatever he desired. They say that by manipulating the doll he forced them to have sex with him, and with each other, and to do horrible, brutal things to their own bodies. And though I wasn't there that night, I think I can assure you that what they say is true, because it all happened right in the living room—right there amid the well-stocked bookcases and the sofas and the fireplace—of a house I've come to think of as my second home.

Call me Dr. Bombay. Some months ago—let's say about halfway between the first time you heard the words *information superhighway* and the first time you wished you never had—I found myself tripping with compulsive regularity down the well-traveled information lane that leads to LambdaMoo, a very large and very busy rustic chateau built entirely of words. Nightly, I typed the commands that called those words onto my computer screen, dropping me with what seemed a warm electric thud inside the mansion's darkened coat closet, where I checked my quotidian identity,

Call me Dr. Bombay.

stepped into the persona and appearance of a minor character from a long-gone television sitcom, and stepped out into the glaring chatter of the crowded living room. Sometimes, when the mood struck me, I emerged as a dolphin instead.

I won't say why I chose to masquerade as Samantha Stevens's outlandish cousin, or as the dolphin, or what exactly led to my mild but so-far incurable addiction to the semifictional digital otherworlds known around the Internet as multi-user dimensions, or MUDs. This isn't my story, after all. It's the story of a man named Mr. Bungle, and of the ghostly sexual violence he committed in the halls of LambdaMOO, and most importantly of the ways his violence and his victims challenged the thousand and more residents of that surreal, magic-infested mansion to become, finally, the community so many of them already believed they were.

That I was myself one of those residents has little direct bearing on the story's events. I mention it only as a warning that my own perspective is perhaps too steeped in the surreality and magic of the place to serve as an entirely appropriate guide. For the Bungle Affair raises questions that—here on the brink of a future in which human life may find itself as tightly enveloped in digital environments as it is today in the architectural kind— demand a clear-eyed, sober, and unmystified consideration. It asks us to shut our ears momentarily to the techno-utopian ecstasies of West Coast cyberhippies and look without illusion upon the present possibilities for building, in the on-line spaces of this world, societies more decent and free than those mapped onto dirt and concrete and capital. It asks us to behold the new bodies awaiting us in virtual space undazzled by their phantom powers, and to get to the crucial work of sorting out the socially meaningful differences between those bodies and our physical ones. And most forthrightly it asks us to wrap our late modern ontologies, epistemologics, sexual ethics, and common sense around the curious notion of rape by voodoo doll—and to try not to warp them beyond recognition in the process.

In short, the Bungle Affair dares me to explain it to you without resort to dime-store mysticisms, and I fear I may have shape-shifted by the digital moonlight one too many times to be quite up to the task. But I will do what I can, and I can do no better, I suppose, than to lead with the facts. For if nothing else about Mr. Bungle's case is unambiguous, the facts at least are crystal clear.

The facts begin (as they often do) with a time and a place. The time was a Monday night in March, and the place, as I've said, was the living room— which, due to the inviting warmth of its decor, is so invariably packed with chitchatters as to be roughly synonymous among LambdaMOOers with a party. So strong, indeed, is the sense of convivial common ground invested in the living room that a cruel mind could hardly imagine a better place in which to stage a violation of LambdaMOO's communal spirit. And there was cruelty enough lurking in the appearance Mr. Bungle presented to the virtual world—he was at the time a fat, oleaginous, Bisquick-faced clown dressed in cum-stained harlequin garb and girdled with a mistletoe-and-hemlock belt whose buckle bore the quaint inscription "KISS ME UNDER THIS, BITCH!" But whether cruelty motivated his choice of crime scene is not among the established facts of the case. It is a fact only that he did choose the living room.

The remaining facts tell us a bit more about the inner world of Mr. Bungle, though only perhaps that it couldn't have been a very comfortable place. They tell us that he commenced his assault entirely unprovoked, at or about

10 P.M. Pacific Standard Time. That he began by using his voodoo doll to force one of the room's occupants to sexually service him in a variety of more or less conventional ways. That this victim was legba, a Haitian trickster spirit of indeterminate gender, brown-skinned and wearing an expensive pearl gray suit, top hat, and dark glasses. That legba heaped vicious imprecations on him all the while and that he was soon ejected bodily from the room. That he hid himself away then in his private chambers somewhere on the mansion grounds and continued the attacks without interruption, since the voodoo doll worked just as well at a distance as in proximity. That he turned his attentions now to Starsinger, a rather pointedly nondescript female character, tall, stout, and brown-haired, forcing her into unwanted liaisons with other individuals present in the room, among them legba, Bakunin (the well-known radical), and Juniper (the squirrel). That his actions grew progressively violent. That he made legba eat his/her own pubic hair. That he caused Starsinger to violate herself with a piece of kitchen cutlery. That his distant laughter echoed evilly in the living room with every successive outrage. That he could not be stopped until at last someone summoned Zippy, a wise and trusted old-timer who brought with him a gun of near wizardly powers, a gun that didn't kill but enveloped its targets in a cage impermeable even to a voodoo doll's powers. That Zippy fired this gun at Mr. Bungle, thwarting the doll at last and silencing the evil, distant laughter.

These particulars, as I said, are unambiguous. But they are far from simple, for the simple reason that every set of facts in virtual reality (or VR, as the locals abbreviate it) is shadowed by a second, complicating set: the "real-life" facts. And while a certain tension invariably buzzes in the gap between the hard, prosaic RL facts and their more fluid, dreamy VR counterparts, the dissonance in the Bungle case is striking. No hideous clowns or trickster spirits appear in the RL version of the incident, no voodoo dolls or wizard guns, indeed no rape at all as any RL court of law has yet defined it. The actors in the drama were university students for the most part, and they sat rather undramatically before computer screens the entire time, their only actions a spidery flitting of fingers across standard QWERTY keyboards. No bodies touched. Whatever physical interaction occurred consisted of a mingling of electronic signals sent from sites spread out between New York City and Sydney, Australia. Those signals met in LambdaMOO, certainly, just as the hideous clown and the living room party did, but what was LambdaMOO after all? Not an enchanted mansion or anything of the sort—just a middlingly complex database, maintained for experimental purposes inside a Xerox Corporation research computer in Palo Alto and open to public access via the Internet.

To be more precise about it, LambdaMOO was a MUD. Or to be yet more precise, it was a subspecies of MUD known as a MOO, which is short for "MUD, Object-Oriented." All of which means that it was a kind of database especially designed to give users the vivid impression of moving through a physical space that in reality exists only as descriptive data filed away on a hard drive. When users dial into LambdaMOO, for instance, the program immediately presents them with a brief textual description of one of the rooms of the database's fictional mansion (the coat closet, say). If the user wants to leave this room, she can enter a command to move in a particular direction and the database will replace the original description with a new one corresponding to the room located in the direction she chose. When the new description scrolls across the user's screen it lists not only the fixed features of the room but all its contents at that moment—including things (tools, toys, weapons) and other users (each represented as a "character" over which he or she has sole control).

As far as the database program is concerned, all of these entities—rooms, things, characters—are just different subprograms that the program allows to interact according to rules very roughly mimicking the laws of the physical world. Characters may not leave a room in a given direction, for instance, unless the room subprogram contains an "exit" at that compass point. And if a character "says" or "does" something (as directed by its user-owner), then only the users whose characters are also located in that room will see the output describing the statement or action. Aside from such basic constraints, however, LambdaMOOers are allowed a broad freedom to create—they can describe their characters any way they like, they can make rooms of their own and decorate them to taste, and they can build new objects almost at will. The combination of all this busy user activity with the hard physics of the database can certainly induce a lucid illusion of presence—but when all is said and done the only thing you *really* see when you visit LambdaMOO is a kind of slow-crawling script, lines of dialogue and stage direction creeping steadily up your computer screen.

To the extent that Mr. Bungle's assault happened in real life at all, it happened as a sort of Punch-and-Judy show, in which the puppets and the scenery were made of nothing more substantial than digital code and snippets of creative writing.

Which is all just to say that, to the extent that Mr. Bungle's assault happened in real life at all, it happened as a sort of Punch-and-Judy show, in which the puppets and the scenery were made of nothing more substantial than digital code and snippets of creative writing. The puppeteer behind Bungle, as it happened, was a young man logging in to the MOO from a New York University computer. He could have been Al Gore for all any of the others knew, however, and he could have written Bungle's script that night any way he chose. He could have sent a command to print the message "Mr. Bungle, smiling a saintly smile, floats angelic near the ceiling of the living room, showering joy and candy kisses down upon the heads of all below"—and everyone then receiving output from the database's subprogram #17 (a/k/a the "living room") would have seen that sentence on their screens.

Instead, he entered sadistic fantasies into the "voodoo doll," a subprogram that served the not exactly kosher purpose of attributing actions to other characters that their users did not actually write. And thus a woman in Haverford, Pennsylvania, whose account on the MOO attached her to a character she called Starsinger, was given the unasked-for opportunity to read the words

"As if against her will, Starsinger jabs a steak knife up her ass, causing immense joy. You hear Mr. Bungle laughing evilly in the distance." And thus the woman in Seattle who had written herself the character called legba, with a view perhaps to tasting in imagination a deity's freedom from the burdens of the gendered flesh, got to read similarly constructed sentences in which legba, messenger of the gods, lord of crossroads and communications, suffered a brand of degradation all-too customarily reserved for the embodied female.

"Mostly voodoo dolls are amusing," wrote legba on the evening after Bungle's rampage, posting a public statement to the widely read in-MOO mailing list called *social-issues, a forum for debate on matters of import to the entire populace. "And mostly I tend to think that restrictive measures around here cause more trouble than they prevent. But I also think that Mr. Bungle was being a vicious, vile fuckhead, and I . . . want his sorry ass scattered from #17 to the Cinder Pile. I'm not calling for policies, trials, or better jails. I'm not sure what I'm calling for. Virtual castration, if I could manage it. Mostly, [this type of thing] doesn't happen here. Mostly, perhaps I thought it wouldn't happen to me. Mostly, I trust people to conduct themselves with some veneer of civility. Mostly, I want his ass."

Months later, the woman in Seattle would confide to me that as she wrote those words posttraumatic tears were streaming down her face—a real-life fact that should suffice to prove that the words' emotional content was no mere playacting. The precise tenor of that content, however, its mingling of murderous rage and eyeball-rolling annoyance, was a curious amalgam that neither the RL nor the VR facts alone can quite account for. Where virtual reality and its conventions would have us believe that legba and Starsinger were brutally raped in their own living room, here was the victim legba scolding Mr. Bungle for a breach of "civility." Where real life, on the other hand, insists the incident was only an episode in a free-form version of Dungeons and Dragons, confined to the realm of the symbolic and at no point threatening any player's life, limb, or material well-being, here now was the player legba issuing aggrieved and heartfelt calls for Mr. Bungle's dismemberment. Ludicrously excessive by RL's lights, woefully understated by VR's, the tone of legba's response made sense only in the buzzing, dissonant gap between them.

Which is to say it made the only kind of sense that *can* be made of MUDly phenomena. For while the *facts* attached to any event born of a MUD's strange, ethereal universe may march in straight, tandem lines separated neatly into the virtual and the real, its meaning lies always in that gap. You learn this axiom early in your life as a player, and it's of no small relevance to the Bungle case that you often learn it between the sheets, so to speak. Netsex, tinysex, virtual sex—however you name it, in real-life reality it's nothing more than a 900-line encounter stripped of even the vestigial physicality of the voice. And yet, as many a player can tell you, it's possibly the headiest experience the very heady world of MUDs has to offer. Amid flurries of even the most cursorily described caresses, sighs, and penetrations, the glands do engage, and often as throbbingly as they would in a real-life assignation— sometimes even more so, given the combined power of anonymity and textual suggestiveness to unshackle deep-seated fantasies. And if the virtual setting and the interplayer vibe are right, who knows? The heart may engage as well, stirring up passions as strong as many that bind lovers who observe the formality of trysting in the flesh.

To participate, therefore, in this disembodied enactment of life's most body-centered activity is to risk the realization that when it comes to sex, perhaps the body in question is not the physical one at all, but its psychic double, the bodylike self-representation we carry around in our heads. I know, I know, you've read Foucault and your mind is not quite blown by the notion that sex is never so much an exchange of fluids as it is an exchange of signs. But trust your friend Dr. Bombay, it's one thing to grasp the notion intellectually and quite another to feel it coursing through your veins amid the virtual steam of hot netnookie. And it's a whole other mind-blowing trip altogether to encounter it thus as a college frosh, new to the net and still in the grip of hormonal hurricanes and high-school sexual mythologies. The shock can easily reverberate throughout an entire young worldview. Small wonder, then, that a newbie's first taste of MUD sex is often also the first time she or he surrenders wholly to the slippery terms of MUDish ontology, recognizing in a full-bodied way that what happens inside a MUDmade world is neither exactly real nor exactly make-believe, but profoundly, compellingly, and emotionally meaningful.

A sense was brewing that something needed to be done—done soon and in something like an organized fashion—about Mr. Bungle, in particular, and about MUD rape, in general.

And small wonder indeed that the sexual nature of Mr. Bungle's crime provoked such powerful feelings, and not just in legba (who, be it noted, was in real life a theory-savvy doctoral candidate and a longtime MOOer, but just as baffled and overwhelmed by the force of her own reaction, she later would attest, as any panting undergrad might have been). Even players who had never experienced MUD rape (the vast majority of male-presenting characters, but not as large a majority of the female-presenting as might be hoped) immediately appreciated its gravity and were moved to condemnation of the perp. legba's missive to *social-issues followed a strongly worded one from Zippy ("Well, well," it began, "no matter what else happens on Lambda, I can always be sure that some jerk is going to reinforce my low opinion of humanity") and was itself followed by others from Moriah, Raccoon, Crawfish, and evangeline. Starsinger also let her feelings ("pissed") be known. And even Jander, the Clueless Samaritan who had responded to Bungle's cries for help and uncaged him shortly after the incident, expressed his regret once apprised of Bungle's deeds, which he allowed to be "despicable."

A sense was brewing that something needed to be done—done soon and in something like an organized fashion—about Mr. Bungle, in particular, and about MUD rape, in general. Regarding the general problem, evangeline, who identified herself as a survivor of both virtual rape ("many times over") and real-life sexual assault, floated a cautious proposal for a MOO-wide powwow on the subject of virtual sex offenses and what mechanisms if any might be put in place to deal with their future occurrence. As for the specific problem, the answer no doubt seemed obvious to many. But it wasn't until the evening of the second day after the incident that legba, finally and rather solemnly, gave it voice: "I am requesting that Mr. Bungle be toaded for raping Starsinger and I. I have never done this before, and have thought about it for days. He hurt us both."

That was all. Three simple sentences posted to *social*. Reading them, an outsider might never guess that they were an application for a death warrant. Even an outsider familiar with other MUDS might not guess it, since in many of them "toading" still refers to a command that, true to the gameworlds' sword-and-sorcery origins, simply turns a player into a toad, wiping the player's description and attributes and replacing them with those of the slimy amphibian. Bad luck for sure, but not quite as bad as what happens when the same command is invoked in the MOOish strains of MUD: not only are the description and attributes of the toaded player erased, but the account itself goes too. The annihilation of the character, thus, is total.

And nothing less than total annihilation, it seemed, would do to settle LambdaMOO's accounts with Mr. Bungle. Within minutes of the posting of legba's appeal, SamIAm, the Australian Deleuzean, who had witnessed much of the attack from the back room of his suburban Sydney home, seconded the motion with a brief message crisply entitled "Toad the fukr." SamIAm's posting was seconded almost as quickly by that of Bakunin, covictim of Mr. Bungle and well-known radical, who in real life happened also to be married to the real-life legba. And over the course of the next 24 hours as many as 50 players made it known, on *social* and in a variety of other forms and forums, that they would be pleased to see Mr. Bungle erased from the face of the MOO. And with dissent so far confined to a dozen or so antitoading hardliners, the numbers suggested that the citizenry was indeed moving toward a resolve to have Bungle's virtual head.

There was one small but stubborn obstacle in the way of this resolve, however, and that was a curious state of social affairs known in some quarters of the MOO as the New Direction. It was all very fine. you see, for the LambdaMOO rabble to get it in their heads to liquidate one of their peers, but when the time came to actually do the deed it would require the services of a nobler class of character. It would require a wizard. Masterprogrammers of the MOO, spelunkers of the database's deepest code-structures and custodians of its day-to-day administrative trivia, wizards are also the only players empowered to issue the toad command, a feature maintained on nearly all MUDS as a quick-and-dirty means of social control. But the wizards of LambdaMOO, after years of adjudicating all manner of interplayer disputes with little to show for it but their own weariness and the smoldering resentment of the general populace, had decided they'd had enough of the social sphere. And so, four months before the Bungle incident, the archwizard Haakon (known in RL as Pavel Curtis, Xerox researcher and LambdaMOO's principal architect) formalized this decision in a document called "LambdaMOO Takes a New Direction," which he placed in the living room for all to see. In it, Haakon announced that the wizards from that day forth were pure technicians. From then on, they would make no decisions affecting the social life of the MOO, but only implement whatever decisions the community as a whole directed them to. From then on, it was decreed, LambdaMOO would just have to grow up and solve its problems on its own.

Faced with the task of inventing its own self-governance from scratch, the LambdaMOO population had so far done what any other loose, amorphous agglomeration of individuals would have done: they'd let it slide. But now the task took on new urgency. Since getting the wizards to toad Mr. Bungle (or to toad the likes of him in the future) required a convincing case that the cry for his head came from the community at large, then the community itself would have to be defined; and if the community was to be convincingly defined, then some form of social organization, no matter how rudimentary, would have to be settled on. And thus, as if against its will, the question of what to do about Mr. Bungle began to shape itself into a sort of referendum on the political future of the MOO. Arguments broke out on *social and elsewhere that had only superficially to do with Bungle (since everyone agreed he was a cad) and everything to do with where the participants stood on LambdaMOO's crazy-quilty political map. Parliamentarian legalist types argued that unfortunately Bungle could not legitimately be toaded at all, since there were no explicit MOO rules against rape, or against just about anything else—and the sooner such rules were established, they added, and maybe even a full-blown judiciary system complete with elected officials and prisons to enforce those rules, the better. Others, with a royalist streak in them, seemed to feel that Bungle's as-yet unpunished outrage only proved this New Direction silliness had gone on long enough, and that it was high time the wizardocracy returned to the position of swift and decisive leadership their player class was born to.

And then there were what I'll call the technolibertarians. For them, MUD rapists were of course assholes, but the presence of assholes on the system was a technical inevitability, like noise on a phone line, and best dealt with not through repressive social disciplinary mechanisms but through the timely deployment of defensive software tools. Some asshole blasting violent, graphic language at you? Don't whine to the authorities about it—hit the @gag command and the asshole's statements will be blocked from your screen (and only yours). It's simple, it's effective, and it censors no one.

But the Bungle case was rather hard on such arguments. For one thing, the extremely public nature of the living room meant that gagging would spare the victims only from witnessing their own violation, but not from having others witness it. You might want to argue that what those victims didn't directly experience couldn't hurt them, but consider how that wisdom would sound to a woman who'd been, say, fondled by strangers while passed out drunk and you have a rough idea how it might go over with a crowd of hardcore MOOers. Consider, for another thing, that many of the biologically female participants in the Bungle debate had been around long enough to grow lethally weary of the gag-and-get-over-it school of virtual-rape counseling, with its fine line between empowering victims and holding them responsible for their own suffering, and its shrugging indifference to the window of pain between the moment the rape-text starts flowing and the moment a gag shuts it off. From the outset it was clear that the technolibertarians were going to have to tiptoe through this issue with care, and for the most part they did.

Yet no position was trickier to maintain than that of the MOO's resident anarchists. Like the technolibbers, the anarchists didn't care much for punishments or policies or power elites. Like them, they hoped the MOO could be a place where people interacted fulfillingly without the need for such things. But their high hopes were complicated, in general, by a somewhat less thoroughgoing faith in technology ("Even if you can't tear down the master's house with the master's tools"—read a slogan written into one anarchist player's self-description—"it is a damned good place to start"). And at present they were additionally complicated by the fact that the most vocal anarchists in the discussion were none other than legba, Bakunin, and SamIAm, who wanted to see Mr. Bungle toaded as badly as anyone did.

Needless to say, a pro-death-penalty platform is not an especially comfortable one for an anarchist to sit on, so these particular anarchists were now at great pains to sever the conceptual ties between toading and capital punishment. Toading, they insisted (almost convincingly), was much more closely analogous to banishment; it was a kind of turning of the communal back on the offending party, a collective action which, if carried out properly, was entirely consistent with anarchist models of community. And carrying it out properly meant first and foremost building a consensus around it—a messy process for which there were no easy technocratic substitutes. It was going to take plenty of good old-fashioned, jawbone-intensive grass-roots organizing.

So that when the time came, at 7 P.M. PST on the evening of the third day after the occurrence in the living room, to gather in evangeline's room for her proposed real-time open conclave, Bakunin and legba were among the first to arrive. But this was hardly to be an anarchist-dominated affair, for the room was crowding rapidly with representatives of all the MOO's political stripes, and even a few wizards. Hagbard showed up, and Autumn and Quastro, Puff, JoeFeedback, L-dopa and Bloaf, HerkieCosmo, Silver Rocket, Karl Porcupine, Matchstick—the names piled up and the discussion gathered momentum under their weight. Arguments multiplied and mingled, players talked past and through each other, the textual clutter of utterances and gestures filled up the screen like thick cigar smoke. Peaking in number at around 30, this was one of the largest crowds that ever gathered in a single LambdaMOO chamber, and while evangeline had given her place a description that made it "infinite in expanse and fluid in form," it now seemed anything but roomy. You could almost feel the claustrophobic air of the place, dank and overheated by virtual bodies, pressing against your skin.

I know you could because I too was there, making my lone and insignificant appearance in this story. Completely ignorant of any of the goings-on that had led to the meeting, I wandered in purely to see what the crowd was about, and though I observed the proceedings for a good while, I confess I found it hard to grasp what was going on. I was still the rankest of newbies then, my MOO legs still too unsteady to make the leaps of faith, logic, and empathy required to meet the spectacle on its own terms. I was fascinated by the concept of virtual rape, but I couldn't quite take it seriously.

In this, though, I was in a small and mostly silent minority, for the discussion that raged around me was of an almost unrelieved earnestness, bent, it seemed, on examining every last aspect and implication of Mr. Bungle's crime. There were the central questions, of course: thumbs up or down on Bungle's virtual existence? And if down, how then to ensure that his toading was not just some isolated lynching but a first step toward shaping LambdaMOO into a legitimate community? Surrounding these, however, a tangle of weighty side issues proliferated. What, some wondered, was the real-life legal status of the offense? Could Bungle's university administrators punish him for sexual harassment? Could he be prosecuted under California state laws against obscene phone calls? Little enthusiasm was shown for pursuing either of these lines of action, which testifies both to the uniqueness of the crime and to the nimbleness with which the discussants were negotiating its idiosyncrasies. Many were the casual references to Bungle's deed as simply "rape," but these in no way implied that the players had lost sight of all distinctions between the virtual and physical versions, or that they believed Bungle should be dealt with in the same way a real-life criminal would. He had committed a MOO crime, and his punishment, if any, would be meted out via the MOO.

On the other hand, little patience was shown toward any attempts to downplay the seriousness of what Mr. Bungle had done. When the affable HerkieCosmo proposed, more in the way of a hypothesis than an assertion, that "perhaps it's better to release . . . violent tendencies in a virtual environment rather than in real life," he was tut-tutted so swiftly and relentlessly that he withdrew the hypothesis altogether, apologizing humbly as he did so. Not that the assembly was averse to putting matters into a more philosophical perspective. "Where does the body end and the mind begin?" young Quastro asked, amid recurring attempts to fine-tune the differences between real and virtual violence. "Is not the mind a part of the body?" "In MOO, the body is the mind," offered HerkieCosmo gamely, and not at all implausibly, demonstrating the ease with which very knotty metaphysical conundrums come undone in VR. The not-so-aptly named Obvious seemed to agree, arriving after deep consideration of the nature of Bungle's crime at the hardly novel yet now somehow newly resonant conjecture "All reality might consist of ideas, who knows."

On these and other matters the anarchists, the libertarians, the legalists, the wizardists—and the wizards—all had their thoughtful say. But as the evening wore on and the talk grew more heated and more heady, it seemed increasingly clear that the vigorous intelligence being brought to bear on this swarm of issues wasn't going to result in anything remotely like resolution. The perspectives were just too varied, the meme-scape just too slippery. Again and again, arguments that looked at first to be heading in a decisive direction ended up chasing their own tails; and slowly, depressingly, a dusty haze of irrelevance gathered over the proceedings.

It was almost a relief, therefore, when midway through the evening Mr. Bungle himself, the living, breathing cause of all this talk, teleported into the room. Not that it was much of a surprise. Oddly enough, in the three days since his release from Zippy's cage, Bungle had returned more than once to wander the public spaces of LambdaMOO, walking willingly into one of the fiercest storms of ill will and invective ever to rain down on a player. He'd been taking it all with a curious and mostly silent passivity, and when challenged face to virtual face by both legba and the genderless elder statescharacter PatGently to defend himself on *social, he'd demurred, mumbling something about Christ and expiation. He was equally quiet now, and his reception was still uniformly cool. legba fixed an arctic stare on him—"no hate, no anger, no interest at all. Just . . . watching." Others were more actively unfriendly. "Asshole," spat Karl Porcupine, "creep." But the harshest of the MOO's hostility toward him had already been vented, and the attention he drew now was motivated more, it seemed, by the opportunity to probe the rapist's mind, to find out what made it tick and if possible how to get it to tick differently. In short, they wanted to know why he'd done it. So they asked him.

And Mr. Bungle thought about it. And as eddies of discussion and debate continued to swirl around him, he thought about it some more. And then he said this:

"I engaged in a bit of a psychological device that is called thought-polarization, the fact that this is not RL simply added to heighten the affect of the device. It was purely a sequence of events with no consequence on my RL existence."

They might have known. Stilted though its diction was, the gist of the answer was simple, and something many in the room had probably already surmised: Mr. Bungle was a psycho. Not, perhaps, in real life—but then in real life it's possible for reasonable people to assume, as Bungle clearly did, that what transpires between word-costumed characters within the boundaries of a make-believe world is, if not mere play, then at most some kind of emotional laboratory experiment. Inside the MOO, however, such thinking marked a person as one of two basically subcompetent types. The first was the newbie, in which case the confusion was understandable, since there were few MOOers who had not, upon their first visits as anonymous "guest" characters, mistaken the place for a vast playpen in which they might act out their wildest fantasies without fear of censure. Only with time and the acquisition of a fixed character do players tend to make the critical passage from anonymity to pseudonymity, developing the concern for their character's reputation that marks the attainment of virtual adulthood. But while Mr. Bungle hadn't been around as long as most MOOers, he'd been around long enough to leave his newbie status behind, and his delusional statement therefore placed him among the second type: the sociopath.

And as there is but small percentage in arguing with a head case, the room's attention gradually abandoned Mr. Bungle and returned to the discussions that had previously occupied it. But if the debate had been edging toward ineffectuality before, Bungle's anticlimactic appearance had evidently robbed it of any forward motion whatsoever. What's more, from his lonely corner of the room Mr. Bungle kept issuing periodic expressions of a prickly sort of remorse, interlaced with sarcasm and belligerence, and though it was hard to tell if he wasn't still just conducting his experiments, some people thought his regret genuine enough that maybe he didn't deserve to be toaded after all. Logically, of course, discussion of the principal issues at hand didn't require unanimous belief that Bungle was an irredeemable bastard, but now that cracks were showing in that unanimity, the last of the meeting's fervor seemed to be draining out through them.

People started drifting away. Mr. Bungle left first, then others followed—one by one, in twos and threes, hugging friends and waving goodnight. By 9:45 only a handful remained, and the great debate had wound down into casual conversation, the melancholy remains of another fruitless good idea. The arguments had been well-honed, certainly, and perhaps might prove useful in some as-yet-unclear long run. But at this point what seemed clear was that evangeline's meeting had died, at last, and without any practical results to mark its passing.

It was also at this point, most likely, that JoeFeedback reached his decision. JoeFeedback was a wizard, a taciturn sort of fellow who'd sat brooding on the sidelines all evening. He hadn't said a lot, but what he had said indicated that he took the crime committed against legba and Starsinger very seriously, and that he felt no particular compassion toward the character who had committed it. But on the other hand he had made it equally plain that he took the elimination of a fellow player just as seriously, and moreover that he had no desire to return to the days of wizardly fiat. It must have been difficult, therefore, to reconcile the conflicting impulses churning within him at that moment. In fact, it was probably impossible, for as much as he would have liked to make himself an instrument of LambdaMOO's collective will, he surely realized that under the present order of things he must in the final analysis either act alone or not act at all.

So JoeFeedback acted alone.

He told the lingering few players in the room that he had to go, and then he went. It was a minute or two before ten. He did it quietly and he did it privately, but all anyone had to do to know he'd done it was to type the @who command, which was normally what you typed if you wanted to know a player's present location and the time he last logged in. But if you had run a @who on Mr. Bungle not too long after JoeFeedback left evangeline's room, the database would have told you something different.

"Mr. Bungle," it would have said, "is not the name of any player."

The date, as it happened, was April Fool's Day, and it would still be April Fool's Day for another two hours. But this was no joke: Mr. Bungle was truly dead and truly gone.

They say that LambdaMOO has never been the same since Mr. Bungle's toading. They say as well that nothing's really changed. And though it skirts the fuzziest of dream-logics to say that both these statements are true, the MOO is just the sort of fuzzy, dreamlike place in which such contradictions thrive.

They say that LambdaMOO has never been the same since Mr. Bungle's toading. They say as well that nothing's really changed.

Certainly whatever civil society now informs LambdaMOO owes its existence to the Bungle Affair. The archwizard Haakon made sure of that. Away on business for the duration of the episode, Haakon returned to find its wreckage strewn across the tiny universe he'd set in motion. The death of a player, the trauma of several others, and the angst-ridden conscience of his colleague JoeFeedback presented themselves to his concerned and astonished attention, and he resolved to see if he couldn't learn some lesson from it all. For the better part of a day he brooded over the record of events and arguments left in *social,* then he sat pondering the chaotically evolving shape of his creation, and at the day's end he descended once again into the social arena of the MOO with another history-altering proclamation.

It was probably his last, for what he now decreed was the final, missing piece of the New Direction. In a few days, Haakon announced, he would build into the database a system of petitions and ballots whereby anyone could put to popular vote any social scheme requiring wizardly powers for its implementation, with the results of the vote to be binding on the wizards. At last and for good, the awkward gap between the will of the players and the efficacy of the technicians would be closed. And though some anarchists grumbled about the irony of Haakon's dictatorially imposing universal suffrage on an unconsulted populace, in general the citizens of LambdaMOO seemed to find it hard to fault a system more purely democratic than any that could ever exist in real life. Eight months and a dozen ballot measures later, widespread participation in the new regime has produced a small arsenal of mechanisms for dealing with the types of violence that called the system into being. MOO residents now have access to a @boot command, for instance, with which to summarily eject berserker "guest" characters. And players can bring suit against one another through an ad hoc arbitration system in which mutually agreed-upon judges have at their disposition the full range of wizardly punishments—up to and including the capital.

Yet the continued dependence on death as the ultimate keeper of the peace suggests that this new MOO order may not be built on the most solid of foundations. For if life on LambdaMOO began to acquire more coherence in the wake of the toading, death retained all the fuzziness of pre-Bungle days. This truth was rather dramatically borne out, not too many days after Bungle departed, by the arrival of a strange new character named Dr. Jest. There was a forceful eccentricity to the newcomer's manner, but the oddest thing about his style was its striking yet unnameable familiarity. And when he developed

the annoying habit of stuffing fellow players into a jar containing a tiny simulacrum of a certain deceased rapist, the source of this familiarity became
obvious:

Mr. Bungle had risen from the grave.

In itself, Bungle's reincarnation as Dr. Jest was a remarkable turn of events,
but perhaps even more remarkable was the utter lack of amazement with
which the LambdaMOO public took note of it. To be sure, many residents
were appalled by the brazenness of Bungle's return. In fact,
one of the first petitions circulated under the new voting system was a request for Dr. Jest's toading that almost immediately gathered 52 signatures (but has failed so far to reach
ballot status). Yet few were unaware of the ease with which
the toad proscription could be circumvented—all the toadee
had to do (all the urBungle at NYU presumably had done)
was to go to the minor hassle of acquiring a new Internet
account, and LambdaMOO's character registration program
would then simply treat the known felon as an entirely new and innocent
person. Nor was this ease generally understood to represent a failure of toading's social disciplinary function. On the contrary, it only underlined the truism (repeated many times throughout the debate over Mr. Bungle's fate) that
his punishment, ultimately, had been no more or less symbolic than his crime.

*Mr. Bungle
had risen from
the grave.*

What *was* surprising, however, was that Mr. Bungle/Dr. Jest seemed to
have taken the symbolism to heart. Dark themes still obsessed him—the
objects he created gave off wafts of Nazi imagery and medical torture—but
he no longer radiated the aggressively antisocial vibes he had before. He was
a lot less unpleasant to look at (the outrageously seedy clown description had
been replaced by that of a mildly creepy but actually rather natty young man,
with "blue eyes . . . suggestive of conspiracy, untamed eroticism and perhaps a
sense of understanding of the future"), and aside from the occasional jar-
stuffing incident, he was also a lot less dangerous to be around. It was obvious he'd undergone some sort of personal transformation in the days since I'd
first glimpsed him back in evangeline's crowded room—nothing radical
maybe, but powerful nonetheless, and resonant enough with my own experience, I felt, that it might be more than professionally interesting to talk with
him, and perhaps compare notes.

For I too was undergoing a transformation in the aftermath of that night
in evangeline's, and I'm still not entirely sure what to make of it. As I pursued
my runaway fascination with the discussion I had heard there, as I pored over
the *social debate and got to know legba and some of the other victims and
witnesses, I could feel my newbie consciousness falling away from me. Where
before I'd found it hard to take virtual rape seriously, I now was finding it difficult to remember how I could ever not have taken it seriously. I was proud
to have arrived at this perspective—it felt like an exotic sort of achievement,
and it definitely made my ongoing experience of the MOO a richer one.

But it was also having some unsettling effects on the way I looked at the
rest of the world. Sometimes, for instance, it was hard for me to understand

why RL society classifies RL rape alongside crimes against person or property. Since rape can occur without any physical pain or damage, I found myself reasoning, then it must be classed as a crime against the mind—more intimately and deeply hurtful, to be sure, than cross-burnings, wolf whistles, and virtual rape, but undeniably located on the same conceptual continuum. I did not, however, conclude as a result that rapists were protected in any fashion by the First Amendment. Quite the opposite, in fact: the more seriously I took the notion of virtual rape, the less seriously I was able to take the notion of freedom of speech, with its tidy division of the world into the symbolic and the real.

Let me assure you, though, that I am not presenting these thoughts as arguments. I offer them, rather, as a picture of the sort of mindset that deep immersion in a virtual world has inspired in me. I offer them also, therefore, as a kind of prophecy. For whatever else these thoughts tell me, I have come to believe that they announce the final stages of our decades-long passage into the Information Age, a paradigm shift that the classic liberal firewall between word and deed (itself a product of an earlier paradigm shift commonly known as the Enlightenment) is not likely to survive intact. After all, anyone the least bit familiar with the workings of the new era's definitive technology, the computer, knows that it operates on a principle impracticably difficult to distinguish from the pre-Enlightenment principle of the magic word: the commands you type into a computer are a kind of speech that doesn't so much communicate as *make things happen,* directly and ineluctably, the same way pulling a trigger does. They are incantations, in other words, and anyone at all attuned to the technosocial megatrends of the moment— from the growing dependence of economies on the global flow of intensely fetishized words and numbers to the burgeoning ability of bioengineers to speak the spells written in the four-letter text of DNA—knows that the logic of the incantation is rapidly permeating the fabric of our lives.

And it's precisely this logic that provides the real magic in a place like LambdaMOO—not the fictive trappings of voodoo and shapeshifting and wizardry, but the conflation of speech and act that's inevitable in any computer-mediated world, be it Lambda or the increasingly wired world at large. This is dangerous magic, to be sure, a potential threat—if misconstrued or misapplied—to our always precarious freedoms of expression, and as someone who lives by his words I do not take the threat lightly. And yet, on the other hand, I can no longer convince myself that our wishful insulation of language from the realm of action has ever been anything but a valuable kludge, a philosophically damaged stopgap against oppression that would just have to do till something truer and more elegant came along.

Am I wrong to think this truer, more elegant thing can be found on LambdaMOO? Perhaps, but I continue to seek it there, sensing its presence just beneath the surface of every interaction. I have even thought, as I said, that discussing with Dr. Jest our shared experience of the workings of the MOO might help me in my search. But when that notion first occurred to me, I still felt somewhat intimidated by his lingering criminal aura, and I hemmed and hawed a good long time before finally resolving to drop him MOO-mail requesting an interview. By then it was too late. For reasons known only to himself, Dr. Jest had stopped logging in. Maybe he'd grown bored with the MOO. Maybe the loneliness of ostracism had gotten to him. Maybe a psycho whim had carried him far away or maybe he'd quietly acquired a third character and started life over with a cleaner slate.

Wherever he'd gone, though, he left behind the room he'd created for himself—a treehouse "tastefully decorated" with rare-book shelves, an operating table, and a life-size William S. Burroughs doll—and he left it unlocked. So I took to checking in there occasionally, and I still do from time to time. I head out of my own cozy nook (inside a TV set inside the little red hotel inside the Monopoly board inside the dining room of LambdaMOO), and I teleport on over to the treehouse, where the room description always tells me Dr. Jest is present but asleep, in the conventional depiction for disconnected characters. The not-quite-emptiness of the abandoned room invariably instills in me an uncomfortable mix of melancholy and the creeps, and I stick around only on the off chance that Dr. Jest will wake up, say hello, and share his understanding of the future with me.

He won't, of course, but this is no great loss. Increasingly, the complex magic of the MOO interests me more as a way to live the present than to understand the future. And it's never very long before I leave Dr. Jest's lonely treehouse and head back to the mansion, to see some friends.

I won't pretend I knew what I was doing when I wrote "A Rape in Cyberspace." I thought, to be honest and if you can believe it, that I was setting down little more than an engaging true-life fable, played out in a realm of experience so circumscribed and so unique that no one (except perhaps the residents of LambdaMOO itself) could possibly take it as anything but a curiosity, a traveler's tale brought back from strange climes and only barely pertinent to the world as we know it. The philosophical excursions woven into the piece reached for a certain universal relevance, to be sure, but they were almost an afterthought, added at the last moment in hopes of teasing from the story a broader significance I wasn't entirely sure it had.

I needn't have bothered, though. For in the deluge of online responses to which I was soon exposed, very few readers remarked directly on my transparent attempts at intellectual provocation. It was the story itself that provoked them, or elements of the story anyway. And it was the story seen not as a piece of exotica but as a dispatch from a place maybe a little too close to home: the busy intersection of sex, violence, and representation around which late twentieth-century American culture hovers like a soul obsessed.

That the story tapped such a deep vein of anxieties is a development I look on now with some sense of gratification, yet I can't say I was exactly enjoying myself as those anxieties began flooding in my general direction. Opinions ran strong, and those that reflected not-so-very-well on me—or on the acts and attitudes of the tiny, textual world I had tried to represent as accurately as possible—seemed to run strongest. "Media culture keeps blurring the line between real offense and imaginary offense, but this is ridiculous," wrote one participant in a lengthy discussion on the haut-cachet New York bulletin-board system ECHO. "That article had no journalistic value whatsoever" added another ECHO-dweller, fuming at what many in that virtual community saw as crass exploitation of the unsettling and admittedly problematic notion of "virtual rape": "It was just using the RAPE catchphrase to SELL PAPERS . . . and it brutally trivializes people who have suffered through the real thing."

This hurt. The trivialization charge was an argument I recognized as part of the rhetorical arsenal of pro-sex feminists in their righteous battle against legal scholar Catharine MacKinnon's creepy redefinitions of porn as rape (and more broadly, of word as deed), and I didn't feel at all good about being placed conceptually in her camp. Compared to this insult, one Echoid's crudely worded announcement that he had used a copy of my article to tidy himself after a bowel movement seemed a friendly chuck under the chin. So I was relieved when West Coast feminist pornographer (and disaffected former MacKinnon-ite) Lisa Palac posted on ECHO in the article's favor, downplaying any fuss over its use of the word *rape* as essentially semantic, and finding in it an effective illustration of "how online worlds and identities reflect . . . RL socialization":

I can't tell you how often I am interviewed by reporters who are under the assumption that taking on an online identity is "risk-free." And that for some reason, going online will be free from the social/cultural shapes as we know them. . . . [The subject of] this article may be extreme, but it disproves the "all is safe in cyberspace" notion.

Palac's note signaled, or so I thought, that the debate was mellowing and would soon enough be off my screen and out of my life. In fact, though, what it mainly signaled was that the debate had reached the other side of the country and would soon become fodder for the topic-hungry habitués of the WELL, a Bay Area bulletin-board system even more vigorously literate than ECHO. Once there, the discussion grew a notch more thoughtful, though no less contentious. Even more than the ECHO conference, the WELL's discussion seemed haunted by the ghosts of nearly every nineties polemic to have grappled with the issue of dangerous expression, from Anita Hill to the campus curriculum battles to the *succès de scandale* of "Beavis and Butt-head." The twists and turns of the arguments grew so convoluted that at one point, if I followed correctly, my account of Mr. Bungle's fate was determined to imply that Shakespeare, Sophocles, and Ibsen should also have been lynched on grounds of subjecting countless audience members to the emotional violence of catharsis.

More effectively critical, though, were the comments of R. U. Sirius, cofounder and guiding light of the magazine *Mondo 2000*. "The conflation of language and mediated activity with real activity seems to be more or less complete," wrote Sirius, in a formulation not at all surprising to anyone familiar with *Mondo 2000*'s reputation as a nest of giddy, pop-Baudrillardian armchair prophets stoned out of their minds on the ascendancy of digital simulation. What might have surprised those unable or unwilling to look past that caricature, however, was the entirely characteristic moral rigor Sirius then brought to bear on LambdaMOO's own giddy romp through the conflations of the hyperreal:

These people all volunteered to act in a theater of the imagination and then got scared. Do we want Disney World? As the simulacrum becomes a bigger part of our lives, do we demand that people clip their imaginations at the place where it feels comfortable? . . . I think that freedom would be well served by simple toughening up.

And this hurt too. It was bad enough feeling like a rhetorical football, after all, without feeling part of me wanting to agree with some of those landing the hardest kicks.

Days of online discussion started piling up into weeks, and I began to wonder: How long could this go on? And how long would it be before the turbulence of the debate spilled over into less neatly compartmentalized venues for social interaction, like my more casual online encounters on the MOO, or the offline interactions I still respectfully referred to as real life? The WELL conference slowed down eventually, but controversy over the tale of Mr. Bungle spread into other online conferencing forums: Internet mailing lists, Usenet newsgroups, Compuserve. To this day, in fact, four months after its original publication, the story (stripped down to ASCII and turned loose to wander the nets) continues to find new pockets of interest and to gather online discussion around itself. Yet in the end, what I had dreaded most—the general irruption of the controversy into other areas of my life—has failed to materialize. LambdaMOOers, for the most part, seem to have accepted my interpretation of their world as true to their own experiences and left it at that. Most real-lifers unacquainted with any form of cyberspace, on the other hand, have found in the story a fascinating glimpse of a realm too distant from their own to pass judgment on—a parallel universe perhaps, or maybe a hint of their own future.

Which leaves only the denizens of the bulletin-board cybercosm to argue over the meaning of the life and crimes of Mr. Bungle. And, frankly, the fact that they have done so with such vociferous gusto remains something of a puzzle to me. Certainly, arguing is what people mainly do in such settings, and certainly, as I suggested earlier, the bleedthrough from larger cultural concerns about texts and violence has fed much of the fracas. Yet the more I ponder the furious online response to my story, the more I suspect the real object of that fury is neither LambdaMOO nor America's latest culture wars, but the ambiguous nature of online discourse itself.

Perched on a tightwire between the reasoned deliberation of text and the emotional immediacy of conversation, online communication sets itself up for a fall that is constantly realized. Fooled by the cool surface of electronic text, people lob messages cast in aggressively forensic impersonality into the midst of this combustibly personal medium, and the result, routinely, is just the sort of flame war I found myself embroiled in: a heatedly antagonistic exchange fueled by the most livid of emotions yet pretending in its rhetorical strategies to the most rational of dialogue. And in some sense, I think, the two sides of the Bungle war have taken up the two sides of this basic tension: the rational recognition (on the part of those who found the story ridiculous) that ultimately anything that happens online is "only words on a screen" countered by the emotional understanding (on the part of those who found the story compelling) that words can have powerful and deeply felt effects. It's too much to hope, I suppose, that this tension will ever really be resolved. Still, it's comforting to think that the noisy dialogue sparked by my article has not been only sound and fury. On its surface, of course, the discussion has provided more than its share of insight into a story I myself didn't fully understand when I wrote it. But deeper down, in the very structure of the debate, I have sometimes imagined I can hear the sound of cyberspace groping toward an end to flame wars.

■ QUESTIONS FOR REREADING

1. Plot out, as well as you can, the events that take place in Dibbell's account of a virtual rape at LambdaMOO and his account of how the members of that virtual community responded to it.

2. Once you have plotted out the events, take up the general issue of what constitutes rape. See if you can determine a difference between *actual* and *virtual* rape. Is there a difference between real action and symbolic action?

3. What might be the difference between sexual harassment in actuality, over the telephone, in e-mail messages, or at a MUD/MOO? What might be the consequences for the person being harassed or assaulted?

4. In considering the first three groups of questions, take note of how males and females answer them. If you are a male, listen carefully to what the females say, and vice versa.

■ WRITING ASSIGNMENTS FOR REREADING

1. If you are a male, *go to* a MUD/MOO and sign on with a female name and pretend to be female. (Bruckman, in "Gender Swapping on the Internet," suggests that we do such a thing.) If you are a female, do the opposite. (Go to the Web site for instructions.) Save a record of all of your discussions as a pretender, so that you can study them later. After attempting this exercise, write an account of your experiences and discuss them in class. Then return to Dibbell's article and read it again.

2. Go back and read the writing assignments for Bruckman's article. Now that you have gone to a MUD or MOO, attempt to answer the questions in essay form and share your written experiences with your classmates.

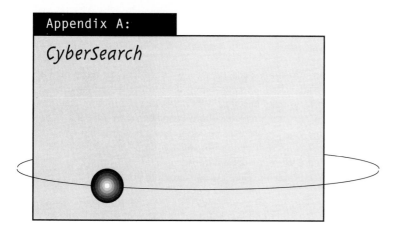

Appendix A:

CyberSearch

- Netiquette
- How To Use E-mail and Subscribe to Lists
- How To Do Research (and Surf) on the Net/www: Some Pointers
- How To Avoid Copyright Problems (Citing Electronic Discourse)
- On-Line Writing Labs (OWLS)

This appendix is basically a *general* guide to doing research on the Net and World Wide Web (www). Therefore, if you already have an e-mail account and some knowledge of the Net and Web, this section may not be very helpful, though it would do you well to review the material discussed here and to look at the material on copyright problems and on OWLS.

So as not to be redundant, I have not included here much information about virtual libraries, which can be found in chapter 5 of *CyberReader*. I have not discussed FTP or Gopher or many other ways of getting around on the Web; instead, I have concentrated on some very powerful search engines (and search engines of search engines) that include ftp and gopher sites as well as other sources. Again, this appendix is only a general guide. Once you are capable of navigating around on the www, you will find many free sources to help you in much greater detail. For example,

- *Electronic Freedom Foundation's Guide to the Internet,* v. 3.20 (formerly *The Big Dummy's Guide to the Internet*), with text without links. <http://www.eff.org/pub/EFF/netguide.eff>

- *John December's Web Text Index.* <http://www.december.com:80/web/text/index.html>

- *Big Dummy's Guide to the Internet,* by Adam Gaffin with Jvrg Heitkvtter, table of contents with links. <http://www.cs.yale.edu/HTML/WORLD/org/eff/bdgtti-1.04/bdgtti-1.04_toc.html>

■ N E T I Q U E T T E

Netiquette is a combination of two words, namely, the *Net* and *etiquette.* Hence, netiquette, which has to do with the basic rules of how to behave in cyberspace.

When you first get into cyberspace, whether you are sending out e-mail or attending a MUD, you are called a *newbie*. Being new to the virtual environment means that you may make mistakes. When we travel to foreign countries, for example, we discover often that the rules of behavior are very different from the ones that we are used to. Cyberspace is a different country! Netiquette, therefore, has been developed to warn you of the problems that you will be confronted with in virtual environments and to instruct you in ways of avoiding these problems. Here are some simple guidelines:

1. Always remember that though you are typing into a monitor, there are human beings on the other end receiving the message. It may be wise at first to just observe and study by reading different posts on newsgroups or discussion groups. In another word, be a *lurker*.

2. Avoid *flaming* someone. In other words, do not attack another person online. If you do, be prepared to be attacked. Don't be afraid to apologize. Understand that as a newbie you can send out a message that unbeknownst to you will be received as a flame (an attack). Until you learn the basic conventions of communicating in this environment, you can easily make a mistake such as responding to someone, say, in an ironic tone (as far as you are concerned) but having it not perceived as ironic (as far as the other person is concerned). Irony or any other similar tone is difficult enough in real life (IRL) to detect. Don't expect someone staring into a monitor reading your text to know that you are being ironic. Tone will usually get interpreted in a negative way.

3. Since face-to-face (F2F) communication is replaced by words typed across a monitor, you will need to learn some of the basic graphic conventions that suggest tone. For example, learn what are called *smileys* and *emoticons*. Here are a few:

:-)	smiling or happy
.)>=	(this is my own smiley . . . pirate + vampire + beard)
:-(	sad
:,(	crying
;-)	wink
:-&	tongue-tied
:-X	lips are sealed
:-o	shocked, incredulous
:-#	my lips are sealed
:D	laughter
:|	Hmmm
>:->	Devilish
(8-o	It's Mr. Bill!

etc.

Or if you know basic but mock hypertext markup language (HTML), you can use what are now being called *emotags*. They will allow you to get away with a certain amount of sarcasm. For example, you can use <SMILE>, <FALLING DOWN LAUGHING>, <CRYING>, <WINK>, etc. Here's how:

```
<IRONIC>John and Joan, I have missed your sarcasm so
much.</IRONIC>
```

Or you could write,

```
<WINK>Grrl, if you only knew what I knew!</WINK>
```

You are limited only by your imagination with this approach.

Along the same lines, if you TYPE YOUR MESSAGE IN ALL CAPS you will be read as being *angry*.

4. Never send a message or say something in private that you would not want the entire world to read. Nothing is secure in cyberspace. And we human beings make mistakes! I have; you will!

   A special caveat: If you are replying to someone's message by way of a reply-command, be very careful; make sure that the address is the correct destination for your message. If someone has forwarded a message to you and you return a message by the reply-command, your message will most likely go out to a lot of people you don't even know. :-(

5. Keep messages, if possible, brief. This rule holds in most cases. But again, when on a list, lurk (observe) for awhile so as to learn what is and is not acceptable. If your message is too long or if you send out far too many messages, brief or long, you may be accused of *spamming*. By the way (BTW), you can shorten your messages by using abbreviations, as I have done a number of times in the preceding paragraphs. Here are some more that are commonly accepted:

   IMHO   in my humble opinion

   IOW   in other words

   FYI   for your information

   TNX   thanks

   ROFL   rolling on the floor laughing

   RTFM   read the f***ing manual . . .

Often, one way to get flamed on a discussion list is to start asking basic questions that you could find the answers to elsewhere. Don't waste other people's time. If you do, you may get a shorthand response such as RTFM. In general, never get on a list as a newbie and start asking people to help you with your homework or making similar requests unless you want to get flamed.

There are many other considerations, but these will get you started. If you want to know more about netiquette, try EINet Galaxy <http://www.einet. net/> and search for the term or any other terms. Also, see *The Net: User Guidelines and Netiquette,* <http://www.fau.edu/~rinaldi/net/index.htm>; or, *I'm Not Miss Manners of the Internet,* <http://www.fau.edu/rinaldi/netiquette. html>. (Often when a URL or address is given, it is placed in <>; understand that you are *not* to type or include these right/left angles when using a URL or an address.)

There are many ways to get yourself on the Net by way of commercial providers, but I am going to assume here that your school or university provides access for you. Moreover, I am going to assume that your access will be by way of what is called a VAX account. (Usually, faculty or more "serious" users of the Net have UNIX accounts, which you may want later to have.)

Getting On-line

The very first thing that you should do is visit the academic computing services on your campus. (In some schools, as at my university, every student is automatically given an account, but it is necessary to request that it be activated.) When you request an account, computing services will most likely give you a pamphlet explaining the use of their system. You will also be given an address, which is composed of these generic parts: your *user name or userid @ domain address*. For example: *jsmith@utarlg.uta.edu*. And you will have to establish a password, which you will have to change intermittently. (You should never, ever give your password to anyone! And when establishing your new password, you should not use your name, initials, or anything obvious to someone who would want to crack into your account and use it for illegal purposes.)

If the computer that you are using is connected directly to the server, then simply follow the instructions given to you by your academic services. (If you have access by way of the web browsers known as Netscape or Internet Explorer, and so on, then forget these instructions altogether and just follow the graphics intuitively. Usually, you will find an icon for an envelope at the lower right of the browser interface.) If you are using a telephone and a modem, however, you will have to make sure that the software you are using is configured correctly and that you have the correct telephone number to dial in for the size of your modem (2400 baud, 14,400 baud, 28,000 baud). Essentially what you are doing is making a telephone call to the university's host computer, which will tell you on your monitor when you have connected. At this point, you will need to know how to log on to a particular service, which would be a particular address to the VAX account (or to the university library address, and so on), and you will need in some cases to establish a terminal emulation setting, which is usually VT100. Again, all of this information has to be obtained from your on-campus computer services, because it can vary from campus to campus, from system to system.

Sending E-mail

Once you get on-line and to the $ or % or equivalent prompt, then you can begin sending and eventually reading mail. This may be done in many cases by typing the word *mail* after the $ prompt and pressing the Return key. Then you will get the *EMAIL>* prompt, after which you type *send* and the Return key. Then you will be asked to type the e-mail address. The way that you do this can vary from service to service. Sometimes you have to put in a lengthy procedure such as IN%"userid@domaine.address". If any of this is missing, you will immediately get a message saying, "illegal address specified." A shorter version of this long procedure does away with IN% and the quotation marks. After typing the full address, again press the Return key. Next, you fill in the *Subject:* heading with a phrase designating specifically what the message is about. In sum, with the longer version:

```
$ mail

EMAIL> send

To: IN%"jsmith@utarlg.uta.edu"

CC:IN%"jbrown@utarlg.uta.edu"

Subject:tomorrow's exam
```

(Notice here, as is found in some software, that there is a *CC:* prompt, giving you an opportunity to send yourself or another person a copy of the message. What you simply do is include the correct address following the same procedure as for the *To:* prompt.) After setting up the complete address, you then again press the Return key and begin your message. Be very careful to type about three-fourths of the way across the space provided and then press the Return key. You should do this with every line. If you do not, there is a chance that the message will be received as an unevenly distributed set of typed lines. Once you have finished your message and want to send it, usually you press *Control-Z.* (Again, check the manual supplied by your academic computer services.) If you want to cancel your message, usually you press *Control-C.*

If you want to delete mail that you have received, simply type *d* (or *delete*) after reading the specific post that you want to delete, or type *d* and the number of the post or posts—for example, d 1–4 or d 1, 2–3—and press Return. All other posts are automatically saved. When you are given an account, you are allotted what are called a number of *blocks;* if you want to check how much space you have remaining, type at the $ or % prompt *show quota* and then press Return.

Once you have sent and read all the messages, you will want to disconnect from the host frame. You do this while you are still in mail mode by typing *exit.* Once in exit, you usually type *logoff.* At this point, use your software command (usually in the *dial* menu) to *hang up* (often Control-H will do, and then Control-Q to quit the application).

Some universities have a mail program called Pine, which is easy to use and allows you to do all kinds of things you cannot do with the method that I've just described. Pine has so many features that I cannot describe them here, but the directions in the software that you will access are very clear. Instead of typing *mail* at the $ or equivalent prompt, you will type *pine* and then press Return, which will get you to the index and the help files:

```
? HELP—Get help using Pine

C COMPOSE MESSAGE—Compose and send a message

I FOLDER INDEX—View messages in current folder
```

L FOLDER LIST—Select a folder to view

A ADDRESS BOOK—Update address book

S SETUP—Configure or update Pine

Q QUIT—Exit the Pine program

Take the time to learn this mail and editing program; it definitely will be worth your effort.

Be aware that the preceding instructions may not be absolutely precise for you. Learning how to get logged on will require some patience and, in many cases, some help from your instructor or a friend.

Subscribing to and Reading Usenet

After sending private mail, you might be interested in looking over what is available in terms of *newsgroups* (on Usenet). Having made this suggestion, however, I must tell you that newsgroups have become more and more controversial because of some of the topics. Many colleges and universities restrict what groups you can have access to. The issue of censorship has been raised. (A famous case is that of the restriction of newgroups at Carnegie-Mellon University. You can go to *The English Server* <http://english-server. hss.cmu.edu/>, CMU, and find information on the controversy.) I mention this issue because you may not have access to Usenet, or you may have access to only a limited version of it. There are many other reasons why your local institution may not provide this service. One is simply space/bandwidth.

In any case, here are the basics: Usenet is not by way of e-mail and is separate from what is called the Net but is nonetheless available on the Net. There are many, many Usenets sending information to each other. Each discussion group on a given topic is called a newsgroup, and there are thousands of such groups, which fall into a variety of categories such as *alt* (alternative), *comp* (computers), *info, misc, news, rec* (recreational activities), *soc* (social issues), *sci* (science), *tx* (Texas), and so on. Such lists might be designated as <alt.cyberpunk>, <comp.os.msdos>, <rec.wine.making>. (In the various parts or sections of *CyberReader,* you will find references to particular newsgroups that you may want to start reading or even contributing to.)

There are several ways *to access newsgroups,* but I will refer to *Tin* and graphic browsers such as Netscape and Internet Explorer.

By way of Tin: In order to see what is available to you and simply to read the discussions, you will access software in your university's computer that is most often Tin. (Of course, your university may not have this program but may use another one. Again, if you wish, check with academic computer services to see if Usenet is available and how to access it.) When you get to the $ or % prompt, simply type *tin*. If the program is available, it will begin searching for available lists. This may take a while. (If you are using the browser Netscape, all this is much easier.) Eventually, you will see printed on your screen the beginning of a list of the <alt.> newsgroups. Understand that you are automatically subscribed to *all* the lists available to you, and that you can go through all several hundred or thousand and unsubscribe to the ones you are not interested in. But nothing could be more time-consuming! However, if you want to do that, then you will get a list of items (here's one such item) that looks like this:

```
Subscribe to new group alt.cyberpunk (y/n/q) [n]:
```

If you are not interested, type *n* or press the Return key. Otherwise, type *y*. Again, I would not recommend this approach. I took the opposite approach and unsubscribed from the kinds of lists that do not interest me. All you would have to do, when you are in Tin, to unsubscribe to multiple groups such as <rec> or <sci>, is to type *U.* (Tin is case sensitive.) Then you will receive the following prompt at the lower left of your screen:

```
Enter regex unsubscribe pattern>
```

If you want to unsubscribe to all of the <rec> lists, type *rec.** and all the lists in this grouping will be eliminated from showing up on your screen the next time you access Tin. (If you ever want to see them on your screen again, simply type *y,* the yank command.) If you want to unsubscribe to particular groups within the hierarchy of <rec.>, then type, for example, <rec.arts> or <rec.arts.comics>, and so on.

Later, if you change your mind, you can resubscribe by typing *S,* which will give you the following prompt:

```
Enter regex subscribe pattern>
```

If you want to resubscribe to all the <rec> lists or whatever, then type: *rec.**.

You might want to save for later any decision about what you want to keep and discard and just start reading. To read on the first time around, you can simply move down the list by following the directions at the bottom of the screen:

```
<n>=set current to n, TAB=next unread, /=search pattern,
c)atchup, g)oto, j=line down, k=line up, h)elp, m)ove, q)uit,
r=toggle all/unread, s)ubscribe, S)ub pattern, u)nsubscribe,
U)nsub pattern, y)ank in/out
```

Instead of using *j* or *k* you can use your arrow keys. If you want to search, type </> and then the key word. The directions are easy to follow. What I do is navigate on newsgroups the same way that I do on the Web, using arrows and the Return key to move up and down one level, or using the Return key to read what has been posted on a particular newsgroup. The space bar will allow you to skip down the lists of pages. You will catch on quickly. If you want to add a point to the discussion, then type *r,* and type your message, following the instructions again. To exit from Tin, simply type *q.* (Again, if you use Netscape, it is all just a matter of clicking on the button for Newsgroups and following the simple instructions by way of pointing and clicking.)

By way of *graphic browsers:* The best source of information for each browser is the Help menu. In Netscape, for example, go to the Help menu and pull it down to On Usenet News. There you will find links to detailed information. For other Web sites with information go to:

Tile.Net <http://tile.net/>

Listz, the mailing list directory <http://liszt.com/>

Deja News (http://www.dejanews.com/) Looks where people chat on Newsgroups.

Usenet FAQs <http://www.cis.ohio-state.edu/hypertext/faq/bngusenet/top.html>

Subscribing to Listservs (Academic Discussion Groups)

It is hard to know what to say about these lists, which can be more formal and academic in tone, but you should know about them. It would be best to discuss with your instructor the appropriateness of your subscribing to a *particular* academic list. If you are interested in finding a list of lists, point your browser to the Directory of Scholarly Electronic Conferences <http://www.mid.net/KOVACS/>. There are lists that are nonacademic, and you can find them at Tile.Net and Listz (see the preceding discussion for the addresses).

Downloading and Printing Electronic Discourse

When you find a document on the www that you would like to save a copy of, all you have to do, if on Lynx, is type *p.* You are then usually given three options:

Save to a local file

Mail the file to yourself

Print to the screen

I tend to use the second and third options. If you want to e-mail the file to yourself, you simply press the down-arrow key to that link and then press the right-arrow key. You will be asked for your e-mail address. After giving it, you press Return and the file will be sent to you. If you want to print and save the file on your monitor (in your hard disk), then you press the down-arrow to the third option. However, to save the file, you will have to use your e-mail software, the commands for which are different from software to software. If I use *Z-Term,* I go to the File menu and pull down to Start Capture, then I name the file, and press the right-arrow key or press Return twice, and the file is printed and captured on my screen. I have to return to the File menu and Stop Capture. Later, if I wish and if it is legal (and it usually is), I can print out the file. If I use Pine, I first pull the Session menu down to Capture Session to File and name that file. When I have finished and have quit Pine, I just open the file and print it. When I use Netscape, I simply point to print and click for either the mail option or the Web page. (See the last section of this appendix about copyright problems.)

■ HOW TO DO RESEARCH (AND SURF)
ON THE NET/WWW: SOME POINTERS

Do you have any idea about how to *point your browser,* as I suggested that you do in the previous paragraph? If not, then you will learn how in this section. I will spend most of the time, however, introducing very briefly the various *search engines.* In the first edition of *CyberReader,* I gave instructions for conducting research primarily on Lynx (the text-based Web program); for the sake of equity (many people are still limited to or would rather use Lynx), I will give instruction for both Lynx and graphic browsers such as Netscape and Internet Explorer.

Lynx

If your university makes Lynx available, then at the $ or % prompt, type either <www> or <lynx> and press return. You should or will usually find on your screen your university's Web site. From here you can navigate to any number of places (on campus, throughout your state, or elsewhere), depending on the links that have been established locally for you. However, if you want to discover information outside what is immediately available to you on your university Web site, then type *g,* and you will see in the lower left of the box

URL to open:

It is at this point that you type the URL (uniform resource locator). The URL is composed of <access method://host.domain/path/filename>. It can begin with the access method *http://* and then become a unique address—for example, <http://www.abacon.com/>. When this is accurately typed, press the Return key (or the right-arrow key) and you are on your way to a Web site. Follow the same procedure for the access methods such as FTP or gopher, which I will not discuss here for reasons given earlier.

Graphic Browsers Such as Netscape

It is so easy! Once your browser has been launched and settled at its main page, which at your college or university will be the college page, simply type the URL in the Net site or Show Location rectangular strip close to the top of the page. Then press return, and off you go. The graphic interface for all this is so intuitive that you will see immediately what needs to be done to get on down the road.

Knowing how to http is one thing; knowing how to find a URL for what you want is quite another. When you go to the library and use the computers to check the holdings and to determine whether particular books are on the shelves, you are simply engaging in a database search. When you use the World Wide Web (www), you are checking databases as well by using a variety of what are called search engines. In what follows I am going to quickly survey some of the engines and include the directories of each so that you will know what to expect. (Remember that once you get to each of these sites, there will be help links to assist you. Once you begin to feel comfort-

able with one, you will be comfortable with the others. They are set up for
you to use them intuitively.)

The Major Search Engines

A. *HotBot* ‹h t t p : / / w w w . h o t b o t . c o m / ›
HotBot is one of my favorites and is generally considered to be the best all-
purpose search engine. Remember, after getting into Lynx, to type *g* and then
the URL, and finally, press the Return key. (If you are on Netscape or other
graphic browsers, you will type the URL in the rectangular space provided and
then click the appropriate button or press the Return key. Also, if you are
using these browsers, you will have immediate access to all of the search
engines by simply clicking on the *Net Search* director button. All you have to
do is click on the icons and follow the directions.) When you arrive at Hot-
Bot, you will see in screen 1 of 4 the following:

```
Help | Wired News | HotWired | Wired Magazine

       Usenet | Top News Sites | Classifieds | Domain Names | Stocks |
                 Discussion Groups | ShareWare | The Web
              Find: Businesses | People | Email Addresses

—H o t B o t—    The WIRED Search Center     Click here for Tripod

Search: The Web

look for [all the words_____]

_____     Search

Additional Search Terms:
[must contain____][the words_]

_____

[must not contain][the words_]

_____

(NORMAL LINK) Use right-arrow or <return> to activate.
   Arrow keys: Up and Down to move. Right to follow a link; Left to
go back.
   H)elp O)ptions P)rint G)o M)ain screen Q)uit /=search
[delete]=history list
```

By typing the right arrow → you will arrive at screen 2 of 4 and will see:

```
The Wired search engine

   HotBot [INLINE]

   Help Directory

   Getting Started
   Learn the basics and find tips to get the most out of HotBot.

   Frequently Asked Questions
   Get answers to all your questions about HotBot.

   Add URL to HotBot
   New web site? Let us know, and we'll add it to the HotBot index.
```

```
     Advertise on HotBot
     We'll send you all the information you need to advertise your
     site on HotBot.
-press space for next page-
    Arrow keys: Up and Down to move. Right to follow a link; Left to
go back.
    H)elp O)ptions P)rint G)o M)ain screen Q)uit /=search
[delete]=history list
```

Back to 1 of 1: On your keyboard, press the down-arrow key until you reach *Look For [All the Words]*. Here just type what you want to search for. Let's say we will search for—vanity of vanities—*victor j vitanza*. Simply type that name or your own name into the space. Notice that I used all lowercase letters and that I did not put a period after my initial. Then, on your keyboard, press the down-arrow key again until you reach *Look For*. At this point, press the right arrow $\rightarrow$ and you will have opened up a number of options. Look here (at a detail of the page):

```
Search : The Web
                   **********************
    look for   * all the words      *
               * any of the words   *
   _____   * exact phrase       *_    Search
               * the page title     *
    Additional * the person         *
    [must cont * links to this URL   *
   _____   * the Boolean phrase *
    [must not  **********************
```

Now you have the options to decide what kind of limited and focused search you would like to try. If you are looking for a person, as we are, then simply push the arrow key down $\downarrow$ to *The Person,* and once that selection is made, press the arrow key back to the left $\leftarrow$, closing the options. All that remains now in this short instruction is to press the the down-arrow key $\downarrow$ to Search and then press the Return key. You will get the number of sources or "hits" available at which this name is located. If you want to regulate the number of hits for each return, you can do so between 10 and 100; if you want to regulate the amount of information, you can do so from the URL with three or so line descriptions or just the URL. (Remember: You navigate up and down with arrows in those directions, $\uparrow$ and $\downarrow$, even if you have a column of links that are set alongside each other. Your tendency will be to use the right arrow, which will send you, however, out on a link. Learning how to navigate with Lynx is like learning how to use a standard transmission. If you want to move to the next page down, press the space bar; move up to the prior page, type - [a hyphen]. It's simple.) Going for the results, which were set at lots of 100 and only one-liners with URLs, our return shows:

```
HotBot Search Results

Returned: 842 matches.
```

Breakdown: victor: 416669, j: 1–100 Next

    9254144, vitanza: 1262, victor:
    416669, vitanza: 1262, vitanza:

1. English 5351 (History of Rhetoric I)—99%
2. Foundations of Rhetoric—97%
3. Writing the Paradigm—95%
4. (alternate)http://altx.com/ebr/ebr2.vitanza.html
5. Victor J. Vitanza Uncanny Page—95%
6. T H E. I N T E R N E T. U N I V E R S
   I T Y—Works Cited—95%
7. PRETEXT, REINVW, Eberly/2—93%
8. PRE/TEXT: Electra(Lite) 1.1A: Print/Electronic Pubs.:
   Polylogue—93%
9. (alternate)http://www.utdallas.edu/pretext/PT1.1A/
   PT1.1A.html
10. U. T. A. English Dept. Graduate T. A. Homepage: Projects,
    etc.—92%
11. The Mental Blender—Whip—92%
12. English 5336 (Critical Pedagogy)—92%
13. PRETEXT, REINVW, ULMER, July/1

etc.

What the results indicate is that the HotBot search engine found 842 instances in its data bank of the name <victor j vitanza>. Many of the hits, as is often the case, are the same. Each of these is a title for a Web site. When you arrow up and down this list (↑ and ↓) and decide to arrow right →, you are going to the virtual destination of the Web site, gopher, or ftp site. Often, attempting to get to a search engine requires patience, since each is often being used and is overloaded. If this is the case you will receive the message "Unable to connect." The best thing to do, then, is to try again or try another link. You may type into the search space whatever key terms you have an interest in knowing more about. (As you go through each part, or section, of *CyberReader*, you will see at the accompanying Web site that I have given instructions in using HotBot as well as other search engines and have suggested key terms that come from the readings and that you might search for. I have also given a number of URLs that you might try.)

At this point you should go to *HotBot* on Netscape and take a look at the graphical interface that is so much easier to use than the text-based Lynx. But to do this you will have to go to the accompanying Web site, where the graphic interface is best experienced. Go specifically to Appendix A at the site and follow the instructions provided.

When making a detailed search, here are some strategies to help you to further refine and narrow your search:

Quotes: One of the most powerful ways to put together a search is to use *quotes* around the word or phrase. Hence, if you were searching for information on "bell hooks" you would put her name in quotes as I have done here. It would also be good to keep all names, words in general, in *lowercase,* because if you use uppercase (capital letters) the engine is directed to look only for those items in caps. (Since "bell hooks" represents her name in lowercase, you would never find it on the Web unless someone had stuck to the convention of capital letters for proper names when writing about "hooks.") This is a very general way to search for "hooks," but since she is relatively new in the history of literature and criticism, you would be wise to start at a general level.

Boolean logic: If you were to search for "William Shakespeare," you might start out by typing his name in quotes just to see the number of hits you might get. Remember that just because Shakespeare has been read and written about longer than bell hooks does not mean that on the Web you will find more about Shakespeare than about hooks. The Web, unlike the actual library, is so new to us (four to five years) that it is hard to tell what might be available on it. Therefore, it pays to begin with a general search and then narrow things down. To make detailed searches, you should use boolean logic—in other words, use the terms AND, OR, NEAR, and NOT. (These may be used in upper- or lowercase.) What do they mean? AND allows for a combination search; OR for one or the other; NEAR for the two items appearing within ten words of each other; and NOT (always represented as AND NOT and never NOT by itself) is an exclusion.

   Let's say that you would like to search for any Web pages on Shakespeare's sonnets and not the plays. To retrieve such sites (if any are available), you would then type into the search form: *Shakespeare AND sonnet* AND NOT plays.* What does this search for? Well, it searches for any information, if available in the AltaVista databank, on Shakespeare's sonnets *and not* his plays. Note that the symbol * is used. When this is inserted into the middle of a word or at the end, it allows the search to find variable spellings or forms of the word, which in this case would be, besides the singular form *sonnet,* the plural form *sonnets.* It is possible, since the Web often has material on it that is not proofread in any professional way, that there will be variations in the spellings. In Shakespeare's own day, there were many ways to spell his name! It would be wise, therefore, to add an asterisk to *Shakespear** and not type *Shakespeare.* And it would be wise to try both first and last names spelled differently. The NEAR command may appear to be puzzling, but what if on a page there is a rendering of our author's name as "Shakespeare, William"? It is possible that a conventional search of "William Shakespeare" (in quotes) might miss "Shakespeare, William." Hence, it would pay to type into the search form: William NEAR Shakespear* AND sonnet* AND NOT play*.

   These two approaches—quotes and boolean—should make your searching successful, for the most part. Now let's turn to a list of other search engines. (Remember that on any graphical browser, all you have to do is click on Net Search, or whatever is comparable, and you will find all of these, if not more, search engines.)

B. OTHER SEARCH ENGINES

Other Search Engines and Directories: Global Search:

   Infoseek <http://guide.infoseek.com/>

Excite <http://www.excite.com/>. "Excite Live" allows you to set up your own Excite page according to your preferences.

Lycos <http://www.lycos.com/>. "My Yahoo" allows you to set up your own Yahoo page according to your preferences.

Whole Internet Catalog <http://nearnet.gnn.com/gnn/wic/index.html>

Yahoo, Directory <http://www.yahoo.com/>

Telephone Numbers and Mailing Addresses and Electronic Addresses:

For *White Pages,* to help locate people on the Internet:

Bigfoot, e-mail forwarding service, good for when you change your number or provider. <http://bigfoot.com/>

Four11, e-mail, current addresses, and telephone numbers. <http://www.Four11.com/>

WhoWhere?, e-mail addresses, home pages, URLs, internet phone numbers. <http://www.whowhere.com/>

For *Yellow Pages* (businesses):

BigBook <http://www.bigbook.com/On'Village>

On'Village <http://www.onvillage.com/>

GTE Superpages: Yellow Pages <http://superpages.gte.net/>

FAQ: How to Find E-mail Addresses <http://www.cis.ohio- state.edu/hyper-text/gaq/usenet/finding-addresses/faq.html>

■ HOW TO AVOID COPYRIGHT PROBLEMS (CITING ELECTRONIC DISCOURSE)

Copyrights

The best discussion on copyright problems that I know of is *10 Big Myths about copyright explained,* by Brad Templeton <http://www.clarinet.com/brad/>, to be found at <http://www.clarinet.com/brad/copymyths.html>. If you have any doubts whatsoever about things on the Net/www, generally assume you should *not* think or act as if material there is free to disseminate. And you *should* have doubts! Alway look for copyright statements at Web sites and gopher/ftp sites and specifically attached to any article, chapter or book, or graphic found in cyberspace. Along the same lines, you should be very sensitive to the fact that e-mail sent to you personally should *never* be disseminated (forwarded, cited, or published, in part or in whole) without the written permission of the poster (author). It is generally understood, however, that posts sent to newsgroups and to listservs (discussion groups) are disseminated to everyone and are often archived and in that sense published. If you want to cite any of this material, you should be guided by the "fair use" principle; in other words, as a student or academic, you have the right to quote a limited amount from electronic works just as you do from printed works. However, you must give correct and full references (see the following). And yet, remember that there is no "fair use" principle for private e-mail!

Additional information about copyrights on the Net:

Copyright FAQ <http://www.netmeg.net/faq/law/copyright-faq/>

Copyright, Intellectual Property, and Publishing on the WWW
<http://www.pitt.edu/~hypertch/copyright.html>

The Copyright WebSite <http://www.benedict.com/index.html>

Copyright Act of 1976, as amended <http://www.law.cornell.edu/usc/17/>

Copyright Clearance Center Online <http://www.openmarket.com/copyright/>

A Visit to Copyright Bay
<http://www.nmjc.cc.nm.us/copyrightbay/default.html>

Copyright and Multimedia Law for Webbuilders and Multimedia Authors:
<http://www.lib.uiowa.edu/proj/webbuilder/copyright.html>

UT System Crash Course in Copyright:
<http://www.utsystem.edu/ogc/intellectualproperty/cprtindx.htm>

WATCH, Writers, Artists, and Their Copyright Holders:
<http://www.lib.utexas.edu/Libs/HRC/WATCH/>

Electronic Discourse and How to Cite It

What, in part, contributes to people not citing what they find on the Net or www is that there is not yet a standardized (that is, widely accepted) bibliographical form for citing electronic discourse. The Modern Language Association in the *MLA Handbook for Writers of Research Papers* (Fourth Edition) recommends several formats (in section 4.9–10, Citing Online Databases). They have recently updated their suggestions: <http://www.mla.org/set_stl.htm>. Also, you might want to check the American Psychological Association's (APA) *Publication Manual* (Fourth Edition).

However, there are other competing—and much refined—sources for documenting electronic discourse. For example, there is Janice R. Walker's "Columbia Online Style: MLA-Style Citations of Electronic Sources" (endorsed by the Alliance for Computers & Writing and which I recommend) <http://www.cas.usf.edu/english/walker/mla.html>; and Andrew Harnack and Eugene Kleppinger's "Beyond the MLA Handbook: Documenting Electronic Sources on the Internet" <http://english.ttu.edu/kairos/1.2/inbox/mla_archive.html>. Harnack and Kleppinger are updating their format in *Online! A Reference Guide for Using Internet Sources.*

Both of these refinements of the MLA style are received better than any other formats, including the MLA itself. Moreover, neither at this date has eclipsed the other in use. And at times, it is difficult to tell if there is any substantive difference between the two, but on close examination, there *are* differences. The issue, however, is not that one would eclipse the other, but that when working and citing material in electronic environments, you will have to be flexible. As I said in the preface to the first edition of *CyberReader,* the environment of electronic media is all about change. Therefore, I will give some examples from both (stating in parentheses whose is being emulated), leaving you, along with your instructor, to select which format you are going to follow or perhaps even combine. When in doubt, remember to ask your instructor what he or she wants you to follow. Here are a few of the general yet varied recommendations for citing electronic discourse:

A 1. WWW SITES, AN ARTICLE OR DOCUMENT THAT CAN BE VIEWED OR PRINTED (WALKER)

Author's name

Full title of the work (in quotes)

Title of the complete work (in italics)

Document date

Full http address

Date of visit (in parentheses)

Example:

Stivale, Charles J. " 'help manners': Cyber-Democracy and its Vicissitudes." 20–21 May 1996 http://wwwpub.utdallas.edu/~cynthiah/lingua_archive/help_manners.html (4 January 1998).

A 2. WWW SITES, AN ARTICLE OR DOCUMENT THAT CAN BE VIEWED OR PRINTED (HARNACK AND KLEPPINGER)

Author's name

Title of document (in quotes)

Title of complete work (in italics)

Date of publication or revision

URL (in angled brackets)

Date of access (in parentheses)

If any of these elements is not available, then skip to the next. You can only give the information that is available to you.

Example:

Stivale, Charles J. " 'help manners': Cyber-Democracy and its Vicissitudes." 20–21 May 1996 <http://wwwpub.utdallas.edu/~cynthiah/lingua_archive/help_manners.html> (4 January 1998)

Question and comment: What do you see to be the differences between the two styles? What it comes down to in this particular format is the angled brackets.

B1. E-MAIL, LISTSERV, AND NEWSGROUP CITATIONS (WALKER)

Author's name or alias

Subject line (in quotes)

Date of the message (if different from access)

Address of the listserv or newslist

Date of access (in parentheses)

For personal e-mail listings, omit the email address.

Example:

Moore, Dinty W. "dm>vv: followup." Personal e-mail (9 Dec 1997).

Davis, Diane D. "Theory vs. Practice." Pretext@jefferson.village.virginia.edu (22 October 1997).

B2. E-MAIL MESSAGE (HARNACK AND KLEPPINGER)

Author's name

Author's e-mail address (in angled brackets)

Subject line (in quotes)

Date of publication

Type of communication (personal e-mail, general announcement, call for papers, etc.)
>   Or if listserv, then address of listserv (in angled brackets)
>   Or if newsgroup, then address of newsgroup (in angled brackets)

Date of access (in parentheses)

Example:

Moore, Dinty W. <Dinty@psu.edu> "dm>vv: followup." 9 Dec 1997. Personal e-mail. (9 Dec 1997).

Comment: The differences in this format are more significant—for example, in terms of giving or not giving a personal e-mail address. Walker suggests prudently that the address should not be given.

C1. GOPHER SITES (WALKER)

Author's name

Title of the paper (in quotes)

Date of publication if different from the date accessed

Print publication information

Gopher search path followed to access the information

Date that the file was accessed (in parentheses)

Example:

"puptcrit." gopher://jefferson.village.Virginia.EDU:70/11/pubs/listservs/
spoons/puptcrit.archive. (5 January 98).

C2. GOPHER SITES (HARNACK AND KLEPPINGER)

Author's name

Title of the paper (in quotes)

Date of publication

Print publication information

URL (in angled brackets)

Date accessed (in parentheses)

Example:

"puptcrit." <gopher://jefferson.village.Virginia.EDU:70/11/pubs/
listservs/spoons/ puptcrit.archive> (5 January 98).

Building on Walker's basic format—let's project the outcome—we would
most likely cite an article in an *electronic journal* in the following way:

Moulthrop, Stuart. "You Say You Want a Revolution?: Hypertext and the
Laws of Media." *Postmodern Culture.* 1.3 (1991): 53 par. 21. http://
jefferson.village.virginia.edu/pmc/contents.all.html (4 January 1998).

The examples given and a sample projection by way of Walker's
paradigm—which can obviously be done with Harnack and Kleppinger's
also—should cover most instances in which you might have to cite electronic
discourse. If you need others, then visit the Web sites.

On-Line Writing Labs (OWLS)

There is one more major source for help about any problems that you might
be having with writing or citing references, which is your local writing center
or laboratory. But if your local lab resources are not the best or the lab is not
on-line, you can point your browser to a number of really excellent OWLs,
where you can find information about and help for the most basic writing
problems (such as with punctuation, developing a thesis sentence, basic
grammar, and so on) and help for writing in various genres (such as letters
of application and resumes); but also you will find information about citing
electronic references in MLA and APA formats. Here are a few OWLs that
you might want to visit and browse. Note that many of the sites are linked
to other sites, so when you are at one, you are only a click away from
another:

- The Purdue Univ. On-Line Writing Lab <http://owl.trc.purdue.edu/>.

- The Writery (Univ. of Missouri)
  <http://www.missouri.edu/~wleric/writery.html>.

- Roane State Community College Owl
  <http://fur.rscc.cc.tn.us/OWL/OWL.html>.

- The Univ. of Texas-Austin, Undergraduate Writing Center
  <http://www.utexas.edu/depts/uwc/.html/main.html>.

- Bowling Green Univ. Writing Center
  <http://www.bgsu.edu/departments/writing-lab>.

- The Dakota State Univ. Online Writing Lab
  <http://www.dsu.edu:80/departments/liberal/cola/OWL/>.

- Michigan Tech. Univ. Writing Center
  <http://www.hu.mtu.edu/~jdcolman/wc/welcome.html>.

- The Univ. of Michigan OWL
  <http://www.umich.edu/~nesta/OWL/owl.html>.

- Rennselaer Writing Center
  <http://www.rpi.edu/dept/llc/writecenter/web/home.html>.

- Taft Community College Online Writing Lab
  <http://www.taft.cc.ca.us/www/tc/tceng/owl.html>

- Writing Online Resource Directory
  <http://darkwing.uoregon.edu/~jcross/word.html>.

These, then, are some of the most basic introductions to the Net and the www. Remember that you will learn as you go; remember that you should share what you know; and remember that it should be our purpose to build an actual community and virtual ones as well. Have phun, for the surf's up.

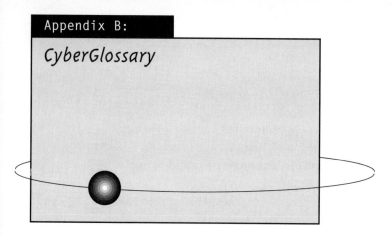

The list of terms in this glossary is *only* a beginning that supplements the individual key terms found in each chapter. I have excluded from this glossary those terms that are already listed and discussed in each chapter, and I have included only those words and proper names that might be of additional help to you while reading *CyberReader*. You will find on many occasions, therefore, that you will need additional reference sources. When this happens, you might check these on-line glossaries, which you can find at the *CyberReader* Web site:

- *NetLingo: The Internet Language Dictionary:* <http://www.netlingo.com/>
- *Babel: A Glossary of Computer Related Abbreviations and Acronyms, Ver. 98A:* <http://www.access.digex.net/~ikind/babel.html>
- *Computing Dictionary:* <http://wombat.doc.ic.ac.uk/>
- *Cyberpoets Guide to Virtual Culture* (see Lexicon of Virtual Culture) <http://www.seas.upenn.edu/~mengwong/cyber/cgvc1.html#1.2>
- *Jargon File 3.0.0.* <http://www.phil.uni-sb.de/fun/jargon/index.html>

Also, magazines such as *Wired* (Gareth Brandwyn's "Jargon Watch") will include updates on the growing number of new words.

ABRAHAM, RALPH: Author of *Chaos, Gaia, and Eros,* which is about three different views of history. The title corresponds to the mind, the body, and the spirit of evolution. The book has had a profound influence on people who write about cyberspace. It has an excellent glossary.

ACKER, KATHY (CF. APPROPRIATION): Novelist. See her *Empire of the Senseless* (1988), which is a cyberpunk-textual appropriation of Gibson's *Neuromancer*. In her novels, Acker takes large chunks of other authors' works and reworks them.

AGRIPPA: A BOOK OF THE DEAD: William Gibson's (and Dennis Ashbaugh's and Kevin Begos's) electronic book that can be read only once, because it is consumed by a virus as it is read. A copy of the decoded, nondestroyed version can be found at <http://sfbox.vt.edu:10021/J/jfoley/gibson/gibson.html>.

A G E N T :   Software that can change and learn in virtuality. A typical agent might be coded with a user's preferences and made to search the Web, until recalled, with the user's interests in virtual mind.

A P P R O P R I A T I O N :   The borrowing of other artists' works for use in one's own work in dis/order to play with it and make something new. Appropriation, according to Kathy Acker, is not plagiarism. But it *is* pla(y)giarism!

A R P A n e t :   Advanced Research Projects Agency, a wide-area network, was developed by the federal government during the Cold War. It has become the U.S.'s contribution to the World Wide Web.

B A N D W I D T H :   The amount of information that can be transferred per second through copper wires or fiber optic cables, and so on.

B A R L O W ,   J O H N   P E R R Y :   Lyricist for the Grateful Dead, cofounder of the Electronic Freedom Foundation, and "Cognitive Dissonant." Home page: <http://www.eff.org/~barlow/barlow.html>.

B A U D R I L L A R D ,   J E A N :   French sociologist-cultural theorist who is best known for his discussions of simulation replacing "reality." See his *Simulacra and Simulation* (1981).

B I T S   &   B Y T E S :   Units of computerized information. A bit is the binary 0/1. A byte is group of 8 such bits.

B U R R O U G H S ,   W I L L I A M   S . :   Novelist. See his *Nova Express* (1965) and other novels. First known as a "beat" novelist. Burroughs's fiction is part of what is now called "Slipstream," cyberpunk fiction written/published prior to 1984 that has influenced, say, the authors published in Sterling's *Mirrorshades* collection. Burroughs has recently been used in commercials for Nike.

C R A S H   C U L T U R E   (C F .   P O S T M O D E R N) : Perhaps best explained in a simile: . . . is like speeding up in your car, passing everyone else, only to have to stop for the traffic light. A term coined by Arthur Kroker: "Contemporary society as it undergoes a simultaneous fatal acceleration and terminal shutdown" (*Data Trash*). Or like Crash TV, 500 channels and nothing to see.

C T H E O R Y :   A listserv and Web site edited by the Krokers: <http://www.freedonia.com/ctheory/>.

C Y B E R C R U D   (C Y B E R B A B B L E) :   Computer talk, jargon.

C Y B E R N E T I C S :   The study of systems of communications and control in living organisms and machines. See "Principia Cybernetica Web" <http://pespmcl.vub.ac.be>.

C Y B E R R E A D E R : This book, edited and written by Victor J. Vitanza. Home page: <http://www.uta.edu/english/V/Victor_.html>.

E L E C T R O N I C   B O O K : Simply put, a book formatted in an electronic medium. However, such a book is really no longer a book as generally thought of. The electronic medium is not only the message, but it also changes the message in the book that has been changed. (See chapter 5 of this book.)

E - M A I L : Electronic mail, which is distributed over the Net.

E X C R E M E N T A L   C U L T U R E : Reruns on television. Recycling. Grunge. (See Kroker, *Data Trash*.)

F A Q S : Frequently asked questions.

F L E S H M E E T : An event at which on-line participants who have never previously met in real life (IRL) finally agree to meet face to face (F2F). There of course may be subsequent meetings or none at all, even on-line. .)>=

F R E E W A R E   (C F .   S H A R E W A R E) : Software that is free of charge.

F R I N G E : The opposite of mainstream. Meaning *on the edge*. Fringe science, such as nanotechnology.

F T P   (C F .   G O P H E R ,   H T T P) : File transfer protocol, which allows for the transference of complete files from a remote computer to one's own computer.

G A T E S ,   B I L L : The man from (president of) Microsoft. See John Seabrook's "E-Mail from Bill."

G I B S O N ,   W I L L I A M   (C F .   *N E U R O M A N C E R*) : Along with Bruce Sterling, the cyberpunk science-fiction writer. His home page: <http://sfbox.vt.edu:10021/J/jfoley/gibson/gibson.html>. (See chapter 6 of this book.)

G L O B A L   V I L L A G E : A phrase popularized by Marshall McLuhan, referring to, for example, television as the medium unifying the various societies and cultures of the world.

G O P H E R   (C F .   F T P ,   H T T P) : A protocol and program that searches and retrieves documents from remote databases. Gopher allows you to access ftp sites as well as other sites. (More and more of these sites, gopher or ftp, are being transferred to the www, which are accessed by way of http.)

G R A T E F U L   D E A D : The group. See home page: <http://www.cs.cmu.edu/afs/cs.cmu.edu/user/mleone/web/dead.html>.

G U T E N B E R G   G A L A X Y :   A term and title of a book (subtitled *The Making of Typographic Man* [1962]), by Marshall McLuhan, in
which the author discusses the various technologies, but especially print
technology (literacy), and the influences on shaping culture and society.
McLuhan speaks of "waves," such as electronic waves, and surfing on them!

H A R D W A R E   (C F .   S O F T W A R E) :   Machine.

H T M L   (C F .   H Y P E R T E X T) :   Hypertext markup language, which is used to establish nonsequential discourse.

H T T P :   Hypertext transfer protocol, which specifies sites that are part
of the World Wide Web. A URL begins with http:// and the rest of the
address follows. Similarly, an ftp or gopher will begin with ftp://.

H Y P E R R E A L I T Y :   Extended reality, which is more real than
reality. It is real/ity that has been simulated to such a high degree that it
often seduces its viewers/participants to prefer it to reality. (This term is
extremely complicated in its philosophical ramifications.)

I S D N :   Integrated services digital network. Changes information on-
line into digital packets (groups of 1's and 0's) that are capable of traveling
at high speeds. ISDN travels through fiber-optic cables. In contrast, POTS
(plain old telephone service) transfers information by way of analog, by
sound waves boosted continuously by amplifiers. POTS travels though copper wires.

K A P O R ,   M I T C H :   Cofounder of the Electronic Frontier Foundation. See his home page: <http://www.kei.com:80/homepages/
mkapor/>.

K R O K E R ,   A R T H U R   A N D   M A R I L O U I S E :
Cultural critics, known for a number of books such as *The Panic Encyclopedia,* and for their electronic list C Theory.

L A N I E R ,   J A R O N :   Coiner of the term *virtual reality* and
developer of VPL (virtual programming language). Home page:
<http://www.well.com/Community/Jaron.Lanier/index.html>.

L E A R Y ,   T I M O T H Y :   Often referred to as the philosopher
professor and "LSD guru" of the 1960s. (See chapter 6.)

L U R K   (L U R K E R) :   To frequent a discussion list or BBS but
never contribute to the discussion.

L Y N X :   A text-based application that allows users to browse the
World Wide Web.

M C K E N N A ,   T E R E N C E :   Like Timothy Leary, known as a
pyschedelic-philosopher. McKenna has published *Food of the Gods* (1992).
(See chapter 1 of *CyberReader.*)

MCLUHAN, MARSHALL: (See *Gutenberg Galaxy.*)

MEMES (A.K.A. META-VIRUS):   Ideas are like viruses as they spread from host-mind to host-mind. (Memes is a word based on *mimesis,* imitation.) This idea of memes is based on Richard Dawkins's book *The Selfish Gene.* (See chapter 2 of *CyberReader.*)

MIRRORSHADES: A collection of cyberpunk short fiction, edited by Bruce Sterling.

MONDO 2000:   A much-celebrated magazine that has been in part perceived as focusing on things on the edge or things fringe, such as cyberpunk, virtual reality, wetware, designer aphrodisiacs, artificial life, techno-erotic paganism, and so on. See *Mondo 2000: A User's Guide to the New Edge,* in which such topics are stressed. Those behind the magazine—especially Queen Mu—however, have been devoted to producing a work of art in an age of mechanical reproduction.

MORPH(ING):   Metamorphosis; changing shapes.

MUDrape: Virtual rape. (See chapter 7.)

NANOTECHNOLOGY: *Nano-* is a prefix meaning *one-billionth.* Yes, technology reduced to the size of molecules and atoms. The possibilities, in medicine alone, are staggering. See Eric Drexler's *Engines of Creation.*

NELSON, THEODOR H.:   Founding genius, among other things, of the Xanadu project, which would be the connectability of all libraries and publishers and their holdings on the World Wide Web and which would allow them to sell books to buyers. The project is more complicated and richer than suggested here. Nelson's site: <http://xanadu.net/the.project>. (See chapter 5.)

NETIQUETTE: *Etiquette* plus *net.* Manners on the Internet. (See Appendix A.)

NEURAL CHIPS: First the book became flesh; now the flesh becomes a chip, as Kroker says, "when flesh goes electronic." (See Kroker, *Data Trash.* See William Gibson's SF short story "Johnny Mnemonic.")

NEUROMANCER (CF. GIBSON):   Title of Gibson's cyberpunk novel.

NEW EDGE: On the fringes of culture, knowledge, or science. *Mondo 2000* represents the new edge.

NEWSGROUPS: Discussion groups on a wide variety of subjects that are delivered by a network called Usenet. Unlike discussion groups on a listserv (or mailserv), which deliver each contribution in the form of e-mail to its subscribers, newsgroups have their subscribers virtually go to the individual group and sort and read the posts. (See Appendix A.)

N O M A D   (C F .   P O S T M O D E R N) :   One who lives in a group that has no set place or territory, but drifts from place to place, depending on needs and desires.

O P E R A T I O N   S U N   D E V I L   (O S D) :   The Secret Service name for a group of raids on alleged crackers. The OSD and related raids are discussed fully in Bruce Sterling's *The Hacker Crackdown*. (See chapter 3 of *CyberReader*.)

P H   (F O R   F / f) :   The *ph* replacing *F/f* is often used by hackers as a sign of their interests in tele*ph*ones and how to hack them.

P H I B E R   O P T I C K :   A hacker. (See chapter 3.)

P H R A C K :   An electronic zine, mostly for hackers and computer enthusiasts. The name *Phrack* is a neologism based on phone, freak, and hack. *Phrack* <http://freeside.com/phrack.html> has a full archive of articles.

P H R E A K :   Tele*ph*one plus *freak*.

P I N E :   A program, situated in a provider's mainframe, that allows for reading and filing of e-mail and for setting up a directory of "addresses." (See Appendix A.)

P I X E L S :   Tiny electronic dots, configured to represent information.

P L A G I A R I S M   (C F .   A P P R O P R I A T I O N) : Theft of another's ideas without giving credit. A concept that is getting more and more difficult to define.

P O S T M O D E R N / I S M   (P O M O ;   C F .   C R A S H C U L T U R E ,   S I M U L A T I O N) :   Cannot be defined, but has competing definitions, depending on one's ideological position. For Jean-François Lyotard, POMO is incredulity toward metanarratives; that is, POMO carries with it a predisposition toward not believing in such major concepts as origination and progress and liberation (emancipation). (See *The Postmodern Condition*.) Hence, a postmodernist is not predisposed toward particular goals to be arrived at, but toward drifting; is not predisposed toward searching for the way of accomplishing an end, but toward taking what is ready-at-hand to achieve what is tentatively decided on or presented; is not predisposed to believe in origin or original but that all is simulation or copies of copies forever. Surfing on the Net or www (or rhizome, that which has no beginning or end, but all middle) can be and has been seen as a postmodernist form of drifting. Again, the term is a complicated one and must be studied from many ramifications. (See Thomas Docherty, ed.: *Postmodernism: A Reader*.)

P O S T M O D E R N   C U L T U R E :   An electronic journal <http://jefferson.village.virginia.edu/pmc/contents.all.html>.

QUEEN MU: "Domineditrix" on the editorial staff of *Mondo 2000*.

RANT: On-line histrionics in content and style. (I myself enjoy ranting!)

RAVE: An all-night dance party.

RHIZOME: A vegetable configuration that is everywhere on its surface and innards *a middle*. A configuration that is nonhierarchical. The rhizome has been popularized by Gilles Deleuze and Félix Guattari in their book *A Thousand Plateaus*. The Internet and the World Wide Web have been compared to a rhizome.

RUCKER, RUDY.   Another cyberpunk science-fiction author. See *Live Robots*, which includes *Software* (1982) and *Wetware* (1988). Rucker is associated with R. U. Sirius and Queen Mu and the magaZine *Mondo 2000*.

SHAREWARE (CF. FREEWARE):   A software program written and developed usually by an individual instead of by a company and which its user can try out for a while and then pay a fee to the programmer.

SIMULATION (CF. POSTMODERN, RHIZOME):   A sham representation of the real. However, this is a heavily laden ideological term and needs to be carefully considered from various vantage points. One view of simulation is that there is no original (or traceable origin) but only copies. See Plato, *Republic* (Book X); Baudrillard, *Simulacra and Simulation*.

SIRIUS, R. U.:   Cultural critic, and cofounder and editor-in-chief of *Mondo 2000*.

SMILEYS (EMOTICONS):   Conventional graphical representations for on-line discussions that suggest the poster's tone (voice, attitude) such as :-) for smiling or :D for laughing. (See Appendix A.)

SNAIL MAIL (CF. E-MAIL):   Regular postal system, akin to the pony express.

SOFTWARE (CF. HARDWARE):   Information.

SPAM (SPAMMING, PASTE BOMBING):   A load of nasty or worthless posts dumped by way of e-mail to an individual or to subscribers to a discussion list.

SPASM: "The state of living with absolutely contradictory feelings all the time, and really loving it: fascinated yet bored/panicked yet calm/ecstatic yet terminal/apathetic yet fully committed" (Kroker, *Data Trash*).

S P R A W L :   A term used by William Gibson (in *Neuromancer*), indicating the accumulation of cities. Sprawl is taking place in many MUDs and MOOs such as ChibaMOO and LambdaMOO. (See chapter 7 of this book.)

S T E R L I N G ,   B R U C E :   Along with William Gibson, a cyberpunk science-fiction writer. Sterling is editor of *Mirrorshades,* the anthology of cyberpunk SF authors. He is also the author of several novels such as *Islands in the Net* and the author of *The Hacker Crackdown.* (See chapter 6 of this book.)

S T E V E   J A C K S O N   G A M E S :   The name of the company—named after its owner, in Austin, TX—that was raided by the Secret Service (SS). Read all about it in Sterling's *The Hacker Crackdown.* The URL for SJGames: <http://www.io.com/sjgames/>.

T E C H N O C U L T U R E   (C Y B E R C U L T U R E) :   A culture with a style of thinking founded on technology, often new edge and fringe. In extreme form, technoculture manifests *techno-paganism,* a belief in new technology as an agent of change.

T H R E A D :   A particular topic of discussion on a newsgroup or listserv.

T I N :   The name of a program for reading newsgroups, which is usually found in a university server's mainframe.

U R L :   Uniform resource locator, a type of address that allows surfers on the Net to locate sites. It begins, for example, with <http://> (hypertext transfer protocol), which is one type of "access method." A complete URL is composed of <access method://host.domain/path/filename>. Other access methods are file transfer protocol (ftp), gopher protocol (gopher), and wide area information servers (wais).

V I R T U A L   E L I T E   (V I R T U A L   C L A S S) :   A term used by Arthur Kroker and Michael Weinstein in reference to a new economic and social class that lives partially in but completely transacts its business in virtual space. See *Data Trash: The Theory of the Virtual Class* (1994). The phrases *virtual elite* and *virtual class* most likely parallel Thorstein Veblen's "leisure class."

V I R T U A L   S E X   (C Y B E R S E X ,   C Y B E R -
E R O T I C S ,   D I L D O N I C S ,   T E L E D I L D O N I C S) :
Sex in virtual reality. (See chapter 4.)

V I R U S   (C F .   M E M E) :   Will infect your software and wipe out your information in your hardware. A famous virus is "Friday the 13th." (See chapter 1.)

W E T W A R E   (L I V E W A R E) :   Protoplasm as software. DNA (codes) in a cell is wetware. See Rudy Rucker, *Wetware.*

W I R E D :   A slick magazine and one that must be read! The company has an electronic version known as "HotWired," which can be subscribed to at no charge: <http://www.hotwired.com/Login/>.

W O R L D   W I D E   W E B   (A . K . A .   w w w ,   W 3) : The application, developed in 1990 in Switzerland at the European Laboratory for Particle Physics, which provides a hypertext/multimedia interface for all those connected to it, whether on the Internet, Bitnet, and so on.

W O R M :   A computer virus that geometrically folds and squares (replicates) itself across the Net.

X A N A D U   (See Nelson, Theodor H.)

Z I N E S :   Mostly, but not by any means limited to, electronic magazines. (See chapter 5.)

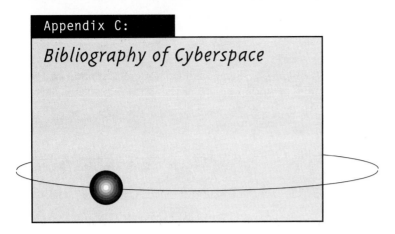

Appendix C:

Bibliography of Cyberspace

This is a very select set of references. It does not include references to works given in the text. As you begin to read, you will find other references, whether in a print medium or an electronic one on the www.

Abraham, Ralph H. *Chaos Gaia Eros.* NY: HarperCollins, 1994.

Acker, Kathy. *Empire of the Senseless.* NY: Grove Weidenfeld, 1988.

Baker, John F. "Electronic Art Book . . . For One Read Only." *Publishers Weekly* (June 29, 1992): 28.

Barlow, John Perry, Sven Birkerts, Kevin Kelly, Mark Slouka. "What Are We Doing On-line?" *Harper's Magazine* (August 1995): 35–46.

Bender, Gretchen, and Timothy Druckrey, ed. *Culture on the Brink: Ideologies of Technology.* Seattle: Bay Press, 1994.

Benedikt, Michael, ed. *Cyberspace: First Steps.* Cambridge, Mass.: MIT Press, 1991.

Benjamin, Walter. "The Work of Art in the Age of Mechanical Reproduction." In *Illuminations,* ed. Hannah Arendt. NY: Schocken, 1969.

Birkerts, Sven, and Kevin Kelly. "The Electronic Hive: Two Views." *Harper's Magazine* (May 1994): 17–21, 24–25.

Brand, Stewart. *The Media Lab: Inventing the Future at MIT.* NY: Viking, 1987.

Brockman, John. *Digerati: Encounters with the Cyber Elite.* San Francisco: Hard-Wired, 1996.

Bukatman, Scott. *Terminal Identity: The Virtual Subject in Post-Modern Science Fiction.* Durham, NC: Duke Univ. Press, 1990.

Cavazos, Edward A. *Cyberspace and the Law: Your Rights and Duties in the On-line World.* Cambridge, Mass.: MIT Press, 1994.

Conley, Verena Andermatt, ed. *Rethinking Technologies.* Minneapolis: Univ. of Minnesota Press, 1993.

Dawkins, Richard. *The Selfish Gene.* Second Edition. Oxford: Oxford Univ. Press, 1989.

De Landa, Manuel. *War in the Age of Intelligent Machines.* Cambridge, Mass.: Zone/MIT Press, 1991.

Deleuze, Gilles, and Félix Guattari. *A Thousand Plateaus.* Trans. Brian Massumi. Minneapolis: Univ. of Minnesota Press, 1987.

Dery, Mark, ed. *Flame Wars: The Discourse of Cyberculture.* Durham, NC: Duke Univ. Press, 1994.

Downing, David, and James Sosnoski, ed. Special Issue: The Geography of Cyberspace. *Works and Days* 23/24 or 12.1–2 (spring/fall 1994).

Drexler, Eric. *Engines of Creation.* Garden City, NY: Doubleday, 1986.

Gibaldi, Joseph. *MLA Handbook for Writers of Research Papers.* Fourth Edition. NY: MLA, 1995.

Germain, Ellen. "In the Jungle of MUD." *Time* (September 13, 1993): 61.

Hafner, Katie. "Get in the MOOd." *Newsweek* (November 7, 1994): 58–59.

Hafner, Katie. "Kevin Mitnick, Unplugged." *Esquire* (August 1995): 81–88.

Haraway, Donna. "A Manifesto for Cyborgs: Science, Technology, and Socialist Feminisim in the 1980s." *Socialist Review* 15, No. 80 (1985): 65–107.

Heidegger, Martin. *The Question Concerning Technology and Other Essays.* Trans. William Lovitt. NY: Harper and Row, 1977.

Heim, Michael. *Electric Language: A Philosophical Study of Word Processing.* New Haven: Yale Univ. Press, 1987. (This book is being published in a new edition.)

Hollinger, Veronica. "Cybernetic Deconstructions: Cyberpunk and Postmodernism." *Mosaic* 23 (spring 1990): 29–44.

Holtzman, Steven R. *Digital Mantras: The Languages of Abstract and Virtual Worlds.* Cambridge, Mass.: MIT Press, 1994.

Johnson-Eiloa, Johndan. *Rearticulating Hypertext Writing.* Norwood, NJ: Ablex, 1997.

Joyce, Michael. *Of Two Minds: Hypertext, Pedagogy, and Poetics.* Ann Arbor: Univ. of Michigan Press, 1995.

Kelly, Kevin. *Out of Control: The New Biology of Machines, Social Systems, and the Economic World.* NY: Addison-Wesley, 1994.

Kramarae, C., ed. *Technology and Women's Voices: Keeping in Touch.* NY: Routledge, 1988.

Kroker, Arthur, and Marilouise Kroker. *Digital Delirium.* New York: St. Martin's Press, 1997.

_____. "Excremental TV." *Mediamatic* 7.2 (1993): 147–53.

Kroker, Arthur, Marilouise Kroker, and David Cook. *Panic Encyclopedia: The Definitive Guide to the Postmodern Scene.* NY: St. Martin's Press, 1989. On-line: <http://www.freedonia.com/panic/>.

Kroker, Arthur, and Michael A. Weinstein. *Data Trash: The Theory of the Virtual Class.* NY: St. Martin's Press, 1994.

Landow, George P., ed. *Hyper/Text/Theory.* Baltimore: The Johns Hopkins Univ. Press, 1994.

Lyotard, Jean-François. *The Postmodern Condition.* Trans. Geoff Bennington and Brian Massumi. Minneapolis: Univ. of Minnesota Press, 1984.

Markley, Robert, ed. Special Issue: Dreaming Real: Cyberspace, Virtual Realities, and Their Discontents. *Configurations* 2.3 (fall 1994).

Markoff, John. "Hacker and Grifter Duel on the Net." *The New York Times* (The Late Edition, February 19, 1995): A1, 3.

Markoff, John. "A Most-Wanted Cyberthief Is Caught in His Own Web." *The New York Times* (The Late Edition, February 16, 1995): A1, D17.

Morton, Donald. "Birth of the Cyberqueer." *PMLA* 110.3 (May 1995): 369–81.

Nunberg, Geoffrey. "The Places of Books in the Age of Electronic Reproduction." *Representations* 42 (spring 1993): 13–37.

Ong, Walter J. *Orality and Literacy: The Technologizing of the Word.* NY: Methuen, 1982.

Poster, Mark. *The Mode of Information.* Cambridge: Polity Press, 1990.

Postman, Neil. *Amusing Ourselves to Death: Public Discourse in the Age of Show Business.* NY: Penguin, 1986.

Postman, Neil. *Technology: The Surrender of Culture to Technology.* NY: Vintage, 1993.

Quittner, Joshua. "Johnny Manhattan Meets the Furry Muckers." *Wired* 2.03 (March 1994): 92–97, 138. On-line. HotWired. http://vip.hotwired.com/wired/2.03/features/muds.html (21 January 1998).

Rheingold, Howard. *Virtual Reality.* NY: Simon & Schuster, 1991.

Roszak, Theodore. *The Making of a Counter Culture: Reflections on the Technocratic Society and Its Youthful Opposition.* NY: Anchor, 1969.

Schoemer, Karen. "Seriously Wired." *The New York Times* (The Late Edition, August 8, 1993): sec. 9: 1, 9–10.

Schwenger, Peter. "*Agrippa,* or, The Apocalyptic Book." In *Flame Wars.* Durham, NC: Duke Univ. Press, 1994: 61–70.

Seabrook, John. "E-Mail from Bill." *The New Yorker* (January 10, 1994): 48–61.

Seabrook, John. "No E-Mail from Bill." *The New Yorker* (February 7, 1994): 8–9.

Shah, Rawn, and James Romine. *Playing MUDs on the Internet.* NY: John Wiley, 1995.

Shapiro, Andrew L. "Cyberscoop!" *The Nation* (March 20, 1995): 369–70.

Slatalla, Michelle, and Joshua Quittner. *Masters of Deception: The Gang That Ruled Cyberspace.* NY: HarperCollins, 1995.

Sponsler, Claire. "Beyond the Ruins: The Geopolitics of Urban Decay and Cybernetic Play." *Science-Fiction Studies* 20 (1993): 251–64.

Stephenson, Neal. *Snow Crash.* New York: Bantam, 1993.

Sterling, Bruce. *The Hacker Crackdown: Law and Disorder on the Electronic Frontier.* NY: Bantam, 1992. On-line: http://gopher.well.com:70/1/Publications/authors/Sterling/ or at http://cec.wustl.edu/~cs142/books/hacker_crackdown/The-Hacker-Crackdown,-Part-1%3 a-Crashing-the-System-(112K) (21 January 1998).

Taylor, Mark C., and Esa Saarinen. *Imagologies: Media Philosophy.* NY: Routledge, 1994.

Turkle, Sherry, *The Second Self: Computers and the Human Spirit.* NY: Simon and Schuster, 1984.

Ulmer, Gregory. *Teletheory: Grammatology in the Age of Video.* NY: Routledge, 1989.

Uncapher, Willard. "Trouble in Cyberspace." *Humanist* 51 (September/October 1991): 5–14.

Van Der Leun, Gerard. "This Is a Naked Lady." *Wired* (1993, Premiere Issue): 74, 109. On-line. HotWired. http://vip.hotwired.com/wired/1.1/features/cybersex.html (21 January 1998).

Virilio, Paul. *Speed and Politics.* Trans. Mark Polizzotti. NY: Semiotext(e), 1986.

Virilio, Paul, and Sylvère Lotringer. *Pure War.* Trans. Mark Polizzotti. NY: Semiotext(e), 1983.

Wajcman, J. *Feminism Confronts Technology.* University Park, PA: The Pennsylvania State Univ. Press, 1991.

Wertheim, Margaret. "Electronic Café." *Omni* (January 1993): 66–68, 70.

Woolley, Benjamin. *Virtual Worlds: A Journey in Hype and Hyperreality.* NY: Penguin, 1992.

I would like to express appreciation for permission to reprint the following:

Barker, Gerry. "Computers Should Supplement Textbooks, Not Replace Them," *Fort Worth Star-Telegram,* December 7, 1997: Sec. D, page 3. Permission granted by the author, manager, InterActive Content.

Barlow, John Perry. "Crime and Puzzlement." Reprinted by permission of the author.

Barlow, John Perry. "The Economy of Ideas: A Framework for Rethinking Patents and Copyrights in a Digital Age." Copyright 1993–1998 Wired Magazine Group, Inc. All rights reserved. Reprinted by permission.

Bey, Hakim. "The Net and the Web" from *TAZ.* Anti-copyright, 1985, 1991. Permission given.

Birkerts, Sven. "Into the Electronic Millennium" from *The Gutenberg Elegies: The Fate of Reading in an Electronic Age* by Sven Birkerts. Copyright © 1994 by Sven Birkerts. Reprinted by permission of Faber and Faber Publishers, Inc.

Bolter, Jay David. "The Computer as a New Writing Space" (Chapter 2) from *Writing Space.* Copyright 1991. Reprinted by permission of the publisher, Lawrence Erlbaum Associates, Inc., and the author.

Bombay, Dr. Emilio. "Would You View This with Your Mother?" (Mike Gerst, *Star-Telegram* systems editor), Aug. 21, 1997. Reprint courtesy of *The Fort Worth Star-Telegram.*

Borges, Jorge Luis. "The Library of Babel" in *Ficciones,* translated by Anthony Kerrigan. Copyright © 1962 by Grove Press. Used by permission of Grove/Atlantic, Inc.

Bruckman, Amy S. "Gender Swapping on the Internet." From *Proceedings of INET '93,* copyright by The Internet Society, 1993. Reprinted by permission of the author.

Critical Art Ensemble. "Utopian Plagiarism, Hypertextuality, and Electronic Cultural Production," *Critical Disturbances.* Anti-copyright 1994 Autonomedia & Critical Art Ensemble. Permission given.

Dibbell, Julian. "A Rape in Cyberspace." Village Voice, December 21, 1993. Reprinted by permission of the author.

Ebnet, Matthew. "Vigilantes Patrol Cyberspace: Cleaning up the Internet is the Mission of Many Web Users Across the U.S." June 8, 1997. Reprinted by permission from *The Kansas City Star.*

Elmer-Dewitt, Philip. "Cyberpunk." Copyright 1993, Time Inc. Reprinted by permission.

Exon, Sen. James. "Keep Internet Safe for Families." Permission granted by J. James Exon, U.S. Senator (D-NE).

Gup, Ted. "The End of Serendipity." *The Chronicle of Higher Education,* November 21, 1997: A52. Permission given by the author.

Hackers (roundtable). "Is Computer Hacking a Crime?" Copyright © 1990 by *Harper's Magazine.* All rights reserved. Reproduced from the March issue by special permission.

Harrington, James. "Beware of Chilling Freedom of Expression." Dallas Morning News, April 9, 1995, 1J, 10J. Permission granted by the author.

Heim, Michael. "The Essence of VR," from *The Metaphysics of Virtual Reality.* Copyright © 1994 by Michael Heim. Used by permission of Oxford University Press.

Herring, Susan. "Bringing Familiar Baggage to the New Frontier: Gender Differences in Computer-Mediated Communication." Originally delivered as a speech to the American Library Association, panel entitled "Making the Net*Work*: Is there a Z39.50 in Gender Communication?," Miami, June 27, 1994. Permission granted by the author.

Jonas, Gerald. "The Disappearing $2,000 Book." Reprinted by permission of the author.

Kantrowitz, Barbara. "Men, Women, and Computers." From *Newsweek,* May 16, 1994, copyright © 1994, Newsweek, Inc. All rights reserved. Reprinted by permission.

Kurzweil, Raymond. "The Future of Libraries: Parts I, II, and III." Reprinted from *Library Journal,* January 15th, 1992, February 15, 1992, and March 15, 1992. Copyright 1992 by Reed Publishing, USA. Reprinted by permission of the author.

Leary, Timothy. "The Cyberpunk: The Individual as Reality Pilot" and "Evolution of Countercultures" (chart), from *Chaos & Cyber Culture,* by Timothy Leary, copyright 1994: Timothy Leary. Permission to reprint granted by Ronin Publishing, Berkeley, California. All rights reserved.

Leslie, Jacques. "MUDroom." Copyright © 1993, Jacques Leslie, as first published in *The Atlantic Monthly.* Reprinted by permission of the author.

Lewis, Peter H. "No More 'Anything Goes': Cyberspace Gets Censors." Copyright © 1994 by the New York Times Company. Reprinted by permission.

on the impact of computer technology on individuals, organizations, and society.

Turkle, S. "Identity Crisis" from *Life On the Screen: Identity in the Age of the Internet* by Sherry Turkle, copyright © 1995 by Sherry Turkle. Reprinted with the permission of Simon & Schuster.

Woolley, Benjamin. "Cyberspace" Ch 6, *Virtual Worlds*. Permission granted by Blackwell Publishers and the author, who holds the copyright.